E. EARLE ELLIS

Tradition
and
Interpretation
in the
New Testament

Essays in Honor of

E. Earle Ellis

for His 60th Birthday

Edited by

Gerald F. Hawthorne

with

Otto Betz

WILLIAM B. EERDMANS PUBLISHING COMPANY
Grand Rapids, Michigan

J. C. B. MOHR (PAUL SIEBECK)
Tübingen

Copyright © 1987 by Wm. B. Eerdmans Publishing Co.
255 Jefferson Ave. S.E., Grand Rapids, Mich. 49503
This edition published 1987 jointly by Wm. B. Eerdmans Publishing Co.
and J. C. B. Mohr (Paul Siebeck), Tübingen, Germany

Library of Congress Cataloging-in-Publication Data

Tradition & interpretation in the New Testament.

English and German.
1. Bible. N.T.—Criticism, interpretation, etc.
2. Ellis, E. Earle (Edward Earle)
I. Ellis, E. Earle (Edward Earle)
II. Hawthorne, Gerald F., 1925– .
III. Betz, Otto.
IV. Title: Tradition and interpretation in the New Testament.
BS2395.T73 1987   225.6   87-22367

ISBN 0-8028-3644-5

CIP—Kurztitelaufnahme der Deutschen Bibliothek

Tradition & [and] interpretation in the New Testament:
essays in honor of E. Earle Ellis for his 60th birthday
ed. by Gerald F. Hawthorne with Otto Betz.
Grand Rapids, Michigan;
Tübingen: Mohr, 1987

ISBN 3-16-145306-9

NE: Hawthorne, Gerald F. [Hrsg.]; Ellis, Edward Earle: Festschrift

CONTENTS

PREFACE

It is a great pleasure for me to share together with some of the many distinguished colleagues of Earle Ellis in this expression of admiration of and appreciation for him on his 60th birthday. For more than a quarter of a century he has given to us, and to the world of scholars and pastors and teachers, the benefits of his own diligent pursuit of knowledge and of his own fervent desire to understand and interpret the Bible.

His numerous books and articles published by prestigious publishing houses and in significant journals testify to the quality of his scholarship, and the value of his intellectual insights. They testify not only to his dedication to careful learning, but of equal importance, to his faith-commitment and to the surrender of himself to enriching the church in the world of today.

He is an able teacher, a diligent student, a distinguished scholar, a Christian gentleman, a loyal friend, a man of the church, a *kosmopolites*. It is, therefore, with delight that we honor him with this collection of essays that is itself representative of his international and ecumenical interests and his own breadth of scholarly pursuits.

Many thanks are due to too many people and organizations to mention them all. But it would be inappropriate not to single out a few of these as representative of the whole. First, a great debt is owed to each contributor to this volume who so readily assented to write, and for the promptness with which the articles were submitted. Second, I owe a special debt of thanks to Professor Dr. Otto Betz, Emeritus Professor of New Testament, University of Tübingen, who so kindly accepted the task of editing the German and French articles in this volume, and doing this with such care. Surely his name deserves a place on the title page. Third, Mr. William B. Eerdmans, Jr., President of Wm. B. Eerdmans Pulishing Company, deserves hearty thanks for making this project possible. Without his courteous help and ready willingness this venture would have failed. Fourth, a debt of gratitude is owed to Wheaton College, to the Wheaton College Alumni Association, and to the administrators of the Norris Alden Fund for generous financial help which made it possible to put this volume together. Fifth, and finally, many thanks for the gracious and generous help of Mrs. Karen Mason, our departmental secretary, the Wheaton College Library staff, and Jane Hawthorne, my wife, who spent hours in proofreading and indexing.

GERALD F. HAWTHORNE

EDWARD EARLE ELLIS:
CURRICULUM VITAE

Background

E. Earle Ellis was born in Fort Lauderdale, Florida, March 18, 1926, and grew up in the neighboring town of Dania. At the age of eleven he confessed Christ as Savior and Lord, was baptized and received into the church. After graduation from high school he spent two years in the United States Army, serving as a Private and Second Lieutenant in America and in Europe. While pursuing the study of law, he received a call from Christ to the ministry. He completed his theological education and, perceiving his gifts to be primarily in the area of teaching, was ordained to the gospel ministry in 1959 with that end in view. During the succeeding years he has held ecclesiastical orders in three denominations: Southern Baptist, American Baptist, and Reformed Church in America.

Education

Diploma	South Broward High School, Dania, Florida, 1944
B.S.	University of Virginia, 1950
	(University of Virginia Law School, 1949-50)
M.A., B.D.	Wheaton (Illinois) Graduate School, 1953
Ph.D.	University of Edinburgh, 1955
Post-graduate Studies:	University of Tübingen, 1954
	University of Göttingen, 1955
	University of Marburg, 1961-62
	University of Basel, 1962

Academic Honors

University of Virginia: Beta Gamma Sigma
Wheaton Graduate School: Honor Society
University of Göttingen: von Humboldt Scholar (1968-69)
University of Tübingen: von Humboldt Scholar (1975-76)
John Simon Guggenheim Fellow (1975-76)
Juniata College: J. Omar Good Visiting Distinguished Professor (1978-79)
Wheaton College: Doctor of Divinity Degree (1982)
Robinson College, Cambridge University: Visiting Fellow (1982-83)

Teaching Posts

1952-53 Instructor in Business Law
    Wheaton College, Wheaton, Illinois

1955-58 Assistant Professor of Bible and Philosophy
Aurora College, Aurora, Illinois
1958-60 Assistant Professor of New Testament
Southern Baptist Theological Seminary, Louisville, Kentucky
1960-61 Visiting Professor of New Testament
Bethel Theological Seminary, St. Paul, Minnesota
1962-70 Associate Professor of Biblical Studies
1970-77 Professor of Biblical Studies
1977-85 Research Professor of New Testament Literature
New Brunswick Theological Seminary, New Brunswick, New Jersey
1985-87 Visiting Professor of Theology
1987— Research Professor of Theology
Southwestern Baptist Theological Seminary, Ft. Worth, Texas

Professional Societies

Institute for Biblical Research (Founder; Chairman, 1970-81)
The Society of Biblical Literature
Studiorum Novi Testamenti Societas (Executive Committee, 1967-69; Editorial Board, 1987-89)

Publications

1956
1. "A Note on Pauline Hermeneutics," *NTS* 2 (1955-56) 127-133.

1957
2. *Paul's Use of the Old Testament*. Edinburgh and Grand Rapids, 1957.
3. "A Note on I Cor 10:4," *JBL* 76 (1957) 53-56.
4. " 'Saith the Lord,' " *EvQ* 29 (1957) 23-28.

1958
5. *Paul's Use of the Old Testament*. Grand Rapids, 1958. Reprint of #2.
6. "The Problem of Authorship (of) First and Second Timothy," *RE* 56 (1959) 343-354.

1959
7. Review: A. R. C. Leaney, *The Gospel According to St. Luke*, New York, 1958, in *RE* 56 (1959) 30-31.
8. Review: H. Riesenfeld, *The Gospel Tradition and Its Beginnings*, London, 1957 in *RE* 56 (1959) 31-32.

1960
9. "Consecrate," "Cornerstone," "Earnest," "Enemy," "Example," *Dictionary of Theology*, ed. E. F. Harrison, Grand Rapids, 1960, 137-138, 140-141, 175, 182, 204.
10. "Jude," *The Biblical Expositor*, ed. C. F. H. Henry, Philadelphia, 1960, 1241-1246.
11. "II Cor 5:1-10 in Pauline Eschatology," *NTS* 6 (1959-60) 211-224.
12. Review: J. Munck, *Paul and the Salvation of Mankind*, Richmond, 1960, in *RE* 57 (1960) 342-343.

13. "The Authorship of the Pastorals," *EvQ* 32 (1960) 151-161. Reprint of #6.

1961

14. *Paul and His Recent Interpreters,* Grand Rapids, 1961.

1962

15. "Colossians," *The Wycliffe Bible Commentary,* ed. E. F. Harrison, Chicago, 1962, 1333-1346.
16. "Paul," "Life," "Quotations" ("Annunciation," "Benedictus," "Gloria in Excelsis," "Kneel," "Light," "Magi," "Magnificat," "Mammon," "Nunc Dimittis," "Rock," "Vow"), *New Bible Dictionary,* ed. J. D. Douglas, London & Grand Rapids, 1962, 943-955, 735-739, 1071 (39, 140, 471-472, 702, 739, 765-766, 772, 775, 901, 1098, 1313).
17. "O Pensamento Teológico e Rudolfo Bultmann," *Revista Teológica* 1 (1962) 15-18.

1963

18. "Luke 11:49-51: An Oracle of a Christian Prophet?" *ExpTim* 74 (1962-63) 157-158.
19. Review: B. Rigaux, *Saint Paul et ses lettres,* Bruges, 1962, in *JBL* 82 (1963) 453-454.

1964

20. "Jesus, the Sadducees and Qumran," *NTS* 10 (1963-64) 274-279.

1965

21. *The World of St. John,* London & Nashville, 1965.
22. Review: D. E. H. Whiteley, *The Theology of St. Paul,* Philadelphia, 1964 in *JBL* 84 (1965) 454-456.

1966

23. *The Gospel of Luke (New Century Bible),* London, 1966.
24. "Present and Future Eschatology in Luke," *NTS* 12 (1965-66) 27-41.
25. Review: C. H. Talbert, *Luke and the Gnostics,* Nashville, 1966, in *JBL* 85 (1966) 264-266.

1967

26. *Paul and His Recent Interpreters,* Grand Rapids, 2nd edition, 1967. Reprint of #14.
27. "The Authority of Scripture: Critical Judgments in Biblical Perspective," *EvQ* 39 (1967) 196-204.

1968

28. " 'Those of the Circumcision' and the Early Christian Mission," *Studia Evangelica IV,* ed. F. L. Cross (= TU 102), Berlin 1968, 390-399.

1969

29. *Neotestamentica et Semitica. Studies in Honour of Matthew Black,* Edinburgh, 1969 (editor).
30. "Midrash, Targum and New Testament Quotations," *Neotestamentica et Semitica,* eds. E. E. Ellis and M. Wilcox, Edinburgh, 1969, 61-69.
31. "Die Funktion der Eschatologie im Lukasevangelium," *ZTK* 66 (1969) 387-402.
32. Review: H. A. Wilcke, *Das Problem eines messianischen Zwischenreich bei Paulus,* Zürich, 1967, in *JBL* 88 (1969) 100-103.

1970

33. "Midrashic Features in the Speeches of Acts," *Hommage au Professeur B. Rigaux*, ed. A. Descamps, Gembloux, 1970, 303-312.
34. "The Role of the Christian Prophet in Acts," *Apostolic History and the Gospel: Essays presented to F. F. Bruce*, ed. W. W. Gasque, Exeter and Grand Rapids, 1970, 55-67.
35. Review: P. Richardson, *Israel in the Apostolic Church*, Cambridge, 1969, in *Christianity Today* 14 (1969-70), 832-833.

1971

36. "Paul and His Co-Workers," *NTS* 17 (1970-71) 437-452.
37. "Midraschartige Züge in den Reden der Apostelgeschichte," *ZNW* 62 (1971) 94-104. Revision and translation of #33.

1972

38. *Eschatology in Luke*, Philadelphia, 1972.
39. Review: H. Schürmann, *Das Lukasevangelium, Erste Teil*, Freiburg, 1969 in *Bib* 53 (1972) 143-146.

1973

40. *Paul and His Recent Interpreters*, Grand Rapids, 3rd edition, 1973. Reprint of #14.
41. "Christ and Spirit in I Corinthians," *Christ and Spirit in the New Testament. Studies in Honour of C. F. D. Moule*, ed. B. Lindars, Cambridge, 1973, 269-277.
42. "La fonction de l'eschatologie dans l'evangile de Luc," *L'evangile de Luc. Memorial L. Cerfaux*, ed. F. Neirynck, Louvain, 1973, 141-155. Translation of #31.
43. "Jude," *The Biblical Expositor*, Philadephia, 1973. Reprint of #10.
44. Review: O. Kuss, *Paulus: Die Rolle des Apostels in der Theologischen Entwicklung der Urkirche*, Regensburg, 1971, in *JBL* 92 (1973) 141-142.

1974

45. *The Gospel of Luke*, London 1974. Revised ed. of #23.
46. "Christ Crucified," *Reconciliation and Hope. Presented to L. L. Morris*, ed. R. Banks, Exeter & Grand Rapids, 1974, 69-75.
47. "Die Funktion der Eschatologie im Lukasevangelium," *Wege der Forschung* CCLXXX, ed. G. Braumann, Darmstadt, 1974. Reprint of #31.
48. "Saint Luke," *Encyclopedia Britannica*, 15th ed., Chicago, 1974.
49. "Situation and Purpose in Acts," *Int* 28 (1974) 94-98.
50. " 'Spiritual' Gifts in the Pauline Community," *NTS* 20 (1973-74) 128-144.
51. " 'Wisdom' and 'Knowledge' in I Corinthians," *TynBul* 25 (1974) 82-98.

1975

52. *Jesus und Paulus. Festschrift für W. G. Kümmel*, Göttingen, 1975 (co-editor).
53. "Adultery," "Childlikeness," *Dictionary of Christian Ethics*, ed. C. F. H. Henry, Grand Rapids, 1975, 9-10, 94.
54. "The Composition of Luke 9 and the Sources of Its Christology," *Current Issues in Biblical and Patristic Interpretation. Studies (for) M. C. Tenney*, ed. G. F. Hawthorne, Grand Rapids, 1975, 121-127.
55. Review: C. K. Barrett, *The Second Epistle to the Corinthians*, New York, 1973, in *JBL* 94 (1975), 466-467.
56. Review: C. K. Barrett, *New Testament Essays*, London, 1972, in *JAAR* 43 (1975) 423-424.

57. "La composition de Luc 9 et les sources de sa christologie," *Jésus aux origines de la christologie,* ed. J. Dupont, Gembloux, 1975, 193-200. Translation of #54.
58. "Exegetical Patterns in I Corinthians and Romans," *Essays in Honor of Prof. L. J. Kuyper,* ed. J. I. Cook, Grand Rapids, 1975, 137-142.
59. "New Directions in Form Criticism," *Jesus Christus in Historie und Theologie, Festschrift für H. Conzelmann,* ed. G. Strecker, Tübingen, 1975, 299-315.
60. "Paul and His Opponents," *Christianity, Judaism and Other Greco-Roman Cults. (Studies for) Morton Smith,* 4 vols., ed. J. Neusner, Leiden, 1975, 1.264-298.
61. "'Weisheit' und 'Erkenntnis' im 1. Korintherbrief," *Jesus und Paulus. Festschrift für W. G. Kümmel,* eds. E. E. Ellis and E. Grässer, Göttingen, 1975, 109-128. Translation of #51.
62. "Reformed Preaching—An Exegetical Response," *Reformed Review* 28 (1974-75) 85-86.

1976
63. "Prophecy," "Spiritual Gifts," "Tongues," *Interpreter's Dictionary of the Bible: Supplement,* ed.K. Crim, Nashville, 1976, 700-701, 841-843, 908-910.
64. Review: H. W. Shires, *Finding the Old Testament in the New,* Philadelphia, 1974 in *Int* 30 (1976) 90-91.

1977
65. "How the New Testament Uses the Old," *New Testament Interpretation,* ed. I. H. Marshall, Exeter & Grand Rapids, 1977, 199-219.
66. "Prophecy in the New Testament Church—and Today," *Prophetic Vocation in the New Testament and Today,* ed. J. Panagopoulos, Leiden, 1977, 46-57.

1978
67. *Prophecy and Hermeneutic in Early Christianity* (Vol. 18 in WUNT), Tübingen, 1978.
68. *Prophecy and Hermeneutic in Early Christianity,* Grand Rapids, 1978. Paperback edition of #67.

1979
69. *Paul and His Recent Interpreters.* Grand Rapids, 1979, 4th ed. Reprint of #14.
70. "Lord's Supper and a Public Confession of Faith," *The Church Herald* 36 (19 Oct 1979) 9-11.
71. Review: K. G. Sandelin, *Die Auseinandersetzung mit der Weisheit in 1 Korinther 15,* Åbo, 1976, in *JBL* 98 (1979) 305-306.

1980
72. *Prophecy and Hermeneutic in Early Christianity,* Grand Rapids, 2nd edition, 1980. Reprint of #68.
73. "Dating the New Testament," *NTS* 26 (1980) 487-502.
74. Review: B. T. Viviano, *Study as Worship: Aboth and the New Testament,* Leiden, 1978, in *TLZ* 105 (1980) 674.
75. Review: B. Gerhardsson, *Die Anfänge der Evangelientradition,* Wuppertal, 1977, in *TLZ* 105 (1980) 894-895.
76. "Paul," "Life," . . . *The Illustrated Bible Dictionary* 3 vols., ed. N. Hillyer, Leicester, UK & Wheaton IL, 1980. Revisions of articles in #16.

1981
77. *The Gospel of Luke,* Grand Rapids, 1981. Revised paperback edition of #45.

78. *Paul's Use of the Old Testament,* Grand Rapids, 3rd edition, 1981. Paperback edition of #2.
79. "The Silenced Wives of Corinth," *New Testament Textual Criticism. Essays in Honor of B. M. Metzger,* ed. E. J. Epp, Oxford 1981, 213-220.
80. "The Old Testament in the Early Church," *NBTS Newsletter* 10, 3 (Mar. 1981) 11-13.
81. Review: G. Hughes, *Hebrews and Hermeneutics,* Cambridge, 1979, in *TLZ* 106 (1981) 418-419.

1982
82. "La datation du Nouveau Testament," *Communio* 7 (1982) 75-89. Translation of #73.
83. "Foreword" to L. Goppelt, *TYPOS: The Typological Interpretation of the Old Testament in the New,* Grand Rapids, 1981 (1939), ix-xx.

1983
84. *The Gospel of Luke,* Grand Rapids, 4th edition, 1983. Reprint of #77.
85. "Gospels Criticism: A Perspective on the State of the Art," *Das Evangelium und die Evangelien. Festschrift für O. Betz,* ed. P. Stuhlmacher, Tübingen, 1983.

1984
86. *The World of St. John,* Grand Rapids, 2nd edition, 1984. Reprint of #21.
87. "If Only a Secularist Religion is Taught," *The Wall Street Journal* 203 (60 = 27 Mar 1984) 34.
88. Review: R. Riesner, *Jesus als Lehrer,* Tübingen, 1981, in *JBL* 103 (1984) 656-658.

1985
89. *Paul's Use of the Old Testament,* Grand Rapids, 3rd edition, 1985. Reprint of #2.
90. "Paul's Missionary Journeys," *New Bible Atlas,* ed. J. Paterson et al., Leicester, UK, 1985, 80-81.

1986
91. "Gospel according to Luke," *International Standard Bible Encyclopedia,* ed. G. W. Bromiley, Grand Rapids, 1986, 3.180-186.
92. "Traditions in I Corinthians," *NTS* 32 (1986) 451-502.
93. "Die Datierung des Neuen Testaments," *TZ* 42 (1986) 409-430. Revision and translation of #73.

Forthcoming
94. "Quotations," *International Standard Bible Encyclopedia, Volume Four,* ed. G. W. Bromiley, Grand Rapids, 1987.
95. "Traditions in the Pastoral Epistles," *Early Jewish and Christian Exegesis: Studies in Memory of William Hugh Brownlee,* ed. C. A. Evans, Decatur GA, 1987.
96. "The Conception of the Old Testament in Early Christianity," *Compendia Rerum Judaicarum ad Novum Testamentum, Section Two, Volume I,* ed. M. J. Mulder, Assen and Philadelphia, 1988.

Guest Lectures

Western Theological Seminary (Spring Lectures 1965)
University of Zürich (Theological Faculty Club Lecture, Summer 1965)
Oxford University (Congress on the Gospels 1965)

Catholic University of Louvain (Journées Bibliques 1968)
Cambridge University (New Testament Seminar Lecture 1969)
University of Uppsala (New Testament Seminar Lecture 1969)
University of Göttingen (New Testament Seminar Lecture 1969)
Smith College (Religion Department Lecture 1969)
Studiorum Novi Testamenti Societas (Main Paper 1970)
University of Bergen (University Lectures 1971)
Northwestern College (Spring Lectures 1973)
Tyndale House, Cambridge (New Testament Lecture, 1973)
Catholic University of Louvain (Journées Bibliques 1973)
Oxford University (Congress on Biblical Studies 1973)
Williams College (Chaplain's Lectures 1973)
Drake University (Staley Lectures 1974)
Montclair (NJ) State College (Religion Department Lecture 1974)
The Ecumenical Institute, World Council of Churches, Bossey, Switz. (Consultation
    of New Testament Scholars, September 1975)
U.S. Army in Europe (Chaplains' Conference Lectures, 1976)
Schloss Mittersill (International Students Conference Lecturer, Spring 1975 and
    1976)
Princeton Theological Seminary (Theological Forum Lecture 1976)
Yale University (Intervarsity Lectures 1977)
Wheaton (IL) Graduate School (Theological Society Lecture 1977)
Princeton Theological Seminary (Theological Forum Lecture 1978)
Juniata College (Spring Lecture 1978)
Trinity Episcopal School for Ministry (Fall Lectures 1978)
Cambridge University (Divinity School Lecture 1979)
King's College, London (New Testament Seminar Lecture 1979)
St. John's College, Nottingham (Spring Lecture 1979)
Studiorum Novi Testamenti Societas (Short Paper 1979)
Oxford University (International Conference on Patristic Studies 1979)
North Park Theological Seminary (Nils W. Lund Memorial Lectures 1979)
Trinity Evangelical Divinity School (Fall Lecture 1979)
Wheaton (IL) Graduate School (Theological Society Lecture 1979)
Princeton Theological Seminary (Theological Forum Lecture 1981)
Trinity Episcopal School for Ministry (Trinity Lectures 1982)
Trinity Evangelical Divinity School (Spring Lecture 1982)
University of Tübingen (Conference on the Gospels 1982)
University of Birmingham (New Testament Seminar Lecture 1982)
Oxford University (Origen Society Lecture & New Testament Seminar Lecture
    1982)
Cambridge University (Divinity School Lecture 1982)
University of Kent at Canterbury (New Testament Seminar Lecture 1983)
Cambridge University (New Testament Seminar Lecture 1983)
Ridley Hall, Cambridge (Guest Lecture 1983)
University of Durham (University Lecture & New Testament Seminar Lecture 1983)
University of Manchester (New Testament Seminar Lecture 1983)
Tyndale House, Cambridge (Guest Lecture 1983)
Concordia Theological Seminary (Faculty Forum Lecture 1983)

Institute for Biblical Research (Annual Lecture 1983)
Reformierte Pfarrergesellschaft of Basel (Guest Lecture 1984)
Cedar Campus (Summer Conference Lectures 1984)
International Conference of Theists & Atheists (Dallas 1985)
Church of God School of Theology (ETS Conference Addresses 1985)
Emmanuel School of Religion (Kershner Memorial Lectures 1985)
Yale Divinity School (Christian Study Center Lectures, Spring 1986)
University of Ft. Hare, Ciskei (Guest Lectures 1986)
The Baptist Theological College, Cape Town (Guest Lecture 1986)
University of Cape Town (Religious Studies Department Lecture 1986)
University of the Orange Free State (New Testament Department Lecture 1986)
University of South Africa (Religious Studies Department Seminar Lectures 1986)
University of Pretoria (Theological Faculty A Guest Lecture 1986)
University of Pretoria (Theological Faculty B Guest Lectures 1986)
University of Witwatersrand (SCA Guest Lecture 1986)
Southwestern Baptist Theological Seminary (Day-Higgenbotham Lectures, 1987)
Evangelical Theological Society, Southwest Region (Guest Lectures, 1987)

Visiting Lectureships & Fellowships

Drew University (Visiting New Testament Lecturer 1967-68)
Princeton Theological Seminary (Spring Semester Doctroral Seminar 1970) (Summer School Lecturer 1974, 1976, 1978) (Visiting New Testament Lecturer 1976-1977)
University of Tübingen (Winter Semester Seminar 1975-76)
Juniata College (J. Omar Good Visiting Distinguished Professor 1978-79)
Robinson College, Cambridge University (Visiting Fellow 1982-83)
University of Stellenbosch (Winter Semester Visiting Lecturer 1986)

THE CONTRIBUTORS

C. K. BARRETT, Emeritus Professor of Divinity, University of Durham, England.

OTTO BETZ, Professor of New Testament, i. R., University of Tübingen, West Germany.

PEDER BORGEN, Professor of New Testament and Religions in the Graeco-Roman World, Department of Religious Studies, University of Trondheim, Norway.

F. F. BRUCE, Emeritus Professor in the University of Manchester, England; formerly Rylands Professor of Biblical Criticism and Exegesis in the University of Manchester.

DAVID R. CATCHPOLE, Professor of Theological Studies, University of Exeter, England.

DAVID DAUBE, Emeritus Professor of Law, University of California, Berkeley, California, USA.

JAMES D. G. DUNN, Professor of Divinity, Department of Theology, University of Durham, England.

DOM JACQUES DUPONT, Monastere Saint-André, Ottignies, Belgique.

JOSEPH A. FITZMYER, S.J., Professor Emeritus of New Testament in the Biblical Studies Department, The Catholic University of America, Washington, DC, USA.

LARS HARTMAN, Professor of New Testament Exegesis, Department of Theology, University of Uppsala, Sweden.

GERALD F. HAWTHORNE, Professor of Greek and New Testament Exegesis, Wheaton College, Wheaton, Illinois, USA.

MARTIN HENGEL, Professor of New Testament and Early Judaism, University of Tübingen, West Germany.

SEYOON KIM, Professor of New Testament at the Asian Center for Theological Studies, Seoul, Korea; Visiting Associate Professor of New Testament, Calvin Theological Seminary, Grand Rapids, Michigan, USA.

RICHARD N. LONGENECKER, Ramsay Armitage Professor of New Testament, Wycliffe College, University of Toronto, Toronto, Ontario, Canada.

U. LUZ, Professor of New Testament, Evangelical-Theological Faculty, University of Bern, Switzerland.

I. HOWARD MARSHALL, Professor of New Testament Exegesis, University of Aberdeen, Scotland.

RALPH P. MARTIN, Professor of New Testament and Director of Graduate Studies Program, Fuller Theological Seminary, Pasadena, California, USA.

WAYNE A. MEEKS, Woolsey Professor of Biblical Literature, Department of Religious Studies, Yale University, New Haven, Connecticut, USA.

C. F. D. MOULE, Lady Margaret's Professor Emeritus in the University of Cambridge; Fellow of Clare College, Cambridge, England.

PETER RICHARDSON, Professor of Religious Studies and Principal of University College, University of Toronto, Toronto, Ontario, Canada.

WILLY RORDORF, ordentlicher Professor für Patristik und Alte Kirchengeschichte, Theologische Fakultät, Universität Neuenburg, Schweiz.

D. MOODY SMITH, Professor of New Testament Interpretation, The Divinity School, Duke University, Durham, North Carolina, USA.

GRAHAM N. STANTON, Professor of New Testament Studies, King's College, University of London, London, England.

GEORG STRECKER, ordentlicher Professor für Neues Testament am Fachbereich Theologie der Georg-August-Universität Göttingen, West Germany.

PETER STUHLMACHER, Professor of New Testament at the Protestant Faculty of Theology, University of Tübingen, West Germany.

TABULA GRATULATORIA

Paul J. Achtemeier
James B. Adamson
S. T. Ola. Akande
Barbara Aland
Kurt Aland
Ralph H. Alexander
Joseph M. Alexanian
Hugh Anderson
Sasagu Arai
Carl E. Armerding
David E. Aune

Tjitze Baarda
Heinrich Baarlink
J. Arthur Baird
William Baird
David W. Baker
David Balch
Andrew J. Bandstra
Robert Banks
R. S. Barbour
S. Scott Bartchy
Markus Barth
Freeman Barton
Richard A. Batey
Richard Bauckham
William A. Beardslee
Paul Beasley-Murray
Pier Franco Beatrice
Linda L. Belleville
Arthur J. Bellinzoni
Ernest Best
Hans Dieter Betz
Gilbert Bilezikian
Hermann Binder
Peter Blaeser
Daniel I. Block
Craig Blomberg
Otto Böcher
G. H. Boobyer
Gerald L. Borchert
M. Eugene Boring
Günther Bornkamm
Michel Bouttier
Gijs Bouwman
John Bowker
Manfred T. Brauch
Paul L. Bremer
Ingo Broer
James A. Brooks

Raymond E. Brown
Schuyler Brown
George Wesley Buchanan
Christoph Burchard
U. Busse

Allen Cabaniss
P. J. Cahill
Charles E. Carlston
G. Lloyd Carr
G. P. Carras
D. A. Carson
Frank G. Carver
Thomas Scott Caulley
Knox Chamblin
David J. A. Clines
Gareth Lee Cockerill
James I. Cook
Bruce Corley
Lorin L. Cranford

Peter Davids
James A. Davis
Christoph Demke
Albert -M. Denis, O.P.
J. L. de Villiers
P. G. R. de Villiers
Christian Dietzfelbinger
Raymond B. Dillard
Angelico-Salvatore Di Marco
Karl Paul Donfried
D. Dormeyer
John Drane
Dennis C. Duling
Marcel Dumais
William J. Dumbrell
Robert L. Duncan
David L. Dungan
I. J. Du Plessis
Jan A. Du Rand

Robert Eisenman
J. Keith Elliott
John H. Elliott
Walter Elwell
David H. Engelhard
S. I. Enoch
Eldon Jay Epp
Norman R. Ericson
Josef Ernst

Christoffer F. Evans
Craig A. Evans
David Ewert

William R. Farmer
Hobert K. Farrell
Gordon D. Fee
Elisabeth Schüssler Fiorenza
P. Bonifatius Fischer, O.S.B.
Fred L. Fisher
J. Terence Forestell
Robert T. Fortna
Jarl Fossum
Dan Fraikin
R. T. France
Hubert Frankemölle
Majella Franzmann
Hermann Josef Frede
Edwin D. Freed
A. Fuchs
Reginald H. Fuller
Victor Paul Furnish

Richard B. Gaffin, Jr.
Harry Y. Gamble, Jr.
W. Ward Gasque
Birger Gerhardsson
John G. Gibbs
Soren Giversen
T. Francis Glasson
Mark E. Glasswell
Joachim Gnilka
Paul W. Gooch
Victor R. Gordon
Michael Goulder
Michel Gourgues, O.P.
Erich Grässer
Prosper Grech
Michael Green
Guy Greenfield
D. Heinrich Greeven
Pierre Grelot
James C. G. Grieg
Douglas M. Gropp
Wayne Grudem
Robert A. Guelich
Robert H. Gundry

Klaus Haacker
Donald A. Hagner

xix

Ferdinand Hahn
S. G. Hall
Robert G. Hamerton-Kelly
Paul L. Hammer
Raymond J. Hammer
K. Hanhart
A. T. Hanson
Douglas R. A. Hare
Daniel J. Harrington, S.J.
J. Gordon Harris
Murray J. Harris
Victor Hasler
Günter Haufe
E. Haulotte
David M. Hay
Charles W. Hedrick
James D. Hester
C. J. A. Hickling
Earle Hilgert
David Hill
Verlin O. Hinshaw
Edward C. Hobbs
Robert Hodgson
Harold W. Hoehner
Robert G. Hoerber
Paul Hoffmann
Otfried Hofius
Carl R. Holladay
Mike Holmes
T. Holtz
Morna D. Hooker
J. Leslie Houlden
George Howard
David Hubbard
Robert L. Hubbard
H. Hübner
Robert B. Hughes
P. E. Hughes
Arland J. Hultgren
Harry B. Hunt, Jr.
W. Bingham Hunter
Claus-Hunno Hunzinger
L. W. Hurtado

Marie E. Isaacs

Seynaeve Jaak
G. Jeremias
Jacob Jervell
Richard L. Jeske
Robert Jewett
Alan F. Johnson
Dennis E. Johnson
Jakob Jónsson
E. A. Judge

Walter C. Kaiser, Jr.
Robert J. Karris, O.F.M.
Howard C. Kee
Karl Kertelge
Leslie R. Keylock
René Kieffer
Jack Dean Kingsbury
Simon J. Kistemaker
Hans-Josef Klauck
Hans Klein
William W. Klein
George W. Knight III
Otto Knoch
John Knox
Robert A. Kraft
Jacob Kremer
Edgar Krentz
Heinz-Wolfgang Kuhn
Werner Kümmel

J. Lambrecht, S.J.
William L. Lane
Friedrich Lang
Paul-Emile Langevin, S.J.
Hugolin Langkammer
W. J. Larkin, Jr.
Edvin Larsson
William Sanford La Sor
Bernard C. Lategan
Michael Lattke
Sophie Laws
Thomas W. Leahy, S.J.
A. R. C. Leaney
R. Le Déaut
Simon Legasse
Ragnar Leivestad
Fritzleo Lentzen-Deis, S.J.
Xavier Leon-Dufour, S.J.
Paul E. Leonard
Herbert Leroy
William H. Leslie
John R. Levison
H. Lichtenberger
Walter Liefeld
Andrew T. Lincoln
Barnabas Lindars, S.S.F.
Henrik Ljungman
D. Eduard Lohse
Tremper Longman, III
Thomas R. W. Longstaff
Evald Lövestam
J. Luzarraga

Donald Madvig
Abraham J. Malherbe
C. S. Mann

W. Harold Mare
Stanley B. Marrow, S.J.
Brice Martin
Michael Martin
Cardinal Carlo Maria Martini
J. Louis Martyn
Kikuo Matsunaga
Ulrich Mauser
B. Mayer
John Mbiti
Harvey K. McArthur
Davis McCaughey
Terence P. McGonigal
John McHugh
R. J. McKelvey
Edgar V. McKnight
Martin McNamara, M.S.C.
John McRay
David G. Meade
Richard R. Melick, Jr.
Helmut Merklein
Bruce M. Metzger
Robert P. Meye
B. F. Meyer
Khoza Elliot M. Mgojo
J. Ramsey Michaels
Otto Michel
Berkeley Mickelsen
Watson E. Mills
Paul S. Minear
L. Monsengwo-Pasinya
Hugh Montefiore
Robert Morgan
Leon Morris
Robert H. Mounce
Halvor Moxnes
Paul-Gerhard Müller
Robert Murray, S.J.
Franz Mussner

Frans Neirynck
Poul Nepper-Christensen
Fritz Neugebauer
Eugene A. Nida
D. E. Nineham
Brian M. Nolan
Stephen F. Noll
John Nolland

P. T. O'Brien
Birger Olsson
J. C. O'Neill
Bernard Orchard
E. F. Osborn
Peter von der Osten-Sacken
R. F. O'Toole, S.J.

John Panagopoulos
James Parker, III
Pierson Parker
Priscilla Patten
Rebecca Patten
Arthur G. Patzia
Henning Paulsen
Philip Barton Payne
Birger A. Pearson
Rudolf Pesch
Romano Penna
Charles Perrot
Josef Pfammatter
Antonio Pinero-Saenz
Clark H. Pinnock
Eckhard Plümacher
Petr Pokorny, CSC
Wiard Popkes
E. A. C. Pretorius

Emilio Rasco, S.I.
Bo Reicke
Marty L. Reid
Jannes Reiling
C. R. Renowden
Martin Rese
James L. Resseguie
John Reumann
J. K. Riches
Hans-Friedemann Richter
Herman Ridderbos
Harald Riesenfeld
Rainer Riesner
Hubert Ritt
Donald Robinson
Cyril S. Rodd
Wayne G. Rollins
Kazimierz Romaniuk
John M. Ross
Eugen Ruckstuhl

Leopold Sabourin, S.N.
Karl-Gustav Sandelin
E. P. Sanders
James A. Sanders
Akira Satake
Zdenek Sázava

Wolfgang Schenk
Gottried Schille
Jacques Schlosser
Walter Schmithals
Rudolf Schnackenburg
Bernardin Schneider, O.F.M.
Sandra M. Schneiders
David M. Scholer
Wolfgang Schrage
Thomas R. Schreiner
David Schroeder
Heinz Schürmann
B. Schwank
Eduard Schweizer
J. Julius Scott, Jr.
Giuseppe Segalla
Russell P. Shedd
Philip L. Shuler
Lou H. Silberman
Robert Bryan Sloan, Jr.
Stephen S. Smalley
Elmer B. Smick
Charles W. F. Smith
Klyne Snodgrass
Cerlas Spicq
Robert A. Spivey
Robert H. Stein
William Richard Stegner
James S. Stewart
Alfred Suhl
J. P. M. Sweet
Jan Szlaga

Alan Thalhuber
Gerd Theissen
Walter Thiele
Frank S. Thielman
Anthony C. Thiselton
John Christopher Thomas
Marianne Meye Thompson
Margaret E. Thrall
John E. Toews
Stephen H. Travis
Kurt Treu
Wolfgang Trilling
Allison A. Trites
Karl-Wolfgang Tröger

Andrew H. Trotter, Jr.
Kiyoshi Tsuchido
Christopher Tuckett
George Allen Turner
Joseph B. Tyson

Pieter W. van der Horst
Bastiaan Van Elderen
William A. Van Gemeren
A. Vanhoye, S.J.
B. M. F. van Iersel
Raymond C. Van Leeuwen
Beltrán Villegas
James W. Voelz
Willem S. Vorster
Christos Sp. Voulgaris

Günter Wagner
Larry Lee Walker
William O. Walker, Jr.
Andrew F. Walls
Bruce Waltke
Joseph S. Wang
A. J. M. Wedderburn
Alfons Weiser
David Wenham
Walter W. Wessel
Stephen Westerholm
D. E. H. Whiteley
Allen Wikgren
Max Wilcox
William C. Williams
R. McI. Wilson
S. G. Wilson
Walter Wink
Christian Wolff
N. T. Wright
Wilhelm Wuellner

Edwin Yamauchi
Frances Young
Norman H. Young
Ronald Youngblood

J. A. Ziesler
Jean Zumstein

PART I

Proclamation and Response[1]

C. K. Barrett

New Testament Christianity was a proclaimed faith. "Faith comes as a result of hearing, and hearing comes through the word of Christ" (Rom 10:17). It is this that makes it distinctive among the cults of antiquity, and, it may be added, of the modern world also. Not wholly distinctive, of course; Judaism also is a proclaimed faith, and its proclamation resembles that of primitive Christianity in that it relates the saving deeds of God. Its credo is in the form of a story. "A wandering Aramaean was my father . . ." (Deut 26:5-10). But Judaism is more than a proclamation; it is life lived in accordance with Torah, and as long as the Temple stood Torah included a sacrificial cultus which all those who took their religion seriously were called upon to practice. Even if they lived too far from the Holy Place themselves to take part in worship there they paid the temple tax and consoled themselves with the thought that they were part of a people that offered the appointed sacrifices in the appointed place. Christianity carried with it no such cultic obligation. In this respect there is a closer parallel in the gnostic proclamation as we see it in, for example, the Hermetic literature, where the preacher appeals to the earth-bound race of men to hear and believe the truth he proclaims and offers a way of rebirth that does not depend upon the ritual acts of the mysteries. Here however the proclamation is different in that it depicts in mythical terms a metaphysical account of the universe and of the meaning of human life. To emphasise in this way the uniqueness of New Testament Christianity as a proclaimed faith does not therefore mean to ignore the partial parallels that exist in the contemporary world; on the contrary, they must be kept in mind. All over the ancient world preachers were seeking to win converts to various religious and philosophical ways of life and, at least at first sight and first hearing, the Christian evangelists must have resembled them closely, and to some extent they will have been understood and responded to in similar terms.

This observation leads to another preliminary point. It is of the essence of the New Testament proclamation that it must be made; response is a secondary matter. Peter and John declare, "We cannot but speak the things that we have seen and heard" (Acts 4:20). That is (they are speaking to the Council), You may believe what we say, ignore it, or kill us for saying it; that does not concern us. We must say it. The theme is repeated throughout the New Testament: "Preach the word; be at it in season, out of season" (εὐκαίρως, ἀκαίρως; 2 Tim 4:2). To say this is not to say that the New Testament preachers were indifferent to the results of their work; it means that the proclamation has an objectivity which makes it independent of both preacher and repsonse, and that the response that occurs is not wholly dependent on either preacher or hearer.

First however we must consider the form and contents of the preaching. Only one book of the New Testament purports to tell us what the first Christians said when they set out to commend the Gospel, and it is well known that the narrative of Acts poses serious problems in this as in other respects. I shall consider it later. All the books of the New Testament are related, though not always directly, to the work of preaching; and many of them are earlier than Acts. Earliest of all are the Pauline epistles; and that Paul was a great evangelistic preacher stands beyond doubt. I have already quoted his conviction that faith comes by hearing; and out of the same context I draw attention to the often overlooked rhetorical question of Rom 10:14: "How are they to believe in one whom they have not heard?" In Christian preaching men not only hear about Christ; they hear Christ, who himself speaks when the word is faithfully preached. The preaching of the Gospel is itself part of the event that constitutes the Gospel. One might therefore expect Paul to give an account of the way he himself conducted the process that was obviously of such vital importance to him. He does not do this, though the letters do contain hints of great importance. There is, for example, the passage in Rom 10 to which I have already referred. This contains in v 9 the formulation, "If with your mouth you confess Jesus as Lord, and if with your heart you believe that God raised him from the dead, you will be saved." This is often regarded as a baptismal confession, and it may have been used for this purpose, but Paul describes it as "the word of faith which we preach"—that is, it summed up the content of his preaching. This is consistent with 1 Cor 2:2, "I resolved that in the midst of you I would know nothing but Jesus Christ, and him crucified," and with other passages such as Gal 3:1. The passage however in which Paul comes nearest to describing the way in which he preached to those who were not Christians or even Jews (1 Thess 1:9, 10) describes the result—no doubt the intended result—of his preaching in Thessalonica: "You turned to God from idols to serve a God who is living and true and to await his Son from heaven, whom he raised from the dead, Jesus, who rescues us from the coming wrath." Here we learn nothing about Christ crucified; Jesus' act of deliverance relates to the future, and as a sort of propaedeutic the Thessalonians have been taught to forsake idolatry for the true God—that is, the God of the Old Testament, the God of Judaism. How Paul persuaded them of this he does not tell us. Was it by an argument from natural theology? Was it by argument based on the Old Testament? Or did he combine the two, as Hellenistic Jews had done before him? This is a question to which I must return.

While Paul was at work, though he tells us nothing of it, the material that we read in the Synoptic Gospels was in oral circulation. In the use of this material various motives were at work, and the narratives and sayings of the gospels were used in ethical instruction, in debate, and in the administrative discipline of the churches. But some of them at least, probably many of them, were used in preaching, and all of them—with the single exception of material about John the Baptist[2]—are, or purport to be, accounts of things said or done by Jesus. This appears in summary form in Acts: "Jesus of Nazareth, a man approved of God unto you by mighty works and portents and signs which God did through him in the midst of you, as you yourselves know, this man, I say, who was handed over by the determinate foreknowledge and counsel of God, you nailed up and killed. God raised him up by loosing the pangs of death" (2:22, 23); ". . . Jesus of Nazareth, how God anointed him with the Holy Spirit and power, who went about doing good and healing all who were oppressed by the devil, for God was with him" (10:38). These summaries are expanded in detail in the gospels. It is probably correct to say that the gospels grew backwards from the stories of the crucifixion and resurrection. If this is so they reflect Paul's preaching of Christ crucified and risen, which, central as it is, requires elucidation; the reasonably intelligent reader will inevitably ask, But why did they crucify him? Was there not some good reason? If there was, and he deserved his fate, he is no savior. It was necessary therefore to narrate the debates of Jesus with the Jews and their growing antipathy to him. All this constituted a part, or a form, of preaching, for the public proclamation of the market place will often turn into dispute and argument, without which the preacher could not effectively make his point.

Dispute and argument fill up a good deal of the Fourth Gospel and to some extent play the same role as dispute and argument in the Synoptic Gospels. There is a difference, however, and one gains the impression of a church engaged in standing argument with its environment, so that it is harder to detach preaching material, or the evidence for preaching material. This would be true if we follow J. L. Martyn's attractive picture of the gospel as written on two levels, the *einmalig*, which hands on the old traditions about what Jesus did in his earthly life, and the contemporary, in which the evangelist relates these to the life of the church.[3] Preaching indeed is not far away; thus chapter 9, which on the *einmalig* level tells the story of the cure of a blind man and the subsequent dispute between Jesus and the Synagogue, on the contemporary level presupposes the conversion—the illumination—of a Jew and the troubles that he and the preacher run into through the objections of the local Jews. This presupposes rather than describes preaching and its results. And I do not myself think that it leads to an adequate account of John's aim and method. That which distinguishes him from the other evangelists is not that he set out to adapt the gospel tradition and gospel message to an environment different from those in which the Synoptists worked but rather that he absolutized the tradition and the message, setting them out in a form that was independent of particular environments and thus capable of being adapted to all.[4] The rest of the Johannine literature seems to take up an ambiguous attitude to preaching. "He that is unrighteous let him be unrighteous still, and he that is filthy let him be filthy still, and he that is righteous let him practise righteousness still, and he that is holy let him be holy still" (Rev 22:11) does not sound like a call to evangelism. It is true that the time is near (22:10), but this fact might well be a ground for added urgency. "We know that we are of God and the whole world lies in the evil one" (1 John 5:19) suggests a static situation, in which "we" know who and where we are, and have given up the rest of mankind to its fate. Those to whom the world listens are those of whom the author of 1 John disapproves because they have learned the world's language (1 John 4:5). The Fourth Gospel itself, however, is proof enough that it is possible to put the language of gnosticism to good use; perhaps we ought to say that the writers of the epistles had had unfortunate experiences with less successful "modernists". That which distinguishes the Fourth Evangelist is that he chooses to set out the gospel message in terms of the gospel story. Certainly it is his own treatment of the gospel story that he gives us and many factors have contributed to his book. But it contains a story of what Jesus did and said, and what happened to him. I pass no judgment here on the historical value of what John narrates; for the moment the important thing is that what he offers us has the form of a narrative.

With this we may return to Acts, of which preaching is an important part. I have already pointed out that Acts shares the interest, which appears most clearly in the Synoptic Gospels, in the story of Jesus of Nazareth. With the Synoptic Gospels and with Paul too it shares a concentration of interest upon the story of the cross and resurrection. In the early addresses to Jewish audiences the repeated refrain is, "Whom you crucified, whom God raised from the dead" (e.g. 4:10). This is true of the great speeches of Peter, and of Paul's address in the synagogue at Pisidian Antioch (13:16-41); it is not so true of the other speeches in Acts. For our purpose we may set aside Paul's speech in 20:18-35, since this is not public proclamation of the Gospel but an edifying charge to the Ephesian elders. One would be inclined to set aside also Paul's legal defence speeches given in Jewish and Roman courts in the concluding chapters were it not that these are models of evangelistic zeal; see especially 26:29. But Stephen's speech in chapter 7 and Paul's Areopagus address in chapter 17 differ markedly. What is most remarkable in Stephen's speech[5] is that it is only in the last sentence that it becomes specifically Christian. Before this point Stephen has given a summary of parts of Old Testament history, and though there are matters, especially in his description of Moses as a rejected but vindicated and returning redeemer, that cried aloud for Christological application, his main argument is that his people have consistently rejected the prophetic word of God in the interests of their own religious institutions. This, he adds at the end, they have continued to do in regard to Jesus. In this respect Stephen's speech before the Council resembles Paul's on the Areopagus;[6] here too Jesus is mentioned (and that not by name) only at the end. The main body of the speech uses the Epicurean attack on popular superstitious religion and the Stoic notions of the unity of the race and of its duty to seek after the omnipresent deity and to unite itself with his will; all this, however, or most of it, is expressed in the language of the Old Testament. And it is not easy to reconcile some of it with the thought of the epistles, especially of Rom 1. My own view of these two speeches is that they belong within the church's mission to the gentile world but not within Paul's wing of it. Both, I believe, represent the kind of propaganda used among the Gentiles by Hellenistic Jews—of whom, it seems, Stephen was one. They did not find it necessary to jettison all their old arguments; they introduced Jesus at the end. Luke sees in the earlier speech the cue for the church to move out of Judaism, in the latter the way in which a great evangelist approached the Gentiles.

The great interest of Stephen's speech and of Paul's Areopagus address[7] must not blind us to the fact that these are in a sense foreign bodies in New Testament proclamation. When this is surveyed as a whole, and in all its variety, two characteristics stand out. The first is its objectivity. Briefly or at length it concentrates on the facts of the story of Jesus, making especially the point of his crucifixion and resurrection. It does not, in general, appeal to human need and make offers of remedies for the human condition. It does indeed offer the forgiveness of sins, but this is an objective rather than a subjective matter. There is no address to a guilt-ridden conscience; the preachers in Acts and elsewhere are not represented as promising relief to the sufferers, to the anxious, and so forth. Of course, they are not simply historians or legend-mongers with an interesting tale to tell, and the second characteristic of their proclamation is that they set the objective facts about Jesus in an interpretative setting. Throughout the greater part of the New Testament this interpretative framework is eschatology. The events of the life, death, and resurrection of Jesus are regarded both as fulfilling divine promises, and thus as themselves "last things", and also as reaffirmations of the divine promises, and thus as pointing forward to "last things" still to come. They place the hearer in a unique situation, between unrepeatable divine acts of judgment and mercy and the final divine act of judgment and mercy which lies in the future. The acts of Jesus are given their meaning by this setting, and the hearer too, if he accepts the Christian message as true, finds the meaning of his own existence determined in this way. All of this requires something of a background in Judaism and the Old Testament, and is bound up with the affirmation that Jesus was the Jewish Messiah. It would not do for every audience; hence perhaps the use of Greek thought (mediated by Hellenistic Judaism) in Acts 17, the contact with gnosticism in John, and with popular Platonism in Hebrews. All of these are attempts to explain the facts about Jesus in terms of a prescribed setting. All of them acknowledge his place in the particularity of history, and at the same time claim for him universal significance.

This leads to the question, What kind of response is called for by these various ways of presenting Jesus? In the first place, the hearer is asked to accept certain alleged historical truths about a person called Jesus of Nazareth. The modern student of the New Testament is immediately aware of a problem here, for he too is presented in his New Testament with the same alleged facts, and his immediate reaction, if he has been trained in the methods of historical criticism, is not necessarily scepticism but at least suspense of judgment. He will not accept the alleged facts without investigating them by all the means that his critical faculty can suggest. In addition, he will bring to bear presuppositions of a non-historical kind; he may for example rule out *a priori* any kind of miracle, and thus from the beginning subtract a good deal from the claims of Acts 2:22, 23; 10:38. This reaction appears already in Acts 17:32. Here we must make a distinction. What was claimed in the early years in Galilee and Judaea was open to the test of living memory. There were those who could of their own knowledge test at least the question whether Jesus had during his lifetime been believed to work miracles. If it had been known that he had not died at the hands of his opponents, or if it had been known that there had been no talk about a messianic claim, the preaching of the cross must have failed. If any one had been able to prove, and had proved, that his body was still rotting in the grave the preaching of the resurrection could never have been repeated, at least, in the terms used in the New Testament. Outside Palestine the position was different. What means were open to Paul in Corinth, for example, to prove even that Christ was crucified, not to mention that he had been raised from the dead? Perhaps it mattered less than we think. We cannot suppose that historical criticism was diligently practised among the "not many wise" of Corinth; on the other hand, some of them may have been shrewd enough to grasp that no preacher would have told so repulsive a story as the crucifixion—to the Jews a stumbling-block, to the Greeks foolishness—if he had not been obliged by the facts to do so. The Christian will not have been slow to point out a pragmatic verification of the preacher's claims: somehow the message worked. "That is what you were, some of you; but you were washed, you were sanctified, you were justified, in the name of the Lord Jesus Christ and in the Spirit of our God" (1 Cor 6:11). The fornicators and idolaters were fornicators and idolaters no more. But at some stage there must have been a readiness to accept the preacher's word: there was a person called Jesus, and he had lived, died, and come to life again in an extraordinary way.

The last of these propositions called for another step. That a person called Jesus had lived was no problem; there was nothing unprecedented in the claim that he had worked miracles. And why should he not have been crucified? Judaea was a troublesome province, and Pilate was not the man to stand nonsense from the Jews.

Resurrection however was bound to raise the question of the interpretative framework. This would raise fewer problems in a Jewish environment than elsewhere. There was no difficulty in accepting the framework itself, only the difficulty of accepting the place of Jesus within it, and the distorting effect in a program for the future of supposing that part of what ought to belong to that future was now already in the past. If others, at Qumran for example, could believe that they were themselves part of eschatological history perhaps the Christians might be right. But how were listeners to be persuaded that the Christians were in fact right (with the consequence that the people of Qumran, and others, were wrong)? This, it seems, must have depended on what one made of the resurrection. If the story was true and Jesus was really alive, it must be because God had raised him from the dead, and this God would have done only if he had been right, certainly not if he had been making, or even tolerating on the lips of others, blasphemous claims. The positive response, then, will have been: Yes, Jesus was all you say; we are sorry for our share in responsibility for his death; we believe he is alive, and accept the consequence that God is beginning to fulfil his promises.

But what would all this mean in a Hellenistic city, such as Corinth or Ephesus? It would mean something. The odd beliefs and practices of Jews were not unknown; and prophecy of a kind was significant enough for Augustus to have more than two thousand prophetic books destroyed—they could disturb the populace and lead to revolt.[8] Some new frame of reference however was needed, and it was not hard to find. 1 Cor 16:22 (μαράνα θά) is enough to show that for the Semitic-speaking church Jesus was already Lord, and *mar* became κύριος, and κύριος was not an unfamiliar term in the world of religion. The κύριος was a supernatural being, and there were parallels even to the notion of suffering and death followed by a kind of resurrection. Parallels do not mean identity; but one must try to get into the skin of a man in the Corinthian street who heard Paul speaking of a crucified Lord who was now alive and offered a new life in a new fellowship, and with a new hope. What induced the Corinthian to abandon, let us say, the Lord Sarapis in favor of the Lord Jesus? This is a question with a theological aspect to which I shall return; it would be wrong however to overlook the fact that it has also a human aspect, and that human thoughts and motives (whatever may have been behind them) must have passed through human heads. Historical realism will have played a part. The Corinthian may not have questioned the historical truth of the Sarapis myth, but if it happened at all it happened a long time ago, when the world was young. But the story of Jesus belonged to his own world; the crucifixion happened only twenty years ago. There were (unless we are thinking of Stephanas, the firstfruits of Achaea—1 Cor 16:15) those who had already accepted the new faith and manifested the kind of change referred to in 1 Cor 6:9-11. There was the personality of Paul himself, who must have been one of the most formidable and most engaging of the preachers who swarmed through the Hellenistic world. And though one had never read the Old Testament one could believe that there were ancient books whose predictions were now being fulfilled. In any case, though Paul certainly did not require one to become a Jew he did presuppose the Jewish doctrine of the righteous God in whose eyes men were sinners; he would judge the world, and that soon; it would be well to receive forgiveness now and to begin to observe the moral laws. So one did. Out of the old world in which there were κύριοι πολλοί one came into the new, in which there was but one (1 Cor

8:5, 6); and from this one κύριος one accepted, in the company of his other servants, both protection and direction.

The rest is specialization, bound to arise as the preachers came into contact with fresh hearers, and as inquiring minds found themselves compelled to work out a theology corresponding to the proclaimed faith. I have mentioned gnosticism. The core of the Fourth Gospel is a statement in absolutely pure gnostic form: "This is eternal life, to know thee, the only true God, and Jesus Christ whom thou didst send" (John 17:3). One could substitute the name of any other gnostic revealer. Of course, the name makes all the difference, not only to the being of the one true God, but also to what knowing him implies, in trust, love, and obedience. But those who belonged to the world of developing gnosis will have known what John meant, and may, or may not, have abandoned other revealers for the one who claimed to be himself the way, the truth, and the life. I referred also to the popular Platonism of Hebrews; it was the simple idealist structure of apocalyptic that opened the way to this,[9] but it provided a way (which could be combined, as it was by Philo, with the Old Testament—"Moses endured as seeing him who is invisible", Heb 11:27) of understanding the meaning of faith, with which, focused upon the now unseen Christ, the Christian life both begins and is consummated (Heb 12:2).

So much for Christian preaching and the kind of response it might be expected to elicit. It is now time to begin at the other end and examine such direct evidence as we have about the response as it was in fact made. This means studying both the language and the narratives of response.

Our earliest evidence is that of the Pauline epistles, and we must return to some of the most important passages. There is 1 Thess 1:9, 10: "You turned to God from idols, to serve a God who is living and true and to await his Son from heaven, whom he raised from the dead, Jesus, who rescues us from the coming wrath." There is the "word of faith which we preach" in Rom 10:8, 9: "If with your mouth you confess Jesus as Lord, and if with your heart you believe that God raised him from the dead, you will be saved." There is the summary phrase, "obedience of faith" (Rom 1:5; 15:26). In 1 Cor 2:1-4 Paul describes his unvarnished preaching as made "that your faith might not depend on men's wisdom, but on God's power". It was the "hearing of faith" that led to the gift of the Spirit and the working of miracles in Galatia (Gal 3:2, 5). It is clear that for Paul the fundamental word is faith (πίστις). This characterizes not only the beginning of the Christian life but its whole content from beginning to end: "everything that is not of faith is sin" (Rom 14:23). As response it may be said to contain three elements:

(1) It means starting from the Christian conception, which is the Old Testament conception, of the one true God. If the potential converts are Jews, what is required of them is that they take their own ancestral belief seriously—as, of course, many of their ancestors did not, for the Old Testament is full of the records of those who believed in a God who would be satisfied by due performance of Temple rituals—a God who might as well be Baal. God is living and active; and is true—not only real (as opposed to idols who had no real existence as gods at all) but faithful, that is, one who keeps his word and executes his promises. This matter has a logical priority and Paul himself mentions it first in 1 Thess 1:9. Whether in fact it came first in Paul's preaching, and in the response of his hearers, is another question. I have already referred to his Areopagus speech in Acts 17. Is Luke correct in suggesting that Paul

approached the matter in the manner of Hellenistic Judaism, using as a praeparatio evangelica the convergence of Greek critical theology and Old Testament prophecy? There is little in his epistles (except 1 Thess 1:9) to suggest that he did so, and in Rom 1 a good deal to suggest that he saw the claims of natural theology in a different light. Did he adopt the alternative method of beginning (not finishing, as in Acts 17:31) with Jesus, and moving from him to his doctrine of God? Did he follow sometimes the one, sometimes the other method? On the whole, and especially in view of 1 Cor 2:1-5, it seems likely that he did not begin with philosophical argument, and that we must ascribe Acts 17 to a different line of evangelistic preaching, other than Paul's; he may however have used, and to some extent hellenized, the Old Testament material that lies under the surface in Acts 17:24-26.

(2) Faith means accepting Jesus as κύριος. It seems clear from 1 Cor 8:5, 6 that Paul used this word, not as is often asserted as the LXX's rendering of the tetragrammaton, but in the context of Hellenistic religion. There are (in popular estimation) many gods (θεοί) and many lords (κύριοι) but for us there is only one God and one Lord. About the one God enough has been said; the one Lord is Jesus Christ. The κύριοι of Hellenistic religions were saviors, protectors, perhaps revealers, and masters (the correlate of κύριος is δοῦλος). For Paul, Jesus was all of these, and confessing him as Lord meant to accept him in all these capacities, and to do so publicly. For the meaning of his saving work we may turn to the traditional formula quoted by Paul at 1 Cor 15:3, "Christ died for our sins according to the Scriptures." It was Christ crucified that Paul preached at Corinth (1 Cor 2:2), Christ crucified who was placarded before the eyes of the Galatians (Gal 3:1).

(3) Faith also includes believing that God raised him from the dead; thus the concept of Jesus Christ was integrated with the concept of God. It is precisely because they belong together in this way that Paul could have approached the doctrine of God by way of the proclamation of Jesus. On the one hand, Jesus was not a divine rebel, a Prometheus-like figure, who brought man salvation against the will of a reluctant and opposed supreme deity. There was no division; it was the action of the Father that caused the dead Crucified to become the living and ever-present Crucified. On the other hand, Paul here takes up the eschatological framework of interpretation. The resurrection had begun, following upon the period of suffering. God had anticipated his final act of renewing his creation. This was unexpected. For one person he had done what it had been expected that he would do at the last day; and he had done it (as Paul went on to teach) that others might in Christ enter into the process, dying with Christ to sin that with him they might walk in newness of life (Rom 6:4). Paul's understanding of the interpretative eschatological framework made possible the understanding of Christian life in terms of personal renewal, which made it formally comparable with the mysteries, but consisting not only, not so much in the conferment of immortality as in moral conversion. All this was on offer; the question was whether the hearer was prepared to respond, Jesus is Lord. If he did, he would be saved (Rom 10:9), salvation being understood in the terms described.

Acts reflects the Pauline language. In Athens (Acts 17:18) Paul preached Jesus and the resurrection, which recalls Rom 10:9. To the Philippian jailer he says (Acts 16:31), "Believe on the Lord Jesus, and thou shalt be saved." I say that this is Pauline language; it probably was, as it has always remained, common Christian language, and no doubt not every reader of Acts put into the word faith the radical content Paul gave it. It appears however on the lips of Peter (especially 15:7, 9, referring back to the story of Cornelius); Christians are referred to as those who believe. With this, and again calling to mind the Pauline language quoted above, we may put Luke's description of those who received the word (e.g. 2:41); they not only heard it but accepted it as true and acted upon it. Acts uses one word, repentance, which occurs only seldom in Paul. Peter, asked on the day of Pentecost by his hearers what they should do, answers, "Repent" (2:38), and the word is frequently repeated. Except where there seems to be a special reference to repenting of the sin of crucifying the Messiah this word includes most of the first two elements in the Pauline understanding of response. It is repentance towards God (20:21), and is immediately coupled with faith in the Lord Jesus Christ. Repentance emphasizes turning from false gods to the true one, but already includes a more than academic belief in him.

The language of response leads to the narrative of response; for this we are mainly dependent on Acts, though most of what is described in Acts finds nearer or more remote parallels in the epistles. I have just quoted "Repent" from Peter's Pentecost speech (Acts 2:38); it is followed immediately by "Let each of you be baptized". Here at least (see 2:41) it is taken for granted that those who hear the word in faith will, as their first Christian action, get themselves baptized. It is often assumed that baptism was universally practiced in the early church and that all believers were baptized. This is perhaps not quite so certain as appears at first sight. In chapter 2 of Acts Peter requires baptism; in chapter 3 in a similar speech he does not mention it, and from this point in Acts onward it appears only here and there. Notwithstanding the enormous expansion of the church in chapters 4, 5, 6, 7 it is not mentioned. It returns in chapters 8, 9, 10, but in the First Missionary Journey (chapters 13, 14) it drops out again. There are baptisms in chapter 16, none in chapter 17 (in Thessalonica, Beroea, Athens), a number in chapter 18 (Corinth). After this there is only the curious fact that Apollos (who knew only the baptism of John) was, apparently, not baptized, wheareas the (about) twelve in Ephesus (who knew only the baptism of John) were baptized.[10] It seems that some of Luke's sources took the view that all must be baptized on conversion, but that others were, at least, less interested. It is probable that most members of the Pauline churches were baptized, but here too the evidence is not unambiguous. 1 Cor 1:14-17 is a relative depreciation of the importance of baptism, and the difficult verse 15:29 is best explained by the suggestion that some members of the church in Corinth died before baptism, which others then received in their place. The dead were penitent believers, and baptism on their behalf was not an attempt to make dead heathen Christian by magical means, but a powerful representation of the resurrection, in which they would doubtless in any case share. But Rom 6 alone is sufficient to show that Paul could argue from the assumption that baptism was a universal Christian practice. What did it mean? Such a believing and obedient closeness to Christ meant that one shared his death and looked forward to sharing his resurrection. Whether or not Paul was the first Christian to associate baptism with death and resurrection it was characteristic of him to do so, and the association belongs intimately with the eschatological interpretative framework of the work of Jesus. The believer, though still living in this age, passed in union with Christ through the messianic affliction and into the resurrection life. Baptism into the name of Christ meant becoming his property, his slave, and thus manifested and expressed the believing obedience which constituted response to the Gospel.

To the acted response of baptism must be added that the believers continued in the apostles' teaching and the (Christian) fellowship, in the breaking of bread and the prayers (Acts 2:42). All that can be said here about the important details in this verse is that together the four imply one, the church, and that responding to the Gospel, though in one sense entirely personal and individual, meant at the same time joining a community. This is as clear in the Pauline epistles as it is in Acts. Even the letter commonly described as addressed to an individual—Philemon—is in fact addressed to a church: "Paul, prisoner of Christ Jesus, and Timothy our brother, to Philemon, our dear friend and fellow worker, and to Apphia our sister, and to Archippus our fellow soldier, and to the church at your house" (Phlm 1). It is at this point that all those social and religious parallels that I have alluded to should be dealt with in detail, for the community of Christians took shape as other communities did and under the same principles of sociological development, except that they were always (but especially by Paul) exposed to a theological criticism which inverted the will to power, and the readiness to use any means to obtain power, which characterize human society.[11] Not that the Christian groups were faultless; they were not, and in the first century as now the potential convert, the man attracted by the truth he had begun to perceive in Jesus, might well have found himself repelled as much as attracted by the company he was called upon to keep. If one had only to describe reformed adulterers and thieves (1 Cor 6:9-11) all would be well—very well; but one had also to reckon with a church that could pride itself upon a case of incest (1 Cor 5:1, 2), with greedy gluttons who got drunk at what should have been the Lord's Supper (1 Cor 11:21), with preachers who preached with the intention of making Paul's sufferings in prison yet more bitter (Phil 1:17). Local churches were divided, and the whole church was divided; Paul saw it threatened by those whom he felt obliged to describe as false apostles, deceitful workers, servants of Satan (2 Cor 11:13, 14). They probably used the same language of him.[12] But there was no getting away from the church, for it was God's intention to have a people, and if it was nothing else it was a school for character. Wherever, and under whatever perverse forms, it existed, it lived, or professed to live, under the authority of Jesus and therefore could never wholly forget what he had said about discipleship and leadership.[13]

It is right here to mention that response to the Gospel, and especially admission to the people of God, evoked the sharpest controversy in the first-century church. "Certain people came down from Judaea and began to teach the brothers, 'Unless you are circumcised in accordance with the custom of Moses you cannot be saved'" (Acts 15:1). The Pauline epistles prove that these persons were not overcome at a blow but continued to propagate their opinion and by doing so to break up the Pauline churches. Their attitude did not affect the response of Jewish hearers of the Gospel who were already circumcised and were called upon only to render trust and obedience to Jesus as the Christ—whether thereafter they continued to observe Torah or not was not a matter of initial response to the preaching; but it did affect the response of Gentiles, for if Paul's opponents were right, Gentile response to the Gospel must begin with or at least include circumcision and the taking up of life under the Torah. We stand here on the verge of historical and theological problems which cannot be discussed in this place. I mention them, however, because they will enable me to bring this paper to a close.

The hearer of the message accepts it, receives the word that he has heard. He repents, he puts his trust in Christ and accepts him as the redeeming and authoritative Lord. Probably he is baptized, and by this rite of initiation becomes a member of the people of God. But what is the people of God? We read the Old Testament, and it appears to be virtually identical, notwithstanding apostasy, with the racially determined people of Israel. We read the New Testament, and it appears to be constituted by those, of whatever racial origin, who have accepted the Gospel; unbelieving Jews remain outside. How are the two "peoples" related to each other, and what—if now anything—is the position of the Jews? This was in the New Testament church, and remains today, a most practical question. The decision—a decision to receive or not to receive—asked of the hearer is also a practical question, as all decisions are. But these two practical questions both point in the direction of a theological question. Reduced to simple matter-of-fact terms the question is twofold. (1) If God called Israel to be his servant and made promises to the family of Abraham, what becomes of these promises now? Has the word of God failed? Has he revoked his election of the Hebrew people? (2) Does it lie within the power of man, whether Jew or Gentile, to say Yes or No to God? Granted that it may seem to a man that he is making his own decision, how does he come to make it and what is God's part, if any, in the process? Does God still act in terms of his own election? It is inevitable that such questions should be set in the context—indeed, in the words—of Rom 9-11, though there are other passages that must also be borne in mind.

In the light of 1 Cor 1:18 and 2 Cor 2:15 ("those who are perishing") it is impossible to maintain that Paul was in any simple sense a universalist. What then are we to make of Rom 11:25 ("the full number of the Gentiles"), 26 ("all Israel will be saved"), 32 (". . . that he may deal with all men in mercy")? First, it is important to note the "almost intolerable eschatological tension"[14] of the context, especially of the second *now* in v 31 (". . . that they too may now receive God's mercy"). Paul is not writing of a long-extended friction between church and synagogue but believes that God's purposes will reach their fulfilment soon, probably in his own lifetime. This means that if God is to act he must act catastrophically. There will not be time for a long period of persuasion in which one Gentile after another, one Jew after another, is persuaded to accept the Christian message. Secondly, the future is set in the context of a positive activity on God's part. "Out of Zion shall come a deliverer, and he shall remove from Jacob all his impieties; and this is the covenant I will make with them, when I take away their sins" (Rom 11:26, 27; a composite quotation, for which see Isa 59:20; 27:9; Ps 14:7; Jer 31:33). From this one will infer that when in the next verse (11:28) Paul writes of Israel that "in terms of the Gospel they are enemies on your account, but in terms of the election they are beloved on account of the fathers" he does not mean by "on account of the fathers" that all that is necessary for salvation is to have Abraham, Isaac, and Jacob among one's ancestors. He means that the offer of delivering love is assured to Israel, that the promise and election are on God's side sure; he does not change his mind (11:29). His offer of mercy is made to all (11:32), and he will deal with men in no other way—he will not trade favor for works. But what if man insists on some other way?

The mercy of God is antecedent to man's salvation and is antecedent also to his response to the Gospel; and it is put into effect by the work of the Holy Spirit. This is apparent in Paul's references to preaching and to conversion. "My argument and my proclamation were not enforced by persuasive words of wisdom but by a manifestation of Spirit and power" (1 Cor 2:4). "Our Gospel did not come to you in word only but in power and in the Holy Spirit and in much assurance" (1 Thess 1:5). The same thought is expressed in various ways in Acts. The conversion of Saul is evidently due not to his initiative but to God's (9:4). The gift of the Spirit to Cornelius anticipates even the end of Peter's speech (10:44). At Pisidian Antioch it was those who were appointed to eternal life who believed (13:48). At Philippi the Lord opened Lydia's heart to attend to what Paul was saying (16:14). That there is a predestinarian element in New Testament theology seems unquestionable; that it is possible to misunderstand this element with a mechanical rigidity that perverts its meaning is also true. Its true meaning is expressed in the fact that the preaching of the Gospel is part of the Gospel, part of the objective facticity of which the Gospel consists.[15] "I am not ashamed of the Gospel, since it is the operation of God's power working towards salvation, effective for everyone who has faith . . . for in it (the Gospel) God's righteousness is revealed" (Rom 1:16, 17). In the Gospel the voice of Christ himself is heard (Rom 10:14), and it is this that creates its contact with the hearer.

Notes

1. An earlier form of this paper was given to the Methodist pastors of Scandanavia at their meeting in Trondheim in August 1985. I do not think that Earle Ellis will object to a paper which attempts to make some practical use of New Testament study.

2. Perhaps we should add the account of Peter's denial.

3. J. L. Martyn, *History and Theology in the Fourth Gospel,* New York and Evanston, 1968.

4. C. K. Barrett, *Essays on John,* London, 1982, 131.

5. I have written about this speech in the Festschrift for H. Greeven: *Studien zum Text und zur Ethik des Neuen Testaments, Festschrift zum 80. Geburtstag von H. Greeven,* ed. W. Schrage, Berlin, 1986, 57-69.

6. *New Testament Christianity for Africa and the World: Essays in Honour of Harry Sawyerr,* ed. M. E. Glasswell and E. W. Fasholé-Luke, London, 1974, 69-77.

7. With which 1 Thess 1:9, 10 should be compared.

8. Suetonius, *Augustus,* 31.

9. *The Background of the New Testament and its Eschatology: Studies in Honour of C. H. Dodd,* ed. W. D. Davies and D. Daube, Cambridge, 1956, 363-393.

10. *The New Testament Age: Essays in Honor of Bo Reicke,* ed. W. C. Weinrich; Macon, 1984, 29-39.

11. C. K. Barrett, *Church, Ministry, and Sacraments in the New Testament,* Exeter, 1985, 38-40.

12. *Mélanges Bibliques en hommage au R. P. Béda Rigaux,* ed. A. Descamps and A. de Halleux, Gembloux, 1970, 377-396.

13. Similar remarks could be made with reference to other parts of the New Testament. Thus the reader of the gnostic formula of John 17:3 discovers at the end of the chapter (17:26) that the distinguishing mark of the quasi-gnostic Johannine church is after all not gnosis but love.

14. K. Barth, *The Epistle to the Romans,* E.T. by E. C. Hoskyns, Oxford, 1933, 417.

15. See above pp. 3, 4, 6.

Example and Precept:
From Sirach to R. Ishmael

David Daube[1]

I have repeatedly commented on the adoption by other sects of the Sadducean postulate that a rule, to be fully binding, must have its basis in a Scriptural precept and that a mere example, set by however high an authority, will not do.[2] The Zadokite Fragments,[3] combating polygamy and probably also divorce, adduce three verses from the Pentateuch: "Male and female created he them", at the time understood to describe the ideal, androgynous *Ur*-Adam;[4] "The beasts, clean and unclean, went in two and two";[5] and "The king shall not multiply wives to himself".[6] The first two offer examples. The third, a precept, is really not a good text for general consumption; it is appended, *faute de mieux,* in response to the new demand. Similarly, both Matthew[7] and Mark,[8] in the controversy about divorce, begin with "Male and female created he them" and then add "And the twain shall be one flesh".[9] No doubt in this case, too, the example once stood by itself but time came when it was found inadequate in the debate with opponents. Whereas in this instance the critical moment antedates the two gospels, in the Sabbath dispute caused by the disciples plucking corn it lies between them. Mark,[10] followed by Luke,[11] is content with the example of David and his band who, as they were hungry, ate the priests' shewbread.[12] Matthew[13] supplements this defence by what the fault-finders ought to "have read in the Law", namely, the Book of Numbers:[14] the Temple service overrides the Sabbath restrictions. Since the task in hand is even weightier, that precept applies all the more.

The matter is, of course, more complicated. To single out just two points—to a present-day expert, quite often what is looked on as a precept by ancient exegetes does not appear to be that at all. Of this, "the twain shall be one flesh" is an illustration, not, to a historian, a commandment in the ordinary sense.[15] Again, in general, ancient exegetes—in this much like modern ones—conceive of a precept as covering, beyond its literal scope, a great deal that careful study, they hold, will reveal as implied. The extension of the law in Numbers to Jesus' ministry is a specimen of this approach. However, I do not propose to follow up these and similar questions. What I want to draw attention to here is that the successive stages example and precept are preserved for the approval of medicine.

The condemnation in 2 Chronicles[16] of Asa who, in his last illness, "consulted not the Lord but with the physicians", shows the writer—fourth century B.C.—to be a 'Jewish Scientist'. He would have been displeased even had the king recovered: just before this final scene he has a seer censure the king for calling on an ally when his country was invaded instead of trusting solely in God, and this though the war was won. Substantial remnants of a rigorist attitude are noticeable around A.D. 300, when a Talmudic sage contends that, both before and after a blood-letting, the patient should invoke God alone as healer; the doctor contributes nothing, one turns to him from habit only.[17] In between Chronicles and this warning, we can trace the argumentation of the liberals who, not surprisingly, prevailed.

Sirach[18]—early second century B.C.—strenuously advises recourse to the physician and his prescriptions, supplying, indeed, an elaborate theological framework. It is God who endows the physician with his insights and God who calls forth beneficent plants and elements. Accordingly, the medical art is pursued for God's glory and the perpetuation and well-being of his world. Nor may the sick neglect prayer, sacrifice and renunciation of sin. More than that, the doctor himself must pray for diagnosis and treatment to succeed. The part of specific interest in this context is where 'Jewish Science' is directly attacked and refuted. The line opening with God's creation of remedies from the earth goes on, "and let not a discerning man reject them", against the kind of doctrine found in Chronicles. (I am not claiming that it is an allusion to that work; it may be but need not.) There follows the evidence for this stand: "Was not the water made sweet by the wood, that he might make known to all men his power?"—a reference, as is well-known, to a miracle soon after the crossing of the Red Sea.[19] The people journeyed three days before coming upon a pool, and then the water was "bitter", undrinkable. God, however, showed Moses a wood to throw into it and the water turned "sweet". The forceful, proud style Sirach employs, a rhetorical question, "Was not the water made sweet?", underlines the confidence he puts in the quote.

It does furnish strong support—so long as example is good enough. God, though he could have changed the nature of the water in a trice, had it done through a human agent and, besides, with the aid of a curative shrub.[20] Let us note that, while the patient could have behaved better, the doctor prayed and his intervention very much redounded to the honor of his Master. That, strictly speaking, the object in need of improvement was not a person but water is immaterial. Its quality had a vital impact on persons; and we should bear in mind that on several occasions the restoration of unwholesome water figures as a "healing".[21] Actually, ancient interpreters would be particularly inclined to treat this episode as illuminating the subject of medicine since, immediately afterwards, God vowed, if the people proved obedient, to bring on them none of the diseases he brought on their oppressors, ending up with, "I am the Lord your healer". For Sirach, the whole forms one coherent scheme with, above all, God the ultimate ruler delegating some saving work to men pious and wise and using such means as he puts at their disposal.

Whether he is the first to think of appealing to this precedent I leave open. There seems to be no comparable exposition which might help to decide anywhere in his treatise. And what conclusions, if any, may be drawn from this very uniqueness I am not sure. Anyhow, we do know that it is the School of R. Ishmael which, about the middle of the second century A.D., manages to discover a precept sanctioning the doctor's services.[22] Above I mentioned a scholar of around A.D. 300 who despises them. A more down-to-earth colleague, in tune with the need of ordinary mortals, cites that School's exegesis of a statute in Exodus[23] according to which, if you injure a man, you must, among other things, "get him healed". Already the LXX speaks of payment for physician or remedies, and naturally, this is how all Rabbis understand it.[24] Here, then, the School of R. Ishmael infers, authority is conferred on the profession by—to use Matthean language—"what we read in the Law". It may be asked how, once this verse was given publicity, 'Jewish Science' could go on. A proper answer would lead too far afield. It must suffice to name a simple counter-argument the idealists might resort to: the provision in Exodus is a concession of which the truly faithful will not avail himself. In passing—though I have enormous respect for ancient medicine, I suppose the proportion of cases it could successfully treat was lower than nowadays. Hence, statistically, avoidance of treatment was less perilous.

Genesis Rabba,[25] expanding on the completion by God of all the hosts of heaven and earth, adduces the section of Sirach under discussion but, strikingly, omits anything indicative of doubts about the physician's office. All we hear is: "Ben-Sira says, God called forth medicines from the earth. With them the healer heals the infliction and the druggist prepares the drug". The exhortation not to refuse this help and its justification from the miracle in the desert are cut out; neither is there any hint at precept. Presumably, in the world of whoever is responsible for the version before us acceptance of medicine may be taken for granted.

A few observations by way of appendix. *Duo cum faciunt idem non est idem.* When the Sadducees confined sacrosanctity to precept, they did so in order to preserve elbow-room. Even in handling precept, they knew how to cope by means of bold interpretation; that they were literalists is a myth. (An old *a fortiori* of theirs, for example, extends an owner's liability for damage done by his animal—decreed in the Bible—to damage done by his slave[26].) It is a far cry to the Pharisaic enterprise, initiated in earnest by Hillel, of tying every must and must-not to a Pentateuchic ordinance no matter by how strained a reasoning process. One aim was indeed to render the many traditional regulations of the sect defensible against attack by the rival: they would turn out possessed of that Scriptural legitimacy which, in the eyes of the Sadducees, was a condition of bindingness. But there was another, more general motive: by contrast with the Sadducees, the Pharisees wished for certainty, steadiness, rather than elbow-room, and the solid, thorough underpinning of the entire system greatly contributed to this end. Significantly, a day in January 100 B.C., when a Sadducean Sanhedrin unable to reach decisions was replaced by a Pharisaic one, became a festival in the Pharisaic calendar.[27] Patricians wanting freedom and plebeians security is a pretty frequent phenomenon.

Here a word about Eliezer ben Hyrcanus, the maverick disciple of Johanan ben Zaccai, may be in order.[28] He, a wealthy aristocrat, deplored exclusive reliance on statutes and what might be derived from them, and equally the deadly cutting off of disagreements by a vote; and he favored some revival of the once-all-powerful respect for opinions coming down from the great masters. But he was defeated. The Talmud[29] tells of a session when he dissented from his confreres. He requested Heaven for one miracle after another to back him up and they all were vouchsafed him. A stream, for example, flowed backwards. Finally a Heavenly Voice sided with him in so many words. His opponents nonetheless carried the day. The Law itself, it was pointed out to him, professed that "it is not in heaven".[30] Any who wonder how a deeply religious culture could deny regulative force even to examples held out by the Lord—his androgynous Adam, his healing through humans and plants—may find some building bricks at least for an explanation in this legend.

It is scarcely accidental that a somewhat related development—somewhat related despite enormous differences both all round and in detail—takes place in the Rome of the New Testament period. Peter Stein[31] recently solved the age-old puzzle concerning the respective characteristics of the two law schools of the Principate: the

Sabinians were conservative, relying on experience, averse to too rigid a framework, the Proculians innovative, envisioning a scientific, consistent set of rules. It is the founder of the latter faction, Labeo, who proclaimed *ratio* to be a source of law and assigned a special role to *regula*.[32] Incidentally, we might class him as yet another underdog valuing security: he remained a Republican under Augustus. Years ago, I examined[33] an unsuccessful attempt of the Sabinians to get barter recognized as sale; more precisely, to get an agreement to give an object for an object put on the same level with one to give an object for money. In the course of the struggle, Sabinus made use of lines from the Iliad which—as he understood them—show "the long-haired Achaeans procuring wine, some for money, some for iron, some for hides, some for cattle, some for slaves": no distinction here between payment by means of coin and payment by means of goods like iron or a hide.[34] At the time, I took the view that this reference was probably little more than an elegant adjunct to the jurist's substantial argumentation. By now I suspect that, in his camp, the wisdom of the famous bard and the example of those Greek heroes still commanded a degree of serious consideration.

Notes

1. The invitation to this Festschrift reached me late, so my paper is somewhat sketchy. But I am too eager to participate to hold it back.

2. See D. Daube, *The New Testament and Rabbinic Judaism*, London, 1958, repr., New York, 1973, 67-89; "Responsibilities of Master and Disciples," *NTS* 19 (1972), 4-7; "Das Alte Testament im Neuen—aus jüdischer Sicht," translation by W. Schuller of an as yet unpublished lecture, "The Old Testament in the New: a Jewish Perspective," *Xenia*, 10 (1984), 10, 11; "Zukunftsmusik: Some Desirable Lines of Exploration in the New Testament Field," *Bulletin of the John Rylands Library of Manchester*, 68, No. 1 (1985-86), 56, 57; "Temple Tax," in the forthcoming Festschrift for W. R. Farmer; and "Two Jewish Prayers," to appear shortly.

3. *Fragments of a Zadokite Work* 7.1-4 in *Apocrypha and Pseudepigrapha of the Old Testament*, ed. by R. H. Charles, 1913, 2.810.

4. Gen 1:27; 5:2; Genesis Rabba on 1:26, 27; Mekhilta on Exod 12:40; Philo, *Creation* 24.76; *Allegorical Interpretation* 2.4.13; *Who is the Heir* 33.164.

5. Gen 7:9.

6. Deut 17:17.

7. Matt 19:3-9.

8. Mark 10:2-9.

9. Gen 2:24.

10. Mark 2:23-28.

11. Luke 6:1-5.

12. 1 Sam 21:3-6.

13. Matt 12:1-8.

14. Num 28:9-10.

15. In some cases, such as that of "Be fruitful and multiply", even moderns are tempted to assume a commandment where, originally, there is none. These words began as a sheer blessing. See my *The Duty of Procreation*, Edinburgh, 1977, 2-4.

16. 2 Chron 16:12.

17. Babylonian Berakoth 60a.

18. Sir 38:1-15. It has been suggested that his extraordinary enthusiasm for the work of physicians owes something to his acquaintance with Egyptian views. See J. T. Sanders, *Ben Sira and Demotic Wisdom*, Chico, CA., 1983, 75.

19. Exod 15:25. See e.g. G. H. Box and W. O. E. Oesterley, "Sirach," in Charles, *Apocrypha and Pseudepigrapha, 1.449*.

20. Reminds me of a joke that was current among young students (the less earnest sort) at East-European Jewish seminaries. The Rebbe tells the story of the saintly man who, in the course of a persecution, is thrown into a dungeon together with a newborn. By heaven's grace, overnight he grows female breasts so he can nurse the child. One of the pupils asks why God did not simply send milk. "Fool", replies the Rebbe, "should God waste good milk when he can make the man provide it?"

21. 2 Kings 2:21, 22; Ezek 47:8, 9, 11.

22. Babylonian Berakoth 60a; Baba Qamma 85a.

23. Exod 21:19 adduced in Bab. Ber. 60a, B.Q.85a.

24. See my "Zur frühtalmudischen Rechtspraxis," *ZAW* 9 (1932), 154.

25. Genesis Rabba 10.6 on Gen 2:1. The passage resurfaces in Yalqut Job 7.901.

26. Exod 21:35, 36; Mishnah Yadaim 4.7; see my "Texts and Interpretation in Roman and Jewish Law," *Jewish Journal of Sociology*, 8 (1961), 12.

27. Megillath Taanith; see my article cited in the preceding footnote.

28. See W. Bacher, *Die Agada der Tannaiten*, Strassburg, 2nd ed., 1903, 1.96-155, and Y. D. Gilat, "Eliezer ben Hyrcanus," in *Encyclopedia Judaica*, New York, 1971, vol 6, cols. 619-21. By the way, a clause in his death-bed counsel (Babylonian Berakoth 28b) is understood in so many different ways that one more conjecture cannot do much harm. Just conceivably, it is directed against the new fashion in education, with the emphasis on rational deduction and systematization—*hagha*

and its derivatives can signify this—and recommends, instead, the good, old method of learning by close attachment to teachers, by reverently taking in what they say and do.

29. Babylonian Ba Metia 59a-b.

30. Deut 30:12.

31. See P. Stein, "The Two Schools of Jurists in the Early Roman Principate," *Cambridge Law Journal*, 31 (1972), 8-31, and "Sabino Contro Labeone," *Bullettino dell'Istituto di Diritto Romano*, 19, 3rd ser. (1977), 55-67.

32. Both notions are taken over by the second-century anti-Roman sage Simeon ben Johai; see my "Jewish Law in the Hellenistic World," *Jewish Law Annual*, Suppl. 2 (1980), 58-60. From a text adverted to on p. 55 of this article—Digest 4.8.19.2, Paul XIII ad edictum—it appears that Sabinus' penchant for elbow-room could go too far even for his successor Cassius. (Ironically, the former was an exception among the leading jurists of his time in not belonging to the senatorial nobility. Still, he did come from a prominent Veronese family. See W. Kunkel, *Herkunft und Soziale Stellung der Römischen Juristen*, Weimar, 1952, 119, 120, 272- 289, 341-344; *Roman Legal and Constitutional History*, transl. by J. M. Kelly, Oxford, 1966, 107.)

33. See "The Three Quotations from Homer in Digest 18.1.1.1," *Cambridge Law Journal*, 10 (1949) 213-215.

34. Digest 18.1.1.1, Paul XXXIII ad edictum; Iliad 7.471-74.

Three Ways of Understanding Relations between the Testaments: Historically and Today

Richard N. Longenecker

Understanding relations between the Old Testament (the Jewish Scriptures) and the New Testament (the Christian canonical writings) has always been of great importance in Christian hermeneutics. Any discussion of Gospel and Law, for example, rests heavily on how one views the relation of the testaments, as does also every analysis of how the New Testament writers use the Old. In fact, one's understanding of relations between the testaments—whether articulated or not; assumed or consciously explicated—determines in large measure what kind of Christian theology one espouses, what kind of Christian gospel one proclaims, and what kind of Christian lifestyle one practices.

Often we hear of the differences between Marcionism and catholic Christianity; in certain quarters, of the polarities between Reformed and Dispensational theologies. In actuality, however, the discussion as to the relation of the testaments has historically been tripartite (i.e., related to or executed by three parties), not simply bipartite—with a similar tripartite discussion continuing in full vigor today. In what follows, I would like to sketch out in rather broad strokes the major lines in the discussion, dealing first historically with the three main streams of thought in the early Church (Marcionite, Alexandrian, Antiochean) and then indicating how and where similar features corresponding to those three basic approaches continue today.

Marcion

Marcion of Sinope (a village of Pontus in northeastern Asia Minor, along the southern shore of the Black Sea) was in second- and third-century Christendom "like a figure standing just off-stage but casting his shadow over every player on it."[1] While we know of him mainly through Irenaeus' *Adversus Haereses* (against both Gnostics and Marcion) and the third edition of Tertullian's *Adversus Marcionem* (the third edition of A.D. 208 being the only extant edition; the first probably appeared in A.D. 198 without Book 5)—together, of course, with passing references to him by such diverse writers as Origen, Cyril of Jerusalem, and Pelagius—Marcion's influence on the Christianity of second-century Asia Minor seems to have been immense and his impact on the theology of most Christian writers elsewhere in the empire is evident at almost every point in their works.

Claiming fidelity to Paul, Marcion laid stress on Paul's critique of the Mosaic law and concluded (1) that the revelation that came in Jesus Christ is opposed to the teaching of the Jewish Scriptures, (2) that the God of the New Testament is entirely other than the God of Judaism, and (3) that therefore Christians must repudiate everything associated with the Jewish law and everyone "too close kindred with Judaism,"[2] including even the Jerusalem apostles. Sometime around A.D. 140 Marcion compiled a truncated version of the New Testament that contained only ten letters of Paul (minus the Pastorals, and, of course, Hebrews) and the Gospel according to Luke—all with omissions and alterations to suit his understanding of Christianity. At the head of his *Apostolikon* ("Apostolic Writings") stood Galatians, which Marcion saw as the interpretive key to the Christian religion vis-à-vis Judaism and the Mosaic law.

As Marcion understood it, Galatians was directed against Judaism and everything Jewish. It declares the abolition of the Jewish law and repudiates the Creator God of the Jewish Scriptures. Thus as Marcion read Galatians, he saw, for example, 1:6-9 as settting up a sharp contrast between Paul's preaching and the tenets of Judaism, with the angel from heaven of 1:8 who preached another gospel being a messenger of this Jewish Creator God, whom Paul opposed. He interpreted the Hagar-Sarah allegory of 4:21-31 as representing two distinctly different "revelations" (not "testaments"), the former being the Jewish religion that Paul directs his converts to cast out. And he insisted that Paul's words of 6:14—that through the cross of Christ "the world has been crucified to me and I to the world"—have reference to the renunciation of the Jewish God and the Jewish law.[3] Nor did the Jerusalem apostles fare any better with Marcion, for they, as he saw it, proclaimed an entirely different gospel, which is why Paul says in 2:11-21 that he censured Peter at Antioch for not walking uprightly according to the truth of the Christian gospel.[4]

Marcion's radical separation of the gospel from the Jewish Scriptures and the Mosaic law, which Tertullian labels "his special and principal work,"[5] struck at the very roots of the fundamental Christian conviction as to the continuity of God's revelation in Jesus of Nazareth with God's earlier revelations and actions as recorded in the Jewish Scriptures. It was, therefore, of vital concern to the Church at large, and Christian writers of Marcion's day and following often took great pains to deny any such separation and to affirm the positive features of Paul's attitude toward the law.

Early Responses to Marcion

Irenaeus (A.D. 130–200) and Tertullian (A.D. 160–after 220) wrote refutations of Marcion's position. Neither of them, of course, was from Alexandria, but they laid the foundations for an approach to the Scriptures that would be carried further by the Alexandrian Fathers, particularly Origen. Irenaeus was from the Roman province of Asia (in the area of Asia Minor) and had been instructed as a youth by Polycarp of Smyrna. Most of his adult ministry, however, was carried on in Gaul, where in A.D. 178 he became Bishop of Lyons. Tertullian was born in Carthage, the city-state port on the north coast of Africa (nine miles northeast of modern Tunis). He was trained in Roman legal rhetoric and only became a Christian as an adult. After his conversion he wrote apologetic works defending Christianity, polemical works attacking various heresies, and a variety of works on moral and ethical subjects. Jerome speaks of him as a presbyter,[6] but most modern scholars doubt that he belonged to the clergy. Ultimately he became a Montanist and used the same vigor in attacking orthodox Christianity as he had previously exhibited in defending it.

Tertullian's *Adversus Marcionem*, as the title suggests, is given over entirely to a refutation of Marcion—his general position in Books 1-4; his exegesis of the ten letters of Paul in Book 5. It is probably the most representative and certainly the most devastating polemic against Marcion of the day. Tertullian agreed with Marcion on the importance of Galatians vis-à-vis Judaism: "We too claim that the primary epistle against Judaism is that addressed to the Galatians."[7] But Tertullian went on to insist that Marcion was terribly wrong to renounce the Creator God and set aside the Jewish Scriptures, for both the abolition of the law and the establishment of the gospel derive from the Creator's own ordinance and are rooted in the prophecies of the Jewish Scriptures.[8] So Tertullian argued that it is the same God as preached in the gospel who had been known in the law, though "the rule of conduct" is not the same.

Specifically, Tertullian insisted that Galatians must be understood to teach that the Christian renunciation of the law stems from the Creator's own will and came about through the work of the Creator's Christ. As for the Jerusalem apostles, he saw them as basically one with Paul in soteriology and christology, though he says that their faith in those early days was "unripe and still in doubt regarding the observance of the law"—just as Paul's practice was inconsistent at times (e.g., in circumcising Timothy, Acts 16:3), though only "for circumstances' sake." As for the "false brothers brought in unawares," they were Jewish Christians who perverted the gospel by their retention of the old rule of conduct. Their endeavors, however, Tertullian held, came to an end when Peter, James and John officially sanctioned the legitimacy of Paul's mission by giving to him and Barnabas "the right hand of fellowship."

So Tertullian, on the basis of his reading of Galatians, taught that the law was meant by God for the early instruction of his people; but that with the fulfilment of his redemptive purposes in the coming of Christ, God abolished the law that he himself had appointed ("Better he than someone else!")—though God also confirms the law (i.e., the moral law) in society to the extent that he must.[9] As for Marcion's deletions in Galatians (deleting 1:18-24; 2:6-9a; 3:6-9; and parts of 3:10-12, 14a, 15-25; 4:27-30, with extensive alterations in 4:21-26), Tertullian exclaimed: "Let Marcion's eraser be ashamed of itself."[10] And as for Marcion's theology generally, Tertullian's attitude is epitomized at the very beginning of his work: "The most barbarous and melancholy thing about Pontus [dismal as the region is of itself] is that Marcion was born there."[11]

The Alexandrian Fathers

Building on the deep desire of early Christians to keep the Jewish Scriptures for the Church (*a la* Irenaeus and Tertullian)—which meant, in turn, minimizing the negative and maximizing the positive features of Paul's attitude toward the Mosaic law— the Alexandrian Fathers developed a distinctive approach to matters having to do with the relation of the testaments, particularly Clement of Alexandria and Origen. We often think of the Alexandrians as simply allegorist. But allegorical exegesis was only a tool they picked up from certain Jewish teachers of their city to enhance their own approach to the Scriptures[12]—a tool which was eventually discarded by their successors, though their basic approach found rootage extensively within catholic Christendom.

Clement of Alexandria was a convert to Christianity in adult life, and, after a long spiritual pilgrimage, settled in Alexandria as a pupil of Pantaenus, whom he succeeded as head of the Catechetical School there during A.D. 190–202. He left Alexandria when severe persecution of Christians broke out under Septimus Severus, and died in Asia Minor about A.D. 214. While Clement's extant works are far fewer than those of his extremely prolific successor, Origen, there can be no doubt as to how he viewed the Mosaic law and the relation of the Old and New Testaments. Most succinct is the following quotation from "The Rich Man's Salvation":

> Now the works of the law are good—who will deny it? For "the commandment is holy" [Rom 7:12], but only to the extent of being a kind of training, accompanied by fear and preparatory instruction, leading on to the supreme lawgiving and grace of Jesus [cf. Gal 3:24]. On the other hand, "Christ is the fulfilment [πλήρωμα, not τέλος] of the law unto righteousness to every one who believes [Rom 10:4], and those who perfectly observe the Father's will he makes not slaves, in the manner of a slave, but sons and brothers and joint-heirs [cf. Gal 3:26–4:7].[13]

Thus, contra Marcion, as to the nature of the law, it is "good" and "holy"; as to the purpose of the law, it was given to be "a kind of training, accompanied by fear and preparatory instruction"; as to the focus of the law, that is to be found in its "leading on to the supreme law-giving and grace of Jesus"; as to Christ's work in relation to the law, "Christ is the fulfilment of the law"; as to the Christian's status before God, it is one of being righteous apart from the law—no longer slaves under the law but "sons and brothers and joint-heirs"; and as to the Christian's responsibility to God, it is to believe and perfectly observe the Father's will. All of this, in general, sounds eminently Christian. In the hands of Origen, however, such affirmations received an explication that sets them apart as being distinctive.

Origen (A.D. 185-254), the precocious and pious son of the Greek grammarian and Christian martyr Leonides, became head of the Catechetical School in Alexandria at the youthful age of eighteen in A.D. 203, at a time of great persecution and when the Church in Egypt lacked leadership. During his lifetime he published a prodigious number of critical, exegetical, theological, apologetic and practical writings. There is extant among all these materials, however, no commentary on Galatians, so we are left without direct knowledge of how Origen specifically interacted with Marcion. Yet we are not left to wonder how Origen understood the issues dealt with in Galatians, for there are several direct statements and numerous hints on these matters in the many Greek fragments we have of his commentaries on Matthew, John and Romans, in the Latin portions (admittedly few) of his Galatians commentary preserved by Pamphilus and Jerome, and in the two hundred or so extant homilies we have from Origen on various biblical passages. In addition, in *De Principiis* Origen spells out quite explicitly his principles of biblical interpretation.

In *Contra Celsum*, which was written near the end of his life, Origen uses Gal 5:17 in support of his sharp distinction between the flesh and the spirit—with primacy, of course, being given to the spirit.[14] Earlier in *De Principiis* he made this same distinction, using Gal 5:17 there in support as well.[15] So it seems safe to say, though without access to his Galatians commentary itself, that Galatians with its flesh-spirit dichotomy was foundational for Origen's thought. Likewise, the Hagar-Sarah allegory of Gal 4:21-31 seems to have been foundational for his exegetical method, for in *Contra Celsum* it is that passage which he uses to justify his allegorical or spiritual exegesis.[16] And in that same work, Gal 2:15 is used to buttress his evaluation of Paul vis-à-vis the Jerusalem apostles (he was "mightier than they")[17] and Gal 2:12 to support his understanding of their character (they had "not yet learned from Jesus to ascend from the law that is regulated according to the letter to that which is interpreted according to the spirit").[18]

It is in his extant Romans commentary, however, where we find Origen dealing extensively with Paul's teaching on the law. There he notes that not every reference to law in Paul's writings has the Mosaic law in view, and so insists that distinctions must be made in Paul's usage if we are to understand his meaning.[19] He lists six ways in which the word "law" is used and illustrates them from Romans and Paul's other letters: (1) the Mosaic law according to the letter (Gal 3:10, 19, 24; 5:4); (2) the Mosaic law according to its spiritual sense (Rom 7:12, 14); (3) natural law (Rom 2:14); (4) Mosaic history (Gal 4:2); (5) the prophetic books (1 Cor 14:21); and, though this sense is suggested only somewhat tentatively, (6) the teachings of Christ (1 Cor 9:21).[20] With regard to distinguishing between the Mosaic law and natural law, Origen posits that the presence or absence of the article with νόμος is of help, though he never claims this to be an invariable rule.[21]

More particularly, when commenting on Paul's teaching regarding the Christian's relation to the law, Origen—in concert with Irenaeus, Tertullian, and the Alexandrians generally—separated the law into two parts: (1) the ceremonial laws of Leviticus, which, interpreted according to the flesh, have come to an end with Christ; and (2) the moral requirements of the law, which have been retained and amplified by Christ.[22] And when relating law and gospel, while not without an understanding of the gospel as the historical fulfilment of the law, "his main emphasis," as Maurice Wiles points out, "was placed on the more static and less dynamic conception of the already present but hidden spiritual meaning of the law."[23] For example, commenting on Rom 6:14 Origen interprets "you are not under law but under grace" as a contrast between the letter of the law and the spirit of the law, without any attention to historical developments either within or between the testaments.[24] It is, in fact, this separation of law into its ceremonial and moral parts that characterizes Origen's thinking. And it is no exaggeration to say that this same general approach to relations between the testaments and many of these same features of interpretation have become ingrained in much of Christian theology.

The Antiochean Fathers

At Antioch of Syria, however, another brand of Christian interpretation arose—one which owed much to Origen for its critical spirit and grammatical precision, but also stood in opposition to many of the Alexandrian exegetical tenets and to their general hermeneutical approach. John Chrysostom (A.D. 345-407), who became famous in his native Antioch as a great Christian leader and outstanding preacher ("John the Golden Mouth") and who then served as Archbishop of Constantinople from A.D. 398 to his death in A.D. 407, is certainly one of the most important of the Antiochean Fathers. Theodore of Mopsuestia (died A.D. 429), who was born in Tarsus but lived in Antioch, was a colleague of Chrysostom, and became Bishop of the ecclesiastical see of Mopsuestia, is likewise important. Also Theodoret (A.D. 393-460), a native of Antioch and a disciple of Theodore, who later became Bishop of Cyrrhus in Syria.

Chrysostom and his Antiochean colleagues, of course, shared a common Christian faith with Origen and the Alexandrian Fathers. But they differed widely in their general hermeneutical approach to the Scriptures and on many exegetical matters. For while the Alexandrians, in concert with Irenaeus and Tertullian, did everything they could to assure that Paul's opposition to the law was kept to a minimum—and so tended to view relations between the testaments in somewhat static fashion—the Antiochean Fathers emphasized historical developments and redemptive fulfilment, and so understood differently Paul's teaching on such matters as Gospel and Law and the Christian's relation to the Mosaic law. Likewise, the Antiochean Fathers stood diametrically opposed to allegorical exegesis and denied the legitimacy of separating the law into two unequal parts—viz, the ceremonial law, which came to an end with Christ, and the moral law, which was reaffirmed by Christ. And while they acknowledged that Paul used the word law differently in his writings to refer at times to natural law or to the whole Old Testament, as well as to the Mosaic law, they tended not to appeal to these distinctions in explicating difficult passages, but preferred to interpret such passages along the lines of only one sense per passage for the word law. So, for example, whereas Origen held that Paul's use of law changed frequently and without notice in Romans 7, Chrysostom insisted that the interpretation of Romans 7 must be in terms of the Mosaic law throughout, with other ideas about natural law and/or a paradisal command to be ruled out altogether.[25]

Themes of development and fulfilment come to the fore at many places in the Antiochean Fathers' treatment of the New Testament. For example, though he refused to separate gospel and law into opposing forces, Chrysostom was not prepared to see the Mosaic law as an ethical guide for Christians. Thus on Paul's statement, "Now that faith has come, we are no longer under the supervision of the law; for you are all sons of God through faith in Christ Jesus" (Gal 3:25-26), Chrysostom writes:

> The Law, then, as it was our tutor, and we were kept shut up under it, is not the adversary but the fellow-worker of grace. But if when grace is come it continues to hold us down, it becomes an adversary; for if it confines those who ought to go forward to grace, then it is the destruction of our salvation. If a candle which gave light by night kept us, when it became day, from the sun, it would not only not benefit, it would injure us. And so does the Law, if it stands between us and greater benefits. Those then are the greatest traducers of the Law who still keep it, just as the tutor makes a youth ridiculous by retaining him with himself when time calls for his departure.[26]

And though he failed to apply the verse either to the anti-Semitism prevalent in his day or to male chauvinism, in a remarkable sermon delivered at Constantinople toward the end of his life Chrysostom interpreted Gal 3:28 as having relevance for the question of slavery. Thus while agreeing generally with Christians of his day that slavery is "the penalty of sin and the punishment of disobedience," Chrysostom went on to assert:

> But when Christ came he annulled even this, for in Christ Jesus "there is no slave nor free". Therefore, it is not necessary to have a slave; but if it should be necessary, then only one or at most a second. . . . Buy them and after you have taught them some skill by which they may maintain themselves, set them free.[27]

In so speaking, Chrysostom was knowingly breaking away from a common Christian view that since slavery arose because of sin it could only be eradicated in the eschaton when God deals finally with sin.[28] Based on a more dynamic understanding of redemption, Chrysostom argued for an application of the gospel to the question of slavery even here and now—not just reserving such matters for the future.[29]

It is fair to say, then, that the Antiochean Fathers, while not denying continuity with the redemptive activities of God throughout history, had a livelier sense of historical development and redemptive fulfillment than did their Alexandrian counterparts. For while the concept of continuity between the testaments was important for both the Alexandrian and Antiochean Fathers (contra Marcion), the Alexandrians tended to understand continuity in terms of identity and sameness whereas the Antiocheans saw it in terms of development—a development that retained the essence of the gospel throughout, but with genuine growth of understanding and varieties of expression both within and between the testaments. So because of their more dynamic approach to the Scriptures, the Antiochean Fathers treated questions concerning Gospel and Law, relations between the two testaments, and the place of the Mosaic law in the Christian life differently from the Alexandrians.

The Situation Today

It would be presumptuous to attempt to draw straight lines between the three approaches we have sketched out above and what we see today. Much has transpired in the intervening centuries to break down the lines of distinction and even to muddle the issues. Yet similar tendencies exist in various contemporary theologies. And while it may seem to some more meddling than illuminating to do so, I would like to indicate here how and where features similar to Marcionite, Alexandrian and Antiochean approaches to the Scriptures exist today—though, of course, in different dress and called by other names.

Taking as the central feature of Marcion's approach the dichotomy between the testaments, at least two systems of interpretation today may be said to exhibit Marcionite tendencies. On the left of the theological spectrum, Bultmannianism, with its understanding of revelation as historically unconnected and momentary in nature, has little interest in the Jewish Scriptures as prolegomena for the Christianity of the New Testament. It considers the use of the Jewish Scriptures to demonstrate a promise-fulfillment theme and the attempt to link the two testaments together in terms of some overarching salvation-history scenario to be innovations on the part of the New Testament evangelists and other writers, and not intrinsic to the consciousness of Jesus or his earliest followers. It prefers, rather, to focus on the theological anthropology of Paul and John, interpreting their writings in ways that incorporate certain gnostic and dualistic features. On the theological right, Dispensationalism, too, exhibits Marcionite tendencies—particularly in its sharp distinctions between Israel and the Church, the dispensations of Law and Grace, Kingdom Ethics and Gospel Ethics, and even Jesus and Paul. Building on a distinctive ecclesiology, it tends to make Paul's letters the essential Christian canon within the Scriptures, viewing these writings in ways that likewise often are reminiscent of gnostic and dualistic thought. In effect, interpreters on both the left and the right of today's theological spectrum share certain Marcionite tendencies in their respective approaches to the question of the relation of the testaments, even though they are hardly on speaking terms theologically.

An Alexandrian approach to the Scriptures (apart from its use of allegorical exegesis, which tended to drop off) became dominant in catholic Christendom, and can be seen rather clearly in the more traditional forms of Roman Catholicism, Reformed Theology, and Puritan Theology—diverse as these forms of theology are from one another in specific doctrinal formulation. In Alexandrian thought the relationship between the testaments is taken to be essentially one of identity or sameness, with what appear to be innovations in later formulations only seen as more precise explications and applications of what was already implicit in the earlier statements. The analogy to be drawn is that of a syllogism, where what appears to be an innovation in the conclusion is really only the logical deduction already contained in the major and minor premises, and so new only in the sense that it had not been explicitly seen to have been the case before. Thus all doctrinal and ethical issues are argued first on the basis of the Old Testament and then from the more explicit data of the New (believing, thereby, to demonstrate the oneness of biblical teaching). Likewise, balance between the testaments is sought in both the Church's liturgy and its canon law (whether or not these terms are used). Extremes of an Alexandrian approach are to be found in the "Free" Presbyterians of Scotland and the "Theonomy" advocates of the Bible Belt in the States, though these are only two extreme examples of an approach to the Scriptures that has deep rootage in the Christian Church today.

With the surging tide of Alexandrian thought flooding Christendom, an Antiochean approach to the relation of the testaments has often been relegated to the backwaters of the Church's consciousness. Martin Luther, however, at least in his Galatians commentary of 1535-38 (though seemingly without being aware of it himself),[30] stood firmly in the Antiochean tradition, with this approach to the relation of the testaments being carried on by many Lutherans (where the "young" Luther is looked to more than Melanchthon) and revived by many in the modern Biblical Theology movement. In somewhat extreme form it can also be seen in Mennonite theology and ethics. In effect, this approach stresses both continuity and genuine innovations in redemptive history. It appeals by way of illustration to the growth of a plant, where stalk, leaves and flower are not just reproductions of an original seed, yet where growth is always controlled by—and to be judged by—what is inherent in the seed itself. Yet it calls on us to appreciate the fulness of growth by looking first of all at the flowering plant itself, and only then to go back to an analysis of the seed. Thus, on such an approach, doctrinal and ethical issues are dealt with first of all on the basis of the data of the New Testament and then related to that of the Old Testament—recognizing genuine growth of understanding and variations of expression both within each of the testaments and between the testaments. Likewise, liturgy and canon law are constructed to reflect the supremacy of God's revelation in Christ and the present working of the Spirit, without denying the importance of God's past revelations and activities as contained in the Jewish Scriptures.

Lines of demarcation cannot always be clearly drawn, either between ecclesiastical groups or within them. For example, Anglicans with their broad ecclesiastical structures and Baptists with their aversion to many such structures seem to be able to countenance the alliance of all three approaches. Yet while lines cannot always be clearly drawn, tendencies can be recognized and ingrained presuppositions (even my own Antiochean proclivities) must be tested.

Without doubt our presupposed approaches influence our hermeneutics and exegesis. Hermeneutical theory and exegesis, however, must not be allowed to be simply controlled by our presuppositions. Rather, analyses of the biblical data must be allowed constantly to test, challenge and correct (where necessary) our ingrained approaches. So it is necessary to recognize how relations between the testaments have been understood historically and what mental baggage we each have inherited in order that we may be properly critical in carrying out the work of biblical interpretation today.

Notes

1. M. F. Wiles, *The Divine Apostle. The Interpretation of St Paul's Epistles in the Early Church*, Cambridge, 1967, 49.

2. Cf. Tertullian, *Adv Marc* 5.3.1.

3. Ibid. 5.2-4. Marcion's dualism, while not developed, was evidently implicit throughout his treatment of Galatians, if Tertullian's account represents Marcion aright.

4. Ibid. 5.3.6-7.

5. Ibid. 1.19.4.

6. Jerome, *De Vir Ill* 53.

7. Tertullian, *Adv Marc* 5.2.1.

8. Tertullian even argued that Paul is prefigured in the Old Testament: "Among those figures and prophetical blessings over his sons, when Jacob had got to Benjamin he said, 'Benjamin is a ravening wolf; until morning he will still devour, and in the evening will distribute food' [Gen 49:27]. He foresaw that Paul would arise from the tribe of Benjamin, a ravening wolf devouring until the morning, that is, one who in his early life would harass the Lord's flock as a persecutor of the churches, and then at evening would distribute food, that is, in declining age would feed Christ's sheep as the doctor of the Gentiles. Also the harshness at first of Saul's pursuit of David, and afterwards his repentance and contentment on receiving good for evil [cf. 1 Sam 18] had nothing else in view except Paul in Saul according to tribal descent, and Jesus in David by the Virgin's descent from him" (ibid. 5.1.5- 6). And again: "For he [Isaiah] says, 'I will take away from Judaea,' among other things, 'even the wise master-builder' [Isa 3:3]. And was not that a presage of Paul himself, who was destined to be taken away form Judaea, which means Judaism, for the building up of Christendom? For he was to lay that one and only foundation which is Christ" (ibid. 5.7.10).

9. Ibid. 5.2.1-4. On Tertullian's views on God as having both abolished and confirmed the law, caution is needed. Only here does he speak in an unqualified manner of God having abolished the law. Usually he distinguishes between (1) the ceremonial aspect of the law, which was abolished, and (2) the moral aspect, which was confirmed and heightened by Christ (cf. *De Pudicitia* 6.3-5; *De Monogamia* 7.1; *De Oratione* 1.1).

10. Ibid. 5.4.2.

11. Ibid. 1.1.4.

12. C. Siegfried, *Philo von Alexandria*, Jena, 1875, 16-37, and H. A. A. Kennedy, *Philo's Contribution to Religion*, London, 1919, 32- 34, have shown that "there can be little question that Philo stood in a long succession of allegorical interpreters of the Old Testament. The practice had been reduced to a kind of science" (quoting Kennedy, p. 32). Clement reveals his awareness of this line of interpreters in referring to a second- century B.C. Alexandrian Jew named Aristobulus who used allegorical exegesis in a series of works on the Mosaic law (cf. *Stromata* 5.14.97).

13. Clement, *Quis Dives Salvetur?* 9.2; cf. *Strom* 4.130.3 for the other occasion where Clement uses πλήρωμα in commenting on Rom 10:4.

14. Origen, *Contra Cels* 8.23.

15. Origen, *De Prin* 1.3.4; 3.2.3; 3.4.1-5.

16. *Contra Cels* 4.44: "Scripture frequently makes use of the histories of real events in order to present to view more important truths, which are but obscurely intimated; and of this kind are the narratives relating to the 'wells' and to the 'marriages' and to the various acts of 'sexual intercourse' recorded of righteous persons, which, however, it will be more seasonable to offer an explanation in the exegetical writings referring to those very passages. But that wells were constructed by righteous men in the land of the Philistines, as related in the book of Genesis, is manifest from the wonderful wells which are shown at Ascalon, and which are deserving of mention on account of their structure, so foreign and peculiar compared to that of other wells. Moreover, that both young men and female servants are to be understood metaphorically, is not our doctrine merely, but one which we have received from the beginning from wise men, among whom a certain one [Paul] said, when exhorting his hearers to investigate the figurative meaning: 'Tell me, you that read the law, do you not hear the law? For it is written that Abraham had two sons: the one by a bond maid; the other by a free woman. But he who was of the bond woman was born after the flesh; he of the free woman was by promise. Which things are an allegory, for these are the two covenants: the one from

Mount Sinai, which genders to bondage, which is Agar' [Gal 4:21-24]. And a little after, 'But Jerusalem which is above is free, which is the mother of us all' [Gal 4:26]. And anyone who will take up the Epistle to the Galatians may learn how the passages relating to the 'marriage' and the 'intercourse with the maid-servants' have been allegorized—the Scripture desiring us to imitate not the literal acts of those who did these things, but (as the apostles of Jesus are accustomed to call them) the spiritual."

17. Ibid. 7.21.

18. Ibid. 2.1; though Origen goes on to offer a partial justification for Peter and his associates, arguing that "certainly it was quite consistent that those should not abstain from the observance of Jewish usages who were sent to minister to the circumcision."

19. Origen, *Comm ad Rom* on Rom 3:19 (*PG* 14.958).

20. Origen, "Fragments on Romans," ed. H. Rambsbotham, *JTS* 13 (1912) 216-218 (on Rom 2:21-25) and 14 (1913) 13 (on Rom 7:7).

21. *Comm ad Rom* on Rom 3:21 (*PG* 14.959).

22. Ibid. on Rom 8:3 and 11:6; cf. Irenaeus, *Adv Haer* 4.16.4; Tertullian, *De Pud* 6.3-5; *De Mono* 7.1; *De Orat* 1.1; *Apostolic Constitutions* 6.20.

23. Wiles, *The Divine Apostle*, 65.

24. Origen, *Comm ad Rom* on Rom 6:1 (*PG* 14.1035).

25. Chrysostom, *Hom in Rom* 12.6, on Rom 7:12; though in treating Rom 2:14-15 he distinguished between written law, natural law, and law as revealed in action.

26. Chrysostom, *Comm on Gal* on Gal 3:25-26.

27. Chrysostom, Homily 40 on 1 Corinthians 10, in *The Homilies of S. John Chrysostom on the First Epistle of St. Paul the Apostle to the Corinthians*, Part II, Oxford, 1839, 580.

28. Ibid.: "I know I am annoying my hearers, but what can I do? For this purpose I am appointed and I will not cease speaking so."

29. Cf. R. N. Longenecker, *New Testament Social Ethics for Today*, Grand Rapids, 1984, 60-65.

30. In 1519 Luther published a commentary on Galatians that was largely dependent on Jerome and Erasmus, who, in turn, were largely dependent on Origen and the Alexandrian tradition. Then in 1523 he produced an abbreviated and revised form of his 1519 work, which in its omissions and changes began to depart from both (see *Luthers Werke*, 2, Weimar, 1884, 436-758; *Luther's Works*, 27, ed. J. Pelikan, St. Louis, 1964, 151-410). During the fall semester of 1531, however, Luther gave another series of lectures on Galatians at the University of Wittenburg. That series was taken down in full by three of his students and published in 1535. It was then republished with revisions in 1538 as his definitive exposition of Galatians (*Luthers Werke*, 40[1] and 40[2a]; *Luthers Works*, 26 and 27a; see Luther's Preface in the Weimar edition [40[1]] where he acknowledges all that his students have taken down from his lectures as his own [pp. 33-37]). In the 1535-38 Galatians commentary Luther frequently opposes Jerome on matters of exegesis and interpretation, occasionally taking issue with Erasmus' *Paraphrase on Galatians* [1518 or 1519] as well.

Is Apocalyptic the Mother
of Christian Theology?

I. Howard Marshall

It was in 1960 that E. Käsemann originally published an essay which subsequently appeared in English with the title "The Beginnings of Christian Theology" in which he affirmed, "Apocalyptic was the mother of all Christian theology". The essay aroused controversy, and the author wrote a second essay in which he attempted to clarify and defend his position under the title "On the Subject of Primitive Christian Apocalyptic."[1]

The Thesis Stated

According to Käsemann primitive Christian apocalyptic is to be defined as "the expectation of an imminent parousia";[2] that is to say, it is the form of early Christianity which is dominated by the expectation of the impending return of Jesus. Käsemann begins from an analysis of certain sayings in Matthew which show the existence of two groups in the early church, which shared belief in possessing the Spirit of God, but which differed in what they believed in other respects and attacked each other sharply, measuring each other by their lack of signs of the Spirit. One group was engaged in mission to the Gentiles and was associated with Stephen and his followers; it moved out to Antioch and prepared the way for Paul. The other was strongly Jewish Christian; it too was concerned with mission but only to the Jews so as to bring about the restoration of Israel, and it insisted on strict adherence to the law. Both groups used what Käsemann calls "sentences of holy law"[3] to set out their rules; these were sayings which set side by side earthly conduct and heavenly reward or judgment and were promulgated by Christian prophets. And behind the concern for mission and the promises and threats in the holy law stood a fervent expectation of the coming of Jesus. The communities where this type of Christianity was to be found were "the little congregations on the borders of Palestine and Syria".[4]

Thus the marks of this type of Christianity were:

a. Fervent expectation of the coming of Jesus.
b. Enthusiastic Christianity associated with the presence of the Spirit.
c. Leadership by prophets who were the bearers of the Spirit.
d. Strong Jewish legalism.
e. Fierce opposition to the group of Christians who sought to convert Gentiles and who consequently took a less rigid attitude to the law.

Some comments must now be made on further details of this thesis.

a. Käsemann largely builds it on his understanding of various texts in Matthew in the light of what he calls "form criticism", by which I take it that he means that from these texts we can discern their life-setting in the early church. He draws attention to the polemical features in Matt 7:22, 23 (a group of enthusiastic prophets attacked by Matthew for failure to do the will of God); 23:8-10 (an attack on a Judaistic Christian rabbinate developing in the church); 5:17-20 (an insistence on keeping every detail of the law, which Matthew himself does not share and has modified); 10:5, 6 (an attack by Jewish Christians on an ongoing mission to the Samaritans and Gentiles); 10:41 and 13:16, 17 (evidence for a division of the community into prophets and righteous men). The community saw itself as having the presence of the Spirit to such an extent that, whereas speaking against the Son of man was a venial offence, to speak against the Spirit working in the church was unpardonable (Matt 12:32). So too in Matt 10:13, 14 the tremendous authority of the missionary as the representative of Christ is portrayed. And overarching all is the authority of Christ who sits on the throne as the Son of man, the sign of the triumph of the righteousness of God. He will come again before the church has completed its mission to Israel.

b. All the evidence which has been cited comes from the early church and not from Jesus himself. When Käsemann says that apocalyptic is the mother of Christian theology, he adds, "since we cannot really class the preaching of Jesus as theology".[5] There are two points here. One is that the real beginning of Christian theology is after Easter—and here Käsemann is being loyal to the verdict of his teacher, R. Bultmann. But the other point is that the teaching of Jesus was not in fact apocalyptic. His teaching "did not bear a fundamentally apocalyptic stamp but proclaimed the immediacy of the God who was near at hand."[6] Although Jesus had links with John the Baptist whose message was apocalyptic, yet his own message was different. "At the decisive point it reverses the message of the Baptist by orientating the repentance which it, too, requires, not towards wrath but towards grace; consequently it calls man to the service of God in his daily life as if no shadow lay upon the world and God were not inaccessible. This service of God is then coupled with love of one's brother man as if there were no necessary distinction of cultus and ethic, and creation remained yet undisturbed. Love of one's brother, however, actually includes the far-off unknown and the enemy as if there were no world-renouncing piety required as the sign of the ineluctable will of God and no one could flee from this will. Though man may be in flight from God, yet God has never withdrawn himself from man. No 'works' are therefore required to call him back, just as there is no assurance in the face of his judgment. On the basis of this remarkable 'eschatology', which views all life as lived 'before God', it is easy to understand how Jesus, so far as we can see, did not baptize, built up no community as a holy remnant and as the nucleus of the messianic people of God and recognized no sharpening of the Torah other than the demand for obedience and love."[7] Consequently Käsemann can conclude, "I am convinced that no one who took this step can have been prepared to wait for the coming Son of Man, the restoration of the Twelve Tribes in the Messianic kingdom and the dawning of the Parousia (which was tied up with this) in order to experience the near presence of God. To combine the two would be, for me, to cease to make any kind of sense."[8]

Thus for Käsemann the picture of Jesus is a non-apocalyptic one—but this is a picture which rests on the judgment that a considerable amount of gospel material does not go back to Jesus. However, it must be noted that Käsemann still wants to argue for some kind of continuity between the church and Jesus: "By designating Jesus as its Lord and as the Son of Man who was to come and by its consciousness of itself as being sent 'in his name', the primitive community was laying claim to a continuity of history and of content. But this can only mean that after Easter eschatology, christology and ecclesiology were and are bound up with the message and activity of Jesus."[9]

c. Käsemann argues that in the Hellenistic church and Paul one can see opposition to the earlier enthusiasm of the Jewish church. Paul shows a certain reserve against the eschatology of the enthusiasts, in that while they believed that they were experiencing the resurrection life of Jesus, Paul believed that Christians possessed "the reality of sonship only in the freedom of those under temptation—the freedom which points forward to the resurrection of the dead as the truth and the completion of the reign of Christ."[10] Thus the apocalyptic enthusiasm of the Jewish church was shared by the Hellenistic church but in a different form, and Paul had to respond to it.

d. Finally, Käsemann has to allow that the theology of apocalyptic Christianity has been discredited by the delay of the parousia: "We have to state clearly and without evasion that this hope proved to be a delusion and that with it there collapsed at the same time the whole theological framework of apocalyptic of the time after Easter, at the heart of which was the restoration of the Twelve Tribes but which also fought for the Mosaic Torah and against the practice of the Gentile mission."[11] Nevertheless, Käsemann wants somehow to maintain this delusive hope, for he concludes his first essay by saying that the central motif of apocalyptic was "in fact the hope of the manifestation of the Son of Man on his way to enthronement; and we have to ask ourselves whether Christian theology can ever survive in any legitimate form without this theme, which sprang from the Easter experience and determined the Easter faith."[12]

I hope that this is a fair and adequate summary of Käsemann's position. It has certainly proved stimulating to subsequent scholars. As I have already indicated, Käsemann was moved to reply at some length to critical comments from some of his German colleagues. But, whatever else he achieved, he certainly contributed to the development of a fresh look at the nature of apocalyptic and its place in early Christianity. Consequently, when James Dunn came to write about the diversity of theological viewpoint in the NT he singled out four main areas for discussion, namely Jewish Christianity, Hellenistic Christianity, Apocalyptic Christianity and Early Catholicism. Dunn admits that these four areas are not the only ones that might be listed and emphasizes that they do not indicate separate segments but rather what he calls "dimensions and emphases within first-century Christianity which all overlap and interact to some degree."[13] Thus, when he talks about apocalyptic Christianity, he is talking about a particular strand of thought which might be found in many places.

Dunn begins by examining the characteristics of apocalyptic thinking and the apocalyptic writings, and this is a valuable point in his discussion when compared with that of Käsemann whose attempt at definition is really quite inadequate. He then proceeds to look for apocalyptic features in the NT, and he finds them in three areas: the teaching of John the Baptist, of Jesus, and of the earliest Christians. John looked forward to imminent judgment in the shape of a baptism by fire possibly carried out by a heavenly being, and only those who genuinely repented could hope to survive. Jesus too announced the coming of God's kingdom, but saw its power already at work in his ministry. He anticipated a period of trials before the imminent End of the world, and his outlook was centered on Israel. But he refrained from detailed speculation and the drawing up of an apocalyptic calendar, and he emphasized that the kingdom was already present in some way. With regard to the earliest church Dunn argues that they saw the resurrection of Jesus as the beginning of the resurrection of the dead, that they lived in daily expectation of his parousia, and their common life centered round the temple and was thus Israel-centered. He sums up: *"Christianity began as an apocalyptic sect within Judaism, a sect which in its apocalypticism was in substantial continuity with the messages both of John the Baptist and of Jesus.* And since this is where Christianity all began, to that extent Käsemann is correct: apocalyptic *was* 'the mother of all Christian theology'."[14]

But apocalyptic did not disappear without trace, and Dunn proceeds to look at its literary deposit in the NT, which he finds at three points in particular. First, the earliest NT documents in his opinion, 1 and 2 Thess, demonstrate that Paul's teaching has strong apocalyptic features; some of the converts clearly thought that they were living in the last day itself, and Paul had to temper their enthusiasm. There is a note of sobriety alongside the hope of the imminent End. (We may note in parenthesis that the extent of apocalyptic thinking in the writings of Paul may in fact be much greater. See the work of J. C. Beker cited in n. 1.) Second, there is Mark 13, a composite document in which the author suggests that the imminent desecration of the temple in Jerusalem will be the beginning of the End. But, as in 1 and 2 Thess, the center of the imminent expectation is the coming of Jesus as the Son of man, and the exposition is marked by sobriety and earnestness. Finally, there is the Revelation of John which is a genuine apocalyptic document with a clear Christian content.

From this survey Dunn concludes that apocalyptic was an integral part of first-century Christianity. It has continued within the church, though it has always been a somewhat uncomfortable companion to orthodox theology. Positively, Dunn says, it is a valid part of Christianity, setting reality on a wide canvas, seeing history as having a purpose, and thus giving a proper evaluation to the present time and leading the believer to a new sense of responsibility to the world.

The Thesis Examined

So much by way of exposition of the case for apocalyptic as the mother of Christian theology. It is now time to cast a critical eye over it and to see what we are to make of it. The question, we remind ourselves, is whether apocalyptic is the mother of Christian theology.

The first point to be made is that the answer must depend to a great extent on the definition of the term "apocalyptic". We must start with Käsemann's definition, since it is primarily his statement that is under scrutiny. The obvious and necessary criticism is that he has given rather a special sense to the term apocalyptic. If we rewrite his thesis, then it would take the form that "the expectation of an imminent parousia is the mother of Christian theology." We shall examine that statement in a moment, but first of all I think that it is fair to say that this is not necessarily the meaning that most people would draw from the original statement. What is apocalyptic? Here Dunn is a much more sure guide when he distinguishes between the type of thinking we call apocalyptic and the sort of literature which belongs to this literary classification. For Dunn apocalyptic theology is characterized by: belief in two ages with a sharp break between them; an attitude of pessimism towards the present age and hope with regard to the age to come; belief in an eschatological climax involving a time of severe tribulation, judgment on God's enemies, salvation for God's people, and resurrection; the belief that the End is imminent; a vision of reality that is cosmic in scope; and finally belief in the sovereignty of God who will bring about the fulfilment of his people's hopes. It thus emerges that the End which is imminent is an End which has certain specific characteristics. Now I do not see that Käsemann would want to quarrel with this definition. What he has done is to draw attention to the characteristically Christian element, the parousia or coming of the Son of Man, that is—for Christians—of Jesus. That is perhaps fair enough, but I shall suggest in a moment that simply to talk of an imminent parousia can open the door to a wrong emphasis.

However, it would be wrong to pass over the fact that another, rather different definition of apocalyptic has been given by C. Rowland. He agrees with G. Bornkamm that "the disclosure of divine secrets is the true theme of later Jewish apocalyptic,"[15] and cites other authors to the same effect. In his own words: "Apocalyptic, therefore, is a type of religion whose distinguishing feature is a belief in a direct revelation of the things of God which was mediated through dream, vision or divine intermediary."[16] Adopting this definition, he is able to show that apocalyptic did not have a special view of eschatology, and that, while apocalyptic is often concerned with eschatological issues, there is not a distinctive apocalyptic eschatology. Hence eschatology should not be made the basis of a definition of apocalyptic, and consequently some texts which are often said to be apocalyptic are not really so at all. However, this definition does do justice to a body of literature which can properly be called apocalyptic.

This is not the place to evaluate Rowland's work in detail, but I must confess that I find it generally persuasive. The point which emerges is that Käsemann has produced a definition of apocalyptic in terms of eschatology which is inappropriate. However, the effect of this point is not to make Käsemann's or Dunn's presentation immediately untenable. For we can still ask whether it is the case that "the expectation of an imminent parousia is the mother of Christian theology", and obviously this statement may be true or false quite independently of whether this expectation has been incorrectly labeled as apocalyptic. We can also of course ask the separate question whether eschatology would be a better candidate for the motherhood of theology.[17]

Thus we find that Käsemann has really raised three possible questions. First, the place of the expectation of an imminent parousia in early Christianity. Second, the place of apocalyptic ideas and imagery in the traditional sense of that term. And, third, the place of apocalyptic understood as belief in the direct revelation of the things of God.

The second point which I wish to make concerns the place of expectation of the imminent parousia in early Christianity. We saw that Käsemann reached his conclusions about this on the basis of a form-critical analysis of certain materials in Matthew which understood the texts primarily as witnesses to a life-setting in the early church and denied that they brought us into direct contact with the historical Jesus. Let me make three comments on this point.

First, we observed that Dunn was able to show the presence of an apocalyptic, or, as we should better say, an eschatological strand in early Christianity which emphasized the imminence of the parousia without resorting to the sceptical estimate of the gospel material as authentic Jesus-tradition which was advocated by Käsemann. It is not necessary to share Käsemann's excessively sceptical attitude to the gospel tradition in order to show the presence of expectation of the imminent return of Jesus in the early church.

Second, the evidence assembled by Dunn does demonstrate the existence and importance of this belief. There is no way in which the significant position of the hope of the imminent parousia in the early church can be denied. There have certainly been attempts to do so, but they can hardly be pronounced successful.[18]

Third, in particular Käsemann's attempt to deny that Jesus shared a belief in the parousia is a failure. Even if the texts which he discusses from Matthew were church-creations, there remains a sufficient basis of material in Mark and Q to disprove his contention. Dunn has pointed out the unlikelihood of a non-apocalyptic Jesus standing between an apocalyptic John the Baptist and an apocalyptic primitive church. He has also argued that Jesus' message of the immediacy of God is integrally related to his doctrine of the imminent future of the kingly rule of God which is already being manifested in his own ministry. In short, the hope of the parousia is to be found right through the teaching of Jesus and of the early church.[19]

But this conclusion raises the third point that I want to make. Granted that the imminent parousia was part of early Christian thinking, did it occupy such a place that it can rightly be called the mother of Christian theology? Again the question of definition comes up, because Käsemann has used the metaphor of motherhood without indicating unambiguously what it is meant to convey. He could mean that this hope was the central, the most significant belief in early Christianity. He could also mean that it was thinking about this belief which was the earliest kind of theological thinking carried on by the early Christians and that it was out of this thinking that more developed theology arose. To prove the latter point Käsemann would need to give some kind of demonstration of how Christian theology developed in this womb, and he has not done this. But the two questions need to be answered: a. Was the imminent parousia the central motif in early Christian theology? b. Can early Christian theology be shown to have developed from this matrix?

I should want to argue that, while the imminent parousia was an important motif in early Christian theology, it did not occupy the central position that Käsemann claims for it. First of all, E. Lohse has remarked how the earliest expressions of the gospel which we possess make little or no reference to the parousia. 1 Cor 15:3-5 is generally recognized to be a very early summary of the gospel, and it is concerned with the death, burial, resurrection and appearances of Christ, and not with his future coming. The same is true of other passages such as Rom 1:3, 4; 4:25; 10:9, 10. If there is an eschatological event which is proclaimed here, it is the resurrection of Jesus, not his parousia. But this was an eschatological belief which was common to most of Judaism, and the Christian novelty was in believing that in the case of Jesus the resurrection had already happened.

From this fact Lohse concludes: "It is clear that the origin of Christian theology is not to be found in apocalyptic—be it in Jewish expectation, or be it in primitive Christian enthusiasm—but it lies in the kerygma that preaches the crucified Christ as the risen Lord. Käsemann's thesis . . . receives no confirmation from the oldest expressions of Christian preaching and the confession of the earliest church. The origin and center of primitive Christian theology lies rather from the beginning in the word of the cross."[20]

Second, there is a lot of evidence to show that the beginnings of Christian theology lie in study of the OT Scriptures, a study that was much broader than being confined simply to the apocalyptic parts of the OT. Although it is true that Daniel was an important text for the early church, it was probably not the most important—even if M. Casey goes too far in playing down its influence.[21]

Third, we ask just how important a place expectation of the imminent parousia had in the thinking of the early Christians. Following Käsemann various scholars have argued that the very earliest stage in Christianity was one of hoping for the return of Jesus as the Son of man, and that, for example, the earliest use of the christological titles was in connection with the parousia. F. Hahn in particular has argued for an evolution in christological thinking along these lines.[22] But what is the evidence? If we turn back to Dunn's summary, we note that first he mentions the apocalyptic category of resurrection by the early Christians to express their new faith.[23] What this shows, however, is that the early church was confronted by an experience for which there was no other explanation, rather than that they deliberately chose a category which arose out of their conviction that the End was at hand. One might say that their conviction that Jesus was risen led them to believe that they were living in the last days.[24] We may add to this the fact of their experience of the Spirit, which according to Acts 2:17, 18 was seen as a sign of the fulfilment of prophecy and as a token that the last days had dawned. Second, Dunn mentions the daily expectation of the parousia. He cites as evidence the "Maranatha" cry, the hope expressed in Acts 3:19-21, the sayings about the coming of the Son of man preserved in Q, and, we may add, the evidence of 1 Thess about the content of Paul's preaching. This evidence certainly points to the hope of the parousia as imminent. The question is whether it signifies that there was a "daily" expectation. Third, Dunn mentions the Israel-centeredness of the early Christians with their hopes of eschatological renewal at the temple. But this evidence surely suggests rather that the early Christians regarded Jesus as establishing true Judaism and that they naturally used the temple as he did, as the place for true worship of God and teaching about his kingdom. To deduce that they had a "very narrow" outlook[25] is unjustified.

What we may take from this evidence is that the expectation of the parousia must be seen in the context of belief in the resurrection and consequent vindication and exaltation of Jesus and in the context of the present experience of the Spirit. One can certainly conclude that the early Christians were apocalyptically-minded in that they believed that they were living in the last days, but their horizon was not formed exclusively by the hope of the imminent parousia. The resurrection of Jesus and the gift of the Spirit as immediate experiences must have been of basic importance, and it was out of their present experience of Jesus that they were led to cry "Maranatha".

We may strengthen this argument further by observing that the parousia and the associated events are rarely the occasion of specific teaching in the NT. On the whole the references are incidental and they occur in contexts which suggest that they may have had their home in Christian worship. We do not get the impression that teaching about the parousia was the central element in Christian instruction or in evangelism. Of course we do have the apocalyptic material in the Gospels and the teaching of Paul about the parousia. But it must be noted that it is difficult to know just how the gospel material was related to the kerygma and catechetical instruction of the early church. There are in fact two opposing errors in this area. On the one hand, Käsemann tends to emphasize the importance of the gospel material and to play down the kerygma in his discussion of the earliest church. On the other hand, W. Schmithals has argued that the gospel tradition exerted little or no influence in the early church and is largely a literary creation from a period later than Paul.[26] Somehow a balance between these extreme viewpoints must be achieved. As regards the Pauline evidence, it is noteworthy that his discussions of eschatology are largely concerned with the problem of the resurrection (1 Thess 4; 1 Cor 15; 2 Cor 5), and when he does discuss the parousia specifically (2 Thess 2) it is to correct people who imagined that it would happen immediately. The gospel apocalyptic material in its present form has a twofold concern to warn people to be ready for what may take them unawares and to warn them equally not to be misled by suggestions that the Day of the Lord is already present. The problems are how far the intense expectations which are combatted here represent any kind of "main stream" Christian thinking, and whether this element of caution goes back to the earliest days or reflects a later stage at which the delay of the parousia was a problem. I would claim that there is evidence in the Gospels that Jesus did allow for an interval before the parousia and hence that the early church had this element of caution right from the start.[27]

When all this has been said, it is of course undeniable that the gospel tradition contains statements—perhaps one should say numerous statements—which are future-related in one way or another. Whether or not they were spoken by Jesus exactly as we have them, they were handed down in the church and known to the church. It is important not to play down their significance, perhaps because we find them strange and want to construct a Jesus and an early church that fit in with our preconceptions of what they ought to be like. However, the conclusion that I would want to draw at this stage is that, while the hope of the parousia formed an important part of the horizon of early Christianity, to speak of it as the mother of Christian theology is unjustified. Rowland puts the point well: "What Dunn has indicated is the way in which eschatology dominated early Christian theology. Most of the ideas he collects point to early Christianity as an eschatologically-orientated community, whose expectation about the future is distinguished, not so much by the so-called 'apocalyptic' elements, but by the earnest conviction that the hopes of Judaism were already in the process of being realized. They believed that the final climax of history was imminent, not because they had utilized a particular brand of eschatology, but because their beliefs about Jesus and their experience of the Spirit had led them to understand their circumstances in this particular way."[28]

Fourth, we saw that Käsemann regarded the apocalyptic theology of early Christianity as discredited by the fact that the parousia never happened. At the same time he wanted to hold on to this hope. Käsemann goes astray because he assumes a. that the expectation of the early church was delimited, i.e. one could set a kind of *terminus ante quem* for its occurrence, and b. that a hope which has dragged out for 1900 years must surely be a mistaken one. Various comments can be made about this. The first is that the fact that the time of waiting has turned out to be long is no indication that the early church would have regarded the hope as unreal or illusory. It has often been pointed out that the hope still burns brightly in what are probably among the latest books of the NT, such as 2 Tim, 2 Pet and Rev. If we bear in mind that the early Christians regarded the prophecies of Isaiah and others as not finding fulfillment until their own time, centuries after they were given, we can assume that they may have been prepared for a period of waiting. There is, to be sure, a difference in that the early Christians did believe that they were living in the era of fulfillment, and one might ask just how long the time would have to drag on before Christians would regard the coming of Jesus not as the beginning of the End time but rather as the middle or center point of history—and Käsemann would presumably argue that precisely this did happen. But I am dubious whether the idea of "the middle of time" is a NT idea, and my impression is that the early Christians thought of themselves as living in the last days. Further, it is important to ask whether A. L. Moore is not right in arguing that the time of the parousia is not delimited in the NT; there is no place in which it is categorically affirmed that it must come within a definite time interval.[29] The real question is whether an interval of 1900 years is not so far beyond the horizon of the NT writers as to alter seriously the whole content of the hope: can we in fact proclaim the imminence of the parousia in the same way as the first Christians did? May we sing "Soon and very soon we are going to see the King" with the parousia rather than our own death and resurrection in mind?

It lies beyond the scope of this essay in NT criticism to defend the view that in the hope of the parousia we have an element of Christian faith and hope which we are too easily led to surrender or to keep quiet about. The passage of time has not disproved the hope of his coming. If the hope of the imminent parousia of Jesus is not the mother of Christian theology, it is certainly the near horizon. "For now is our salvation nearer than when we first believed. The night is far gone; the day is at hand" (Rom 13:11, 12).

Notes

1. E. Käsemann, "The Beginnings of Christian Theology" and "On the Subject of Primitive Christian Apocalyptic", in *New Testament Questions of Today*, London, 1969, 82-107, 108-37. See the excellent summary and analysis of his work by W. G. Rollins, "The New Testament and Apocalyptic," *NTS* 17 (1970-71) 454-76. For the original responses to Käsemann's views see R. W. Funk (ed.), *Apocalypticism, JTC* 6, New York, 1969, which includes essays by G. Ebeling, E. Fuchs and other scholars together with reprints of Käsemann's two essays. See also the critical comments by R. Bultmann, "Ist die Apokalyptik die Mutter der christlichen Theologie? Eine Auseinandersetzung mit Ernst Käsemann," in *Exegetica*, Tübingen, 1967, 476-82. The more recent work by J. C Beker, *Paul the Apostle: The Triumph of God in Life and Thought*, Edinburgh, 1980, is important for its claim that the theology of Paul is thoroughly apocalyptic in character; the issues raised by it are too wide to be discussed here, especially since our topic is the origin of Christian theology rather than its Pauline development.

2. Käsemann, *Questions*, 109 n. 1.

3. Käsemann, "Sentences of Holy Law in the New Testament", in *Questions*, 66-81.

4. Käsemann, *Questions*, 92.

5. Käsemann, *Questions*, 102.

6. Käsemann, *Questions*, 101.

7. Käsemann, *Questions*, 113-14.

8. Käsemann, *Questions*, 101-102.

9. Käsemann, *Questions*, 121.

10. Käsemann, *Questions*, 137.

11. Käsemann, *Questions*, 106.

12. Käsemann, *Questions*, 107.

13. James D. G. Dunn, *Unity and Diversity in the New Testament*, London, 1977, 236.

14. Dunn, *Unity, 325*.

15. G. Bornkamm, *TDNT* 4, 815.

16. C. Rowland, *The Open Heaven*, London, 1982, 21.

17. Rowland, *Heaven*, 355.

18. For attempts to play down the existence of the hope of the parousia in some areas of the early church see T. F. Glasson, *The Second Advent: The Origin of the New Testament Doctrine*, London, 1945, 1963[3]; *His Appearing and His Kingdom: The Christian Hope in the light of its History*, London, 1953; J. A. T. Robinson, *Jesus and His Coming: The Emergence of a Doctrine*, London, 1957.

19. The fact that Jesus believed in the imminent future coming of the End and the kingdom of God seems to me to be well-established despite the critical doubts that exist about the authenticity of some of the sayings about the future activity of the Son of man.

20. E. Lohse, "Apokalyptik und Christologie," *ZNW* 62 (1971) 48-67; citation from 58. Cf. W. Schneemelcher, *Das Urchristentum*, Stuttgart, 1981, 113-14.

21. M. Casey, *Son of Man: The Interpretation and Influence of Daniel 7*, London, 1980.

22. F. Hahn, *The Titles of Jesus in Christology*, Guildford, 1969.

23. Dunn, *Unity, 323*.

24. G. Lohfink, "Der Ablauf der Osterereignisse und die Anfänge der Urgemeinde," *TQ* 160 (1980) 167-76.

25. Dunn, *Unity, 324*.

26. W. Schmithals, *Das Evangelium nach Markus*, Gütersloh and Würzburg, 1979.

27. G. R. Beasley-Murray, *Jesus and the Kingdom of God*, Grand Rapids, 1986.

28. Rowland, *Heaven*, 355.

29. A. L. Moore, *The Parousia in the New Testament*, Leiden, 1966.

Jesus, Judaism, and Paul

C. F. D. Moule

In another paper[1] I have argued against S. G. F. Brandon and many others, that Jesus of Nazareth was not acceptable to Judaism, and that, over and above merely political and prudential considerations, opposition from Judaism was a decisive factor in bringing him to his death. In agreement with E. P. Sanders and others, I have argued that the sequel to the death of Jesus is an important part of the evidence which helps to establish the conclusion. But I have argued also that the grounds for the unacceptability of Jesus to Judaism lie deeper and extend further than Sanders seems to suggest. The real gravamen against Jesus was, I believe, the sheer immediacy of his relation with God. Although it seems to have been none of Jesus' intention to attack Judaism as such (even if he attacked aspects of the Judaism of his day in favor of an eschatological renewed Judaism of the future), yet he appears to have, as it were, burst its bounds, to have been too big for it, and to have transcended and superseded it.[2] In so arguing, I appealed to the Pauline epistles as the earliest evidence for the nature of the sequel to the death of Jesus. The Fourth Gospel, probably at a later date, points in its own different way, in the same direction.

In the present paper, I attempt to fill out in rather more detail certain aspects of the Pauline sequel to the death of Jesus, and, in particular, to consider the much-debated question of Paul's understanding of Jesus' relation to Moses, to the Torah, and to Israel. I offer this sketch in appreciation of a good friend who has devoted much of his skill to the elucidation of Paul's mind and ministry.

Those who are disposed to ignore Paul in reaching their estimate of Jesus see him as ignorant, wilfully or otherwise, of both typical Judaism and typical Christianity. This is unjustified. On the Christian side, to deduce a lack of interest in the origins of the Christian movement from the paucity of references in the epistles to the historical traditions is, considering the nature and purpose of the epistles, a patently false argument from silence; to belittle such passages as do hark back to tradition (1 Cor 7:10, 11:23-25, 15:1-8 especially) is tendentious; and to appeal to 2 Cor 5:16 (Paul no longer knowing Christ according to the flesh) in support of the theory is bad exegesis.[3] Equally, it is perverse, in the light of Gal 1:13, 14 and Phil 3:4-6, even if one ignores the Acts, to hold that Paul was not an informed Jew. That he was a well-informed Jew and Christian, and that he never ceased to wish to see himself as a patriotic Jew is difficult to deny, though it is all too clear that his Christian convictions led him beyond anything that an observant Jew could approve; and in Phil 3:3-11 he virtually admits as much.

In short, if opposition from Judaism was an essential factor in bringing Jesus to the cross, Paul's alienation from his fellow Jews, and probably in the end his death, was due to the corresponding fact—that belonging to Jesus meant bursting the bounds of Judaism. The two halves of the picture dove-tail exactly.

How, then, did Paul, as a Christian, understand the relation of Jesus to Judaism? Jesus had, as I believe, been deemed by certain Jews, including Pharisees such as

Paul was, to be a threat to Judaism, and had, to their satisfaction, been put to death by the Romans in the most degrading way possible. When Paul became convinced that this Jesus was vindicated by God, and in transcendent glory, this meant nothing less than a revolution in his thinking about the Mosaic Law and in his way of life as a Jew.

Moreover, belonging to this vindicated and glorious one, who was not only Messiah (which need imply no more than a human dignity) but transcendently exalted and uniquely close to God, Paul found communities which included gentiles as well as Jews. Whether or not there were mixed communities of this sort in Damascus or in Jerusalem, no doubt he found them in Antioch; and they belonged to Jesus Christ; indeed, they were, so to speak, contained in him: Jesus was the very environment in which they lived. "Those who are in Christ" (or "in the Lord", etc.) was a common designation for them.

If so, then Paul is bound to acknowledge that these mixed communities are, somehow, God's chosen people. He uses *klētos,* "called" (e.g. in Rom 1:6), to describe them, and speaks of their "election", *eklogē* (1 Thess 1:4). Very significantly, he calls them *hoi hagioi,* "the dedicated ones". The Semitic equivalents, $q^e d\bar{o}$šîm, qaddîšîn are normally, in the Scriptures and, for instance, in the Qumran literature, a designation for supernatural beings; but a good case can, in my belief, be made for its referring, in certain contexts, to humans (see Dan 7, 1QM 10.10, and perhaps, Deut 33:3, Pss 16:3, 34:10, CD 20.8, 4Qps Dan^a)[4]; and in these contexts the term seems to refer to Jewish groups which set themselves to be ultra-observant—sectarian *ecclesiolae in ecclesia,* as it were. It is amazing that such a term came to be applied to groups containing gentiles who were not observant at all, in any normal sense, and containing Jews who, if they were to participate fully in common meals and worship, were bound to make concessions to a gentile way of life: but so it was. The same outlook seems to be reflected incidentally in 1 Cor 10:2, where the Israelites in the wilderness are referred to as having been "baptized into Moses", a curious phrase which seems best explained as a retrojection from and a parallel to the characteristically Christian locution, "baptized into (the name of) Jesus" (or "Christ" or "the Lord", etc.).[5] If so, then the implication is that those who are baptized into Jesus are the counterpart of the Israel of Moses' following.

This is extraordinary, but it is something that Paul found himself bound to come to terms with. It comes to expression in a spectacular way when, wrestling with the new phenomena as a trained interpreter of Scripture, Paul succeeds in finding Scriptural warrant for a people of God which includes unproselytized gentiles. In Gen 15:6, Abraham found access to God and acceptance with him (God "reckoned" it as "rightness") by taking God at his word—by implicit faith; and this, in the chronology of the Genesis narrative, was before Abraham received the circumcision-law (Gen 17). As the archetypal believer, therefore, even when not circumcised, Abraham was promised that all the tribes of the earth would in him find blessing (Gen 12:3, *nibr^{e}ku*), a promise which, in Gen 22:18, is repeated in the form that all the "nations" *(gôyyîm)* of the earth would "bless themselves" *(hithbār^{e}ku)* in his "posterity". The reflexive verb (if not, indeed, the straight passive)[6] probably in fact signifies the use of Abraham's name in formulae of blessing (that someone may be "blessed as Abraham was blessed"); but the words are sufficient for the expositor: out of them, building on the position of the initial promise, *before* circumcision, Paul draws the conclusion that in Abraham's posterity will be found blessing for all the gentiles, without the requirement of circumcision. And who is this "posterity" (in the singular) but Jesus? Thus by incorporation in Jesus Christ and without circumcision, the gentiles become Abraham's posterity, and so Israelites—Israelites by faith even when not by circumcision. This argument is presented in Gal 3:7-22 and Rom 4. This, Paul seems to be telling himself, is not bypassing the election of Israel: it is only making intelligible the phenomenon of the uncircumcised becoming members of the community which undoubtedly belongs to the one who has been vindicated as God's Chosen One.[7] Paul remains convinced that God's election of Israel cannot fail (Rom 9:6, 11:2), but he is driven to re-define Israel. There are those who maintain that "children of Abraham" was already a wider term than "Israel";[8] but a good case can be made for its being a synonym for Israelites,[9] and it certainly seems that Paul's argument depends on this. By choosing to use the phrase "children of Abraham" for God's people, he is able to authenticate God's long-standing intention to include those whose faith in Jesus Christ makes them children of the faith which Abraham showed before he was circumcised (Rom 4:11).

In the same way, using an analogy to suit his meaning, Paul declares in Rom 11 that gentiles may be grafted, by virtue of faith (verse 20), into the olive tree which is Israel, and become authentic branches of that rich and fruitful plant whose roots go deep into Israel's history.

Virtually, then, Jesus Christ epitomizes Israel—indeed, is Israel— since to be incorporated in him by faith means inheriting the blessings promised to Abraham's posterity. It is as though Paul might have started his Christian life with his thinking moving in an ellipse round two fixed foci—Israel the elect people (his antecedent, Jewish conviction) and Jesus the elect one (the new conviction, brought about by the experiences which showed him Jesus as Christ and as the glorified and vindicated Son of God). If so, then in course of time he found that these two had one and the same axis—and that Jesus was the larger, the more inclusive: indeed, Jesus includes, is, not only Israel but all Adam, all humankind (Rom 5:12-21; 1 Cor 15:22, 45); he is, as it were, Israel universalized. There is no direct evidence for a progression in Paul's thought from two foci to one: that is mere speculation on my part; but the conclusion, with one focus, is, I think, clear enough; and its implications are summed up in Eph 2:11-22 (whether by the apostle or by a disciple)—a new humanity in which Jews and gentiles are fellow-citizens with *hoi hagioi* because the cross of Jesus Christ has annulled the divisiveness and exclusiveness of the law.[10]

An observer may be forgiven for seeing Paul's use of Scripture as a tour de force—an anticipation of the preposterous "talking for victory" in Justin's *Trypho*; and his opponents must have been quick to retort that, when the circumcision law is given (Gen 17), it is stringently enjoined on all Abraham's posterity. But, however little his case may be "proved" from Scripture, the fact remains that he is convinced by his experiences that entry into the destiny of Israel at its fullest and most developed is now through the new covenant inaugurated by the death and resurrection of Jesus Christ. For this conviction he uses Scripture simply as a vehicle. It is clearly Paul's intention to insist on the continuity of Israel, as Abraham's descendants, right through to the Christian communities of mixed, Jewish and gentile composition—Abraham's descendants by virtue of their incorporation, by faith, in Abraham's "posterity", Jesus Christ. There is, he wants to maintain, no *New* Israel. But about the newness of the New Covenant inaugurated by Jesus Christ Paul is uncompromising. Echoing the language of Jer 31:31-34, he holds that the New Covenant there spoken of is now in force and actually supersedes the Mosaic Covenant. In Jesus Christ, as their climax and summation, the ancient people of Israel are brought within this New Covenant, and it is blindness on their part if they fail to recognize it.

This radical doctrine of the supersession of the Old Covenant is, of course, prominently associated with the writer to the Hebrews, from whom the collective title of the Christian Scriptures *(the New Testament)* is perhaps derived.[11] To this writer it is brutally clear that the New Covenant has made the Old obsolete. In Heb 8:13, the writer declares that when God, in Jer 31:31, speaks of a new covenant, he is pronouncing the first covenant old; and being old means getting close to disappearance. But in fact the doctrine is no less clear in Paul. To be sure, Rom 10:4 is notoriously ambiguous. It could mean that Christ was the climax of the Torah. It could mean that he terminated it. It has been suggested that it may mean both bring to fulfilment and supersede, though there are those who declare this compromise to be the least defensible of the proposals.[12] But, whatever is made of Rom 10:4, 2 Cor 3 is unambiguous, and so is Gal 4:21-31. In 2 Cor 3, the radiance on Moses' face (in the story in Exod 34) is transitory. The radiance accompanying the New Covenant belongs, by contrast, to the era of the constant spiritual presence of God (v 18) in Jesus Christ, and it is permanent and increasing, not oscillating or transitory. Those Jews are blindfolded who fail to realize this and to come to terms with it (vv 14, 15). Similarly, in the allegory of Gal 4:21-31 the covenant from Mount Sinai is harshly likened to Hagar, the slave-girl, the mother of servitude, and to "the present Jerusalem" and her "children", who are in servitude. It is the "Jerusalem above" which corresponds to Sarah, the free woman, whose child, Isaac, was born in accordance with God's promise, and she is the mother of Christians. It is they who are accepted by God, whereas Hagar's child is expelled (Gen 21:10, 12)!

So, in the end, "God's Israel" (Gal 6:16) seems to be only those, both Jews and Gentiles, who are incorporated by faith (and, no doubt, baptism) in Jesus Christ.[13] This is a harsh conclusion; but it helps to explain something that has been interpreted as inconsistency in Paul.[14] Paul is at one moment fiercely intolerant of Judaizing Christians, while, at another moment, he is endlessly tolerant of the vagaries of practice within the Christian communities. The outbursts of Galatians are in strong contrast to the gentle tolerance of Rom 14 and 1 Cor 8-10. But is there not a clear principle behind his varying attitudes? What makes him fierce and abusive, indeed "unprintable", is the claim that circumcision is *necessary,* as well as faith in Jesus Christ (and baptism, one supposes, into Jesus Christ), for entry into the people of God and into the Covenant. That claim, on the face of it, sounds reasonable enough: if Israel is indeed God's elect, then does it not follow that circumcision is the logical and necessary antecedent to entering the people of God, even if faith and baptism into Jesus may follow as the way into the Christ-sect of Judaism? But the very wording of that question explains Paul's explosion. It implies that to enter the Christian Church is *only* to enter a sect of Judaism, *only* an extra step, whereas Paul is convinced that Jesus Christ contains the whole of Israel, and more. One cannot go further into the people of God than by being in Jesus Christ. To suggest the need for something further is to impugn the sufficiency of Jesus Christ.

Conversely, for a Jew to stop short of faith in Jesus Christ means falling short of God's full design for Israel. In the olive tree analogy in Rom 11, native branches had been broken off because of unbelief (vv 19-23): harsh again, but logical in the light of the Christology of the Christian Church.

It has been argued that, in the confrontation between Paul and Peter reflected in Gal 2, Peter is no more inconsistent than Paul, and that it is unfair of Paul to represent him as going back on his declared position. Peter, it is said, is only making concessions to Judaism, where Paul is making concession to gentiles.[15] But this is not so, if being a Christian at all means accepting the finality and all-inclusiveness of Jesus Christ. What Peter is criticized for is basing his priorities on diplomacy rather than Christology. Paul may have been inconsistent in sometimes behaving as an observant Jew and sometimes not (1 Cor 9:19-22), but at least these variations were controlled by a consistently held conviction about Jesus Christ.

Returning to the matter of the New Covenant, a proposal made by many Christians today is that they should recognize that the Old Covenant has never been revoked. The Pope has voiced this view, and it is represented by Christians in other communions also.[16] But this is an unjustified deduction from the optimistic words of Rom 9:6 and 11 *passim*. There Paul is emphatic about the impossibility of God's revoking his *election* of Israel. But he nowhere says that the *Old Covenant* is not revoked; and his hopes for Israel seem to lie either in his identification of Christians as the growing-point of "God's Israel", the "remnant" from which God's future for Israel will spring (Rom 11:5), or in his expectation of a "land-slide" of Israelites into the New Covenant by faith in Jesus Christ.[17] In the former case, *pas Israel* in Rom 11:26 has to be interpreted very loosely—"Israel as an entity"?—while even in the latter case, it would presumably have to mean a majority rather than literally every individual without exception. There is no reason to believe that, had Paul lived to see centuries of alienation between Synagogue and Church, he would have been content to reckon that the separated followers of two different covenants (one of which, in his belief, was superseded) were both equally fulfilling God's election of Israel. Even in Rom 11:13-24, where Paul is concerned to drive home, for gentile Christians, the lesson that they depend on the stock of the olive tree which is Israel, he makes clear what he sees to be the converse, that the "natural" Jewish branches are broken off unless they have faith in Jesus Christ. They are like the branches in John 15:6, which are detached from the "true" vine. In proportion as Jesus Christ is seen as all-inclusive, faith in him becomes exclusively the only *full and complete* way of inclusion. Melito is one of the Church Fathers who carried this principle to its harshest extreme.[18] Those who, like myself, dare not and cannot speak in terms of "breaking off" (Rom 11:17, 19, 22), even allowing for the possibility of re-grafting (Rom 11:23), still less of "withering" and "being burned" (John 15:6), may nevertheless have to come to terms with the idea that there is something less than the fulfilment of God's *full* purpose when a Jew fully hears and understands the Christian message but rejects it. Otherwise, where is the distinctiveness and finality of Paul's Christology? (It need hardly be said that it is Christians who must bear much of the blame for such rejection. The Christian message is too often presented in ways which guarantee that it shall not be heard or understood and must be unacceptable—sometimes because of bad articulation, but more often because of the Chruch's failure to live it.)

If this is a painful conclusion for anyone who today loves and admires Jewish friends, so it was for Paul of Tarsus. The result of Paul's conviction that Jesus is Messiah and Lord and that, as the inaugurator of a new covenant, he transcends Israel of the Old Covenant and includes all who put their faith in God through him, is that Paul is torn between his allegiance to the Law and his recognition of its supersession in Jesus Christ. It is tempting to try to reconcile his statements by saying that what he abandons is not the Torah itself but a "legalistic" abuse of it. I am myself among those who have asked: May not all his adverse statements about *nomos* refer to "*nomos* used 'legalistically' for a person's own satisfaction", while all his favorable judgments fall under the rubric "*nomos* used correctly, to illuminate the nature and claims of God"?[19] Unfortunately, it is doubtful whether this proposal can be sustained. There are passages where one is almost driven to translate *nomos* not as Torah under any aspect but as "principle" or "system"—a meaning which, as H. Räisänen shows, can easily be illustrated from contemporary non-biblical documents.[20] It seems that we have to accept the conclusion that Paul uses *nomos* in a variety of senses and is not entirely consistent in his statements. He wins his argument in Galatians by disparaging the Law, but, in Romans, declares that he is establishing and revering it.

It may be, further, that the standard "Reformers' interpretation" of Paul's Gospel as a declaration of freedom from "legalism" and from the struggle to justify oneself needs to be qualified, at least in the case of Galatians. Was Paul, perhaps, concerned there to establish that no legal requirements (such as circumcision, sabbath, and kosher food) must be added, as of necessity, to faith in Christ, rather than to meet psychological needs for liberation from self-justification?[21] Yet, is it so easy to disabuse oneself of the sense that, at least for Romans, the "Reformers' interpretation" still holds water?[22] Whereas E. P. Sanders is surely right[23] in scouting the notion that Judaism was a religion of anxious "book-keeping", and in observing that a Jew was in the Covenant-area by no merit but by the grace of God, it must not be overlooked that Sanders does, nevertheless, agree that obedience to the Torah was necessary for staying within the Mosaic Covenant, within which one is initially placed by the sheer grace of God. If the Jew was "in " (i.e. within the Covenant) unless he deliberately put himself "out" by flagrant transgression, this does not alter the fact that "staying in" does therefore depend on observance: a code of laws does play an essential part, though not in the initiation of "salvation", which is by pure grace, yet in its maintenance. If, then, by contrast, Paul (while agreeing that the initial offer of salvation is purely by the grace of God) holds that both its acceptance and its maintenance are by faith rather than by adherence to any law-code, and that conduct such as, he believes, in fact fulfils the Law (in its spirit, if not in its letter) is an *effect* of this faith-union but in no way its *cause,* then he is not only setting up a sharp contrast between faith and Torah religion (which Dr Sanders agrees he is doing), but is, by implication, contrasting the maintenance of the convenantal relation for Christians by faith with the maintenance of it in Judaism by "works"; and this latter does seem to me not far off from the "legalism" (convenient though unbiblical term!) which Dr Sanders holds that Paul is not attacking.[24] Thus Sanders, if I understand him rightly, is denying that the Reformers' salvation by unmerited grace *versus* salvation earned by "works" ("legalism") is the issue with which Paul is concerned, and is saying, rather, that the issue is simply salvation (for Jew and gentile alike) by faith in Jesus Christ *versus* "covenantal nomism"; but I am asking whether "covenantal nomism" itself is so far from implicit "legalism". That both the Jew (according to "covenantal nomism") and the Christian (according to Paul) are "out" if "good works" do not follow is certainly true, but this is no proof that "good works" play the same role in both systems of salvation. In the one they are part of the *means* of "staying in", in the other they are a *symptom* of "staying in".[25]

If there is any truth in this contention, it throws some light on the tortured ambiguity of Paul's relation to the Law, which has already been mentioned and which E. P. Sanders and H. Räisänen so impressively uncover.[26] One of the results of Paul's confrontation with Jesus Christ as the love of God embodied, is a new attitude to law-keeping. It seems to have come home to him that only when one is "put right" with God by the response of faith to the antecedent grace of God does it become possible to fulfil the real demands of the Law, when these are formulated in terms of its "spirit" rather than its "letter". This is a paradox which, in fact, the observation of personal relations anywhere confirms. A trustful response to love is the only means of getting anywhere near to meeting the demands of love. Thus, Paul's "no" to the Law and "yes" to faith turns out to be, in fact, his "yes" to the "law of love" (all the deeds requred by love—see Rom 13:8, Gal 5:14), a "yes" made possible only because it is the result of faith; which helps to illuminate 1 Cor 7:19, which Sanders rightly describes[27] as one of the most amazing sentences that Paul ever wrote: "Neither circumcision nor uncircumcision counts for anything, but keeping the commandments of God". Is this Paul's "no" to the Torah as a salvation-system and "yes" to it as a revelation of God's nature? (Cf. Gal 6:15.) Perhaps Dr Sanders is right in denying that Paul's reason for rejecting the Torah is that it is too difficult to perform; but, if so, neither is Paul rejecting its performance as undesirable—provided it is interpreted as the performance, arising from faith, of what he believes to be the essential demands of the Torah. This, perhaps, is how Rom 6:14 should be read: sin shall not dictate to you (i.e. you *will* be able to keep the Law) precisely *because* you are not "under" Law but "under" grace.

This leads to the observation that a great deal is going on beneath the surface of Paul's argumention. It is because of Paul's understanding of Jesus Christ—because he has found in him the revelation and embodiment and mediation of the love of God—that faith in Jesus Christ is for him thenceforward the way to God. This may lead him to contradictory statements about the Law; but it is not by some adventitious or arbitrary decision to choose Jesus Christ that his Torah-religion is replaced, but because, in Jesus he is confronted by a living embodiment of that forgiveness and liberation by the mercy of God which, for both Judaism and Christianity, is at the heart of faith. For Paul, the glorification of Jesus Christ is more than merely his vindication against the verdict that sent him to death. It is the creative power of God's forgiveness, manifested in the death of Jesus and operative in his risen life: "God was in Christ, reconciling the world to himself" (2 Cor 5:19). If Paul's use of *nomos* is ambiguous, and perhaps inconsistent, it is because he is tenaciously faithful to the paradox of continuity and discontinuity, of fulfilment and yet supersession, which he finds in Jesus, and which is too big for fully coherent talk. It is the belief that Jesus is God's elect and the climax of Israel, and that, in a unique sense, he is one with God and with Adam, and so God's mercy and humankind's response embodied and implemented—it is these Christological convictions that bring the pain of the tension between continuity and discontinuity to Paul the Jew who has become part of the body of Jesus Christ. When Paul accepts the death of Jesus Christ as "for our sins" (1 Cor 15:3), he sees the whole sacrificial system summed up but also transcended; and my belief is that it was precisely because Jesus was, in fact, what Paul articulates, that

Jesus himself clashed with Judaism. Jesus was emphatically Jewish in his recognition and preaching of the great verities for which the Torah stands—the compassion and grace of God, the call to repentance and to resulting good deeds. But it was his tacit assumption that he had direct knowledge of the will of God and that where he was, there God's sovereignty was in action—it was this immediateness and directness of the representation of the Divine in the human—that seemed blasphemy. And it is exactly this that Paul articulates and that leads to the conviction that Jesus fulfills and transcends Torah and brings in the New Covenant. This is the real "scandal".

The all-inclusiveness of Jesus Christ was the conviction that determined Paul's thinking and practice. He seems never to have given up his conviction that, although the Old Covenant was transcended, God's election of Israel remained unrevoked; but his conception of what constituted Israel is hard for any Jew to recognize as valid; and his Christology led him to such views of the Law and such selective observance of it that, in the end, his claim to remain a loyal Jew could scarcely be maintained—as he virtually confesses in 1 Cor 9:19-22 and Phil 3:7-11. Paul was caught in the explosion that was the Person of Jesus, and so, I believe, is all that may be distinctively called Christian; a fact which needs to be recognized as significant evidence about Jesus himself as a historical person.

Notes

1. "The Gravamen against Jesus" in Festschrift for W. R. Farmer, ed. by E. P. Sanders, forthcoming.

2. In this connexion see A. J. M. Wedderburn, "Paul and Jesus: The Problem of Continuity," *SJT* 38 (1985) 189-203; and B. F. Meyer, *The Aims of Jesus*, London, 1979.

3. See C. F. D. Moule, "Jesus in New Testament Kerygma" in *Verborum Veritas, Festschrift für Gustav Stälin*, ed. by O. Bocher and K. Haacker, Wuppertal, 1970, 15-26.

4. C. F. D. Moule, *The Origin of Christology*, Cambridge, 1977, 13, 14.

5. C. K. Barrett, *The First Epistle to the Corinthians*, London, 1968, 221.

6. LXX has *eneulogēthēsontai* for both forms alike.

7. Paul does not actually apply *klētos* or *eklektos* to Jesus; and it is only in the Captivity Epistles that the closely related terms *ho ēgapēmenos* (Eph 1:6) and *ho huios tēs agapēs autou* (Col 1:13) occur; but *ho huios autou* (Gal 4:4) is, in its context, close to the same meaning.

8. See, e.g., D. W. B. Robinson, *Faith's Framework: the Structure of New Testament Theology*, Sutherland, Australia, 1985, 101-123, against Earle Ellis and others.

9. Dr W. Horbury of Corpus Christi College, Cambridge, has kindly communicated the following considerations in a letter (March 18, 1986). I am paraphrasing: 1. It is true that there is evidence for Abraham as father of many nations, including gentiles (Gen 17:5); indeed, it seems sometimes to be treated as a matter for pride that Abraham included so many nations among his descendants (Gen 25:1-26; 1 Chr 1:27-33, 34-54). See *Jub.* 15:6-8, 1 Macc 12:21, Jos. *Ant.* 2.238-41, Job 42:17c (LXX; cf. 1 Chr 1:44). On the borderline stands the thought that Abraham is the father of proselytes: *j. Bik.* 1.4, 64a, on Gen 17:5; cf. *Tanḥ.* ed. Bub., Lek leka, f.32a on Gen 14:1. 2. However, this well-marked gentile interpretation of Gen 17:5 could combine with, or disappear before, a yet stronger Israelite interpretation (see Gen 17:8-14). Sir 44:19-21 begins with an allusion to Gen 17:5, but—like the Genesis narrative—swiftly lays emphasis on circumcision and the Israelite seed (Gen 17:10), ending with a reference to Ps 72:8. Hence "seed of Abraham" and "children of Jacob" seem to be identical in Ps 105:6. (The parallel in 1 Chr 16:13 has "Israel" for "Abraham", but this need not be a deliberate correction, since "Abraham" is used in 2 Chr 20:7 apparently as a parallel to "Israel", and the interchangeability of the two may reflect a current usage in prayer.) "Abraham" is definitely the Israelite ancestor at Isa 51:1, 2; Ezek 33:24; and the force of Isa 63:16 depends on the assumption that Abraham and Israel alike are "our" fathers. See also Isa 41:8; 2 Chr 20:7; Tob 4:12; Pss Sol 9:9, 10; 18:3; 3 Macc 6:3 (all prayers); 4 Macc 6:17, 22, etc. This line of thought, whereby Abraham is pre-eminently Israelite, is obviously encouraged by the triple formula, "Abraham, Isaac, Jacob", Exod 2:24, etc., cf. Luke 1:54, 55, 73. Note further: *Tg. Isa* 41:8, 9 (where the Israelite particularity of MT "seed of Abraham" is further emphasized), *m.Ned.* 3.11 ("children of Noah" in a vow thought to mean gentiles, but "seed of Abraham" thought to mean Israelites), *m.B.Qam.* 8.6, in name of Akiba (even the poorest in Israel are sons of Abraham, Isaac, and Jacob; cf. John 8:33), *m.'Abot* 3.12, in name of Eleazar of Modiim (circumcision the covenant of "Abraham our father"). 3. The importance of interpretation 2. seems to be indicated not only by Paul's use of it when he attests his own Israelite descent (Rom 11:1, 2 Cor 11:22), but also by its prominence in the environment of early Christians (Matt 3:9; John 8:33; the Lucan canticles). [Add Luke 13:16; 19:9.]

10. Are the *dogmata* of Eph 2:15; Col 2:14 intended as a synonym for the Torah?

11. Robinson, however, traces the title rather to Justin and Melito, who got it, he thinks, "by direct extrapolation from the Old Testament" (*Faith's Framework*, 47, cf. 99).

12. E.g. H. Räisänen, *Paul and the Law*, Tübingen, 1983, 53; R. Jewett, "The Law and the Coexistence of Jews and Gentiles in Romans," *Int* (1985) 341-356 (349-354).

13. *Contra* E. D. Burton, *The Epistle to the Galatians*, Edinburgh, 1921, 358; P. Richardson, *Israel in the Apostolic Church*, Cambridge, 1969, 81, 82; Robinson, *Faith's Framework*, 102, cf. 113. For a good survey of views, see F. F. Bruce, *Commentary on Galatians*, Grand Rapids, 1982, 274-75.

14. E.g. P. Richardson, "Paul's Inconsistency: 1 Corinthians 9:19-23 and Galatians 2:11-14," *NTS* 26 (1979-80) 347-362; E. P. Sanders, *Paul, the Law, and the Jewish People*, Philadelphia, 1983, 101-102.

15. Cf. Sanders, ibid. 177.

16. The Pope is reported in an anonymous leader in *The Times*, 1 July 1985, as speaking of ". . . the people of God of the Old Covenant, which has never been revoked". So J. Koenig argued for a similar position in "The Jewishness of the Gospel: Reflections by a Lutheran," *JES* 19 (1982) 57-68. H. W. Montefiore, Bishop of Birmingham, wrote: ". . . we should reject the view that . . . the Second or New Covenant abrogates the Old . . .", *The Church and the Jews: a Lent Lecture given to the Clergy of the Stepney Area on 24 February 1983*, Birmingham, 10. He firmly rejects, however, the relativism that claims that all religions are culturally conditioned, and he recognizes that either Jesus is the Christ or not (ibid., 11).

17. J. Pelikan called attention, in a popular article, "The Enduring Relevance of Martin Luther", *New York Times Magazine*, 18 Sept 1983, to the fact that Martin Luther's commentaries on the Hebrew Bible are filled with extravagant praise for the Jewish people before Christ, but that, when his hope that the "rediscovery" of the authentic Gospel through the Reformation would cause a large-scale return of the Jews to the true faith, which was the faith of Abraham, "the father of all believers", Christians and Jews alike, was disappointed, he lashed out at the Jews and reverted to an endemic anti-Semitism. We all deplore the anti- Semitism and vehemently repudiate it; but Luther's hope of a land-slide may be comparable to that which Paul cherished.

18. Cited by Robinson, *Faith's Framework*, 100.

19. See C. F. D. Moule, "'Justification' in its Relation to the Condition *kata pneuma* (Rom 8:1-11)" in *Battesimo e Giustizia in Rom 6 e 8*, ed. by L. De Lorenzi, Rome, 1974, 177-201; C. E. B. Cranfield, "Some Notes on Romans 9:30-33" in *Jesus und Paulus, Festschrift für W. G. Kümmel*, ed. by E. E. Ellis and E. Grässer, Göttingen, 1975, 35-43; *Romans*, Edinburgh, 2 Vols., 1975, 1979, *passim;* H. Hübner, "Pauli Theologiae Proprium," *NTS* 26 (1979-80), 445-473 (464-466).

20. Räisänen, *Paul and the Law*, 50 n. 34; "Sprachliches zum Spiel des Paulus mit *nomos*" in *Glaube und Gerechtigkeit in mem. R. Gyllenberg*, PFES 38 (1983), 131-154. And for a refutation of the position indicated in n. 19, see Räisänen, *Paul and the Law, passim;* Sanders, *Paul, the Law, and Jewish People*, 15 n26, etc. In "Paul, the Lawyer, on Law," *Journal of Law and Religion* 3 (1985) 1-49, J. Hall proposes that Paul's inconsistencies are those of a lawyer, deliberately manipulating his arguments to suit his cause.

21. E. P. Sanders, *Paul and Palestinian Judaism*, London, 1977, *passim*, and *Paul, the Law, and Jewish People, passim;* J. D. G. Dunn, "The New Perspective on Paul," *BJRL* 65 (1983) 95-122; "The Incident at Antioch (Gal 2.11-18)," *JSNT* 18 (1983) 7-11; "Works of the Law and the Curse of the Law (Galatians 3:10-14)," *NTS* 31 (1985-6) 523-542.

22. That Paul's view of *nomos* changed between Galatians and Romans is maintained by H. Hübner, *Das Gesetz bei Paulus. Ein Beitrag zum Werden der paulinischen Theologie*, FRLANT 119, Göttingen, 1978, [2]1980; see a review by J. M. G. Barclay, *JTS* ns 37 (1980) 183-187.

23. Especially in *Paul and Palestinian Judaism, passim*.

24. See *Paul, the Law, and Jewish People*, 154-160.

25. See further M. D. Hooker, "Paul and 'Covenantal Nomism'" in *Paul and Paulinism, Essays in honour of C. K. Barrett*, ed. by M. D. Hooker and S. G. Wilson, London, 1982, 47-56; R. H. Gundry, "Grace, Works, and Staying Saved in Paul," *Bib* 66 (1985) 1-38; K. R. Snodgrass, "Justification by Grace—to the Doers: an Analysis of the Place of Romans 2 in the Theology of Paul," *NTS* 32 (1986) 72-93.

26. Sanders, *Paul, the Law, and Jewish People*, 143-167; Räisänen, *Paul and the Law, passim*.

27. *Paul, the Law, and Jewish People*, 103.

Gottes- und Menschenliebe in Neuen Testament

Georg Strecker

Das Christentum gilt als Religion der Liebe. In keiner anderen Religionsgemeinschaft steht das unbedingte Bekenntnis zur Wirklichkeit und Notwendigkeit der Gottesliebe und der Liebe zum Mitmenschen so sehr im Zentrum. So zeigt es das Neue Testament als die älteste Urkunde des Christentums, in der die Anfänge des christlichen Glaubens und Denkens in bleibender Verpflichtung für die Christen aller Zeiten schriftlich niedergelegt worden sind. Ohne Parallele in anderen Religionen findet sich nur hier der Satz "Gott ist Liebe" (1 Joh 4,8). Um zu verstehen, was es mit dem christlichen Glauben auf sich hat, ist es notwendig zu erfragen, was der Begriff "Liebe" (griechisch: "Agape") im Neuen Testament an historischen und theologischen, an dogmatischen und ethischen Inhalten einschließt und was er als Gabe und Aufgabe zum Ausdruck bringen will.

I

Das Wort Ἀγάπη (und Derivate) ist nicht eine christliche Schöpfung. Auch wenn sein Ursprung in der griechischen Sprache nicht eindeutig ist,[1] so ist es doch im vorbiblischen Griechisch gelegentlich nachzuweisen. So ist das Verb ἀγαπᾶν in Bezug auf das Verhältnis des Höhergestellten zum Geringeren belegt.[2] Solche "herabsteigende Liebe" wird auch von der Gottheit gegenüber den sterblichen Menschen ausgesagt.[3] Von besonderer Bedeutung ist, daß möglicherweise das Wort "Agape" als Kultname der Fruchtbarkeitsgöttin Isis überliefert wurde; diese ägyptische Mysteriengottheit wird auch als Stifterin der Liebe gefeiert.[4] Allerdings ist das Wortfeld insgesamt nicht häufig vertreten. Es steht hinter den äquivalenten Begriffen ἐρᾶν, φιλεῖν und στέργειν zurück. Es hat nichts von dem naturhaften Trieb des "aufsteigenden" Eros an sich, der in der dionysischen Religion den Menschen ekstatisch mit der Gottheit eint, andererseits in der platonischen und nachplatonischen Philosophie der Sinnenwelt entrückt und zum Maßstab des wahrhaft Schönen und Guten wird.[5] Demgegenüber hat ἀγαπᾶν im Griechentum eine vergleichsweise geringe Bedeutung. Es kann mit dem verhältnismäßig farblosen Ausdruck "jemanden gern haben" oder "jemandem Ehre erweisen" übersetzt werden.[6] Von einer solchen blassen Ausdrucksweise ist der neutestamentliche Sprachgebrauch weit geschieden. Daher ist es notwendig, zum Verständnis des Hintergrunds des neutestamentlichen Agapebegriffs auf die nichtgriechische Vorstellungswelt zurückzugreifen.

Die griechische Übersetzung des Alten Testaments (LXX) gibt das hebräische 'hb mit dem Verb ἀγαπᾶν wieder.[7] Anders als in der griechischen Literatur hat hier "Liebe" einen profilierten, exklusiven Sinn, wie denn der Begriff oftmals durch Gegenüberstellung zum "Haß" eine spezifische Schärfe erhält: Wie der König Israels "die Gerechtigkeit liebt und den Frevel haßt" (Ps 45,8 MT = 44,8 LXX), so "liebt" auch "der Herr das Recht und haßt frevlerischen Raub" (Jes 61,8). Schon hierdurch ist deutlich, daß ἀγαπᾶν in der LXX sich umfassend auf das Tun Gottes und der Menschen bezieht und kein Bereich göttlicher oder menschlicher Zuwendung ausgeklammert ist. So wird auch das geschlechtliche Leben mit dem Wort ἀγαπᾶν bezeichnet (Hos 3,1; 4,18; Jer 2,25; Ez 16,37), aber auch die Liebe von Freunden im ungeschlechtlichen Sinn; zum Beispiel kann das Freundschaftsverhältnis von Jonathan und David durch das Wort Ἀγάπησις umschrieben werden.[8] Nicht zuletzt gilt dies für die ethische Zuwendung zum Mitmenschen, wie sie in der grundlegenden ethischen Forderung "Liebe deinen Nächsten wie dich selbst" (Lev 19,18) ausgesprochen ist.

Die alttestamentliche Gotteslehre ist zwar nicht durch den Begriff "Liebe", vielmehr durch den Gedanken der Erwählung des Volkes Israel durch Gott-Jahwe bestimmt, aber diese Erwählung kann als Handeln der Liebe Gottes gegenüber seinem Volk interpretiert werden: "Weil der Herr euch liebte und weil er den Eid hielt, den er euren Vätern geschworen hatte, darum hat euch der Herr mit starker Hand . . . herausgeführt und aus dem Sklavenhaus befreit, aus der Hand des Pharao, des Königs von Ägypten" (Dtn 7,8). Erweist sich in der heilvollen Herausführung aus der ägyptischen Gefangenschaft Jahwe als Liebender, so kann schon der Prophet Hosea das Verhältnis Jahwes zu seinem Volk mit dem Bild einer Ehe beschreiben (2, 19ff). Dieses Bild ist von den späteren Propheten aufgenommen worden (Jer 2,2; Jes 24,4ff). Im Dtn wird es mit der ethischen Weisung verbunden, daß das Volk Israel seinerseits Liebe gegenüber seinem Gott üben (6,5) und seine Gebote halten soll (20,12f; vgl. Ex 20,6). Hiermit sind Grundstrukturen des neutestamentlichen Agapeverständnisses vorweggenommen worden. Allerdings hat "Liebe" im Alten Testament noch nicht—wie dies später im Judentum und im Neuen Testament der Fall sein wird—die Funktion eines summierenden Prinzips, in dem alle Gebote zusammengefaßt sind. Vielmehr steht das alttestamentliche Gebot der Liebe auf einer Ebene neben zahlreichen anderen Weisungen. Ein weiterer Schritt in Richtung auf das Neue Testament wird in der Literatur des hellenistischen Judentums außerhalb der Septuaginta getan. Hier ist neben dem griechischen Alten Testament die entscheidende Grundlage zu finden, auf der sich Sprache und Vorstellungswelt der griechisch- sprachigen Gemeinden des Neuen Testaments gestalten. In erheblich größerem Ausmaß als das hebräische Alte Testament und das aramäischsprachige Judentum und Judenchristentum hat das hellenistische Judentum und das hiervon beeinflußte griechischsprachige Judenchristentum auf die Entstehung des frühchristlichen Denkens eingewirkt. Dies ließ auch für genuin-griechische Einflüsse Raum, auch wenn diese im wesentlichen nicht literarisch geprägt waren und durch das Zwischenstadium der zeitgenössischen Denkweise hindurchgegangen sind. Der Göttinger Gelehrte Emil Schürer hat zu Anfang dieses Jahrhunderts in dem klassischen Werk "Die Geschichte des jüdischen Volkes im Zeitalter Jesu Christi"[9] die Geschichte und Literatur vor allem des hellenistischen Judentums eingehend dargestellt. Für dieses Diaspora-Judentum, das sich um die Zeitwende in der römisch-hellenistischen Welt zu orientieren suchte, ist bezeichnend, daß Vorstellung und Begriff der Agape einen zentralen Raum einnehmen. Hier ist eine dreifache Aussagerichtung zu unterscheiden:[10]

1. die Liebe von Mensch zu Mensch; sie wird z.B. in dem im 2. Jahrhundert vor

Christus geschriebenen Aristeasbrief als "Gabe Gottes" und als Kraft (τὸ δυνατόν) der Frömmigkeit (εὐσέβεια) bezeichnet.[11] Neben der Liebe des Menschen zum Menschen steht

2. die Liebe des Menschen zu Gott. Sie ist nach Philo von Alexandria die Hinwendung zu Gott als dem "wahrhaft Seienden"; durch sie überwindet der Mensch alle Furcht und erhält den Zugang zum wahren Leben.[12] Schließlich erscheint die Agape

3. als Liebe Gottes zu den Menschen, wodurch der ursprüngliche Charakter der Agape als einer "herabsteigenden Liebe" zum Ausdruck kommt. Denn Gott neigt sich in Liebe zu seinem Volk herab und verheißt ihm das Kommen seines Gesalbten, des Messias (PsSal 18,4ff). Seine Liebe zeigt sich auch in der Gabe der Tora, die seine Weisung offenbart; sie wurde vor der Welt geschaffen und ist nicht nur dem erwählten Volk Israel, sondern der Menschheit insgesamt zugesprochen (Prov 8,22ff). Daher ist Gottes Liebe mit dem Erbarmen identisch, das er "aller Welt" zuwendet (PsSal 18,3).

Solche göttliche Gabe äußert sich in einer Vielzahl von einzelnen Anweisungen, die mit rationalen Begründungen verbunden sind. Besonders die jüdische Weisheitsliteratur, die schon in ihren Anfängen griechische Einflüsse nicht verleugnet,[13] ist durch ethisches, rationales Spruchgut geprägt und durch vernunftgemäße Überlegungen, etwa durch die Vorstellung von einer innerweltlichen Entlohnung des gerechten Menschen motiviert. Hierher gehört auch das die neutestamentliche Anweisung vorwegnehmende Gebot, dem Feinde Gutes zu tun. Es wird nicht nur durch den Vergeltungsgedanken begründet, sondern auch durch die Feststellung: "Dann wirst du feurige Kohlen auf sein Haupt sammeln", d.h. du wirst dir deinen Feind zum Freunde machen (Prov 25,21). So hat es Paulus in die Paränese des Römerbriefes aufgenommen (Röm 12,20). Auch im Aristeasbrief hat die Empfehlung an den ägyptischen König, daß er seinen Widersachern seine Gunst bereitwillig schenken solle, eine utilitaristische Ausrichtung; denn hierdurch vermag der Herrscher seine Untertanen zu ihrer Pflicht zurückzuführen und zu seinem eigenen Nutzen zu gewinnen (Arist 227).

II

Wie im Judentum, aber auch im Griechentum, so ist besonders im neutestamentlichen Schrifttum das Motiv von der "herabsteigenden Liebe" Gottes bekannt.[14] Diese Liebe manifestiert sich im Kreuzestod Jesu Christi. Im Anschluß an ältere christliche Tradition bezeugt dies Paulus mit den Worten: "Gott beweist seine Liebe gegen uns dadurch, daß Christus für uns gestorben ist, als wir noch Sünder waren" (Röm 5,8). Gottes Liebe ist nicht nur eine abstrakte Idee, die lediglich gedacht werden könnte, auch ist sie nicht durch mystische Einwohnung zu erlangen, sondern sie ereignet sich in einem historischen Geschehen, im Kreuzestod Jesu von Nazareth. Ein historisches Faktum stiftet die Urbeziehung zwischen Gott und Mensch, die dem Menschen die Fülle Gottes und das Ziel seines Lebens erschließt. Am Ende des Weges der Glaubenden steht das, was ihnen zugesagt ist, daß sie erfahren werden, daß Gott alles in allem sein wird (1 Kor 15,28).[15] Paulus verweist im unmittelbar voraufgehenden Text darauf, daß die Christen im Glauben an das verkündigte Wort und an die Wirksamkeit der Taufe den Geist Gottes empfangen haben und daß die

Gabe des Geistes Ausgießung der Liebe Gottes in den menschlichen Herzen bedeutet.[16] Daher können die Glieder der christlichen Gemeinden in der Frühzeit der Kirche allgemein als Ἀγαπητοί, d.h. als von Gott Geliebte bezeichnet werden (1 Thess 1,4; vgl. Kol 3, 12). Sie sind von Gott geliebt, weil Gott seine Liebe in seinem Sohn offenbart hat, weil solche Liebe in der Taufe erfahren und im glaubenden Hören auf das Wort Gottes angeeignet wird.

III

Die Erfahrung des eschatologischen Heils ereignet sich nicht allein darin, daß die christliche Gemeinde die Liebe Gottes in Jesus Christus sich glaubend aneignet, sondern nicht zuletzt in der Weise, daß sie ihrerseits auf das Geschenk der Gottesliebe mit Liebe zu Gott antwortet. Dieses Verhältnis der Glaubenden zu Gott beschreibt Paulus mit den Worten: "Wir wissen aber, daß denen, die Gott lieben, alle Dinge zum Guten zusammenwirken; denen, die nach seiner zuvor getroffenen Entscheidung berufen worden sind" (Röm 8,28). Die Liebe Gottes gegenüber den Menschen ist mit der "zuvor getroffenen Entscheidung" Gottes identisch. Sie weist auf einen vorzeitlichen göttlichen Heilsratschluß zurück. Solche den Menschen vorgegebene, existenzbegründende Erwählung muß in das menschliche Leben bestimmend eingreifen: die erwählende Liebe Gottes bewirkt, daß sich Menschen in Liebe Gott zuwenden und in solcher Zuwendung zu Gott Gewißheit und Zuversicht haben (vgl. 2 Kor 3,4; Eph 3,12).

Ist die christliche Gemeinde die Gemeinschaft derer, die als von Gott Geliebte ihrerseits Gott Liebe entgegenbringen, so kann sich dies auch als Liebe gegenüber Jesus Christus äußern; denn das, was dem Gottessohn entgegengebracht wird, ist auch auf seinen Vater ausgerichtet, wie besonders im johanneischen Schrifttum bezeugt wird: "Jesus sprach, wenn Gott euer Vater wäre, würdet ihr mich lieben; denn ich bin von Gott ausgegangen" (Joh 8,42; vgl. 1 Petr 1,8). Die Liebe zu Gott ist zugleich Liebe gegenüber Jesus Christus. Der christliche Glaube anerkennt die Einheit zwischen Vater und Sohn (Joh 10,30: "Ich und der Vater sind eins"). Verwirklicht er die aufsteigende Agape als Antwort auf die ihm gewährte herabsteigende Gottesliebe, so ist solche Agape auf den Sohn und den Vater in eins bezogen.

Hiermit ist der dogmatische Grundbestand im Neuen Testament skizziert. Das Wort Ἀγάπη wird im Neuen Testament sowohl auf das Verhältnis Gottes zum Menschen als auch auf das Verhältnis des Menschen zu Gott angewendet. Es ist nach dem Gesagten deutlich geworden, daß dieses Verhältnis nicht mit mystischen Kategorien sachgemäß zu beschreiben ist. Denn die Offenbarung Gottes in Jesus Christus ist ein personales Geschehen. Dies hat zur Konsequenz, daß der Mensch, der sich im Glauben an Gottes Offenbarung in Jesus Christus als von Gott Geliebter begreift, sich ebenfalls als ein personhaftes, in seiner Welt und für seine Welt verantwortliches Wesen versteht.

IV

Daß der Mensch unter der Agape in das Spannungsverhältnis zwischen Gott und Mensch gestellt ist, kommt in dem Streitgespräch zur Sprache, das nach der evangelischen Überlieferung Jesus mit einem jüdischen Schriftgelehrten führt, in dem ihm die Frage nach dem ersten von allen Geboten (Mk 12,28) oder nach dem großen bzw. größten Gebot im Gesetz (Mt 22,36) vorgelegt wird. Die Antwort Jesu verweist nicht auf ein bestimmtes erstes oder größtes Toragebot, das allen anderen übergeordnet wäre, sondern weicht scheinbar aus, indem der Eingang des alttestamentlichen Gebetes "Schema Israel" zitiert wird: "Höre Israel, der Herr unser Gott, ist ein Gott" (Mk 12,29: Dtn 6,4). Bevor die Frage nach dem Maßstab für das rechte Tun des Menschen beantwortet wird, ist es notwendig, sich des Grundes zu vergewissern, auf dem menschliches Tun, wenn es sinnvoll sein soll, sich realisieren kann. Das altisraelische Bekenntnis zu dem erwählenden Gott, dessen Handeln allem menschlichen Tun vorausgeht, leitet unmittelbar zu dem Gebot über: "Du sollst den Herrn deinen Gott lieben . . ." (Mk 12,30: Dtn 6,5). Diesem Gebot der aufsteigenden Liebe des Menschen zu Gott stellt Jesus nun ein zweites, gleichwertiges[17] parallel: "Du sollst deinen Nächsten lieben wie dich selbst" (Mk 12,31: Lev 19,18).

Man kann die kritische Frage stellen, ob dieses Streitgespräch, so wie es in den Evangelien überliefert wird, tatsächlich von Jesus geführt worden ist. Nach rabbinischem Verständnis sind nicht die Gebote des Alten Testaments in eine Skala einzuordnen, die mit einem ersten Gebot beginnt, sondern man unterscheidet allenfalls zwischen leichteren und schwereren Geboten.[18] Freilich, Jesus stammt aus dem sprachlich und kulturell gemischten Galiläa, so daß nicht nur genuin palästinisch-jüdische, sondern auch hellenistische Einflüsse sich auf seine Sprache und Vorstellungswelt ausgewirkt haben können.[19] Aber wie auch die Einzelheiten der Überlieferungsgeschichte dieses Streitgespräches beurteilt werden mögen, sicher ist, daß hier eine authentische Aussagerichtung der Verkündigung Jesu zur Sprache kommt: Jesus fordert nicht nur die Liebe zum Mitmenschen, sondern er stellt neben die zwischenmenschliche Dimension die Perspektive Gott—Mensch und Mensch—Gott. Die vertikale und die horizontale Dimension bedingen einander. Die Liebe zum Mitmenschen ist getragen von der Liebe zu Gott, und das Gebot der Liebe zu Gott realisiert sich nur dort, wo man sich in Liebe den Mitmenschen zuwendet. Da Jesus keine Eindimensionalität des menschlichen Verhaltens lehrt, hat er nicht einer weltflüchtigen Mystik das Wort geredet, aber sich auch nicht für ein sozialpolitisches Engagement ausgesprochen, wonach die wesentliche Aufgabe der Christen darin bestehe, die gegebenen Verhältnisse zu ändern. Wenn Jesus in der Logienüberlieferung als "Freund der Zöllner und Sünder" bezeichnet wird (Mt 11,19 par, Lk 7,34), so steht dies im Zusammenhang mit seiner Verkündigung von der nahenden Gottesherrschaft. Er ist einem Propheten der Endzeit vergleichbar, der seine Botschaft an das ganze Volk Israel richtet und sich besonders den sozial Deklassierten, den Entrechteten und gesellschaftlichen Randsiedlern zuwendet. Die nachösterliche Gemeinde hat seine Botschaft von dem Kommen der Gottesherrschaft mit seiner Person verknüpft, indem sie ihn nicht nur als den künftigen, sondern zugleich als den schon gekommenen Menschensohn und Gottessohn anrief und verehrte. Von diesem christologischen Bewußtsein sind die auf Jesus zurückgeführten ethischen Weisungen getragen.

In der Beispielerzählung vom barmherzigen Samariter konkretisiert sich das Tun der Liebe, wie es nach der Verkündigung Jesu dem Willen Gottes entspricht. Es ist der verachtete Samariter, der das Gebot der Liebe erfüllt, indem er sich dessen annimmt, der unter die Räuber gefallen ist, im Unterschied zum Priester und zum Leviten, die achtlos an dem Verwundeten vorübergehen (Lk 10, 29-37). Gemeint ist auch hier die Zweidimensionalität der Agape. So wird es in der späteren Parabel vom

Weltgericht ausgesagt, wo der Weltrichter die indirekte Mahnung ausspricht, sich der Hungrigen, der Fremden, der Kranken und Gefangenen anzunehmen: "Was ihr getan habt einem unter diesen meinen geringsten Brüdern, das habt ihr mir getan" (Mt 25,40). Das dem Nächsten erwiesene Werk der barmherzigen Liebe ist dem Christus selbst getan. Das Gebot der Liebe erschöpft sich nicht in seinem ethischen Sinn, sondern es ist nur von seinem Ursprung her zu verstehen, von der Offenbarung der Agape Gottes im Christusgeschehen.[20]

V

Die Zweidimensionalität des Liebesgebotes in der Verkündigung Jesu gewinnt eine besondere Schärfe in der unbedingten Forderung: "Liebet eure Feinde!" Diese Weisung gehört zu den ethischen Radikalismen Jesu. Diese werden (wie z.B. das absolute Ehescheidungsgebot oder das Verbot des Eidgebrauchs) in der Reihe von sechs Antithesen der Bergpredigt überliefert, also in einem matthäischen Kontext. Erst nach Ablösung späterer mündlicher oder schriftlicher Überlagerungen ist es möglich, ihren ursprünglichen Sinn zu entdecken, so wie Jesus ihn gesagt und gemeint hat.[21] Schon in der vorsynoptischen Überlieferung, in der Q-Quelle, ist das Feindesliebegebot mit dem Gebot der Gewaltlosigkeit und dem Verbot der Vergeltung verbunden (Mt 5,38ff par; Lk 6,27ff). Und Lukas erläutert das Gebot, die Feinde zu lieben, mit der (gegenüber Matthäus vermutlich primären) Forderung: "Segnet die euch fluchen, und betet für die, die euch beleidigen" (6,28).

Die kompromißlose Forderung Jesu, die Feinde zu lieben, wird aus ihrem ursprünglichen Zusammenhang mit der Ankündigung Jesu vom nahenden Gottesreich verständlich. Jesus geht über die überlieferten alttestamentlich-jüdischen ethischen Weisungen weit hinaus. Das Gebot der Liebe gilt nicht nur dem Volksgenossen (wie dies im Gebot der Nächstenliebe Lev 19,18 vorausgesetzt ist), auch wird nicht (wie Ex 23,4f) verlangt, dem persönlichen Feind in besonderen Notlagen Beistand zu leisten. Jesu Gebot leidet keine Eingrenzung. Es spart nicht einmal den Kriegsgegner aus. Jesu Forderung ist absolut: Wer auch immer euch in feindlicher Absicht gegenübertritt, sagt Jesus zu seinen Nachfolgern, der soll auf eure Liebe und auf eure Fürbitte stoßen! Hier gibt es nichts, was man zwischen sich und Gottes Forderung stellen könnte. Keine rationalen Überlegungen oder missionarische Zielsetzungen motivieren das Gebot der Feindesliebe. Es ist allein begründet in der kommenden Gottesherrschaft, die im Auftreten Jesu ihren Anfang genommen hat. Die Hörer Jesu, die diesen Ruf vernehmen, können nichts anderes tun, als einzugestehen, daß sie solche unbedingte Forderung nicht erfüllt haben. Darum ist das Gebot der Feindesliebe wie die übrigen ethischen Radikalismen Jesu letztlich mit dem Umkehrruf Jesu identisch, der sich aus dem Nahen der Gottesherrschaft ableitet. Das Feindesliebegebot darf daher auch nicht mit Leo Tolstoi in dem Sinn ausgelegt werden, daß Jesus mit dieser Forderung die Position eines Pazifismus vertreten habe, sondern es ist konkret gewordener Umkehrruf, die Aufforderung, sich abzuwenden von dem falschen Lebensweg und hinzuwenden zur kommenden Gottesherrschaft. Ähnlich wie Johannes der Täufer seine Hörer zur Umkehr rief und zur Bußtaufe leitete, so fordert auch Jesus mit seiner Botschaft seine Nachfolger auf, das Heil nicht bei sich selbst zu suchen und nicht auf eigene Leistungen zu gründen, sondern sich dem Kommen Gottes zu öffnen. Jesus gibt mit dem Gebot der Feindesliebe also keine Verhaltensregel, die das Verhältnis von Mensch zu Mensch allgemein ordnen soll, sondern er ruft zur Umkehr auf, die das Eingeständnis des eigenen Versagens und des Angewiesenseins auf den Kommenden einschließt und sich zur Solidarität der Sünder vor dem richtenden und begnadigenden Gott bekennt.

Die urchristliche Kirche, der der erste Evangelist Matthäus angehört, steht nicht mehr in der ungebrochenen Erwartung des kommenden Gottesreiches. Sie weiß, daß mit dem Auftreten, dem Tod und der Auferstehung Jesu Christi die Gottesherrschaft sich schon ereignet hat, auch wenn ihre Vollendung noch aussteht. In dieser veränderten Situation, in der mit einem unabsehbaren Ablauf einer künftigen Weltgeschichte gerechnet wird, versucht diese Kirche, die Worte Jesu neu zu verstehen. Das Gebot der Feindesliebe wird nun in einer Zeit aktuell, in der die christliche Gemeinde Verfolgungen ausgesetzt ist und wegen ihrer Zugehörigkeit zu Christus Nachstellungen ertragen muß (Mt 5,10-12). Die Feinde, denen Liebe entgegengebracht und für die Fürbitte getan werden soll, sind also zur Zeit des Evangelisten Matthäus die Christenverfolger. Solche Haltung der uneingeschränkten Agape verwirklicht die "Imitatio Dei", die Nachfolge, die sich das Handeln Gottes zum Vorbild nimmt, der seine Sonne über Böse und Gute aufgehen und über Gerechte und Ungerechte regnen läßt (Mt 5,45). Die matthäische angefochtene Gemeinde orientiert sich an der Forderung, die als Zusammenfassung des ersten Abschnittes der Bergpredigt formuliert ist: "Ihr sollt vollkommen sein, wie euer himmlischer Vater vollkommen ist!" (5,48).

VI

Hat Matthäus das Gebot der Feindesliebe in der Form einer Antithese dem alttestamentlich-jüdischen Gebot der Nächstenliebe und des Feindeshasses gegenübergestellt (5,43), so will er damit das Neue anzeigen, das durch die Botschaft Jesu in die Welt der Religionen gebracht worden ist. Diese Botschaft radikalisiert das alttestamentliche Gesetz und setzt es zu einem Teil außer Kraft. Mehr einen Ausgleich stellt demgegenüber die Goldene Regel dar, die Matthäus als abschließende Zusammenfassung der Bergpredigt zitiert: "Alles nun, was ihr wollt, das euch die Menschen tun, ebenso sollt auch ihr ihnen tun; denn dies ist das Gesetz und die Propheten." (7,12)

Lukas bezeugt die Goldene Regel in der Feldrede (Lk 6,31). Sie hat demnach vorsynoptische Ursprünge; aber sie reicht über christliche Überlieferung weit zurück. Schon im chinesischen Konfuzianismus (um 500 v. Chr.) ist die Goldene Regel belegt: "Tzu-Kung fragte und sprach: 'Gibt es ein Wort, nach dem man sein ganzes Leben handeln kann?' Der Meister (Konfuzius) sprach: 'Ist es nicht die Gegenseitigkeit? Was du nicht wünschest, das man dir tue, das füge auch keinem anderen zu.'" Seit Konfuzius ist die Goldene Regel in den asiatischen und orientalischen Kulturkreisen verbreitet, und sie ist in der hellenistischen und römischen Literatur häufig zitiert worden. Seit dem 4. Jahrhundert v. Chr. ist sie ein wesentlicher Bestandteil der antiken Vulgärethik. Über das griechischsprechende Judentum ist sie zum hebräischsprechenden Judentum und zum Rabbinismus gelangt. So wird sie von Rabbi Hillel (um 20 v. Chr.) als Zusammenfassung der Tora zitiert: "Einmal kam ein Heide zu Rabbi Schammai und sprach zu ihm: Nimm mich als Proselyten auf, unter der einen Bedingung, daß du mich die ganze Tora lehrst, während ich auf einem Bein stehe. Da stieß ihn Rabbi Schammai mit dem Baumaß fort, das er gerade in der Hand hatte. Der Heide ging zu Rabbi Hillel. Dieser nahm ihn als Proselyten auf. Er sprach zu ihm: Was dir unlieb ist, das tue keinem anderen. Das ist die ganze Tora, und das andere ist Auslegung. Gehe und lerne!"[22]

Es scheint beachtenswert zu sein, daß Rabbi Hillel nur die negative Fassung der Goldenen Regel lehrte ("Was dir unlieb ist, das füge keinem anderen zu") und nicht die positive Fassung, wie wir sie aus der Bergpredigt kennen ("Alles, was ihr wollt, das die Menschen euch tun, das sollt auch ihr ihnen tun"). Schon bei Konfuzius ist die negative Form der Goldenen Regel belegt. Ist also die positive Fassung spezifisch christlich? Soll hierdurch ausgesagt sein, daß die christliche Gemeinde den Mitmenschen nicht nur vor Schaden bewahren, sondern sich tatkräftig für ihn einsetzen soll? Jedoch: Schon Konfuzius hat die negative Fassung positiv interpretiert; das Prinzip der Gegenseitigkeit besagt danach nicht nur, jemandem keinen Schaden zufügen, sondern auch, "für jemanden sein Bestes wollen" oder "Gütigkeit gegen andere üben". Für Rabbi Hillel ist die negative Fassung die Zusammenfassung der ganzen Tora, also nicht nur der Verbote, sondern auch der Gebote des alttestamentlichen Gesetzes bis hin zum Gebot der Nächstenliebe.[23] Auch der Aristeasbrief verbindet die negative mit der postiven Fassung. Zur Zeit des entstehenden Christentums ist also zwischen beiden Fassungen nicht wirklich unterschieden worden. Sowohl die negative als auch die positive Aussage geben der ethischen Zielsetzung Ausdruck, daß sich der Mensch in seinem Handeln von der Rücksichtnahme auf den Mitmenschen leiten lassen soll.

Scheinbar ist die Goldene Regel Bestandteil einer egoistischen Volksethik. Sie scheint dem do-ut-des Prinzip zu folgen, einer Ethik auf Gegenseitigkeit, wonach man dem Mitmenschen das zufügen soll, was man von ihm selbst erleidet, im guten wie im schlechten Sinn. Doch darf die Goldene Regel nicht in der Weise verstanden werden, daß das eigene Verhalten von dem des anderen abhängig gemacht werden soll, vielmehr fordert sie, daß das, was man für sich selbst wünscht, die Grundlage des eigenen Verhaltens gegenüber den Mitmenschen sein soll. Die Goldene Regel richtet sich also weder nach der Reziprozität noch nach der Realität aus, sondern sie ist eine Forderung, die das eigene reale Verhalten an den idealen Vorstellungen und Wünschen orientiert, wie sie das eigene Ich gegenüber den Mitmenschen hat. Daher ist die Goldene Regel offen für unterschiedliche Inhalte, je nach dem, welche Vorstellungen und Wünsche für wichtig gehalten werden. Der Königsberger Philosph Immanuel Kant ist der letzte große Interpret der Goldenen Regel gewesen, als er den kategorischen Imperativ formulierte: "Handle so, daß die Maxime deines Willens jederzeit zugleich als Prinzip einer allgemeinen Gesetzgebung gelten kann." Im Zusammenhang mit der Bergpredigt nimmt die Goldene Regel das Thema auf, das Mt 5,20 lautet: "Eure Gerechtigkeit soll besser sein als die (Gerechtigkeit) der Pharisäer und Schriftgelehrten." Die Goldene Regel ist nichts anderes als die Forderung der Gerechtigkeit; sie faßt das Gebot der Vollkommenheit (5,48), der Barmherzigkeit (5,7) und der Feindesliebe (5,44) zusammen; sie ist die Summe des alttestamentlichen Gotteswillens, wie ihn der matthäische Jesus in der Bergpredigt autoritativ auslegt und zum "vollen Maß" bringt (5,17).

VII

Die johanneische Literatur enthält eine Agape-Aussage, die nahezu zur Quintessenz christlicher Theologie geworden ist: Ὁ θεὸς ἀγάπη ἐστίν = "Gott ist Liebe" (1 Joh 4,8). Eine ontologische Feststellung, wie sie in nichtchristlichen Religionen auch nicht angenähert bekannt ist. Gottes Sein wird als Sein der Liebe gekennzeichnet. Scheinbar eine Definition, ein Versuch, objektivierend von Gott zu sprechen. Doch ist die Feststellung "Gott ist Liebe" untrennbar mit dem Bekenntnis des Glaubens verbunden, wonach die Liebe Gottes in Jesus Christus offenbart worden ist. So wird in johanneischer Fortführung der urchristlichen Tradition[24] der Heilsindikativ durch das Wort Agape umschrieben: "Darin ist die Liebe Gottes unter uns offenbar geworden, daß Gott seinen einzigen Sohn in die Welt gesandt hat" (1 Joh 4,9). Der nicht aufzulösende Zusammenhang mit dem christologischen Bekenntnis macht deutlich, daß der Satz "Gott ist Liebe" nicht als eine Tautologie verstanden werden darf, als ob das Subjekt "Gott" mit dem Prädikat "Liebe" vertauschbar und beides miteinander identisch wäre. Es ist nicht gemeint, daß die Liebe Gott ist, so daß Gott zu einer "Art von Mitmenschlichkeit" würde;[25] vielmehr wird Gott deswegen als Agape bezeichnet, weil er sich in seinem vergebenden Handeln als Liebender gezeigt hat.[26]

Die von Gott gesetzte Wirklichkeit der Agape drängt zur Realisierung auf seiten des Menschen. Sie enthält die Forderung, daß die Menschen untereinander Liebe üben sollen: "Wenn Gott uns so geliebt hat, dann müssen auch wir einander lieben" (1 Joh 4,11). Wie dies der paulinischen Zuordnung von Indikativ und Imperative entspricht, so begründet auch in der johanneischen Theologie der eschatologische Indikativ den ethischen Imperativ.[27] Gottes Liebe ist der bleibende Grund für das Gebot, einander zu lieben. Solche gegenseitige Liebe ist nichts anderes als die Liebe zum Bruder, die selbstverständlich eine geschwisterliche Liebe ist, also die Liebe zur christlichen Mitschwester einschließt.[28]

Solche Liebe unter Christen wird im ersten Johannesbrief das alte und das neue Gebot genannt (2,7f). Es ist "alt", weil es von Anfang war und die Gemeinde seit ihrer Gründung darauf verpflichtet worden ist (vgl. 2 Joh 6). Dieses in der johanneischen Tradition verankerte Gebot verbürgt die Kontinuität der Gemeinde. Das Gebot der gegenseitigen Liebe ist zugleich ein "neues" Gebot, weil es durch Christus offenbart und beispielhaft praktiziert worden ist (Joh 13,34f). Christi Gebot der Bruderliebe ist die Weisung der neuen Heilszeit, verbindlich für alle, die sich zu Gott bekennen, die aus Gott, also im Licht und im Leben sind (1 Joh 2,9f; 3,14f); denn wer nicht liebt, der hat Gott nicht erkannt und bleibt im Tode (1 Joh 3,14; 4,8).

Ist der Tatsache, daß im johanneischen Schrifttum die zwischenmenschliche Liebe nur als gegenseitige Liebe oder als Bruderliebe genannt wird, zu entnehmen, daß sich der johanneische Kreis zu einer Konventikelethik bekennt und das Liebesgebot gruppenspezifisch begrenzt worden ist? Dies würde besagen, daß sich die johanneische Ethik wesentlich von der Weisung Jesu, den Nächsten zu lieben, unterscheidet. Ein Unterschied würde auch zur Ethik des Paulus bestehen, wonach nicht nur Liebe der Christen untereinander, sondern auch die Liebe gegenüber allen Menschen gefordert wird.[29] Es mag kein Zufall sein, daß in der johanneischen Literatur weder das Gebot der Nächsten- noch das der Feindesliebe bezeugt ist. Der johanneische Christus spricht mit dem Gebot der Liebe unmittelbar seine Jünger an (13,34f), und in den Johannesbriefen richtet sich die gleiche Forderung an die angesprochene christliche Gemeinde (1 Joh 2,7ff; 2 Joh 6). Zur Bruderliebe wird ebenso aufgerufen wie zur Gottesliebe und zum Halten der Gebote, ist doch die Einheit der Gemeinde durch die Verbreitung von falschen Lehren bedroht (1 Joh 5,1ff). Dennoch ist aus diesem Befund schwerlich die Schlußfolgerung zu ziehen, daß in den johanneischen Schriften "das Gebot der Nächstenliebe nicht nur eingeschränkt, sondern schlicht außer Kraft gesetzt" sei;[30] denn die johanneische Theologie kennt nicht die Alternative Bruderliebe oder Nächstenliebe, sondern den grundsätzlichen Gegensatz von Bruderliebe und Bruderhaß (1 Joh 2,9-11; 3,14f). Sie schließt daher ein, daß die christliche Verwirklichung der Agape sich nicht allein auf das Verhältnis der Gemeindeglieder untereinander beschränkt, sondern daß die johanneischen Christen sich verantwortlich in der Welt und zur Welt verhalten, so daß sie auch ihr Sein in der Agape gegenüber Nichtchristen bewußt wahrnehmen (vgl. 1 Joh 2,15ff; 5,4). Denn wenn auch die Welt im Bösen liegt (1 Joh 5,19), so ist doch Jesus Christus als "Retter der Welt" gesandt worden (1 Joh 4,9. 14; Joh 3,16f), und der Offenbarer wird in seiner unumschränkten Liebe gegenüber den Menschen (1 Joh 3,16; Joh 15,13) der christlichen Gemeinde zu einem verpflichtenden Beispiel; denn "wie Christus ist, so sind auch wir in der Welt" und müssen uns wie jener als unumschränkt Liebende erweisen (1 Joh 4,17).

Obwohl der johanneische Kosmosbegriff weitgehend negativ bestimmt ist, weiß die johanneische Gemeinde um einen missionarischen Auftrag. So geht es aus dem zweiten und dritten Johannesbrief als den möglicherweise ältesten Dokumenten des johanneischen Kreises hervor. In der Nachfolge Jesu ist diese Gemeinde in die Welt gesandt (Joh 17,18; vgl. 10,16; 20,21). Indem sie das Gebot der gegenseitigen Liebe verwirklicht, erfüllt sie ihren Auftrag; so scheint sie als das wahre Licht in der Welt (1 Joh 2,8ff).

Daß das Gebot der Bruderliebe nicht einer konventikelhaften Abgeschlossenheit Vorschub leisten soll, ergibt sich schließlich aus der Tatsache, daß sich die johanneische Gemeinde zu dem Satz "Gott ist Liebe" bekennt (1 Joh 4,8.16). Ist Gott der unumschränkt Liebende, so ist seine Agape nicht auf den Kreis der Christen zu begrenzen, sondern schließt Christen und Nichtchristen ein. Die Menschheit insgesamt hat die Möglichkeit, solche Liebe zu erfahren und sich anzueignen. Ist doch das Ziel der Sendung des Sohnes an die Welt, allen, die Gott ihm gegeben hat, dies meint: allen, die glaubend seine Botschaft annehmen, ewiges Leben zu bringen (Joh 17,2f).

Wir kehren zum Ausgangspunkt zurück: Ist also das Christentum eine Religion der Liebe? Man sollte diese Frage nicht zu schnell bejahen; denn der christliche Glaube ist nicht monoman und hat nicht nur eine Antwort auf die Wechselfälle des Lebens zur Hand. Gerät der Mensch in Konfliktsituationen, so zeigt sich rasch, daß der Rückgriff auf das "Prinzip Agape" nicht auf sämtliche Probleme des geschichtlichen Lebens eine konkrete Antwort bereithält. Hier ist der Christ aufgerufen zu unterscheiden und zu entscheiden, was jeweils das Rechte ist, das zu tun der Wille Gottes von ihm verlangt. Solche Entscheidung vollzieht sich im Raum der Freiheit, wie er durch die Offenbarung der Liebe Gottes in Jesus Christus begründet worden ist. Hierdurch gewinnt der Christ die Freiheit des Urteilens und Handelns, eine Freiheit, die immer aufs neue aufs Spiel gesetzt und immer wieder neu zu bedenken ist. Trotz dieser Einschränkung läßt sich im Vergleich mit anderen Weltreligionen das Christentum als "Religion der Liebe" bezeichnen, solange es Christen gibt, die sich zu dem Satz "Gott ist Liebe" bekennen und bemüht sind, daraus konkrete Folgerungen für ihr Handeln in der Welt abzuleiten. Auch wenn die christliche Agape nicht sämtliche Fragen des konkreten Lebens beantwortet, so bezeichnet sie doch nicht nur die Art und Weise, wie ein Christ sich in der Welt zu verhalten hat, sondern sie gibt nach neutestamentlichem Verständnis auch den Inhalt des christlichen Tuns an. Dies meint: Die Forderung der Agape drängt darauf, im christlichen Leben konkret zu werden; denn als der durch Jesus Christus erschlossene Grund ist die Agape das intendierte Ziel des christlichen Glaubens und des christlichen Lebens. Sie ist Zuspruch und Anspruch an den Menschen zugleich. So gilt es im Sinn des Paulus: "Nun aber bleiben Glaube, Hoffnung, Liebe, diese drei, aber die Liebe ist die Größte unter ihnen" (1 Kor 13,13).

Notes

1. Gegen E. Peterson (Ἀγάπη, BZ 20, 1932, 378-382), der die von H. Lietzmann (*An die Korinther I.II*, HNT 9, Tübingen, [3]1931, 68), E. Stauffer (Art. ἀγαπάω, *ThWNT*, 1.37f) und W. Bauer (*WB*, [2]1928, 7) angeführten Belege als durchweg nicht sicher ansah und es für "geradezu unwahrscheinlich" hielt, "daß das Wort ἀγάπη außerhalb der christlich-jüdischen Kreise geschaffen oder gebraucht worden ist" (a.a.O. 382), kann die Existenz des Substantivs in der paganen Gräzität aufgrund damals noch nicht ausgewerteter Texte und neuer Funde inzwischen als erwiesen angesehen werden (Belege bei Bauer, *WB*, [5]1958, 9, und O. Wischmeyer, "Vorkommen und Bedeutung von Agape in der außerchristlichen Antike," *ZNW* 69 (1978) 212-238). Nach Wischmeyer handelt es sich bei den ältesten Belegen um nichtliterarische Bezeugungen des Frauennamens Ἀγάπη aus dem 6. bzw. dem 5. Jh. v. Chr. Wie Στοργή und Φιλία sei Ἀγάπη ein "Abstraktname", dessen Entstehung das Vorhandensein des Substantivs ἀγάπη voraussetze (a.a.O. 226f). Aus der Tatsache, daß einer dieser ältesten Belege einen Hetärennamen wiedergibt, könne gefolgert werden, daß ἀγάπη "als 'Liebe' in einem ähnlichen allgemein erotisch gehaltenen Sinne wie in den Parallelnamen Στοργή und Φιλία zugrunde lag" (a.a.O. 237).

2. Z. B. gegenüber Fremden: Hom Od VIII 33; ἀγαπητός bezeichnet den von den Eltern geliebten (einzigen) Sohn: Hom Il VI 401; Od II 365 u.ö.

3. So erzeigt der Gott seine Liebe gegenüber den Sterblichen, wenn er sie mit seinem Besuch ehrt: Hom Il 24, 464; auch CIG 5119; DioChrys Or 33,21.

4. Die hierfür als Belege angeführten Stellen aus P Oxy 1380, einem als "Isis-Litanei" bekanntgewordenen Text aus dem 2. nachchristl. Jahrhundert, sind jedoch umstritten. Nach der Ausgabe von B. P. Grenfell u. A. S. Hunt (*P Oxy XI*, 1915, p. 196.198) ist in Z. 27f ἐ]ν Θώνι ἀγάπ[ην . . .], in Z. 109f ἐν Ἰταλίᾳ ἀ[γά]πην θεῶν zu lesen. Demnach wäre die Göttin Isis in Thonis als ἀγάπη, in Italien als ἀγάπη θεῶν angerufen worden. Diese Lesart hat starken Widerspruch hervorgerufen, da von den durch die Herausgeber zu ἀγάπην vervollständigten Worten jeweils nur drei Buchstaben klar zu identifizieren sind. Am schärfsten hat sich Peterson gegen die Auswertung dieser Stellen als Belege für die außerchristliche Bezeugung von ἀγάπη ausgesprochen; er ging dabei freilich von der heute nicht mehr haltbaren Annahme aus, daß das Wort in der außerbiblischen Literatur überhaupt nicht vorkomme (a.a.O. 382 [s.o. Anm. 1]). Selbst bei den Forschern, die P Oxy 1380 als Beleg für das außerchristliche Vorkommen von ἀγάπη anerkennen, herrscht im Detail Unsicherheit: E. Stauffer nimmt für Z. 109 G. Manteuffels Konjekturvorschlag auf, wonach ἐν Ἰταλίᾳ ἀ[γα]θήν ἄθολον zu lesen ist (*Revue de philologie* 54 (1928) 163), hält aber das ἀγάπην in Z. 28 aufgrund der Parallelität zu φιλίαν in Z. 94 für "einigermaßen gesichert" (*ThWNT*, 1.38). Zu dem umgekehrten Ergebnis gelangt C. H. Roberts (*Journal of Egyptian Archeology* 39 [1953] 114) aufgrund eigener Prüfung des Originals. Während er ἀγάπην in Z. 28 als Zweifelhaft ansieht und die Lesarten ἀγάπησιν oder ἀγαθήν für wahrscheinlich hält, sei für Z. 109 Grenfalls und Hunts Rekonstruktion zu folgen; das erste ἀ des ἀγάπην gelesenen Worts bedürfe nicht einmal des Unsicherheitsvermerks. Ihm haben sich die meisten neueren Forscher angeschlossen, so daß sich die im *JThS* über mehrere Jahrgänge hinweg geführte Auseinandersetzung zwischen S. West u. R. E. Witt (*JThS* 18 [1967] 142f; 19 [1968], 209-211; 20 [1969], 228-230; rekapituliert von J. G. Griffiths, *JThS* 29 [1978] 147-151) nurmehr um Z. 109, insbesondere um die religionsgeschichtliche Möglichkeit der Lesarten ἀγάπη θεῶν bzw. ἀγαθή θεός als Isis-Titel drehte. Eine befriedigende Klärung kann jedoch auch auf diesem Weg nicht erreicht werden, da Isis in der Spätantike als universale Gottheit verehrt wurde, als "una quae es omnia dea Isis" (Dessau, Inscr. Lat. Select. 4362), die mit allen möglichen orientalischen und griechischen Gottheiten gleichgesetzt werden konnte und daher als die "tausendnamige" (μυρόνυμα) bezeichnet wurde (vgl. J. Leipoldt—W. Grundmann, *Umwelt des Urchristentums I [Darstellung]*, Berlin, 1979, 123f.). Isis wurde mit Demeter (= bona dea) und auch mit Aphrodite identifiziert, so daß "Beziehungen sowohl zu einer Titulatur ἀγάπην θεῶν als auch ἀγαθὴ θεός vorhanden sind" (Wischmeyer, a.a.O. 220. Nm. 41). In beiden Fällen würde es sich allerdings um einen einmaligen Beleg handeln. Wird man mit Wischmeyer Z. 109 "wegen der mangelhaften Überlieferung und wegen der zusätzlichen Schwierigkeit, ἀγάπην θεῶν sinnvoll zu übersetzen" (a.a.O. 220f), nicht als sicheren Beleg ansehen können, so ist eine solche Titulatur angesichts der Prädikationen φιλία in Z. 94 und φιλόστοργος in Z. 12 und Z. 131 und der Belege, in denen Isis als Subjekt von ἀγαπᾶν erscheint

(CIG 5119 und Wilcken, Chrest 109, 12), jedenfalls nicht unwahrscheinlich. So entspricht es auch der Verwendung von στέργειν in Bezug auf Isis in der Aretalogie v. Kyme 19f.27 (veröffentlicht von W. Peek, "Hymnus in Isim Andrius," Diss. Berlin, 1929, 18ff; deutsche Übersetzung in: J. Leipoldt—W. Grundmann, *Umwelt des Urchristentums II [Texte]*, Berlin ⁵1979, 96ff, dort Z. 25f. 34) und der allgemeinen Charakteristik der Göttin (vgl. dazu F. Cumont, *Die orientalischen Religionen*, Leipzig, ³1931, 83f).

5. Vgl. Stauffer, a.a.O.⁵ 35f (mit Hinweis auf die spätere humanistische Kultivierung des Erosbegriffes bei Maximus und die mystische Sublimierung durch Plotin).

6. Vgl. Stauffer, a.a.O. 36.

7. Zum Vorkommen von ἀγαπάω κτλ. in der Septuaginta:

ἀγαπάω	258x	(167x 'āhēb)
ἀγάπη	19x	(6x 'ah^{a}bâ)
ἀγάπησις	10x	(6x 'ah^{a}bâ)
ἀγαπητός	22x	(1x 'āhēb)

8. 2Reg 1,26 (Überordnung über die ἀγάπησις γυναικῶν).

9. E. Schürer, *Die Geschichte des jüdischen Volkes im Zeitalter Jesu Christi*, I-III, Leipzig, ³/⁴1901-1909.

10. Vor allem in der stoisch geprägten Gräzität bedeutet φιλέω 1. die Liebe von Mensch zu Mensch im "herabsteigenden" Sinn (so Anthol. graec. VII, 378,2: Ehepartner; Pind., Pyth. 10,66: Freunde; Hom Od XIV 146; XV 370: Herren und Gesinde), 2. die Liebe der Götter zu den Menschen (Hom Il II 197; XI 94; Od XV 245f). Dagegen wird die Liebe des Menschen zu Gott nicht mit φιλέω bezeichnet.

11. Arist 229.

12. Deus imm 69; vgl. de migr Abr 169; Weish 3,9; Philo Fr. bei Joh Damsc, zit. bei J. Wettstein, *Novum Testamentum Graecum II*, Graz, 1962 (Nachdr. von 1752) p. 715 zu 1 Joh 2,15 (= Th. Mangey [Hg.], Philonis Judae; Opera II, 1742, p. 649).

13. So z.B. Prov 1-9: A. Weiser, *Einleitung in das Alte Testament*, Göttingen, ⁴1957, 219.

14. Belege für "herabsteigende Liebe" im NT: Röm 5,5ff; 8,32.39; Joh 3,16f; 1 Joh 4,9f u.a.

15. Trotz dieser scheinbar pantheistischen Formulierung steht Paulus im Traditionsstrom der jüdischen Eschatologie, in der nicht eine endzeitliche Identifikation Gottes mit dem All, sondern die künftige endgültige Ausübung seiner herrscherlichen Gewalt erwartet wird, wie H. Conzelmann zu Recht betont hat (KEK V, 1969, S. 326f)—dies unterscheidet das ntl. Denken von der Auffassung des Zen-Buddhismus, wonach die Vollkommenheit darin besteht, daß "eins in allem und alles in einem" erkannt wird (vgl. die knappe, aber eindringende Charakteristik bei H. Thielicke, *Zu Gast auf einem schönen Stern. Erinnerungen*, Hamburg, ³1984, 343).

16. Röm 5,5; vgl. noch Joh 3,16 ("also hat Gott die Welt geliebt . . ."); 1 Joh 4,9 ("darin ist die Liebe Gottes zu uns offenbar geworden, daß Gott seinen einzigen Sohn in die Welt gesandt hat, damit wir durch ihn leben"); siehe unten.

17. Mt 22,39 antwortet auf die Frage des Schriftgelehrten nach dem großen Gebot, indem das zweite gleichrangig neben das erste Gebot gestellt wird (ὁμοία). Vgl. A. C. Burchard ("Das doppelte Liebesgebot in der frühen christlichen Überlieferung," in: *Der Ruf Jesu und die Antwort der Gemeinde, FS J. Jeremias*, hrsg. v. E. Lohse, Göttingen, 1970, S. 39-62; S. 61): V 39 zeige Gleichordnung der beiden Gebote trotz Differenz, d.h. das "Gebot der Nächstenliebe ist . . . hermeneutisches Prinzip und kritischer Kanon" des Gesetzes.—Ohne jegliche Verbindung werden in Lk 10,27 die beiden Gebote unter dem sachlichen Imperativ ἀγαπήσεις nebeneinandergeordnet.—In Mk 12,31 wird durch die Numerierung δευτέρα αὕτη (vgl. V 29: πρώτη) eine kurze Verbindung zwischen dem Gebot der Gottesliebe und dem der Nächstenliebe hergestellt. V 33 zeigt aber in der Antwort des Schriftgelehrten, daß die beiden Gebote wie bei Mt als gleichrangig angesehen werden.

18. Nachweise bei G. Strecker, *Die Bergpredigt. Ein exegetischer Kommentar*, Göttingen ²1985, 59 Anm. 105.

19. Nach Burchard wäre "das doppelte Gebot als solches oder in seiner Funktion gegenüber der tora ein Novum" (a.a.O. 55). Die Zitatenkombination Dtn 6,5 + Lev 19,18 sei in jüdischen Texten nicht belegt, der Substanz und der Funktion nach aber im jüdisch-hellenistischen Bereich vorgebildet (Test Iss 5,2; Test Dan 5,3; Philo, De spec leg II 63; De decal 18f). R. A. Fuller ("Das Doppel-

gebot der Liebe. Ein Testfall für die Echtheitskriterien der Worte Jesu," in: *Jesus Christus in Historie und Theologie, FS H. Conzelmann,* hrsg. v. G. Strecker, Tübingen 1975, 317-329) dagegen verankert das Doppelgebot in der hellenistischen Weisheitstradition Palästinas. Mit dem Verweis auf den Semitismus in Test Dan 5,3 (ἐν mit Dativ) und in den aramäischen Fragmenten des Test Levi sieht er den Beginn der Testamentenüberlieferung eher in Palästina als im hellenistischen Judentum. Die Verbindung des Doppelgebotes mit der Weisheit in Test Naph 8,9f und Test Levi 13, 7 deute darauf hin, daß die hellenisierte Weisheitsüberlieferung und die Jesustradition aus derselben Weisheitstradition stammen. Das würde bedeuten, "daß es zwei Seiten in Jesu Gedankenwelt gab, die eine apokalyptisch, die andere weisheitlich" (a.a.O. 29).

20. Vgl. auch das Gleichnis vom verlorenen Sohn bzw. von den verlorenen Söhnen in Lk 15,11-32.

21. Da am Anfang der neutestamentlichen Überlieferung weitgehend isolierte Einzelstücke stehen, ist es nicht gut möglich, eindeutig den ursprünglichen "Sitz im Leben" des Gebotes der Feindesliebe zu bestimmen; dies gilt auch für die vorsynoptische Zwischenüberlieferung. So ist versucht worden, die "Feinde" mit zelotischen Aufständischen gleichzusetzen, die um das Jahr 66 die Christen bewegen wollten, sich in den Wirren des jüdischen Krieges auf ihre Seite zu stellen. Oder man hat an die Gegner der urchristlichen Missionare gedacht, welche die dem Gebot der unbedingten Armut verpflichteten christlichen Wanderprediger verfolgten—doch sind dies sozialethische oder soziologische Interpretationen, die im Text selbst keinen sicheren Anhaltspunkt haben und zudem über die Situation im Leben Jesu keine Auskunft geben. A. L. Schottroff ("Gewaltverzicht und Feindesliebe in der urchristlichen Jesustradition. Mt 5, 38-48; Lk 6,27-36," in: *Jesus Christus in Historie und Theologie, FS H. Conzelmann,* hrsg. v. G. Strecker, 1975, 197-221), die Mt 5,39-41 im Zusammenhang der Geschichte des frühen Christentums sieht: Es liege eine politische Apologie vor, die "—nach innen gewendet—die Forderung, keine Pläne für einen Aufstand oder einen gewaltsamen Widerstand zu machen und—nach außen gewendet—die Beteuerung der friedlichen Absicht" aufzeige (219).

22. b Schabb 31a (P. Billerbeck I 460); zu Konfuzius: Lin-Yü XV 24; vgl. auch Herodot III 142; Hom Od V 188f.

23. Vgl. zum Verhältnis positiver und negativer Fassung auch Did 1,2f; Arist 207; Einzelheiten bei G. Strecker, a.a.O. 157.

24. S.o. IIf.

25. Gegen A. Nygren, *Eros und Agape,* Gütersloh, [2]1956, 97f; H. Braun, "Die Problematik einer Theologie des Neuen Testaments," in: ders, *Gesammelte Studien zum Neuen Testament und seiner Umwelt,* Tübingen, [3]1971, 341; E. Jüngel, *Gott als Geheimnis der Welt,* Tübingen, 1977, §20f; dagegen zu Recht M. Rese, "Das Gebot der Bruderliebe in den Johannesbriefen," *ThZ* 41 (1985) 52, Anm. 37 und schon R. Bultmann, *Die Johannesbriefe,* KEK 14, Göttingen, [2]1969, 71.

26. Entsprechend sind die verwandten Aussagen "Gott ist Licht" (1 Joh 1,5) und "Gott ist Geist" (Joh 4,24) nicht in einem distanzierten definitorischen Sinn gemeint, sondern als Bekenntnisaussagen zu verstehen, die das Handeln Gottes an den Menschen umschreiben.

27. Problematisch D. Bonhoeffer: "Es ist die Liebe Gottes und keine andere . . . , mit der der Mensch Gott und die Nächsten liebt" (*Ethik,* hrsg. v. E. Bethge, [8]1975, 58). So sehr auch die inhaltliche Beziehung der gegenseitigen Liebe zur Liebe Gottes vorausgesetzt ist, die Liebe Gottes bleibt doch eine Vorgabe, die—obwohl in Jesus Christus erschlossen—dem Menschen nur nachahmbar, nicht aber erreichbar ist. Andererseits gehört zum ethischen Imperativ die Verklammerung mit dem Indikativ unaufgebbar hinzu, so daß die Liebe zum Mitmenschen die andere Seite des von Gott Geliebtwerdens darstellt.

28. Zu Rese, a.a.O. 44.—In den Johannesbriefen wird die Anrede παιδία bzw. τεχνία unterschiedslos gebraucht:

τεχνία θεοῦ   1 Joh 3,1f; 3 Joh 4; vgl. 2 Joh 1.4.13
τεχνία   1 Joh 2, 1.12.28; 3,7.18; 4,4; 5,21; vgl. Joh 13,33
παιδία   1 Joh 2,14.18

29. Röm 13,8-10; Gal 5,14; 6,10; 1 Thess 3,12.

30. Rese, a.a.O. 57 (vgl. a.a.O. 54f zu 1 Joh 4,21). Es geht nicht an, für diese These "die Verweigerung der Gastfreiheit in den johanneischen Gemeinden" nach 2 Joh 10 zu zitieren; es handelt sich hierbei nicht um die Verweigerung von Gastfreiheit, sondern um die Abweisung von falschen Lehrern.

Part II

Paul's Use of the Old Testament in Acts

F. F. Bruce

Nearly thirty years ago Earle Ellis made his entrance into the field of international New Testament scholarship with the publication of his monograph, *Paul's Use of the Old Testament*. When the invitation to contribute to a *Festschrift* in his honor came to me, I was engaged on a fresh study of the Acts of the Apostles; it seemed to me, therefore, that an examination of the way in which the Lukan Paul uses the Old Testament would be an appropriate contribution.

If, by some disastrous mischance, none of the Pauline letters had survived, we should still have in the Acts of the Apostles a picture of Paul as he appeared to one of his admirers—an impressive character, a devoted missionary, a forthright and versatile speaker, but not (so far as Luke's record goes) a letter-writer. How far the impression of the man given by his own letters matches the impression of him that we receive from Acts is a question which has engaged the attention of many readers, who have given widely divergent answers to it. Here one limited aspect of the question may be provided with some evidence leading to an answer, if the use of the Old Testament in Paul's speeches in Acts (outlined in this paper) is compared with Dr. Ellis's intensive study of the use of the Old Testament in his letters.

1. *The Use of the Old Testament in a Synagogue Homily.* In Acts 13:16-41 Luke reports Paul as delivering a "word of exhortation" to a congregation of Jews and God-fearing Gentiles in the synagogue of Pisidian Antioch, by invitation of the rulers of the synagogue. Before he received the invitation, the lessons from the Law and the Prophets for that sabbath day had been read; it is possible, then, that the homily was based on one or both of those lessons. Some scholars, indeed, have undertaken to deduce from the homily what the lessons were on this occasion.[1] Unfortunately, they do not all agree. We may ignore this question and concentrate on the homily itself.

Whoever composed the homily, wrote J. V. Doeve, "must have had an excellent command of hermeneutics as practised in rabbinic Judaism."[2] More specifically, J. W. Bowker has recognized in it a "proem homily" form, starting with a text which does not come from either of the lessons, but which may serve as a bridge between them. The proem text at Pisidian Antioch Bowker takes to have been 1 Sam (LXX 1 Kgdms) 13:14, which is quoted in a targumic form in Acts 13:22.[3]

The homily begins with a summary of the mighty acts of God in the history of Israel from the Exodus to the establishment of David as king. In the earlier days of the settlement, the Israelite worshipper, when presenting his firstfruits at the sanctuary, acknowledged the good hand of God on his people from Jacob's descent into Egypt to Israel's occupation of the promised land (Deut 26:5-10). As time went on, there were further mighty acts of God to recall: in Ps 78, for example, the review covers God's "marvels in the land of Egypt" and moves on to its climax with God's choice of Judah as the favored tribe, Zion as the site for his sanctuary, and David as "the shepherd . . . of Israel his inheritance" (vv 12-72). This is the scope of the first part of Paul's homily.

71

Since it deals with a period of Old Testament history, it is not surprising that its language echoes that of the Old Testament, but there is no formal quotation until Paul reaches the accession of David to the throne; then he quotes God's testimony regarding David: "I have found in David the son of Jesse a man after my heart, who will do all my will" (Acts 13:22). These words conflate Ps 89:20 (LXX 88:21), "I have found David my servant", with Samuel's announcement to Saul in 1 Sam (LXX 1 Kgdms) 13:14, "the LORD has sought out a man after his own heart." The added clause, "who will do all my will", appears in the Targum of Jonathan (in the form ". . . his will") as a paraphrase of "after his own heart".[4] Here both the literal rendering (as in LXX) and the paraphrase are found together; they were probably joined in the testimony tradition used both by the Lukan Paul and by Clement of Rome (1 Clem 18:1). (In the testimony tradition ἄνδρα as against LXX ἄνθρωπον is a closer equivalent of Heb. 'îš, used in 1 Sam 13:14.)

This text, then, forms the climax of the first part of the homily—both because, as Paul goes on to announce, Jesus has come in fulfilment of God's promise to David, and also perhaps because, like David, so great David's greater Son is the man of God's choosing—preeminently so.

Jesus' Davidic descent is not a central theme in Paul's teaching (it plays no part in the recorded teaching of Jesus himself). When it is mentioned in Paul's letters, it comes in a summary of the common stock of Christian belief, as in Rom 1:3 (cf. 2 Tim 2:8), or in a biblical quotation, as in Rom 15:12, where Isa 11:10 is cited as a prophecy of the Gentiles' placing their trust in Christ. But it was a central theme in much early Christian teaching, and Luke gives prominence to it in the nativity narrative of his Gospel and in the reports of speeches of Peter and Paul in Acts.

In the present homily it is David who provides the transition from the kerygma of days gone by to the kerygma of the new age.[5] The mighty acts of God in Israel's history have culminated in the mightiest act of all, the resurrection of Jesus. Jesus has come in the line of descent from David. For the Lukan Paul, as for the Paul of his letters, the leading motif of the earlier revelation is promise, not law, even if it is the promise to David, not the promise to Abraham, that is in view.

The gospel kerygma, as outlined here, covers the same ground as Peter's preaching in the house of Cornelius (the same ground, it might be said, as the Gospel of Mark): it begins with John's baptismal ministry and goes on to the appearance of the risen Christ. Not only the resurrection of Christ but his execution took place in fulfillment of prophetic utterances which were unwittingly brought to realization by those who were responsible for his death. By putting him to death, they "fulfilled all that was written of him" (Acts 13:29): no specific scriptures are mentioned. But when his rising from the dead is introduced, one scripture after another is called in evidence. The first to be quoted, "Thou art my Son; today I have begotten thee" (Ps 2:7), may not refer exclusively to the resurrection: it illustrates God's fulfilling the promises made to the forefathers by raising up Jesus, and "raising up" may be used in the sense which it bears in v 22, where God "raised up David to be their king".[6] It is quoted, however, in a resurrection context, and the next two quotations are expressly linked to the resurrection. "I will give you the holy and sure blessings of David" (Isa 55:3) is interpreted in the sense that Jesus' resurrection fulfills the promises made to David and guarantees the perpetuity of his throne (cf. Acts 2:30-36). And as in Peter's Pentecostal speech, so at Pisidian Antioch, the assurance of Ps 16 (LXX

15):10, "Thou wilt not let thy Holy One see corruption", is treated as a prophecy of Jesus' resurrection, and the use of the LXX, with the word "corruption" (διαφθορά), seems to imply the empty tomb (from which Jesus' body was raised in new life, instead of being left to undergo decomposition).

Paul in his letters can string together a catena of biblical quotations, or combine two or more quotations to make a composite prophecy. He knows that Christ was raised from the dead "in accordance with the scriptures" (1 Cor 15:4); what scriptures had he in mind? When he emphasized the resurrection of Christ in his preaching, did he use biblical quotations to illustrate or confirm his statements? If so, what were they? They need not have been peculiar to Paul's preaching: whether he himself was the preacher or one of the Jerusalem leaders, he tells the Corinthians, "so we preach, and so you believed" (1 Cor 15:11). It would not be surprising if, in preaching the same resurrection faith, he and they adduced the some prophetic scriptures as, in some degree, Paul and Peter are represented as doing in Acts. No matter how much the selection and application of these Old Testament texts owe to Luke, there is no sound reason to doubt that he is reproducing the general sense of Paul's preaching.

The quotation of Hab 1:5 ("Behold, you scoffers, and wonder, and perish . . .") in the peroration comes from a prophet of whom Paul in his letters makes notable use (cf. the quotation and explanation of Hab 2:4b in Gal 3:11 and Rom 1:17). Habakkuk's words in their original setting pointed to the Chaldaean invasion of Judah. The author of the Qumran commentary on Habakkuk applied them to the Roman occupation of 63 B.C. Paul refers them to the final judgment. For Paul, as for the Qumran commentator, the "scoffers" are those who do not take the word of God seriously, and this is not inconsistent with Habakkuk's intention, although he addresses himself to Gentiles and not explicitly to "scoffers" (but that LXX καταφρονηταί had a Hebrew *Vorlage* is evident from the text cited by the Qumran commentator).[7]

One further quotation must be mentioned before we leave Pisidian Antioch: when Paul and Barnabas encounter the opposition of the synagogue authorities the next sabbath day, they announce that they will present their message direct to the Gentiles, and justify this action in words drawn from the second Isaianic Servant Song (Isa 49:6): "I have set you to be a light for the Gentiles, that you may bring salvation to the uttermost parts of the earth" (Acts 13:47). The person addressed is the Servant of Yahweh. When the words of Isa 49:6 are echoed in Luke 2:32, they are referred personally to Jesus; now his messengers are associated with him in their fulfillment. Both Luke and Paul himself recognize that whatever the missionaries achieve is achieved by Christ working with or through them (Acts 14:27; cf. Rom 15:17, 18, where Paul speaks of "my work for God" as being "what Christ has wrought through me").

2. *The Use of the Old Testament in Evangelizing Pagans.* When Paul (or any one else) made use of the Old Testament in addressing a synagogue congregation, certain assumptions could be made. It could be assumed that many, perhaps most, of the hearers would recognize an Old Testament quotation, or an allusion to the Old Testament, and that they would unhesitatingly acknowledge its authority, even if they did not accept the conclusions which a Christian preacher drew from it.

But no such assumptions could be made in the evangelizing of pagans. They had no knowledge of the Old Testament, and would neither recognize Old Testament quotations nor acknowledge their authority.

Again, it could be assumed that members of a synagogue congregation, whether Jews or "God-fearing" Gentiles, worshiped the living and true God, the creator of heaven and earth. They had no need to be introduced to him. What they needed to know was that this God, in fulfillment of his promises recorded in the Jewish scriptures, had sent his Son Jesus. With pagans the situation was different. They worshiped gods that were no gods. The first lesson they had to learn concerned "the living and true God"; only when they had come to know about him could they be told about "his Son from heaven, whom he raised from the dead". It is plain from 1 Thess 1:9, 10 that this was the twofold theme of Paul and his colleagues when they addressed the pagans of Thessalonica, and the evidence of Acts confirms that the message which Paul communicated to pagans in other places emphasized the same twofold theme.

When the people of Lystra were about to pay divine honors to Barnabas and Paul, the two missionaries tried to bring them to a better understanding of the divine nature by telling them of the "living God who made the heaven and the earth and the sea and all that is in them" (Acts 14:15). This form of words is taken straight from the Old Testament—from the Fourth Commandment, for example, where it is stated that "in six days the LORD made heaven and earth, the sea, and all that is in them" (Exod 20:11). This is not a formal quotation, of course, but on what would the preachers base their instruction about the true God if not on those writings in which his self-revelation is recorded? When Barnabas and Paul go on to speak of this God as the one who has not only created all things but also makes continuous provision for his creatures, they tell the Lystrans how "he gave you from heaven rains and fruitful seasons, satisfying your hearts with food and gladness" (Acts 14:17). This is not such a word-for-word echo of Old Testament language as their proclamation of God as Creator, but behind it can be recognized the terms of God's promise to Noah and his descendants in Gen 8:22 and the psalmists' joyful celebration of the goodness of God who supplies his people's need with seasonal rains and plentiful harvests.

The short summary of *praeparatio evangelica* to pagans in Lystra is amplified in Paul's speech before the court of the Areopagus at Athens (Acts 17:22-31). The members of that august court were as much pagans as the unsophisticated idolaters of Lystra, but they were cultured pagans, who would be expected to recognize and appreciate references to Greek poets and philosophers. So in Paul's speech we find allusions to insights of the leading philosophical schools which would be intelligible to them, and at least one quotation (probably two) from Hellenistic poetry, with which they would be familiar.

It would be wrong, however, to say that quotations from Greek poets play in Paul's *Areopagitica* the part which quotations form Hebrew psalmists and prophets play in his address at Pisidian Antioch. This may be so, in limited measure, from the viewpoint of literary form; but materially their role is different. The quotations from Pseudo-Epimenides and Aratus have only illustrative force: when the nature of the supreme God has been set forth on a more secure basis, then it can be pointed out that pagan thinkers have used language about him which shows that they had not been left without witness regarding his nature. But the knowledge of God communicated in this speech is derived from higher authority than theirs.

After finding his point of contact with the audience in the altar dedication "To the Unknown God", Paul begins his exposition by speaking of "the God who made the world and everything in it" (Acts 17:24)—practically the same words as form the exordium of the address at Lystra. God the Creator of all is also God the Lord and Possessor of all: God Most High, whom Melchizedek served as priest, is designated *qônēh šāmayim wā'āreṣ*, both maker and owner of heaven and earth (Gen 14:19, 22). Because he is Lord of heaven and earth, says Paul, he does not inhabit material sanctuaries. Euripides might have been cited to this effect, but Paul is echoing successive Old Testament statements—1 Kgs 8:27, for example, or Isa 66:1, 2.

Because God is Lord of heaven and earth, moreover, he needs nothing from his creatures: "It is not because he lacks anything that he accepts service at men's hands" (Acts 17:25, NEB). Far from our being able to satisfy any need of his, it is he who satisfies every need of ours—life and breath and all else. It is strange that Martin Dibelius should find Jewish antecedents to this insight only in writings of Hellenistic type: he cites 2 Macc 14:35 and 3 Macc 2:9.[8] That God's only requirement of human beings is a just, merciful and humble life is emphasized in Mic 6:6-8; why should they think it necessary to please or propitiate him with animal sacrifices and libations of oil? It is because, as he himself declares in Ps 50:12, "the world and all that is in it is mine", that he has no need of gifts or offerings like these. That is exactly the reason adduced in the *Areopagitica* for God's having no need of anything that human hands can bring him. One of Plato's dialogues, the *Euthyphro,* had been devoted to this theme, and a reference to Plato might have gone down well in Athens, but Paul's thought (or Luke's) moves along Old Testament lines, even if the wording and the presentation are Hellenistic.

If "from one man God has made every nation to inhabit the earth," is the correct translation of ἐξ ἑνός (Acts 17:26), there is no need to look beyond the first two chapters of Genesis for the identity of that one man: he is Adam. How his descendants were spread abroad "over the face of all the earth" is described in detail in Gen 10 and 11. The "allotted periods" which God has appointed for them are probably the "fruitful seasons" mentioned in the speech at Lystra; another suggestion is that they are the epochs fixed by the divine decree for the rise and fall of world empires, as seen in the visions of the book of Daniel. The "boundaries of their habitation" might be, as Dibelius thought, the habitable zones of the earth;[9] more probably they are the areas apportioned to the various nations by the Most High when he gave them their inheritance, according to the Song of Moses (Deut 32:8).

According to the first chapter of Genesis, the earth was formed and furnished to be a home for humanity before humanity was brought into existence to occupy it; so, according to J. H. Moulton, the tenses of the Greek verbs in Acts 17:26 indicate that "the determination of man's home *preceded* his creation, in the Divine plan".[10]

God's purpose in thus arranging time and place for the accommodation and wellbeing of men and women was "that they should seek God" (Acts 17:27). Paul affirms in Rom 1:20 that the visible things which God has made are pointers to "his everlasting power and divinity"; if human beings, seduced and confused by false worship, have failed to discern his true nature, "they are without excuse." But if God's purpose in all his works is that men and women should seek him, this is an echo of a call which recurs throughout the Old Testament: "Seek me and live" (Amos 5:4); "Seek the LORD while he may be found" (Isa 55:6). The Paul of the epistles takes up the same theme when he applies, paradoxically, to Gentiles the words of God in Isa 65:1, "I have been found by those who did not seek me; I have shown myself to those who did not ask for me" (Rom 10:20).

It is beside the point to contrast Paul's insistence on new life in Christ with the exposition of natural life "in God" presented in the *Areopagitica*. The quotations from the poets come in the part of the speech which is still *praeparatio*. Natural life is bestowed by God on all living things, especially on the human family into whose nostrils he "breathed the breath of life" (Gen 2:7). When he takes away their breath, they die; when he sends forth his Spirit, they are created (Ps 104: 29, 30); it is, in fact, in him that they "live and move and have their being". If Daniel can remind a pagan king of "the God in whose hand is your breath, and whose are all your ways" (Dan 5:23), the Lukan Paul is at liberty to say as much to a pagan court in Athens. This is no "God-mysticism" to be set against Paul's "Christ-mysticism";[11] it is the biblical doctrine of God the creator, whose image and likeness have been reproduced in humanity. It is monstrous, therefore, for human beings to suppose that they can represent him by any device of their own "art and imagination" (Acts 17:29).

This is good Old Testament teaching transposed into terms that were calculated to be intelligible to the Areopagites. Only when this instruction about the true God has been imparted does the speaker move on to the new thing that God is doing on the earth in the gospel age, through the "man whom he has appointed": the "but now . . ." of Acts 17:30 has its counterpart in the "but now . . ." of Rom 3:21. But the statement that through this man God, on a fixed day to come, "will judge the world in righteousness" is taken *verbatim* from the Old Testament (Pss 96:13; 98:9).

3. *The Use of the Old Testament in Ministry to Christians.* In an address to Christians one might have expected to find one or two quotations from the Old Testament. In Paul's only address to Christians recorded in Acts—his exhortation at Miletus to the elders of the Ephesian church—there is, in fact, not one Old Testament quotation or even reference. The only quotation in the speech is of an otherwise unrecorded saying of Jesus: "It is more blessed to give than to receive" (Acts 20:35).

There is nothing surprising in the absence of Old Testament quotations or references from Paul's words of exhortation to a Christian audience. Commenting on the distribution of Old Testament quotations in the Pauline epistles, Dr. Ellis has pointed out that there are none in those to the Thessalonians, Philippians or Colossians, and only one in Ephesians.[12]

There are, as might be expected, Old Testament parallels to passages in the Miletus address. A farewell address such as this will show resemblances to other farewell addresses, and resemblances can be recognized between this address and Samuel's words in 1 Sam (LXX 1 Kgdms) 12:1-5 in particular. If Samuel challenges his hearers, "Whose ox have I taken? . . . Or whom have I defrauded? Whom have I oppressed? Or from whose hand have I taken a bribe . . .?" (1 Sam 12:3), so Paul can count on his audience's assent when he says, "I coveted no one's silver or gold or apparel" (Acts 20:33).

When Paul charges the Ephesian elders to "feed the church of the Lord which he obtained (περιεποιήσατο) with his own blood" (Acts 20:28), there is perhaps an echo of Ps 74 (LXX 73):2, "Remember thy congregation, which thou hast gotten (ἐκτήσω) of old", or of Isa 43:21, "the people whom I formed (περιεποιησάμην) for myself." Again, Paul's declaration that he is "innocent of the blood of all of you" (Acts 20:26; cf. Acts 18:6) may be an echo of God's word to Ezekiel about his responsibility as a watchman for the house of Israel (Ezek 33:7-9). But echoes like these, probabably undesigned, are in a very different category from direct quotations.

4. *The Use of the Old Testament in Apologetic Speeches.* Paul's remaining speeches in Acts are apologetic in character: he makes his defense in a variety of settings—to a hostile crowd in the outer court of the temple (Acts 22:3-21), to the Sanhedrin (23:1-6), before the Roman procurators Felix and Festus (24:10-21; 25:8-11), before the younger Agrippa (26:2-23, 25-27, 29), and to a gathering of Roman Jews (28:23-28).

We shall not expect to find Old Testament quotations in speeches for the defense made before Roman procurators. Paul does indeed claim Old Testament backing when he tells Felix how he worships the God of the fathers, "believing everything laid down by the law or written in the prophets, having a hope in God which these themselves accept, that there will be a resurrection of both the just and the unjust" (24:14, 15). This statement of belief in a twofold resurrection, based presumably on Dan 12:2, has a parallel elsewhere in the Lukan writings (Luke 14:14) but not in Paul's letters, where the only resurrection in view is that of "those who belong to Christ" (1 Cor 15:23).

There is no Old Testament quotation in the speech to the crowd in the outer court; there is one in the proceedings before the Sanhedrin, but it is not a gospel *testimonium;* Paul observes that he would have been deterred from deliberately insulting the high priest by the commandment in Exod 22:28 (LXX 27): "You shall not speak evil of a ruler of your people."

He does not quote the Old Testament in addressing Agrippa, but maintains that the message which he proclaims amounts to "nothing but what the prophets and Moses said would come to pass" and expresses his assurance that Agrippa himself believes the prophets (26:22, 27). Even if Agrippa did believe the prophets, there was a difference between believing the prophets and accepting Paul's interpretation of them.

Paul's last speech in Acts, addressed to the Jews who came to see him in his lodgings soon after he arrived in Rome, concludes with a formal quotation—the words from Isa 6:9, 10, about unseeing eyes, unhearing ears and uncomprehending hearts, which were used from early days in the church as a *testimonium* for Israel's rejection of the gospel (Acts 28:25-27). Those words are not formally quoted in Paul's letters when he deals with the problem of Israel's unbelief, although other texts to very much the same effect are cited. But they are introduced (in a targumic form) at the end of the parable of the sower in Mark 4:12, and the parallel passage in Matt 13:13-15 quotes the Isaianic text more fully and formally. The Lukan parallel, on the other hand, abbreviates the Markan reference (Luke 8:10). (In John 12:39, 40, the record of Jesus' public ministry is rounded off with a quotation of Isa 6:10.) Luke reserves the formal quotation of the text to the end of Acts, where it is introduced "with devastating effect".[13]

This exemplifies a practice attested several times in Luke-Acts: Luke will omit altogether, or pass over lightly, a Synoptic theme from the appropriate context of his Gospel in order to introduce it later, in an appropriate context in Acts. One is led to the conclusion that, while composing his first volume, Luke already had the second volume in view, and decided where, in the plan of the twofold work, a particular theme should appear.

Of Paul's Old Testament quotations in Acts, as for Paul's speeches in general, one may say that the composition is Luke's, but that he worked with Thucydidean conscientiousness, so as to reproduce the total purport of what was actually said.[14]

*   *   *

These desultory observations are offered to Earle Ellis as a small tribute of thirty years' friendship and admiration, and in the confident hope that he will continue to enrich us for a long time to come with the warmth of his personality and the depth and breadth of his learning, so that he will go on leading us to a fuller understanding of the New Testament documents.

Notes

1. A. E. Guilding, *The Fouth Gospel and Jewish Worship*, Oxford, 1960, 78, suggests that the *seder* was Deut 1 and the *haphtarah* Jer 30. J. W. Bowker, "Speeches in Acts: A Study in Proem and Yelammedenu Form," *NTS* 14 (1967-68) 101-110, suggests Deut 4:25-46 and 2 Sam 7:6-16.

2. *Jewish Hermeneutics in the Synoptic Gospels and Acts*, Assen, 1954, 175-6.

3. "Speeches in Acts," 104.

4. "All my will" renders πάντα τὰ θελήματά μου. It is possible that *r'wth* in the Targum should be pointed *ra'wāt̄eh*, lit. "his wills", rather than *r^e'ût̄eh*, "his will". See M. Wilcox, *The Semitisms of Acts*, Oxford, 1965, 21-24.

5. Cf. G. E. Wright, *God Who Acts*, London, 1952, 76-81.

6. The verb in verse 22 is ἐγείρειν, whereas in verse 33 it is ἀνιστάναι, but the verbs are used interchangeably.

7. In 1QpHab 2.1, 3, 5 *habbôg^edîm* is read where MT has *baggôyîm* ("among the nations"). In several places in OT LXX renders *bgd* by καταφρονεῖν (cf. Prov 13:15; Hos 6:7; Hab 1:13; 2:5; Zech 3:4).

8. *Studies in the Acts of the Apostles*, E.T., London, 1956, 45.

9. *Studies in the Acts of the Apostles*, 33-34, 37.

10. *Grammar of New Testament Greek*, I, Edinburgh, [2]1906, 133.

11. Cf. A. Schweitzer, *The Mysticism of Paul the Apostle*, E.T., London, 1931, 5-8.

12. *Paul's Use of the Old Testament*, Edinburgh, 1957, 30.

13. K. Lake and H. J. Cadbury, *The Acts of the Apostles: Translation and Commentary* = *The Beginnings of Christianity*, Part 1, Vol. 4, London, 1933, 347.

14. ἐχομένῳ ὅτι ἐγγύτατα τῆς ξυμπάσης γνώμης τῶν ἀληθῶς λεχθέντων (Thucydides, *History* 1.22.1).

John and the Synoptics: Can Paul Offer Help?

Peder Borgen

I. An Independent Oral and/or Written Tradition?

The relationship of John to the Synoptic Gospels is a problem yet to be solved in New Testament research. Until World War II the predominant view was that John used one, two or all Synoptic Gospels. After the research done on this material by P. Gardner Smith shortly before the outbreak of the War, a trend away from that position gained momentum. A new consensus seemed to emerge: John was independent of the Synoptics.[1]

Many scholars who followed this trend assume that John utilizes an ancient oral tradition independent of the other gospels.[2] A major work along this avenue of research was C. H. Dodd's book, *Historical Tradition in the Fourth Gospel* (Cambridge, 1963, repr. 1965). Dodd attempted to uncover the traditional material in John by comparing it with what is most obviously related to the Synoptic Gospels, namely the passion narratives. He then proceeds with the analysis to the materials where there are fewer and fewer apparent synoptic contacts: the narratives of Jesus' ministry, those regarding John the Baptist and the first disciples, and finally, the discourse materials.

In recent years the view that John is dependent upon the Synoptic Gospels has gained new impetus. For example, F. Neirynck rejects theories of "unknown" and "hypothetical" sources behind John, whether they are supposed to be written or oral.[3] He writes, ". . . not traditions lying behind the Synoptic Gospels but the Synoptic Gospels themselves are the sources of the Fourth Evangelist."[4]

Against this background it seems pertinent to look afresh on Paul's letters in order to gain insight into pre-synoptic usage of gospel materials. In this way we may find evidence as to the form and the method employed in the transmission of tradition and thus make the hypothesis of oral tradition less hypothetical.

Among the passages containing traditional gospel material in Paul's letter, those passages on the Lord's supper in 1 Cor 10:3, 4, 16, 17, 21 and 11:23-29 (34) stand out. Only here does Paul use a unit of gospel tradition of some length.[5] What can we learn from these passages about agreements with the Synoptics and about the nature of the pre-synoptic use of gospel materials?

Paul and Mark. Paul (1 Cor 11:23-26) and Luke (22:15-20) represent a version of the institution of the Last Supper different from the one in Mark 14:22-25 and Matt 26:26-28.[6] Nevertheless, a comparison between Paul and Mark/Matt is of importance, since we can see in this way what kind of agreement might exist between two mutually independent versions of the same unit of tradition.[7]

The correspondences between eucharistic traditions in 1 Cor and Mark 14:22-25 are as follows:

PAUL AND MARK

Sentences (almost verbatim agreement)

1 Cor 11:24— τοῦτό μού ἐστιν τὸ σῶμα

Mark 14:22—τοῦτό ἐστιν τὸ σῶμά μου

Scattered Parts of Sentences (phrases)

1 Cor 11:25— τοῦτο . . . ἡ . . . διαθήκη
    . . . τῷ αἵματί μου
1 Cor 11:23— ἔλαβον ἄρτον
1 Cor 11:24— ἔκλασεν καὶ εἶπεν

Mark 14:24—τοῦτο . . . τὸ αἷμά μου τῆς
    διαθήκης
Mark 14:22—λαβὼν ἄρτον
Mark 14:22—ἔκλασεν . . . καὶ εἶπεν

Word Sets

1 Cor 11:26— ἐσθίῃ τὸν ἄρτον . . . τὸ
    ποτήριον πίνητε
1 Cor 11:27— ἐσθίῃ τὸν ἄρτον . . . πίνῃ
    τὸ ποτήριον . . . τοῦ σώματος . . .
    τοῦ αἵματος
1 Cor 11:28— τοῦ ἄρτου ἐσθιέτω . . .
    τοῦ ποτηρίου πινέτω
1 Cor 11:29— ἐσθίων . . . πίνων . . .
    ἐσθίει . . . πίνει . . . τὸ σῶμα
1 Cor 11:25— τὸ ποτήριον . . . πίνητε
1 Cor 10:3-4— ἔφαγον . . . ἔπιον
1 Cor 10:16— τὸ ποτήριον . . . τοῦ
    αἵματος . . . τὸν ἄρτον . . . κλῶμεν
    τοῦ σώματος . . .
1 Cor 10:17— ἄρτος . . . σῶμα . . . ἄρτου
1 Cor 10:21— ποτήριον . . . πίνειν . . .
    ποτήριον

Mark 14:22-24—ἐσθιόντων . . ἄρτον . . .
    τὸ σῶμα . . . ποτήριον . . .
    ἔπιον . . . τὸ αἷμα

Single Words

1 Cor 11:24— εὐχαριστήσας
1 Cor 11:24— ὑπέρ
1 Cor 11:23— παρεδίδετο
1 Cor 10:16— εὐλογίας/εὐλογοῦμεν
1 Cor 10:17— οἱ πολλοί . . . πάντες

Mark 14:23—εὐχαριστήσας
Mark 14:24—ὑπέρ
Mark 14:21—παραδίδοται
Mark 14:22—εὐλογήσας
Mark 14:23-24—πάντες . . . πολλῶν

Variant Words (corresponding in meaning)

1 Cor 11:24—εὐχαριστήσας
1 Cor 11:25—ἐμῷ
1 Cor 11:23—ἐν τῇ νυκτί
1 Cor 11:26—ἄχρι οὗ

Mark 14:22—εὐλογήσας
Mark 14:24—μου
Mark 14:17—ὀψίας
Mark 14:25—ἕως τῆς ἡμέρας ἐκείνης
    ὅταν

There are 68 words in 1 Cor 11:23b-26. Of these, 25 words are also used in Mark 14:22-25. Out of 49 words in 1 Cor 11:23b-25, 21 are found in Mark 14:22-25. Thus, 1/3 to almost 1/2 of the number of words used here are the same coming from two mutually independent versions of this unit of tradition.

This comparison makes possible the following generalization: Between mutually independent versions of units of oral and/or written traditions there may be close verbal agreements in the form of sentences, word-pairs and sets, single words, and corresponding variant terms. At the same time there are differences which give each version its distinctive character. There is no specific agreement found in the contexts of the passages in Paul and the passage in Mark except that Paul seems to presuppose a passion narrative, corresponding to the passion narratives in the Gospels.

After having examined the agreements between the eucharistic traditions in 1 Cor and Mark, our analysis also raises the question: What insights can these passages in 1 Cor 10 and 11 give us into the nature of the pre-synoptic traditions?

II. Tradition Received and Handed on: Commentary Attached

It is commonly recognized that Paul in 1 Cor 11:23-26 cites the institution of the Lord's supper as a unit of tradition. This is made clear by Paul's introductory sentence: "I have received (παρέλαβον) from the Lord that which I have given (παρέδωκα) to you."[8] 1 Cor 11:23 then indicates that the chain of tradition goes back to the words of Jesus, and that as the Lord, Jesus' institution of the supper had juridical (binding) authority for the congregation at Corinth.[9]

By an interpretative formulation in v 26—"to eat the bread and drink the cup"—Paul sets the theme within the perspective of the eschaton. This perspective dominates the subsequent verses.[10]

Before analysing 1 Cor 11:27-34, we will first present the text:

"The text":

23 Ἐγὼ γὰρ παρέλαβον ἀπὸ τοῦ κυρίου, ὃ καὶ παρέδωκα ὑμῖν, ὅτι ὁ κύριος Ἰησοῦς ἐν τῇ νυκτὶ ᾗ παρεδίδετο ἔλαβεν ἄρτον

24 καὶ εὐχαριστήσας ἔκλασεν καὶ εἶπεν, τοῦτό μού ἐστιν τὸ σῶμα τὸ ὑπὲρ ὑμῶν. τοῦτο ποιεῖτε εἰς τὴν ἐμὴν ἀνάμνησιν.

25 ὡσαύτως καὶ τὸ ποτήριον μετὰ τὸ δειπνῆσαι, λέγων, τοῦτο τὸ ποτήριον ἡ καινὴ διαθήκη ἐστὶν ἐν τῷ ἐμῷ αἵματι. τοῦτο ποιεῖτε, ὁσάκις ἐὰν πίνητε, εἰς τὴν ἐμὴν ἀνάμνησιν.

Theme:

26 ὁσάκις γὰρ ἐὰν ἐσθίητε τὸν ἄρτον τοῦτον καὶ τὸ ποτήριον πίνητε, τὸν θάνατον τοῦ κυρίου καταγγέλλετε, ἄχρις οὗ ἔλθῃ.

Commentary:

27 Ὥστε ὃς ἂν ἐσθίῃ τὸν ἄρτον ἢ πίνῃ τὸ ποτήριον τοῦ κυρίου ἀναξίως, ἔνοχος ἔσται τοῦ σώματος καὶ αἵματος τοῦ κυρίου.

28 δοκιμαζέτω δὲ ἄνθρωπος ἑαυτόν, καὶ οὕτως ἐκ τοῦ ἄρτου ἐσθιέτω καὶ ἐκ τοῦ ποτηρίου πινέτω·

29 ὁ γὰρ ἐσθίων καὶ πίνων κρίμα ἑαυτῷ ἐσθίει καὶ πίνει μὴ διακρίνων τὸ σῶμα.

30 διὰ τοῦτο ἐν ὑμῖν πολλοὶ ἀσθενεῖς καὶ ἄρρωστοι καὶ κοιμῶνται ἱκανοί.

31 εἰ δὲ ἑαυτοὺς διεκρίνομεν, οὐκ ἂν ἐκρινόμεθα·

32 κρινόμενοι δὲ ὑπὸ τοῦ κυρίου παιδευόμεθα, ἵνα μὴ σὺν τῷ κόσμῳ κατακριθῶμεν.

33 Ὥστε, ἀδελφοί μου, συνερχόμενοι εἰς τὸ φαγεῖν ἀλλήλους ἐκδέχεσθε.

34 εἴ τις πεινᾷ, ἐν οἴκῳ ἐσθιέτω, ἵνα μὴ εἰς κρίμα συνέρχησθε.

1 Cor 10:16-17, 21:

16 τὸ ποτήριον τῆς εὐλογίας ὃ εὐλογοῦμεν, οὐχὶ κοινωνία ἐστὶν τοῦ αἵματος τοῦ
    Χριστοῦ; τὸν ἄρτον ὃν κλῶμεν, οὐχὶ κοινωνία τοῦ σώματος τοῦ Χριστοῦ ἐστιν;

17 ὅτι εἷς ἄρτος, ἓν σῶμα οἱ πολλοί ἐσμεν, οἱ γὰρ πάντες ἐκ τοῦ ἑνὸς ἄρτου μετέχομεν.

21 οὐ δύνασθε ποτήριον κυρίου πίνειν καὶ ποτήριον δαιμονίων·

By using technical terms for the transmission of tradition—i.e.
παρέλαβον/παρέδωκα—Paul introduces in v 23 a quote of the Institution of the
Lord's supper (11:23b-25).

In vv 27-34 Paul gives a paraphrasing commentary on the quoted unit of tradition.
From this fact we see that (already) in the middle of the fifties the Jesus-tradition was
so fixed that it was quoted and used as basis for an added exposition. As can be seen
from the words underscored with a single line in vv 27-34, Paul utilizes fragments—
words and phrases—from the quoted tradition and builds them into a paraphrasing
exposition which applies it to a case-situation. In Paul's exposition the genitive τοῦ
κυρίου (v 27) serves as a clarifying addition to the fragments from the quoted tradition, . . . τὸ ποτήριον and . . . τοῦ σώματος. As can be seen from the words underscored by a double line, legal terms are woven together with these fragments from the
tradition of the Lord's Supper. Such legal terms are: ἀναξίως, ἔνοχος ἔσται (v 27),
and κρίμα . . . διακρίνων in v 29. In vv 30-32 Paul elaborates upon these legal terms,
without drawing on fragments from the eucharistic tradition. Finally, in vv 33-34 he
returns to the explicit discussion of the eucharistic meal. Here he refers back to the
institution of the Lord's Supper, vv 23-27, and even back to the situation in Corinth
pictured in vv 17-22. In these concluding verses 33-34, we again, as in vv 27-29, find
terminology from the (eucharistic) meal (τὸ φαγεῖς/ἐσθιέτω) woven together with a
legal term (κρίμα).

Although Paul writes the exposition himself and applies the eucharistic tradition
to a specific case, he nevertheless uses traditional ethical/legal forms. The form of
casuistic legal clauses is especially evident:[11]

27 ὃς ἂν ἐσθίῃ . . . ἔνοχος ἔσται . . .
29 ὁ γὰρ ἐσθίων . . . κρίμα ἑαυτῷ ἐσθίει . . .[12]

The exposition is in argumentative form. The case of eating unworthily is stated
in v 27. An exhortation then follows in v 28, followed by the rationale in v 29 (γάρ).
The negative effect which this has (διὰ τοῦτο) on the Corinthian church is narrated
in v 30. In vv 31-32 the opposite alternative is presented, and then in vv 33-34 the
conclusion is drawn.

This analysis shows that Paul uses a variety of forms in his elaboration and that
he changes style from third person singular to first and second person plural, and
from indicative to imperative, etc. Paul's style is, moreover, argumentative. He draws
logical conclusions.

This analysis also indicates that the help to be gained from an author's own particular style, and other individual characteristics, is limited. On the basis of such
criteria one can hardly draw the conclusion that 1 Cor 11:27-29 is produced by Paul
himself, since traditional style and terminology are used there. The section is, nevertheless, composed by Paul, and the following guide rule can be formulated: In the ex-

pository paraphrasing of gospel traditions, both words and phrases are fused together into traditional forms.[13]

Moreover, Paul does not indicate that he uses a novel approach when he comments on a given unit of tradition. From this one can assume that there were two activities running parallel in the church communities: (a) gospel tradition was being received, preserved and handed on, exemplified by 1 Cor 11:23-26, and (b) it was commented upon, paraphrased and applied to relevant concerns and situations as exemplified by 1 Cor 11:27-29.

Fragments: Eucharist and Manna. After we have analysed 1 Cor 11:23-34, some remarks should be added on 1 Cor 10:3, 4, 16, 17 and 21. It is significant that Paul here uses an expository paraphrase of fragments from the eucharistic tradition without first quoting the tradition itself.[14]

16 τὸ ποτήριον τῆς εὐλογίας, ὃ εὐλογοῦμεν, οὐχὶ κοινωνία ἐστὶν τοῦ αἵματος τοῦ Χριστοῦ; τὸν ἄρτον, ὃν κλῶμεν, οὐχὶ κοινωνία τοῦ σώματος τοῦ Χριστοῦ ἐστιν;

17 ὅτι εἷς ἄρτος, ἓν σῶμα οἱ πολλοί ἐσμεν, οἱ γὰρ πάντες ἐκ τοῦ ἑνὸς ἄρτου μετέχομεν.

21 οὐ δύνασθε ποτήριον κυρίου πίνειν καὶ ποτήριον δαιμονίων.

The words underscored by a single line are taken from the eucharistic tradition, as quoted in 1 Cor 11:23-26. The terms underscored with a dotted line—τῆς εὐλογίας, ὃ εὐλογοῦμεν—raise the question whether Paul also draws on other versions of the tradition,[15] since the corresponding term in 1 Cor 11:24 is εὐχαριστήσας, just as in Luke 22:17, 19. On the other hand, Matt 26:26 and Mark 14:22 have εὐλογήσας.

In 1 Cor 10:16-17, 21 the fragments from the eucharistic tradition occur within the context of 1 Cor 10:14-22. The heading of the passage is Paul's parenetic imperative in v 14: φεύγετε ἀπὸ τῆς εἰδωλολατρίας ("Flee from idolatry"). The reference to the Lord's Supper (vv 16-17, 21) and to the Law of Moses (Lev 7:6, 15; Deut 18:1-4) in v 18 serves as the argumentative basis for the warning against idolatry. The conclusion in vv 21-22 has the form of a rule for mutually exclusive alternatives:

v 21 οὐ δύνασθε ποτήριον κυρίου πίνειν καὶ ποτήριον δαιμονίων
οὐ δύνασθε τραπέζης κυρίου μετέχειν καὶ τραπέζης δαιμονίων.

("You cannot drink the cup of the Lord and the cup of demons.
You cannot partake of the table of the Lord and the table of demons.")

The same form is found in Matt 6:24 (Luke 16:13):

οὐ δύνασθε θεῷ δουλεύειν καὶ μαμωνᾷ.

("You cannot serve God and Mammon.")

Thus, in 1 Cor 10:21a Paul's paraphrase of a fragment from the eucharistic tradition has been given a traditional form, a form which also occurs in the Gospels, i.e. in Matt 6:24 par.[16] The passage from 1 Cor 10:14-22 reflects its oral nature. Paul exhorts the Corinthian church by means of a letter in lieu of appearing in person. The oral style is especially evident when Paul in v 15 addresses the church as if he were speaking to them: "I speak (λέγω) as to sensible people; judge for yourselves what I say (ὅ φημι)."

Formulations from the eucharistic tradition are also reflected in the haggadic reference to the manna and the well in the desert in 1 Cor 10:3-4, where it is said:

"They all ate the same spiritual food, and they all drank the same spiritual drink." In this passage Israel typifies the Christian people of God. Thus the events of the journey through sea and desert are applied to baptism (v 2) and the Lord's Supper (vv 3-4). The formulation in 1 Cor 10:3-4 seems even to reflect eucharistic phrases, as can be seen from the similarity to the wording in 1 Cor 11:26, which is an expansion of the institution of the Lord's Supper (1 Cor 11:23-26).

I Cor 10:3: τὸ αὐτὸ πνευματικὸν βρῶμα ἔφαγον . . .
10:4: τὸ αὐτὸ πνευματικὸν ἔπιον πόμα . . .
I Cor 11:26: ἐσθίητε τὸν ἄρτον . . .
τὸ ποτήριον πίνητε . . .

The conclusion to be drawn from these observations, is that already in the mid-fifties the biblical stories about the manna and the well were being applied to the Lord's Supper.[17]

III. Eucharistic Traditions in John, Paul and the Synoptics

Paul's usage of eucharistic gospel traditions in 1 Cor 10:3-4, 16-17, 21 and 11:23-34 can further our understanding of John's use of tradition. It can strengthen the hypothesis that John draws on oral traditions and is independent of the Synoptic Gospels. Such a theory does more than just allude to unknown and hypothetical sources behind John. Paul makes it possible to provide dated evidence for analogous use of gospel tradition independent of the Synoptics.

The best starting point for the examination of this hypothesis is found in John 6:51b-58, since John here draws on eucharistic tradition in a way which comes very close to Paul's handling of it. John has closer agreements with Paul than with the Synoptics.

The agreements between John and Paul are:

Word Sets

John 6:53— φάγητε τῆς σάρκα—πίητε αὐτοῦ τὸ αἷμα	1 Cor 11:24-25— τὸ σῶμα . . . ἐν τῷ ἐμῷ αἵματι
John 6:54— ὁ τρώγων μου τὴν σάρκα καὶ πίνων μου τὸ αἷμα	Cor 11:27— τοῦ σώματος καὶ τοῦ αἵματος
John 6:55— ἡ . . . σάρξ μου—καὶ τὸ αἷμά μου	1 Cor 10:16— τοῦ αἵματος . . . τοῦ σώματος
John 6:56— ὁ τρώγων μου τὴν σάρκα καὶ πίνων μου τὸ αἷμα	1 Cor 11:26— ἐσθίητε . . . πίνητε
John 6:52— τὴν σάρκα φαγεῖν	1 Cor 11:27— ἐσθίῃ . . . πίνῃ
John 6:57— ὁ τρώγων με	1 Cor 11:28— ἐσθιέτω . . . πινέτω
John 6:58— ὁ τρώγων τοῦτον τὸν ἄρτον	1 Cor 11:29— ὁ . . . ἐσθίων . . . πίνων. . . ἐσθίει καὶ πίνει
John 6:55— βρῶσις . . . πόσις	1 Cor 10:3-4— ἔφαγον . . . ἔπιον
	1 Cor 10:3-4— βρῶμα . . . πόμα

Sentences (in parts)

John 6:51— ὁ ἄρτος . . . ὃν ἐγὼ δώσω ἡ σάρξ μού ἐστιν ὑπὲρ . . .	1 Cor 11:24— ἄρτον . . . τοῦτό μού ἐστιν τὸ σῶμα τὸ ὑπὲρ . . .
	Luke 22:19—ἄρτον . . . ἔδωκεν . . . τοῦτό ἐστιν τὸ σῶμά μου τὸ ὑπέρ . . .

Subject Matter, not Words

John 6:53— οὐκ ἔχετε ζωὴν ἐν ἑαυτοῖς	1 Cor 11:29— κρίμα . . .
John 6:54— ἔχει ζωὴν αἰώνιον, κἀγὼ	1 Cor 11:34— μὴ εἰς κρίμα . . .
ἀναστήσω αὐτὸν ἐν ἐσχάτῃ ἡμέρᾳ	1 Cor 11:32— μὴ σὺν τῷ κόσμῳ
	κατακριθῶμεν

M.-E. Boismard[18] emphasizes the agreements between John 6:51b and 1 Cor 11:24. John reflects a liturgical tradition here which is represented by Paul's version of the institution of the Lord's Supper. (Boismard thinks that Luke 22:19b is probably an addition by a scribe.) Moreover, Boismard suggests that John's term "my flesh" instead of "my body" in the Synoptic and Pauline versions of the institution, translates Jesus' own words in Aramaic. Thus, John here renders a tradition which is independent of the Synoptics in spite of the verbal similarities which exist. Boismard's view that John has stronger kinship with Paul than with the Synoptics, should be more thoroughly investigated.

1. John presupposes the institution of the Lord's Supper and paraphrases parts from it, without quoting the story of the institution itself. Similarily, Paul in 1 Cor 10:16-17, 21 selects words from the eucharistic tradition without quoting it. The story of the institution is presupposed as known, so that the commentary in 1 Cor 11:(26) 27-29 is also a close parallel, although the institution is quoted in 11:23-25 (26).

2. John and Paul use tradition in the same way. They make expository paraphrases of fragments. The fragments consist of word sets. The sets in John 6:51b are ὁ ἄρτος/βρῶσις—ἡ σάρξ, πόσις—τὸ αἷμα and φαγεῖν (τρώγειν)—πίνειν. Correspondingly, the Pauline words sets in 1 Cor 10:3-4, 16-17, 21 and 11:27-29 are ὁ ἄρτος /βρῶμα—τὸ σῶμα, ποτήριον / πόμα—τὸ αἷμα and ἐσθίειν/φαγεῖν— πίνειν.

3. There are similarities between John and Paul with regard to the form given to the expository paraphrases. In John 6:53 the eucharistic fragments are built into a sentence where a conditional clause (ἐάν) is followed by the main clause. Correspondingly, in 1 Cor 11:27 Paul paraphrases words from the tradition to a sentence where a conditional relative clause (ὃς ἄν) is followed by a main clause. In John 6:54, 56-58 a participial phrase tied to the subject takes the place of the subordinate clause, as also is the case in 1 Cor 11:29 (ὁ . . . ἐσθίων καὶ πίνων). In both places there is variation of style between second and third person.

Moreover, both John and Paul use argumentative style. For example, negative and positive alternatives are presented to the readers (John 6:53-54; 1 Cor 11:27-28), and the rationale (γάρ) is given (John 6:55; 1 Cor 11:29). Then a conclusion is drawn (John 6:58; 1 Cor 11:33).

4. Both John and Paul apply the biblical story of the manna and the well to the eating and drinking in the Lord's Supper. In John 6:(31) 51b-58 words from the eucharistic tradition are made part of the midrashic exposition of the Old Testament text on the manna, cited in v 31. In 1 Cor 10:3-4 the Israelites' eating and drinking in the desert typify the Lord's Supper. Against this background, it is probable that John 6:55 ("for my flesh is food [βρῶσις] indeed, and my blood is drink [πόσις] indeed"), refers to the manna and the well, just as do the corresponding terms—βρῶμα— πόμα —in 1 Cor 10:3-4.[19]

5. Furthermore, both John 6:41, 43 and 1 Cor 10:10 refer to murmurings by the Israelites in the desert.

6. The formulation in John 6:51b—ὁ ἄρτος δὲ ὃν ἐγὼ δώσω ἡ σάρξ μού ἐστιν ὑπὲρ τῆς τοῦ κόσμου ζωῆς—is similar to 1 Cor 11:24—τοῦτό μού ἐστιν τὸ σῶμα τὸ ὑπὲρ ὑμῶν and Luke 22:19—τοῦτό ἐστιν τὸ σῶμά μου τὸ ὑπὲρ ὑμῶν διδόμενον, and reflects the wording in the presupposed institution story in the Johannine community.

The fact that the verb δίδωμι is used in John 6:51b-52 and Luke 22:19, but not in 1 Cor 11:23-26, cannot undermine the view that John 6:51b-58 is in closest agreement with 1 Cor 10:3-4, 16-17, 21; 11:23-34, especially since the term in John 6:51-52 is but a repetition of the word ἔδωκεν from the Old Testament quotation in John 6:31.[20]

What in our analysis indicates that John draws on oral tradition? First, the close agreement between John (6:51-58) and Paul (parts of 1 Cor 10 and 11) make it probable that John is not dependent upon the Synoptics. Neither can it be maintained that John is dependent upon Paul's letter in 1 Cor. Thus, Paul and John most probably draw on oral eucharistic traditions, combined with the biblical/haggadic stories about the manna and the well. Second, the common celebration of the eucharist supports the view that John, not only Paul, also utilizes liturgical traditions. Third, 1 Cor 10:17, 21 shows that the story of the institution was already known in the mid-fifties to readers in the Corinthian church, and expository elaboration could therefore presuppose this story of institution. John 6:51-58 has the same usage of word-sets, etc, from the institution of the Lord's Supper, the same form, the same argumentative style, etc. There are, therefore, strong arguments in favor of drawing the conclusion that John 6:51-58, just as 1 Cor 10:16-17, 21, presupposes the oral tradition about the Lord's Supper and develops an expository paraphrase on parts of it.

"Text" and Commentary. In the preceding sections we discussed the expository use of fragments of the tradition in John 6:51b-58 where the unit of tradition was presupposed and not stated. Using 1 Cor 11:23-34 as a model we shall now examine some of the passages in John where a unit of tradition is followed by an expository commentary. Passages such as John 2:13-22; 5:1-18; 9:1-41 and 12:44-50 fall into this category. In this paper, John 5:1-18 will be in the center of the discussion. The author, however, has analysed John 12:44-50 in a recent publication.[21]

This kind of commentary is identified on the basis of the following criterion: Words and phrases from the quoted tradition are repeated and paraphrased in the commentary.[22]

John 5:1-18. In John 5:1-18, vv 1-9 quote a story about healing from the tradition, and the commentary then follows in vv 10-18.

Dodd and other scholars have shown that the story about healing, vv 1-9, has the same form as several stories about healing in the Synoptics.

Dodd deals only with John 5:10-18 in a summary fashion without examining it.[23] In these verses phrases from the quoted unit of tradition (vv 1-9) are repeated and paraphrased. This commentary has a systematic outline: In vv 10-13 the sentence ἆρον τὸν κράβατόν σου καὶ περιπάτει from v 8 (also in v 9) is repeated and paraphrased. In vv 14-16 the phrase ὑγιὴς γένεσθαι/ἐγένετο ὑγιής(vv 6 and 9) is repeated and paraphrased. Finally in vv 17-18 the speaking and acting person in the story of healing, Jesus himself, becomes the explicit focal point of the commentary. The term σάββατον in v 9 is repeated in each of the three parts of the commentary— in vv 10, 16 and 18 respectively. These repetitions of words and phrases from the quoted story of healing end in v 18, which thus marks the close of the combined quotation and commentary in 5:1-18. The Evangelist elaborated upon the christological theme of 5:1-18 in the discourse of 5:19-47. Up to this point John 5:1-18 is in accord with the model form of quoted tradition and attached commentary found in 1 Cor 11:23-34. Is the paraphrastic commentary in John 5:10-18, like the one 1 Cor 11:27-34 put into traditional form?

There is little in common formally between John 5:10-18 and 1 Cor 11:27-34 apart from the expository paraphrase. In both cases, however, narrative stories are interpreted, viz. the act of healing (John and the story of a meal [1 Cor]). While the exposition in 1 Cor 11:27-34 is a didactic monologue, the exposition in John 5:10-18 has the form of a dialogue, more precisely of a legal debate on a controversial action (miracle) performed on the sabbath.

The differences between John and Paul should not be exaggerated, however. In 1 Cor 10:14-22 questions are also formulated (vv 16, 18) as well as questions *and* answers (vv 19-20). Similarly, the exposition of the eucharist in John 6:51-58 includes the schema of question and answer (vv 52-58).

Nevertheless, concerning traditional forms there are closer agreements between John 5:1-18 and passages which state a case followed by a judicial exchange. Consequently, with regard to form, Matt 12:1-8 (plucking grain on the sabbath), and Luke 13:10-17 (the healing of a crippled woman on the sabbath), parallel in an interesting way John 5:1-18. A synoptic presentation of these three passages makes the agreement of form evident. Since a comparison between Matt 12:1-8 and Mark 2:23-28 is also of interest for our discussion, the Markan version is included in the presentation. The agreement of form raises the question of John's dependence on (or independence of) the Synoptic Gospels, and therefore agreements of content are included in the survey on pages 90-91.

The strongest argument in favor of John's dependence is the verbatim agreement between John 5:8 (ἔγειρε ἆρον τὸν κράβατόν σου καὶ περιπάτει, etc.) and Mark 2:9 (ἔγειρε καὶ ἆρον τὸν κράβατον σου καὶ περιπάτει, etc.). As for this phrase, "take up your mat and walk," etc., it should be noted that another stereotyped phrase from the gospel tradition has also been worked into the paraphrase of the commentary, namely μηκέτι ἁμάρτανε (John 5:14) which also occurs in the non-Johannine pericope of John 7:63-8:11.[24] By analogy, the use of this stereotyped phrase in these two mutually independent stories also supports the view that the expression, "take up your pallet and walk" (John 5:8, etc., Mark 2:9, etc.) is a stereotyped phrase as well, and could occur in various contexts in stories which are independent of each other.[25] Apart from this phrase the two stories of healing, John 5:1-9 and Mark 2:1-12, are very different with hardly any further verbal agreement. Thus, the stories are much more different than are the Pauline (1 Cor 11:23-26) and Markan (Mark 14:22-25) stories of the Lord's Supper, where there is a close agreement between sentences, phrases and words, although they are mutually independent.

The other agreements listed in the survey also call for comment. The agreement between John 5:10 (. . . οὐκ ἔξεστιν . . .) and Matt 12:2 (. . . οὐκ ἔξεστιν . . .) is due to the fact that a traditional form corresponding to Paul's use of traditional (gospel) forms in 1 Cor 10:21 and 11:27-29 is used in John's paraphrase.

The references to the persecution of Jesus (John 5:16), and the seeking to kill him (v 18), are all features which have a basis in the gospel tradition. The persecution of

Jesus and the search to kill Jesus are elements which are central in John as can be seen from 5:16, 18; 7:19-20, 25; 8:37, 40; 11:53; 15:20. They are also central to the Johannine community since a direct correlation is made between the persecution of Jesus and attempts to kill him, and the persecution of the disciples/the Christians and attempts to kill them (John 15:20; 16:2).[26] The passion narratives and the killing of Jesus show that these elements have a firm basis in the gospel tradition and in history.

John 5:16, 18 and Mark 3:6 par., connect this motif in the gospel tradition with Jesus' apparent violation of the sabbath in different ways. There is no verbal agreement between Mark 3:6 and John 5:16, 18, and thus it seems arbitrary to draw the conclusion that John here is dependent on Mark as indicated by Neirynck. John's independence is supported by the observation that the expository commentary in John 5:10-18 is attached to the story (the case) just as in Matt 12:18 and Luke 13:10-17, while the corresponding discussion in Mark 3:1-6 precedes the story of healing.

The motif of blasphemy in John 5:18 ("making himself equal with God") has a distinctive use that is different from the corresponding use of this motif in Mark 2:7 par and 14:64 par. Thus, these parallels do not prove that John is dependent upon the Synoptics.

Arguments based on form can also be advanced against John's dependency on the Synoptics. In spite of the similarity of form between John 5:1-18, on the one hand, and Matt 12:1-8 and Luke 13:10-17, on the other, John has a distinctive use of this common form. The form can hardly be said to be taken from the synoptic passages. Only in John 5:10-18 does the legal debate have the function of changing the stage (vv 10-13, the Jews and the person healed; v 14, Jesus and the person healed; vv 15-18, the person healed, the Jews and Jesus). Moreover, only in John 5:10-18 are phrases from the story (the case) repeated quite mechanically in the subsequent legal debate. Only John has, therefore, an extensive paraphrase of parts of the case/story used as a "text".

The conclusion is that not only John 5:1-18 and Matt 12:1-8 but also Luke 13:10-17 follow a traditional structure for a controversial case which is subsequently followed by a judicial dialogue.

The question still remains as to whether the passage comes from an oral tradition or whether it is based on a written document. Three points suggest that John 5:1-18 not only draws on oral tradition, but is itself an oral unit which has been written down.

1. The story of healing (John 5:1-9) has the same form as have the stories of healing in the Synoptics. Consequently, John here seems to reproduce transmitted tradition corresponding to Paul's rendering of the eucharistic tradition in 1 Cor 11:23-25 (26). The expository commentary in John 5:10-18 corresponds to Paul's commentary in 1 Cor 11:(26) 27-34. John 5:1-18, as a whole, is therefore a unit parallel to 1 Cor 11:23-34, and results from a corresponding expository activity in the Johannine community.

2. This hypothesis is supported by a consideration of the *Sitz im Leben* of John 5:1-18. The life setting of the passage concerns the controversy between the church and the synagogue, in which Christology, the sabbath and the Law of Moses were central issues. The importance of these questions for understanding the actual situation of the Johannine community is evident from John 9:1-41. The studies of J. L. Martyn and S. Pancaro have shown that the history of the Johannine community is reflected in these two passages.[27]

John 5:1-18

The case, vv 1-9

Μετὰ ταῦτα ἦν ἑορτὴ τῶν Ἰουδαίων, καὶ ἀνέβη Ἰησοῦς εἰς Ἱεροσόλυμα. ἔστιν δὲ ἐν τοῖς Ἱεροσολύμοις ἐπὶ τῇ προβατικῇ κολυμβήθρα ἡ ἐπιλεγομένη Ἑβραϊστὶ Βηθζαθά, πέντε στοὰς ἔχουσα. ἐν ταύταις κατέκειτο πλῆθος τῶν ἀσθενούντων, τυφλῶν, χωλῶν, ξηρῶν. ἦν δέ τις ἄνθρωπος ἐκεῖ τριάκοντα καὶ ὀκτὼ ἔτη ἔχων ἐν τῇ ἀσθενείᾳ αὐτοῦ· τοῦτον ἰδὼν ὁ Ἰησοῦς κατακείμενον, καὶ γνοὺς ὅτι πολὺν ἤδη χρόνον ἔχει, λέγει αὐτῷ· θέλεις ὑγιὴς γενέσθαι; ἀπεκρίθη αὐτῷ ὁ ἀσθενῶν· Κύριε, ἄνθρωπον οὐκ ἔχω, ἵνα ὅταν ταραχθῇ τὸ ὕδωρ βάλῃ με εἰς τὴν κολυμβήθραν· ἐν ᾧ δὲ ἔρχομαι ἐγώ, ἄλλος πρὸ ἐμοῦ καταβαίνει. λέγει αὐτῷ ὁ Ἰησοῦς· ἔγειρε ἆρον τὸν κράβαττόν σου καὶ περιπάτει. καὶ εὐθέως ἐγένετο ὑγιὴς ὁ ἄνθρωπος, καὶ ἦρεν τὸν κράβαττον αὐτοῦ καὶ περιεπάτει. ἦν δὲ σάββατον ἐν ἐκείνῃ τῇ ἡμέρᾳ.

Expository dialogue, vv 10-18

ἔλεγον οὖν οἱ Ἰουδαῖοι τῷ τεθεραπευμένῳ· σάββατόν ἐστιν, καὶ οὐκ ἔξεστίν σοι ἆραι τὸν κράβαττον. ὃς δὲ ἀπεκρίθη αὐτοῖς· ὁ ποιήσας με ὑγιῆ ἐκεῖνός μοι εἶπεν· ἆρον τὸν κράβαττόν σου καὶ περιπάτει.

Matthew 12:1-8

The case, v 1

ἐν ἐκείνῳ τῷ καιρῷ ἐπορεύθη ὁ Ἰησοῦς τοῖς σάββασιν διὰ τῶν σπορίμων· οἱ δὲ μαθηταὶ αὐτοῦ ἐπείνασαν, καὶ ἤρξαντο τίλλειν στάχυας καὶ ἐσθίειν.

Expository dialogue, vv 2-8

οἱ δὲ Φαρισαῖοι ἰδόντες εἶπαν αὐτῷ· ἰδοὺ οἱ μαθηταί σου ποιοῦσιν ὃ οὐκ ἔξεστιν ποιεῖν ἐν σαββάτῳ. ὁ δὲ εἶπεν αὐτοῖς· οὐκ ἀνέγνωτε τί ἐποίησεν Δαυὶδ ὅτε ἐπείνασεν καὶ οἱ μετ' αὐτοῦ; πῶς εἰσῆλθεν εἰς τὸν οἶκον τοῦ θεοῦ καὶ τοὺς ἄρτους τῆς προθέσεως ἔφαγον, ὃ οὐκ ἐξὸν ἦν αὐτῷ φαγεῖν οὐδὲ τοῖς μετ' αὐτοῦ, εἰ μὴ τοῖς ἱερεῦσιν μόνοις; ἢ οὐκ ἀνέγνωτε ἐν τῷ νόμῳ ὅτι τοῖς σάββασιν οἱ ἱερεῖς ἐν τῷ ἱερῷ τὸ σάββατον βεβηλοῦσιν καὶ ἀναίτιοί εἰσιν; λέγω δὲ ὑμῖν ὅτι τοῦ ἱεροῦ μεῖζόν ἐστιν ὧδε. εἰ δὲ ἐγνώκειτε τί ἐστιν· ἔλεος θέλω καὶ οὐ θυσίαν, οὐκ ἂν κατεδικάσατε τοὺς ἀναιτίους. κύριος γάρ ἐστιν τοῦ σαββάτου ὁ υἱὸς τοῦ ἀνθρώπου.

Mark 2:23-28

The case, v 23

καὶ ἐγένετο αὐτὸν ἐν τοῖς σάββασιν παραπορεύεσθαι διὰ τῶν σπορίμων καὶ οἱ μαθηταὶ αὐτοῦ ἤρξαντο ὁδὸν ποιεῖν τίλλοντες τοὺς στάχυας.

Expository dialogue, vv 24-28

καὶ οἱ Φαρισαῖοι ἔλεγον αὐτῷ· ἴδε τί ποιοῦσιν τοῖς σάββασιν ὃ οὐκ ἔξεστιν; καὶ λέγει αὐτοῖς· οὐδέποτε ἀνέγνωτε τί ἐποίησεν Δαυὶδ ὅτε χρείαν ἔσχεν καὶ ἐπείνασεν αὐτὸς καὶ οἱ μετ' αὐτοῦ; πῶς εἰσῆλθεν εἰς τὸν οἶκον τοῦ θεοῦ ἐπὶ Ἀβιαθὰρ ἀρχιερέως καὶ τοὺς ἄρτους τῆς προθέσεως ἔφαγεν, οὓς οὐκ ἔξεστιν φαγεῖν εἰ μὴ τοὺς ἱερεῖς, καὶ ἔδωκεν καὶ τοῖς σὺν αὐτῷ οὖσιν; καὶ ἔλεγεν αὐτοῖς· τὸ σάββατον διὰ τὸν ἄνθρωπον ἐγένετο καὶ οὐχ ὁ ἄνθρωπος διὰ τὸ σάββατον· ὥστε κύριός ἐστιν ὁ υἱὸς τοῦ ἀνθρώπου καὶ τοῦ σαββάτου.

Luke 13:10-17

The case, vv 10-13

ἦν δὲ διδάσκων ἐν μιᾷ τῶν συναγωγῶν ἐν τοῖς σάββασιν. καὶ ἰδοὺ γυνὴ πνεῦμα ἔχουσα ἀσθενείας ἔτη δεκαοκτώ, καὶ ἦν συγκύπτουσα καὶ μὴ δυναμένη ἀνακύψαι εἰς τὸ παντελές. ἰδὼν δὲ αὐτὴν ὁ Ἰησοῦς προσεφώνησεν καὶ εἶπεν αὐτῇ· γύναι, ἀπολέλυσαι τῆς ἀσθενείας σου, καὶ ἐπέθηκεν αὐτῇ τὰς χεῖρας· καὶ παραχρῆμα ἀνωρθώθη, καὶ ἐδόξαζεν τὸν θεόν.

Expository dialogue, vv 14-17

ἀποκριθεὶς δὲ ὁ ἀρχισυνάγωγος, ἀγανακτῶν ὅτι τῷ σαββάτῳ ἐθεράπευσεν ὁ Ἰησοῦς, ἔλεγεν τῷ ὄχλῳ ὅτι ἓξ ἡμέραι εἰσὶν ἐν αἷς δεῖ ἐργάζεσθαι· ἐν αὐταῖς οὖν ἐρχόμενοι θεραπεύεσθε καὶ μὴ τῇ ἡμέρᾳ τοῦ σαββάτου. ἀπεκρίθη δὲ αὐτῷ ὁ κύριος καὶ εἶπεν· ὑποκριταί, ἕκαστος ὑμῶν τῷ σαββάτῳ οὐ λύει τὸν βοῦν αὐτοῦ ἢ τὸν ὄνον ἀπὸ τῆς φάτνης καὶ ἀπαγαγὼν ποτίζει; ταύτην δὲ θυγατέρα Ἀβραὰμ οὖσαν, ἣν ἔδησεν ὁ σατανᾶς ἰδοὺ δέκα καὶ ὀκτὼ ἔτη, οὐκ ἔδει λυθῆναι ἀπὸ τοῦ δεσμοῦ τούτου τῇ ἡμέρᾳ τοῦ σαββάτου; καὶ ταῦτα λέγοντος αὐτοῦ κατῃσχύνοντο πάντες οἱ ἀντικείμενοι αὐτῷ, καὶ πᾶς ὁ ὄχλος ἔχαιρεν ἐπὶ πᾶσιν τοῖς ἐνδόξοις τοῖς γινομένοις ὑπ' αὐτοῦ.

Sentences (almost verbatim agreement)

John 5:8—ἔγειρε ἆρον τὸν κράβατόν σου καὶ περιπάτει
Mark 2:9—ἔγειρε καὶ ἆρον τὸν κράβατόν σου καὶ περιπάτει

John 5:9—εὐθέως ... ἦρεν τὸν κράβατον αὐτοῦ καὶ περιπάτει
Mark 2:11—ἔγειρε ἆρον τὸν κράβατόν σου καὶ

John 5:10—ἆραι τὸν κράβατον
Mark 2:12—ἠγέρθη καὶ εὐθὺς ἄρας τὸν κράβατον

John 5:11—ἆρον τὸν κράβατόν σου καὶ περιπάτει

John 5:12—ἆρον καὶ περιπάτει

John 5:14—μηκέτι ἁμάρτανε
(John 8:1— μηκέτι ἁμάρτανε)

Parts of Sentences

John 5:10—σάββατόν ... οὐκ ἔξεστίν σοι (ἆραι)
Matt 12:2 (cf. Mark 2:24)—ὃ οὐκ ἔξεστιν (ποιεῖν) ἐν σαββάτῳ

Words

John 5:6—... ἰδὼν ὁ Ἰησοῦς ... λέγει
Mark 2:5—ἰδὼν ὁ Ἰησοῦς ... λέγει

John 5:10—... ἔλεγον ... οἱ (Ἰουδαῖοι)
Mark 2:24—οἱ (Φαρισαῖοι) ἔλεγον

John 5:3D—παραλυτικόν
Mark 2:3—παραλυτικόν

Subject Matter, not Words

John 5:18—making himself equal with God
Mark 2:7—It is blasphemy. Who can forgive sins but God alone

John 5:14—Sin no more

John 5:16—the Jews persecuted Jesus
Mark 3:6—the Pharisees went out and immediately held counsel with the Herodians against him, how to destroy him

John 5:18—the Jews sought all the more to kill him

John 5:17—My father is working still, and I am working
Matt 12:8 (cf. Mark 2:27; Luke 6:5)—For the Son of Man is Lord of the Sabbath

ἠρώτησαν αὐτόν· τίς ἐστιν ὁ ἄνθρωπος ὁ εἰπών σοι· ἆρον καὶ περιπάτει. ὁ δὲ ἰαθεὶς οὐκ ᾔδει τίς ἐστιν· ὁ γὰρ Ἰησοῦς ἐξένευσεν ὄχλου ὄντος ἐν τῷ τόπῳ. μετὰ ταῦτα εὑρίσκει αὐτὸν ὁ Ἰησοῦς ἐν τῷ ἱερῷ καὶ εἶπεν αὐτῷ. ἴδε ὑγιὴς γέγονας· μηκέτι ἁμάρτανε, ἵνα μὴ χεῖρόν σοί τι γένηται. ἀπῆλθεν ὁ ἄνθρωπος καὶ εἶπεν τοῖς Ἰουδαίοις ὅτι Ἰησοῦς ἐστιν ὁ ποιήσας αὐτὸν ὑγιῆ. καὶ διὰ τοῦτο ἐδίωκον οἱ Ἰουδαῖοι τὸν Ἰησοῦν, ὅτι ταῦτα ἐποίει ἐν σαββάτῳ. ὁ δὲ ἀπεκρίνατο αὐτοῖς· πατήρ μου ἕως ἄρτι ἐργάζεται, κἀγὼ ἐργάζομαι. διὰ τοῦτο οὖν μᾶλλον ἐζήτουν αὐτὸν οἱ Ἰουδαῖοι ἀποκτεῖναι, ὅτι οὐ μόνον ἔλυεν τὸ σάββατον, ἀλλὰ καὶ πατέρα ἴδιον τὸν θεόν, ἴσον ἑαυτὸν ποιῶν τῷ θεῷ.

3. The evangelist has more interest in the Christological aspect as such than in the sabbath question. Accordingly, in the discourse which follows in John 5:19-47 phrases and terms about the sabbath and the sabbath controversy are not repeated any more, whereas the Christological idea in John 5:17 ("My Father is at work even till now, and so I am at work too") *is* developed.[28]

Conclusion. John 5:1-18 follows a traditional structure in which a controversial state of affairs concerning the sabbath is followed by judicial dialogue. Paul in 1 Cor 11:23-34 uses the same basic form of a story from the gospel tradition followed by an expository commentary of legal nature. Since the similarities between the two mutually independent traditions of 1 Cor 11:23-25 (26) and Mark 14:22-25 are much more extensive and clearer than they are between John 5:1-18 and the Synoptics, the Johannine passage is certainly independent of the Synoptic Gospels. John 5:1-18 is probably an oral unit transmitted through the activity of the Johannine community. This view is supported by the parallel structure of "text" and "commentary" in 1 Cor 11:23-34 and by the life setting of John 5:1-18 where we find conflicts between church and synagogue about the sabbath and the Law of Moses in relation to Christology. By adding John 5:19-47 to the sabbath controversy, the evangelist seems to want to develop the Christological aspect more independently of the sabbath controversy.

Notes

1. Cf. D. M. Smith, Jr., "John and the Synoptics: Some Dimensions of the Problem," *NTS* 26 (1980) 425-26; F. Neirynck, "John and the Synoptics," in M. de Jonge, ed., *L'Evangile de Jean. Bibliotheca Ephemeridum Theologicarum Lovaniensum,* 44 (Leuven, 1977) 73-75.
2. Similar views are held by R. Bultmann, "Zur johanneischen Tradition," *TLZ* 60 (1955) 524; P. Borgen, "John and the Synoptics," *NTS* 5 (1959) 246-59, reprinted in P. Borgen, *'Logos was the true Light' and other Essays on the Gospel of John,* Trondheim, 1985, 67-80; D. M. Smith, Jr., "The Source of the Gospel of John: An Assessment of the Present State of the Problem," *NTS* 10 (1963-64) 336-51; E. Haenchen, "Johanneische Probleme," *ZTK* 56 (1959) 19-54; R. E. Brown, *The Gospel According to John,* 2 vols., Garden City, New York, 1966, 1970; B. Lindars, "Two Parables in John," *NTS* 16 (1969-70) 318-29; *Behind the Fourth Gospel,* London, 1971; *The Gospel of John,* London, 1972; R. Schnackenburg, *Das Johannesevangelium,* 3 vols, Freiburg, 1965, 1971, 1975; C. H. Dodd, *Historical Tradition in the Fourth Gospel,* Cambridge, 1965; A. Dauer, *Die Passionsgeschichte im Johannesevangelium,* München, 1972. See also the critical comments by R. Kysar, *The Fourth Evangelist and His Gospel,* Minneapolis, MN, 1975, 66-67.
3. F. Neirynck, "John and the Synoptics," 103-106; *Jean et les Synoptiques. Examen critique de l'exégèse de M.-E. Boismard,* Leuven, 1979; see also M. Sabbe, "The Arrest of Jesus in Jn 18, 1-11 and its Relation to the Synoptic Gospels," in *L'Evangile de Jean,* ed. by M. de Jonge, Leuven, 1977, 205-34, esp. p. 233: "For better understanding of the relation between John and the Synoptic Gospels and for a more homogeneous explanation of John's text as a whole, the awareness of the redactional creativeness of John combined with a direct dependence upon the Synoptics, is more promising."
4. Neirynck, "John and the Synoptics," 106.
5. Concerning Paul and the gospel tradition in general, see the recent works by D. L. Dungan, *The Sayings of Jesus in the Churches of Paul,* Philadelphia, 1971; B. Fjärstedt, *Synoptic Tradition in 1 Corinthians,* Uppsala, 1974; D. C. Allison, Jr., "The Pauline Epistles and the Synoptic Gospels: The Pattern of Parallels," *NTS* 28 (1982) 1-32; P. Stuhlmacher, "Jesus Tradition im Römerbrief," *Theologische Beiträge* 14 (1983) 240-50; *id.* (ed.), *Das Evangelium und die Evangelien,* WUNT 28, Tübingen, 1983, 16-20, 157-82.
Some scholars regard 1 Cor 11:23-26 as a unique liturgical tradition, not representative for the transmission of gospel material in general; so recently N. Walter, "Paulus und die urchristliche Tradition," *NTS* 31 (1985) 500-501, 505. I have argued against this view in "Nattverd-tradisjonen 1 Kor 10 og 11 som evangelietradisjon" ("The Eucharistic tradition in 1 Cor 10 and 11 as Gospel Tradition"), *Svensk exegetisk årsbok,* 51-52 (1986-87) 32-39.
6. G. Bornkamm, *Studien zu Antike und Christentum, Gesammelte Aufsätze,* München, 1963, 2.152; H. Schürmann, *Der Einsetzungsbericht,* Münster, 1955, 1 (Luke 22:19-20 is halfway between Mark/Matt and Paul).
7. About Mark's independence of Paul, see Schürmann, *Einsetzungsbericht,* 8.
8. Cf. J. Jeremias, *The Eucharistic Words of Jesus,* New York, 1955, 128-29; H. Riesenfeld, *The Gospel Tradition,* Philadelphia, 1970, 15-18; B. Gerhardsson, *Memory and Manuscript,* Uppsala, 1961, 288-90, 305, 321-22; *Die Anfänge der Evangelientradition,* Wuppertal, 1977, 27.
9. Cf. H. Conzelmann, *Der erste Brief an die Korinther,* Meyerk, Göttingen, 1969, 230-31; Gerhardsson, *Memory,* 322; Stuhlmacher, *Das Evangelium und die Evangelien,* 19; Bornkamm, *Studien,* 146-48; E. Käsemann, *Essays on New Testament Themes,* Naperville, IL, 1964, 120-32. Concerning interpretive elements in v 26, see Conzelmann, *An die Korinther,* 237; cf. Jeremias, *Eucharistic Words,* 115; Käsemann, *Essays,* 121; Bornkamm, *Studien,* 148.
10. Cf. Käsemann, *Essays,* 121-32.
11. See especially E. Käsemann, "Sätze heiligen Rechtes im Neuen Testament," *NTS* 1 (1954-55) 248-50; *Essays,* 122-25; Bornkamm, *Studien,* 168.
12. For such casuistic statements see Matt 5:21,22, etc. See examples from the OT and from the Qumran writings in W. Nauck, *Die Tradition und der Charakter des ersten Johannesbriefes,* WUNT 3, Tübingen, 1957, 29-33. Examples from rabbinic writings and Philo are given by P. Borgen, *Bread from Heaven: an Exegetical Study of the Concept of Manna in the Gospel of John and*

the Writings of Philo, Leiden, 1965, 88-89; see further P. Fiebig, *Der Erzahlungsstil der Evangelien,* Leipzig, 1925, 3-20.

13. Cf. A. G. Wright, "The Literary Genre Midrash," *CBQ,* 28 (1966) 110-11: "What the ancient writer was aware of was that he wrote within a particular tradition: it was this that largely decided the literary form to which we have given a name. He was a Deuteronomist, a priestly writer, a follower of the sages, an anthologist of the prophets, or the like"—quoted from B. Vawter, "Apocalyptic: Its Relation to Prophecy," *CBQ* 22 (1960) 33; R. Le Déaut, "Apropos a Definition of Midrash," *Int* 25 (1971), 270: "The authors were conscious of writing in a *tradition* rather than in a certain literary form." Cf. also Borgen, *Bread,* 59.

14. Cf. H. Schürmann, *Ursprung und Gestalt,* Düsseldorf, 1970, 86; Conzelmann, *An die Korinther,* 201-202; J. Héring, *Le Royaume de Dieu et sa venue,* Neuchatel, 1959.

15. Such a version of the eucharistic tradition would draw on the Jewish technical term for the cup of wine over which the thanksgiving after the meal has been said. See Str-B 4.72, 628, 630-31; Conzelmann, *An die Korinther,* 202; C. K. Barrett, *The First Epistle to the Corinthians,* New York, 1968, 231.

16. Cf. A. Resch, *Der Paulinismus und die Logia Jesu. Texte und Untersuchungen zur Geschichte der altchristlichen Literatur.* N.F. 12, Leipzig, 1904, 53.

17. Cf. Käsemann, *Essays,* 114; Schürmann, *Ursprung, 173.*

18. M.-E. Boismard, *L' Evangile de Jean,* in *Synopse de quatre évangiles en francais,* ed. by P. Benoit and M.-E. Boismard, Paris, 1977, 204-205.

19. Cf. Borgen, *Bread from Heaven,* 91-92, where reasons are given for the preference of the reading ἀληθῶς instead of ἀληθής.

20. Ibid., 86-90.

21. P. Borgen, "The Use of Tradition in John 12:44-50," in Borgen, *'Logos Was the True Light',* 49-66 (first published in *NTS* 26 [1979] 18-35).

22. Such commentaries are also found in the Synoptics, as shown by J. Wanke in his study, "Kommentarworte. Älteste Kommentierungen von Herrenworten," *BZ,* N.F. 24 (1980), 208-33, and G. N. Stanton, "Matthew as a Creative Interpreter of the Sayings of Jesus," in Stuhlmacher, *Das Evangelium und die Evangelien,* 273-87.

23. C. H. Dodd, *The Interpretation of the Fourth Gospel,* Cambridge, 1968, 320. He characterizes briefly vv 10-18 as the transition from the narrative of the healing at Bethesda to the discourse which follows.

24. Lindars, *John,* 312, seems to think that the phrase in John 8:11 is taken from 5:14. If so, it shows how a stereotyped phrase may be extracted from a story, leaving the rest of the story intact. Against Lindars it may be said that the phrase has a more natural place in the context of 8:11, while it is used rather abruptly in 5:14.

25. Cf. Haenchen, *Johannesevangelium,* 269: "'wandernde' Einzelzüge."

26. Cf. S. Pancaro, *The Law in the Fourth Gospel,* Leiden, 1975, 45-46.

27. J. L. Martyn, *History and Theology in the Fourth Gospel,* New York, 1968; Pancaro, *The Law,* 497-512.

28. An additional note on John 5:9: Did the point about the sabbath belong to the story of the healing in the oral transmission, or was it added to form a basis for the expository dialogue found in John 5:10-18? This question has been much debated, since the reference to the sabbath in v 9b seems to be an addition to the story about healing. R. E. Brown, in discussing E. Haenchen's view that the reference to the sabbath and the sabbath controversy in vv 9b-13 constitutes a secondary addition to the healing narrative, says: "One almost needs the Sabbath motif to give this story significance" (Brown, *John,* 1.210). A further observation supports the view of Brown. The story of healing (John 5:1-9) is a tradition with legal authority (cf. 1 Cor 11:23-25[26]) which legitimates the attitude of the Johannine community towards the Sabbath (the Law of Moses).

The Law and the Prophets in Q

David R. Catchpole

Within the diversity of early Christian belief it is clear that purposeful appeal to "the law and the prophets" was at least one focus of unity. It is no surprise, therefore, to find just such an appeal in Q, an appeal which is made on several occasions and effected with a notably uniform pattern and argument. The investigation of the most prominent Q traditions in which this appeal is documented will hopefully be an appropriate tribute to a scholar whose friendship is prized and whose many studies of the use of the OT in the NT have brought profit and insight.

Matt 11:12-13/Luke 16:16

First and foremost among the relevant traditions must stand the programmatic statement of principle in Matt 11:12-13/Luke 16:16. This provides the theoretical basis upon which appeal is made elsewhere to heroic figures such as Abel, Noah, Abraham, Lot, Isaac, Jacob, Solomon, Jonah and Zechariah. The actual wording of the saying has to be recovered, however, from two strikingly different renderings: πάντες γὰρ οἱ προφῆται καὶ ὁ νόμος ἕως Ἰωάννου ἐπροφήτευσαν (Matt 11:13), diff ὁ νόμος καὶ οἱ προφῆται μέχρι Ἰωάννου (Luke 16:16a). Not only is the study of the theology of Q facilitated, but also the defence of the very existence of Q enhanced, by the fact that in this single saying no fewer than four Matthaean features seem to be less primitive than their Lukan counterparts. (1) The word πάντες would not only fit the Lukan tendency to generalize but would also in association with 'the prophets' fit a well-established Lukan trend.[1] Mark nowhere, and Matt nowhere apart from 11:13, uses the phrase πάντες οἱ προφῆται, and we would expect Luke to have adopted it with enthusiasm if it had been in his source. (2) The word γὰρ is present only in order to make v 13 explain the preceding v 12. But the sequence from v 12, describing the post-Johannine period, to v 13, describing the pre-Johannine period, must be secondary.[2] No such bipartite saying would exist in isolation in so artificial a form, and its existence thus in the Matthaean context clearly derives from a redactional concern with the John/Elijah equivalence affirmed in v 14. Again Luke's rendering is more primitive. (3) The order οἱ προφῆται καὶ ὁ νόμος must be secondary,[3] since it serves the MtR purpose of highlighting the prophets, whereas Luke's phrase is more idiomatic (cf. 4 Macc 18:10) and supported by Matt 5:17, which H Schürmann has shown to be an alternative variant of the same saying.[4] (4) The verb προφητεύειν again fits the purpose of Matthew,[5] but it is artificial when its subject includes the law. Luke's version without any verb at all appears more original. This conclusion, together with the three previously drawn, leaves us with just one remaining discrepancy, i.e. ἕως/μέχρι. This time the vote may be cast in favor of Matthew's ἕως[6] since this word is attested elsewhere in Q,[7] whereas μέχρι is not. Given the comparative rarity of μέχρι (2-1-1+2) and its employment elsewhere in

MtR[8] and Lukan narrative[9] passages, it might have been retained by Matthew, while it could certainly have been introduced by Luke. So the Q original underlying Matt 11:13/ Luke 16:16a probably ran: ὁ νόμος καὶ οἱ προφῆται ἕως 'Ιωάννου.

The meaning of this saying in the context of Q depends in part on its inter-relationship with the complementary Matt 11:12/Luke 16:16a and in part on the effect of related sayings further afield in Q. A full investigation of the *Stürmerspruch* lies beyond the scope of this study, but a partial discussion is essential. For this purpose it is germane that in three instances Luke again appears to preserve more primitive wording. (1) The phrase ἀπὸ τότε is notably simpler than Matthew's ἀπὸ δὲ τῶν ἡμερῶν 'Ιωάννου τοῦ βαπτιστοῦ ἕως ἄρτι, which was itself partly demanded by Matthew's presentation of the post-Johannine period first and partly expressive of his concern to establish parallelism between John and Jesus.[10] The provenance of ἀπὸ τότε from Q[11] is supported also by there being no parallels in Luke-Acts, and by a remarkable agreement with Matt 4:17, where there is the same presentation of Jesus' succeeding John and preaching the near kingdom in fulfillment of scripture.[12] (2) Matthew's qualification of the kingdom as τῶν οὐρανῶν is normally regarded as secondary in relation to τοῦ θεοῦ, which happens to be Luke's wording. (3) In spite of the prevalent tendency to attribute εὐαγγελίζεται to LkR,[13] and this verb is of course beloved of Luke, consideration must be given to the possibility that this time the evangelist drew it from his source. Attacks on the kingdom in Matt 11:12 must be understood in the light of similar laments by the author of 1QH 2:10, 11, 21, 22 as attacks on the proclaimers and the proclamation of the kingdom, which is an agreed theme in Luke 16:16. The double βιάζεται/βιασταί reference in Matt appears tautologous, while εὐαγγελίζεται as a description of Jesus' activity, specifically marking him out from John, is exactly the language of Q in Matt 11:5/Luke 7:22. That Matthew should avoid using the same verb twice within a mere eight verses is not at all surprising: he avoided a double use of εὐαγγέλιον in the two near summary statements in Matt 4:17, 23/Mark 1:14-15, 39. We thus arrive at the provisional conclusion that in Q the saying began ἀπὸ τότε ἡ βασιλεία τοῦ θεοῦ εὐαγγελίζεται . . . , and, if that is so, it integrated both the proclamation of the future kingdom to the poor in the first Q beatitude (Matt 5:3/Luke 6:20b) and the declaration to John that the poor were being evangelized (Matt 11:5/Luke 7:22).

Given that "the law and the prophets" stands for an existing corpus of sacred scripture from which instruction may be given and received, it is the extraordinary attachment of the phrase ἕως 'Ιωάννου which attracts attention. The absence of a defining verb increases the level of ambiguity which, however, is fortunately diminished by associated material. In theory, we might be faced here with a devaluation of the authority of the law and the prophets, a possibility which was so real to Matthew that he attacked it fiercely in his first recension of the saying in Matt 5:17. Such a possibility may already have occurred to the editor of Q and may be responsible for his juxtaposing Matt 11:12-13 (5:17)/Luke 16:16 and Matt 5:18/Luke 16:17. Whether the juxtaposition was theologically motivated or merely an accidental by-product of a catchword connection using νόμος, it remains plain that no one could simultaneously accept the permanence of each κεραία of the law and infer from ὁ νόμος καὶ οἱ προφῆται ἕως 'Ιωάννου any devaluation of authority. Certainly the law goes on for ever. What then is the relevance of ἕως 'Ιωάννου? Perhaps we should begin by noting the ambiguity of the preposition ἕως which in itself could have an inclusive or an exclusive effect on the Baptist. This ambiguity, as far as Q is concerned, is a help and not a hindrance. For in relation to the prophets it is clear that Q regards John's position with ambivalence. First, the effective realization of prophetic hope and expectation takes place in activities of Jesus which are listed in Matt 11:5/Luke 7:22 and which are not activities of John. Indeed, they form a basis for viewing Jesus as the coming one who is announced by, separate from, and superior to, John (Matt 3:11/Luke 3:16)—the coming one who is in Q the Son of man (Matt 24:44/Luke 12:40).[14] Secondly, and for all that much is true in relation to Jesus which is not true in relation to John, it remains firm that John's status is defined by Q as the realization of scripture, specifically law (Exod 23:20) and prophecy (Mal 3:1) in Matt 11:10/Luke 7:27. There one person (God) speaks to a second (Jesus) about a third (John): "Behold, I send my messenger before your face, who shall prepare your way before you." Furthermore, it is important to take seriously the combined effect of Matt 11:4/Luke 7:22, where the disciples of John "see and hear," and Matt 13:17/Luke 10:24, where an undefined audience is informed that "seeing and hearing" is an experience which marks an advance on prophetic experience and full participation in what will bring future blessedness. John and his disciples, therefore, quite evidently share in what was anticipated by the prophets of old and now presently activated in the new era of Jesus. Thus it comes about that the ambivalence towards the Baptist which is articulated in the phrase ἕως Ἰωάννου is matched by a certain bifocal view of the law and the prophets. In one sense, everything has changed: events set in train by, and involving, John have fulfilled the law and the prophets. In another sense, nothing has changed: the law and the prophets retain their supreme status and remain available powerfully to reinforce the preaching of the kingdom of God by him who is the Son of man.

This last observation can be reinforced. There is evidence that in Q the mission charge (Matt 10/Luke 10) was followed by "The Blessedness of the Disciples" (Matt 13:16-17/Luke 10:23-24), which was in turn followed by "The Baptist's Question" (Matt 11:2-6/Luke 7:18-23).[15] Moreover, the framework with its question, "Are you ὁ ἐρχόμενος . . . ?" is probably a secondary editorial interruption[16] in a sequence which would otherwise pass smoothly from the acclamation in Matt 13:16-17/Luke 10:23-24 to the list in Matt 11:5/Luke 7:22. The evidence begins to emerge when we uncontroversially assign to MtR the position of Matt 13:16-17 and also recall that disparate Q traditions are often juxtaposed on the basis of shared subject-matter. Matt 11:2-19/Luke 7:18-35 as a whole is a good example of this. Now commentators discussing Matt 11:2-6 frequently find themselves alluding to Matt 13:16-17 as the closest parallel, and vice versa.[17] In both there is "seeing and hearing" and in both the highlighting of the fulfillment of prophetic expectations. Positionally, there are three other hints that in Q the one unit immediately preceded the other. (1) Matt·11:2-19 and 11:25-27 occur immediately after the mission charge in Matthew's Q sequence, while Luke 10:21-22/Matt 11:25-27 and 10:23-24 do the same in Luke's Q sequence. Can this be coincidence? (2) The προφήτης + δίκαιος combination in the MtR saying 10:41[18] is a combination which occurs nowhere else apart from 13:17 diff Luke 10:24 and 23:29 diff Luke 11:47. Is this a coincidence or, more probably, a MtR reminiscence of what originally stood before Matt 11:2-19? (3) Nowhere in Q apart form Matt 11:2/Luke 7:18 do the disciples of John appear. But in Luke 11:1 there is a very curious allusion to John and his disciples,[19] which happens to introduce the Q tradition which, in Luke's Q sequence, follows 10:23-24. Is this a coincidence or a LkR reminiscence of what originally stood after "The Blessedness of the Disciples", i.e. Luke 7:18-35/Matt 11:2-19?

On such a foundation we can proceed to build by observing the very probably secondary character of John's question about 'the coming one.' For Q the coming one is the Son of man, as already noted, and for the John of Q the coming one is a transcendent heavenly judge and eschatological savior, a profile to which the earthly Jesus can scarcely conform.[20] Furthermore, there is no natural engagement between the credentials of Jesus,[21] listed in response to John's question, and the Son of man-oriented question itself. Therefore, the latter is most likely a secondary insertion by the editor of Q who thus discloses his purpose of making fulfilled prophecy attest the Son of man.

* * *

When Jesus ben Sirach looked back on the work of his grandfather he saw above all devotion to "the law and the prophets" as the source of great teachings, instruction and wisdom which redounded to the credit of Israel (Sir, prol. 1,8). When Judas Maccabeus set about stabilizing the faith of his army and their confidence that the Gentiles would be worsted and Israel made victorious, it was "the law and the prophets" which he used for encouragement (2 Macc 15:9). When the father of the seven famous martyrs educated his children he taught them "the law and the prophets" (4 Macc 18:10), from which raw material their mother was able to compile, first, a list of named heroes who had faced testing, suffering and/or death (Abel, Isaac, Joseph, Phineas, Hananiah, Azariah, Mishael and Daniel: vv 11-13) and, secondly, a sequence of quotations from named persons confirming the conviction that the inevitable sufferings of the righteous will lead to life (Isaiah, David, Solomon, Ezekiel and Moses: vv 14-19). Unsurprisingly, there comes to expression in these lists a strong Israel-consciousness and a strategy of encouragement. In Q, however, the situation is not quite the same. The panorama of Israel's history from Abel to Zechariah in Matt 23:34-36/Luke 11:49-51 is a critical accusation, using the Deuteronomic view of history and affirming an identification of those addressed with the killers rather than the killed. The note sounded when the memory of Solomon and Jonah (Luke 11:31-32/Matt 12:41-42), or of Noah and Lot (Matt 24:37-39/Luke 17:26-30), is revived is certainly not a note of encouragement. Just what sort of note is being sounded requires careful definition, and therefore it is to a study of these last two traditions that we shall shortly turn. Before we do that, however, the presence of a formal scheme must be noted.

Several times in Q we encounter the phenomenon of a tradition or collection of traditions shaped so as to consist of a heading, a pair of illustrative arguments, and a concluding summary. The age of the various components of such schemes varies from case to case, so while the scheme exhibits a more or less uniform tendency, the history of the tradition or traditions may not conform to a uniform process of development. One example of this Q phenomenon is the "Love your Enemies" complex (Luke 6:27-35) where the demand is set out at beginning (vv 27-28) and end (v 35), and supported by illustrative arguments (vv 32-33), but formally interrupted in between by related material (vv 29-31). In this case, the Q editor probably received from pre-Q tradition, which may well in turn have derived from Jesus, the demand for love and the associated promise of heavenly sonship, but he himself created the two illustrations.[22] Another example is the "Cares about Earthly Things" complex (Luke 12:22-31), where interruptions (vv 22b, 25, 26, 30a) suggest that the Q editor received from pre-Q tradition a total unit consisting of the twice-stated demand for no anxiety, with two illustrative arguments in between. This unit presupposes a context of such short-term eschatological expectation that again attribution to the historical Jesus arguably involves no great risk.[23] A third example is the "Prayer for Food" complex (Luke 11:2-13) in which the Lord's Prayer in general and the petition for necessary bread in particular functions as a heading (vv 2-4), and the two parables featuring the friend and the father (vv 5-9, 11-13) function as illustrative arguments, separated by an editorial interruption (v 10). Like the second example, but unlike the first, this third example almost certainly gives us authentic Jesus material in both the "heading" and the illustrations.[24] The existence of such a scheme, sometimes antedating Q and sometimes the creation of the Q editor, gives us an angle on both the complexes we are going to investigate. In each we have a pair of illustrations with matching argument and shared appeal to "the law and the prophets".

Matt 12:38-42/Luke 11:16, 29-32

The broad outline of the underlying Q tradition can be discerned from the Matt/Luke agreements, i.e. a request for a sign; a criticism of the contemporary sign-seeking generation as evil; a declaration that the only sign which will be provided is the sign of Jonah, understood with reference to the Son of man; and a pair of illustrative examples from "the law and the prophets".[25] This broad outline can be given sharp definition by observing once again that Luke's version is substantially more primitive. (1) The order Solomon + Jonah (Luke 11:31, 32) appears more primitive than the order Jonah + Solomon (Matt 12:41, 42) since it conforms to the Biblical sequence. It is certainly possible in principle that the non-Biblical sequence in Matt was derived from Q and employed by that source in order to bring the Jonah illustration immediately next to the "sign of Jonah" saying. On that showing Luke would have corrected the order of the source. Whether or not that is the case it is evident that in the history of the tradition the two argumentative illustrations belong to an earlier stage than the sign saying. *Either* the saying about the men of Nineveh belonged originally with the saying about the sign of Jonah, in which case the Solomon saying is a secondary imitation of the Jonah saying, which is in turn more unlikely, *or* the saying about the sign of Jonah is a secondary heading imposed upon two already existing argumentative illustrations, at least one of which it manifestly did not suit. Existing in isolation at the pre-Q stage, the Solomon + Jonah pairing must have been in that order, which therefore Luke either recognized and restored, in spite of what had been the case in Q, or simply retained from Q. (2) The unspecific sign of Jonah in Luke must be more primitive than the very specific passion-orientated sign of Jonah in Matt. The latter is typically Matthaean in its conscious appeal to OT wording and its allusion to the death, burial and resurrection of Jesus; it is untypical of Q which lacks any parallel elsewhere for such an allusion: and it is unlikely to have been dropped by Luke, had he known it,[26] in view of his contrary tendency, confirmed by Luke 17:25 (Mark 8:31),[27] to insert passion allusions into a Q context.

This does not however, exhaust the interest which the student of Q has in the MtR κοιλία τοῦ κήτους. For the fact is that the word κοιλία, used rather sparsely in the synoptics (3-1-8+2), crops up in the tradition which immediately precedes the "sign of Jonah" in the Lukan sequence, namely "The Blessedness of Christ's Mother" (Luke 11:27-28). How are we to account for this curious phenomenon? Coincidence is an implausible explanation. Lukan reminiscence of Matt 12:40 is impossible, since κοιλία was absent from the Q Vorlage of that saying. The only remaining possibility is that there is Q tradition underlying "The Blessedness of Christ's Mother" and that Matt 12:40 contains a redactional reminiscence.[28] Additional support for this inference can be adduced. The phrase θέλειν ἰδεῖν occurs in the synoptics only in Matt 12:38 diff Luke 11:29 and Luke 8:20 diff Mark 3:32, apart from Luke 10:24 diff Matt 13:17 and Luke 23:8. The incidence of the first two is notable, in that the first belongs to the tradition immediately following Luke 11:27-28 and the second is part of LkR revision of the Markan doublet of Luke 11:27-28. This is most easily explained as LkR reminiscence of the sequence Luke 11:27-28, 29 in the source.[29]

For this proposal to be viable, Luke 11:27-28 must not be merely a LkR remodelling of the "Christ's Real Brothers" pericope in Mark 3:31-35, to which it is obviously related. This is indeed unlikely[30] since, first, as doublets Luke 8:19-21 and 11:27-28 should be assigned to separate sources; secondly, the formulation of the blessing pronounced on Jesus' mother recalls such thoroughly Jewish formulations as "the blessings of the breasts and the womb" promised to Joseph (Gen 49:25), or the doom-laden rejection of pregnancy in the setting of judgment, "Blessed are the barren, and the wombs that never bore, and the breasts that never gave suck" (Luke 23:29, cf. Mark 13:17), or the exclamation of Baruch (2 Bar 54:10):

> Blessed is my mother among those who bear,
> and praised among women is she who bore me.[31]

If it is correct that Q contained a sequence consisting of material underlying Luke 11:27-28, 29-30, 31-32, then it next becomes clear that the first and the second units are rival introductions to, or headings for, the third. Indeed one might almost say that the first has a stronger claim than the second! Luke 11:27-28 contains an exceedingly sharp contrast between the hearers of Jesus and the mother of Jesus. Since an acclamation of Jesus' mother is an implicit acclamation of Jesus, this unit describes a Jesus who is more concerned with what he says and how he is heard than with who he is.[32] In short there is here every discouragement from reflection on the person of Jesus and every encouragement for concentration on total and unreserved response to the words of Jesus. That rings very true to the historical Jesus, and rather less true to typical early Christian tendencies. Luke 11:31-32 contains a pair of illustrations of unreserved response to authoritative speech, whether the form be σοφία or κήρυγμα. The mode of argument is *a minore ad maius,* just as it was in the two complexes dealing with anxiety and prayer, and by all the normal canons of authenticity, this pair of sayings should be assigned to the historical Jesus. (1) The use of Gentile persons in an antithesis which works to the disadvantage of Jewish persons is striking. In the case of the men of Nineveh the argument runs counter to the trend evinced in Tob 14:4, 8, 15, where Nineveh's doom is predicted by Jonah and realised without relief. (2) The *a minore ad maius* argumentation produces concluding declarations καὶ ἰδοὺ πλεῖον Σολομῶνος/'Ιωνᾶ ὧδε. These are not designed to be personal and christological, as the neuter πλεῖον confirms.[33] They are affirming with all possible strength that there is all the more reason to make a similar response now because there is an ultimacy about the contemporary presentation of wisdom and proclamation of judgment. His placing of himself within, and at the climax of, the succession of the wise men and the prophets; the style and content of his teaching as conforming to those of wisdom and prophecy; the emphasis upon response to what is said, rather than on reflection on the person of him who says it—all these are surely major features of the historical Jesus. Luke 11:29-30 contains a reference to Jonah and the Ninevites, which formally links it with Luke 11:31-32, but a smooth passage from the one to the other is prevented by the severe internal tensions evident in the former. The declaration that θέλομεν σημεῖον ἰδεῖν belongs in the context of the mission of a charismatic-eschatological leader with its promise of signs of liberation before the final crisis.[34] Jesus' denunciation of the sign-seeking generation as evil leads us to expect that signs in the customary sense will be refused and therefore that his concern is with the ultimate crisis event, not with any pre-crisis events. Also, the use of the οὐ ... εἰ μὴ form would normally introduce an exception, but this time the entity specified must be an exception which in no way weakens the general rule. This suggests as the wording of the most appropriate response to the initial request: καὶ σημεῖον οὐ δοθήσεται αὐτῇ εἰ μὴ τὸ σημεῖον τοῦ υἱοῦ τοῦ ἀνθρώπου. The word σημεῖον would thus be used in a transferred sense to denote the coming one (as in Matt 24:30), and the saying as a whole would be a refusal of a sign in the conventional sense (as in Mark 8:12). The present form of Luke 11:29-30 suggests a superimposition of a different, and indeed alien, scheme, i.e. the parallelism involving Jonah/the Ninevites and the Son of man/this generation. This parallelism modifies the Son of man, so that he is now no longer the eschatological coming one but the pre-eschatological preacher of judgment, that is, in the present generation none other than Jesus. Important for our study is a two-fold corollary. First, the earliest and pre-Q stage of the tradition underlying Luke 11:29-30 takes a detached view of the Son of man, deals with a problem which fits convincingly into the mission of Jesus, but lacks any direct internal connection with Luke 11:31-32. Secondly, the secondary and Q-editorial stage of the tradition can claim to pick up and reflect upon a Jonah-Jesus comparison in Luke 11:32, even though to do so involves a personalizing shift, i.e. it imposes a Son of man = Jesus equation upon the traditions which is by no means warranted by either. We have seen precisely this happening elsewhere on the level of Q-editorial activity.

The conclusion is therefore that in Luke 11:27-28, 29-30, 31-32 there are Q traditions, each of which with varying degrees of immediacy stems from the historical Jesus. The first and the third might well have belonged together at the pre-Q stage and showed a use of precedents drawn from "the law and the prophets" to reinforce the pressure for immediate response to the multi-faceted word of Jesus. Whether or not that was the case, the Q editor was responsible for the position of the second tradition and at the same time for its adaptation, so that it not only continued the fight against customary expectations associated with charismatic figures but also articulated his own conviction that the coming Son of man was Jesus himself.

Matt 24:26-28, 37-39/Luke 17:23-24, 26-30, 37

Once again the broad outlines of the Q tradition underlying Matt and Luke are discernible, i.e. a warning against localized eschatological expectation, a comparison of the Son of man with lightning, and an appeal to precedent derived from "the law and the prophets". An initial problem, however, concerns the provenance of the saying about Lot (Luke 17:28-30). In principle this might be assigned to "sayings newly formed within the sphere of Q tradition"[35] or even attributed to L,[36] but in practice it is much more likely to stem from Q, for the following reasons. (1) We have already cited examples of Q's predilection for pairs, and more examples could have been cited.[37] (2) Judgment by fire, which is the theme of the Lot episode, is important to Q as the preaching of John at the outset shows, cf. Matt 3:7-12/Luke 3:7-9, 16-17. (3) The grim precedent of judgment upon Sodom has already been invoked in Q, cf. Matt 10:15/Luke 10:12. (4) The occasional omission of Q material by Matt should surprise us no more than his occasional omission of Markan material. (5) The tendency to combine the examples of Noah and Lot is so firmly entrenched in Jewish tradition that pre-Lukan origin in this instance appears much the more probable option. The relevant Jewish texts include Wis 10:3-4, 6-8, which includes Noah and Lot as the second and fourth in a list of those who were saved by wisdom; Sir 16:7,8 which uses the generation of the flood and the Sodomites to head a list of those whose rebellion and sin incurred the flaming wrath of God; 3 Macc 2:4, 5 which mentions the flood and the destruction of Sodom as prime examples of the fate in store for the proud and insolent; Jub 20:5, 6 which refers to the giants and the Sodomites as those judged for wickedness and uncleanness; T Naph 3:4; 4:16 and 3:5 which cites the Sodomites and the watchers as examples of persons veering away into idolatry and changing the course of nature; Sanh. 10:3 which follows the generalization that "all Israelites have a share in the world to come" with a list of those who do not, a list in which the generation of the flood and the men of Sodom figure in first and third places respectively, with a parenthesis quoting the view of R Nehemiah that these two groups correspond to "the wicked" and "the sinners" in Ps 1:5.

The conclusion that Q contained the pairing of Noah and Lot can be followed up with the observation that while the original wording has been very little altered by either evangelist, Luke several times stands closer to it than Matt does.[38] (1) The substantial introduction, unique to Matt, ὡς γὰρ ἦσαν ἐν ταῖς ἡμέραις ἐκείναις ταῖς πρὸ τοῦ κατακλυσμοῦ (24:38a), spoils the dramatic effect of suddenly introducing the flood after the list of human activities and is probably secondary.[39] (2) The phrase ἐν ταῖς ἡμέραις is, however, present in almost exactly the same place in Luke i.e. in the time note ἐν ταῖς ἡμέραις τοῦ υἱοῦ τοῦ ἀνθρώπου, where Matt prefers to speak of the παρουσία. Since the latter term is MtR at 24:3/Mark 13:4 and is clearly being used by this evangelist to integrate the whole discourse (see vv 3, 27, 37, 39), while never being used by any other evangelist, it is not too difficult to infer that Luke is again more faithful to Q. This also enables us to explain the well-known variation between "day" and "days".[40] The pair of precedents began by comparing the days of Noah and the days of the Son of man, and clearly had in mind in each case the period before the crisis; it then moved directly into the reference to the similar period in the life of Lot, but only mentioned the Son of man and his day after referring to the day of Lot's exit from Sodom, i.e. the day of the crisis itself. Thus the whole unit consisting of the two examples is coherent and symmetrical. (3) The allusion to the ignorance of Noah's contemporaries (οὐκ ἔγνωσαν ἕως. . .) is secondary[41] and a MtR intrusion, since content-wise it differs, and position-wise it is distanced, from the list of activities "eating and drinking, marrying and giving in marriage". It prepares for the following separate section Matt 24:42–25:13, framed by exhortations to watchfulness in view of ignorance.

What then were the two examples drawn from "the law and the prophets" intended to convey? When Luke 17:26-30 is set alongside the other texts cited above which belong to the same family, a number of form-critical observations become possible. First, statements of principle accompany and appear to be a normal control on such lists.[42] Secondly, the flood and Sodom serve to illustrate judgment themes. Thirdly, a statement of the reason for judgment is normally provided.[43] Fourthly, when personal references to Noah and Lot are included, the main theme of judgment is tempered by a subordinate theme of salvation. In terms of these parameters Luke 17:26-30 is, first, in need of a heading (which will bring us back to consider Matt 24:26-28/Luke 17:23-24, 37); secondly, entirely in line by highlighting judgment; thirdly, quite remarkable in listing purely inoffensive activities on the part of notorious offenders (another point to which we shall return); fourthly, not at all incapable of conveying a hint of divine rescue. Two items, therefore, emerge for our agenda.

The inoffensive activities of the contemporaries of Noah and Lot should clearly not be adjusted by assimilating "eating and drinking" to allegations of gluttony, or "marrying and giving in marriage" to the doubtful liaisons of Gen 6:1-4,[44] or "buying and selling" and "planting and building" to undue prosperity and wealth.[45] To the contrary, all four pairings are repeatedly attested, more or less idomatic, and in content entirely honorable. Elsewhere in Q, however, equally innocent and honorable pairings, "sowing and reaping" or "toiling and spinning" or work "in the field (and) . . . at the mill" are employed to describe life which is ordinary, everyday, but unaligned to the great and near eschatological crisis.[46] That the contemporary generation should be addressed as it is in the Noah + Lot pairing can only mean that its own life-patterns have been superimposed upon the ancient examples, so that it is not being accused of precisely the same ancient offences, but that it is at the same time being reminded of the danger in which it stands through complacent inattention to the imminent occurrence of judgment. When we enquire what form uncomplacent attention would have taken, we have to call in aid the tradition attested by Josephus,[47] Philo,[48] and the Targums[49] that the days of Noah and the days of Lot were days of opportunity for repentance.[50] And the *Sitz im Leben* of Luke 17:26-30 thus emerges as the preaching *of* near judgment and *for* repentance and *to* the unrestricted general public. The complacent and settled are warned of the implications of an event which to them will be shocking in its suddenness and disastrous in its finality unless, that is, they open themselves to the message of the contemporary counterpart of Noah and of Lot.

This leads us to, and leaves us with, the discussion of whether the two precedents from "the law and the prophets" were preceded in Q by a heading. Such a discussion must center on the saying comparing the Son of man to the lightning, which Matt and Luke agree in placing shortly before the two precedents (Matt 24:27/Luke 17:24). It must also draw on the proverbial saying "Where the corpse is there will the eagles be gathered together", which comes next in Matthew's Q sequence although a little later in Luke's Q sequence (Matt 24:28/Luke 17:37). This is because the evidence favors the originality of Matthew's placing:[51] we can well understand Luke's shifting the saying to the end of his section on "The Day of the Son of man", partly because of its unclear connection with the preceding saying, and partly because of his wish to insert a different intrusive saying concerned with the passion (Luke 17:25). Moreover, the disciples' question about place in the typically Lukan[52] introduction (ποῦ, κύριε, Luke 17:37a) suggests a reminiscence of the topic of place which had figured in the saying about those who point to this or that location for the eschatological event (Matt 24:26/Luke 17:23). If, then, the transition from the Son of man-lightning saying to the Son of man-orientated sayings about Noah and Lot was interrupted by the eagles saying, what did it mean and why was it there? Biblical tradition had frequently used eagles/vultures to represent speed[53] and heavenliness,[54] often (because of adverse associations) as imagery of divine judgment.[55] If the risk of taking context into account be not too great, then it may be worth observing that the closest parallel for our saying is part of a determined argument that the eagle's movement to the heights and then, so rapidly, to the corpse below is something wholly outside human control:

> Is it at your command that the eagle mounts up and makes his nest on high?
> On the rock he dwells and makes his home in the fastness of the rocky crag.
> Thence he spies out the prey; his eyes behold it from afar.
> His young ones suck up the blood; and where the slain are, there is he.

> Job 39:27-30

The proverbial saying is therefore peculiarly well-suited to a context of judgment and a concern with a being whose coming will be from heaven to earth and with notable immediacy.[56] Secondly, its dealing with the issue of place by means of the affirmation of immediacy makes it interlock with the warning against contemporary tendencies to locate the ultimate intervention of God in particular places. In short, editorial activity seems to be injecting an extra answer to the question posed at the beginning, an answer which is relevant but secondary. However, by its secondariness in its Q context it makes us ask whether at the pre-Q stage a line of continuity may have joined the lightning saying to those about Noah and Lot, with the former serving as the heading for the latter.

In Q the lightning saying ended οὕτως ἔσται τοῦ υἱοῦ τοῦ ἀνθρώπου, since παρουσία (Matt 24:27) has already been assigned to MtR, and the qualifying phrase ἐν τῇ ἡμέρᾳ αὐτοῦ is textually insecure in Luke 17:24 and probably a later assimilation to the wording of Luke 17:30. It is noticeable that in that way the saying corresponds to the putative pre-Q version of Matt 12:39/Luke 11:29.[57] A comparison between the lightning and the Son of man presents few problems though there is some difficulty about the two versions of the phrase qualifying the lightning: ἐξέρ—χεται ἀπὸ ἀνατολῶν καὶ φαίνεται ἕως δυσμῶν (Matt) diff ἀστράπτουσα ἐκ τῆς ὑπὸ τὸν οὐρανὸν εἰς τὴν ὑπ' οὐρανὸν λάμπει (Luke). Matthew's attachment of an indicative form of a verb to each of the allusions to east and west, together with the use of ἐξέρχεσθαι in the first case, yields a description which would fit the sun rather better than the lightning.[58] It is possible that Luke's clearer version, which speaks about light shining on the whole world, is an improvement,[59] though surely more probable that the original form of the saying was unconfusing. If so, Luke is once again more primitive and the verb ἐξέρχεται a secondary MtR distortion. Its removal allows the verb "to shine", whether φαίνειν (Matt) or λάμπειν (Luke), to relate to the whole unified phrase meaning "over all the world", whichever formulation be preferred. A case could be made for λάμπειν, for which Luke shows no special fondness,[60] rather than φαίνειν, which is often employed by Matt;[61] equally a case could be made for ἀπὸ ἀνατολῶν ἕως δυσμῶν as more traditional[62] or concrete[63] and matched in Q by Matt 8:11/Luke 13:29; again, the double formulation ἀστραπὴ ἀστράπτουσα need not be dismissed as LkR in view of precedent in Ps 144:6.[64] These sub-decisions would yield an original

> ὥσπερ ἡ ἀστραπὴ ἀστράπτουσα ἀπὸ ἀνατολῶν ἕως δυσμῶν λάμπει,
> οὕτως ἔσται ὁ υἱὸς τοῦ ἀνθρώπου,

though the verbal minutiae do not at all affect the main thrust of the saying. That thrust is unequivocally plain in the light of established associations of lightning in Biblical tradition.

Again and again in Biblical tradition lightning represents judgment, often in the setting of theophany.[65] As a component of storm, lightning is often associated with thunder and wind, fire and flood.[66] It is thoroughly understandable, therefore, that in spite of there being no explicit reference to lightning in Gen 6-7 or 19, Philo should include it in his descriptions of the flood (*De Abr* 43) and the judgment of Sodom (*De Mos* 2.56). Similar implicit recognition of the congruence of lightning with what happens in Gen 19 is shown by Josephus, who uses in his narrative (*Ant* 1.203) the term βέλος which various OT texts use as a synonym for lightning.[67] Within the broader range of lightning passages the association of suddenness or speed[68] merits attention. Speed conveys a sense of the decisiveness, the forcefulness, the finality of judgment (cf. Mal 3:5). Thus it begins to emerge that the imagery of the Son of man-lightning saying makes it a suitable heading for the Noah + Lot complex.

As such a heading, was the Son of man-lightning saying from the beginning organically linked with the Noah + Lot complex? Did that complex never exist separately from it, in the same way as the ravens + lilies complex probably never existed separately from the prohibition of anxiety, and the tax collectors + Gentiles complex never existed separately from the demand for love? The answer is almost certainly No. For the affirmation of suddenness in the Son of man saying is more the premise than the main concern, the latter being found in the words ἀπὸ ἀνατολῶν ἕως δυσμῶν λάμπει. These words are wholly appropriate to a lightning saying, since similar passages elsewhere speak of universal effect when contrasting the earth and the heaven from which God intervenes, comes and reigns. Thus it is that God's "lightnings lighten the world" (Ps 96:4), or "the lightning when it flashes is widely seen" (Ep Jer 60-61), or "the lightning shone exceedingly, so as to illuminate the whole earth" (2 Bar 53:9). In the Q saying the universal scope of the lightning-like appearance of the Son of man answers the problem of location mentioned in Matt 24:26/Luke 17:23. It rounds off a complete and self-contained unit which needs no amplification, a unit which matches the pre-Q unit which arguably underlay Matt 12:38-40/Luke 11:29-30. Both confront critically ideas associated with the movements of the charismatic-eschatological leaders, and both do so by recourse to the coming of the Son of man. At the same time we observe that the Noah + Lot complex has no interest in questions of location. Instead, it corresponds with the Solomon + Jonah complex in a shared warning that the present indifferent generation is in grave danger by virtue of the imminent eschatological crisis. The likelihood is therefore that the Q editor has acted in both contexts in the same way as he acted in placing before the two parables of the friend (Luke 11:5-8,9/Matt 7:7) and the father (Matt 7:9-11/Luke 11:11-13) one heading consisting of a warning against an outlook he rejected (Matt 6:7-8) and another heading consisting of the Lord's Prayer (Matt 6:9-13/Luke 11:2-4). Disparate units have been brought together according to the same formal pattern.

Our study therefore suggests that in the Noah + Lot and Solomon + Jonah complexes we are able to reach back to traditions which antedate Q. The theological concerns are in each case identical. Famous OT precedents are adduced to reinforce public proclamation of judgment but at the same time to place "the law and the prophets" at the service of the gospel. The Q editor, it seems, had no reservation in using these two complexes. Nor did he diminish in any way the critique of contemporary eschatological movements which had previously been mounted by diverse pre-Q traditions. His contribution was one, not of diminution but of definition, a determined clarification that the Son of man is Jesus. This was his way of assimilating the proclaimer and the proclaimed.

Notes

1. See Luke 11:50 diff Matt 23:35; Luke 13:28 diff Matt 8:11; Luke 24:27; Acts 3:18, 24; 10:43.
2. J. Schmid, *Matthäus und Lukas*, Freiburg, [2]1930, 284-85; S. Schulz *Q—Die Spruchquelle der Evangelisten*, Zürich, 1972, 261.
3. Schulz, *Spruchquelle*, 261.
4. H. Schürmann, *Traditionsgeschichtliche Untersuchungen zu den synoptischen Evangelien*, Düsseldorf, 1968, 130-132; also "Das Zeugnis der Redenquelle für die Basileia-Verkündigung Jesu", in J. Delobel, ed., *Logia* Mémorial J. Coppens, Leuven, 1982, 121- 200, esp. 169-173.
5. Schulz, *Spruchquelle*, 261.
6. Schulz, *Spruchquelle*, 261.
7. Matt 5:26/Luke 12:59; Matt 11:23/Luke 10:15; Matt 13:33/Luke 13:21; Matt 23:35/Luke 11:51; Matt 23:39/Luke 13:35.
8. Matt 11:23; 28:15.
9. Acts 10:30; 20:7.
10. The formulation of the saying may be compared with that of Mark 13:19, where ἀπὸ . . . ἕως τοῦ νῦν attaches no unique significance to the present.
11. Similarly Schulz, *Spruchquelle*, 262; otherwise, P. Hoffmann, *Studien zur Theologie der Logienquelle*, Münster, [2]1975, 52.
12. I owe this suggestion to Professor F. Neirynck.
13. Cf. Schürmann, in *Logia* (note 4), 172; Schulz, *Spruchquelle*, 262; Hoffmann, *Studien*, 51; M. D. Goulder, *Midrash and Lection in Matthew*, London, 1974, 359. The phrase ἡ βασιλεία τοῦ θεοῦ εὐαγγελίζεται certainly does match Luke 4:43; 8:1; Acts 8:12.
14. J. A. Fitzmyer, *The Gospel according to Luke I-IX*, New York, 1981, argues that "the coming one" is *Elias redivivus* on the basis of the combined evidence of Luke 3:7-9, 15-17; 7:18-23 (Q). But Matt 11:10/Luke 7:27 shows that in Q the Baptist was regarded as having performed the role of Elijah.
15. This involves modifying minimally the standard view that the order of Q has been preserved by Luke: see recently, P. Vassiliadis, "The Original Order of Q. Some Residual Cases", in *Logia* (note 4), 379-387. This view is probably correct most of the time, but one recalls that even the order of his basic source, Mark, was occasionally varied by Luke, cf. Luke 6:17-19; 8:19-21.
16. Whereas "The Blessedness of the Disciples" and the list of Jesus' activities (Matt 11:5/Luke 7:22) probably contain, at least in part, historical tradition, the inherent unlikelihood that the Baptist should even consider the possibility that the transcendent, heavenly figure (=God?) he proclaimed was Jesus is widely noted. Cf. C. H. Kraeling, *John the Baptist*, New York, 1951, 129; E. Schweizer, *The Good News according to Matthew*, London, 1976, 255; P. Hoffmann, *Studien*, 201. Rather, "the identification of Jesus on earth and the Judge to come takes place by reason of a post-Easter cognition which emphasizes in particular what Jesus' activity on earth means for salvation". H. E. Tödt, *The Son of Man in the Synoptic Tradition*, London, 1965, 256.
17. See, for example, J. Schmid, *Das Evangelium nach Lukas*, Regensburg, [4]1960, 189; R. H. Fuller, *The Mission and Achievement of Jesus*, London, 1963, 34.
18. Cf. R. H. Gundry, *Matthew. A Commentary on his Literary and Theological Art*, Grand Rapids, 1982, 202.
19. That Luke 11:1 is LkR is convincingly argued by Schweizer, *The Good News according to Luke*, London, 1984, 190-91.
20. H. Schürmann, *Das Lukasevangelium I*, Freiburg, 1969, 409, 412.
21. Cf. W. Grimm, *Die Verkündigung Jesu und Deuterojesaja*, Frankfurt, [2]1981, 124-130.
22. For detailed argument see D. R. Catchpole, "Jesus and the Community of Israel. The Inaugural Discourse in Q," *BJRL* 69 (1986), 296-316.
23. See D. R. Catchpole, "The Ravens, the Lilies and the Q Hypothesis", in A. Fuchs, ed., *Studien zum Neuen Testament und seiner Umwelt* 6-7 (1981-82), 77-87.
24. See D. R. Catchpole, "Q and 'The Friend at Midnight' (Luke xi.5-8, 9)," *JTS* 34 (1983), 407-424.
25. Schulz, *Spruchquelle*, 251-52; B. Lindars, *Jesus Son of Man*, London, 1983, 39.
26. J. A. Fitzmyer, *The Gospel according to Luke X-XXIV*, New York, 1985, 931.

27. The words δεῖ... πολλὰ παθεῖν καὶ ἀποδοκιμασθῆναι are common to Luke 17:25 and Mark 8:31/Luke 9:22; Luke's αὐτόν corresponds to Mark's τὸν υἱὸν τοῦ ἀνθρώπου, since that term has just been used in Luke 17:24; πρῶτον gives the saying a salvation- historical perspective and schematically recalls Mark 13:10, which could be influencing Luke here; ἀπό here matches the change from ὑπό to ἀπό in Mark 8:31/Luke 9:22; while τῆς δενεᾶς ταύτης is a feature which is certainly typical of Q (Matt 11:16/Luke 7:31, etc) but cannot by itself establish that Luke 17:25 is derived from that source, and could easily be a reminiscence of Mark 13:30 or of Mark 8:38 (which, of course, stood near to Mark 8:31).

28. Schürmann, *Untersuchungen*, 231.

29. That is not to deny the presence of Lukanisms in 11:27-28. But the presence of Lukanisms in Luke/Mark parallels is sufficient warning against an inference of total Lukan creativity.

30. Fitzmyer, *Luke X-XXIV*, 926-27, resists both Lukan composition and derivation from Q, and instead ascribes the tradition to L.

31. Cf. Aboth 2:8, the blessing on the mother of R. Joshua b. Hananiah.

32. The formulation ἀκούειν τὸν λόγον (τοῦ θεοῦ) could be LkR, cf. 10:39; Acts, *passim*, but it also stands close to Q usage in Matt 7:24, 26/ Luke 6:47, 49 and is certainly derived from a source elsewhere (Mark 4:15-20/Luke 8:12-15).

33. E. E. Ellis, *The Gospel of Luke*, London, 1966, 168: "The neuter form rules out a reference to Jesus." It may be too specific to refer instead to "the Spirit in his eschatological function", though if Isa 61:1-2 be seen as a keynote of Jesus' mission the Spirit would certainly have a place in a broader context.

34. Josephus, *Ant* 20:97-99; *B J.* 2:258-260/*Ant* 20:167- 68; *B J.* 2:437-439; *B J.* 6:285-287.

35. Tödt, *Son of Man*, 65; cf. D. Lührmann, *Die Redaktion der Logienquelle*, Neukirchen, 1969, 74: 'die Tradition aus der Lk Q übernimmt'.

36. Fitzmyer, *Luke X-XXIV*, 1165, regards vv 28-32 as deriving from L, with the statement about Lot's wife in vv 31b-32 forming an *inclusio* with vv 28-29. However, v 31, upon which v 32 depends, is more likely to derive from Mark 13:15-16, while the formal correspondence between vv 26-27 and vv 28-30 is impressive enough to suggest common origin.

37. See Matt 11:18-19/Luke 7:33-34; Matt 13:31-33/Luke 13:18-21; Matt 24:40-41/Luke 17:34-35.

38. Cf. Lührmann, *Redaktion*, 75-83.

39. Schulz, *Spruchquelle*, 279.

40. Cf. Fitzmyer, *Luke X-XXIV*, 1168-69.

41. Rightly, Schulz, *Spruchquelle*, 279.

42. Wis 9:17-18; Sir 16:4, 6; 3 Macc 2:3; Jub 20:5f; T Naph 3:2.

43. Wis 10:3; Sir 16:7; 3 Macc 2:4-5; Jub 20:5; T Naph 3:3, 5.

44. So, Fitzmyer, *Luke X-XXIV*, 1170-71.

45. Compare Josephus, *Ant* 1:170-71, 194.

46. Matt 6:26, 28/Luke 12:24, 27; Matt 24:40-41/Luke 17:34-35.

47. *Ant* 1:74.

48. *Questions on Genesis* 1:91; 2:13.

49. Tg. Onkelos Gen 6:3; Tg. Pseudo-Jonathan Gen 6:3; 19:24; Tg. Neofiti I Gen 18:21.

50. See J. Schlosser, "Les jours de Noé et de Lot. A propos de Luc, XVII, 26-30," *RB* 80 (1973), 13-36, esp. 18-19.

51. Similarly, Schulz, *Spruchquelle*, 278, 280; Lührmann, *Redaktion*, 72.

52. J. M. Creed, *The Gospel according to Saint Luke*, London, 1931, 221.

53. Deut 28:49; 2 Sam 1:23; Job 9:25-26; Hab 1:8.

54. Prov 23:5; Lam 4:19.

55. Prov 30:17; Jer 4:13; Hos 8:1; Hab 1:8.

56. Cf. T. W. Manson, *The Sayings of Jesus*, London, 1971, 147: "One characteristic of the vulture is the almost incredible swiftness with which it discovers and makes its way to its prey. The saying here draws attention to . . . the swiftness and suddenness of the coming of the day of the Son of man."

57. See above, p. 101.

58. Cf. Pss 50:1; 113:3; Mal 1:11.

59. A. Harnack, *The Sayings of Jesus,* London, 1908, 106; Schulz, *Spruchquelle, 279.*
60. Elsewhere in Luke-Acts it occurs only in Acts 12:7.
61. The statistics are 13-1-2+0. Note the parallelism between ὡς λαμπάδες πυρός and ὡς ἀστραπαί in Nah 2:4 LXX; similarly Ezek 1:13; Dan 10:6; Ep Jer 60-61.
62. See 1 Chr 12:15; Pss 50:1; 113:3; Bar 4:36-37. Luke's form of words would normally include the term ἄκρον, cf. Deut 4:32; 30:4; Ps 19:6.
63. Tödt, *Son of Man,* 49.
64. The LXX runs ἀστραψον ἀστραπήν.
65. Exod 19:16; Deut 32:41; Pss 18:14; 144:6, etc.
66. Hab 3:8-12; Wis 5:20-22.
67. Ps 144:6 is typical.
68. Cf. the comment on Luke 10:18 by W. Foerster, ἀστραπή, *TDNT* 1, 505: "In Lk 10:18 the point of the comparison is the suddenness of the divine working."

Aramaic Evidence Affecting the Interpretation of *Hosanna* in the New Testament

Joseph A. Fitzmyer, S.J.

The Jewish background of NT writings has often been of interest to Professor E. Earle Ellis, and I am happy to contribute an article on such a topic to a volume honoring him, as he reaches an important stage in his career. We have been friends for many years, and I make this contribution with respect and esteem.

Three of the evangelists preserve the Semitic word *hōsanna* in their Greek accounts of Jesus' entry into the city of Jerusalem. The earliest occurence is found in Mark 11:9-10: *hoi proagontes kai hoi akolouthontes ekrazon, hōsanna, eulogēmenos ho erchomenos en onomati kyriou. eulogēmenē hē erchomenē basileia tou patros hēmōn Dauid. hōsanna en tois hypsistois*—"Those who went before and those who followed kept crying aloud, 'Hosanna! Blest be he who comes in the name of the Lord! Blest be the kingdom of our Father David that is coming! Hosanna in the highest!'"

Matthew has a redacted form of the same acclamation in 21:9: *hoi de ochloi hoi proagontes auton kai hoi akolouthontes ekrazon, legontes, hōsanna tō huiō Dauid. eulogēmenos ho erchomenos en onomati kyriou, hōsanna en tois hypsistois*—"The crowds that went before him and those following kept crying aloud, saying, 'Hosanna to the son of David! Blest be he who comes in the name of the Lord! Hosanna in the highest!'" Matthew also repeats the first part of the acclamation as he recounts the reaction of the chief priests and the scribes to Jesus' purging of the temple and the children crying aloud in the temple precincts, *hōsanna tō huiō Dauid*, "Hosanna to the son of David!"

The third and last evangelist who records the cry is not the Synoptist Luke,[1] but John in his account of Jesus' entry into Jerusalem (12:13): *elabon ta baia tōn phoinikōn kai exēlthon eis hypantēsin autō kai ekraugazon, hōsanna, eulogēmenos ho erchomenos en onomati kyriou, [kai] ho basileus tou Israel*—"They took branches of palm trees and went out to meet him, crying aloud, 'Hosanna! Blest be he who comes in the name of the Lord, the King of Israel!'"

Commentators recognize that the acclamation quotes in part the Greek translation of Ps 118:25-26,[2] *ō kyrie, sōson dē, ō kyrie euodōson dē, eulogēmenos ho erchomenos en onomati kyriou*, "O Lord, save (us); O Lord, make prosperous (our) way! Blest be he who comes in the name of the Lord!" This translation renders well the sense of the Hebrew original, *'annā' Yhwh hôšî'āh nā'*, *'annā' Yhwh haslîḥāh nā'*, *bārûk habbā' běšem Yhwh*.[3] The acclamation is derived from that part of Psalm 118 in which thanks are expressed to Yahweh for deliverance from distress, as the psalmist makes a summons for a procession of gratitude. The acclamation itself is a cry for help addressed to Yahweh, whose blessing of salvation and success is being invoked on those who process in his name. The imperative *hôšî'āh* is elsewhere addressed to

Yahweh, especially in the psalter (Ps 12:2; 20:10; 28:9; 60:7; 86:16; 108:7); a shorter form *hôša'* is addressed to him in Ps 86:2 and possibly in Jer 31:7.[4] The long imperative *hôšî'āh* is further addressed by a woman of Tekoa to King David (2 Sam 14:4; cf. 2 Kgs 6:26) and by the men of Gibeon to Joshua (Josh 10:6). In every instance the imperative is translated into Greek in the LXX by *sōson*, except in Josh 10:6, where *exelou* is found instead. Nowhere in the Greek version does a transliterated Semitic word occur for *hôšî'āh* or *hôša'*, and only in Ps 118:25 does the precative particle *nā'* follow the imperative *hôšî'āh*, which is translated *sōson dē*.

Even if one has to recognize that Ps 118:25-26 lies behind the acclamation in the Gospels, it is noteworthy that the Semitic form *hōsanna* occurs here in its earliest attestation; none of the evangelists has used the Greek translation from the LXX. It stands, for that reason, a good chance of representing a genuine primitive Christian recollection of what was shouted to Jesus on the occasion of his entry into Jerusalem—or at least of what was often shouted to persons like him coming to the city of Jerusalem.

The later rabbinic tradition associated Ps 118:25-26 with the feast of Tabernacles and its liturgy.[5] Indeed, it used the term as a name in Aramaic for the seventh day of that feast, *yômā' děhôša'nā'*, "the day of Hosanna" (*Leviticus Rabbah* 37.2).[6] Moreover, the term was even used of the branches, otherwise called *lûlāb*, waved in the rain-making ceremony, which was part of the liturgy (*b. Sukkah* 30b, 37b; cf. *Tg. Esther II* 3:8).[7] By the time these rabbinic texts were composed in the fifth century A.D.,[8] the sense of the original cry of help to Yahweh had disappeared; the term had undergone a semantic shift and become "a fixed formula in the procession round the altar of burnt offering."[9] How early did this shift in meaning take place? Before we try to answer that question, there are other aspects of the word *hōsanna* that have to be considered.

When Origen (A.D. 185-254) commented on Matt 21:9, he realized that the Gospels were written (copied?) "by Greeks . . . who did not know the language" (*hypo Hellēnōn . . . mē eidotōn tēn dialekton*) and were confused by what was written in Psalm 118. He transliterated the Hebrew of vv. 25-26 thus *anna adonai osianna anna adonai aslianna barouch abba bsaim adonai*.[10] He understood the psalm correctly, but made no attempt to explain the Greek transliteration in the Gospels, *hōsanna*, or how it differed from Hebrew *hôšî'āh nā'*. Eusebius (A.D. 260-340) did not understand *hōsanna* at all, when he wrote about "the great crowd of men and children (who) went before him, shouting with joy *hōsanna tō huiō Dauid*." He commented that "instead of *ō kyrie, sōson dē*, which is found in the (Greek) Psalm, they shouted in a more Hebraic (form) *hōs anna*," writing the word as two and wrongly dividing it.[11] Later, when Jerome (A.D. 342-420) wrote to Pope Damasus about the term, he cited Hilary's expalnation of *hōsanna* as meaning "redemptio domus David" (redemption of the house of David), written "hebraico sermone," and rejected that explanation, along with that of other unnamed interpreters who said that *hōsanna* was Hebrew for "glory" or "grace."[12] Jerome then cited the Hebrew of what he called Psalm 117 in a form almost identical with Origen's transliteration given above. He further noted that the Hebrew word is *osianna*, which "we in ignorance corruptly pronounce *osanna*," and he further interpreted Hebrew *anna* (with inital aleph) as "obsecro" and *osianna* as "salvifica" or "salvum facere."[13] He also explained the difference between *hosanna* and *osianna* as an elision of a medial vowel.[14]

When E. J. Goodspeed was preparing his English translation of the NT, he surveyed older English versions of Matt 21:9 and published a note that gave many of the variant ways in which English translators had handled *hōsanna*—from "Osanna (that is I preye save)" of Wyclif (1382), to "hosaianna" of Tyndale (1525) and Coverdale (1535), to "Hosanna the sonne of Davie" of Geneva (1560), to "Hosanna to the Son of David" of many subsequent versions. Goodspeed himself maintained that the cry had lost its liturgical character and had become a spontaneous outburst like "Vive le roi!" or "God save the King!" He explained, "The pilgrims called down blessings upon Jesus as he went by: 'God bless the Son of David! . . . God bless him from on high!'"[15]

When E. Kautzsch discussed the Aramaic words in the NT, he recognized that commentators rightly explained the relation of the acclamation in the Gospels to Psalm 118, but that "the form *hōsanna* cannot be identified with *hôšî'āh nā'*"; he quoted Elias Levita's explanations that the Greek form was a "shortened pronunciation of the prayer cry = *hôša'nā'* and compared Syriac *'awša'nā'*, citing A. Hilgenfeld's suggestion that Greek *hōsanna* reflected "Aram. *'ôša'nā'*."[16]

The problem with this explanation has always been the lack of any evidence that the root *yš'* was ever used in Aramaic prior to or contemporary with the NT.[17] The root appears abundantly in Hebrew,[18] and it is attested in Moabite,[19] but neither C. F. Jean–J. Hoftijzer,[20] I. N. Vinnikov,[21] nor K. Beyer[22] give any evidence of its use in Aramaic, apart from the proper name *Yš'yh* (*AP* 5:16; 8:33; 9:21),[23] which is undoubtedly a Hebrew name, identical with that of the famous OT prophet. Because of this situation scholars have at times called attention to the short form of the imperative *hôša'* used in Ps 86:2 and possibly in Jer 31:7.[24] This does not help, however, since there is no evidence that the *hôša'* was ever used with the precative particle *nā'* in Hebrew; it occurs only with the long imperative, and then only in Ps 118:25.

Now, however, two instances of the root *yš'* have come to light in Aramaic texts, and even though *hôša'nā'* has not yet been found, the instances lend support to the interpretation of Greek *hōsanna* as a transcription of Aramaic *hôša'nā'*. The first bit of evidence is found in the recently discovered Old Aramaic inscription from Tell Fachariyah. In it a "king of Gozan" *(mlk Gwzn)* sets up a statue of himself before the god Hadad of Sikan. The king's name is written as *hdys'y*. Line 1 of the Aramaic text reads: *dmwt' / zy / hdys'y : zy : šm : qdm : hddskn*, "The likeness of Hadduyith'i, which he erected before Hadad of Sikan . . . ."[25] Thus begins the long Aramaic inscription from the ninth century B.C., from the phase of Old Aramaic. It is a translation, not exact in all details, of an accompanying Assyrian inscription; the latter is inscribed on the front skirt of the statue of the king, and the Aramaic on the back skirt. The Assyrian text has no counterpart of line 1 of the Aramaic, but in line 8 of the Assyrian text the name of the king is given as ^{I}*U-it-'i GAR.KUR* ^{URU}*gu-za-ni*, i.e., ^{I}*adad2-it-'i šakin* ^{uru}*Gu-za-ni*, "H., governor of Gozan."[26] The striking thing about this name is the newly attested preservation of an effort to represent in the borrowed Phoenician alphabet the interdental *t*, still being pronounced by the Arameans of this period, by the consonant *samekh*. In other Old Aramaic inscriptions this interdental was usually represented by *šin* (e.g., in the Sefire inscription: *šwb*, Sf III 6,20,24,25; *yšb*, Sf III 7,17; *šm*, Sf III 6).[27] In this new inscription, however, it appears as *samekh*. The king's name appears to be Aramaic; its theophoric element is that of Hadad, the storm-god of the Aramean pantheon. His name means "Hadad is my salvation." The second half of the name is a form of the root *yṯ'* and is related to the Hebrew noun *yeša'* (see Mic 7:7; Hab 3:18; Ps 18:47 for the same suffixal form in Hebrew). The primary editors vocalize the king's Aramaic name as "Hadad-yis'i" (and the Assyrian form as "Adad-it'i"). S. A. Kaufman vocalizes the Aramaic name as "Had-Yiṯ'i," explaining it as "Had(du) is my help." He notes that the name of the god is otherwise spelled *hdd* in the Aramaic inscription (lines 1,15,17), that Haddu is the Amorite form of the name, and that the Akkadian form is sometimes 'Ad.[28] But the form *Had-Yiṯ'i* is strange for an Aramaic name, and I should prefer to read it as *Haddu-yiṯ'i*. In any case, it shows that the Proto-Semitic root *yṯ'*, "save," is attested in Aramaic.

Kaufman further commented, "The root *yṯ'*, well known in its Hebrew guise of *yš'*, is found in Aramaic only in proper names from this early period."[29] This comment leads to my second instance. In a fragmentary text from Qumran Cave 4, which J. T. Milik has partially published and provisionally labeled Pseudo-Daniel[a], there is an instance of *yš'* in an Aramaic text written in Herodian script.[30] In fragment D, line 2 one reads, *[mlkwt'] dh rbt' wywš' 'mw[n]*, "this great [kingdom], and he will rescue the[m]."[31] Here the root *yš'* clearly appears, but in a form that is again striking. One would have expected it to appear as *ywt'* in the Middle Phase of the language, but instead it appears as in Hebrew as *yš'*. This is, however, not the only instance of *š* instead of *t* in the Aramaic of this period, since *'šwr*, "Asshur, Assyria," appears in 1QapGen 17:8,[32] whereas *'twr* is regularly the form in *Ahiqar* (lines 3-5, 8, 10-14, 20, 32 etc.). In any case, it seems that *yš'* was occasionally used in Aramaic, even outside of proper names.

Granted, *hôša' nā'* as such has not yet been found in Aramaic, but the two instances noted above show that the root *yṯ'/yš'* was not completely unknown in Aramaic, even if only rarely attested. Moreover, the precative particle *n'/nh* is likewise attested in the Middle Phase of the language: 11QtgJob 30:1; 34:3, 6, 7; 37:6 (used after an imperative in each instance); 1QapGen 20:5 (used after a jussive).[33] It should also be noted that there is no long form of the imperative in Aramaic and that *hôša'* would be the normally expected form. Indeed, one wonders whether the short Hebrew form in Ps 86:2 and Jer 31:7 (if imperatival) is not really Aramaized.[34]

Such, then, is the new Aramaic evidence that affects the interpretation of *hōsanna* in the Greek accounts of Jesus' entry into Jerusalem. It makes plausible that *hôša' nā'*, and not *hôšî'āh nā'*, was the current Aramaic form of the cry shouted to Jesus, as a greeting, the first evidence of which is, strangely enough, preserved in the Greek text of the Gospels.

The evidence for the relation of *hôša' nā'* to the feast of Tabernacles in the later rabbinic tradition has been cited above. The shift in meaning thus attested is clear, but is there any evidence that this shift had already taken place in the first century A.D.? Was it being used then as a cry to greet pilgrims coming to Jerusalem for the feast of Tabernacles, or some other feast? In other words, had it already lost its original meaning of a cry for help addressed to Yahweh, as in Ps 118:25? No little debate has surrounded this question in modern times. I turn to a review of some of the suggestions because some of them are farfetched. As far as I can see, the evidence for the shift having taken place in the first century is found in the Greek of the Gospel texts themselves.

If we had only the Johannine form of the tradition about Jesus' entry into Jerusalem, the debate would probably not arise, since there (John 12:13) Ps 118:25-

26 is quoted and modified only by the addition of *[kai] ho basileus tou Israel*—
"[even] the King of Israel." However, both Mark 11:10 and Matt 21:9 record the cry
hōsanna en tois hypsistois, "Hosanna in the highest," which suggests that the cry had
acquired a stereotyped meaning no longer that of the original sense of the psalm;
otherwise how could *hōsanna* be joined to the following phrase? This meaning is further suggested by the cry twice used by Matthew alone, *hōsanna tō huiō Dauid,*
"Hosanna to the son of David!" (Matt 21:9, 15). The dative is clear in the Matthean
Greek. If *hōsanna* were felt as reflecting the original sense of transitive *hôšíʻah nāʼ*
of Ps 118:25 or even of Greek *sōson dē,* why would the dative be used? Hence, it must
have carried the sense of "Hail to the son of David," or something like the forms suggested by E. J. Goodspeed above.

Attempts have been made to explain the dative by citing OT examples of *hôšíaʻ*
followed by *lě-* (e.g., Ps 72:4, *yôšíaʻ libnê ʼebyôn,* "may he save the poor"; 86:16,
wěhôšíʻah lěben ʼamātekā, "and save the son of your handmaid"; 116:6, *wělî
yěhôšíaʻ,* "and he saves me"). G. Dalman appealed to such instances to show that
Hebrew *hôšíaʻ* could be construed with *lě-,* and so *hōsanna* would not mean "give
greeting to."[35] Apparently unaware of Dalman's treatment, C. T. Wood repeated the
argument, regarding the examples from the psalms as cases of "Dative in late
Hebrew": "*a fortiori* must the dative follow in Aramaic." Hence he translated Matt
21:9: "Oh save the Son of David."[36] If the Hebrew of the psalms cited is, indeed,
"late," would not the more logical explanation of *lě-* in such passages be that it represents Aramaic influence, with *lě-* being the sign of the accusative?[37] For the LXX
has rendered these phrases as *sōsei tous huious tōn penetōn* (71:4); *sōson ton huion
tēs paidiskēs sou* (85:16); and *esōsen me* (114:6). If this be correct, one would have
to claim either that Matt 21:9 is an overliteral translation of *hôšaʻ nāʼ lě-* or that the
Greek *hōsanna* there reflects the semantic shift of *hôšaʻ nāʼ* from a cry for help to a
greeting. The reason why the latter is preferred is the form that the cry eventually
takes in *Did.* 10:6, where one finds *hōsanna tō theō Daueid.* This hardly means,
"Save David's God." It is rather, "Hosanna (Hail) to the God of David!"

The debate, however, continues in another fashion, since F. D. Coggan tried to insist on the association of *hōsanna* with the meaning of Jesus' own name (*Yesúaʻ
Yehôšúaʻ,* related by him to the root *yšʻ*): "Do now that which your name implies—
that for which we have been so long waiting, namely, be a modern Joshua and bring
about a national deliverance and *save* us from our enemies . . . . 'Save, we pray thee'
goes up the cry. 'Jesus, live up to the honored name "Joshua" and be at once deliverer
and King.'"[38] Coggan squirmed, however, in seeking to get around the formulation
of Matt 21:9, 15 with its dative, by claiming their originality and suggesting the translation, "Save (us) we pray! (Hither) to the Son of David!"[39] Such an explanation of
hōsanna may seem to suit the Matthean Gospel, since the evangelist records the
popular etymology of Jesus' name in 1:21, *kai kaleseis to onoma autou Iēsoun, autos
gar sōsei ton laon autou apo tōn hamartiōn autōn*—"You shall name him Jesus, for
he will same his people from their sins." That the real etymology of the name of
Jesus, however, is a form of *yšʻ* is another matter. I shall not repeat here all the reasons
why the form *Yěhôšúaʻ,* of which Jesus is an abbreviation, is to be related to the root
šwʻ and why the full name really means "Yahweh, help!"[40] Consequently, I am highly skeptical about the import of Coggan's suggestion. The best explanation of the dative *tō huiō Dauid* remains that *hôšaʻ nāʼ* had lost its original meaning of a cry for

help and had become a cry of greeting to pilgrims coming to Jerusalem for feasts.[41] If this be correct, then the other cry, *hōsanna en tois hypsistois* is equally explicable: Let the greeting being given to the Son of David extend even to the heights of the heavens (where God himself dwells)![42]

What had been originally a cry for help in pre-Christian Judaism (Ps 118:25) thus became in first-century Palestine a spontaneous cry of greeting or a cry of homage.[43] That *hōsanna* was a prayer addressed to God for help to be shown to the Messiah, as E. P. Gould once sought to explain it,[44] is unlikely. That the greeting is extended to him who is the Messiah in Christian belief in Mark 11:10 or Matt 21:9 is clear. But there is simply no evidence for the association of the cry *hôša' nā'* with a messianic expectation in pre-Christian Judaism. The same has to be said for E. Werner's interpretation of *hōsanna* as a "messianic supplicaiton," which was later suppressed by both Jews and Christians. Werner tried to show further that "in apostolic times, Ps 118 was considered a direct prophecy of the coming of Christ," and he cited 1 Pet 2:4-7 as an indication of such an interpretation.[45] That it was so considered may be right, but it is a Christian interpretation of the psalm, and does not say anything about how the Jews of the time would have understood it. Moreover, Werner's evidence for the "messianic" interpretation of Psalm 118, when Jewish sources are brought forth, is drawn from *b. Pesahim* 117b; *y. Megilla* 2.1; and *Midrash Hallel*, documents that do not antedate the fifth century and none of which can be associated with pre-Christian Palestinian Judaism. Similarly, E. Lohse has claimed that Psalm 118 was "sometimes interpreted Messianically," citing *Midr. Ps.* 118:22 (on Ps. 118:24-29),[46] but Jewish scholars themselves date this text to the middle period of midrashic literature, between A.D. 640 and 900![47]

The upshot of this discussion is that, though there is now evidence that Greek *hosanna* could well represent an Aramaic form *hôša' nā'*, and though that form would merely be an Aramaized form of the imperative in Ps 118:25, the term undoubtedly represents a cry that Jerusalemites used to greet pilgrims coming to Jerusalem for feasts like that of Tabernacles and perhaps even Passover. That the original sense of the term (a cry for help addressed to Yahweh in Ps 118:25) was in the course of time lost is clear. The Gospel texts of Mark and Matthew themselves suggest that the term was already a cry of greeting or homage, and this NT evidence remains the oldest available for such a semantic shift. It is, indeed, confirmed by later Christian usage (*Did.* 10.6) and by later Jewish usage, but none of the latter can be used to show that *hôša' nā'* was per se a "messianic supplication" in pre-Christian Judaism.

Notes

1. Luke undoubtedly omitted *hōsanna* because its significance would have been missed by his predominantly Gentile Christian readers; see F. D. Coggan, "Note on the Word *hōsanna*," *ExpTim* 52 (1940-41), 76-77; also E. Lohse, "Hosianna," *NovTest* 6 (1963) 113-19, esp. 114.

2. See A. Rahlfs, *Psalmi cum Odis,* Göttingen Septuaginta 10, Göttingen, 1931, 287.

3. Other discussions of this term can be found in L. S. Potvin, "Words in New Testament Greek Borrowed from the Hebrew and Aramaean," *BibSac* 33 (1876) 52-62; F. Spitta "Der Volksruf beim Einzug Jesu in Jerusalem," *ZWT* 52 (1910) 307-20; F. C. Burkitt, "W and Θ: Studies in the Western Text of St Mark (Continued): *Hosanna,*" *JTS* 17 (1916) 139-52; E. F. F. Bishop, "Hosanna: The Word of the Joyful Jerusalem Crowds," *ExpTim* 53 (1941-42) 212-14; J. S. Kennard, Jr. "'Hōsanna' and the Purpose of Jesus," *JBL* 67 (1948) 171-76; T. Lohmann, "Hosianna," *Biblisch-Historisches Handwörterbuch,* 4 vols., ed. by B. Reicke and L. Rost, Göttingen, 1962-79, 2.752; B. Sandvik, *Das Kommen des Herrn beim Abendmahl im Neuen Testament,* ATANT 58, Zürich, 1970, 37-51; W. Rebell, "Hosanna," *EWNT,* 3.1217-18.

4. In this case the LXX (38:7) understood it not as an imperative, but as a perfect and rendered it *esōsen.*

5. See Str-B, 1.845-50. Cf. Lohse, "Hosianna" (see n. 1 above) 114-16.

6. See *Midrash Rabbah,* 10 vols., ed. M. Freedman and M. Simon, London, 1951, 4.466: "*Hosha'na Rabbah*" as the name of the seventh day of the feast of Tabernacles.

7. See L. Goldschmidt, *Der babylonische Talmud,* 9 vols., Berlin, 1897-1935, 3.83. Also A. Sperber, *The Bible in Aramaic,* Leiden, 1968, IVA.189 or P. de Lagarde, *Hagiographa chaldaice,* Osnabrück, 1967, 247. Cf. J. J. Petuchowski, "Hoshi'ah na' in Psalm cxviii 25—A Prayer for Rain," *VT* 5 (1955) 266-71.

8. The first two of these writings date from about A.D. 450. See M. D. Herr, "Midrash," *EncJud,* 16 vols., New York, 1972, 11.1507-14; he dates *Lev. Rabb.* among the classical Amoraic midrashim of the early period (400-640). E. Berkovits dates the Babylonian Talmud "from the days of Abba Aricha . . . and Samuel, in the first half of the third century, to the end of the teaching of Ravina in 499" ("Talmud, Babylonian," *EncJud,* 15.755-68, esp. 755). *Tg. Esther II* would come from a still later date. See Y. Komlosh, "Targum Sheni," ibid., 15.811-15: "at the end of the seventh or the beginning of the eighth century."

9. See E. Lohse, "*Hōsanna,*" *TDNT,* 9.682.

10. Origen, *Comm. in Matth.* 16.19 (GCS 40.541-42).

11. Eusebius, *Dem. evang.* 6.8,2 (GCS 23.258). E. Lohse analyzes the Eusebian form as Greek *hōs* (= *eis*) *ana* (*TDNT,* 9.683, n. 14).

12. Jerome, *Ep.* 20.1 (Ad Damasum, CSEL 54.104)

13. Jerome, *Ep.* 20.3 (CSEL 54.106).

14. Jerome, *Ep.* 20.5 (CSEL 54.109): "'osianna' sive, ut nos loquimur 'osanna' media uocali littera elisa."—For other ancient uses of the cry, see A. Resch, *Ausserkanonische Paralleltexte zu den Evangelien gesammelt und untersucht,* TU 10/1-5, Leipzig, 1893-97, 3.533-35.

15. See E. J. Goodspeed, *Problems of New Testament Translation,* Chicago, 1945, 34-35. See also *The Complete Bible: An American Translation,* Chicago, 1960, NT 21.

16. A. Hilgenfeld, *Grammatik des Biblisch-aramäischen mit einer kritischen Erörterung der aramäischen Wörter im Neuen Testament,* Leipzig, 1884, 173. Cf. A. Hilgenfeld, *ZWT* 27 (1875) 358 (non vidi); also *Evangeliorum secundum Hebraeos . . . quae supersunt,* 2d ed., Leipzig, 1884, 25. He translates Aramaic '*ôša'nā*' as "serva nos."

17. Cf. P. Joüon, *L'Évangile de Notre-Seigneur Jésus-Christ,* VS 5, Paris, 1930, 128: "totalement inconnue en araméen." J. Jeremias, "Die Muttersprache des Evangelisten Matthäus," *ZNW* 50 (1959) 270-74, esp. 274.

18. See W. Baumgartner, *Hebräisches und aramäisches Lexikon zum Alten Testament,* 3d ed., Leiden, 1967—, 427-28.

19. See H. Donner and W. Röllig, *Kanaanäische und aramäische Inschriften,* 2d ed., Wiesbaden, 1966-69, §181:3-4.

20. C. F. Jean—J. Hoftijzer, *Dictionnaire des inscriptions sémitiques de l'ouest,* Leiden, 1965, 112.

21. I. N. Vinnikov, "Slovar arameyskich Nadpisey," *Palestinskii Sbornik* 7/70 (1962) 236.

22. K. Beyer, *Die aramäischen Texte vom Toten Meer samt den Inschriften aus Palästina, dem Testament Levis aus der Kairoer Genisa, der Fastenrolle und den alten talmudischen Zitaten,* Göttingen, 1984, 601.

23. See A. Cowley, *Aramaic Papyri of the Fifth Century B.C.*, Oxford, 1923; repr., Osnabrück, 1967, 11, 23, 26.

24. See n. 4 above for the problem of *hôša'* in Jer 31:7.

25. See A. Abou-Assaf, P. Bordreuil, and A. R. Millard, *La statue de Tell Fekherye et son inscription bilingue assyro-araméenne,* Etudes Assyriologiques, cah. 7, Paris, 1982, 23. Cf. S. A. Kaufman, "Reflections on the Assyrian-Aramaic Bilingual from Tell Fakhariyeh," *Maarav* 3/2 (1982) 137-75.

26. *La statue,* 13, 15; cf. Kaufman, "Reflections," 159.

27. See J. A. Fitzmyer, *The Aramaic Inscriptions from Sefîre,* BibOr 19, Rome, 1967, 149.

28. Kaufman, "Reflections," 163-64.

29. Ibid., 164.

30. J. T. Milik, "Prière de Nabonide et autres écrits d'un cycle de Daniel: Fragments araméens de Qumrân 4," *RevBib* 63 (1956) 407-15, esp. pp. 411-15. However, Milik has published no photograph of the Pseudo-Danielic fragments.

31. See J. A. Fitzmyer and D. J. Harrington, *A Manual of Palestinian Aramaic Texts: (Second Century B.C.–Second Century A.D.),* BibOr 34, Rome 1978, §3D2 (correct the translation to what is used here).

32. Ibid., §29B:17.8. Cf. N. Avigad and Y. Yadin, *A Genesis Apocryphon: A Scroll from the Wilderness of Judaea,* Jerusalem, 1956, 22.

33. See J. P. M. van der Ploeg and A. S. van der Woude, *Le targum de Job de la grotte xi de Qumrân,* Leiden, 1971, 70, 78, 84. Cf. Fitzmyer and Harrington, *A Manual* (see n. 31 above), §5.

34. See n. 4 above.

35. G. Dalman, *The Words of Jesus Considered in the Light of Post-Biblical Jewish Writings and the Aramaic Language,* Edinburgh, 1909, 220-23, esp. p. 221.

36. C. T. Wood, "The Word *hosanna* in Matthew xxi.9," *ExpTim* 52 (1940-41) 357.

37. See GKC §117n; P. Joüon, *Grammaire de l'hébreu biblique,* 2d ed., Rome, 1947, §125k. C. C. Torrey (*Documents of the Primitive Church,* New York, 1941, 77-78) had recognized this feature earlier.

38. Coggan, "Note" (see n. 1 above), 77.

39. Coggan thinks that the Matthean form is more original, despite the fact that *tō huiō Dauid* is absent from the earlier Marcan form and the independent Johannine tradition.

40. See my commentary, *The Gospel according to Luke I-IX,* AB 28, Garden City, NY, 1981, 347. Cf. W. Baumgartner, *HALAT* (see n. 18 above), 379-80; M. Noth, *Die israelitischen Personennamen,* Stuttgart, 1928; repr., Hildescheim, 1966, 101-10, 154.

41. See H. Bornhäuser, *Sukka (Laubhüttenfest),* Die Mischna II/6, Berlin, 1935, 106-7.

42. Jerome's interpretation: "Denique Matthaeus, qui euangelium Hebraeo sermone conscripsit, ita posuit: 'osianna barrama'. Id est 'osanna in excelsis', quod saluatore nascente salus in caelum usque, id est etiam ad excelsa peruenerit pace facta non solum in terra, sed et in caelo" (*Ep.* 20.5 [CSEL 54.110]). W. C. Allen interprets it thus: "Let those in the heights of heaven say, 'Hosanna'" (*A Critical and Exegetical Commentary on the Gospel according to St. Matthew,* ICC, 3d ed., Edinburgh, 1912, 221). To what extent has Ps 148:1 affected the interpretation of this phrase?

43. *Pace* E. Werner, "'Hosianna' in the Gospels," *JBL* 65 (1946) 97-112. He claims, "Yet in all Hebrew literature no passage in which *Hōsanna* expresses exultation occurs."

44. E. P. Gould, *A Critical and Exegetical Commentary on the Gospel According to St. Mark,* ICC, Edinburgh, 1907, 208-9.

45. "Hosianna" (see n. 43 above), 112-14. In Ps 20:17 one reads '*attāh yāda'tî kî hôšîa' Yhwh měšîhô*), where the verb is used of an anointed one saved by God. But to read that into the *hôšî'āh nā'* of Ps 118:25 or even into the Gospel use of *hōsanna* is another matter. This is hardly the basis for the interpretation of the latter as a "messianic supplication."

46. E. Lohse, *TDNT,* 9.683; cf. "Hosianna" (see n. 1 above), 116. There is no evidence for

Lohse's claim that this specifically messianic shift had taken place "in pre-Chr. Judaism . . . when the temple was still standing, i.e. prior to 70 A.D."

47. See Herr, "Midrash," *EncJud* (see n. 8 above) 11.1511-14; W. G. Braude, *The Midrash on Psalms*, 2 vols., New Haven, 1959, xi-xxxi. Cf. C. Burger, *Jesus als Davidssohn: Eine traditionsgeschichtliche Untersuchung*, FRLANT 98, Göttingen, 1970, 48; he recognizes the same defect in Lohse's argument.

The Role of Christian Prophets in the Gospel Tradition

Gerald F. Hawthorne

The purpose of this paper[1] is to ask once again whether or not the origin of some of the sayings of Jesus that are recorded in the gospels may be traced to the work of early Christian prophets.[2] It is my hope that in re-opening this discussion I may make a further small contribution to the on-going discussion, and at the same time to extend my congratulations to a distinguished scholar, who himself has written on this subject, and express my deep appreciation to a highly respected, highly distinguished, longtime friend.

I. Introduction

An introduction is in order to alert readers to a personal bias and to inform them of my own understanding of the early Christian prophets—who they were and what they did.

1. I admit to being voluntarily within a creedal tradition that holds as one of its important beliefs, a high view of Scripture. I affirm at the outset, therefore, that Holy Scripture is God's special revelation to mankind, that it is the trustworthy authoritative message of God, essential for a correct understanding of God and his acts and of ourselves and the meaning of our existence and that it was inspired by the Spirit of God, given to be obeyed as the voice of the living God (2 Tim 3:15-17).

Nevertheless, I also affirm that this sacred text was written down by human beings in human language at specific junctures in time and in particular geographical locations, with all the limitations that humanness, language, space and time, societies and their cultures impose upon it. I affirm, therefore, that the Bible is a joint effort of both God and man in time and space—a product initiated by God and under his control, so that every part and form of it can be labeled "God breathed" (*theopneustos*, 2 Tim 3:16; 2 Pet 1:21), but also a product of different men, living at different times and in different places, having differing personalities and outlooks, fears, and aspirations, etc., so that every part and form also bears the stamp of humanness: *omnia ex deo; omnia ex hominibus*. It is my belief, therefore, that the Bible is both a word from God to be heard and obeyed, which stands above me and is my critic, and at the same time that it is a human word to be analyzed and subjected to the most thorough historical and literary criticism. My understanding of the Christian prophets' role in the formation of the gospel tradition, will of course be colored by this creed.

2. By Christian prophet I have in mind a powerful authority-figure in the early church who was inspired by the Holy Spirit and impelled by the Spirit to speak his message to individuals and to the church with authority and power. He was a person who received and proclaimed divine revelations, not merely a person who preached "good news" in a traditional way.

The Christian prophet was anticipated and announced by Jesus (Matt 5:11, 12; 7:21, 22; 10:40; cf. Mark 9:41; Matt 23:24-37; Luke 13:34). But the first Christian prophet to step out of the shadows and be named was Agabus, whose prophecies seem to have been of local application (Acts 11:27, 28; 21:10, 11). Judas and Silas were also called prophets (Acts 21:30-32). Several prophets had their home-base in Antioch, Syria (Acts 13:1-3). The four virgin daughters of Philip the Evangelist were prophetesses (Acts 21:10). In all likelihood Paul was numbered among the prophets (cf. Acts 13:1 with 9:3-9; 2 Cor 12:1-3; Gal 1:11, 12; 2:2).[3] John, the writer of the Apocalypse, was a prophet (Rev 1:10; 17:3; 21:10), and the woman he calls "Jezebel" and "false", was a prophetess of prominence and authority in Ephesus (Rev 2:20-21). Polycarp, Bishop of Smyrna, was termed "the apostolic and prophetic teacher" (*Mart. Pol.* 12:3; 16:2), and both Barnabas, Ignatius and Hermas appear to have been self-styled prophets (*Barn.* 16:9; Ign. *Phld.* 7; *Herm. Vis.* 1.3).

Although the names of early Christian prophets are few, there is, nevertheless, a good deal to be learned about their character, activity, message, destiny and importance by a study of the New Testament and the early Fathers.

a. Apparently the presence and activity of Christian prophets was quite widespread (cf. Acts 20:23 with 21:10, 11).

b. Early Christian prophets worked within the framework of the Christian community. Quite possibly they only became active when the church was at worship or when intercession was being made to God from this assembly of the godly who had the "faith of the Divine Spirit" (*Herm. Mand.* 11.9; Acts 13:1, 2). Their place within the structure of the church was one of great importance, ranking second only to the apostles (1 Cor 12:28-29; Eph 4:11; cf. Matt 10:40, 41). In all likelihood a congregation would be addressed on the Lord's day by its prophets speaking in the Spirit and giving it both exhortation *and* revelation (1 Cor 14).[4]

c. Seemingly early Christian prophets belonged to and worked together in bands or brotherhoods of prophets (Acts 11:27; 13:1; Rev 19:10; 22:9), which can be considered as elite or exclusive groups. For not every one was a prophet (1 Cor 12:29; contrast *Barn.* 16:9).[5]

d. The early Christian prophet was a person of the Scripture, whose mind was saturated with the Old Testament text. As a consequence prophetic utterances were often couched in the language of the Bible. Stephen's famous prophetic review of Israel's history is a classic example of this phenomenon (Acts 7). Thus new prophetic insight may have been prompted by meditation upon the ancient texts (compare Rom 11:27 with Isa 27:9; 1 Cor 15:51, 54, 55 with Isa 25:8; Hos 13:14)—new insight and meaning that was authoritative and powerful, for, like Stephen's arguments which came through the Spirit, they could not be refuted (cf. Acts 6:10).

e. The early Christian prophet was a person of the Spirit[6] whose words and actions on occasion were *especially* prompted by the Spirit (διὰ τοῦ πνεύματος, Acts 11:27, 28; 13:2; cf. Rev 1:10; 4:2), so that at a particular moment he could say, "The words which I am going to speak (τάδε) are *the words* of the Holy Spirit" (Acts 21:11; *Herm. Mand.* 11.8, 9; *Did.* 11.7; cf. Rev 1:8).[7] It was this experience of inspiration that separated the one role of the Christian prophet (1 Cor 14:31) from the other, i.e. his role as preacher,[8] and made what he said under inspiration take precedence over what he said otherwise. This, it seems to me, is what Paul meant when he wrote the Corinthian church that two or three [of their prophets] could speak while the rest of the prophets (οἱ ἄλλοι) exercised their judgment upon what was said. *But* if another [prophet] *received a revelation,* the first speaker must give way to him (1 Cor 14:29, 30).

Prophecy, therefore, was of more than one kind. It included what could be called "ministry"—prophetic words given for the improvement, encouragement, consolation and general benefit of the Christian community (1 Cor 14:3-4). This was closely tied with teaching (Acts 13:1; 1 Cor 14:31; Rev 2:20; *Herm. Sim.* 9.15.4) and with a lively interest in and a knowledge of the Gospel tradition and the words of the earthly Jesus.[9]

But it also included another dimension, a "higher" dimension, related directly to a special work of the Spirit upon the prophet by which the Spirit revealed to him a word form the risen exalted Christ (cf. Rev 1:10 with 4:1, 2a)—a word that did not come whenever the prophet wished, but only when God wished, whenever the prophetic Spirit rested on him and filled him (2 Pet 1:20, 21; Rev 22:6; cf. *Herm. Mand.* 11.8).

This part of the prophet's ministry was the result of a direct revelation given to him of an aspect of the divine mind hitherto unknown (Eph 3:5; Rev 10:7; 22:6)—something that transcended a Christian's previous knowledge. The prophet was "let in," so to speak, on the secret counsel of God by the Holy Spirit, and commissioned to share this secret (μυστήριον) by prophesying it to the church, not only orally but possibly in written form as well (cf. Col 1:26, 27 with Rom 16:26).[10] Like Old Testament prophecy this prophetic message was an immediate communication of God's (Christ's) word to his people through human lips. There are times in fact when the risen Christ speaks in the first person and the figure of the prophet fades into the background—"Behold," says the exalted Christ, "I am coming as a thief" (Rev 16:15; 22:7), so that it becomes clear that the words that are spoken are indeed the words of the heavenly Lord of the church (Rev chaps. 2 and 3).

f. In the New Testament the ministry of the prophet was clearly distinguished from that of apostle, teacher, miracle worker, evangelist, etc. (1 Cor 12:28-29; Eph 4:11).[11] Even though his functions may have, in actuality, overlapped those of other charismatic figures within the church,[12] yet he was nonetheless considered in a class by himself, and his ministry pneumatic, "given by the Spirit." Indeed, his ministry was considered to be the chief of attainable pneumatic gifts (1 Cor 14:1, 3-5).

g. Hence, early Christian prophets were highly valued, important, pneumatic, awesome figures within the early church. As a result whatever they said was received by the community as the command of the Lord (1 Cor 14:29, 30, 37). At this point David Hill quite correctly took issue with an over-statement made by me in the original form of this paper: The prophet's word was looked upon "as the command of the Lord to be obeyed *without question.*"[13]

I readily concede to him that the phrase, "without question," should be stricken, for it is true that from the earliest period of the church's history regulations and controls, if only self-imposed controls, were placed upon Christian prophets (1 Cor 11:4; 14:29, 32), and critical evaluations of all their utterances by persons qualified to judge them were required (1 Cor 14:29). But this fact, that the prophet's prophecies were subject to examination, is not, in my judgment, sufficient reason to say so emphatically, as Hill does, that the prophets' words, their prophetic statements, were thus less than divinely authoritative. Nor is it sufficient reason to say that only Paul and the writer of the Revelation enjoyed unquestioning authoritative status, whereas the congregational prophets did not.[14] Consider the following:

(1) Even the Old Testament prophets, who boldly proclaimed, "Thus says the Lord," and whose proclamations were taken as the authoritative word/command of God, were themselves subject to critical evaluation (cf. Deut 13:1-5; 18:21, 22).

(2) Paul's own prophetic word seems on more than one occasion to have been challenged, evaluated, if you please, and was not always taken at first as the true word of the Lord by all people who heard it (cf. 2 Cor 1:18; 6:8; 12:11, 12 and numerous other places where he defends his right to speak as the mouthpiece of the Lord, the Lord's apostle-prophet).

(3) Finally, even the most "prophetic" book of the New Testament, the book of Revelation, was not accepted wholly without critical evaluation and challenge by the church, not only in respect to its authorship, but also in respect to its contents (cf. Eusebius, *H.E.* 3.28; 7.24, 25). Hence, the discovery that the words of "congregational prophets" were to be tested does not mean, therefore, that they "did not enjoy the authoritative status of Paul or of the unknown 'John' who wrote Revelation."[15]

In this connection it is surprising to note that Hill himself defines the early Christian prophet as follows—"a Christian who functions within the Church, occasionally or regularly, as a divinely called and divinely inspired speaker who receives intelligible *and authoritative* [italics mine] revelations or messages, which he is impelled to deliver publicly, in oral or written form, to Christian individuals and/or the Christian Community."[16]

h. It was the awe-inspiring nature of the Christian prophets, and the fact that their word had the potential of being the authoritative word of the Lord to the congregation, that opened the door for abuses to set in and for false prophets to arise (cf. Matt 7:15; 24:11). Thus there arose the need for the creation of criteria by which genuine prophets could be distinguished from the counterfeit. Hence, we begin to see statements like this—"if your gift is prophecy, prophesy in agreement with the faith" (Rom 12:6), meaning that all prophetic utterances must conform to a given body of truth and any prophecies which contradict such basic teachings of the church as preserved in its traditions, are false prophecies. Still other tests were devised and applied to those who presumed to speak in the Spirit: all true prophecies had to be fixed to the once-for-all historic act of God through the man Jesus (1 John 4:1-3).

Abuses had a tendency to lower the prophet and his ministry in the eyes of the people. This perhaps was why Paul had to warn the Thessalonians not to stifle inspiration nor to despise prophecies (1 Thess 5:20), and why, though establishing guidelines for distinguishing the true prophet from the false, the writer of the Didache strongly urges his readers, nevertheless, to hold the true prophet in awe (*Did.* 11).[17]

II. Traces of the Christian Prophet's Creative Role

That certain sayings attributed to Jesus are in reality the result of the creative activity of early Christian prophets is considered by many today as one of the assured results of gospel criticism.[18]

How can this be, since in reality there seems to be no "hard" proof for a phenomenon like this occurring? Professor F. F. Bruce remarks that "the role of prophets in the formation of the tradition has been greatly exaggerated. *We simply have no concrete evidence* to indicate that prophets in church meetings uttered words in the name of the exalted Lord which were preserved in the tradition as sayings of Jesus 'in the days of his flesh'."[19] And Professor David Aune after an extraordinarily careful and thorough examination of prophecy in the early church, comes to much the same conclusion. It is his studied opinion that the critical methodology for detecting and demonstrating that oracles of Christian prophets were uttered in the name of the exalted Lord and became mingled with the sayings of the historical Jesus has not yet been developed.[20]

I am willing, in fact, I am compelled to agree with Professors Bruce and Aune— there is no "concrete evidence" for such a role played by Christian prophets in the formation of the gospel tradition, and no critical methodology has as yet been developed by which such a role can be detected and demonstrated. But to dismiss the Christian prophet completely from playing such a role in the history of the tradition, and then to say, as Aune does, that early Christianity did in fact exercise a *creative role* in the formulation, reformulation and transmission of the sayings of Jesus, leaves one without a clue as to who, or what group was responsible for "these creative additions and modifications in the tradition."[21] This is highly unsatisfactory to me, and therefore I wish once again, on the basis, not of hard evidence, but of "soft" evidence, the accumulation of data—some of which I presented in my earlier paper, some of which I add now, not all of which is of equal weight—to at least suggest the possibility that early Christian prophets did play some significant role in the formation of the gospel tradition. I have no illusions of being able *to prove* that a single utterance of the risen Lord spoken by a prophet actually became part of the dominical sayings—Professor Hill is quite right in challenging any such claim whether made by me or anyone else.[22] All I shall be attempting to do, and no more, is to provide a reasonable case for the *possibility* of some such intermingling, however slight.

1. Seemingly, the New Testament does not make a sharp distinction between Jesus' own spoken words and those of his apostles. Notice that it records Jesus as himself saying, "the one who hears you, hears me" (Luke 10:16; cf. Matt 10:40; John 13:20; Gal 4:14). The apostles, therefore, were fully authorized spokesmen for Jesus, and to hear their message was to hear Christ's, was to hear his word of truth (Eph 4:20, 21).

2. And even if the early church was, on occasion, concerned to distiguish between the Jesus of history and the Christ of faith, to use modern terminology (cf. 1 Cor 7:10, 12), it nevertheless, without question, believed firmly that these two titles belonged to the same person: "Let all Israel be assured of this," Peter proclaimed, "that God has made this *Jesus* whom you crucified both *Lord and Christ*" (Acts 2:36). Hence, the risen Lord of the church was not a different person from that of the Jesus who lived and taught in Palestine during the days of his flesh, but one and the same.

3. Furthermore, the early church considered itself a community of the Spirit— people living in the ecstasy of the fulfilment of Joel's prophecy, living in those last days when God would pour out his Spirit on all mankind so that men and women would rise up and prophesy (Acts 2:16-21). This meant that the church *expected* people to prophesy, to speak the word of the Lord to them, and that therefore they not only looked back to a past time when Jesus *was* with them, but to the exciting present moment of Jesus' immediate presence as their living Lord—Christ-with-them-today. For the Holy Spirit in the church was none other than the Spirit of Christ in the church

(cf. Acts 16:6, 7—τὸ ἅγιον πνεῦμα . . . τὸ πνεῦμα Ἰησοῦ—with John 14:15-18; Rom 8:9b, 10; 2 Cor 3:17). It was the fulfilment of Jesus' own promise that where two or three would meet together in his name there he would be with them (Matt 18:20).

4. This implies, then, that the interest of the early Christians lay not only in what their Lord once has said to a basically Jewish audience, but also in what the living Lord of the church was saying to them (Palestinian and non-Palestinian Christians) right now! It is a fact of Scripture that these Christians took for granted that the heavenly Christ *would reveal* to them further truths about himself: "I have still many things to tell you," Jesus said to his disciples, "but you cannot grasp them now. When he comes, the Spirit of Truth, he will guide you into all truth . . . what he hears (will hear) he *will speak,* and he *will tell* you what is yet to come. He will bring glory to me by taking from what is mine and making it known to you" (John 16:12-15).[23] A textual variant to John 14:26, although probably not original, at least indicates the kind of expectation that was abroad in the church: where the accepted text states that the Holy Spirit will remind the disciples of all things Jesus *had said* (ἃ εἶπον ὑμῖν ἐγώ), *the variant indicates that the Spirit would bring to their minds whatever things he might say* (ἃ ἂν εἴπω ὑμῖν ἐγώ).

5. The place and practice of the prophet in the pneumatic-community is also an important consideration. It should be clear from the introduction, and should be kept in mind, that from this writer's perspective *the Christian prophet was no ordinary individual but one who spoke with authority.* He was a person especially inspired by the Spirit, that all-important identifying power which made the prophets' words, one and the same with the words of Christ. The prophet, thus inspired, was the earthly voice, so to speak, by which the heavenly Lord expressed in propositional form those promised revelations of himself and of his will to individuals and/or groups in the early history of the Christian church.

Mark 13:11 (= Matt 10:19 = Luke 21:15) is interesting in this connection. Mark (and Matthew) quote Jesus as saying *to his disciples* that the Holy Spirit (the Spirit of your Father) at some future time, no doubt after his own death-resurrection-ascension, would be the one to speak through (ἐν) them. But Luke has Jesus say, "*I* myself will give you the ability to speak," i.e. "*I* will be speaking through you." By this important change Luke makes clear, therefore, that the Spirit which was to inspire Jesus' disciples was none other than Jesus himself! Thus what the disicples would say would in reality be what Jesus would be saying through them.

Now although it is clear from these texts (both from John [16:12-15] and from Mark 13:11 par.) that the risen Christ would yet speak to his own (or to the world), it is not completely clear how or through whom he would do this. It might be argued, therefore, that these promises apply to all Christians, and hence all Christians are potentially or actually prophets, thus eliminating any need for positing a special group of pneumatics (prophets) to receive and transmit words from the risen Lord.

Using these same texts, however, the opposite idea can also be argued and with even greater force, especially if they are considered in light of what has been said above about the Christian prophet's role—that unique role of receiving revelations from the risen Lord and proclaiming them to the church. Is it not true that John 16:12-15 was addressed to a select body (apostles) that had a certain succession and that, at least on one occasion, was identified with prophets (*Did.* 11.4, 5)? And was not Mark

13 also spoken to a special group of people who would be facing death as *martyrs* ("witnesses," a term also used to describe the early Christian prophet [Rev 19:10 with 17:6])? In fact, *prophets* occupied such a place in the number of *martyrs* that James, in encouraging his readers to hold on to the end, "cites not Jesus' sufferings, but that of the [Christian?] prophets" (James 5:10)![24]

6. The words of the exalted Jesus spoken through his prophets are very like in form and content to the word of Jesus recorded by the evangelists in the gospels. This can be tested by comparing the latter with the former as found in the Apocalypse. Granting the fact that the apocalyptic genre[25] is quite different from the gospel genre, and granting, too, that at the end of the first century A.D., the "sayings" in Revelation are still acknowledged for what they are—sayings of the exalted Lord spoken through a prophet by the Spirit, yet the similarity between gospel-sayings and Revelation-sayings is striking nonetheless. Take the Lord's words in Rev 2:10, for example: "Do not be afraid of the suffering to come. The devil will throw some of you into prison to put you to the test . . . only be faithful till death, and I will give you the crown of life," and compare them with the words of Jesus to his disciples that are recorded in the gospels: "Do not be afraid of those who kill the body. . . . You will be hated by all for my sake. But the one who endures to the end will be saved" (Matt 10:28, 22). Compare also Rev 3:20 with John 14:23, and Rev 16:15 with Matt 24:43, 44; Luke 12:39, and Rev 3:5 with Luke 17:8, 9, etc. If one removes the contexts surrounding the sayings of Jesus, the character of those preserved in the tradition are not radically different from those sayings of the exalted Lord pronounced through his prophet. Surely it is not too much to say that *all* words of this Blessed One, whether spoken in Galilee by his own lips or from heaven through his prophets, would be heard by the church as instruction, encouragement, chastening or promise from the living Lord. (Would the sayings of Jesus in Rev 1-3 be any less "authentic" than those in the gospels?) If this is so then is it not possible to imagine that some of the risen Lord's words could have been included perhaps unconsciously among the pre-resurrection sayings of Jesus?

7. Paul, however, seems to make a distinction between the words spoken by the earthly Jesus and preserved in the tradition of the church, and those that were not, i.e. from those that might have been spoken by the risen Lord through a prophet, e.g. through Paul himself (1 Cor 7:10, 12, 25, 40). It is this distinction that has made some scholars cautious—and rightly so—about claiming that words received from the heavenly Jesus found their way into the gospels and were regarded by the early church as having equal validity with the pre-resurrection sayings found there.[26]

Without throwing caution to the winds, let us nevertheless consider some important factors in this matter of Paul's seeming desire to make such distinctions:

a. Paul may have been familiar with the tradition and used it (cf. 1 Cor 15:3), but we should not forget that he also asserted his independence from it, claiming that the message he preached was no human invention, that he did not take it over from any man, that no man taught it to him, but that he received it through revelation from Jesus Christ (Gal 1:11, 12; 2:6).

b. If, however, we grant that Paul did distinguish words spoken by Jesus on earth from those spoken by him from heaven, it does not follow that he considered the latter of less importance or any less authoritative. If Paul, because of a lack of traditional information, had to rely on his own opinion (1 Cor 7:25, 40), it made no authoritative difference, because he believed that as an apostle-prophet he had the mind/Spirit of God/Christ (1 Cor 7:40; cf 2:11-15).[27]

c. There are, on the other hand, instances of where Paul's general instructions to the churches contain elements of what has been thought of as traditional sayings of Jesus, or at least allusions to them, but where Paul felt no compulsion to point out this fact or to distinguish between them and his own demands as apostle-prophet for the conduct of the churches to which he wrote (cf. Rom 12:14 with Matt 5:24; Rom 13:9 with Mark 12:31; Rom 14:12 with Luke 16:2; Rom 14:3 with Matt 7:2; Rom 14:20 with Mark 7:19; Rom 16:19 with Matt 10:16; 1 Cor 13:2 with Mark 11:23; 1 Thess 5:2, 4 with Luke 12:39.[28] [Could it by any chance be possible that instead of Paul drawing from traditional material as the source of his parenesis, the traditional material drew from Paul? That is to ask, did some of the words of Jesus now contained in the gospels come from the parenesis, i.e. from the words of admonition and encouragement originating with the risen Lord and channeled through his prophet, Paul?]).

d. According to the Book of Acts it was Paul who asked the Ephesian elders to remember "the words of the *Lord Jesus* who said, 'It is more blessed to give than to receive'" (Acts 20:35). But this is a statement not found in our four gospels. Paul also wrote to the Thessalonian Christians, "We can tell you this from the *Lord's* own teaching, that any of us who are left alive until the Lord's coming will not have any advantage over those who died" (1 Thess 4:15, JB). Where does one find this "teaching of the Lord"? Certainly not in the canonical gospels,[29] although it is not unlike what Jesus might have said. It is possible, of course, that these sayings might also be words of the exalted Christ spoken through a prophet by revelation—in this case through Paul himself. Whether or not this latter statement could be true, *it is true,* and this is important, that these sayings in Acts and Thessalonians were regarded by the early church as dominical as any of the sayings of Jesus in the gospels!

e. Finally, in this connection, there is one saying of Jesus in Luke (assuming that the text is correct) that is not found in the sources Mark or Q—the eucharistic word of Jesus, "Do this in remembrance of me" (Luke 22:20 = Mark 14:22 = Matt 26:26). The only other place it occurs is in Paul's teaching on the Last Supper (1 Cor 11:24), teaching he claims to have received *from the Lord* (1 Cor 11:23). Is it possible that here is a concrete example of a word received from the risen Lord, transmitted to the Corinthian church through the prophet, Paul, and which later found its way into the gospel narrative as a word of Jesus through Paul's close associate, Luke?

8. It is very possible that early Christian prophets functioned as interpreters of Old Testament Scripture. Perhaps the Old Testament was a key catalyst for their prophetic insight and utterances (cf. Acts chaps. 2 and 15) since many of their oracles were derived from interaction with the sacred text. But this interaction with the text was done in a manner characteristic of the prophetic mind. The Old Testament was not always quoted verbatim. Often it was shortened or enlarged upon or modified in other ways,[30] but never was the Old Testament treated as a past authority merely to be commented upon by the prophet; it was spoken fresh as the present word of the living Lord. Paul's own revelations apparently came in conjuction with his exegesis of the Old Testament (cf. Rom 11:25-27; 1 Cor 15:51, 52), and it is most instructive to see how he shaped the text to express the new inspired vision he received as a prophet.[31]

Could this treatment of the Old Testament by the Christian prophet have been a model for the prophet's working with the traditional sayings of Jesus in the period before they took written form in the gospel?[32] Is it not possible that a *peshered* saying of Jesus (or even a saying *de novo*) from a Christian prophet would readily have had an authoritative status and as such been given a place within the gospel tradition? For example, while Matt 19:9 refers only to instances where the husband divorces his wife, this is expanded in Mark 10:11, 12 to include dual divorce terminology, i.e. to include those instances where a woman could divorce her husband as well as where the husband could divorce his wife. Jewish law, however, *only* allowed the husband to initiate divorce proceedings, while Graeco-Roman law allowed the wife as well as the husband to initiate such proceedings. As Mark 10:1-12 stands, therefore, it seems to reflect the reformulation of the Jewish-oriented message of Jesus so as to apply it to a new historical-cultural situation of the Christian church and in the process the creation of a new saying of Jesus—"And if a woman divorces her husband and marries another she commits adultery." This reformulation (or creation) is certainly in keeping with the spirit of Jesus' original teaching, but it may very well not have been an actual part of that teaching.

9. A further point, while considering the relation of the Christian prophet to the Old Testament, is the following: If one should concede that not all the sayings of Jesus in the gospels were actually spoken by him between his birth and ascension, but later by him though his prophets, it is possible that the book of Hebrews may give a hint as to how this was done. The Christian prophet (here the writer *To the Hebrews*) takes words from the Old Testament, quotes them exactly or freely, and places them in the mouth of Jesus so that they become his words. Note carefully the wording of 2:11-13 (NIV)—"Both the one who makes men holy and those who are made holy are of the same family. So Jesus is not ashamed to call them brothers. *He says, 'I* will declare your name to my brothers . . .' And again, '*I* will put my trust in him.'" [italics mine]. Of special interest is Hebrews 10:5-7. Do not the words here, put on Jesus' lips by the prophetic writer quoting Psalm 40:7-9—". . . '*I* have come to do your will (θέλημα) O God'" (10:5-7) sound very like the Gethsemane words of Jesus in Luke's gospel—"Not my will (θέλημα) but yours be done" (Luke 22:42)?

10. It is a fact that sayings of Jesus which are today not considered part of the text of the traditional four gospels were, nevertheless, accepted as authentic sayings of Jesus, and therefore canonized, by certain segments of the early church. One of these is the variant to Luke 6:5 found in Codex D and used by Marcion. What of the words of Jesus in John 7:53–8:11? Or of those in the longer ending of Mark? Certainly the words of Jesus here were accepted as part of the canon and they appear even today in many Bibles. Do these sections contain authentic words of Jesus? What of the Freer logion, a noteworthy insertion into Codex W near the close of the longer ending of Mark's gospel (after 16:14)? It too includes additional words of the resurrected Christ. And what of the shorter ending to Mark?

The sayings here could all have been drawn from oral tradition. But is it not also possible that they could have been oracles of Christian prophets which solved particular problems that the early church faced—concern over the abrupt ending of Mark's gospel on a note of fear, worry over why the message of Christ was making such slow progress in the world and why the chosen showed unbelief and hardness of heart[33] (the Freer logion[34])? If so, then, it appears that there was indeed an openness on the part of early Christians to supplement the tradition by the prophetic word.

11. In the gospel of John there are places where it is difficult, if not impossible, to say where the words of Jesus end and the words of the evangelist begin. John 3:10-21 is a classic example.[35] Here there seems to be an imperceptible change from the words of Jesus addressed to Nicodemus to the words of the exalted Christ addressed to the world and spoken through John (note the translations that make use of quotation marks and observe where they place the closed-quotes to indicate the end of Jesus' words). Why was there not greater care taken on the part of the writer of the Fourth Gospel to make the kind of sharp distinction between what Jesus actually said in the days of his flesh and what he said after his ascension through the evangelist (prophet) that we twentieth century people would like to see? Perhaps the answer is that in the thinking of this evangelist, a first century man, inspired by the Spirit of God, it made no significant difference. He viewed his gospel as a prophetic gospel,[36] himself as a prophet and his task, guided and validated by the Spirit of truth (the Spirit of Jesus, John 16:12-25), to work creatively with the tradition.[37] Only in this way could the facts be put in proper perspective and the whole truth of God about Jesus Christ be set forth. Hence, quite naturally there would be this blending of tradition and inspired (prophetic) interpretation. "And if John were asked to justify the freedom he has exercised in handling the tradition of Jesus' words and deeds, he could appropriately reply: 'Who but Jesus has the authority to interpret Jesus? The risen Lord is not another Jesus; he is the same one who lived among us in the flesh . . . [and] still teaches us through the Spirit.'"[38]

12. What seems strange to many of us—the possibility that the words of the risen Lord Jesus are equally authentic with those of the earthly Jesus—seems not to have been strange at all to Christians of the early centuries of the church's history. The Didache is a case in point. Not only does it teach about prophets (Did. 11), but it itself may have been the work of a prophet. Dating from about A.D. 110[39] it claims to be "The Teaching of the Lord Through the Twelve Apostles to the Gentiles," and was thus accepted as an authoritative document, at least by the Syrian church.[40] How did it gain this acceptance? If Professor Aland is correct, it was not because the author pretended that he had discovered it as a holy book of the past, or because he had it sent off to distant friends to make its way in a place where the author was unknown. "The only conceivable hypotheseis is that the author of the writing introduced it first to his own congregation . . . in the service of worship. Indeed the congregation knew that this address was written by its elder . . . But when he claimed his work to be the message of the Lord through the Apostles and when his own congregation . . . acknowledged this to be valid, they did this only because it was but the written version of what hitherto had been orally delivered in any congregational meeting: a prophet got up and preached the Word of the Lord. Everyone knew the prophet and his human affairs. But when he spoke with inspired utterance it was not he that was heard but the Lord or the Apostles or the Holy Spirit himself. The writer of the Didache knew himself to be a charismatic and was acknowledged as such, because the content of the message confirmed the claim. Accordingly the written word received the same credence as the charismatically spoken word and thus the Didache achieved recognition in the church of those days."[41] It became the word of the Lord for them, and traditional words of Jesus (Did. and passim) and the words of their own charismatic figure (their prophet-preacher) were mingled together without distinction and with equal weight.

The writings of Justin Martyr (d. *ca.* A.D. 165) should also be considered in this connection. The "prophetic Spirit" looms large in his thinking[42] and prophecies for him are more trustworthy than human reports. How naturally he takes the prophetic word of the Old Testament—any part of it—and like the writer of Hebrews applies it to Jesus Christ (*Dial.* 38.3, *passim*) or puts its words into his mouth (*Dial.* 37.1-3) to form new sayings of Jesus. Justin writes: "Therefore, our Lord Jesus Christ said: 'In whatsoever I overtake you, in that will I also judge [you]'" (*Dial. 47.5*).[43]

For Justin the gift of prophecy, found everywhere in the Old Testament, came to rest at last in Christ. As a consequence no prophet now exists among the Jews, but they abound among believers in Christ (*Dial.* 52.4; 82.1; 87.2, 3; 88.1). It is possible that Justin even thought of himself as a prophet. In any case he feels free, when quoting Jesus' words from the gospels, to alter them, summarize them, combine them in new ways (see 1 *Apol.* 16 for a surprising combination of Matt 4:10 and Mark 12:30) or even add to them. Of special interest is *Dial.* 35.2, 3. Here Justin is talking to Trypho about the Lord Jesus and says: "For he [Jesus] said: Many shall come in my name clothed without in sheep skins, but within they are ravaging wolves [Matt 24:5 combined with 7:15]. And: there shall be divisions and heresies [1 Cor 11:18, 19]. And: beware of false prophets, who will come to you . . . [Matt 7:15]." (Note the easy inclusion of words from Paul among the words of Jesus so that they too become *verba Domini.*) Again Justin writes, "For Christ did not call the righteous . . . to repentance, but the ungodly . . . So *he said,* I have not come to call the righteous but sinners to repentance [Mark 2:17 = Matt 9:13 = Luke 5:32]. For the heavenly Father wishes the repentance of a sinner rather than his punishment" (1 *Apol.* 15.8). Where would Justin have placed the quotation marks in the text here cited—after "repentance" or after "punishment"? From what I can observe of his thought it was of no consequence to him. Even though the latter sentence cannot be traced to a saying of Jesus in the gospels, it is for Justin, nevertheless, a correct "prophetic" interpretation of the former saying which can be traced to Jesus in the gospels. Therefore, in his thinking, the latter has every right to rank equally with the former.

Melito of Sardis (d. *ca.* A.D. 190), though perhaps a bishop,[44] nevertheless belonged to this same pneumatic milieu. It is possible that his prophet-like characteristics were the very characteristics that projected him into a leadership role in the church. In any case, his recently discovered sermon, *On the Passover,* shows him to be a charismatic. Like the New Testament prophet described above in the introduction his ministry was played in two keys: (1) an ordinary key where his message was presented in language intended to scrutinize, judge, encourage, inform, etc., and (2) an extraordinary key, an "apocalyptic"/revelational key where the human instrument fades into the background and the risen Lord alone appears and is heard through the prophet to address the congregation in the first person: "I am the Christ. I am the one who destroyed death . . . and bound the strong one . . . Therefore, come unto me all families of people . . . and receive forgiveness for your sins. I am your forgiveness . . ."[45] How would Melito's audience have heard these words? Would they, could they, have been in a position to distinguish them from any sayings of Jesus they perhaps may have read in or heard from the gospels—assuming, of course, that the gospels were regularly and universally read alongside the Old Testament in the liturgy of the church? (I rather think this is a twentieth century question—one that never would have occurred to them.)

In conclusion, I ask again, did Christian prophets have any part in the creation of dominical sayings? The data marshalled here seem to point in the direction of an affirmative answer.[46]

Granting then even the possibility that this was so, it does not follow that the majority of Jesus-sayings, or even many of them, were created by Christian prophets. I quite agree with Professor Dunn that "while there is good reason to affirm the activity of prophets in earliest Christianity and the acceptance of some of their words as part and parcel of the Jesus-tradition, what we actually know of prophetic utterances and their testing suggests quite strongly that the incorporation of prophetic [words] into the Jesus-tradition was by no means a large-scale affair."[47] Nor does it follow that the early church had no interest in the Jesus of history, in what he did and said during the days of his flesh—only in theologizing about him. Nor does it mean that the early church was incapable of (or disinterested in) distinguishing between the words of Jesus and the words of its exalted Lord.[48] But it seems that, if there was a situation in which the words of the earthly Jesus and the words of the risen Christ existed side by side and circulated together, there at least was the possibility of a mingling of the two together—unconsciously if not consciously.

Neither does the possibility that some of the sayings originating with Christian prophets and later attributed to the earthly Jesus mean that these sayings are "inauthentic" and hence inferior to the "genuine" sayings of Jesus. "Granting the prophet's credentials, [his] saying is as genuine a word of the Lord as a *verbatim* saying form the pre-resurrection ministry. For 'authenticity' has to do with the authority by which a word of Jesus comes to us, not with the ability of scientific historians to give the word a certain ratio of historical probability."[49] These words may not actually have been spoken by Jesus during his earthly life, but then we cannot always be sure we have the *ipsissima verba* of Jesus in any case.[50] But the new saying—the saying through the prophet, granting its possibility—may actually have brought to light, under the guidance of the Spirit, the full meaning of the old saying.[51] Therefore, just because a saying may have originated with a Christian prophet does not mean that it is of secondary importance, without authority or "inauthentic." Only the person who has no doctrine of inspiration can say this. If the Scripture is inspired by the Spirit of God, and if the Scripture includes the words of Christian prophets inspired by the Spirit of God, and if those prophets were led at times by the Spirit of God to transform some of Jesus' words into a new key (John 16:12-15), then it seems we cannot say that there is then a radical distinction to be made in the matter of dominical origin and authority "between sayings of the most unimpeachable authenticity . . . and sayings which were shaped by prophets in the years after the resurrection as the church was directed by the Spirit into new channels of activity and thought."[52]

Notes

1. The underlying idea of this essay was originally presented as an invited paper during the 25th anniversary sessions of the Evangelical Theological Society. Later it was expanded upon and became a discussion paper for a seminar on early Christian prophecy at the Society of Biblical Literature. This document then appeared in a written draft-form in the SBL's 1975 *Seminar Papers*, Vol. 2, 105-129. This seminal idea has been further modified in light of the continuing discussion and is presented once again in this celebration volume.

2. Since my initial work on this topic the following important studies have appeared: D. E. Aune, *Prophecy in Early Christianity and the Ancient Mediterranean World*, Grand Rapids, 1983; M. E. Boring, *Sayings of the Risen Jesus: Christian Prophecy in the Synoptic Tradition*, Cambridge, 1982; J. D. G. Dunn, "Prophetic 'I'-Sayings and the Jesus Tradition: The Importance of Testing Prophetic Utterances Within Early Christianity," *NTS* 24 (1978) 175-98; D. Hill, *New Testament Prophecy*, Atlanta, 1979.

3. For Paul as a prophet see W. D. Davies, *Paul and Rabbinic Judaism*, London, 1948, 177-266; E. Fascher, ΠΡΟΦΗΤΗΣ, 1927, 185; *TDNT*, 6. 828-61; cf. also 812-28; J. M. Meyers and E. D. Freed, "Is Paul Also Among the Prophets?" *Int* 20 (1966) 40-53.

4. See R. Schnackenburg, *La Theologie du Nouveau Testament*, London, 1961, 46.

5. Swete states that "only a relatively small number of believers were 'established to be prophets', forming a charismatic order to which a recognized position was given in the church. Such persons were said ἔχειν προφητείαν (1 Cor 13:2) and were known as οἱ προφῆται (Eph 2:20; 3:5; Rev 18:20; 22:6) being thus distinguished from those who occasionally 'prophesied' (Acts 19:6; 1 Cor 11:4, 5; 14:31)." See H. B. Swete, *the Holy Spirit in the New Testament*, London, 377.

6. Cf. The various translations of Rev 22:6, ὁ κύριος, ὁ θεός τῶν πνευμάτων τῶν προφητῶν . . . The adjective, πνευματικός, is never used to describe the prophet, however. But see E. E. Ellis, "'Spiritual' Gifts in the Pauline Community," *NTS* 20 (1970) 128-44.

7. Cf. the formula τάδε λέγει that is repeated several times over in Rev (2:1, 8, 12, 18; 3:1, 7, 14). This is "John's use of an old traditional formula. The OT prophets had established this formula as the appropriate introduction for God's address to his people" (P. S. Minear, *I Saw a New Earth*, Washington, D.C., 1968, *ad loc.*).

8. Many scholars draw a sharp distinction between prophecy and apocalypse. It seems, however, that both are found at work in the same person. W. Schneemelcher says, "Early Christian prophets who were in fact above all charismatic leaders . . . , used apocalyptic terminology and ideas", in Hennecke, Schneemelcher, Wilson, *New Testament Apocrypha*, Philadelphia, 1963, 2.684. See also P. Vielhauer in Hennecke, Schneemelcher, Wilson, *New Testament Apocrypha*, 2.605-607.

9. G. B. Caird, *The Revelation of St. John the Divine*, New York, 1966, 296, counts at least 14 places in Rev where echoes of the gospel tradition may be detected: Rev 3:3, 5; 6:16; 8:13; 11:2; 14:4, 20; 16:13, 15; 18:21-23, 24; 19:17; 21:3-7.

10. It is the combination of "now" and "prophetic writings" in Rom 16:26 along with the ideas set forth by Paul in Eph 3:5, 6 and elsewhere, that make some believe Paul had *Christian* prophetic writings in mind here—not OT prophetic writings. See E. E. Ellis, "Luke 11:49-51: An Oracle of a Christian Prophet?", *ExpTim* 74, no. 5 (1963) 157.

11. In the Didache apostles and prophets are equated (11.3-6), but the prophet is distinguished from the teacher (13.1-6).

12. See E. E. Ellis, "the Role of the Christian Prophet in Acts," in *Apostolic History of the Gospel*, ed. by W. W. Gasque and R. P. Martin, Grand Rapids, 1970, 55-67; cf. also *Did.* 10.7 where apostle is both identified with prophets and distinguished from them.

13. Hill, *New Testament Prophecy*, 179.

14. *Ibid.*, 179-80.

15. *Ibid.*

16. *Ibid.*, 8, 9.

17. For an excellent essay on prophecy in the NT see the thorough work by E. Cothenet in *Supplément au Dictionnaire de la Bible*, Paris, 1926-, Vol. 8, col 1222-1337.

18. D. E. Aune, *The Cultic Setting of Realized Eschatology in Early Christianity*, Leiden, 1972, 65-73; F. W. Beare, "Sayings of the Risen Jesus in the Synoptic Tradition," in *Christian History and Interpretation: Studies presented to John Knox*, ed by W. R. Farmer, *et al.*, London, 1967, 161-81; R. Bultmann, *History of the Synoptic Tradition*, trans. by J. Marsh, Oxford, 1963, 108-66; Ellis, *ExpTim* 74 (1963) 157-58; J. Jeremias, *New Testament Theology*, London, 1971, I, 2; E. Käsemann, *New Testament Questions of Today*, London, 1969, 66-81; A. Loisy, *Les evangiles synoptiques*, Paris, 1907, 1.195; *The Origins of the New Testament*, London, 1950, 47-49; N. Perrin, *Rediscovering the Teaching of Jesus*, New York, 1967, 15, 16 and passim.

19. F. F. Bruce, *Tradition Old and New*, Grand Rapids, 1970, 64, italics mine. Professor Bruce also cites F. Neugebauer's article, "Geistsprüche und Jesuslogien," *ZNW* 53 (1963) 218-20, who gives a critical evaluation of Bultmann's arguments for the work of the prophet.

20. Aune, *Prophecy in Early Christianity*, 245; He has modified an earlier position he once held. See above, n. 18.

21. *Ibid.*

22. Hill, *New Testament Prophecy*, 180.

23. See also John 14:26; 15:26; 1 Cor 2:16; 7:40; 2 Cor 13:3.

24. P. E. Davies, "Did Jesus Die as a Martyr-Prophet?", *Biblical Research*, 19 (1974) 43.

25. It does not do justice to the Revelation, however, to assign it to the genre "apocalyptic," and thereby to dismiss it from consideration in the discussion of Christian prophecy. Much if not all of the traditional features of apocalyptic are absent from the Revelation, and the writer both calls himself a prophet (1:19, 20) and his writing a prophetic message (1:3; 10:18, 19; 22:7). See G. W. Barker, et al., *The New Testament Speaks*, New York, 1969, 363-70; Vielhauer in Hennecke, Schneemelcher, Wilson, *New Testament Apocrypha*, 2.623-34; M. E. Boring, "The Apocalypse as Christian Prophecy," in *SBL Seminar Papers*, 1974, 2.43-57.

26. See G. N. Stanton's *Jesus of Nazareth in New Testament Preaching*, New York, 1974, where he claims that the early church was more aware of the distinction between the "past" of Jesus and the "present" of the risen Christ than is allowed. See H. A. Guy, *New Testament Prophecy*, London, 1947; J. Lindblom, *Gesichte und Offenbarung*, Lund, 1968, 141-43; V. Taylor, *Formation of Gospel Tradition*, London, 1957, 107; Bruce, *Tradition*, 49, 65; D. Dungan, *The Sayings of Jesus in the Churches of Paul*, Philadelphia, 1971.

27. A. Schweitzer, *The Mysticism of Paul the Apostle*, London, 1931, 172-74, holds that Paul considered communications received directly from Christ through the Spirit to be of greater value than the teaching of Jesus as recorded by tradition.

28. A. Resch, *Der Paulinismus und die Logia Jesu*, in *Texte und Untersuchungen*, NF, 12 (1904), claimed to have discovered 925 allusions to Jesus' teachings in the nine Pauline letters (including Colossians), 133 more in Ephesians, 100 in the Pastorals and 64 in the Pauline speeches in Acts. See Dungan, *The Sayings of Jesus*, xxii.

29. See H. Köster, "Die ausserkanonischen Herrenworte," *ZNW* 48 (1957) 22-37, where he argues that Paul was not concerned to distinguish between the canonical and extracanonical sayings of Jesus.

30. See F. F. Bruce, *The Epistle to the Hebrews* (NIC), Grand Rapids, 1964, xlix.

31. See M. E. Boring, "How may we Identify Oracles of Christian Prophets in the Synoptic Tradition?" *JBL* 91 (1972) 505, n. 11. E. E. Ellis, *Paul's Use of the Old Testament*, Grand Rapids, 1957, 107- 12, argues convincingly that in this kind of interaction with the OT text we have some of the literary remains of early Christian prophets.

32. We know from the Apocalypse that the prophet's mind was saturated not only with the OT, but with the traditions about Jesus (see n. 9 above).

33. Guy, *New Testament Prophecy*, 109.

34. "And they [the disciples] excused themselves saying, 'This age of lawlessness and unbelief is under Satan, who does not allow the truth and power of God to prevail over the unclean spirits. Therefore reveal thy righteousness now'—thus they spoke to Christ." Then Christ replies, "The term of years for Satan's power has been fulfilled. But other terrible things draw near. And for those who have sinned I was delivered over to death, that they may return to the truth and sin no more; that they may inherit the spiritual and incorruptible glory of righteousness which is in heaven."

35. See R. Schnackenburg, *The Gospel According to St. John*, New York, 1980, 1.360. Cf. W. Nicol, *The Semeia in the Fourth Gospel*, Leiden, 1972, 149.

36. Whether or not the writer of the Fourth Gospel is the same as the writer of the Revelation, it does seem that both documents belong to the same "school." The paraclete of John's gospel is none other than the Spirit of Christian prophecy. "Recognition of this fact helps to establish a basic kinship between the Johannine Gospel and Epistles on the one hand, and the Book of Revelation on the other. In none of these works is prophecy confined to the matter of predicting the future; it refers more generally to inspired utterance in the task of making known the very words of the Son of God. In John's Gospel the prophetic function consists in introducing a particular divine perspective on a series of historical events. Prophecy becomes essentially interpretation, and the prophet an inspired interpreter of what Jesus has said and done." Barker, *et al. The New Testament Speaks*, 396.

37. This creative working with the tradition "involves selecting some events and sayings while omitting others (20:30), structuring these according to certain historical and theological considerations and in some instances perhaps even reformulating and rephrasing the words of Jesus handed down in the tradition." Ibid., 396.

38. Ibid., 396. See also Aune, *Cultic Setting*, 65-73; J. L. Martyn, *History and Theology in the Fourth Gospel*, New York, 1968.

39. The most complete study of the Didache is that by J. P. Audet, *La Didaché: instruction des apôtres*, Paris, 1961, but he dates it as early as A.D. 50-70.

40. Apparently Clement of Alexandria also quotes the Didache (3.5) as Scripture (cf. *Misc.* 1.20.100). Eusebius, however, did not consider it so (*H.E.* 3.25.4).

41. K. Aland, "The Problem of Anonymity and Pseudonymity in Christian Literature of the First Two Centuries," *JTS* 12 (1961) 39- 49, especially 43, 44.

42. So much so that one must study Justin's doctrine of the Holy Spirit mainly in connection with prophetic inspiration. See E. R. Goodenough, *The Theology of Justin Martyr*, Amsterdam, 1968, 177.

43. This saying is quoted also by Clement of Alexandria (*Quis dives salvus*, xl, introducing it by "God saith through the prophet," with perhaps a reference to Ezek 33:16-20. Justin alone attributes it directly to Jesus.

44. P. Nautin, *Lettres et Ecrivains chrétiens des IIe et IIIe Siecles*, Paris, 1961, 71, questions the statement made by Eusebius (*H.E.* 4.26.1) that Melito was a bishop.

45. Melito, *On the Passover*, 101-103. See G. F. Hawthorne, "A New English Translation of Melito's Paschal Homily," in *Current Issues in Biblical and Patristic Interpretation*, ed. by G. F. Hawthorne, Grand Rapids, 1975, 173-74.

46. But see D. Hill, "On the Evidence for the Creative Role of Christian Prophets," *NTS* 20 (1974) 262-74. In the present essay I have not merely repeated arguments Hill rejects, but have brought together a chain of thinking that goes beyond his objections and that in my judgment cannot be swept aside as wholly "lacking in substance and authority."

47. Dunn, *NTS* 24 (2, 1978) 197.

48. Against Perrin, *Rediscovering the Teaching of Jesus*, 15. See B. Gerhardsson, *Memory and Manuscript*, Lund, 1964; *Tradition and Transmission in Early Christianity*, Lund, 1964; and even Käsemann, *New Testament Questions*, 46, 47.

49. E. E. Ellis, *The Gospel of Luke*, London, 1966, 172.

50. The Aramaic words of Jesus contained in Mark, however, could be examples of exact expressions of Jesus. See J. Jeremias, *The Prayers of Jesus*, Naperville, IL., 1967. But elsewhere the sayings of Jesus as found in the different traditional sources, are modified, interpreted, rewritten, etc., to reflect the particular theological outlook of those who compiled them. These changes did not conflict with their concept of what the Spirit of Christ was doing in the church, nor do they with mine.

51. Note P. Vielhauer's cautious remarks in Hennecke, Schneemelcher, Wilson, *New Testament Apocrypha*, 181.

52. Beare, "Sayings of the Risen Jesus," 181.

Jesus—The Son of God, the Stone, the Son of Man, and the Servant: The Role of Zechariah in the Self-Identification of Jesus

Seyoon Kim

I

In a study[1] focusing on the *Vollmachtsfrage* of Mark 11:27-33 par, I suggested that in Jesus' preliminary interrogation by a delegation of the Sanhedrin in the wake of his temple action (Mark 11:15-17 par) he implicitly claimed to have performed the temple action with the authority of the Son of God given to him by God at his baptism by John the Baptist. I then argued that this claim of Jesus provides us with a key for interpreting the meaning of his temple action or of his intention in it, while his concern for the sanctity of the temple, his prophecy about the destruction of the temple (Mark 13:1-2 par; 14:58 par; 15:29 par), his promise to build a new temple (Mark 14:58 par; 15:29), and his view of his death provide four more keys.

Interpreting his temple action with the five keys, I suggest that it was intended first of all as a prophetic demonstration of God's impending judgment in the form of the corrupt temple's destruction. Then, in view of Jesus' understanding of his forthcoming death as the atoning and covenant-establishing sacrifice of the Ebed Yahweh (Isa 42–53) whereby he was to gather or create the eschatological people of God and inaugurate the Kingdom of God,[2] I argued that Jesus saw his death as the eschatological fulfilment of the real meaning and purpose of the temple (the atonement of Israel's [and the world's] sins and reconciliation of them with God), and as the work that was to build a new temple because through it the community of the eschatological people of God or the Kingdom of God (which he perceived as the new "temple") was to come into being. I argued further that therefore his temple action was intended to indicate that the temple sacrifices were not only ineffective because of corruption but also redundant because they were about to be superseded by his eschatological sacrifice and that it was also intended as the means of unleashing his atoning death to fulfil the real meaning and purpose of the temple and build a new temple.

In this context, what does it mean that Jesus claimed to have done that temple action *as the Son of God?* It means that precisely *as the Son of God* he saw himself destined to fulfil the real meaning and purpose of the temple and build a new temple—through his atoning and covenant-establishing death. So in the afore-mentioned study, I affirmed Jesus' messianic self-understanding based on 2 Sam. 7:12-16. As the Messiah, i.e. as the Son of David / Son of God, he saw his task in building a "house" (i.e. temple) for God. He interpreted this new temple in terms of God's eschatological people, the community of people atoned and reconciled to God so as to be in the sphere under the gracious kingship or fatherhood of God.[3] The new "temple" was thus God's eschatological people for whom the real meaning and purpose of the temple had already been realized. Jesus saw that as the Son of God he was to build this new "temple" by offering himself as the eschatological atoning sacrifice as the Ebed Yahweh. Through the temple action he deliberately unleashed his atoning death in order to fulfil this task of the Son of God.

I suggested that through the *Vollmachtsfrage* the delegation of the Sanhedrin to some extent grasped Jesus' self-reference as the Son of God, the Messiah, and his intention in his temple action. Hence, the Sanhedrin arrested and tried him precisely on the charge of having threatened to destroy the temple, of having promised to build a new one and of having thereby claimed to be the Son of God (Mark 14:56-61; Matt 26:61-64). For the Sanhedrin he was put to death as a (false messianic pretender; but for Jesus this was precisely the way in which his messianic task was to be accomplished, the task of creating the eschatological people of God or building a new "temple" through his atoning death.

II

In the study on the *Vollmachtsfrage* I also affirmed that the parable of the Wicked Husbandmen (Mark 12:1-12 par) was originally connected with the *Vollmachtsfrage* (Mark 11:27-33 par) and therefore also with the temple action of Jesus (Mark 11:15-17 par) and that in the parable Jesus went on to make his claim to have performed the temple action with the authority of the Son of God a little more explicit. In this parable Jesus alluded to himself as the Son of God whom God sent as his eschatological envoy, only to suffer rejection and death at the hands of the Jewish leaders. At the same time he warned the delegation of the Sanhedrin that God would destroy them.

In the parable, as K. Snodgrass recently has stressed,[4] there is a word-play based on the Hebrew between the "son" *(habbēn)* whom the owner of the vineyards sends as his last envoy and the wicked husbandmen kill (vv 6-8), and the "stone" *('eben)* which the "builders" reject (v 10). By means of this word-play, the "son" and the "stone" are identified with each other, and the "husbandmen" and the "builders" are identified with each other, and the two parts of the parable, the parable proper (vv 1-9) and the Scriptural citation of Ps 118:22-23. Mark 12:10-12 is made to affirm the same point: Jesus' death or rejection as the "son" / "stone" at the hands of the Jewish leaders.[5] So, one of the purposes of citing Ps 118:22-23, in connection with the parable seems to be to provide a scriptural attestation for his destiny of rejection and death as the Son of God which the parable conveys.[6] Yet the emphasis of the citation falls not on the idea of rejection of the "stone" that is found in the first part but on the idea of its vindication or exaltation found in the second part (the "stone" made the head of corner), which is an advancement on the parable proper (vv 1-9). Thus, it seems that Jesus' primary purpose in citing Ps 118:22-23, is to affirm the divine will for his vindication or exaltation after his rejection and death.

But what led Jesus to identify himself with the "stone" of Ps 118:22-23, to produce the word-play, and thereby to speak of his rejection and exaltation in Mark 12:1-12 par? The eschatological interpretation of Ps 118 at the time of Jesus, as evidenced by Mark 11:9 par and some rabbinic literature,[7] is too vague to account for his self-identification with the "stone" of the psalm. The singing of the psalm by his entourage at his entry into Jerusalem (Mark 11:9 par) may have had something to do with it. But Ps 118:22-23 is also reflected in his announcements of the passion of "the 'Son of Man'" (Mark 8:31; Luke 9:22; 17:25; cf. also Mark 9:12). Its quotation in the Parable of the Wicked Husbandmen, then, apparently was not *ad hoc*. Professor E. E. Ellis has analyzed our parable in terms of the pattern of the proem midrash in Judaism and suggested that in its Q version the proem text of Isa 5:1-2, its parabolic exposition, and the concluding texts of Ps 118:22-23, and Dan 2:34-35, 44-45 are all joined together by catchwords— ἀμπελών, λιθοβολεῖν, οἰκοδομεῖν and λίθος.[8] This analysis may be strengthened by the observation of a further tie between the expository parable and the concluding texts through the word-play *habbēn—'eben*. As already pointed out, however, the quotation of Ps 118:22-23 in our parable was no *ad hoc* affair. It is difficult to imagine that it was quoted simply because of some catchword connections with which it provided the initial text Isa 5:1-2 and its parobolic exposition in the parable.

B. Gärtner believes that the Targum's rendering of the *'eben* with *tali'a* in Ps 118:22 and making it refer to David indicate a messianic interpretation of the "stone" in Ps 118:22-29. He further contends that the Targum's paraphrase of Ps 118:29 in terms of binding a "lamb" *(tali'a)* for offering and of sprinkling his blood on the altar indicates the identification of the Davidic Messiah with the Ebed Yahweh.[9] If these are true, it would be easy to explain Jesus' reference to the "stone" of Ps 118:22-23 in Mark 12:1-12. But both points are uncertain. The Targum's interpretation of the "stone" in terms of the historical David is still different from the later clearly messianic interpretation by R. Rashi (d. 1105).[10] It also is not certain whether the *tali'a* in Tg Ps 118:27 refers to the *tali'a* of Tg Ps 118:22 (and therefore to David). The context seems to indicate otherwise.

It is quite possible that Jesus' identification with the "stone" of Ps 118:22-23 is related to his identification with the one "like a son of man" in Dan 7:13. The latter could well have led Jesus to the former *via* the "stone" of Dan 2:34-35, 45, which corresponds closely to the one "like a son of man" in Dan 7 on the one hand and provides a catchword connection with the "stone" of Ps 118:22-23 on the other.[11] The citation of Dan 2:34-35, 45 immediately after Ps 118:22-23 in the Q version of our parable (Matt 21:44 = Luke 20:18) seems to point in this direction.[12] It will be argued below that Jesus' identification with the "stone" of Ps 118:22-23 is indeed related to his identification with the one "like a son of man" in Dan 7:13. But, how, then, was Ps 118:22-23 brought into contact with the tradition of 2 Sam 7:12-16 which is reflected in our parable? Did the opportunity for a word-play *habbēn—'eben* bring them together? Or did Jesus' understanding of the one "like a son of man" in Dan 7 in terms of the Son of God[13] eventually lead him to connect Ps 118:22-23 with 2 Sam 7:12-16? Both may be true. However, there may well have been another reason for his identification with the "stone" of Ps 118:22-23 and his citation of the psalm passage in connection with his allusion to the tradition of 2 Sam 7:12-16 in our parable.

Is it not perhaps significant that the quotation of Ps 118:22-23 is made in the context of a debate sparked off by Jesus' temple action? Would the quotation with its talk of "stone," "builders" and "cornerstone" not have reminded the representatives of the Sanhedrin of Jesus' temple action? In speaking of the "stone" and the "cornerstone" of Ps 118:22 in Mark 12:10 par, may Jesus not have had in mind the temple of

Jerusalem whose edifice of great and beautiful "stones" were proverbial (cf. Mark 13:1; Josephus, *Bell.* 5.5.1-3; *b.* Sukk. 51b)? Since in the rabbinic literature "builders" are often a designation for the Jewish religious leaders and there is a strand of tradition that the Great Sanhedrin was looked upon as the builder of Jerusalem,[14] with the "builders" in Mark 12:10 par (Ps 118:22) may Jesus not have referred to the representatives of the Sanhedrin interrogating him, *as the "temple-establishment,"* i.e., as those who were in charge of the temple and all the privileges—covenant, election, atonement, fellowship, etc.—which the temple symbolized? Since we have already judged that Jesus' temple action was materially related to his prophecy about the destruction of the temple (Mark 13:2 par; 14:58 par; 15:29 par) and his promise to build a new temple (Mark 14:58 par),[15] may we not conjecture that Jesus' warning of the destruction of the temple-establishment in the wake of their rejection of him ("son" / "stone") and his prophecy of his ("son" / "stone") being made the "cornerstone" which he uttered in connection with his temple action in our parable were also related to his prophecy of the destruction of the temple and his promise to build a new temple? We have already judged that his temple action and the *Vollmachtsfrage* reflected the tradition of Nathan's oracle (2 Sam 7:12-16) according to which the Son of David / Son of God was to build a temple for God and that the reference to the "son" in our parable continued this reflection.[16] If this is so, is it not clear that Jesus' identification with the "stone" of Ps 118:22-23 and his citation of the Psalm in connection with the allusion to Nathan's oracle had something to do with his messianic task of building a temple for God? Considering all these we believe we are justified in presuming that he quoted the "stone" passage of Ps 118:22-23 because there he saw himself depicted as the foundation stone of a new temple, i.e. his bringing a new temple into being.[17]

Probably it was not merely for the sake of a vague notion conveyed by the rejection-exaltation scheme nor only for the sake of an oblique allusion to the resurrection that Ps 118:22-23 was quoted in our parable. The context of Jesus' temple action and his allusion to the tradition of Nathan's oracle in our parable seem to suggest that the psalm passage was here cited for a more specific reason than that. They seem also to suggest that neither was the citation just for the sake of the opportunity for a word-play *habbēn-'eben* or the series of identifications the "son of man" of Dan 7 = the "stone" of Dan 2 = the "stone" of Ps 118:22-23 on the one hand and the "son of man" of Dan 7 = the Son of God of 2 Sam 7:12-16 on the other. Jesus seems to have brought Nathan's oracle and Ps 118:22-23 into connection with each other in our parable because in both he saw the common theme of building a temple.

Did his self-understanding as the Son of God who was to build a temple for God, based on the tradition stemming from 2 Sam 7:12-16 (Mark 11:27-33 par; 12:6-7 par), directly lead him to Ps 118:22-23 where he found not only a good opportunity for a word-play *habbēn-'eben* but also an expression of his mission as the Son of God? But where did he then get the idea that it was precisely by way of his rejection by the Jewish leaders or through his atoning and covenant-establishing death as the Son of God that he was to build a new temple? Were the circumstances of conflicts he faced with the Jewish leaders after the execution of John the Baptist the source of the idea? Would it not rather have been the case that Jesus had a scriptural basis for his idea?[18] Then, did Ps 118:22 provide him with the idea? If it did, then it means that Jesus, having originally been attracted to the psalm because of the "stone" and the

idea of its becoming the foundation-stone of a new temple, found in the psalm that as
the "son" / "stone" he was first to be "rejected" by the Jewish leaders before being
made the foundation-stone for a new temple and thus bringing a new temple into
being. But it is not easy to think that from the one word *mā'^{a}ū* / ἀπεδοκίμασαν of
Ps 118:22 Jesus developed the specific idea of his atoning and covenant-establishing
death as the means of his building a new temple.

III

At this point a series of statements in Zechariah are very interesting. In Zech 3:8,
Zerubbabel, the Davidic prince, is called the "servant" of the Lord *(^{a}bdī)* and the
"shoot" *(ṣemaḥ),* and in close proximity (v 9) a reference is made to the "stone"
(h' eben). In Zech 4:7-10 it is said that Zerubbabel will bring forward the "top-stone"
(h' eben hāro'šāh) and, having laid the foundation of the temple, he will complete it.
This is immediately followed by a reference to *h' eben habbdīl* in the hand of Zerubbabel (Zech 4:10). In Zech 6:12-13 Zerubbabel or another Davidic prince to appear[19]
is again called the *ṣemaḥ,* and it is said that "he shall build the temple of the Lord ..."
As in Zech 4:14, so in Zech 6:13 he appears as the anointed and enthroned king. This
series of statements about Zerubbabel, the Davidic prince (or perhaps another
Davidic prince) being the *Ṣemaḥ* and building the temple is clearly a reapplication of
Nathan's oracle (2 Sam 7:12-16) in the post-exilic situation.[20]

Tg. Zech 6:12-13 evidently shows that it was in turn reapplied to the future messiah:

> Thus said Yahweh of hosts: this man, messiah is his name, will be revealed and
> grow and build the temple of Yahweh. He will build the temple of Yahweh and he
> will exalt its splendour and he will sit and rule on his throne, and there will be the
> high priest by his throne, and the kingdom of peace will be between them.[21]

Similarly the Targum also interprets the *Ṣemaḥ* of Zech 3:8 as the messiah. Then
it takes the "stone" of Zech 4:7 as a reference to the messiah and paraphrases the
w^{e}hōṣi' 'et-hā' eben hāro'šāh like this: "he *(sc.* God) will reveal his messiah, whose
name was named since the beginning, and he will rule over all kingdoms."[22] Tan-
huma Toledoth 20 (par Aggadath Bereshith 33a) interprets the "stone" of Zech 4:10
as well as that of Zech 4:7 as the messiah.[23] The Syrian Bishop Aphraates (d. after
345 A.D.) takes the "stone" of Zech 3:9 as well as that of Zech 4:7 as a reference to
the messiah.[24] That such interpretations of the "stones" of Zech 3:9; 4:7, 10 also obtained in the first century A.D. seems to be indicated by Rev 5:6 where the crucified
and risen Christ is referred to as the Lamb "with seven horns and with seven eyes,
which are the seven spirits of God sent out into all the earth." This description of
Christ is clearly drawn from Zech 4:10 (3:9),[25] and it "presupposes the messianic interpretation of Zech 4:10 (3:9) . . . ," as J. Jeremias rightly remarks.[26]

It is interesting to note here that the Targum and a strand of rabbinic and Christian
tradition interpret both the *ṣemaḥ* (Zech 3:8; 6:12) and the "stones" (Zech 3:9; 4:7,
10) as references to the messiah, and that they do so in the context where the building of a new temple is the chief concern. So, apparently the *Ṣemaḥ* and the "stones"
are identified with each other (compare esp. *Tg.* Zech 4:7 with *Tg.* Zech 6:12). The

fact that, in the closely related passages of Zech 3:8-9; 4:7-10; 6:12-13, ṣemaḥ (a concept derived from Nathan's oracle in 2 Sam 7:12-16) and "stone" are found together, both (according to those Jewish and Christian interpretations) referring to the messiah who would build a new temple, provides a remarkable parallel to Mark 12:1-12. There, as we have seen, Jesus, reflecting on his mission as the Son of God (the Son of David) to build a new temple, speaks of himself as the "son" and the "stone."

Since the three passages of Zech directly echo Nathan's oracle in 2 Sam 7:12-16, Jesus' application of the latter to himself[27] makes it probable that he was aware of the references of Zerubbabel the Davidic prince as the "shoot" and the "servant" of the Lord and those to the "stones" in the former.

It is well-known that Zech 9–14 plays an important role in the passion narratives of the Gospels. From Jesus' entry into Jerusalem riding on a colt (Mark 11:1-11 par; Zech 9:9-10)[28] and his shepherd-saying (Mark 14:27 = Matt 26:31; Zech 13:7-9),[29] it can be argued that he identified himself with the Davidic shepherd-king in Zech 9–14 who would be rejected and smitten[30] (cf. also Matt 24:30; Zech 12:12). In the "little flock" of Luke 12:32 and Jesus' perception of the crowds as "sheep without a shepherd" (Mark 6:34), F. F. Bruce sees allusions to Zech 11:11 and 13:7.[31] From these as well as from the theme of Jesus as the shepherd and his people as the flock which pervades most of the Gospel strata,[32] we can presume that Jesus thought of himself in terms of the shepherd (-king) of Zech 9–14. Some exegetes have also seen an allusion to Zech 14:4 in his saying about faith (Mark 11:23 = Matt 17:20)[33] W. Grimm has plausibly suggested that Zech 11:6 exerted a formative influence upon the passion announcement of Mark 9:31 par[34] ("The 'Son of Man'" is delivered [παραδίδοται] into the hands of men . . . .). However, he also believes that the παραδίδοσθαι-sentence is "filled with the spirit of the Deutero-Isaianic message of salvation."[35] In fact, the observation sometimes made that the picture of a lowly shepherd-king in Zech 9:9-10; 11:4-14; 12:10–13:1; 13:7-9 is rather similar to that of the Servant of Yahweh in Isa 42–53[36] also enables us to think that Jesus probably understood himself in terms of the shepherd-king of Zech 9–14 as well as the Ebed Yahweh of Isa 42–53.

In view of this pervasive reflection of the figure of the Davidic shepherd-king of Zech 9–14 on Jesus' part, we may presume that he took the Son of David ("shoot") of Zech 3:8-9; 6:12-13 together with the Davidic shepherd-king of Zech 9–14. The likelihood that Zech 14:21 was part of what lay behind his temple action (Mark 11:15-17 par)[37] would strengthen this conjecture. In my previous essay, I argued that his temple action was a messianic Zeichenhandlung, signaling both the impending destruction of the temple through God's judgment and his building a new temple as the Son of David / Son of God in accordance with the tradition stemming from Nathan's oracle.[38] In as much as he understood himself in terms of the Davidic messiah pictured in Zech 3:8-9; 4:7-10; 6:12-13 and in Zech 9–14, the prophecy in Zech 14:21 ("There shall no longer be a trader—kᵉnaᵃnī—in the house of the Yahweh of hosts on that day") led him to drive traders out of the corrupted temple in order to signal both the impending destruction of the corrupted temple (which was in violation of the will of God manifested in Zech 14:21) and his building of a pure temple, a temple in which there would no longer be a trader.

If Jesus' pervasive reflection on the prophecies of Zech 9–14 thus makes it probable that he (1) interpreted the references to the Davidic prince in Zech. 3:8-9; 4:7-

10; 6:12-13 and the Davidic shepherd-king in Zech 9–11c messianically, (2) identified the two figures and (3) applied them both to himself, then the parallelism which we have observed between Zech 3:8-9; 4:7-10; 6:12-13 (as interpreted by the Targum and some Jewish and Christian authorities) and Mark 12:1-12 makes it probable that like those Jewish and Christian authorities Jesus also interpreted the "stones" and the *Semah* in Zech 3:8-9; 4:7-10; 6:12-13 messianically, identified them with an applied them to himself.

If Jesus thus identified the Son of David of Zech 3:8-9; 4:7-10; 6:12-13 with the Davidic shepherd-king of Zech 9-14 and the Son of David with the "stones" in Zech 3:8-9; 4:7-10; 6:12-13, he may have derived the idea of his rejection as the "son" and the "stone" and the idea of his building a new temple through that rejection in Mark 12:1-12 from those passages of Zech. If so, behind his promise to build a new temple (Mark 14:58 par) there lies Zech 3:8-9; 4:7-10; 6:12-13 as well as 2 Sam 7:12-16, and behind his self-understanding as the "stone" which he expresses in connection with his temple action (Mark 12:1-12 par) there lies Zech 3:8-9; 4:7-10; as well as Ps 118:22-23.

Having obtained the idea of his building a new temple through his rejection as the Son of David / Son of God / "stone" from those passages of Zech, Jesus probably found Ps 118:22-23 expressing them perfectly. For he could see close links between the passages of Zech and Ps 118:22-23: (1) the catchword "stone"; (2) the "stone," "cornerstone" and "builders" of Ps 118:22-23 expressing the idea of building a temple, which is the concern of Zech (3:8-9) 4:7-10; 6:12-13; (3) the idea of rejection (Ps 1118:22; Zech 9–14); (4) Ps 118:22-23 offered a good opportunity for a word-play *habbēn—'eben* and thereby expressed perfectly the identification of the "shoot" (the Son of David / Son of God) and the "stone" of Zech 3; 4; 6; 9–14. So, by using Ps 118:22-23 in connection with the tradition stemming from 2 Sam 7:12-16 in Mark 11:27–12:12, Jesus expressed in a concise and yet puzzling manner his self-understanding as the Son of David / Son of God / "stone" who is to build a new temple through his rejection, a self-understanding which he obtained from the passages of Zech.

If this is so, we may imagine the process of development in Jesus' self-understanding as follows: at his baptism Jesus obtained his messianic self-understanding as the Son of David / Son of God who was to build a temple for God on the basis of 2 Sam 7:12-16.[39] Then he was led to Zech 3:8-9; 4:7-10; 6:12-13 because of the similarity of these pasages to 2 Sam 7:12-16, and to understand himself (in the manner of the Targum) as the "stone" of the temple as well as the Son of David ("shoot") / the "servant" of the Lord. Then, he was led to identify the Son of David the "shoot" (of Zech 3:8; 6:12) with the Davidic shepherd-king of Zech 9–14 and to see in Zech 9–14 a further description of himself as the Davidic shepherd-king who was to be rejected and killed and to mediate a new covenant and create a refined people of God by his martyrdom (Zech 13:7-9).[40] Thus, he came to perceive that it was through his rejection and martyrdom that he was to build a new temple as the son, *habbēn,* of David, Son of God, the "stone." Then, finally, he found in the *'eben* "stone" of Ps 118:22-23 which is rejected by the "builders" but is made by God the "cornerstone" that self-understanding perfectly described.

Thus the series of statements in Zech seem to have built bridges between 2 Sam 7:12-16 and Ps 118:22-23 in Mark 11:27–12:12.

IV

It is sometimes observed that the picture of a lowly shepherd-king in Zech 9:9-10; 11:4-14; 12:10–13:1; 13:7-9, who is rejected and killed by the people to whom he comes, and whose martyrdom causes their repentance and their reconstitution as the new, refined people of God through a new covenant, is rather similar to the picture of the Ebed Yahweh in Isa 42–53.[41] It is possible that Jesus' allusions to the Zech passages (9:9-10; 12:12 [Matt 24:30]; 13:7) were related to his allusions to the Ebed figure (Mark 9:31; 10:45; 14:22).[42]

It is conceivable that, having developed his self-understanding as the Son of David / Son of God who was to build a new temple through his rejection and martyrdom on the basis of 2 Sam 7:12-16; Zech 3:8-9; 4:7-10; 6:12-13; 9–14; Ps 118:22-23, Jesus was led by the similarity between the shepherd-king of Zech 9–14 and the Ebed of Isa 42–53 to see in the latter a further description of his messianic ministry.[43] The reverse is also conceivable: having obtained his self-understanding as the Ebed Yahweh of Isa 42–53, Jesus was led by the similarity between the two figures to understand himself also in terms of the shepherd-king of Zech 9–14, and this led him to identify himself with the "shoot" of Zech 3:8-9; 6:12-13 and then with the Son of David / Son of God of 2 Sam 7:12-16 who is to build a new temple. It is impossible to determine the sequence in the development of his self-understanding.[44] According to the Synoptic accounts of Jesus' baptism (Mark 1:10-11 par), Jesus was led to understand himself as the Son of David / Son of God and as the Servant of Yahweh by the heavenly declaration at his baptism.[45]

What is important to ascertain here is how the figure of the suffering Davidic shepherd-king of Zech 9–14 could have functioned as a bridge between the tradition about the Davidic messiah (2 Sam 7:12-16; Zech 3:8-9; 4:7-10; 6:12-13; 9–14, etc.) and the Ebed Yahweh (Isa 42–53). Through whatever sequence, Jesus was led to think of his messianic role of building a new temple as the Son of David / Son of God also in terms of the role of the Ebed Yahweh. So, he came to understand that the nature of his rejection and martyrdom through which he was to build a new temple as the Son of David / Son of God (2 Sam 7:12-16; Zech 3:8-9; 4:7-10; 6:12-13; 9–14; Ps 118:22-23) was the vicarious, atoning and covenant-establishing death as the Ebed Yahweh (Isa 42–53). In other words, Jesus came to perceive that as the messianic Son of David / Son of God he was to build a new temple for God through his vicarious, atoning and covenant-establishing death as the Servant of Yahweh.

In my earlier work I have attempted to show that from Isa 42–53 Jesus developed his understanding of his mission in terms of creating the eschatological people of God through his atoning and covenant-establishing death.[46] The group of people whose sins are atoned for through his vicarious sacrifice and who are made a new, eschatological people of God through his covenant-establishing sacrifice constitute a new "temple" for God which he, the messianic Son of David / Son of God, builds.[47]

If we may suppose that Jesus was conscious of the series of statements in Zech (3:8-9; 4:7-10; 6:12-13; 9–14), we can explain both how the tradition stemming from 2 Sam 7:12-16 and Ps 118:22-23 were brought together in Mark 11:27–12:12 (the conclusion of the previous section), and how the tradition of 2 Sam 7:12-16 and Isa 42–53 came to be combined in Jesus' self-understanding. If we may suppose that in Jesus' mind the series of statements in Zech acted as bridges between 2 Sam 7:12-16 on the one hand and Ps 118:22-23 and Isa 42–53 on the other, we can explain how Jesus came to understand that as the Son of David / Son of God he was to build a new temple for God through his rejection and martyrdom which was to be the eschatological, atoning and covenant-establishing sacrifice.

V

Jesus' identification of himself as the messianic "stone" of Zech (3:8-9); 4:7-10 and Ps 118:22-23 probably led him to the "stone" in Dan 2:34-35, 44:45, which was also messianically interpreted in Judaism.[48] This is suggested by Luke 20:18 = Matt 21:44 (in the Q version of the Parable of the Wicked Husbandmen)[49] where Dan 2:34-35, 44-45 is alluded to immediately after a quotation from Ps 118:22-23. Since the "stone" in Dan 2 closely corresponds to the "one like a son of man" in Dan 7, Jesus' identificaiton of himself with the "stone" of Dan 2 probably led him to identify himself also with that "son of man" figure in Dan 7. Thus, "the Son of Man" came to be identified with the "stone" of Ps 118:22-23. This identification led Jesus to develop the passion announcements using the self-designation "the Son of Man" from Dan 7 and the idea of rejection from Ps 118:22-23—"The Son of Man" must . . . be rejected (ἀποδοκιμασθῆναι Mark 8:31 par).

As we have seen, Jesus probably identified the Son of David / Son of God (the "shoot") and the "stone" in Zech 3:8-9; 4:7-10; 6:12-13 with each other, both as referring to the messiah, and the Son of David / Son of God / "stone" / the suffering Davidic shepherd-king of Zech 9–14. In the immediately preceding section we suggested that Jesus' identification with the Ebed Yahweh of Isa 42–53 was related to his identification with the Son of David / Son of God / "stone" / the suffering Davidic shepherd-king of Zech. In this section we have just suggested that the "stone" of Zech 3:8-9; 4:7-8 and Ps 118:22-23 led Jesus to the "stone" in Dan 2:34-35, 45, which in turn led him to the "son of man" in Dan 7. If so, we can now explain how the "son of man" of Dan 7 and the Servant of Yahweh of Isa 42–53 came to be identified in Jesus' mind. The series of statements in Zech built bridges between the Ebed Yahweh and the "son of man" as well as between Ps 118:22-23 and the "son of man." The whole network of connections may be shown in a diagram like this:

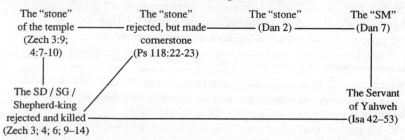

The "stone"   The "stone"   The "stone"   The "SM"
of the temple ——————— rejected, but made——————— (Dan 2) ——————————(Dan 7)
(Zech 3:9;   cornerstone
4:7-10)   (Ps 118:22-23)

The SD / SG /   The Servant
Shepherd-king   of Yahweh
rejected and killed ———(Isa 42–53)
(Zech 3; 4; 6; 9–14)

Jesus' identification with the Son of David / Son of God / shepherd-king rejected and killed (Zech 3:4; 6; 9–14) led him, on the one hand, to identify himself with the Servant of Yahweh in Isa 53, and his identification with the "stone" (Son of David / Son of God [shepherd-king]) of Zech led him, on the other hand, to identify himself with the "stone" / "son of man" of Dan 2 and 7.

But for him as for the Targum and some later rabbinic and Christian authorities, both the "stone" and the "shoot" (the Son of David / Son of God) in Zech 3:8-9; 4:7-10; 6:12-13 referred to the messiah, and so they were identified. Thus he came to identify the Servant of Yahweh and the "son of man" / "stone," and apply both to himself. The fact that both the Servant and the "son of man" are described in Isa 42–53 and Dan 7 respectively as the respresentatives of the real people of God confirmed the correctness of the identification. The understanding that the "son of man" is to be rejected, which Jesus developed through the identification of the "stones" of Zech, Ps 118 and Dan 2 with one another and of them with the "son of man" of Dan 7 further confirmed the unity of the "son of man" and the Servant of Yahweh who is also rejected to suffer vicarious death (Isa 53). So, Jesus identified the two figures and spoke of the passion of "the 'Son of Man'" in terms of the vicarious suffering of the Servant of Yahweh for atonement and covenant (Mark 9:31 par; 14:21 par ["The Son of Man" παραδίδοται . . . Cf. LXX Isa. 53:12; also *Tg*. Isa 53:5, 12: *msr*]; Mark 10:45 = Matt 20:28; Mark 14:21-25 par)[50] as well as in terms of the rejection of the "stone" of Ps 118:22-23 (Mark 8:31 par: ἀποδοκιμασθῆναι —Ps 118:22).[51]

Thus our thesis that the series of statements in Zech functioned as bridges for various self-identifications of Jesus—with the "stone" of Ps 118:22-23; Dan 2:34-35, 44-45, with the "son of man" of Dan 7 and with the Ebed Yahweh of Isa 42–53—explains why his passion announcements of "the Son of Man" reflect both Ps 118:22-23 and Isa 53. This makes irrelevant the dispute over whether Ps 118:22 or Isa 53 stands behind the passion announcements.[52] It is not "either—or," but rather "both—and"!

In our earlier work[53] we suggested that from the "son of man" figure of Dan 7 Jesus obtained his self-undertanding as the Son of God who was to create the eschatological people (children) of God and thus bring about the Kingdom of God (cf. the "stone" of Dan 2:34-35, 44-45). We also suggested that he intended to fulfill that mission of the "Son of Man" / Son of God by taking upon himself the role of the Ebed Yahweh of Isa 42–53, i.e. by means of his atoning and covenant-establishing death. Now we can see that this conclusion which we ascertained from Jesus' "Son of Man" sayings perfectly dovetails with the conclusion we have derived from the present investigation into the theme "Jesus and the Temple" based on his temple action and the ensuing controversy (Mark 11:15-17, 27-33; 12:1-12 and their pars.). The eschatological people of God or the people of the Kingdom of God which he as "the Son of Man" creates are a new temple which he builds as the Son of David / Son of God or whose "cornerstone" he is. He builds the new temple by fulfilling the real function of the temple eschatologically, i.e. by offering his life once for all as the atoning and covenant-establishing sacrifice.

As "the Son of Man" Jesus builds a new temple. Jesus the Son of David / Son of God who is to build a new temple (in accordance with 2 Sam 7; Zech 3:8-9; 4:7-8; 6:12-13; etc.) is "the Son of Man." This confirms the thesis propounded in our previous work:[54] "the Son of Man" is the Son of God! This also helps explain Jesus' assertion that "the Son of Man" has the authority to forgive sins on earth (Mark 2:10 par). As "the Son of Man" who is to build a new temple by fulfilling the real function of the temple, Jesus already exercises the function of the temple, mediation of the divine forgiveness of sins,[55] quite apart from the temple standing in Jerusalem. Hence, the *authority* of "the Son of Man" to forgive sins (Mark 2:10 par) is precisely the *authority* of the Son of God to build a new temple replacing the corrupt one in Jerusalem (Mark 11:27-33 par). That Jesus identified the "Son of Man" with the Son of God who was to build a new temple is confirmed by the combination of the temple, the Son of God and "the Son of Man" in Mark 14:56-62. When Jesus does not respond to the charge of his having threatened to destroy the temple and claimed to build another, the high priest asks him: "Are you the Christ, the Son of the Blessed?" (Mark 14:61 par). Jesus answers affirmatively and speaks of his exaltation and parousia as "the Son of Man." The high priest's two charges—Jesus' temple saying(s) and messianic claim—are closely related on the basis of the tradition stemming from 2 Sam 7:12-16 (Zech 3:8-9; 4:7-10; 6:23-24; etc).[56] In fact, they are but one single charge with two aspects. Jesus' final reply confirms his self-understanding as the Son of David / Son of God who is to build a temple and also his identification of this role of his with his mission as "the Son of Man."

VI

The initial question for our inquiry was how in the Parable of the Wicked Husbandmen (Mark 12:1-12 par) Jesus brought a reference to the "stone" of Ps 118:22-23 and an allusion to the Son of David / Son of God of Nathan's oracle (2 Sam 7:12-16) together, applying them both to himself as the Son of David / Son of God who was to build a new temple through his rejection. We have been struck by the close similarity between a series of statements in Zech 3:8-9; 4:7-10; 6:12-13 (as understood by the Targum and some Jewish and Christian authorities) and Mark 12:1-12 par, and so we have suggested that those Zech passages hold a key for the solution of our question.

It is true that we have not *proved* Jesus' allusion to Zech 3:8-9; 4:7-10; 6:12-13 by means of a direct comparison between the wording of Jesus' sayings and that of the Zechariah passages. Seeing how some motifs in Jesus' teaching are easily explained in the light of those passages, we can only presume that he applied them to himself. The same situation obtains in the case of 2 Sam 7:12-16. There is no direct quotation from or indisputably clear allusion to the passage in his sayings. Yet some of his important sayings and acts are most readily understandable in the light of it and the tradition that stems from it. Hence, we affirm the strong likelihood that he applied 2 Sam 7:12-16 to himself. In this essay, we have suggested that where he reflects Nathan's oracle he reflects not just that oracle, but also the tradition that stems from it, especially Zech 3:8-9; 4:7-10; 6:12-13.

The supposition that Jesus interpreted Zech 3:8-9; 4:7-10; 6:12-13 like the Targum and those Jewish and Christian authorities observed above, and identified the *Ṣemaḥ* / Son of David / Son of God with the Davidic shepherd-king of Zech 9–14, and applied those so understood Zech passages to himself enables us to explain how in the Parable of the Wicked Husbandmen Ps 118:22-23 was brought into connection with the tradition stemming from 2 Sam 7:12-14. In fact, it enables us to explain how 2 Sam 7:12-14; Zech 9–14; Ps 118:22-23; Dan 2:34-35, 45; Dan 7:9-11; Isa 42–45 were brought by Jesus into mutual connection in his various sayings. Zech 3:8-9; 4:7-10; 6:12-13; 9–14 probably functioned as bridges between these OT passages so as to enable Jesus to understand himself as the Son of David / Son of God / "Son of Man" / "Stone" / Ebed Yahweh who was to build a new temple (of the eschatological people of God) for God through his rejection or atoning and covenant-establishing sacrifice.

Notes

1. S. Kim, "Die Vollmacht Jesu und der Tempel: Der Sinn der 'Tempelreinigung' und der geschichtliche und theologische Kontext des Prozesses Jesu," to appear in *Aufstieg und Niedergang der Römischen Welt* 2.26.1, Berlin, 1987.

2. See my book, *"The 'Son of Man'" as the Son of God*, Tübingen, 1983; Grand Rapids, 1985.

3. L. Gaston, *No Stone on Another*, Leiden, 1970, 161-243; E. Lohmeyer, *Kultus und Evangelium*, Göttingen, 1942, 71-101; S. Aalen, "'Reign' and 'House' in the Kingdom of God in the Gospels," *NTS* 8 (1961-62) 215-240; B. Gärtner, *The Temple and the Community in Qumran and the NT*, Cambridge, 1965, 105-122; O. Betz, "Probleme des Prozesses Jesu," *ANRW* 2.25, Berlin, 1982, 630-32; J. Jeremias, *Neutestamentliche Theologie*, Gütersloh, [3]1979, 238; cf. also J. Roloff, *Das Kerygma und der irdische Jesus*, Göttingen, [2]1973, 97-98; B. F. Meyer, *The Aims of Jesus*, London, 1979, 200-201; *pace* G. Klinzing, *Die Umdeutung des Kultus in der Qumrangemeinde und im NT*, Göttingen, 1971, 202-210.

4. K. Snodgrass, *The Parable of the Wicked Tenants*, Tübingen, 1983, 63, 113-118. See also M. Black, "The Christological Use of the OT in the NT," *NTS* 18 (1971/72) 12; P. Carrington, *According to Mark*, Cambridge, 1960, 249-250, 256; R. H. Gundry, *Matthew*, Grand Rapids, 1982, 429.

5. As Snodgrass, *Parable*, 62-65, rightly emphasizes, the word-play is a strong proof for the view that the quotation from Ps 118:22-23 was no secondary addition to the parable but was an original part of it.

6. Cf. Snodgrass, *Parable*, 96.

7. See J. Jeremias, *Die Abendmahlsworte Jesu*, Göttingen, [4]1967, 246-250; cf. J. Jeremias, λίθος, *TDNT* 4.277.

8. E. E. Ellis, "New Directions in Form Criticism," *Prophecy and Hermeneutic in Early Christianity*, Tübingen & Grand Rapids, 1978, 251-52.

9. B. Gärtner, *"tali'a* als Messiasbezeichnung," *Svensk exegetisk årsbok* 18/19 (1953/54) 99-104.

10. Str-B 4.876; Cf. Jeremias, λίθος, *TDNT* 4.277; *Abendmahlsworte*, 246-250.

11. Cf. Snodgrass, *Parable*, 101.

12. Ibid., 41-71 for cogent arguments that Matthew presents the earliest version of the parable and also that Matt 21:44=Luke 20:18 (Dan 2:34-35, 44-45) is an authentic part of the parable.

13. See Kim, *"The 'Son of Man'"*.

14. Str-B. 1.876.

15. Kim, "Vollmacht"

16. Ibid.

17. So, Jeremias, λίθος, *TDNT* 4.277-78; cf. also J. R. Donahue, *Are You the Christ?*, Missoula, 1973, 127, who, however, attributes the quotation of Ps 118:22-23 not to Jesus but to Mark. *Pace* Snodgrass, *Parable*, 73, 102-103. This view may be further strengthened if Jesus' allusion to Isa 5:1, 2 in our parable (Matt 21:33 = Mark 12:1) was inspired by the Targumic interpretation of the "watchtower" (*migdāl*—Isa 5:2) as the temple. Cf. R. H. Gundry, *The Use of the OT in St. Matthew's Gospel*, Leiden, 1967, 44; D. Juel, *Messiah and Temple*, Missoula, 1977, 136-37.

18. This is strongly suggested by the announcements of the passion of "the Son of Man" (e.g. the δεῖ of Mark 8:31 par).

19. There is a dispute as to whom "the man whose name is ṣemaḥ" in Zech 6:12 refers. D. L. Petersen, *Haggai and Zechariah 1–8*, Philadelphia, 1984, 275-78, takes it to refer to Zerubbabel, while W. Rudolph, *Haggai–Sacharja 1-8—Sacharja 9-14–Maleachi*, Gütersloh, 1976, 130-31 thinks it refers to a (future) Davidic prince who will be born in the Holy Land.

20. *Ṣemah* in Zech 3:8; 6:12 refers to the "seed" (*zera'*) of David who is to be made God's "son" in 2 Sam 7:12- 16, as in 4QFlor 1:10-11 (cf. Also Jer 23:5; 33:5). Cf. Rudolph, *Haggai*, 132; D. C. Duling, "The Promises to David and Their Entrance into Christianity—Nailing Down a Likely Hypothesis," *NTS* 20 (1973/74) 55-77.

21. The text in A. Sperber, *The Bible in Aramaic III: the Latter Prophets according to Targum Jonathan*, Leiden, 1962. Cf. similar interpretations of Zech 6:12-13 in Lam. R. I. 16, §51; Pirke de R. Eliezer 48.

22. The text in Sperber, *The Bible in Aramaic III.*

23. Jeremias, λίθος, *TDNT* 4.277.

24. J. Jeremias, κεφαλὴ γωνίας—Ἀκρογωνιαῖος, *ZNW* 29 (1930) 274.

25. R. H. Charles, *The Revelation of St. John*, Edinburgh, 1920, 1.141; H. Kraft, *Die Offenbarung des Johannes*, Tübingen, 1974, 110; G. R. Beasley-Murray, *The Book of Revelation*, Grand Rapids, 1983, 124.

26. Jeremias, λίθος, *TDNT* 4.276.

27. See Kim, "Vollmacht"

28. For its substantial authenticity, see R. Pesch, *Das Markusevangelium* II. Teil, Freiburg etc., ²1980, 187-88; I. H. Marshall, *The Gospel of Luke*, Exeter, 1978, 770-71.

29. For its authenticity, see J. Jeremias, *Theologie*, 270-271; also his ποιμήν, *TDNT* 6.492.

30. For the identification of the shepherd-king of Zech 9-14 as the Davidic messiah, see H. Gese, "Der Messias," *Zur biblischen Theologie*, München (1977) 136-37 (note esp. his comment on Zech 13:7: "... aber sicher ist, dass mit dem geheimnisvollen Titel (sc. der "Mann meiner Sippengenossenschaft"), der auf die Gottessohnschaft hindeutet, der Davidide gemeint ist . . ."); cf. also Rudolph, *Haggai*, 215, n.19; F. F. Bruce, *This is That*, Exeter, 1968, 103; R. T. France, *Jesus and the OT*, London, 1971, 103-110, 188-194.

31. Bruce, *This*, 104-106.

32. Cf. Jeremias, ποιμήν, *TDNT* 6.491-96, 500-501.

33. E.g. W. Manson, *Jesus the Messiah*, London, 1943, 29-30; Bruce, *This*, 108; W. Grimm, *Die Verkündigung Jesu und Deuterojesaja*, Frankfurt, 1981, 161; cf. also Jeremias, *Theologie*, 159, 163.

34. Grimm, *Verkündigung*, 220-21; cf. France, *Jesus*, 157-58, who suggests that καὶ πάντες οἱ ἄγγελοι μετ᾽ αὐτοῦ who are to accompany "the Son of Man" at his parousia (Matt 25:31; cf. also Mark 8:38) reflects *kol-kᵉdošim 'immāk* of Zech 14:5.

35. Grimm, *Verkündigung*, 222.

36. See e.g. P. Lamarche, *Zacharie IX-XIV*, Paris, 1961, 131-147; Rudolph, *Haggai*, 213-215, n. 19; Bruce, *This*, 103; France, *Jesus*, 109-110; cf. also Jeremias, ποιμήν, *TDNT* 6.492, n. 78.

37. C. Roth, "The Cleansing of the Temple and Zechariah XIV.21," *NovT* 4 (1960) 174-81; C. K. Barrett, "The House of Prayer and the Den of Thieves," *Jesus und Paulus, Festschrift für W. G. Kümmel* ed. by E. E. Ellis and E. Grasser, Göttingen, 1975, 19-20; Jeremias, *Theologie*, 145.

38. Kim, "Vollmacht"

39. Ibid.

40. Cf. Gese, "Messias," 137.

41. See the note 36 above. Cf. *ᵃbdi* of Zech 3:8 with *'abdi/'ebed* appearing 18 times in Isa 41-53. Juel, *Messiah*, 186, 192, n. 39, follows P. Seidelin, "Der Ebed Jahweh und die Messiasgestalt im Jesajatargum," *ZNW* 35 (1936) 229-30, in thinking that the Targumic interpretation of (*ᵃbdi* in Isa 42:1; 43:10; 52:13 as a reference to the messiah was derived from the *ᵃbdi semah* of Zech 3:8. Probably the idea in *Tg.* Isa 53:5 that the (Servant-) messiah will build the temple also derived from Zech 6:12-13 (cf. Seidelin, "Der Ebed Jahweh" 212-13). May Jesus also not have been led, as the Targum, to relate the Davidic messiah (*ᵃbdi semah*) of Zech 3:8 and the Servant of Yahweh (*ᵃbdi*) in Isa 42-53 to each other through the hermeneutical principle *gᵉzērāh sāwāh*?

42. According to J. Jeremias, ποιμήν, *TDNT* 6.492, n. 78, the Hebrew imperative *hak* of Zech 13:7 is turned into the 1st person, singular, future, indicative in Mark 14:27 = Matt 26:31 under the influence of Isa 53:6 and this indicates the identification of the shepherd with the Ebed Yahweh.

43. Here the *gᵉzērāh sāwāh* principle could have helped Jesus also to identify the Davidic messiah of Zech 3:8; 6:12-13 with the Ebed Yahweh of Isa 42:53 (see the note 41 above) and apply them both to himself.

44. Although in this article we use the language of "A leading Jesus to B," we are not always trying to determine precisely the sequence in the development of Jesus' self-understanding. Sometimes we use this form of language rather for the sake of the convenience it offers for showing the mutual connection of different OT passages underlying his self-understanding.

45. Cf. I. H. Marshall, "Son of God or Servant of Yahweh?—A Reconsideration of Mk I.11," *NTS* 15 (1968/69) 326-36. Ps 2:7 which is alluded to as well as Isa 42:1 in the heavenly declaration is part of the tradition of 2 Sam 7:12-16. See H. J. Kraus, *Psalmen 1-59*, Neukirchen, 1978, 152.

46. Kim, "The 'Son of Man'", 38-73.

47. Cf. the note 3 above.

48. Josephus, *Ant.* 10.210; Str-B 2.877.

49. Snodgrass, *Parable*, 66-70, 104-106, strongly argues for the view that Matt 21:44 = Luke 20:18 is an integral part of the Parable of the Wicked Husbandmen. Cf. Also Ellis, *Prophecy*, 251-52.

50. For the view that the eucharistic words are the words of "the Son of Man" and reflect Jesus' identification with the figure of the Ebed Yahweh in Isa 42–53, see Kim, *"The 'Son of Man'"*, 38-73.

51. ἐξουδενηθῇ in Mark 9:12 may reflect both Isa 53:3 *(nibzeh)* and Ps 118:22 (*m's*—cf. Acts 4:11). So M. Black, "The 'Son of Man' Passion Sayings in the Gospel Tradition," *ZNW* 60 (1969) 4; J. Jeremias, παῖς Θεοῦ, *TDNT* 5.707. Cf. France, *Jesus*, 123-24; H. E. Tödt, *Der Menschensohn in der synoptischen Tradition*, Gütersloh, ⁴1978, 155-56; Grimm, *Verkündigung*, 215-17.

52. Cf. Jeremias, παῖς Θεοῦ, *TDNT* 5.712; Tödt, *Menschensohn*, 147-57; Black "The 'Son of Man' Passion," 3-4.

53. Kim, "The 'Son of Man'", esp. 15-81.

54. Ibid.

55. Jesus' gathering sinners for table fellowship as "the 'Son of Man'" (Matt 11:19 = Luke 7:34-35; Luke 19:9-10; cf. also Mark 2:15-17 par) also indicates his fulfilling the function of the temple as "the 'Son of Man'". For the purification or forgiveness of sins and the fellowship with God (through his eschatological agent "the 'Son of Man'") which Jesus' gesture imparts to sinners are precisely what the temple is to mediate. Cf. Gaston, *Stone*, 78.

56. Betz, "Probleme," 630-33; Kim, "Vollmacht."

Die Wundergeschichten von Mt 8-9

Ulrich Luz

Die Sammlung matthäischer Wundergeschichten in Kap. 8-9 scheint ein untypisches Beispiel matthäischer Interpretation der Tradition. Matthäus, der sonst so konservative Evangelist,[1] hat sich hier aussergewöhnliche Freiheiten im Umgang mit seinen Quellen erlaubt. Statt, wie sonst üblich, der Abfolge der Markuserzählung zu folgen, hat er zwei verschiedene Abschnitte seiner Markusquelle ineinander verwoben (Mk 1,29–2,22; 4,35–5,43). Deren relative Reihenfolge ist nur im allgemeinen unangetastet geblieben; mindestens zwei auffällige Umstellungen sind festzustellen.[2] Besonders auffällig sind die Verdoppelungen von zwei Wundergeschichten durch den Evangelisten Matthäus (Mt 9,27-31; 20,29-34 = Mk 10,46-52; Mt 9,32-34; 12,22-24 = Lk 11,14f Q). Matthäus erzählt sie als zwei verschiedene Episoden, die zu verschiedenen Zeitpunkten in der Geschichte Jesu sich ereignen. Da solche Verdoppelungen nicht als unbewusste Vorgänge zu denken sind, muss Matthäus bewusst Jesusgeschichten verändert und neu geschaffen haben. Ausserdem fügt er in den Erzählablauf der beiden Kapitel zwei Wundergeschichten aus Q ein (Mt 8,5-13; 9,32-34).[3] Das Ganze verbindet er bewusst eng und gestaltet so eine völlig neue zeitliche und geographische Sequenz der Geschichte Jesu. Das passt schlecht zum Gesamtbild eines konservativen und überlieferungsgetreuen Umgangs mit der Tradition. Das passt auch so schlecht zu der Tatsache, dass der Evangelist Matthäus von Kap. 12 an den Markusfaden kaum mehr ändert, dass man auch schon vermutet hat, er benutze für unsere beiden Kapitel eine besondere Quelle.[4] Dazu kommt, dass Matthäus auch in den Wortlaut der Wundergeschichten insbesondere durch Kürzungen radikal eingreift.[5] So hat man den Eindruck, er zeige sich hier als ein recht massiv die Tradition verändernder Schriftsteller. Nur ab und zu scheint er sich auf das zu besinnen, was er der Tradition schuldig ist: An manchen Stellen scheint er Weggelassenes wieder nachzutragen, Reminiszenzen an Unterdrücktes anzudeuten, fast wie einer, der in seinem Papierkorb noch allerlei brauchbare Schnipsel entdeckt.[6] Kurz, ein auffälliges Verfahren und Grund genug, den Jubilar—und mich selbst—damit zu beunruhigen. Was steckt hinter der matthäischen Freiheit der Tradition gegenüber?

I

Die Wundergeschichten des Matthäusevangeliums waren in den letzten Jahren eher ein Stiefkind der Forschung. Der Hauptgrund dafür dürfte im durchschlagenden Erfolg der bereits mehr als fünfundzwanzig Jahre alten Monographie von H. J. Held über die matthäischen Wundergeschichten liegen.[7] Held bestimmte die Gattung der matthäischen Wundergeschichten als Paradigmen. Entsprechend fragte er nach den durch die diese Paradigmen veranschaulichten oder beleuchteten Themen. Im Vordergrund sah er in Mt 8,1-17 das christologische Thema des Gottesknechts, in 9,18-34 das Thema des Glaubens, und—in dieser Allgemeinheit wenig überzeugend—in 8,18–9,17 das Thema "Jesus als Herr der Gemeinde".[8]

Helds Analyse ging von der redaktionellen Arbeit des Evangelisten Matthäus an den einzelnen ihm überkommenen Perikopen aus. Darum ist sie auch bei der Exegese der einzelnen Perikopen am überzeugendsten. In seiner Analyse spielte das Ganze des Matthäusevangeliums als erzählerischer Rahmen auch der Wundergeschichten und als Schlüssel zu ihrem Verständnis kaum eine Rolle. Die Grundeinsicht von der Uebersummativität des Makrotextes, also des Evangeliums, das den Sinn seiner einzelnen Texte bestimmt, war damals noch nicht bekannt. Nicht ihre Stellung im Evangelium, sondern ihr "Thema" bestimmte den Sinn der Wundergeschichten. Held reflektierte kaum darüber, wie die Wundergeschichten die Matthäuserzählung bestimmen und vorantreiben, sondern er fragte, welchem Thema Matthäus sie unterordnet. So war es prinzipiell egal, wo sie im Matthäusevangelium stehen. Vielleicht ist es nicht unwichtig, auf den theologiegeschichtlichen Hintergrund dieser Wunderdeutung hinzuweisen: Sie ist m.E. ein Musterbeispiel moderner protestantischer Wunderdeutung, die Wundergeschichten nach ihrer kerygmatischen *Bedeutung* und nicht, oder nicht so sehr, nach dem in ihnen berichteten *Geschehen* hin befragt.[9] Matthäus, der die Wundergeschichten paradigmatisiert und zu Exempla des Glaubens, der Christologie, der Jüngerschaft oder der Heilsgeschichte macht, kommt solcher moderner Wunderdeutung von allen Evangelisten scheinbar am weitesten entgegen. Ein Stück des Geheimnisses des Erfolgs von Helds Buch könnte darin gelegen haben, dass die paradigmatisch verstandenen matthäischen Wunder für moderne protestantische Lesser leicht rezipierbar waren.

Auch heute befragen die meisten Exegeten die Wundergeschichten von Mt 8-9 nach ihren "Themen".[10] Weiterführender Gesichtspunkte hat die Forschung seit Held m.E. vor allem an drei Punkten gebracht:

a) Die Einteilung von Mt 8-9 in drei Hauptabschnitte hat weithin nicht überzeugt, zumal sich für den überlangen mittleren Hauptabschnitt Mt 8,18–9,17 kein klares "Thema" finden liess. Burger und Kingsbury sind z.B. zu einer Einteilung in vier Abschnitte zurückgekehrt.[11] Dafür spricht rein formal, dass die vier Hauptabschnitte 8,1-17; 8,18–9,1; 9,2-17 und 9,18-35 annähernd gleich lang sind.[12] Für 8,18–9,1 wurde das Thema in der "Nachfolge",[13] für 9,2-17 in der "Lösung der christlichen Gemeinde aus dem Verband des Judentums" gesehen.[14] Burger hat diese beiden mittleren Abschnitte zum Ausgangspunkt seiner Gesamtdeutung gemacht und damit auch diejenigen Teile von Mt 8-9, die keine Wundergeschichten enthalten (8,18-22; 9,9-17), ernst genommen: Für ihn ist die Gründung der Kirche das eigentliche Thema von Mt 8-9. In Kap. 8-9 habe Matthäus "sein Verständnis der Kirche in die Darstellung des Lebens Jesu zurückgetragen". "Etwas überspitzt" stellt Burger fest: "Die Kapitel 8 und 9 seines Evangeliums bieten den ἱερὸς λόγος, die Gründungslegende der christlichen Kirche".[15] "Ueberspitzt" mag Burger seine These darum genannt haben, weil er sie selber kaum begründet. Man bekommt den Eindruck, hier werde wieder *ein* Aspekt in den Wundergeschichten auf Kosten anderer zum dominanten gemacht. Dennoch meine ich, dass sich diese These begründen lässt, wenn auch anders, als dies bei Burger der Fall war.

b) Unverbunden neben der "thematischen" Interpretation standen immer schon Beobachtungen zum Verlauf der matthäischen *Geschichte:* Auf der Erzählebene sind die Wundergeschichten von Kap. 8-9 unabdingbare Voraussetzung von Kap. 10, wo Jesus den Jüngern die Vollmacht, Wunder zu tun, überträgt (10,1). Mt 10,8 weist auf Mt 8,1-4; 9,18–26.32-34 zurück. Noch deutlicher nimmt Jesus in Mt 11,5f in seiner

Antwort auf die Anfrage der Johannesjünger auf die Kap. 8-9 berichteten Wunder Bezug. Gefragt wurde auch, ob nicht die Ueberfahrt über den See (Mt 8,23-34) ins heidnische Land dem Reflexionszitat über "Galiläa der Heiden" (4,15f) entspreche.[16] Jedenfalls weisen solche Beobachtungen darauf hin, dass nicht nur die lehrhafte, sondern ebenso sehr die Erzählebene der matthäischen Wundergeschichten zu beachten ist. Hier liegt m.E. das Wahrheitsmoment im alten, von Schniewind vorgeschlagenen Stichwort von dem in Mt 8-9 dargestellten "Messias der Tat".[17] Trotz der zahlreichen Kürzungen durch den Evangelisten gerade in den nicht dialogischen Teilen der Wundergeschichten ist der Erzählebene grosse Bedeutung zu schenken.

c) Schliesslich sind die Beobachtungen zur Komposition der beiden Kapitel wichtig. Wenig hilfreich ist es m.E., über die Zahl der Wundergeschichten zu sinnieren. Nicht nur werden dabei die drei Apophthegmen 8,18-22; 9,9–13.14-17 vernachlässigt; es zeigt sich vielmehr auch, dass man sich über die Zahl der Wundergeschichten gar nicht einigen konnte.[18] Viel hilfreicher sind m.E. die Beobachtungen, die vor allem Thompson zur Verklammerung der Wundergeschichten von Kap. 8-9 zusammengetragen hat. Nicht die redaktionelle Bearbeitung der einzelnen Geschichten, sondern ihre Komposition em Rahmen des ganzen Evangeliums ist nach ihm das Wichtigste.[19] Ein Ueberblick ergibt, dass die Stichwortverbindungen nicht nur innerhalb der Einzelgeschichten, sondern auch zwischen den Geschichten und Geschichtengruppen ausserordentlich intensiv sind. Insbesondere im Schlussabschnitt 9,18-34 fallen die vielen sprachlichen und thematischen Reminiszenzen an 8,1–9,17 auf.[20] Zwischen den einzelnen Erzählungen des Abschnittes besteht auf der Erzählebene ein "continuous movement".[21] Das ist besonders auffällig, weil Matthäus ja in Kap. 8-9 Erzählungen aus zwei verschiedenen Abschnitten des Markusevangeliums zusammengestellt und durch Wundergeschichten aus der Logienquelle ergänzt hat. Trotz dieser Verknüpfungen verschiedener Quellenstränge erzählt er einen geschlossenen Ablauf. Er sei hier kurz rekapituliert: Jesus steigt vom Berg, begegnet unterwegs dem Aussätzigen, geht in die Stadt (8,5) und von dort ins Haus (8,14). Der Menschenmenge, die ihn am Abend bedrängt (8,16.18), will Jesus ausweichen und fährt über den See ans jenseitige Ufer ins heidnische Gebiet von Gadara. Dort heilt er einen Besessenen, wird vertrieben und kehrt in seine Stadt zurück (9,1). Auch die Erzählungen von Kap. 9 schliessen chronologisch und örtlich immer unmittelbar an die vorangehende an: In der Stadt heilt Jesus anscheinend unmittelbar nach seiner Ankunft (und nicht, wie Mk 2,1-12, im Haus)[22] den Lahmen, geht dann am Zollhaus vorbei und ins Haus (des Matthäus?) zum Essen (9,9a.10a). Von dort (9,18a) holt ihn der Synagogenvorsteher zu sich ins Haus. Unterwegs zu (seinem eigenen?) Haus begegnen ihm die beiden Blinden (9,27f) und unmittelbar anschliessend bringt man den stummen Besessenen zu ihm (9,32). Kein Zweifel: Matthäus will einen Ablauf schildern, wo eine Geschichte unmittelbar auf die andere folgt. Dabei passieren ihm zwar Ungeschicklichkeiten,[23] aber seine Absicht ist unverkennbar. Der zusammenhängenden matthäischen Erzählung entspricht negativ, dass sich m.E. Mt 8-9 keineswegs nach thematischen Blöcken gliedern lässt: Die "Themen" halten sich vielmehr meist durch verschiedene Abschnitte durch, wobei frühere "Themen" wieder auftauchen, vorbereitete "Themen" dominant werden und früher dominante "Themen" wieder anklingen können. Die matthäische Erzählung von Kap. 8-9 gleicht m.E. am ehesten einem Seil oder einem "Zopf", der bald den einen, bald den anderen thematischen Aspekt an die Oberfläche treten lässt.[24]

Fazit: Es geht Matthäus keineswegs um eine blosse Sammlung von Wundergeschichten, die beispielhaft die Taten des Messias oder gar verschiedene Aspekte seiner Lehre und des christlichen Glaubens erläutern, sondern es geht ihm um eine zusammenhängende *Geschichte*. Davon muss die Interpretation unserer beiden Kapitel ausgehen.

II

Die folgenden Ueberlegungen sind deshalb in lockerer Weise von verschiedenen Erkenntnissen moderner Erzählforschung bestimmt. Zunächst beschäftigen wir uns mit der Funktion der matthäischen Wundergeschichten auf der Erzählebene, bzw, auf der Ebene des matthäischen Diskurses.[25] In einer Erzählung werden "Ereignisabläufe so dargestellt, dass einem Ausgangszustand ein veränderter Endzustand gegenübersteht".[26] Die matthäischen Wundergeschichten von Kap. 8-9 sind im wesentlichen der Anfang eines Erzählgefüges, das auf ein Ende zuläuft und erst von diesem Ende her verstanden werden kann.[27] Versteht man eine Erzählung als Abfolge der drei Grundelemente "Orientierung", "Komplikation" und "Auflösung",[28] so befinden wir uns in Kap. 8-9 wohl am Anfang der "Komplikation". Die Eingangskapitel 1-7 bieten eine "Orientierung", allerdings eine Orientierung besonderer art.[29]

Worauf läuft die Erzählung von Mt 8-9 hinaus? M.E. formuliert Matthäus in 9,33f den Zielpunkt dieses ersten Abschnittes seines Diskurses: Vor dem rahmenden Summar 9,35 (=4,23) erzählt er von der gespaltenen Reaktion des Gottesvolkes Israel auf die Wunder Jesu: Die Volksmengen staunen und sagen: "Noch nie ist solches in Israel erschienen!" Die Pharisäer dagegen lehnen Jesus ab: "Durch den Herrscher der Dämonen treibt er die Dämonen aus!" (9,33f). Verschiedene Hinweise lassen erkennen, dass es sich hier um eine Schlüsselstelle handelt. Sie wird in 12,23f variiert und klingt wieder 21,10f.14-17 an. Sie lässt zwei Hauptpersonengruppen der vorangehenden Geschichten in ihrer charakteristischen Reaktion gegenüber Jesus nachmals zu Worte kommen: die von Jesus beeindruckten Volksmengen (vgl. 8,1.16.18; 9,8, vgl. 9,26.31) und die gegnerischen jüdischen Führer (vgl. 9,2-17). Ausserdem fällt auf, dass der Abschnitt 9,18-34 nicht nur sprachlich, sondern auch inhaltlich noch einmal das Ganze der vorangehenden Geschichten aufnimmt: Die Erwähnungen des Glaubens (9,22.28f) nehmen 8,10.13 auf. Die Nachfolge der Blinden (9,27, vgl. 19) erinnert an 8,18-27; 9,9. Ausserdem greift die Szene der Blindenheilung 9,27 auf 9,9f zurück.[30] Das Schlafen und Auferwecktwerden des Mädchens (9,24f) entspricht dem Verhalten Jesu im Boot (8,25f). Der christologische Titel κύριος 9,28 nimmt das fünfmalige κύριος von 8,2-25 auf. Die Anwesenheit der Jünger 9,19 erinnert daran, dass es es 8,19-27; 9,8-14 um die Jüngerschaft ging. Kurz, man bekommt den Eindruck, dass 9,18-34 nicht in erster Linie eine Zusammenstellung von drei Wundergeschichten unter dem Aspekt des Glaubens sind,[31] sondern dass Matthäus hier fast alle Themen der vorangehenden Abschnitte nochmals anklingen lässt und bündelt. Noch eine weitere Beobachtung ist auffällig: In der Blindenheilung formuliert Matthäus den Schluss, V 30f, mithilfe des früher weggelassenen Schlusses der Heilung des Aussätzigen Mk 1,44f. Diese Geschichte war bei ihm die erste seines ganzen Zyklus (Mt 8,1-4). Man könnte also sagen: Matthäus braucht die markinische

Geschichte 1,40-45 als Rahmen für seinen ganzen Wunderzyklus Mt 8,1–9,34. Auch das deutet darauf hin, dass Matthäus diesen Zyklus nun bewusst abschliessen will. So ist es wohl berechtigt, in 9,33f eine abschliessende Reaktion des Volkes und der Pharisäer nicht nur auf den zuletzt berichteten Exorzismus, sondern auf Jesu Wunder in Israel[32] überhaupt zu sehen. Der Wille, eine solche abschliessende Reaktion zu formulieren, ist dann wohl neben der Absicht, das κωφοὶ ἀκούουσιν von 11,5 zu belegen, das Motiv für die Zufügung und Verdoppelung des kurzen Exorzismus aus Q (Lk 11,14f) gewesen.[33]

Wir können also sagen: Am Ende des Wunderzyklus Mt 8-9 ist es zur Spaltung in Israel gekommen. Die negative Reaktion der Pharisäer, die für Matthäus die wichtigsten und repräsentativsten der Jesus ablehnenden jüdischen Führer sind,[34] steht der neutral-positiven Reaktion der Volksmassen auf Jesus gegenüber. Die Wunder Jesu in Kap. 8-9 haben im Makrotext des Evangeliums die Funktion, diese Spaltung in Israel zu bewirken. Sie bilden die Exposition des später ausbrechenden Konflikts.[35] Von hier aus wird es auch sinnvoll, dass der Evangelist die in Kap. 8-9 berichteten Wunder mehrmals bewusst als Wunder in Israel und als Wunder des Messias Israels[36] kennzeichnet. Die drei Streitgespräche mit den Schriftgelehrten, den Pharisäern und den Johannesjüngern (9,2-17) werden nun innerhalb der Kapitel 8-9 sinnvoll: Sie bereiten die Spaltung in Israel vor. Matthäus ist nicht nur durch seine Markusquelle gezwungen, sie zu bringen—er hat sie im übrigen gerade in diesem Abschnitt recht grosszügig umgestellt—, sondern es zeigt sich hier wie in anderen Abschnitten seines Evangeliums, wie er einen konservativen Umgang mit der Tradition harmonisch mit seinen eigenen schriftstellerischen und theologischen Absichten verbindet. Gerade darin zeigt sich die schriftstellerische Meisterschaft des Redaktors Matthäus.

Es gibt noch ein anderes Resultat des matthäischen Diskurses der Kapitel 8-9, das für das Ganze des Evangeliums wichtig ist: 9,36 sieht Jesus die hirtenlosen Volksmassen und erbarmt sich ihrer, weil sie wie Schafe ohne Hirten sind. Matthäus hat diesen Vers aus Mk 6,34a.b übernommen und hier vorausgestellt. Aus 9,33f ergibt sich, warum: Nachdem die Pharisäer Jesus, im Unterschied zu den Volksmassen, schroff abgelehnt haben, sind sie nicht mehr ihre echten Hirten. Die Volksmassen sind vielmehr durch die Spaltung, die um Jesu willen zwischen ihnen und ihren Führern eingetreten ist, hirtenlos geworden. In dieser Situation bekommen die Jünger den Auftrag, Arbeiter in der Ernte an dem hirtenlosen Volk zu sein. Sie treten nunmehr, nach Kap. 8-9, als Apostel Jesu dem Volk gegenüber.

Damit ist eine gegenüber dem Anfang des Wunderzyklus neue Situation erreicht: Zu Beginn der Bergpredigt traten die Jünger *zusammen* mit dem Volk als Hörer des Evangeliums Jesu von der Gottesherrschaft auf: Sie waren gleichsam der innere Kreis der Volksmassen, die Jesus zuhörten (4,25–5,2; 7,28–8,1). Im ersten Abschnitt der Erzählung von Jesu Wundern in Israel (8,1-17) traten sie nicht in Erscheinung. Dies änderte sich erst mit 8,18. Ist es Zufall, dass Jesus in 8,18—anders als Mk 4,34f—nicht *den Jüngern* den Befehl gibt, ans jenseitige Ufer zu fahren? Vielmehr erblickt Jesus bei Matthäus nur ganz allgemein das Volk um sich herum und gibt den Befehl zum Aufbruch ans jenseitige Ufer. Gilt der Befehl dem Volk, d.h. jedermann, der um Jesus ist? Dann wäre das Volk nicht der Grund für den Rückzug Jesu ans jenseitige Ufer,[37] sondern es wäre zum Aufbruch mit Jesus aufgefordert. Die Erzählung ist an diesem Punkt nicht klar. Immerhin könnte für diese Interpretation sprechen, dass der Erste, der sich bei Jesus meldet und mitkommen will, ein Aussenstehender ist, nämlich der Schriftgelehrte von 8,19.[38] 8,23 taucht dann das Wort μαθητής in Verbindung mit ἀκολουθέω auf: Jüngerschaft bedeutet Nachfolge, und das bedeutet zugleich wieder: Trennung von Israel, Einsteigen ins Schiff. Das Ziel der Ueberfahrt ist wichtig: Es ist die Gadarene, das heidnische Land der hellenistischen Kultur-metropole Gadara.[39] Dort kann Jesus noch nicht wirken, sondern wird von den Be-wohnern vertrieben und kehrt wieder ins Land Israel zurück. Sein καιρός ist noch nicht gekommen. Fortan tauchen die Jünger dem Volk gegenüber auf der Seite Jesu auf: Sie sind nicht nur an Jesu Stelle Ansprechpartner der feindlichen Führer des Volkes (9,11.14), sondern sie werden auch gegenüber den Zöllnern und dem Hilfe suchenden Synagogenvorsteher als *Jesu* Begleiter geschildert. Man könnte sagen: Von dem Moment an, wo die Jünger mit Jesus ins Schiff steigen und vom Volke weg ans jenseitige Ufer fahren, haben sie ihren—für das Matthäusevangelium fortan ein-deutigen—Ort: Sie gehören zu Jesus und stehen dem Volke *gegenüber.* Es ist der Ort, der in der sog. Aussendungsrede Kap. 10 konstitutiv ist.

Dass Matthäus in 8,18 die Jünger sich bewusst vom Volke lösen und zu neuen Ufern aufbrechen lässt, wird durch den folgenden Hauptabschnitt des Matthäusevan-geliums, nämlich 12,1-16,12 bestätigt werden.[40] Dieser Abschnitt schildert in mehr-eren Anläufen den "Rückzug" Jesu und seiner Jünger von Israel. Ein Rückzug Jesu (ἀναχωρέω) ist seine Antwort auf den Todesbeschluss der Pharisäer (12,14f). Wiederum sagt hier Matthäus, dass "viele" aus dem Volk ihm auf diesem Rückzug "folgen" und dass Jesus sie heilt. Wiederum, wie in 9,1-17, führt Jesu Rückzug aus Israel zum Konflikt mit den Pharisäern (12,22-45), der in schroffen Gerichtsworten Jesu endet (12,39-45). Der bösen Generation gegenüber steht die wahre Familie Jesu, über die Jesus segnend seine Hand hält (12,46-50). Nach der Gleichnisrede wieder-holt sich diese Szenenfolge: Auf die Kunde von dem seinen eigenen Tod im voraus andeutenden Tod des Johannes zieht sich Jesus wiederum zurück (14,13; ἀναχωρέω). Wieder folgen ihm die Volksmassen, die Jesus wiederum heilt (14,14c). Es folgen Gemeindetexte: die erste Speisung des Volkes, mit deutlichen Reminiszen-zen an die Abendmahlserfahrung der Gemeinde, und die Sturmstillungsgeschichte, von Matthäus als Nachfolgegeschichte gestaltet. Mit 14,34 setzt eine neue Erzählfolge ein. In ihrem Anfang steht wiederum ein Konflikt mit den Pharisäern und Schriftgelehrten (15,1-20), gefolgt von einem weiteren Rückzug Jesu (15,21), auf dem ihm wohl nur deshalb keine Volksmassen aus Israel folgen, weil er sich ins heid-nische Gebiet von Tyrus und Sidon begibt. Nach einer erneuten Auseinandersetzung mit den Pharisäern und Sadduzäern, die wiederum in einem Gerichtswort endet, verlässt sie Jesus (καταλιπών . . . ἀπῆλθεν 16,4) und geht mit den Jüngern wiederum im Schiff ans jenseitige Ufer (εἰς τὸ πέραν, vgl. 8,18). Und zu allem Ueberfluss zeigt die in diesem Hauptteil stehende Gleichnisrede dieselbe erzähleri-sche Grundstruktur: Sie beginnt am See, wo Jesus die zahlreichen Volksmassen vom Schiff aus lehrt (13,1f). In ihrer Mitte unterbricht Matthäus die Rede durch eine erzählerische Zwischenbemerkung:[41] Jesus verlässt das Volk und geht ins Haus, wohin ihm seine Jünger folgen (13,36a). Wieder haben wir das Grundmotiv der Tren-nung der Jünger von den Aussenstehenden.[42]

Das in 8,18-27 präludierte Motiv der Trennung der Jünger von Israel wiederholt sich also im folgenden Hauptteil so oft, dass es der Leser nicht unbeachtet lassen kann. Durch die Wiederholung wird ihm deutlich: Hier entsteht die Gemeinde. Wer

Jesus aus dem Volk nachfolgt, wird zum Jünger. Die Jünger sind fortan etwas anderes als das Volk Israel: Sie sind bei Jesus, stehen unter seinem Schutz, werden von ihm belehrt und geheilt und erhalten von ihm einen Auftrag. Das Thema "Jüngerschaft" ist also in der Tat in Kap 8-9 nicht ein Thema neben mehreren, sondern in der ganzen Erzählung von Mt 8-9 geht es darum, wie durch das heilende und barmherzige Handeln des Messias Israels, des Gottesknechtes und Davidssohns in seinem Volk (9,9.27) eine Spaltung und eben so die Jüngergemeinde entsteht. Als Antwort auf dieses barmherzige Wirken Jesu entsteht die Gemeinde (vgl. 9,27; 12,15; 14,13; 20,34), die dann weitere Erfahrungen von Jesu heilsamem Handeln macht. An eben diesen Heilungen entstehen aber auch die Konflikte, die zur Spaltung in Israel führen (9,1b-8; 12,9-14.22-45; 14,34–15,1; 21,14-16). Das heilende Handeln des Messias Israels in seinem Volk ist also der entscheidende bewegende Faktor, der den Konflikt und damit die ganze Erzählung vorantreibt.

Wir formulieren ein kurzes *Fazit:* Matthäus erzählt in Kap. 8-9 die Entstehung der Jüngergemeinde aus Israel und die damit verbundene Spaltung in Israel. Die These Burgers, dass es in Mt 8-9 um "die Gründungslegende der christlichen Kirche" gehe, ist also m.E. nicht "etwas überspitzt",[43] sondern richtig. Nur muss man deutlicher als Burger sagen: Es geht nicht—statisch—um eine Zurückprojektion der Wirklichkeit der Kirche ins Leben Jesu und nicht um eine Darstellung der Kirche durch das sprachliche Medium eines Berichts über Jesus, sondern es geht um eine *Erzählung,* die Erzählung nämlich, *wie durch die Wunder des Messias in Israel Gemeinde entstand.*

III

Damit sind wir anhand unserer beiden Kapitel auf das Erzählgerüst des Matthäusevangeliums gestossen, also auf das, was der englischsprachige literary criticism "plot"[44] nennt. Dieses Erzählgerüst ist in seiner Oberflächenstruktur einigermassen verwirrend: Nachdem Jesus eine lange Rede gehalten hat, beginnt er zu heilen (8,1). Er heilt in Kap. 8-9 unentwegt, sozusagen ununterbrochen. Eine Szene jagt die andere. Dass Jesus nach so anstregendem Tun müde auf dem Schifflein einschläft (8,24), vermag auch den nicht zu verwundern, der an der Oberfläche der matthäischen Geschichte bleibt. Warum musste Matthäus diesen kompakten Block von Wundergeschichten schaffen? Warum musste er alle diese Wundergeschichten geographisch und chronologisch so eng miteinander verknüpfen, um unter allen Umständen seinen Lesern deutlich zu machen, dass er eine Geschichte erzählt und nicht eine Zusammenstellung von irgendwann geschehenen Jesuswundern etwa im Stile einer antiken Biographie geben will?[45] Warum der so unmotivierte und dann so schnell abgebrochene Ausflug Jesu ins heidnische Gadarenerland? Warum die un-motivierte Präsenz von Menschen, die Jesu Sturmstillung akklamieren und staunen (8,27)—Matthäus hat ja die "anderen Schiffe" (Mk 4,36b), in denen sie hätten sein können, gestrichen? Und warum der—oberflächlich gesehen—völlig rätselhafte Ausspruch Jesu, dass die Volksmassen keinen Hirten hätten (9,36)? Die Schwierig-keiten der Oberflächenstrukter gehen nach Kap. 10 weiter: Warum der brüske Ab-bruch der Aussendungsrede, ohne dass berichtet wird, wie die Jünger Jesu Gebote ausführen (11,1)? Warum die schroffe Gerichtsankündigung in 11,20-24? Warum das den unmittelbaren Kontext nur an einem einzigen Punkt treffende lange

Erfüllungszitat von 12,18-21, mit dem der Erzähler Matthäus seine Geschichte deutet? Warum der zu den Gleichnissen inhaltlich nicht passende Wechsel der Hörerschaft in 13,36? Warum die dreimalige Wiederholung des Rückzugs Jesu in 13,54–16,12?

Zu den Merkwürdigkeiten der Erzählung kommt ihre Distanz zur Geschichte (history) Jesu: Was auch immer Matthäus über die Geschichte Jesu gewusst, gedacht bzw. nicht gedacht haben mag, er muss gewusst haben, dass *seine* von ihm zusammenhängend und ohne Unterbruch erzählte Geschichte Jesu, d.h. sein Diskurs, fiktiv war. Man kann nicht naiv und diesbezüglich bona fide eine vorgegebene Geschichte, die das Wirken Jesu in chronologischem Abriss erzählt, zertrümmern und sie neu zusammensetzen, durch weitere Ueberlieferungen ergänzen und daraus einen neuen geographisch und chronologisch geschlossenen Ablauf schaffen, ohne zu wissen, dass dieser Ablauf der wirklichen Geschichte Jesu nicht entsprochen haben *kann*. Matthäus dürfte sich für die ihm ja unerreichbare wirkliche Geschichte (history) des irdischen Jesu gar nicht interessiert haben—aber das wissen wir leider nicht. Aber wir wissen, dass er *wusste,* dass seine Geschichte Jesu eine *neue* Erzählung war. Er wusste um ihre Fiktivität, er wusste, dass sie *sein* Entwurf ("plot") war. Man kann z.B. nicht annehmen, dass Matthäus eine ihm einmal überlieferte Geschichte Jesu, dazu noch ihren Helden, verdoppelt und sie als zwei zu verschiedenen Zeiten und an verschiedenen Orten passierte Geschichten erzählt, ohne um die historische Fiktivität seiner Erzählung zu wissen. Wo aber liegt dann der Sinn dieses Unternehmens?

Die matthäische Erzählung wird m.E. nur sinnvoll und das matthäische Erzählgerüst ("plot") ist nur dann in einen verständlichen Diskurs angelegt, wenn man erkennt, dass sie eine *Tiefenstruktur* haben, die der Kommunikation des Autors mit seinen Lesern dient und diese ermöglicht.[46] M.E. ist die matthäische Erzählung so sehr illokutionär, d.h. auf eine Anrede ihrer Leser hinzielend, dass sie nur mithilfe eines kommunikationstheoretischen Textmodells zureichend erfasst werden kann.[47] Die matthäische Geschichte hat unter ihrer Oberfläche eine (oder mehrere!) Tiefenstruktur(en), die u.a. an der Spannung in ihrer Oberflächenstruktur erkennbar wird.[48] Mithilfe dieser Tiefenstruktur kommuniziert der Autor Matthäus mit seinen Lesern. Auf dieser Ebene "sagt" die matthäische Geschichte ihren Lesern etwas, auf dieser Ebene tut sie ihre Wirkung; sie tröstet, bestätigt, ermuntert, ermahnt und fordert.

Rekapitulieren wir nochmals die matthäische Erzählung: Der Evangelist berichtet vom Wirken des Messias Israels in seinem Volk, Er erzählt, wie aus diesem Wirken die Jüngergemeinde entsteht (8-9). Er erzählt dann, wie sich die Spaltung in Israel zuspitzt (11) und wie es zu wiederholten Rückzügen Jesu und der ihm nachfolgenden Jüngergemeinde aus Israel kommt (12,1–16,12). Er berichtet anschliessend über das Leben und die Ordnung der aus Israel heraus entstandenen Gemeinde (16,13–20,34). Er erzählt schliesslich, wie sich der Konflikt in Israel endgültig zuspitzt, von der grossen Abrechnung Jesu mit dem feindlichen Israel in seinen Gleichnissen, seinen Streitgesprächen und seiner Gerichtsrede, die in seinem endgültigen Auszug aus dem Tempel (24,1-3) und in seiner Tötung (26f) gipfelt. An diesem Endpunkt der Geschichte sagt das ganze Volk Nein zu Jesus (27,24f). Darum schickt nach seiner Auferstehung der Messias Israels seine Jünger zu den Heiden (28,16-20).

Das ist das Erzählgerüst der matthäischen Geschichte.[49] Es wird deutlich: *Es ist die Grundgeschichte seiner Kirche, die Matthäus hier erzählt.* Es ist nicht nur die

Geschichte Jesu, sondern im gleichen Zug die Geschichte der ihm nachfolgenden Gemeinde des Matthäus, die selber aus Israel stammt, aus Israel herausgehen musste, von Israel verfolgt wurde, sich von Israel endgültig getrennt hat und nun zur Heidenmission aufbricht. Ihre eigene Geschichte sehen die Leser des Matthäusevangeliums in der Geschichte Jesu grundgelegt. Sie beginnt mit dem heilenden Handeln des Messias Israels in seinem Volk (4,23; 9,35), das alles weitere bewirkt. Die Gemeinde erkennt, dass sie sich selbst dem barmherzigen Handeln des Messias in Israel verdankt (8,1-4.14-17). Sie erfährt, wie aus diesem Handeln heraus Jüngerschaft entstehen kann (8,18-22 nach 8,1-17; 9,9-13 nach 9,2-8; 9,27-31). Sie sieht in der gefährlichen Fahrt der Jünger ans heidnische Ufer sich selbst unterwegs von Israel zu den Heiden (8,23-34). Sie erkennt beispielhaft schon in der Geschichte Jesu, wie Gottes Heilshandeln über Israel hinausdrängt (8,5-13.28-34). Sie sieht, wie durch Jesus die Spaltung in Israel sich anbahnt, die sich immer mehr zuspitzen wird und die später ihre eigenen geschichtlichen Erfahrungen bestimmen wird (vgl. 9,2-17.32-34). Sie erfährt die Geschichte Jesu als ihre eigene Grundgeschichte und so auch die Kontinuität des Handelns Gottes vor und nach Ostern. Akzeptieren wir dies als Grundthese, so werden einige Besonderheiten der matthäischen Erzählung in Kap. 8-9, die auf der Oberfläche der matthäischen Geschichte interpretiert, Schwierigkeiten bieten, durchsichtiger:

1. Matthäus beginnt seine Geschichte von Jesu Handeln in Israel mit einem Block von Wundergeschichten. Dieser zusammenhängende Anfang der Jesusgeschichte darf nicht einfach lehrhaft interpretiert werden, als ob Matthäus z.B. an zehn Beispielen den "Messias der Tat" dokumentieren möchte.[50] Auch wenn dieser Block oberflächlich betrachtet als Schilderung von einem oder zwei Tagen im Leben Jesu merkwürdig anmutet, so hat doch die zusammenhängende Geschichte von Jesu Heilen in Israel im Rahmen des matthäischen Erzählentwurfs ihren guten Sinn: Matthäus deutet so an, dass am Anfang der Geschichte der Gemeinde ein zusammenhängendes, ununterbrochenes Handeln Gottes durch Jesus stand. Die Geschichte der Gemeinde beginnt mit den Taten des Erbarmens des Messias.[51] Alles andere, der Ruf in die Nachfolge, der Glaube der Geheilten, die Konflikte um Jesus, sind Reaktionen auf diese anfängliche Geschichte der barmherzigen Taten des Messias. Die Wundergeschichten von Kap. 8-9 als Anfang der Geschichte der Entstehung der Gemeinde aus Israel haben somit eine ähnliche Funktion wie die Vorordnung von 4,23-25 vor die Bergpredigt: Es geht Matthäus darum zu erzählen, dass die Taten des Messias, resp, die Taten Gottes durch ihn, alles überhaupt erst entstehen liessen.

2. Matthäus durchbricht öfters die zeitliche Retrospektive.[52] Mt 8,11f und 9,15b sind Weissagungen des "omniscienten" Protagonisten Jesus, die sich auf die Zeit der Kirche, resp. des Endgerichts beziehen. Die Verallgemeinerung der ἐξουσία Jesu in 9,8 (die Vollmacht des Menschensohns 9,6 geht auf alle Menschen über) setzt die Erfahrung der Sündenvergebung in der Gemeinde voraus. Proleptischen Charakter hat auch die Ueberfahrt Jesu und der Jünger ins heidnische Land in 8,23-27 und die Heilung der besessenen Gadarener dort. Vom Ganzen der Matthäuserzählung her würde man das πρὸ καιροῦ von 8,29 am liebsten auf die Zeit der Heidenmission deuten, die noch nicht gekommen ist—aber der Text gibt leider keine Hinweise für eine solche Deutung.[53] Schliesslich ist das Präsens historicum zu erwähnen. Wie sonst im Matthäusevangelium, so konzentriert es sich auch in unseren Kapiteln auf das λέγει Jesu (8,4.7.20.22.26; 9,7.9.28). Ohne dass Matthäus hier einen konsequen-

ten Sprachgebrauch entwickelt, wird man doch sagen können, dass das häufige Präsens des Sprechens Jesu mit der Gegenwartsbedeutung der Worte Jesu zusammenhängen dürfte.[54] Unsere Kapitel sind also durchsetzt von direkten und indirekten Hinweisen auf die kommende Zeit der Gemeinde, die in der Jesusgeschichte grundgelegt ist.[55]

Diese Struktur der Grundgeschichte des Evangeliums entspricht dem, was Matthäus bereits in seinem Prolog (1,1–4,22) vorweggenommen hatte. Dort geht es nicht nur um die Vorwegnahme des entscheidenden "evaluative point of view concerning Jesus' identity", nämlich um die Mitteilung von Jesu Gottessohnschaft,[56] sondern es geht um mehr: Es geht um eine proleptische Vor-*Erzählung* der *Geschichte* des Gottessohns "Immanuel". Seine Geschichte beginnt mit der Geburt des davidischen Messias in Israel (1,18-25); sie führt durch die Krise mit dem König Israels (2,1-12) ins heidnische Aegyptenland (2,13-18) und ins Galiläa der Heiden (2,19-23; 4,12-17), wo der Nazoräer[57] Jesus seine Gemeinde berufen wird (4,18-22). Der Prolog erzählt bereits die Grundgeschichte der Gemeinde, die sich von 4,23 an in der Geschichte des Wirkens Jesu vor dem Leser ausführlich ausbreiten wird.

IV

Damit sind aber die Wundergeschichten von Mt 8-9 noch nicht abschliessend gedeutet. *Neben der indirekten Gegenwartsbedeutung der Wunder Jesu als Anfang der eigenen Geschichte der Gemeinde haben sie auch noch eine direkte Gegenwartsbedeutung.* Da sich diese Sinnebene nicht auf die Wundergeschichten von Mt 8-9 als Teil des matthäischen Makrotextes, sondern fast ausschliesslich auf die Einzelgeschichten bezieht, möchte ich auf sie nur noch skizzenhaft hinweisen. Im Unterschied zu Held, der vom paradigmatischen Charakter der Wundergeschichten bei Matthäus sprach, möchte ich lieber von ihrer Transparenz für die Gegenwart sprechen.[58] Der Ausdruck "Transparenz" betont stärker die Unersetzbarkeit der vergangenen Jesusgeschichten. Die vergangenen Taten Jesu ermöglichen ihre Transparenz für die Gegenwart der Gemeinde. Die Transparenz funktioniert dabei verschieden. Die Wunder Jesu können von Erfahrungen berichten, die in der Gemeinde auch noch identisch erfahren werden können: Mt 10,1.8 wird zeigen, dass für Matthäus Heilungen konstitutiv für den Auftrag der Jünger und damit das Wesen der Gemeinde sind. Mt 17,19f bezeugt dasselbe e negativo: Das Ausbleiben von Wundererfahrungen in der Gemeinde ist verhängnisvoll, weil Wunder Ausdruck des Glaubens sind. Die Identität der Erfahrungen ist z.B. auch durch den Wortstamm πιστ- gegeben: Wenn vom Glauben der Geheilten, bzw. wenn vom Kleinglauben der Jünger geredet wird, so ist deutlich, dass damit unmittelbar die eigene Glaubenserfahrung der Gemeinde mit eingeschlossen, ermutigt oder hinterfragt werden soll. Deutlich ist dasselbe auch bei der Erfahrung der Sündenvergebung (9,6.8). An anderen Stellen benutzt Matthäus traditionell vorgegebene Möglichkeiten metaphorischer Deutungen einzelner Ausdrücke und Motive: So lässt sich etwa "blind" und "sehen" metaphorisch deuten:[59] Die physische Heilung von Blinden ist gleichsam nur der Kern oder physische Ausdruck dessen, was mit jedem Menschen geschieht, wenn er Jesus begegnet: Er wird sehend. Auch das Wort ἀκολουθέω ist bei Matthäus übertragen gedeutet und wird zur Chiffre des Unterwegsseins mit Christus auf dem Weg des Gehorsams, des Leidens, aber auch des Getragenseins und der Hilfe. In der Sturmstillungsgeschichte Mt 8,23-27 steht eine ganze Palette traditioneller Metaphern zur Verfügung, die dazu hilft, die Geschichte als symbolische Darstellung von Führungs- und Bewahrungserfahrung der Gemeinde in den Stürmen des Lebens zu verstehen.[60] Zur Transparenz der Wundergeschichten helfen auch Elemente liturgischer Sprache, wie die Gebetsanrede κύριε.[61] Die Geschichte von der Auferweckung der Tochter des Jairus lässt durch die matthäischen Kürzungen die Assoziationen an die eigene kommende Auferweckung von den Toten deutlicher hervortreten.[62]

Drei Bemerkungen sind zu dieser Deutungsebene noch nötig: Einmal ist hervorzuheben, dass sie bei Matthäus nicht neu ist. Der Evangelist führt vielmehr nur weiter, was in der Tradition bereits angelegt war. Auch bei Markus werden gerade die Blindenheilungen schon metaphorisch gedeutet;[63] auch die markinische Sturmstillungsgeschichte ist eine symbolische Verschlüsselung von eigenen Erfahrungen der Gemeinde.[64] Matthäus hat die Transparenz der Wundergeschichten in einzelnen Fällen deutlicher gemacht, etwa durch seine Kürzungen, durch das Weglassen von Namen, die die Einmaligkeit von Geschichten hervorhoben,[65] und vielleicht auch durch die Verdoppelung des blinden Bartimäus. Zweitens: Die meisten Wundergeschichten von Mt 8-9 sind in ihrem Sinn mehrschichtig. Sie haben zugleich eine "indirekte Transparenz" für die Geschichte der Gemeinde im Rahmen des "plot" der ganzen Matthäusgeschichte und eine direkte Transparenz für die Gegenwart. Man kann sich das etwa am Beispiel der Heilung des Knechtes des Hauptmanns von Kapernaum, die einerseits auf das kommende Gericht an Israel und das Heil für die Heiden vorausweist, andererseits aber für den Glauben der Gemeinde direkt transparent ist, verdeutlichen. Ein anderes Beispiel ist die Heilung des Lahmen Mt 9,2-8, die zugleich als Schilderung des Konfliktes mit den Schriftgelehrten Teil der matthäischen Geschichte und durch die Ermöglichung der Sündenvergebung der Gemeinde transparent für die Gegenwart ist. Drittens: Die Transparenz der matthäischen Wundergeschichten ist in keinem Fall mit einer allegorischen Deutung in dem Sinn zu verwechseln, dass die Geschichten von etwas anderem reden wollen als dem, wovon sie vordergründig reden. Vielmehr geht es darum, dass die von ihnen berichtete wirkliche Begebenheit der Geschichte Jesu einen Erfahrungsbereich erschliesst, der weiter ist als sie selbst.[66] Insofern ist gerade die Verbindung der beiden konstitutiven Deutungsebenen, nämlich der bereits traditionell vorgegebenen Transparenz der (Einzel)geschichte für die Gegenwartserfahrungen der Gemeinde und der (auch schon bei Markus, aber in anderer Weise entworfenen) Einordnung der Einzelgeschichten in den Gesamtentwurf der matthäischen Jesusgeschichte für das Verständis entscheidend: *Die matthäischen Wundergeschichten sind Teil der für die Gemeinde grundlegenden Geschichte Jesu und haben gerade als solche transparente Bedeutung.*

V

Nicht nur die damals geschehene Geschichte, sondern auch die durch sie bewirkte Geschichte der Entstehung der Kirche und die durch sie bewirkten und gespiegelten gegenwärtigen Erfahrungen der Gemeinde machen also die Wirklichkeit von Jesuswundern aus. Ich schlage deshalb vor, das Matthäusevangelium, dessen Teil die

Wundergeschichten von Kap. 8-9 sind, eine *"inklusive Erzählung"* zu nennen.[67] Graphisch könnte man sie sich in folgender Darstellung verdeutlichen:

Inklusive Jesus erzählung des Mt

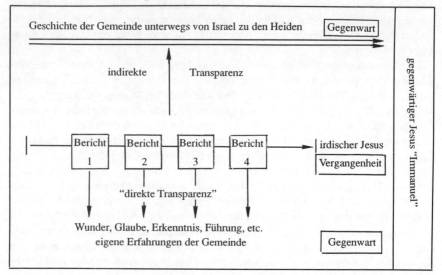

In der Erfahrung ihrer wirkenden Kraft in der Geschichte und im gegenwärtigen Leben der Gemeinde kommen die Wundergeschichten zu ihrer ganzen Wirklichkeit.

Darin, dass ihre Wirklichkeit Teil einer vergangenen Geschichte ist, aber zugleich diese überschreitet und die Gegenwart bestimmt, entsprechen sie der matthäischen Christologie. Jesus, der "damals" Wunder getan hat, ist für Matthäus von Anfang seines Evangeliums an der "Immanuel" (1,24), der alle Tage bei seiner Gemeinde ist bis ans Ende der Welt (28,20). So entspricht die Erfahrung, dass die Wunder Jesu eine über sie hinauszielende Geschichte bewirken und ihre Kraft in den eigenen Erfahrungen der Gemeindeglieder erweisen, der matthäischen Christologie.

Literaturwissenschaftlich müsste über den Erzähltyp, den das Matthäusevangelium repräsentiert, noch weiter nachgedacht werden. Es wird m.E. nicht zureichend erfasst, wenn es einer allgemeinen Theorie "der" Erzählung zugeordnet wird.[68] Das Charakteristikum seiner "inklusiven" Erzählung ist vielmehr, mithilfe ihres direkt oder indirekt transparenten Charakters mit den gegenwärtigen Lesern zu *kommunizieren*, bzw. noch stärker: die Leser in die Erzählung hineinzunehmen. Die für das Verständnis der Evangelien entscheidende Textdimension ist deshalb m.E. die pragmatische, die entscheidende semiotische Frage ist die nach dem Verhältnis von Zeichen und Zeichen*funktion*. Den Evangelien verwandte Erzählungen sind z.B. Mythen, Märchen und vor allem die alttestamentlichen Grundgeschichten Israels.[69] Hilfreich für die literaturwissenschaftliche Beschreibung könnten die Versuche von F. Martinez-Bonati sein, von einer mehrfachen Schichtung des Sinns im Kunstwerk[70] zu sprechen. Hilfreich scheint mir auch die Frage von S. J. Schmidt nach dem "Illokutionspotential" von Texten.[71] Damit ist auch gegeben, dass der Sinn von Wundergeschichten im Rahmen der matthäischen Grundgeschichte nie nur statisch definiert werden kann, sondern immer vom Leser in seiner konkreten geschichtlichen Situation und mithilfe seiner eigenen analogen Erfahrungen neu entdeckt werden muss. Hier bleibt aber noch ein weites, literaturwissenschaftlich-hermeneutisch-theologisches Arbeitsfeld.

Notes

1. Ich teile mit dem Jubilar die Meinung, die Ueberlieferung und Entwicklung der synoptischen Tradition sei im ganzen konservativer und die Treue gegenüber der Tradition grösser gewesen, als dies die klassische deutschsprachige Form- und Traditionsgeschichte annahm. Eben deshalb möchte ich ihn mit Ueberlegungen zu Texten grüssen, die solchen uns wichtigen Meinungen stracks zuwider zu laufen scheinen. In unserer heutigen Forschungssituation, wo z.T. bizarre historische Hypothesen in Magazinen und populären Büchern Schlagzeilen machen, sollten die Schwierigkeiten der eigenen Thesen sorgfältig benannt und offen gehalten werden. Zu meiner allgemeinen Sicht des Mt als eines "konservativen" Evangelisten vgl. U. Luz, *Das Evangelium nach Matthäus* I, EKK I/1, Neukirchen-Zürich, 1985, 56-61.

2. Mk 1,40-45 (= Mt 8,1-4) und Mk 10,46-52 (=Mt 9,27-31) sind vorgezogen. Natürlich kann auch ein antiker Biograph Episoden im Leben seines Helden gegenüber der chronologischen Reihenfolge umstellen, wenn der moralische und literarische Zweck seiner Darstellung dies erfordert. Auffällig ist aber, dass Mt die Umstellungen in einer Quelle vornimmt, die einen geschlossenen chronologisch-geographischen Ablauf darstellen will, und dass er dann selbst wieder einen solchen schafft, aber eben einen anderen als Mk.

3. Anders als der Jubilar nehme ich die Existenz einer schriftlichen Logienquelle Q an. Innerhalb von Mt 8-9 "exzerpiert" Mt Q fortlaufend, d.h. verändert die Reihenfolge von Q nicht. Einzige Ausnahme ist Mt 8,11f (= Lk 13,28f Q). Dieser Spruch steht aber in einer von Mt bereits 7,13f und 7,22f benutzten Q-Sequenz.

4. E. Schweizer, *Das Evangelium nach Matthäus*, NTD 2, Göttingen, 1973, 40 vermutet deshalb, Mt habe für Kap 4-9 eine Zusammenstellung von Jesus worten und -taten benutzt, "die sich auf die Auseinandersetzung mit Israel" konzentrierte.

5. Vgl. bes. H. J. Held, "Matthäus als Interpret der Wundergeschichten," in: G. Bornkamm—G. Barth—H. J. Held, *Ueberlieferung und Auslegung im Matthäusevangelium*, WMANT 1, Neukirchen, 1960, 158-182.

6. Das in 8,1-4 weggelassene Stück Mk 1,44-45a wird Mt 9,30f nachgetragen. Mt 9,28; 20,32 streicht das mk θάρσει (Mk 10,49); steht es darum vorweg in Mt 9,2.22? Mt 9,26 verwendet den weggelassenen Schluss von Mk 1,21-28. Mt 9,20.35 verwenden den später gekürzten Vers Mk 6,56. Vgl. auch u. Anm. 33.

7. Held a.a.O. (o. Anm. 5). K. Gatzweiler, "Les récits de miracle dans l'Évangile selon saint Matthieu," in: M. Didier (ed.), *L'Évangile selon Matthieu. Rédaction et Théologie*, BEThL 29, Gembloux, 1972, 220 urteilt zwölf Jahre später: "On ne peut que le féliciter".

8. Held a.a.O (O. Anm. 5) 236f.

9. Wenige Hinweise müssen genügen: M. Luther kann sagen, dass das eigentlich Bedeutsame am Wunder die Vergebung der Sünden und der Glaube ist (Promotionsdisputation F. Bachofen, 1543 = WA 39/II, 236; Predigt von 1535 = WA 41, 19). Im Anschluss an diese reformatorische Grundauffassung kann R. Bultmann geradezu die Zweideutigkeit von Wundern das theologisch eigentlich Wichtige nennen ("Zur Frage des Wunders," in: ders., *Glauben und Verstehen*, I, Tübingen, 1933, 227). Der in der Forschung dominierenden redaktionsgeschichtlichen Wunderdeutung entspricht ein grundsätzliches Desinteresse an der historischen Fragestellung. Die verbreitete terminologische Unterscheidung zwischen dem (in seiner Faktizität behaupteten) "Mirakel" und dem (geglaubten) "Wunder" dient dazu, beides tendenziell voneinander zu trennen: Die Annahme von Mirakeln ist eine Frage des Weltbildes, das Verstehen der Bedeutung von Wundern erschliesst den Glauben. So zeigen die Mirakel das eigentliche Wunder des durch Jesus geschenkten Glaubens nur an, damals wie heute mit "geringe(r) Ueberzeugungskraft" (G. Klein, "Neues Testament und Wunderglaube," in: ders., *Aergernisse*, München, 1970, 53).

10. Repräsentativ ist etwa J. Gnilka, *Das Matthäusevangelium*, I, HThK I/1, Freiburg 1986, 350: Die mt Wundergeschichten werden für verschiedene "Anliegen benutzt, die für die Adressaten des Evangeliums Aktualität besessen haben müssen". Es gibt also nicht "ein einziges durchgängiges Thema".

11. C. Burger, "Jesu Taten nach Mt 8 und 9," ZThK 70 (1973) 284-287; J. Kingsbury, "Observations on the 'Miracle Chapters' of Mt 8-9," CBQ 40 (1978) 562.

12. Die Abgrenzung zwischen dem zweiten und dritten Abschnitt liegt zwischen 9,1 und 9,2,

nicht, wie man aufgrund der Mk-Quelle oft annahm, zwischen 8,34 und 9,1: ἐμβὰς εἰς πλοῖον 9,1 bezieht sich auf 8,23 διεπέρασεν und ἦλθεν εἰς τὴν... auf 8,18 zurück. Dann ergeben sich drei Hauptabschnitte à je ca 37 Nestlezeilen und ein etwas kürzerer Schlussabschnitt à ca 34 Nestlezeilen.

13. Vgl. Burger a.a.O. (o. Anm. 11) 285.

14. Vgl. Kingsbury a.a.O. (o. Anm. 11) 568.

15. Burger a.a.O. (o. Anm. 11) 287.

16. G. Theissen, *Urchristliche Wundergeschichten*, SNT 8, Gütersloh, 1974, 210.

17. J. Schniewind, *Das Evangelium nach Matthäus*, NTD 2, Göttingen, [8]1956, 36. 106.

18. Sind 10, bzw 2x5 Wundergeschichten zu Zählen (so im Anschluss an E. Klostermann, *Das Matthäuservangelium*, HNT 4, Tübingen, 1927, 72 die meisten, oft verbunden mit einer Exodustypologie, vgl. PA 5,4f)? Oder sind 9 bzw. 3x3 Wundergeschichten zu zählen (so im Anschluss an W. C. Allen, *A Critical and Exegetical Commentary to the Gospel according to St. Matthew*, Edinburgh, [3]1912, 73.80.94 z.B. P. Gaechter, *Das Matthäusevangelium*, Innsbruck, 1963, 259)?

19. W. G. Thompson, "Reflections on the Composition of Mt 8,1-9, 34," *CBQ* 33 (1971) 365-388, bes. 387.

20. Vgl. unten S. 155.

21. Thompson, a.a.O. (o. Anm. 19) 387.

22. Das Fehlen des Dachaufgrabens (Mk 2,4) ist nicht einfach ein Lapsus des Mt. Er hat vielmehr bewusst auf das Haus als Szene von 9,2-8 verzichtet.

23. Ungeschickt is z.B. die Anwesenheit der Volksmenge (8,1) in Verbindung mit dem Schweigegebot (8,4), die Anwesenheit der staunenden Menschen (8,27) trotz des Fehlens der "anderen Boote" (Mk 4,36), die Erzählung der Hirten von "allem", "auch über die Besessenen" (8,33), obwohl ihre Herde weit weg war (8,30).

24. Burger a.a.O. (o. Anm. 11) 283f vergleicht Mt 8-9 mit einem Mosaik oder einem Collage. Ich ziehe das Bild des "Zopfes" vor, weil es die Zielgerichtetheit der mt Erzählung betont: Die mt Wundergeschichten sind nicht als Teile eines Bildes zu verstehen, sondern als Teile eines Ablaufes mit einem klaren Anfang und einem (davon verschiedenen) Ende.

25. Ich verstehe "Diskurs" im Sinne von S. Chatman, *Story and Discourse. Narrative Structure in Fiction and Film*, Ithaca, 1978, 19-27, als die konkrete Art und Weise, wie eine (geschehene) Geschichte erzählt wird. "Diskurs" ist für mich synonym mit "Erzählung". Inhalt der Erzählung ist die "Geschichte".

26. E. Gülich, "Ansätze zu einer kommunikationsorientierten Erzählanalyse (am Beispiel mündlicher und schriftlicher Erzähltexte)..." in : W. Haubrichs (ed.), *Erzählforschung*, I, LiLi Beiheft 4, Göttingen, 1976, 225.

27. Das Ende ist mit der "Ich-bin-bei-euch"-Zusage des erhöhten Gottessohns, der seine Jünger zu den Heiden schickt (28,16-20), erreicht. Im Prolog (1,1–4,22) gibt der allwissende Erzähler Mt seinen Lesern "Signale", die auf dieses Ende hinweisen, z.B. die Immanuelweissagung 1,24f oder die Anbetung des vom König Israels verfolgten Jesuskindes durch die Heiden (2,1-12). Diese Signale können eigentlich erst bei einer zweiten Lektüre des Evangeliums voll verstanden werden und haben zunächst die Funktion, den Leser auf die Tiefendimension der mt Geschichte hinzuweisen. Vgl. dazu Abschnitt III S. 155ff.

28. Gülich a.a.O. (o. Anm. 26) 250-252.

29. Orientierende Funktion hat der Prolog 1,1–4,22 nicht im üblichen Sinn einer Exposition, sondern darin, dass er den Lesern die Geschichte des Jesuskindes als Geschichte des Weges des vom König Israels verfolgten Messiaskindes ins Galiläa der Heiden schildert. Er eröffnet damit den Lesern die Tiefendimension der Geschichte. Orientierende Funktion hat die unmittelbar nach dem Anfang der eigentlichen Erzählung (4,23-25) stehende Bergpredigt in einem ganz anderen Sinn: Sie enthält die bleibend gültigen Gebote des Herrn (vgl. Mt 28,19).

30. Παράγω ἐκεῖθεν, ἀκολουθέω (Aor.), Betreten des Hauses.

31. So Held a.a.O. (o. Anm. 5) 170.236.

32. 9,33, vgl. 4,23: ἐν τῷ λαῷ; vgl. 8,10.

33. In beiden Fällen, 9,33 und 12,23 hat m.E. Mt die "neutrale" Reaktion des Volkes selbst formuliert, und zwar m.E. beidemale unter Verwendung von in 9,8 weggelassenen Teilen von Mk 2,12. Vgl. o. Anm. 6.

34. Luz a.a.O. (o. Anm. 1) 148.

35. Mit J. Kingsbury, *Matthew as Story*, Philadelphia, 1986, 3 bin ich einig, dass "the element of conflict is central to the plot of Matthew".

36. Zu dem in unserem Abschnitt zentralen Davidssohntitel vgl. bes. C. Burger, *Jesus als Davidssohn*, FRLANT 98, Göttingen, 1970, 72-106; D. C. Duling, "The Therapeutic Son of David: An Element in Matthew's Christological Apologetic," *NTS* 24 (1977/78) 392-410; J. D. Kingsbury, "The Title 'Son of David' in Matthew's Gospel," *JBL* 95 (1976) 591-602.

37. So deutet z.B. W. Grundmann, *Das Evangelium nach Matthäus*, ThHK I, Berlin (DDR), 1968, 257f; E. Schweizer a.a.O. (o. Anm. 4) 141 als Möglichkeit.

38. Der Zweite von Mt 8,21f ist wohl deshalb ein Jünger, weil seiner Bitte kein Nachfolgewort voranging (Lk 9,59 vermutlich gegenüber Q ergänzt).

39. Die Dekapolisstadt war als grosse hellenistische Stadt bekannt; Mt wusste sogar, dass ihr Gebiet (im Unterschied zu demjenigen von Gerasa!) bis an den See reichte.

40. Vgl. Luz a.a.O. (o. Anm. 1) 25.

41. Aehnlich in der letzten Rede: 24,1-3a.

42. Durch 13,10-17 wird sie vorbereitet.

43. Burger a.a.O. (o. Anm. 11) 287.

44. Zu den verschiedenen Definitionsmöglichkeiten eines "plot" vgl. A. Culpepper, *The Anatomy of the Fourth Gospel. A Study in Literary Design*, Philadelphia, 1983, 79f.

45. Zum selektiven Charakter antiker Biographien vgl. C. H. Talbert, *What is a Gospel?*, Philadelphia, 1977, 17; P. Shuler, *A Genre for the Gospels*, Philadelphia, 1982, bes. 98f (S. weist auf Tacitus, Agricola, eine dem historischen Ablauf forgende Biographie. Aber diese "Biographie" des a) Römers und b) Historikers Tacitus ist wohl gerade kein typisches Beispiel des genus Biographie). Nach K. Berger, *Hellenistische Gattungen und Neues Testament*, ANRW 25/II, Berlin, 1984, 1239f. berichten bei Biographien nur der Anfang und der Schluss chronologisch. Die übrigen Teile erheben auch keinen Anspruch auf eine chronologische Abfolge.

46. Es geht hier nicht um die Tiefenstruktur im Sinne einer Transformations-Grammatik, sondern um eine "zweite Ebene" des Sinns der Jesuserzählung, in der diese ihre eigene Vergangenheit in Richtung auf den Leser überschreitet.

47. S. J. Schmidt, *Texttheorie. Probleme einer Linguistik der sprachlichen Kommunikation*, UTB 202, München, 1973, 77 versteht "Referenz" als "Anweisung von Textkonstituenten an Kommunikationspartner" und Pragmatik nicht als Teilgebiet der Texttheorie, sondern als Texttheorie überhaupt. Zur pragmatischen Erzählanalyse vgl. auch Gülich a.a.O. (o. Anm. 26).

48. Andere Erkennungsmerkmale dieser Tiefenstruktur sind die "Signale" besonders im Prolog (vgl. Luz a.a.O. [o. Anm. 1] 23), die Durchbrechung der vergangenen Zeitebene durch Weissagungen, die Ueberlagerung der vergangenen Zeitebene durch Aktualisierung traditioneller Logien, die mit der Sprache der Leser identische Sprache Jesu und vor allem die verschiedene Zeitebenen umspannende Christologie des "Gott-mit-uns".

49. Diese Skizze setzt selbstverständlich viele exegetische Entscheidungen voraus, die nicht hier, sondern erst im Kommentar (Bd II, vgl. o. Anm. 1) begründet werden können.

50. Vgl. o. Anm. 17. Ebd 107 gibt Schniewind aber bereits eine beachtenswerte Skizze einer *Erzählung* vom Messias der Tat.

51. Das Zitat aus Hos 6,6 in Mt 9,13 ist m.E. christologisch und nur indirekt paränetisch gemeint. Es interpretiert Jesu Verhalten gegenüber den Zöllnern und—wie 9,27 verdeutlicht— seine Heilungen überhaupt. Anders akzentuiert Gnilka a.a.O. (o. Anm. 10) 333.

52. Vgl. Culpepper a.a.O. (o. Anm. 44) 30f.

53. Vgl. 8,29. Πρὸ καιροῦ kann allerdings nicht sicher so gedeutet werden; der Ausdruck kann auch eine umgangssprachliche Wendung im Sinne von "vorzeitig" sein, vgl. Liddell-Scott s.v. καιρός III 1b.

54. Vgl. Luz a.a.O. (o. Anm. 1) 34.

55. Diese Eigenart mt Erzählweise setzt sich in den folgenden Kapiteln fort: Ich erwähne nur das Ineinander von vergangener Aussendungssituation und gegenwärtiger Gemeindewirklichkeit in Mt 10, den als Weissagung der Auferstehung und der Heidenmission zu lesenden Schluss des Erfülungszitates 12,20c.21, die Weissagungen 12,40-42 etc.

56. Kingsbury a.a.O. (o, Anm. 35) 55. Kingsbury ist (immer noch?) an der Bedeutung und

Rangordnung christologischer Titel interessiert. M.E. müsste dieses Interesse der Frage nach dem Fluss und dem Ziel der Erzählung konsequent untergeordnet werden.

57. Mt 2,23. Ναζωραῖος ist zugleich Selbstbezeichnung der syrischen Gemeinde des Mt, vgl. Luz a.a.O. (o. Anm. 1) 133. So verbindet 2,23 den Sohn Gottes mit den Lesern des Mt und das nächste Erfüllungszitat Mt 4,15f das Ziel des Weges Jesu im Prolog mit der künftigen Aufgabe der mt Gemeinde, der Heidenmission.

58. Vom "Transparenten" spricht bereits K. Barth, KD IV/2, 234 im Anschluss an Heitmüller. Ausgezeichnet formuliert er ebd. 242: Die Wundergeschichten sind, "indem Jesus in den von ihnen berichteten Handlungen Geschichte macht, faktisch zugleich deren Gleichnisse".

59. Vgl. W. Schrage, Art. τυφλός κτλ., ThWNT VIII 276, 4-278,6; 280, 26-281, 34.

60. Vgl. dazu zuletzt Gnilka a.a.O. (o. Anm. 10) 317-319.

61. Psalmensprache! Vgl. Luz a.a.O. (o. Anm. 1) 60.

62. 9,18 geht es um die Auferweckung des bereits toten Mädchens (diff. Mk); 9,25 werden sämtliche mk Einzelheiten, die klar machen, dass es bei dieser Auferweckung um eine Rückkehr ins bisherige Leben geht (das Umhergehen und das Essen), gestrichen.

63. Vgl. E. Schweizer, Das Evangelium nach Markus, NTD 1, Göttingen, [14]1975, 87f. 121.

64. J. Gnilka, Das Evangelium nach Markus, EKK II/1, Neukirchen-Zürich, 1978, 197.

65. Beispiel: Die Identifikation mit dem Synagogenvorsteher Jairos wird der mt Gemeinde, die den Bruch mit der Synagoge erlebt hat, nicht leicht gefallen sein, darum das unspezifische ἄρχων 9,18.

66. Daraus ergibt sich allerdings eine grundsätzliche Nähe des Sinns mt Wundergeschichten zu dem, was später die kirchliche allegorische Auslegung versuchte. Dort soll ja meistens nicht der wörtliche Schriftsinn durch den geistlichen verdrängt werden. Vielmehr ist der geistliche Schriftsinn ein Versuch, verschiedene Aspekte des Gegenwartssinns von Texten (z.B. moralisch oder heilsgeschichtlich) zu erfassen. Gerade das unverbundene Nebeneinander mehrerer Deutungsdimensionen entspricht dem eigenen mt Wunderverständnis.

67. Im Artikel, "Geschichte/Geschichtsschreibung/Geschichtsphilosophie IV. Neues Testament", TRE 12 (1984) sprach ich von "inclusive story" (597f). "Inklusive Erzählung" ist formal richtiger, auch wenn für Mt (und Mk) klar ist, dass es die Geschichte Jesu selbst ist, die die gegenwärtige Existenz einschliesst. Mt unterscheidet zwischen der Gestalt der ihm vorgegebenen Geschichte und der seines Diskurses in bemerkenswerter Weise nicht.

68. Das ist meine wichtigste Frage an Kingsburys (o. Anm. 35) Entwurf, der m.E. die besondere Art des Leserbezugs des Mt.Ev. weithin ausklammert und darum an der Oberfläche des mt Diskurses bleibt.

69. Die alttestamentlichen Geschichtsentwürfe, die in verschiedener Weise eine Identifikation des Lesers mit seiner Grundgeschichte am Sinai voraussetzen (vgl. nur z.B. den geschichtlichen Rahmen des Dtn!), kommen den Evv. besonders nahe.

70. F. Martinez-Bonati. "Erzählungsstruktur und ontologische Schichtenlehre", in: Haubrichs a.a.O. (o. Anm. 26) 175-183.

71. Schmidt a.a.O. (o. Anm. 46) 150: "Ein Text ist jeder geäusserte sprachliche Bestandteil eines Kommunikationsaktes in einem kommunikativen Handlungsspiel, der thematisch orientiert ist und eine erkennbare kommunikative Funktion erfüllt, d.h. ein erkennbares Illokutionspotential realisiert".

John, the Synoptics, and the Canonical Approach to Exegesis

D. Moody Smith

Obviously, John's relationship to the synoptic Gospels is an important issue, with theological as well as literary-historical implications, because they all stand in the same canon of Christian scripture. What their relationship might be if they did not is inconceivable, so closely is their history and interpretation related to their belonging to the New Testament. The historical-critical method of interpretation does not, however, seek to understand the Gospel of John in relation to the synoptics in the New Testament canon. Rather, historical criticism concentrates upon John, or upon any New Testament book, with a view to understanding it in its own right, that is, with respect to its original setting, purpose, and meaning. On these terms the question of John and the synoptics is the question of their historic, literary relationship at the point of origin. Usually this question is cast in terms of whether the Fourth Evangelist knew the other Gospels, since it would be exceedingly difficult to understand any of the synoptics as presupposing, much less derived from the Gospel of John.

The traditional answer to the question of their originative relationship, which was posed as early as the second century, is that John knew and approved of the other gospels, and presumed knowledge of them as he wrote. Thus he wrote to supplement, mildly correct, or interpret the others. Already Origen saw the difficulty of reconciling the differences between John and the synoptics on the historical level; their accounts of Jesus' ministry cannot be made historically consistent and coherent. Therefore, he proposed a reconciliation between John and the synoptics at another hermeneutical level.[1] Thus the justification of Origen's spiritual or allegorical exegesis. In fact, Origen seemed to delight in showing their irreconcilable differences precisely because he wanted to make the hermeneutical move to another level or mode of interpretation. By and large, however, traditional exegesis has throughout most of Christian history sought to minimize the differences between John and the synoptics. Some exegesis continues along this line, even while working on the basis of historical-critical assumptions. This century has, of course, also seen the alternative positions arise as major options: either John rejected the synoptic Gospels and desired to replace them with his own Gospel, or he did not know them. Such views are only conceivable on the basis of historical-critical presuppositions, that is, on the assumption that John is to be interpreted, and its relation to the synoptics is to be understood, in relation to its original context, purpose, and assumptions.

Precisely this perspective in interpretation has been sharply rejected as the starting point of exegesis by some recent critics, who have applied developments in literary criticism to the Fourth Gospel or have insisted that John, like all New Testament writings should be interpreted first of all in its canonical context. It is to this latter view, represented preeminently by Brevard S. Childs that we turn in this essay. In his *The New Testament as Canon: An Introduction,* Childs has specific points to make about the Gospel of John.[2] More basic, however, is his general perspective, which when applied to John, or any New Testament book, has rather far-reaching implications.

For Childs historical criticism cannot be the final arbiter of the meaning of a New Testament writing or text; nor does it afford the initial perspective upon the meaning and shape of a text.[3] In other words, the historical critic asking about a text's origin, historical setting, purpose, and meaning is permitted to have neither the first nor the last word in interpretation. "Historical criticism is an indispensable teacher," writes Childs.[4] But it is a teacher, not judge and jury. Childs does not propose to eliminate traditional historical-critical approaches from the broader task of interpretation, but resists turning over to the historical critic as such the right to say once and for all what a text may mean. To invoke Stendahl's distinction, the historical critic may say what a text meant, but that is not the same as what it means as it now stands in the Christian canon of scripture. But Childs—in his role as churchly, canonical interpreter—will not even agree to allow the historial critic first to say what the text meant, and on that basis take up the further task of stating its theological or canonical meaning.[5] Rather, the canonical shape of the New Testament is the datum with which interpretation *begins*.

I. Childs on the Fourth Gospel

Obviously, such a position and perspective would become extremely important in the interpretation of the Fourth Gospel as part of the Christian canon of scripture. Interestingly enough, in his chapter on the Gospel of John, Childs concentrates on that Gospel itself, and does not deal extensively with the general question of its relation to the synoptics or its position in the canon, both of which could have interesting and important implications for interpretation. He wants to insist primarily upon the final, canonical shape of John, including chapter 21 and any other hypothetical later redactional additions, as the proper object of canonical exegesis. Thus his program is, for example, dramatically opposed to that of Rudolf Bultmann, who takes as the object of exegesis the Gospel of John as he has restored it, i.e., the Gospel in its original order, freed from its later redactional framing or corruption.[6] (Bultmann did not use such pejorative terms, but that is what his theory of redactional restoration comes to.) Childs' program is more in line with the literary-critical work of Alan Culpepper, or the redactional standpoint of Hartwig Thyen, who wants to view the final redactor as the evangelist and to interpret the entire Gospel from his perspective.[7] Yet it is based neither on literary-critical nor on historical-critical grounds, but on the theological and traditional status of the canon as a given for Christian exegesis and interpretation.

While Childs might be interested in John's historical relationship to the synoptic Gospels, and indeed seems to favor John's independence,[8] his own approach is not governed by his position on this question. On his terms, it could not be, for that would be tantamount to handing over the interpretive task to the historical critic, or, to put it another way, allowing the determination of a historical setting or relationship to guide the course of Christian exegesis. Was John dependent on the synoptics? Then John should be read in light of them. Was John intended to displace the synoptics? Then one must choose between them. Was John written in ignorance of the other Gospels? Then they must not be allowed to enter into the exegesis of it. Actually, this final question or position comes closer to representing Childs' own view than the others, but he would not finally embrace it. John after all now finds a place in the canon alongside the other three. Childs rightly calls for more attention to the canonical unity of the four Gospels.[9] Yet each has its integrity. "No one Gospel is made the hermeneutical key, as would have happened had John's Gospel been contructed into an overarching framework and the three synoptics inserted into its story."[10] Interestingly enough, however, when he deals with the John the Baptist accounts in his canonical harmony of the Gospels, Childs does allow the Fourth Gospel to become the key to the others in a way we would not have anticipated given this earlier general statement. In this connection he remarks that "the Fourth Gospel becomes the key to the new hermeneutical function of the fourfold collection," and goes on to "distinguish between the shape of the Fourth Gospel as a literary composition with a discrete integrity and its function within the canonical collection."[11] Focus upon the latter is primary in exegesis.

Thus the canonical approach to the Gospels would not allow a position on the historical relationship of John to the synoptics, whether positive or negative, to assume a determinative role in exegesis. On Childs' terms, the question of John and the synoptics as a historical question of literary and traditional relationships may be interesting, informative, and enriching for exegesis. But it is not the exegetical key, the *sine qua non*, for the interpretation of the Fourth Gospel. The canonical approach to the Gospel must not begin there. To begin there would, in fact, be to surrender to the historical critic the first, and eventually the last, word. Moreover, it would make what could finally be no more than a hypothesis, a hypothetical construct about origins with accompanying implications for setting and purpose, determinative for exegesis. That is exactly what Childs will on no account allow. Thus he sharply rejects Barnabas Lindars's claim that "the effort to get behind the Fourth Gospel to its tradition and sources is not simply a literary-critical game, but an inescapable task in the process of discovering the real meaning" of the Gospel.[12] Whether behind the Fourth Gospel lie the synoptics or other traditional sources, be they oral or written, is an interesting question, but one that cannot finally be decisive in interpretation. Canonical John stands on its own, but it stands in relation to the other Gospels.

Not surprisingly then, Childs names Hoskyns as posing the crucial hermeneutical question and quotes a decisive statement from his commentary:

> The important question is not whether the Fourth Gospel depends upon oral tradition, or upon written documents, or upon both, but whether it is, or is not, a work existing in its own right, and whether it is or is not to be interpreted independently and by itself.[13]

Actually, in the extant, posthumously published text of his commentary, Hoskyns does not clearly espouse John's historical and literary independence of the synoptics, but presupposes that the evangelist knew their tradition in something like the form encountered in them.[14] At the same time he stresses the distinct and in that sense independent theological profile of the Gospel. It is apparently on this latter point of emphasis that Childs so thoroughly agrees with him. When Childs states that "the primary issue turns on the function of the witness to the earthly life of Jesus within the Fourth Gospel,"[15] he is indeed close to Hoskyns. At the same time, the question of the relationship to the synoptics (or to the substance of the specific witnesses), which Hoskyns dealt with at the level of historical criticism, has been removed by Childs in principle to the level of canonical relationship.

In an interesting way Childs' position on the Fourth Gospel, which he can only outline in the context of a general introduction, is analogous to both Culpepper's and Windisch's. The latter are, of course, pursuing different questions and cannot simply be lumped together. Yet their view of the relation of John to the synoptics has striking points of similarity. For both John's Gospel is, on the one hand, independent, in that it is a full and adequate account which is not intended to play a supplementary role and does not require supplementation. On the other, it is clear for both that John presumes knowledge we have from the synoptics. Culpepper characterizes the Johannine narrative as reliable and sufficient, while at the same time noticing that the implied reader is presumed to know many of the major figures and events of the story already.[16] For example, in the Johannine Temple Cleansing it becomes apparent that the implied reader knows that Jesus has risen from the dead (as any Christian would). Windisch speaks of the Gospel of John as a commentary without text or a commentary intended to displace the text.[17] Two things are implied: John's independence of the synoptics, but at the same time his knowledge—and the reader's presumed knowledge—of personages and matters known to us from the synoptic Gospels. Windisch, of course, believes John's knowledge of them came from the synoptics as well and that he intended to displace the other Gospels in the church's use. Culpepper leaves this matter open. With Childs, John's independence is fundamental, although the question of whether or not he used the synoptics is finally not crucial. Initially, with Childs, as with Culpepper and Windisch, knowledge of the synoptics does not seem necessary for understanding and interpreting the Fourth Gospel, which is an independent narrative. Yet in each case, as also with Hoskyns, John is perceived as presupposing the reader's knowledge of either the canonical Gospels or their equivalent tradition. With Windisch and Hoskyns this is a more or less traditional historical-critical judgment. With Culpepper we are in the arena of literary criticism; with Childs canonical criticism. But is there in any case a tension between the affirmation of independence and John's actual relation to the synoptics? If so, this tension, confirmed from different perspectives, may say something about the character of the Fourth Gospel.

II. John's Canonicity in Historical Perspective

There are several other matters related to John's canonical status which, although not at the center of Childs' attention, may be of importance for the issues he is pursuing. These have to do with the history and shape of the Gospel canon, and particularly with John's role in that historical development and shaping process. The remainder of this essay will be devoted, first, to aspects of John's early canonical history that are related to its authority in the church, and then to the matter of the reciprocal roles of John and the synoptics, particularly Matthew, in canonical interpretation. Perhaps even their relative positions say something about how they may be understood. In this connection some interesting implications for the question of John and the synoptics—now once again much discussed—may emerge.

The history of the development of the canon is touched on rather briefly by Childs. There is a chapter on "The Canon as an Historical and Theological Problem," but the canonical approach to exegesis is not based upon a particular understanding of the history and development of the canon. In a discussion of the canonical place and role of the Book of Acts Childs indicates he does not accept the revisionist view of the formation of the canon identified with Sundberg and others, which rejects the once generally held position that the core of the New Testament canon had been established by the end of the second century.[18] Nevertheless, the validity of the canonical approach is not tied to any historical view of the origin and development of the canon. In particular, it does not depend upon the relatively early emergence of the canon as distinctively Christian scripture. More specifically, the canonical status or validity of the Fourth Gospel is not related to the process of its becoming a part of the four-Gospel canon.

Childs chides Westcott, Lightfoot, Zahn, and Lagrange for running in the face of the canonical shaping of the Gospel, in which the author's anonymity is preserved behind the veil of the Beloved Disciple, when they seek to defend Johannine authorship. John the son of Zebedee is never mentioned as the author in the Gospel itself (in fact, never mentioned by name at all), and that is certainly not a matter of chance. Of course, the great conservative scholars were in all probability right in thinking that the Fourth Gospel became a part of the developing canon toward the end of the second century only as it was believed to be the work of that apostle. If so, the canonical process, John's becoming a part of the canon, was in fact intimately related to the determination of authorship. Childs successfully divorces the canonical status of John from the question of specifically Johannine authorship on the authority and at the level of the Fourth Gospel itself. Yet the Gospel's canonicity as an historical process and fact was related to the specific claim of authorship (the Johannine) that has become the church's tradition. And as Childs frequently reiterates, the canonical approach is intimately related to its hearing, i.e., receiving, of these writings. It was heard and received as John's Gospel.

Of course, the question of John and the synoptics is related to the formation of the canon too, for a major part of the resistance to John in the early church was grounded in its unaccountable divergences from the other Gospels that were already playing an authoritative role. John comes in alongside the other three as the work of an apostolic figure of peerless authority and as the Gospel intended to supplement and interpret them. Käsemann pungently and correctly points out that in canonizing John the church domesticated it by divorcing it from its original setting and purpose.[19] For Childs, the questions of canonical authority, as well as canonical interpretation, do not hinge upon reconstructions of historical development or upon the issues which probably played such a large role in the actual unfolding of that development, such as apostolic authorship. Present canonical shape, not reconstructions of the shaping process behind it, is the beginning point and focus of the canonical approach. Nevertheless, these simple observations about the ways in which certain historical and literary questions (authorship and relation to the synoptics) have played a role in John's gaining canonical status and authority are at least worth bearing in mind. If the canonical approach brackets them out, as well it may, one must recognize that the basis for canonical authority is now somewhat different from what it was in antiquity.

III. The Canonical Balance of Matthew and John

The actual shape of the Gospel canon as it confronts us in the New Testament is not central to Child's approach and does not command the center of his attention. He rightly observes that the order of the Gospels has varied historically in canonical lists and manuscripts, although in time the present universally accepted order became firmly established. Because of the flexibility in the process, one should not attach too great importance to the order of the Gospels. Yet the canonical order of the Gospels, like the canonical shape of the individual books makes a certain sense. It seems to bespeak an intention. To speak of "intention" in this regard is uncertain or question begging. Whose intention? How conscious was it? We cannot say. Childs is wary of ascribing too much by way of conscious intention to the redactors of books, and wants instead to speak of their canonical shaping in the church. Moreover, he is aware of the obvious analogy with the canon as a whole. One does not want to ascribe too much to conscious intention in the church's preservation, development, and ordering of the Gospel canon.[20] At the same time the character of the final product, including the final order, projects a kind of intention that can scarcely be ignored.

The positions of Mark and Luke do not appear to be immediately significant or meaningful, yet one could imagine that Mark, if the earliest Gospel, was displaced from its position at the head of the canon by Matthew, which incorporates ninety percent of Mark and was very likely intended to replace it.[21] Luke, it might be argued, was once intended to be followed immediately by Acts, at least by the author, but they were separated when John was accepted into the canon. All this is plausible enough, but scarcely rises above the level of informed speculation, or at best logical inference from the respective texts.

Turning to Matthew, however, several obvious but nevertheless substantial, and I think more significant, observations may be made. Matthew's Gospel stands at the beginning of the New Testament, where it makes meaningful connections forward and backward. Just the fact that Matthew begins with a genealogy, a well-known and ancient Old Testament genre seems to link the new with the old in characteristic ways. (We should remember, of course, that neither the Masoretic text nor the Septuagint ends with the minor prophets, and therefore with Malachi.) The genealogy itself puts Jesus of Nazareth into the Davidic royal line. (Contrast Luke, in which Jesus is a son of David, but otherwise not of the kingly line.) Thus the narrative not only of Matthew, but of the entire New Testament, is linked to Israel's *Heilsgeschichte*, to the drama of God's calling forth and dealing with a people. This is no less important because it is obvious. The birth of Jesus is then described, principally from the standpoint of Joseph, the father, who accedes to God's will in unusual circumstances in order that all righteousness may be fulfilled. The theme of the fulfilling of righteousness then leads like a red thread into the heart of the Gospel According to Matthew. John baptizes Jesus in order that all righteousness may be fulfilled. That Matthew's emphasis on righteousness reaches a high point in the Sermon on the Mount scarcely requires demonstration: "Unless your righteousness exceeds that of the scribes and Pharisees, you shall by no means enter into the kingdom of heaven" (5:20).

Quite plainly the fact that Jesus begins his ministry by delivering the Sermon on the Mount is typical of what we might call the ethical interests of Matthew. It is both legitimate and important to identify those interests. At the same time, that Jesus in his first public appearance announces God's blessedness upon the poor in spirit, those who mourn, the meek, and those who hunger and thirst after righteousness; that he says "You have heard it said to the people of old . . . but I say to you"; that he tells a parable to exhort his followers to build their lives upon his words; all this is significant not just for the interpretation of Matthew, but for the interpretation of the New Testament, the Christian Bible, and Christianity itself. Jesus is defining the righteousness of God. Without overlooking the importance of Christology in Matthew—Jesus is God with us (1:23)—its presentation of Jesus establishes at the beginning of the New Testament the importance of the character of Jesus Christ. He not only fulfills messianic prophecy and expectation, he defines, and redefines, who the Messiah is. That this definition goes on in very close conversation and agreement with the Old Testament and Judaism again makes an important statement. By virtue of Matthew's position this becomes a statement not only of and about Matthew, but about the nature of New Testament Christianity.

One could go on at length, but two further instances of the pivotal role of events in Matthew, which take on added significance because it is the first Gospel, will suffice. Only in Matthew's apocalyptic discourse does Jesus describe the last judgment and the standards according to which it will take place (25:31-46). Fundamental is each believer's relationship to Jesus. (That believers come under eschatological judgment is not to be minimized.) This relationship is not defined so much in terms of faith, certainly not faith as belief, as in terms of obedience. That is, the obedience that unknowingly serves Jesus himself by serving his little ones. Again, in Matthew's account of the risen Jesus' appearance to his disciples on the mountain in Galilee Jesus formally commissions them for their mission, which culminates in the injunction about "teaching them to observe all that I have commanded you; and lo, I am with you always, to the close of the age." Once again the emphasis on Jesus' teaching or word; and now also the promise of his presence. The reader of the New Testament is put on notice that the Jesus about whom he has been informed is not a figure out of the past, but the living and reigning Lord. Doubtless the Christian reader for whom the Gospel was originally intended would have been well aware of this. Nevertheless, whoever picks up the New Testament and reads it through is at the beginning apprised of with what and whom it has to do.

Perhaps enough has been said about Matthew to allow us to turn to John and put it into clearer focus by comparing and contrasting the two. It is obvious, but nonetheless significant and true, that as Matthew properly opens the Gospel canon (and the New Testament) John closes it. Matthew makes entirely clear that the historical and theological roots of the gospel of Jesus Christ lie in Israel, and what kind of Messiah he is.

As Matthew places Jesus in *Heilsgeschichte,* John places him in creation and cosmic history. Although both Gospels reflect hostility between emerging Christianity and its parent religion, Matthew remains conceptually, theologically, closer to Judaism.[22] The message of the opening chapters of Matthew is that the relationship and continuity are close. This impression is due not a little to the genealogy and to the Old Testament formula quotations which punctuate the birth narrative. In some contrast, John's opening reference to Jewish history is sharply negative: "He came to his own home, and his own people did not receive him" (1:11). Despite arguments to the contrary (Bultmann, et al.), that statement is best understood as a reference to Jesus' own nation. With them are contrasted those who believe in his name (1:12), who are defined by that faith and not by human origin. The incarnation and its effects (1:14-18) are then described as events and possibilities available universally. The formula Old Testament quotations, which are encountered immediately in Matthew, with one or two exceptions (6:31; 7:42; cf. 10:34) do not appear in John until the passion narrative and related episodes (12:14-15, 38, 39-40; 13:18; 19:24, 28, 36, 37). Almost certainly their appearance there is to be traced to their existence in the pre-Gospel tradition. In those portions of John which stem from the evangelist, Abraham, Moses, and other heroes of Israel tend to be presented as antitypes; and in chap. 8 descendants of Abraham (8:37) are said to be children of the devil (v 44), not of God (vv 42, 47). As Martyn observes, John does not choose to enter into midrashic debate or discussion with Jewish opponents.[23] Instead, he poses the radical alternative of faith in Jesus as the one whom God has sent. Precisely that possibility is not the culmination of midrashic debate; it is something that only God can give. In this and related ways John establishes not an absolute contradiction, but a significant and creative tension with Matthew. Matthew stands at the beginning of the Gospel canon relating Jesus positively to the Old Testament, and thus to Jewish expectations. John stands at the end, not denying that Jesus is the fulfillment of those expectations, but quite explicitly affirming that he is more than this and setting at the center of his portrayal and emphasizing Jewish rejection of him.

It would be wrong to portray the difference between Matthew and John in terms of a low christology in one and a high christology in the other. Matthew does not have a low christology.[24] He who is "God with us" and who receives "all authority in heaven and on earth" is something more than a young and fearless prophet of ancient Galilee. (Nor should one minimize the obvious tension between Matthew and Judaism.)

But Matthew differs decisively from John in the way in which christology is filled out or explained. Matthew draws deeply upon the Jesus tradition as it is amply reflected elsewhere in the New Testament, and especially upon the tradition of Jesus' logia. It is the teaching Jesus, who proclaims God's rule and will for all humankind, but particularly for his followers, who is messiah and Son of God. Moreover, Jesus' teaching is law, not his law, but the definitive expression and interpretation of Torah. John, on the other hand, virtually ignores this logia tradition and puts the Jewish law in an ambiguous light. As is well-known, there are no parables, no pronouncement stories, no ethical discourses, and no announcements of the imminent in-breaking of God's rule in John. The Fourth Evangelist gives force to Jesus' claim of messiahship and divine sonship in a different way. He has Jesus assert and argue his own case. Thus, as is frequently observed, the Jesus of the Fourth Gospel talks christology explicitly. In Matthew, as in the other synoptic Gospels, christology is very much present, but as the overall framework into which a tradition which obviously arose in Jewish Palestine during Jesus' ministry is fitted. Jesus appealed to Judaism, his fellow Jews, by positive reference to their rich scriptures, traditions, and history. Thus, paradoxically, Matthew's representation of that appeal, which when put alongside John can be seen to be generally true historically, has a more than parochial or ethnic interest. For Judaism, with its national, juridical, and personal, individual dimensions is paradigmatic of human interests and necessities.

John goes another way entirely. In his narrative framework there are striking similarities to Matthew and to the synoptics generally: the encounter with the Baptist, the Feeding of Five Thousand and other incidents about the Sea of Galilee, the events of the Passion. The episodes which John shares with Mark, for example, he has for the most part in the same order. It is primarily John's representation of the speech of Jesus, and secondarily of his healing ministry, that is so different. In the one case Jesus speaks only of himself before the public (and later on before his disciples); in the other his very acts of healing are symbolic not of God's kingdom but of his divine sonship. Through word and deed Jesus points to himself as king and seeks to establish the claim through argument, sometimes exegetical (6:31; 10:34), and demonstration of unheard of supernatural power. The reader either accedes to the claims or is deeply offended. There is almost no way to appreciate what Jesus says and does apart from his imperious claim, for in a real sense that is all Jesus presents. Already within the Gospel of John the Jews, i.e., Jesus' or the church's opponents, take offence, and thus Jewish rejection of Christian claims about Jesus is reflected.

Standing at the beginning of the canon, Matthew represents continuity with, affirmation of, and openness to Jewish tradition, despite clear indications of significant hostility and tension with Judaism (e.g., Matt. 27:25). At the end of the Gospel canon John seems to view these positive relations as mainly terminated (although even, and only, in John we have Nicodemus, the Pharisee and *archōn* of the Jews, who, in my judgment, is still open to and inclined to accept Jesus). Certainly for John allegiance to Jesus means the termination of relations with the synagogue and with Judaism. Discipleship is thus negatively as well as positively conceived. In fact, to say that in John discipleship is conceived positively as believing in Jesus' claims and negatively as separation form the Jewish community may be an oversimplification, but is not an exaggeration. The basis for discipleship is theological belief, dogma, social ostracization and a new community identity. Jesus' teaching about love is not unimportant, but applies primarily, if not only, within the community of his disciples and in any case is not the basis of his challenge to believe in him.

IV. Affinities between John and Paul

At this point there is a clear similarity or parallel between John and Paul, neither of whom presents us with a portrayal of Jesus drawn from the tradition of his words, his teaching. To use the common theological parlance, which in this case is meaningful and appropriate, for John as for Paul Jesus Christ is the eschatological event, the appearance in history of God's salvation and judgment. In both cases faith in Jesus is initially contentless apart from the acknowledgement that in him, or in the event of his crucifixion, God has acted or spoken, revealed himself, decisively in favor of humankind. That is, taken by themselves, Paul and John do not provide a basis in life, history, or tradition for the claim made by Jesus. Thus Bultmann could say—while remaining true to his understanding of Pauline or Johannine theology—that Jesus was not the eschatological or salvation event because he was the Christ; rather he was (understood as) the Christ because he was (experienced or confessed as) the eschatological or salvation event.[25] In other words, for both Paul and John taken alone (or together) the eschatological event requires no traditional or historical accreditation as such. Indeed, the eschatological event cannot tolerate such accreditation, because so to accredit it would be to violate the character of revelation, particularly revelation in Christ, which is *eo ipso* self-authenticating. (This is what is meant by the statement that Jesus is not the eschatological or revelatory event because he is the Christ, he is the Christ because he is—or is the occasion of—that event.)

Probably it is significant, and even crucial, that Bultmann in his work generally, but particularly the *Theology of the New Testament*,[26] lifts Paul and John out from the canon of the New Testament and isolates them as the bearers of this theological insight. In his exegesis of the Pauline letters Bultmann correctly declines to see Paul as presupposing the synoptic Gospels, which did not then exist, and does not see their tradition, which Paul knew in some small part, as important for his kerygma and theology. (The degree to which Paul knew that tradition is still a matter of debate, with Bultmann, or his disciples, and some other scholars minimizing it.) By the same token John is viewed exegetically as independent of the synoptic Gospels and presupposing other traditions and sources. In this he may be correct. Against Windisch, Bultmann does not believe that John intended to displace the synoptics, in part because it is doubtful that he knew them; in part because he cannot find evidence that John was negatively disposed toward antecedent tradition.[27] Nevertheless, in this major landmark of New Testament theology, the twin peaks of theological development within the New Testament are seen as relatively independent of the synoptic tradition, which was at most only partially or fragmentarily known to them. Furthermore, theologically relevant interpretation of Paul and John takes them out of the canon, so to speak. We hear them not as a chorus, not even as a duet, but as successive soloists singing the same basic aria, albeit in different keys. Without denigrating the position or insights of Bultmann, it is almost certainly correct and appropriate to observe that we have here a classic instance of the pressing to a logical conclusion of Luther's criterion of what *preaches* Christ as an hermeneutical key. This criterion has been correlated with a particular existentialist anthropology in a way that has now become familiar. Moreover, it is not surprising that Paul and John should emerge as the two chief exponents or representatives, for at least on Bultmann's terms they are the leading New Testament proponents of Jesus as the eschatological Christ.

The relative isolation of Paul and John from the New Testament canon, and the *de facto* minimizing of canon as a vehicle of authority is, of course, a telling move. (The synoptic Gospels as well as the other and general epistles become in Bultmann's *Theology* a part of the development toward that same early catholicism that later produced the New Testament itself.) The canon, if anything, tends to muffle their highest or sharpest notes, for a canonical reading of John or Paul would require that they be attended to among a broader chorus of voices. The canon has a "both/and" effect, neutralizing theological extremes. Childs has shown quite clearly and well how the framing of the uncontested, genuine Pauline letters with Acts on the one side and the deutero-Pauline letters, particularly the pastorals, on the other has produced a canonical Paul, who stands in a positive relation to, but is not identical with, the historical Paul.

V. The Effect of Canonicity upon the Reading of the Fourth Gospel

Now if one considers the Gospel of John within the canon, especially the Gospel canon, there is a similar effect. That is, there emerges a canonical John. Käsemann, with his typical forcefulness and disdain of compromise, has accurately and acutely described how John was accepted in the church when it was read in light of other, more moderate, views, and its sharp edges were honed down.[28] Of course, the inclusion of the Gospel of John with the other three was well calculated to have precisely this effect. It need not, however, be stated in negative terms, as if the theological value or revelatory significance of John lay solely in its uncompromising and distinctive individuality and brilliance. I would be inclined to argue that John makes sense best, and makes proper theological sense, only when it is viewed in light of the synoptic Gospels. It is the Jesus who presents himself in Matthew, Mark, and Luke who makes intelligible—and I would say legitimizes—the Johannine Jesus.

The canonical status of John, if taken seriously, considerably mitigates the question of John's relationship to the synoptics. If one assumes that John's intended relationship to the synoptic Gospels is crucial for understanding and appropriating the theological message of the Fourth Gospel, a great deal may seem to be at stake in arguing that Windisch, or Gardner-Smith for that matter, was mistaken. John did not intend to displace the synoptics, nor did he write without cognizance of them. On these terms the theological importance of the traditional, churchly or critical position is apparent. John wrote with the synoptics in view and intended to supplement and interpret what he already knew and accepted (Muratorian Fragment, Eusebius). Yet the difficulties of that traditional position are real, as we have already seen. It is still defensible, but certainly not unimpeachable.

On the other hand, if the canonical status and position of John are assumed as significant data to be reckoned with theologically, whether or not John was written in positive cognizance of the synoptics—or in cognizance of them at all—remains an interesting historical theological question, but ceases to require any particular answer. John stands fourth, last, in the Gospel canon, as if it were to be read not only alongside but after the other three. Its traditional position, however arrived at, makes that point rather neatly and clearly. In fact, it is arguable that the traditional viewpoint, that John wrote after the others and in order to supplement and interpret them, is actually derivative from the canonical status of John. That is, it reflects an intelligible and intelligent way of reading John as a canonical book, which would have been read back into its historical origin and purpose. Whether this is the case is somewhat beside the point for our purposes and need not be argued here. The point is that this way of conceiving and understanding John represents a kind of canonical approach to that document that is sensible and not valueless. It has its own hermeneutical justification even if it is dubious or even incorrect historically.

Probably the Christian reader, including the Christian New Testament scholar, whatever his theological or other leanings, would find it really impossible to read John's Gospel and at the same time bracket out completely or effectively the protrayal, image, or *Gestalt* of Jesus formed largely on the basis of the synoptics. It would be difficult to imagine a picture of Jesus formed solely on the basis of the Fourth Gospel. Whether anyone ever had such a picture is an interesting question, for even if neither John nor his intended audience knew one or more of the synoptics they apparently knew related tradition which is not conveyed by the Fourth Gospel (John 20:30; 21:25).[29] Indeed, such a picture would be truncated and distorted, defined as it is so exclusively by dogma, and in all probability dogma already deeply colored and shaped by controversy and conflict within, and later with, the synagogue from which the Johannine community emerged. Important presuppositions are lacking for an acceptable reading of John if the other Gospels are not taken into consideration. The picture of an otherwordly, dogmatic, anti-Jewish Jesus can readily be formed on the basis of the Fourth Gospel alone. That such a protrayal or conception of Jesus does, in fact, inform some modern Christian piety, particularly in America, can scarcely be denied, and is all the more reason for insisting that John not be read by itself but attended to in concert with the New Testament as a whole.

Another danger in reading the Gospel of John in isolation from its canonical context is, however, implicit in the document itself. As in different ways scholars as diverse in their judgments and methods as Windisch, Gardner-Smith, Bultmann, Hoskyns, and Culpepper have argued or shown, John evokes a sense of completeness and adequacy in the reader. It is not necessary to appeal to other writings in order to understand John, after a fashion. Yet what kind of understanding one elicits from it is another matter. Perhaps the great variety of Johannine interpretations that modern criticism has unleashed says something about the real difficulty of understanding John historically as an independent, self-sufficient witness to, and account of, Jesus. It well may be the case that this difficulty existed from the beginning, as John was claimed by interpreters of various theological perspectives or stripes. Certainly Valentinian Gnostics and Montanists early on saw in John a Gospel with the strongest affinities with, or justification of, their own positions. The very recent effort of Raymond E. Brown to understand the early history of the commuity of the Beloved Disciple has led him to view the Johannine Epistles, particularly I John, as bearing witness to a pitched battle over the right interpretation of the Fourth Gospel. According to Brown, the First Epistle is to be understood in relation to its historical context and purpose as a kind of definitive statement, if not commentary, on how the Gospel of John is to be read and understood. Accordingly, the strong emphasis on the flesh and tangibility of Jesus in 1 John (1:1-4) and the polemic against those who apparently denigrate Jesus' fleshliness (4:1-3; cf. 2 John 7) are directed against interpreters within the Johannine community who read the Gospel in a quasi-docetic sense.

Brevard Childs does not find Brown's thesis entirely helpful in discerning the canonical meaning of the Johannine Epistles.[30] However that may be, Brown's carefully and elaborately worked out historical reconstruction is, unless it is far off base, enormously relevant to the canonical reading of the Gospel of John. That is, it illustrates concretely the problem of which we were just speaking, namely, the difficulty in reading the Gospel of John outside a canonical setting, and particularly apart from the other Gospels. Brown's thesis implies that John was not yet being read with any of the other Gospels. In fact, he remarks that the fact that the Epistles do not make use of the synoptic tradition or Gospels as affording handholds for the interpretation of the Gospel probably means that the author(s) does not know them.[31] What evidence we have from the first decade or so of the second century does not support the existence of a Gospel canon, even one consisting only of the synoptics, at that time and thus is consistent with Brown's position. Certainly the ways in which the Gospel was interpreted and misinterpreted later in the second century count on the side of Brown's proposal. But perhaps his most significant contribution is to suggest how open the Fourth Gospel was (and is) for divergent and even contradictory interpretation when it is taken alone, outside any ruling theological or literary context. It is perhaps too much to suggest that John invites heretical readings. Nevertheless, there is an interesting parallel between the second-century and twentieth-century critical readings of that Gospel. In both cases John has been read and interpreted outside the canon, so to speak, first because there was none, and latterly because canon has been ruled out of order on historical-critical grounds. In both centuries interpretations of the Fourth Gospel have tended to diverge widely.

There is little question that the canonical positioning of the Fourth Gospel, which may or may not accord closely with its historically original purpose and setting, affords an important guide or direction for its interpretation within the Christian community. And, of course, the New Testament canon and the church are close correlatives. We need not involve ourselves in the old chicken-egg question of which came first, the canon or the church. Obviously the church was chronologically prior, although it is equally obvious that in establishing a canon of scripture the church intended to say that its source and historic ground of authority was beyond itself. The New Testament as canon commands and endorses the authority of the Gospel of John to the church and to Christians. We have the Gospel of John first of all within the canon, and that, as Childs rightly never tires of insisting, is the primary context for interpretation for Christians who are seeking in that Gospel a word from or about God. We may ask how or why it was written, or about its canonical status and context. When, however, we attend to it as apostolic witness, within the New Testament's witness, we acknowledge it as canon and acknowledge the authority and wisdom of the church that gave it to us as such. John cannot in that setting and for purposes appropriate to it be read otherwise. The historical-critical method may, as Childs agrees, be an indispensable teacher, but it is not the final arbiter of meaning. Standing together in the canon, the Gospels shed light on one another. As one legitimately reads John in light of Matthew, and the synoptics generally, one also reads the latter in the light of John. John may be the key that unlocks the other Gospels, as Calvin confessed, but the other Gospels also lay down necessary suppositions and groundwork on the basis of which John is to be read. Of course, those Gospels too are fundamentally determined by the christologies of their authors and communities. Yet they provide both perspectives and data without which one would read the Gospel of John quite differently and, one must say, to the detriment of the faith that the church wishes to attest in and through the New Testament.

Notes

1. *Commentary on the Gospel of John* 10.2-4. On the differences among the Gospels as a problem in antiquity see O. Cullmann, "The Plurality of the Gospels as a Theological Problem in Antiquity," *The Early Church*, ed. and trans. by A. J. B. Higgins, Philadelphia, 1956, 37-54; also H. Merkel, *Die Pluralität der Evangelien als theologisches und exegetisches Problem in der Alten Kirche*, Traditio Christiana, 3, Bern, 1978, an extremely useful collection of primary sources with an introduction.

2. B. S. Childs, *The New Testament as Canon: An Introduction*, Philadelphia, 1984, 117-42.

3. Ibid., 250.

4. Ibid., 45.

5. Ibid., 250.

6. R. Bultmann, *The Gospel of John: A Commentary*, trans. by G. R. Beasley-Murray, R. W. N. Hoare and J. K. Riches, Philadelphia, 1971; cf. D. Moody Smith, Jr., *The Composition and Order of the Fourth Gospel: Bultmann's Literary Theory*, Yale Publications in Religion, 10, New Haven, 1965, esp. pp. 244-248.

7. See R. A. Culpepper, *Anatomy of the Fourth Gospel: A Study in Literary Design*, New Testament: Foundations and Facets, Philadelphia, 1983; H. Thyen, "Johannes 13 und die 'Kirchliche Redaktion' des vierten Evangeliums," in *Tradition und Glaube: Das Frühe Christentum in seiner Umwelt: Festgabe für Karl Georg Kuhn zum 65. Geburtstag*, ed. by G. Jeremias et al., Göttingen, 1971, 343-356, esp. p. 356.

8. Childs, *New Testament as Canon*, 131.

9. Ibid., 153.

10. Ibid., 155. John Calvin, whom otherwise Childs cites often enough, appears to think otherwise: "The others are certainly not silent on Christ's coming into the world to bring salvation . . . just as John also devotes part of his work to historical narration. But the doctrine that points out to us the power and fruit of Christ's coming appears far more clearly in him than in the others. And since they all had the same object, to show Christ, the first three exhibit his body, if I may be permitted to put it like that, but John shows his soul. For this reason, I am accustomed to say that this Gospel is a key to open the door to the understanding of the others. For whoever grasps the power of Christ as it is here graphically portrayed, will afterwards read with advantage what the others relate about the manifested Redeemer." Calvin adds that John was placed fourth because of when he wrote (presumably last), but reiterates the Fourth Gospel should be read first. Citation from *Calvin's Commentaries: The Gospel of John 1-10*, trans. by H. L. Parker, Grand Rapids, 1961, 6.

11. Childs, *New Testament as Canon*, 169.

12. Ibid., 122, quoting B. Lindars, *Behind The Fourth Gospel*, Studies in Creative Criticism, London, 1971, 22.

13. Childs, *New Testament as Canon*, 132, quoting E. C. Hoskyns, *The Fourth Gospel*, ed. F. N. Davey, London, 1947, 68.

14. Hoskyns, *Fourth Gospel*, 69: "Yet in spite of the simplicity of its form, the Fourth Gospel is not a simple book. One of the causes of this lack of simplicity is that it does not, in fact, exist in its own right and is not in itself adequate for its own understanding."

15. Childs, *New Testament as Canon*, 134.

16. Culpepper, *Anatomy of the Fourth Gospel*, points out that some events, such as Jesus' calling and commissioning of disciples, are presupposed although they are not recounted in the Fourth Gospel (p. 59). The implied reader seems to know of Jesus, most of the named disciples and other major characters in the story, Jewish groups, and the general geography of the story (pp. 213-216). In fact, the story of Jesus himself would seem to be known (p. 222). On the "reliability" of the narrator see p. 32.

17. H. Windisch, *Johannes und die Synoptiker: Wollte der vierte Evangelist die älteren Evangelien ergänzen oder ersetzen?*, UNT 12, Leipzig, 1926, 134. On John's independence cf. also H. Windisch "Die Absolutheit des Johannesevangeliums," *ZST* 5 (1928) 3-54, which is in the main a response to F. Büchsel, "Johannes und die Synoptiker," *ZST* 4 (1926-27) 240-265.

18. Childs, *New Testament as Canon*, 238.

19. E. Käsemann, *The Testament of Jesus: A Study of the Gospel of John in the Light of Chapter 17,* Trans. by G. Krodel, Philadelphia, 1968, 74-76.

20. Childs, *New Testament as Canon,* 172-73.

21. On the evidence of Irenaeus and the Ravenna mosaics for a canonical order of the Gospels in which Mark stood first, see F. C. Grant, *The Gospels: Their Origin and Growth,* New York, 1957, 65-67.

22. On John see J. L. Martyn, *History and Theology in the Fourth Gospel,* rev. ed., Nashville, 1979; on Matthew, W. D. Davies, *The Setting of the Sermon on the Mount,* Cambridge, 1966, esp. pp. 256-315.

23. *History and Theology in the Fourth Gospel,* 127-128.

24. See esp. J. D. Kingsbury, *Matthew: Structure, Christology, Kingdom,* Philadephia, 1975.

25. After insisting that faith in the resurrection is the same as faith in the saving efficacy of the cross, Bultmann goes on to add: "The saving efficacy of the cross is not derived from the fact that it is the cross of Christ; it is the cross of Christ because it has this saving efficacy." See "The New Testament and Mythology," *Kerygma and Myth,* ed. by H. W. Bartsch and trans. by R. H. Fuller, London, 1957, 4.

26. R. Bultmann, *Theology of the New Testament,* trans. by K. Grobel, 2 vols., New York, 1951-55.

27. See Bultmann's review of Windisch's *Johannes und die Synoptiker* in *TLZ* 52 (1927) 197-200.

28. Käsemann, *Testament of Jesus,* 74-76.

29. See n. 16 above.

30. Childs, *New Testament as Canon,* 482-485.

31. R. E. Brown, *The Epistles of John,* AB 30, Garden City, New York, 1982, 98, n. 226.

The Origin and Purpose of Matthew's Sermon on the Mount

Graham N. Stanton

The Sermon on the Mount (SM) has often been studied and expounded in isolation from the rest of Matthew's Gospel. This practice, which can be traced right back to Augustine and Chrysostom, was popular in the sixteenth century. In modern times numerous studies of the SM and several detailed commentaries have been published.[1] But in nearly every case the SM has been treated as a separate entity simply for convenience; there has been no suggestion that the SM has a quite distinctive origin or purpose which sets it apart from the rest of Matthew's gospel and from Mark and Luke.

There are, however, two notable exceptions. In his widely acclaimed book, *The Setting of the Sermon on the Mount,* Cambridge, 1964, W. D. Davies suggests that "one fruitful way of dealing with the SM is to regard it as the Christian answer to Jamnia. Using terms very loosely, the SM is a kind of Christian, mishnaic counterpart to the formulation taking place there." (p. 315)

This hypothesis has often been referred to, but rarely examined in detail. As support, W. D. Davies sets out at length a cumulative case which rests on a large number of observations; he himself recognizes that some of his points are stronger than others. Davies appeals both to the SM and to other parts of Matthew's gospel. Some of the latter passages are undoubtedly significant: for example, Davies is able to show that the evangelist's community was at odds with contemporary Judaism. But the evidence from the SM itself is not compelling: none of the direct links proposed between the SM and the reconstruction taking place within Judaism during the Jamnian period is entirely satisfactory.[2] It is the whole of Matthew, not the SM in isolation, which can plausibly be related (though only indirectly) to the Jamnian period. Although Davies suggests that "there was an outside stimulus for the Evangelist to shape the SM" (p. 315), he does not claim that the SM contains theological emphases which are quite distinct from the rest of Matthew. Davies seems to accept that the SM and the rest of Matthew come from the same *Sitz im Leben,* though he does not discuss this point.

More recently a much bolder explanation of the origin and purpose of the SM has been proposed by H. D. Betz in a set of essays published between 1975 and 1984. Betz claims that the SM and the rest of Matthew contain different theologies: they do not come from the same *Sitz im Leben.* These essays have now been published in one volume, *Essays on the Sermon on the Mount,* Philadelphia, 1985; some have been translated from German into English for the first time. The reader is promised that further support for the author's novel proposals will appear in his forthcoming commentary on the SM in the *Hermeneia* series. But since Betz hopes that his essays will stimulate discussion before his commentary appears, it seems appropriate to consider his hypothesis now. Betz's views raise in an acute form an issue which has nearly always been prominent in modern discussion of the SM, the relationship between "tradition" and "interpretation", the theme of this volume in honor of E. Earle Ellis. In the first part of my essay I shall discuss Betz's hypothesis that the whole of the SM is to be seen as pre-Matthean tradition which has been incorporated without modification by the evangelist and so (presumably) re-interpreted only minimally. I shall then set out some of the reasons why I am convinced that in the SM the evangelist Matthew has shaped and re-interpreted the traditions at his disposal in ways which are completely consistent with the methods and themes developed elsewhere in his gospel. It is a great delight to offer this small piece in honor of Earle Ellis, whose scholarship and friendship I have valued for many years, and whose writings on the relationship between tradition and interpretation in Luke have influenced considerably my own understanding and appreciation of the achievement of the synoptic evangelists.

I. A Pre-Matthean Epitome of the Teaching of Jesus?

On Betz's hypothesis, which either challenges or ignores almost all other current scholarly work on the SM, Matt 5-7 is a pre-Matthean source composed by a redactor of sayings of Jesus in the mid-50s. It derives from a Jewish Christian community which had a strained relationship with its mother faith, Judaism, but which was still very much part of the diverse Judaism of the period. The source has been transmitted intact.

Betz believes that Matt 5-7 contains a theology that is independent of the rest of Matthew's gospel and different at characteristic points. There is a corollary of some theological importance: the Christian community from which the SM stems is distinct but not entirely separate from Judaism, but it has only a minimal Christology and no doctrine of the Cross and Resurrection. Although Betz has not yet set out in full his reasons for accepting that the SM contains a different theology from Matthew's gospel, his case seems to rest primarily on three pillars: hostility in the SM to the Gentile mission—those who do support it are "wolves in sheep's clothing" (Matt 7:15, p. 21); a distinctive eschatology in 7:21-23 and a minimal Christology. We shall return to these points below.

Perhaps the most intriguing part of Betz's theory is the claim that the literary genre of Matt 5-7 is that of an epitome which presents the theology of Jesus in a systematic fashion. In its form as an epitome the Sermon is "a kind of systematic theology" (p. 39). In the opening essay of the collection Betz explores the epitome genre in some detail and suggests that the SM is related in literary form to Epictetus's *Encheiridion*, a philosphical epitome which dates from the middle of the second century. Since this is clearly too late to be of relevance for consideration of the genre of the SM, Betz appeals primarily to what he claims is "the greatest and most famous example of the epitome in antiquity", and the specific prototype of the *Encheiridion*, Epicurus's *Kyriai Doxai* (p. 11). Betz freely acknowledges that Epicurus himself does not use the term epitome. (p. 11)

Few New Testament scholars have done more than Betz to draw attention to the importance of literary genre, but I am not persuaded that Matt 5-7 is analogous in form to the epitomes of the Graeco-Roman rhetorical tradition. In order to elucidate the genre of the SM, Betz appeals to the *Kyriai Doxai* which includes forty sententiae or groupings of sententiae taken from the larger works of Epicurus. But there are substantial differences in form between the *Kyriai Doxai* and Matt 5-7. (a) Whereas the *Kyriai Doxai* is a synopsis of the whole of Epicurus's philosophical system, the SM includes only part of the teaching of Jesus—the ethical teaching. (b) There are a number of verses in the Sermon, especially in the Antitheses, 5: 21-48, which hardly qualify for inclusion in a concise synopsis on the basis of their "primary importance"; they seem to have been included in their present context as illustrations (e.g. 5:39b-42), or as the result either of a catch-word connection or of broadly similar content. (c) Whereas the *Kyriai Doxai* probably contains no literary structure at all, the SM has been carefully composed. Sayings of Jesus have been grouped according to both form and content; in several parts of the SM there is a clear structure.[3]

In my view, Betz's claim that the genre of the SM is analogous with the philosophical epitome is much less plausible than his proposal that Galatians is an apologetic letter in the Graeco-Roman rhetorical tradition. This hypothesis concerning the genre of Galatians is still the subject of keen scholarly discussion and is likely to stimulate further research for some time to come.[4]

A further strand of Betz's theory is equally intriguing. The SM is seen as a pre-Matthean epitome which is critical of the Gentile Christianity known above all from the letters of Paul and the gospels. In particular, Matt 5:17 and 7:15-23 are said to contain anti-Pauline polemic. Tucked away in a footnote is the suggestion that in turning away from the Pauline gospel the Galatians may have been responding to warnings such as those in Matt 7:15-23 (p. 156 n. 124). Betz revives the theory originally proposed by J. Weiss that Matt 5:19 refers to Paul: the 'insignificant person' (ἐλάχιστος) who 'relaxes one of the least of the commandments of the Torah' is none other than Paul, 'the least of the apostles' (ὁ ἐλάχιστος τῶν ἀποσ-τόλων) (1 Cor 15:9).

How strong is this claim that the SM contains anti-Pauline polemic? Betz believes that Matt 5:17 is directed against Pauline law-free Gentile Christians (p. 20). But surely the phrase μὴ νομίσητε is to be interpreted as a rejection of a theoretical possibility. The identical phrase recurs in 10:34 where it is a redactional addition from the hand of the evangelist: "Don't think that I have come to bring peace on earth . . ." In this verse, who is assumed to be thinking along these lines? Surely there is no specific group which is being opposed. Hence it is unlikely that 5:17 is directly polemical.

The suggestion that Matt 5:19 refers to Paul and that 7:24 with its reference to "building on a rock" alludes to Peter will seem plausible only if there are other strong grounds for accepting anti-Pauline polemic in the SM. The references to "false prophets" in 7:15 and to those who say "Lord, Lord" and do not do the will of the Father, 7:21-23, have often been linked with Pauline groups or at least with antinomians in general; in these verses there might seem at first sight to be grounds for accepting Betz's proposal.

But in 7:15-20 the "false prophets" are not described in very precise terms. Even if they are to be linked (as they often are, but not by Betz) with the false prophets of the end-time at 24:11, the comments are very general indeed. As G. Strecker has noted, similar indefinite warnings against false prophecy of the end-time are found in other early Christian writings.[5]

Matt 7:21-23 seems to be more specific. Here the SM refers to "many" who appeal to their charismata, to prophecy and working of miracles. But these verses are not attacking Pauline Christians of any kind: Pauline Christians might have been expected to appeal to πίστις or even (conceivably to γνῶσις as the basis of their libertinism. Scholars have jumped too quickly from the reference to ἀνομία at 7:23 to the view that antinomians are being attacked in this passage; ἀνομία is to be taken as a general reference to disobedience to "the will of the Father". As David Hill has insisted, the condemned charismatics are neither heretics nor antinomians.[6]

In addition to these exegetical observations, there is a more general reason why Betz's theory that Matt 5-7 derives from a Jewish Christian anti-Pauline community in the mid-50s is implausible. He accepts that the community from which the SM comes is suffering persecution from "official" Judaism and notes that 5:11-12 indicates that the community is prepared to take the consequences of the teaching of Jesus, even if it means their lives (p. 21). But why, on this view, would so-called official Judaism want to persecute vigorously the community from which the SM has come?

Betz suggests that its understanding of Torah would have seemed to Paul to involve little more than an abridgement of the law (p. 35). Its soteriology "is none other than that of the Jewish Torah." (p. 92). Its ethical teaching is at home in the context of Jewish piety and theology (p. 123). Christology is largely lacking in the SM which does not include any universalist teaching. "That Jesus was awaited as eschatological defender and intercessor for his followers fits well in the context of contemporary Judaism" (p. 92). In short, according to the author, the community of the Sermon has not differentiated itself sharply from Judaism, but it is opposed to Pauline Christianity. Admittedly in several essays in the collection Betz does draw attention to teaching in the Matt 5-7 which is "striking" in terms of contemporary Judaism.[7] But I still find myself bound to ask, "What was so deeply offensive about this conservative Jewish Christian anti-Pauline community that it attracted persecution?"

A community strongly antagonistic to Paul would seem to me—at least in the mid-50s—to be sufficiently close to Judaism to be unconcerned even about threats of persecution. But since the community of the SM clearly had experienced persecution (5:10-12), the corollary would seem to be that it cannot have been as anti-Pauline as Betz supposes.

On the widely accepted view of the origin of Matt 5-7 (which I share) these difficulties do not arise. Matt 5:10 comes from the hand of the evangelist: this verse strengthens and extends the references in Q to persecution which are used in 5:11-12, and it reflects the later persecution experienced by Matthew's community which had differentiated itself from Judaism.[8] Matthew's gospel as a whole is neither anti-Pauline, nor has it been strongly influenced by Paul's writings;[9] it is simply un-Pauline.

We have already seen that part of Betz's case depends closely on what is virtually an axiom for his hypothesis: Matt 5-7 is a pre-Matthean source which the evangelist has incorporated into his gospel. How could this claim be either verified or falsified? Two tests might be applied. First, if the vocabulary, phrases, syntax and literary form of parts of and of the whole of the SM differ considerably from the rest of Matthew's gospel, then there would be a good case for accepting that the SM is an independent pre-Matthean source. And secondly, if the teaching of the SM and the setting it presupposes both differ from the rest of the gospel, then we may well suspect that the evangelist has integrated intact a source which derives from a very different *Sitz im Leben*. We shall now discuss these two possibilities briefly.

A detailed comparison of the vocabulary and style of the SM and the rest of the gospel would be a considerable undertaking. Betz does not in fact appeal to any arguments along these lines. It would not be difficult to compile a list of Matthean words and phrases which are not found in the SM, but such a list would be of little significance. The absence from the SM of what are usually taken to be "Mattheanisms" may well have more to do with the content of the SM than with the presence of a pre-Matthean source. On the other hand, if a number of distinctively Matthean words and phrases from the rest of the gospel are also prominent in the SM, then the theory that a source has been integrated intact as chapters 5-7 would seem to be called in question.

At least the following fall into that category. (1) ἀνομία: found 4x in Matt, once in the SM at 7:23; probably all four are redactional; not found in Mark or Luke. (2) βασιλεία τῶν οὐρανῶν: 33x in Matt, in many cases redactionally: 7x in the SM— probably all redactional; not found in Mark or Luke (3) δικαιοσύνη: found 7x in Matt, 5x in the SM; probably all 7 are redactional; not found in Mark, only once in Luke. (4) διώκω: found 6x in Matt, 4x in the SM—all four of which are redactional, as also is Matt 10:23; not found in Mark, 3x in Luke. (5) θέλημα: 6x in Matt, 2x in the SM (both redactional); of the other 4x in Matt, 2 or 3 are redactional; 1x Mark, 4x Luke. (6) νόμος καὶ προφῆται:4x in Matt, 3 of which are redactional, 2x in the SM, both redactional; not found in Mark, twice in Luke. (7) πατὴρ (+ σου, ἡμῶν or ὑμῶν) and/or + ἐν (τοῖς) οὐρανοῖς or ὁ οὐράνιος: 29x in Matt, 12 of which are in the SM; many of the 29x are redactional; 2x in Mark, 4x in Luke. (8) πορνεία: Matt 5:32 and 19:9, both redactional as the so-called "exception" in the context of teaching on divorce; the word is used in a very different context at Matt 15:19 = Mark 7:21, but is not found elsewhere in Mark or Luke. (9) τέλειος: Matt 5:48 and 19:21, both redactional; not found in Mark or Luke.

Most of these examples are striking; some reflect Matthean theological themes which are found in the SM and also in the rest of the gospel. So has Betz's case collapsed? It is certainly teetering, but perhaps it has not yet fallen, since it is just conceivable that these words and phrases occurred in the pre-Matthean source and were then developed by the evangelist himself in other parts of his gospel.

This possibility has to be conceded since the evangelist does frequently take a word or phrase which is found just occasionally in one of his sources (especially Mark) and use it very much more often himself. Two important examples are worth noting. (1) The phrase συναγωγαὶ αὐτῶν occurs redactionally five times (Matt 4:23; 9:35; 10:17; 12:9; 13:54) and is often taken as an indication that the evangelist's community is no longer part of Judaism. But the phrase does also occur at Mark 1:23 and 39 and also at Luke 4:15. Matthew seems to have developed considerably a phrase found already in Mark.[10] (2) Matthew's ten-fold use of a "fulfilment formula" to introduce quotations from the prophets as theological comments on his story is well-known as one of the most distinctive features of his gospel. But the evangelist's "formula" is a development and extension of Mark 14:49c, ἀλλ᾽ ἵνα πληρωθῶσιν αἱ γραφαί, as his redaction of this clause at 26:54, 56 confirms.[11]

Are there clear differences in teaching between the SM and the rest of the gospel?

Betz claims that there are (p. 18); two observations are set out briefly, a third more fully:

(a) Unlike the rest of the gospel, the SM is opposed to Gentile Christianity because these chapters are anti-Pauline (p. x and p. 90). But as we have seen, there are insufficient grounds for concluding that Paul or Pauline Christians are attacked in these chapters.

(b) Since the SM contains a minimal Christology and no sign of a Cross-Resurrection theology, the soteriology of this source differs considerably from the evangelist's (pp. 92 and 152-53). But this observation is valid only if we accept as an axiom that Matt 5-7 have been taken intact from a pre-Matthean source.

(c) Betz claims that the distinctive eschatology of 7:21-23 offers strong support for his hypothesis concerning the origin of the SM. Betz insists that in this passage Jesus is portrayed as advocate, and not, as elsewhere in Matthew (16:27; 19:28; 24:30-31; 25:31) as "Son of Man-judge" (p. 147). This exegesis of 7:21-23 runs counter to the almost universally accepted view that in this passage Jesus is the judge. As Betz himself notes, 7:22-23 depicts in briefest scope proceedings at the last judgment (p. 127). Verses 21-23 are set out so tersely that it is not easy to decide whether Jesus is assumed to be advocate or judge.

But even if we allow that Betz's exegesis is just possible, there are difficulties with his view. He has to claim that Luke 6:46 is not the source for Matt 7:21-23; if it were, these verses could be seen more readily as a Matthean development of a Q tradition rather than as part of a pre-Matthean source which comprised the whole of the SM. But there is such a concentration of Matthean vocabulary in 7:21-23 that it is difficult to avoid the conclusion that the evangelist has developed considerably a Q logion. We noted above on p. 185 the following as Matthean words and phrases: βασιλεία τῶν οὐρανῶν, θέλημα, πατὴρ ἐν τοῖς οὐρανοῖς, ἀνομία; to this list we may add πᾶς (often used redactionally) and the three-fold pattern in v 22.

Betz refers to Matt 10:32-33 as a parallel passage in which Jesus appears as "advocate and witness for his own followers" (pp. 142-43). He recognizes that the case for seeing 7:21-23 as un-Matthean and therefore part of a pre-Matthean SM is weakened if there is an important un-Matthean parallel in the Q tradition in 10:32-33. So he boldly suggests that Matt 10:1-42 is also a source which Matthew has taken up into his gospel! The mission discourse is "a work that resembles the pre-Matthean SM in many respects" (p. 142). But if the SM and the mission discourse are both pre-Matthean, are the discourses in 13, 18, (23) 24-25 also pre-Matthean? What has happened to the Q hypothesis? It is easy to pour scorn on some of the arguments which have been used in the past to support Q, but the hypothesis remains much more plausible than any of its rivals.

It is much more preferable to see Matt 7:21-23 and 10:32-33 as Matthean developments of Q traditions. The evangelist would not have been concerned about an apparent contradiction in viewing Jesus in some eschatological scenes as advocate and in some as judge; logical rigor was not the hall-mark of the Jewish apocalyptic tradition to which he was indebted.

Betz has been unable to show that the SM contains a distinctive un-Matthean theology. Although it must remain possible that some Q traditions were expanded and perhaps combined with "M" traditions before the evangelist Matthew composed the SM, it is not easy to suppose that the SM as a whole is pre-Matthean. In Matt 5-7 the evangelist has woven together skillfully his sources into sections which have thematic and structural unity, just as he has done in his other four discourses.

II. The SM as an Integral Part of Matthew's Gospel

The case for isolating the SM from the rest of Matthew's gospel is far from compelling. As we have seen, the SM contains a large number of the evangelist's redactional words and phrases. But there are further reasons for insisting that neither the origin nor the purpose of the SM differs from the other discourses. In the paragraphs which follow we hope to show that in all the discourses the same methods of composition are used, many of the prominent themes of the SM are found, and the same *Sitz im Leben* is presupposed.

Most scholars accept that all five Matthean discourses have been constructed in precisely the same way. Attention has frequently been drawn to the evangelist's careful composition. As examples we may note two points which have rarely been given sufficient attention. (1) Ulrich Luz has recently shown that Matthew frequently indicates his themes through "key" verses which are accentuated through their position. They relate to a larger context; they are not simply headings, but are placed at the beginning or conclusion of a section as generalizations which often function as "transitional" verses. Luz lists as examples: 5:17, 20, 48; 6:1; 7:12, 21; 10:16, 26; 18:10, 14.[12] To this list we might add: 6:33; 10:34, 40. This technique is clearly particularly important and prominent in the SM, but it is also found in some of the other discourses.

(2) Matthew not only re-interprets the sayings of Jesus found in his sources by re-arrangement and modification; he often elucidates them with extra phrases or even (on occasion) whole verses which he himself has composed. The following may be noted as examples: 5:10, 13a, 14a, 16; 6:10b and c, 13b; 7:12, 19, 20, 21; 10:8, 24-25, 41; 18:10a, 14, 35; 23:28, 32-34. The evangelist expounds his sources creatively both in the SM and elsewhere in his gospel.[13]

Neither of these techniques is unique to Matthew; they can both be found elsewhere in the gospels and in other writings of the time. But they are especially characteristic of the evangelist and strongly suggest that the five discourses in his gospel have been composed by the same hand.

We turn now from the evangelist's methods to this theological themes. Several of the main concerns of the SM are found in other parts of the gospel. The opening four chaps. provide a rich theological preface to the SM. Some of the themes of the SM are then developed more fully later in the gospel. In short, Matthew's gospel is a theological story; the five discourses may break up the flow of the narrative, but the evangelist develops his main story-line both in narrative and in discourse.[14] It has sometimes been said that the fourth evangelist is his own best interpreter: the same can be said *mutatis mutandis* of Matthew.

The chaps. which precede and follow the SM are profoundly Christological. But *pace* H. D. Betz, the Christology of the SM itself is not minimal. (a) 5:11 presupposes that disciples will have been persecuted on account of their commitment to the person of Jesus (ἕνεκεν ἐμοῦ). The same theme recurs in 10:17-18: disciples of Jesus will be dragged before governors and kings "for my sake" (ἕνεκεν ἐμοῦ). (b) In 5:17 Jesus claims that he himself fulfills Torah—a profound claim which is elucidated in the antitheses (5:21-48) which follow. The evangelist extends this theme in his introductions to his "formula" quotations of Scripture, all of which comment on the fulfilment of the prophets in the life of Jesus. (c) As we have seen, in 7:21-23 Jesus is almost certainly portrayed as the eschatological judge, as he also is in 16:27; 19:28 and 25:31-46. In short, the Christology of the SM is not unrelated to the rest of the gospel.

If Christology is Matthew's primary concern, discipleship (ecclesiology) is not far behind. The SM is clearly addressed to disciples: Peter, Andrew, James and John are called immediately before the SM. But both at the beginning and the end of the SM reference is made to the presence of crowds (οἱ ὄχλοι). Why are both disciples and crowds mentioned as the audience of the SM? Is this a "loose end"? Are the crowds referred to in 7:28 simply because Matthew has returned to his Marcan source at this point?

The "dual" audience envisaged is quite deliberate. Similar reference to a "dual" audience is made in two of the other discourses. The discourse in chap. 23 is also addressed to "crowds and disciples"; in its continuation in chaps. 24 and 25 Jesus speaks to the disciples in private. Similarly in chap. 13: the parable discourse is addressed to the crowds and the disciples (13:2, 10, 36), though part of it is addressed to disciples alone (13:10 and 36).

In these three discourses the evangelist seems to hint that while all the teaching of Jesus in the five discourses is directed to his disciples, some parts are appropriate for a wider audience. This is confirmed in the closing verses of the gospel. The disciples are told by the Risen Lord to teach those who have been "discipled" from the nations to keep all that Jesus has commanded (28:18-20). Once again the SM is an integral part of the gospel.

In one of the "key" verses in the SM, disciples are told that their ethical conduct must exceed that of the scribes and Pharisees (5:20). In a related "key" verse, 5:48, disciples are told to be perfect or whole-hearted (τέλειοι). In the verses which follow immediately in 6:1-18, their conduct is contrasted starkly with that of the "hypocrites" (6:2, 5, 16) whom the reader naturally assumes to be none other than the scribes and Pharisees of 5:20.

These same points are developed in chap. 23. The crowds and disciples are urged not to follow the example of the scribes and Pharisees (23:2-3) who are then referred to explicitly as "hypocrites" six times. There is even some verbal correspondence between 6:1, 5 and 16 on the one hand, and 23:5 and 28 on the other. Both in chaps. 5 and 6 of the SM and in chap. 23 the evangelist uses the scribes and Pharisees as a foil: disciples are called to "superior" ethical conduct.

In Matthew Christological and ecclesiological concerns are often inter-related. In 4:15-16, immediately before the SM Matthew cites Isa. 9:1-2 in order to portray Jesus as the promised φῶς for Galilee of the Gentiles. At an important point in the structure of the SM, disciples are portrayed similarly: they are called to be φῶς τοῦ κόσμου (5:14). This correspondence between Jesus and the disciples is all of a piece with the evangelist's insistence that the preaching and healing activity of the disciples is patterned closely on that of Jesus himself (10:1, 7, 8).

Matt 5:14 is part of a section in the SM where Matthew's universalist theme is present, a theme already set out in the genealogy,[15] in the coming of the magi, and in the reference to Galilee of the Gentiles at 4:15. Disciples are called to be φῶς τοῦ κόσμου. In illustration of this, disciples are likened to a πόλις: the πόλις is not

Jerusalem, for the article would then surely have been used.[16] The lamp in the further illustration which follows in 5:15 give light for all (πᾶσιν) in the house, a trait not present in the underlying Q logion.

The SM and the other discourses presuppose the same *Sitz im Leben*. The evangelist's community still felt seriously threatened by Jewish opposition at the time the gospel was written: alongside 5:10-12 we may set 10:17-23 and 23:34 and 37.[17] Immediately after the reference to opposition and persecution in 5:11, disciples are warned that the persecution endured by the prophets of old is experienced anew by Christian prophets in the evangelist's own day. This point is made much more explicitly and vigorously in 23:34, where once again the evangelist's own hand can be traced.

While 5:11 does not name the opponents, by 5:20 the reader is left in no doubt as to their identity. By insisting on a superior righteousness the Matthean community is defining itself over against the scribes and Pharisees. It is characteristic of sectarian groups to call in question the integrity of the group from which they have separated. This is precisely what is happening in 5:20, and also in 6:1-18, where "hypocrites" are referred to three times. The reader of 5:20 knows full well that the "hypocrites" of 6:1-18 are the scribes and Pharisees whose religious practices are being gently mocked in order to establish the superiority of the religious practices of the Matthean community. This theme is, of course, extended considerably in chap. 23.

The references to persecution and the polemical passages in the SM and in the rest of Matthew reflect a Christian community coming to terms with the trauma of separation from Judaism and with the perceived continuing threat of hostility and persecution. Matthew's denunciations of the scribes and Pharisees represent in part anger and frustration at the continuing rejection of Christian claims and at the continuing hostility of Jews towards the new community.[18]

Both the SM and other passages in Matthew suggest that the evangelist and his readers were very much at odds, not only with contemporary Judaism, but also with the Gentile world. In the SM there are derogatory references to Gentiles in 5:47, 6:7 and 6:32. In 10:18 and 22 the disciples are told to expect hostility from Gentiles as well as Jews. And in 18:7 and 17 there are two further negative references to the Gentile world "outside" the Matthean community.[19]

We have seen that the SM and the rest of Matthew presuppose the same *Sitz im Leben*. We have also seen that a number of the evangelist's distinctive words, phrases and themes are found both in the SM and in the other parts of the gospel. Indeed, the evangelist has taken pains to link the SM closely to the rest of his gospel. The SM is an important part of a major section which runs from 4:23 to 9:35. Chaps. 5-7, which portray Jesus as "Messiah of Word", are a diptych set opposite chaps. 8 and 9, which portray Jesus as "Messiah of Deed". These five chaps. are introduced and concluded by strikingly similar summaries, 4:23-25 and 9:35-36, which have been composed by the evangelist himself.

Although the SM is often singled out as the center-piece of Matthew's gospel, or even as containing the "essence of Christianity", for the evangelist it is only the first of five discourses to which he attaches equal importance. This is made clear at 26:1, the verse which follows the final discourse. At the end of the earlier discourses (7:28; 11:1; 13:53; 19:1) there is a "transitional" verse: "When Jesus had finished these sayings . . .". At 26:1 the pattern recurs, but πάντας is added: Jesus has now finished all five discourses; the Passion drama unfolds.

The importance Matthew attaches to his five discourses is seen in two further ways. First: at 7:21 we read "Not everyone who says to me 'Lord, Lord,' will enter the kingdom of heaven, but he who does the will of my father in heaven". In the underlying Q logion (Luke 6:46) it is the words of Jesus which are to be obeyed; Matthew reshapes the logion by using his own favorite turns of phrase: "the one who does the will of my Father in heaven." For Matthew, the Q reference to "carrying out the words of Jesus" can be paraphrased by "doing the will of my Father." For the evangelist the words of Jesus are that important.

And secondly, the five discourses are designed as a giant chiasm. The first discourse may be said to correspond to the last; they are both of similar length and much longer than the other discourses. Chaps. 10 and 18 are related: chap. 10 instructs and encourages the community in mission, while chap. 18 considers the internal life of the community. Chap. 13 is central in every sense![20]

The SM is part and parcel of Matthew's gospel. The evangelist has drawn extensively on Q and other traditions, but he has reshaped and re-interpreted them considerably. Only when the SM is wrenched from its present context in Matthew can its theological concerns be contrasted with the evangelist's own. For Matthew the SM is but one part of his attempt to set out the story and teaching of Jesus for the life of his own community. The interpreter of the SM who ignores the rest of Matthew's gospel misunderstands the evangelist's intentions and fails to do justice to the breadth of the evangelist's theological vision. In the SM and in the gospel as a whole, grace and demand are linked inextricably. For Matthew, the Jesus of the SM is the Son of God through whom God is acting for mankind: it is his demanding teaching which is to be central in the life of the community and in its discipling of the nations.

Notes

1. For the history of the interpretation of the SM, see W. S. Kissinger, *The Sermon on the Mount, A History of Interpretation and Bibliography*, Metuchen, 1975; U. Berner, *Die Bergpredigt. Rezeption und Auslegung im 20. Jahrhundert*, Göttingen, 1979. Two major exegetical commentaries have recently been published: R. A. Guelich, *The Sermon on the Mount: A Foundation for Understanding*, Waco, 1982; G. Strecker, *Die Bergpredigt. Ein exegetischer Kommentar*, Göttingen, 1984.

2. In his *Setting of the Sermon on the Mount*, Cambridge, 1964, Davies suggests two possible links between the SM and Jamnia. (1) Matthew presents the teaching of Jesus "in a roughly parallel triadic way" to Johannan ben Zakkai's re-interpretation at the time of Jamnia of the "three traditional pillars" attributed to Simeon the Just in Aboth 1:2. In a discussion with the Emperor Vespasian, Johannan asks permission to go to Jamnia "in order to teach his disciples, establish a prayer house and perform all the commandments." (*Aboth de Rabbi Nathan*, quoted by Davies on p. 306 from J. Goldin's edition). Davies claims that Matthew "confronts the synagogue with a triadic formulation which would not be alien to it" (p. 307). Matt 5:17-48 sets forth the Torah of Jesus; 6:1-18 the true '*bwdh* or worship; and in 6:19–7:12 we have what corresponds to "performance of all the commandments."

But why are the opening and closing sections of the SM omitted? In addition, the re-interpretation of the three pillars cannot be linked with any confidence to the Jamnian period. The dialogue in *ARN* between Johannan and Vespasian looks like a much later idealising both of Jamnia and of Rabbi Johannan ben Zakkai. Josephus (*BJ* VII 216f.) tells us that following Masada Vespasian held on to Jewish land as his own private property, leasing it out. Hence it is hardly likely that Vespasian would have said to Johannan (as in *ARN*) "Tell me, what may I give thee?" To which Johannan replied, "I ask naught of thee, save Jamnia . . ."

(2) Davies suggests that Matthew's re-interpretation of the Lord's Prayer may have been carried out as a counterpart to the main prayer of the synagogue, the *Shemoneh Esreh*, which was being formulated anew at Jamnia (p. 310). This seems unlikely: Matthew's expansions of the original shorter version (as in Luke 11:2-4) can all be explained quite simply as Matthean explanatory or interpretative additions.

3. On the structure of the SM see R. Riesner, "Der Aufbau der Reden im Matthäus-Evangelium," *ThBeitr* 9 (1978) 172-182; G. Bornkamm, "Der Aufbau der Bergpredigt," *NTS* 24 (1977-78) 419-432; U. Luz, *Das Evangelium nach Matthäus* I, *EKK*, Zürich, 1985, 185-87.

4. See, for example, D. Aune's review of H. D. Betz, *Galatians: A Commentary on Paul's Letter to the Churches in Galatia*, Philadelphia, 1979, in *RSR* 7 (1981) 310-28; G. Kennedy, *New Testament Interpretation Through Rhetorical Criticism*, Chapel Hill, 1984, 144-52.

5. G. Strecker, *Der Weg der Gerechtigkeit*, Göttingen, 1962, 276.

6. D. Hill, "False Prophets and Charismatics: Structure and Interpretation in Matthew 7:15-23," *Bib* 57 (1976) 340.

7. See, for example, Betz, *Essays*, 21, 34-35, 68-69, 123.

8. See G. N. Stanton, "The Gospel of Matthew and Judaism," *BJRL* 66 (1984) 267-71.

9. *Pace* M. D. Goulder, *Midrash and Lection in Matthew*, London, 1974, 153-70.

10. G. D. Kilpatrick claims that the αὐτῶν in Mark 1:23 and 39; Luke 4:15 should be omitted as later textual assimilation to Matthew. But the textual evidence he cites for the omissions is slight. *The Origins of the Gospel According to St Matthew*, Oxford, 1946, 110.

11. See G. N. Stanton, "Matthew's Use of the Old Testament", forthcoming.

12. See Luz, *Matthäus* I, 21.

13. For details, see G. N. Stanton, "Matthew as a Creative Interpreter of the Sayings of Jesus," in *Das Evangelium und die Evangelien*, ed. by P. Stuhlmacher, Tübingen, 1983, 273-87.

14. See J. D. Kingsbury, *Matthew as Story*, Philadelphia, 1986. Kingsbury, however, does not discuss the SM in detail.

15. For a thorough discussion, see R. E. Brown, *The Birth of the Messiah*, Garden City, 1977, 71-74.

16. So Luz, *Matthäus, ad loc.*, with reference to G. von Rad.

17. See D. R. A. Hare, *The Theme of Jewish Persecution of Christians in the Gospel According to St Matthew*, Cambridge, 1967, 80-120.

18. For a fuller discussion, see G. N. Stanton, "The Gospel of Matthew and Judaism," *BJRL* 66 (1984) 273-84.

19. Here I am in agreement with H. D. Betz who notes that in the SM "assimilation to pagan culture is sharply rejected throughout," *Essays*, 93, and see also 19 n. 6. Betz also refers to Matt 5:47; 6:7 and 6:32, but fails to note 10:18 and 22; 18:7 and 17 which reflect the same *Sitz im Leben* outside the SM.

20. See J. C. Fenton, "Inclusio and Chiasmus in Matthew," *Studia Evangelica* I, ed. F. L. Cross, Berlin, 1959, 174-79; P. Gaechter, *Das Matthäus-Evangelium*, Innsbruck, 1964.

Part III

Der gekreuzigte Christus, unsere Weisheit und Gerechtigkeit (Der alttestamentliche Hintergrund von 1.Korinther 1-2)

Otto Betz

In seinem lehrreichen Buch, *Prophecy and Hermeneutics in Early Christianity,* hat unser Jubilar die beiden ersten Kapitel des Ersten Korintherbriefes mit besonderer Liebe und Sorgfalt behandelt. Dabei lehnte er die These von R. Bultmann und dessen Schülern U. Wilckens und W. Schmithals, Paulus kämpfe hier gegen gnostische Gegner in der Gemeinde und sei dabei selbst von gnostischen Ideen beeinflußt worden, mit guten Gründen energisch ab. Anders als im 2.Korintherbrief setze sich der Apostel in diesem früheren Schreiben nicht etwa mit einer geschlossenen Gruppe von Gegnern auseinander, sondern behandle seelsorgerlich Probleme der Christen Korinths, die er eher als ein verantwortungsbewußter Vater anspreche (vgl. 1.Kor 4,15.21). Man sollte ferner die leidenschaftliche Stellungnahme zu Weisheit und Torheit, zu Pneumatikern und Psychikern, wie sie der Apostel in 1.Kor. 1 und 2 abgibt, nicht von gnostischen Strömungen und von der Gnosis geprägten Gruppierungen verursacht sehen. Näher stünden auch Paulus *die Weisheit* und die Weisen des *frühen Judentums,* vor allem in Gestalten, wie sie uns in den Lehrern der Qumrangemeinde entgegentreten.[1] Anders als die christliche Gnosis habe die paulinische Botschaft ihre Mitte im *Kreuz des Christus;* E. Ellis hat speziell dem Ausdruck 'Christus als Gekreuzigter' eine seiner Untersuchungen zu 1.Kor 1-2 gewidmet.[2]

1. Das 'Wort vom Kreuz' (1.Kor 1,18) und die Botschaft vom Leidenden Gottesknecht (Jesaja 53)

1.1 Von dieser Mitte der paulinischen Botschaft aus möchte ich in der von E. Ellis gewiesenen Richtung weitergehen und dabei vor allem den *alttestamentlich-jüdischen Hintergrund* der Ausführungen des Apostels in 1.Kor 1-2 aufzeigen. Mit großer Emphase verteidigt Paulus das Thema seiner Botschaft: Nur Christus möchte er gepredigt wissen, und zwar als den Gekreuzigten (2,2; vgl. 1,23)[3]. Das 'Wort vom Kreuz' (1,18) hat eine machtvolle, weil scheidende und die Entscheidung des Endgerichts jetzt schon offenbarende Wirkung: Denen, die in das Verderben gehen, erscheint es als Torheit, für diejenigen aber, die gerettet werden, ist es eine *Gotteskraft* (ibid.) Auch in den darauf folgenden Ausführungen wird die rettende Kraft Gottes ($\delta\acute{u}\nu\alpha\mu\iota\varsigma$ $\theta\epsilon\circ\tilde{u}$) mehrfach erwähnt: Christus ist für die von Gott Berufenen 'die Kraft und Weisheit Gottes' (1,24), und der Glaube beruht nicht auf Menschenweisheit, sondern auf der Kraft Gottes (2,5). Die Verkündigung des Apostels partizipiert an dieser Kraft, denn sie ist vom Erweis des Geistes und der Kraft begleitet

(2,4), und wo sie im Glauben ergriffen wird, wo der Name des Herrn Jesus angerufen wird, weiß man sich dem Verderben entrissen, im Raume des Heils (1,2; 1,18).

1.1.1 Worauf beruht die *Wirkung des Wortes vom Kreuz*, seine rettende, zum Leben mit Gott befreiende Macht? Worauf stützt sich der Apostel, wenn er das Anstoß erregende Kreuz des Messias[4] als Offenbarung der Weisheit Gottes bezeichnet? Eine erste Antwort auf diese Frage muß lauten: Wie die ersten Christen in Jerusalem, so war auch Paulus nach dem Damaskuserlebnis fest davon überzeugt, daß am Kreuz auf Golgatha der Messias gestorben ist und daß er als der vollkommene Gerechte sein Leben stellvertretend für uns sündige Menschen, für unsere Rechtfertigung vor Gott, in den Tod gegeben hat. Dieser Sühnetod des Messias stellte sowohl für die Urgemeinde als auch für Paulus die Erfüllung der Weissagung vom *stellvertretenden Leiden des Gottesknechts in Jes 52,13-53,12 dar*, die in Jes 53,1 ausdrücklich als eine Offenbarung des 'Arms' (d.h. der Macht) Gottes bezeichnet wird. Gerade in 1.Kor 1-2, wo Paulus das Ärgernis und die Torheit des Kreuzes gegen das Macht- und Weisheitsdenken der jüdisch-griechischen Welt verteidigen will, ist ein Rückgriff auf das für die frühchristliche Theologie und Apologetik so bedeutsame Kapitel Jes 53 von vornherein anzunehmen.[5]

1.1.2 Schon das *Evangelium, das der Apostel übernommen* und weitergegeben hat (1.Kor 15,3-5), war von Jes 53 entscheidend geprägt. Das gilt fast für alle gemeinhin als vorpaulinisch bezeichneten Aussagen in den paulinischen Briefen. Vor allem aber ist die Stelle 1.Kor 15,1-5 grundlegend für die Ausführungen in 1.Kor 1-2.

1.1.2.1. Nach 1.Kor 15,4 starb Christus für unsere Sünden; nach Jes 53 wurde der Gottesknecht um unserer Frevel willen durchbohrt (v 5) und gab sein Leben in den Tod (v 12).

1.1.2.2 Nach 1.Kor 15,4 wurde Christus begraben; nach Jes 53,9 fand der Gottesknecht bei Verbrechern und Reichen sein Grab;

1.1.2.3 Nach 1.Kor 15,4 wurde Christus am 3.Tag (vgl. Hos 6,2) von den Toten auferweckt; nach Jes 53,11 wird der Knecht 'Licht sehen' (so 1 QS Jes a und LXX), d.h. aus dem Totenreich in das Leben zurückkehren.

1.1.2.4 Diesen schon bisher beachteten, aber nicht immer als beweiskräftig angesehenen[6] Entsprechungen, die das paulinische κατὰ τὰς γραφάς erklären, möchte ich noch *zwei weitere hinzufügen:*

a) Nach 1.Kor 15,5ff erschien der Auferstandene den Jüngern und zahlreichen Anderen, die er dadurch zu Augenzeugen eines unerhörten, von Gott gewirkten Geschehens machte. So wurde das Wort Jes 52,15 erfüllt: Diejenigen, denen nichts ('von ihm' LXX) erzählt worden war, sehen, und welche nichts hören, verstehen. Auf die Bedeutung dieser Stelle für Paulus werden wir weiter unten näher eingehen.

b) Der Apostel selbst hat in den Sätzen 1.Kor 15,1-2, die auf das von ihm übernommene Credo 1.Kor 15,3-5 *hinführen*, sich deutlich auf Jes 53,1 bezogen. Wie in 1.Kor 1,18 spricht er von der Verkündigung, die rettende Kraft besitzt, aber er nennt sie nun *'Evangelium'* (1.Kor 15,1), das man glauben muß (v 2). Die Begriffe 'Evangelium' und 'glauben', ferner die (rettende) Kraft dieser Botschaft werden zusammen in Jes 53,1 erwähnt.

1.1.2.5 Auch das vielfach als vorpaulinisch bezeichnete Christuslied Phil 2,6-11 mit seinen beiden Strophen 'Erniedrigung-Erhöhung' ist dem Geschick des Gottesknechts nachgebildet (Jes 53; 52,13), und die credo-artige Aussage Röm 4,25 ist von Jes 53,5 (Targum) geprägt.

1.2.1 Ferner ist es wichtig, daß im alten Bekenntnis 1.Kor 15,3-5 der *Messias* (ὁ Χριστός) als das Subjekt des Heilsgeschehens herausgestellt wird: Nicht irgendein jüdischer Zelot, sondern der König der Endzeit starb für unsere Sünden (vgl. auch Röm 6,3f; 7,4f). Auf dieser Tatsache beruht die Heilsbedeutung des Kreuzes. Nach Apg 17,3 hatte Paulus in der Synagoge von der Schrift her zu beweisen, "daß *Christus* leiden und von den Toten auferstehen mußte, und daß dieser Christus der Jesus ist, den ich euch verkündige". Der Machtcharakter des 'Wortes vom Kreuz', die rettende Wirkung des Evangeliums, steht und fällt damit, daß Jesus als der Christus und König der Juden gestorben ist, daß er sich als Messias gesandt wußte und als Menschensohn bewußt sein Leben für Viele dahingab (Mk 10,45; 14,24). Ein unmessianischer Jesus, wie ihn R. Bultmann und seine Schüler annahmen, würde das Evangelium der Urgemeinde schwächen und die theologia crucis des Paulus verderben.

1.2.2 Die Theologie des Kreuzes bezieht aus *Jes 53* ihre argumentative, theologisch-konstruktive und apologetische Kraft. Die ersten Christen haben den Gottesknecht in Jes 52,13-15; 53,1-12 auf den Messias bezogen, so wie das auch der Targum tat und wie der irdische Jesus selbst diese Verse verstanden haben muß. Der Targum, die aramäische Wiedergabe und Deutung von Jes 52,13–53,12, hat ferner mit 1.Kor 15,1-2 die 'Botschaft' in Jes 53,1 (hebr.: shĕmû'ah; LXX ἀκοή) als 'Evangelium' (bĕsôrathana = τὸ εὐαγγέλιον ἡμῶν übersetzt: Sie ist Frohbotschaft, Ansage des Heils, für uns und von uns verkündigt.

1.2.3 Deshalb hat Paulus an Jes 53,1 gedacht, wenn er in 1.Kor 1,18–2,16 das 'Wort vom Kreuz' als die Offenbarung (vgl. 2,10) der Macht und Weisheit Gottes bezeichnet und diese der Weisheit der Welt entgegenstellt. Dafür spricht schon die *1.Pers. plur.*, die in 1,18 plötzlich auftaucht, in 1,23 aufgenommen wird und auch in 2,10.12 noch einmal erscheint. Dieser 'apostolische Plural' der Evangeliumsverkündigung ("wir aber verkündigen" 1.23) hat im prophetischen 'Wir' der Bekenner und Botschafter des Gottesknechts in Jes 53,1 ("Wer glaubt unserer Botschaft?") sein Vorbild.

1.2.4 Noch bedeutsamer ist es, daß wir Jes 53,1 als Stütze für den so stark betonten Machtcharakter der Botschaft annehmen dürfen. Das geht aus *Röm 1,16f* deutlich hervor. Meines Erachtens beantwortet Paulus dort die zweifelnde Frage von Jes 53,1: "Wer aber glaubt unserer Botschaft (=Evangelium), und wem wurde der Arm des Herrn offenbart?" mit dem mutigen Bekenntnis: "Ich schäme mich des Evangeliums (von Christus) nicht, denn es ist eine Kraft Gottes zur Rettung für jeden, der daran glaubt, in erster Linie für den Juden, aber auch für den Griechen". Wie im programmatischen Satz *1.Kor 1,18*, zu dem auch die Verse 1,21; 1,24 und 1,30 gehören, so wird auch in dem allgemein als Thema des Römerbriefs bezeichneten Zeugnis des Apostels 1,16f die Botschaft von Christus als Kraft Gottes, und zwar als eine den Glaubenden rettende Macht, bezeichnet. Das beweist, daß für Röm 1,16f tatsächlich Jes 53,1 das tragende Fundament bildet, genauso wie für 1.Kor 1,18; 15,1f und besonders für 1.Kor 2,5: Der christliche Glaube baut auf die Kraft Gottes. Ein Vergleich zwischen diesen Zentralaussagen der beiden Hauptbriefe ergibt die Äquivalenz der Wendungen 'Wort vom Kreuz' in 1.Kor 1,18 und 'Evangelium' (von Christus) in Röm 1,16; in der Mitte des Evangeliums steht somit das Kreuz.

2. Das Wort vom Kreuz als Evangelium (Jes 53,1)

2.1 Während das schon.für die Verkündigung Jesu gebrauchte Verb εὐαγγελίζεσθαι

(= hebr. bisser) auf *Jes 52,7 und 61,1f* zurückgeht,[7] kann das *neutestamentliche Nomen* εὐαγγέλιον[8] *nur von Jes 53,1 abgeleitet sein.* Für Paulus bilden diese drei Jesajastellen eine feste Einheit;[9] mit ihrer Hilfe hat er in seiner Darstellung des Glaubensweges *(Röm 10)* die apostolische Predigt charakterisiert und legitimiert: a) Die Apostel sind die endzeitlichen Freudenboten von Jes 52,7, das Röm 10,15 zitiert wird; b) mit Jes 52,7 ist Jes 61,1f verbunden. Denn in der das Zitat einleitenden rhetorischen Frage Röm 10,15 a betont der Apostel die Notwendigkeit der Sendung der Freudenboten; diese wird nicht in Jes 52,7, sondern nur in Jes 61,1 ausdrücklich hervorgehoben; c) entscheidend ist, daß Paulus auch Jes 53,1 auf die Verkündigung des apostolischen Evangeliums bezieht. In *Röm 10, 16* wird von ihm die ablehnende Haltung Israels erwähnt und begründet: "Nicht alle sind dem Evangelium gehorsam geworden". Aber das Versagen der Juden wird nicht etwa mit dem Hinweis auf das Verstockungswort Jes 6,9f, sondern mit Jes 53,1 heilsgeschichtlich erklärt: "Jesaja sagt nämlich: 'Herr, wer hat unserer Botschaft geglaubt?'" Dieser Schriftbeweis ist nur dann zwingend, wenn die prophetische Botschaft vom leidenden Gottesknecht und das apostolische Evangelium sachlich eine Einheit bilden und die beiden Verkündigungsbegriffe *'Botschaft'* (shĕmû'ah, ἀκοή) und *'Evangelium'* (εὐαγγέλιον) *das Gleiche besagen.* Wieder wird deutlich, daß das paulinische Evangelium vom Tod und von der Auferstehung Jesu Christi die Erfüllung der auf die messianische Zukunft bezogenen Botschaft vom Leiden und der Erhöhung des Gottesknechts von Jes 53 darstellt. Dieser theologische Bezug läßt sich auch durch ein *sprachliches Argument* bestätigen: Die Deutung der eschatologisch verstandenen 'Botschaft' (shĕmû'ah) in Jes 53,1 als 'Frohbotschaft' (bĕsôrah') im Targum und als 'Evangelium'(εὐαγγέλιον) bei Paulus läßt sich *von Jes 52,7 her rechtfertigen.* Dort stehen die Wendungen 'Freudenbote des Heils' (mĕbasser tôb) und 'Verkündiger des Friedens' (mashmîa' shalôm) in Parallele; sie meinen dieselbe Gestalt;[10] die 'Botschaft' (shĕmû'ah) ist somit 'Evangelium' (bĕsôrah). Dieser Parallelismus ist auch *theologisch wichtig.* Denn Paulus sieht im leidenden Gottesknecht einen 'Friedensstifter' ('oseh shalôm), weil die von ihm stellvertretend übernommene Strafe 'unseren Frieden' bringt (Jes 53,5), unsere Versöhnung mit Gott bewirkt (καταλλαγή = shalôm; vgl. Röm 5,1.10; 2.Kor 5,19). Das Evangelium vom Kreuz des Christus wird so zum 'Wort der Versöhnung' (2.Kor.5,19). Man braucht deshalb nicht anzunehmen, der Targum zu Jes 53 habe in seiner jetzigen Gestalt schon in der Zeit des Paulus existiert; die Deutung von shĕmû'ah = bĕsôrah kann selbständig im Blick auf Jes 52,7 vollzogen worden sein. Nur wurde für den Targumisten die Botschaft vom Gottesknecht deshalb zum 'Evangelium', weil er in Jes 53 den Sieg des Messias und die Erlösung seines jetzt noch unterdrückten Volkes angekündigt sah. Für Paulus hingegen macht das 'pro nobis' des Leidens, der stellvertretende Tod des Gottesknechts, den Heils-und Machtcharakter dieser Botschaft aus und läßt sie als ein Evangelium erscheinen.

2.2 In Röm 10,16 korrespondieren einander ebenso die Wendungen 'dem Evangelium *gehorchen*' und '*an die Botschaft glauben*'. Für Paulus bedeutet das Glauben auch ein Gehorchen; er kann von der ὑπακοὴ πίστεως sprechen (Röm 1,5). Diese von R. Bultmann besonders betonte Eigenart des paulinischen Glaubens[11] läßt sich ebenfalls von Jes 53,1 her erhellen. Denn das glaubende Gehorchen wird dort schon sprachlich durch dessen Gegenstand, die 'Botschaft' (shĕmû'ah = ἀκοή Jes 53,1; Röm 10,16) nahegelegt. Das Verb shama' meint ja sowohl "hören" als auch "gehorchen". Auf beide Bedeutungen legt der Apostel in seinen Ausführungen Röm 10 besonderen Wert: Man kann nicht glauben, ohne (die Botschaft) gehört zu haben (10,14 b), und man sollte sie nicht 'hören', ohne ihr gehorsam zu sein (10,16).

3. Das Geheimnis der Kreuzesbotschaft
(1.Kor 2,9 vgl. Jes 52,15)

3.1 Ist das die Kraft Gottes vermittelnde 'Wort vom Kreuz' in 1.Kor 1,18 von Jes 53,1 maßgeblich bestimmt, so kann man fragen, ob nicht auch in *anderen Aussagen* der beiden ersten Kapitel des 1.Korintherbriefes der *Einfluß des Liedes vom leidenden Gottesknecht* sichtbar wird. In der 26. Auflage des Novum Testamentum Graece von E. Nestle-K. Aland ist er für das problematische Zitat *1.Kor 2,9* registriert:[12] "Was kein Auge gesehen und kein Ohr gehört hat und im kein Herz eines Menschen aufgestiegen ist, was Gott bereitet hat denen, die ihn lieben." Paulus, der hier aus dem Gedächtnis zitiert, hat m.E. primär an die Jes 53,1 unmittelbar voraufgehende Aussage Jes 52,15 gedacht: "So werden viele Völker staunen und Könige ihren Mund verschließen. Denn was ihnen nie erzählt wurde, sehen sie, und was sie nicht hörten, verstehen sie."

Die Verwendung dieser Stelle ist schon deshalb wahrscheinlich, weil der Apostel sie in Röm 15,21 zitiert, ferner, weil er im voraufgehenden Vers (1.Kor. 2,8) von den uneinsichtigen Weltherrschern spricht (vgl. Jes 52,15a) und unmittelbar anschließend (2,10) in emphatischem Wir-Stil an das 'Offenbaren' der Kraft Gottes und damit deutlich an Jes 53,1b erinnert: Was Gott durch den heiligen Geist 'enthüllt' hat, ist eben das unerhörte und zuvor nie bedachte, jetzt aber kraft des Geistes verstandene Geschehen von Kreuz und Auferstehung des messianischen Gottesknechtes. Für Paulus war dies eine 'unter dem Gegenteil' erfolgte Offenbarung des 'Armes' Gottes (Jes 53,1). Er hat sie für diejenigen 'bereitet', d.h. ihrem 'Sehen' und 'Verstehen' (Jes 52,15) zugänglich gemacht, die 'ihn lieben'.[13] So präzisiert Paulus die positiv verstandene Aussage Jes 52,15 im Blick auf das Geheimnis des Kreuzes: Es sind eben nicht viele Völker und Könige, die es recht sehen und verstehen, sondern nur die von Gott Erwählten und vom Geist Erleuchteten. Der Geist läßt sehen und verstehen, was wir mit dem Kreuz an Gaben der göttlichen Liebe empfangen haben (2,13; vgl. Aboth 3,14); Paulus denkt dabei an Jes 55,1-3.

3.2 *Schon Jesus hatte Jes 52,15 aufgenommen,* wie W. Grimm eindrücklich gezeigt hat.[14] Jesus pries seine Jünger: "Selig sind eure Augen, weil sie sehen, und eure Ohren, weil sie hören. Wahrlich, ich sage euch: Propheten und Könige begehrten zu sehen, was ihr seht, und haben es nicht gesehen, und zu hören, was ihr hört, und haben es nicht gehört" (Lk 10,23f/Mt 13,16f). Wie Paulus in 1.Kor 2,9, so hat Jesus das Jesajawort als Verheißung verstanden und frei gebraucht: Das Geheimnis des gegenwärtigen Heilsgeschehens bleibt den Weisen (Lk 10,21) und dem verstockten Israel (Mt 13,13-15) verborgen. Auch bei *Mk 9,9* steht m.E. Jes 52,15 im Hintergrund: Die Jünger sollen vor der Auferstehung des Menschensohns niemand von dem erzählen, was sie auf dem Berg der Verklärung 'gesehen' hatten, weil eben das unerhörte, nie geschaute Ereignis der Auferstehung die volle Enthüllung dessen bringen wird, was mit der Verklärung Jesu zwar angezeigt, von den Jüngern aber nicht verstanden worden war.[15] Nach 1.Kor 2,10-12 wird dieses Geheimnis durch den heiligen Geist verständlich gemacht: Er läßt es 'sehen',[16] 'erkennen' und auch lehren (1.Kor 2,11-13, vgl Joh 2,12; 12,16 nach Jes 52,15), er schafft glaubende Verkündiger des Heils (Jes 53,1; 1.Kor 2,13).

4. Die Wirkung der Kreuzesbotschaft:
Christus als Weisheit und Gerechtigkeit für uns

4.1 Die Maskîlîm und Maṣdîqîm im frühen Judentum

Jes 53,1 und 52,15 bilden somit eine Klammer, die den Abschnitt 1.Kor 1,18–2,13 umschließt. Aber auch innerhalb des umklammerten Teils fehlt der Bezug zum leidenden Gottesknecht nicht. Wie aber 1.Kor 1,18.21.24 sich erst nach der Untersuchung von Röm 1,16; 10,15f fest mit Jesajas Weissagung verknüpfen ließen, so gilt das auch von anderen christologischen Aussagen in 1.Korinther 1: *Man muß weiter ausholen, um den alttestamentlichen Hintergrund deutlich erkennen zu können.* Das betrifft vor allem den *homologischen Schlußsatz 1.Kor 1,30:* "Christus ist für uns zur Weisheit von Gott, zur Gerechtigkeit, Heiligung und Erlösung geworden". Wie kann man ihn dem 'Wort vom Kreuz' und Jes 53 zuordnen? M.E. muß man ihn mit der das Wirken des Gottesknechtes zusammenfassenden, als ein Urteil Gottes formulierten Aussage Jes 53,11 vergleichen: "Durch seine Erkenntnis wird er satt sein, als Gerechter wird mein Knecht die Vielen rechtfertigen". Durch das stellvertretende Leiden des Gerechten wird für andere Gerechtigkeit vor Gott gewonnen, und zwar sind es, wie bei Paulus (vgl. Röm 5,8), die Sünder, die gerettet werden (Jes 53,4f.12). Diese Umwertung der Werte ist *revolutionär, aber auch anstößig.* Sie widerspricht einmal dem allgemein menschlichen und speziell jüdischen Rechtsempfinden, nach dem man den Gerechten für gerecht erklären soll (vgl. Prov 17,15), und zum andern der alttestamentlichen Sühnevorstellung, nach welcher die Sünden durch das Blut geopferter Tiere und durch das Ritual des Großen Versöhnungstages gesühnt werden (Lev 16). Jes 53 wirkt wie ein erratischer Block im Alten Testament. Und will man den Gottesknecht mit dem weggeführten Volk Israel vergleichen, das gleichsam stellvertretend für die sündigen Nationen leidet, so steht solche Deutung im Widerspruch zu Jes 43,3f, wonach Gott Länder wie Ägypten und Äthiopien für Israel als Lösegeld hingeben will. Jesus hat diesen Widerspruch aufgehoben und Jes 43,3f in Jes 53 integriert: Er will sein Leben als Lösegeld für die Vielen hingeben, für sie sein Blut vergießen (Mk 10,45; 14,24).

    4.1.1 Als eine gewisse Vorstufe für diese Auslegung kann man den Gebrauch von Jes 53,11 *in Dan 12,3* betrachten: Der *Menschensohn*—Symbolgestalt für das Volk der Heiligen des Höchsten—*wird als ein leidender Gottesknecht* verstanden (vgl. Dan 7,21). Denn die Märtyrer der großen Religionsnot werden so gepriesen: "Die Weisen (ha-maskîlîm) werden leuchten wie der Glanz der Himmelsfeste, und diejenigen, welche die Vielen zur Gerechtigkeit führen (maṣdîqe ha-rabbîm), wie die Sterne immer und ewig" (Dan 12,3). Hier wird an die Gottesrede angeknüpft, welche die Botschaft vom Leiden des Gottesknechtes (Jes 53,1-10) umgibt. In ihr wird die Rechtfertigung des Knechtes als Errettung aus dem Tod (Jes 53,11), als Triumph über die Feinde (Jes 53,12) und als Erhöhung des Weisen geschildert (Jes 52,13), der von Gott der Welt vor Augen gestellt wird und diese so ins Unrecht setzt: "Siehe, weise sein (jaskîl)[17] wird mein Knecht und erhaben sein, erhoben und sehr hoch sein" (Jes 52,13); "aus der Mühsal seiner Seele wird er (Licht) sehen, er wird sich sättigen an

Erkenntnis, als Gerechter (ṣaddîq) wird mein Knecht die Vielen zur Gerechtigkeit
führen (jaṣdîq), und ihre Sünden wird er tragen" (Jes 53,11); "mit den Starken wird
er Beute teilen" (Jes 53,12). In Dan 12,2f wird dieses Gottesurteil aufgenommen und
auf ein *Kollektiv von Gottesknechten* übertragen: Die zur Auferstehung in Herrlichkeit berufenen Chasidim sind Männer, die der Verbreitung von Weisheit und Gerechtigkeit dienten. Die Verheißungen jaskîl und jaṣdîq für den Gottesknecht werden nun
zu Ehrentiteln für die Getreuen des Gottesvolkes, die eine aktive, und zwar altruisti-
sche, Rolle beschreiben. Die in Jes 52,13 ausgesprochene große Erhöhung wird nun
bildlich-räumlich gefaßt und in einem Vergleich verkündigt: Hoch droben wie die
Sterne am Himmelszelt, werden die Lehrer von Weisheit und Gerechtigkeit leuchten
für immer.[18]

In Dan 12,3 wird ein *neues Ideal von Frömmigkeit* vorgestellt, das von Jes 53 in-
spiriert ist. Die Prädikate 'Weisheit' und 'Gerechtigkeit' sind aus Jes 52,13 und 53,11
gewonnen und miteinander verbunden: Sie sollen wie das Licht der Sterne strahlen
und anderen Menschen zugute kommen. Deshalb wird auch das Partizip ha-
maskîlîm, analog zu den maṣdîqe harabbîm, *kausativ* verstanden (vgl. Dan 11,33);
die Vielen sollen weise gemacht und so zur Gerechtigkeit geführt werden.[19] Aber
nicht durch stellvertretendes Leiden, sondern durch die Lehre der Gebote wird
Gerechtigkeit vor Gott auch bei Anderen gewirkt.

4.1.2 Die *Qumrantexte* zeigen, wie das geschieht. Der 'Lehrer der Gerechtigkeit'
deutet die Worte der Propheten, um die Menschen zur Umkehr zu leiten und sie vor
dem Strafgericht Gottes zu bewahren (1 Qp Hab 2,8-10; CD 1,11f); er führt die
Bußfertigen auf dem Weg nach dem Herzen Gottes (CD 1,8-11). Und der 'Maskil',
ein Lehrer der Gemeinde, soll die 'Kinder des Lichts', 'die Vielen' (1 QS 3,13; 6,8)
unterweisen, ihnen Einblick gewähren in das Geheimnis der Erwählung Gottes zu
Heil und Gericht, in das Wirken der Geister der Wahrheit und der Lüge und in das
von Gott gewollte Ziel der Geschichte (1 QS 3,13–4,26). Die aus dem apokalypti-
schen Buch Daniel entnommenen 'Maskilim' werden in Qumran als Lehrer
apokalyptischer Zukunft etabliert.[20]

4.1.3 *Matthäus* sieht in Johannes dem Täufer einen Mann, der 'auf dem Weg der
Gerechtigkeit kam' (21,32). Durch seine Bußpredigt und Tauftätigkeit wurde dieser
zu einem masdîq ha-rabbîm, zu einem Retter der herbeiströmenden Scharen (Mk
1,4f). Auch Jesus ging diesen Weg, wenn er 'alle Gerechtigkeit erfüllen' (Mt 3,15),
'das Gesetz und die Propheten erfüllen' wollte (Mt 5,17). Er tat dies zwar auch als ein
Lehrer der besseren Gerechtigkeit (Mt 5,17-48), aber inbesondere dadurch, daß er
sein Leben als Lösegeld für die Vielen dahingab (Mt 20,28), sein Blut für 'die Vielen'
vergoß (Mt 26,28). Dadurch wurde Jes 53 in seinem eigentlichen Sinne geschichtlich
verwirklicht und die Weissagung vom Sühneleiden des Gottesknechtes erfüllt; die
Hingabe des Lebens in völligem Gehorsam gegen Gottes Willen macht die Vielen
gerecht.

4.1.4 In der *Weisheit Salomos* wird der Gerechte nach dem Vorbild von Jes 53 und
Dan 12,2f geschildert und der gottlosen Welt gegenübergestellt. Er nennt sich Gottes
Knecht (Sohn 2,13), erregt Anstoß und ist den hochmütigen Gottesleugnern ein
Ärgernis (2,14f). Diese wollen seine Treue testen, indem sie ihn martern und zu
einem schmachvollen Tod verurteilen (2,17-20). Aber von Jes 53 und Dan 12,2 her
werden auch seine Rückkehr zum Leben und seine Rechtfertigung erhofft (3,1-9). Er
ist jedoch nicht der Weise, der zur Gerechtigkeit führt, sondern der Fromme, der die
Andersdenkenden durch seinen Wandel provoziert, aber letztendlich gerechtfertigt

wird und so über seine Gegner triumphiert. Er wird 'Erfolg haben' (jaslah Jes 52,13),[21] ähnlich wie der messianische Gottesknecht im Prophetentargum. Jes 53 wird kollektiv gedeutet und für das Ideal des Gesetzesfrommen in einer gottlosen Welt genutzt. Aber man sollte m.E. *nicht von einem Typos des 'Leidenden Gerechten'* sprechen und diesen auch nicht für die Deutung des Leidens Jesu benutzen. Für einen 'Leidenden Gerechten' konnte es im Alten Testament und frühen Judentum schon sprachlich keinen präzisen Ausdruck geben. Auch ist der Fromme der Sapientia Salomonis, der dem Verlangen nach Typisierung besonders entgegenzukommen scheint, nach dem Bild des leidenden Gottesknechtes in Jes 53 gezeichnet und somit keine typische Größe. Vor allem aber hat sein Tod keine Heilsbedeutung, und das unterscheidet ihn grundsätzlich von Jesus.

4.2 Der maṣdîq ha-rabbîm und der maḥaṭî' ha-rabbîm in Aboth 5,18

4.2.1 Die Rabbinen konnten zwar auch, wie die Weisheit Salomos, den Gegensatz von 'gerecht' und 'gottlos' im Blick auf Jes 53 entwickeln; sie haben aber wie in Dan 12,3 kurze Urteilsformeln gebildet, die sich auf das Bestehen im Gericht Gottes beziehen. Dabei erscheint nur der maṣdîq und die Rechtfertigung der Vielen auf der positiven Seite, jedoch ist die Tätigkeit des maskîl, des weisen Lehrers, in das zur Gerechtigkeit führende Handeln einbezogen.

In den 'Sprüchen der Väter' (Aboth 5,18) wird deklariert: "Jeder, der die Vielen zur Gerechtigkeit führt (köl ha-mezakkeh 'ät harabbîm), für den wird keine Sünde auf sein Konto geschrieben (wörtl.; . . . "kommt in seine Hand", bějadô); jeder, der die Vielen zur Sünde verleitet (kol ha-maḥaṭî' 'ät ha-rabbîm), wird keine Möglichkeit zur Buße haben". Die Stelle *Dan 12,3,* die von der Verherrlichung der Weisen und gerecht Machenden spricht, hat diesem rabbinischen Urteil als Vorlage gedient. Der unmittelbar voraufgehende apokalyptische Satz *Dan 12,2* von der doppelten Auferstehung, entweder zu ewigem Leben oder zu ewiger Schmach, mag das rabbinische Kontrastbild von der unvergebbaren Sünde mit veranlaßt haben. Das Werk des Gerechtmachens anderer hat ein solches Gewicht, daß kein Vergehen es jemals aufheben kann; umgekehrt wird das Verleiten zur Sünde so hart beurteilt, daß das Bestehen im Gericht aussichtslos wird. Zwei biblische Beispiele dienen zur Illustration: "*Mose* war gerecht (zakhā) und führte die Vielen zur Gerechtigkeit (zakhûth); die Gerechtigkeit der Vielen hing von ihm ab".[22] Moses rechtfertigendes Handeln bestand in der Übergabe und im Lehren der Gebote Gottes, deren Erfüllung verdienstvoll ist.[23] Das klassische Gegenstück zu Mose war *Jerobeam*—aufgrund des stereotypen Urteils des Deuteronomisten, dieser König habe gesündigt und Israel zur Sünde verführt (vgl. 1.Kön 15,26 u.a.).[24]

4.2.2 Außer Dan 12,3 hat auch *Jes 53,11* bei dieser Darstellung des rechtfertigenden Handelns als Vorbild gedient. Denn für Mose wird—über Dan 12,3 hinaus—auch das *Gerecht-Sein* eigens erwähnt, das in Jes 53,11 erscheint: "Mein Knecht, der Gerechte, wird die Vielen rechtfertigen" (jaṣdîq ṣaddîq 'abdî 'ät ha-rabbîm); d.h.: der gute Baum bringt gute Früchte (vgl. Mt 7,15-20). In Aboth 5,18 und der ähnlichen Stelle b Joma 87a ist die Wendung ṣaddîq-hiṣdîq durch zakhā-mezakkäh ersetzt. Das Urteil 'gerecht' gründet sich auf verdienstvolles Handeln; die Gerechtigkeit ist eine *iustitia activa,* sie wird durch Werke des Gesetzes erreicht.

4.3 Diese Auffassung erscheint auch *im Targum zu Jes 53,*[25] der den Gegensatz zwischen paulinischer Rechtfertigungslehre und jüdischem Gesetzesgehorsam besonders deutlich erkennen läßt und alle neuerlichen Bemühungen, ein Mißverständnis jüdischer Gesetzeslehre bei Paulus nachzuweisen, zum Scheitern verurteilt. Im Prophetentargum zu Jes 53 tritt der jüdische Nomismus klar zutage, und zwar an einer Stelle, wo man ihn eigentlich gar nicht erwarten dürfte. Der messianische Gottesknecht dieses Targum[26] macht nicht etwa durch sein stellvertretendes Leiden gerecht, sondern als ein *Lehrer der Tora,* die zur Auslegung dieses Textes eigens herbemüht werden muß. Bei der Wiedergabe von Jes 53,11 wird das göttliche Urteil 'saddîq jasdîq' durch ein jasdîq saddîqîn ersetzt: Die Gerechten, die Täter des Gesetzes,[27] werden gerecht gesprochen, nicht die Sünder. Ja, der 'Knecht' ('aebaed) Gottes 'knechtet' die Vielen 'unter das Gesetz' (sha'bed le' orajĕthā' Tg Jes 53,11.12), während er Israel von der 'Knechtschaft' (sha'bûd) der Völker befreit (Tg Jes 53,11).[28] Außerhalb des Gesetzes gibt es kein Heil; diese Maxime gilt auch für den Gottesknecht des Targum: Als masdîq ist er ein maskîl, ein Lehrer des Gesetzes, dem man die Menschen dienstbar machen muß. Im Gegensatz dazu hat Paulus als der Freie sich zu einem 'Knecht' von allen gemacht, um die Vielen zu gewinnen (1.Kor 9,19). Aber das geschah durch den Dienst des Geistes, nicht des Gesetzes (2.Kor 3,6f).

5. Die Rechtfertigung der Vielen durch Gott und Christus im Römerbrief

5.1 Schon vor den Rabbinen hat der Apostel *Paulus den Rechtfertigungstext Jes 53,11* benützt, ihm aber evangeliumsgemäß die Rettung der Verlorenen entnommen. Freilich wird Jes 53,11 nicht direkt zitiert. Aber in Röm 3,25f wird sogar das *rechtfertigende Handeln Gottes* danach beurteilt und formuliert: In aller Öffentlickeit, vor den Toren Jerusalems, hat Gott den Erweis dafür erbracht, daß "er gerecht ist und den rechtfertigt, der aus dem Glauben an Jesus" (lebt). Demnach ist Gott für Paulus hasaddîq jasdîq 'ät ha-rabbîm: Gerecht ist er dadurch, daß er durch das Geschehen von Golgatha sein richtendes, vernichtendes, Urteil über die Sünde gesprochen hat. Aber ebenso rettet er die Sünder, die im Tod des gerechten Gottessohnes die Sühne für ihre Sünden erkennen können (Jes 53,4f) und den Gekreuzigten als den ansehen, der den Fluch des Gesetzes stellvertretend für sie getragen hat (Gal 3,13).

5.2 In *Röm 5,12-21* wird auch die später bei den Rabbinen bedachte Gegenseite des rechtfertigenden Handelns aufgeführt, ja, sie wird sogar an den Anfang gestellt. Während aber die Rabbinen Gestalten der Geschichte Israels wie Mose und Jerobeam einander gegenüberstellen, greift Paulus, dem es um das Angebot der Rechtfertigung für jedermann geht, auf *Adam, den Vater der Menschheit,* zurück: Er ist der 'Typos des Kommenden' (V 14) und als solcher das Gegenbild zu Christus. Dadurch erhält das vergleichende Urteil kosmische Geltung, eine existentielle, für alle Zeit gültige Bedeutung: Wie durch einen Menschen (Adam) die Sünde in die Welt kam und durch die Sünde der Tod . . . so wurde durch den einen Menschen Jesus die Gnade Gottes und das Geschenk der rechtfertigenden Gerechtigkeit für die Vielen=alle in Fülle angeboten (Röm 5,15.17). Die Tatsache, daß Paulus eine *Urteilsformel vor Augen hatte,* läßt begreifen, daß er in Röm 5,12 den Vergleich 'Adam-Christus' beginnt, ohne ihn abzuschließen: Er wußte um Christus als den Gerechten, der die Vielen zur Gerechtigkeit führt (Jes 53,11). Zu ihm gehört Adam, der durch seine Übertretung Sünde und

204 | Der altt. Hintergrund von 1.Korinther 1-2

Tod in die Welt hereinbrachte. Ja, Adam ist nicht nur Kontrastbild, sondern auch Urheber des Unheils und deshalb Ursache der Erlösung; das bedingt die umgekehrte Reihenfolge Sünder-Gerechter und die theologische Diktion: "Wie durch die Übertretung des einen Menschen die Vielen zu Sündern gemacht wurden, so wurden durch den Gehorsam des Einen die Vielen als Gerechten konstituiert." Das in Röm 5,15.18.19 genannte Objekt des heilsgeschichtlichen Handelns, nämlich 'die Vielen', zeigt deutlich, daß der Apostel von Jesus als messianischem Gottesknecht sprach (Jes 53,11), wobei er 'die Vielen' inkludierend als 'alle' ($\pi\acute{\alpha}\nu\tau\epsilon\varsigma$ V 18) verstand. Wie bei den Rabbinen scheint die Tora die Norm für das Urteil 'gerecht-ungerecht' zu sein: Adam hat das Gebot übertreten (V 15), Christus hingegen ist der Gehorsame (V 19). Und doch ist in beiden Fällen nicht das mosaische Gesetz gemeint. Auch hatte Adam nicht direkt zur Sünde verführt, sondern durch seinen Ungehorsam der Sünde die Tür geöffnet (vgl. Gen 4,7), so daß sie in die Welt des Menschen eindringen und den Tod als Sold der Sünde mit sich bringen konnte (5,12).[29] Diesen Mächten stellt sich in Christus die göttliche Gnade entgegen: Als der gehorsame Knecht Gottes hat er die Rechtfertigung der Sünder ermöglicht, durch seinen stellvertretenden Tod ihnen das Leben und die künftige Herrschaft über diese Mächte gesichert (Röm 5,17f); Paulus hat auch die in Dan 12,2 eröffnete Dimension 'ewiges Leben–ewige Schmach' mit bedacht.

5.3 Dabei stellt er einen *'Mehrwert' der Gnadenwirkung* gegenüber dem durch Adam verursachten Unheil[30] fest (Röm 5,15). Er ist etwas anders auch in *1.Kor 15,45 konstatiert und als Urteil ausgebracht:* Der erste Adam war eine lebendige Seele (näphäsh ḥajjah), der letzte Adam aber lebenshaffender Geist (rûaḥ měḥajjeh). Darum starb (mēt) der erste Adam, und alle Menschen sterben durch ihn (mēmît harabbîm). Dagegen wurde Christus als letzter Adam von den Toten auferweckt (hajah); durch ihn werden die Seinen lebendig gemacht (měḥajjeh ha-rabbîm 1.Kor 15,21 f).

Die kreative, 'kausative', Wirksamkeit Christi macht das 'Mehr' der Gnade aus. Dieser Mehrwert erscheint auch in *Jes 53:* Das vom Gottesknecht erwirkte Heil (Shalôm) 'wird viel sein' (Tg Jes 53,5), der davidische Messias wird ein 'Mehrer' sein (marbeh Jes 9,6); er rettet 'die Vielen' (Jes 53). Die Gnade und die Gnadengaben Gottes werden im Alten Testament gern mit dem Prädikat des Reichtums, des Viel-Seins, gerühmt.[31]

6. Christus als Maskîl (unsere Weisheit) und als Maṣdîq (unsere Gerechtigkeit) in 1.Kor. 1-2

6.1 In 1.Kor 1-2 steht die *rettende Weisheit Gottes* der ins Verderben führenden Weisheit der Welt gegenüber (1,18.21-25; 2,5). Weil sie aber 'unter dem Gegenteil', am Kreuz des Messias, geoffenbart wurde, erscheint sie den Juden, die auf wunderbare Machterweise, und den Griechen, die auf einsichtige Demonstrationen von Weisheit bedacht sind (1,22), als Schwäche und Torheit. In Wahrheit ist sie den Verhaltensweisen der Welt weit überlegen (1,25). Gott hat den Weg der *absconditas sub contrario* gewählt, weil seine schöpferische Macht und Weisheit der Welt verborgen blieben, obwohl diese der Weisheit Gottes ihr Dasein verdankt (1,21; 2,7).[32] Dabei greift Paulus wie in Röm 5,12-21 auf den ersten Anfang zurück, und wieder stehen Jes 52,13; 53,12 und Dan 12,3 im Hintergrund. Das *Geheimnis der Heilsgeschichte* war schon im Anfang beschlossen (2,7) und in Jes 53 vorausverkündigt worden. Nach Jes 53, 10 'gefiel es' (haphas) Gott, den Knecht zu 'zermalmen'; nach 1.Kor

1,21 'gefiel es' (εὐδόκησεν) ihm, "durch die Torheit des Kerygmas die Glaubenden zu retten". Auch das uneinsichtige Verhalten der Weltherrscher was schon mitbedacht und in Jes 52, 15 angesagt. Gottes Handeln zum Heil der Menschen ist freilich wunderbar; Nach Jes 53,3f war es zunächst auch den späteren Verkündigern des Gottesknechts unverständlich, so wie der Pharisäer Paulus das Kreuz mißverstand (2.Kor 5,16; Gal 3,13). Deshalb beruft sich der Apostel in 1.Kor 2,10-12 auf die erleuchtende Kraft des heiligen Geistes. Denn Christus als der Gekreuzigte wird den Berufenen als Kraft und Weisheit Gottes verkündigt (1,24), als solcher ist er *"für uns von Gott her zur Weisheit und Gerechtigkeit, zur Heiligung und Erlösung geworden"* (1,30).

6.2 Die prädizierenden, homologischen Nomina dieses Spitzensatzes 1.Kor 1,30 fassen *Jes 52,13-53,12 christologisch zusammen und* machen die heilbringende Wirkung, die in dem maskîl-masdîq Urteil liegt, für die paulinische *theologia crucis* fruchtbar. Vom Kontext her wäre nur das Prädikat "Weisheit" zu erwarten.[33] Daß Paulus weitere Nomina hinzufügt, entspringt nicht etwa einem doxologischen Überschwang; vielmehr stand dem Apostel Jes 53 vor Augen, dessen *interpretatio Christiana er* gegenüber der jüdischen Messiaserwartung zur Geltung bringen mußte. Das Verb ἐγενήθη meint die heilsgeschichtliche Erfüllung[34] von Jes 53 durch Jesu Kreuz; das 'für uns' deutet auf die 'kausative', dienende und rettende, Kraft der Weisheit und Gerechtigkeit, die in den Begriffen 'Heiligung' und 'Erlösung' als solchen bereits zur Sprache kommt.

6.2.1 In Entsprechung zu Jes 52,13; 53,11, sowie Dan 12,3, stehen die Prädikate *Weisheit und Gerechtigkeit* an der Spitze; sie kennzeichnen Christus als maskîl und masdîq in endgeschichtlichem Sinn. Sie werden auch im Judentum als *wesentliche Eigenschaften des Messias* angesehen. Dieser wird die Völker und Nationen richten 'in der Weisheit seiner Gerechtigkeit' (Ps Sal 17,29 vgl. Jes 11,2.4); in Gottes Volk duldet er keine ungerechten Taten (17,27), und er wird es dementsprechend erziehen (17,41.43). Aber für Paulus ist 'Weisheit' nicht so sehr eine Qualität des Christus als eines Herrschers oder auch Lehrers. Vielmehr 'wurde' der Messias Jesus am Kreuz zur 'Weisheit für uns' (Jes 52,13), weil er im Gehorsam des Gottesknechts den Weg ging, durch den sich die heilschaffende Weisheit Gottes der Welt offenbart. Noch mehr gilt das von Christus als 'unserer Gerechtigkeit':[35] Durch sein stellvertretendes Leiden 'wurde' der Gottesknecht als der Gerechte zur Gerechtigkeit für die Vielen (Jes 53,11). Das göttliche Urteil maskîl-masdîq wird kraft des heiligen Geistes in 1.Kor 1,30 homologisch in Substantive gefaßt, die sich auf Gottes Offenbarung in der Geschichte beziehen.

6.2.2 Die beiden letzten Aussagen in 1.Kor 1,30, nämlich *'Heiligung' und 'Erlösung'* waren noch nicht wie 'Weisheit und Gerechtigkeit' begrifflich durch Jes 52,13; 53,11 und Dan 12,3 vorbereitet, sondern sind, diesen entprechend, von Paulus hinzugefügt worden, um den Reichtum der durch Christus geoffenbarten Gnade Gottes zu bekennen. Wie nach jüdischer Erwartung die Weisheit und Gerechtigkeit wichtige Merkmale der messianischen Herrschaft sind, so gehört auch die *Heiligung* wesentlich dazu: Der endzeitliche Davidide wird Jerusalem reinigen und es heilig machen, wie es ganz am Anfang war (Ps Sal 17,30); er wird die Herde Gottes leiten in aller Heiligkeit (17,41; vgl. 17,26). Und die *Erlösung* Israels ist die Hauptaufgabe des Messias; im Vergleich zu Mose wird er der 'zweite Erlöser' genannt. Aber in *1.Kor 1, 30* sind Heiligung und Erlösung auf das Kreuz zu beziehen und mit *Jes 53* zu verbinden: Sie drücken die Wirkung des im Hauptteil von Jes 53 geschilderten

Leidens aus. Die *Heiligung* könnte, sprachlich gesehen, der Aussage Jes 53,10 entnommen werden, wonach es Gott gefiel, den Knecht zu 'zermalmen' (dakk'ô). Dieses seltene Verb haben schon LXX zu dakhā' (Pael) = καθαρίζειν in Beziehung gesetzt (anders in V 5): καὶ κύριος βούλεται καθαρίσαι αὐτόν. Ähnlich mag Paulus in Jes 53,10 einen Hinweis auf die reinigende Wirkung der Lebenshingabe des Gottesknechtes gefunden haben: Die Korinther sind die "in Christus Jesus Geheiligten" (1,2). Nach Jes 53,5 ist der Gottesknecht 'zermalmt' um unserer Sünden willen (mĕdukka' me'ăvônôthenû); auch dies konnte man als Reinigung (mĕdakke') von Sünden verstehen. Christus ist ja das für uns geschlachtete Passahlamm (1.Kor 5,7), und wie Johannes (1,29) könnte auch Paulus die Verbindung von Passahlamm und Gottesknecht (Jes 53,7) hergestellt haben. Justin (Dial. c. Tr. 13,1) findet in Jes 53 den Beweis dafür, daß nicht Wasserbäder und Opfertiere den Menschen von seinen Sünden reinigen können, sondern nur das Blut Christi und die Taufe, die im Glauben an das Kreuz empfangen wird. Zum maskîl und maṣdîq tritt somit der mĕdakke' (mĕtaher und mĕqaddesch), der Christus, der uns reinigt, für unsere Sünden sühnt.

6.2.3 Christus wurde für uns zur *Erlösung,* indem er uns vom Fluch des Gesetzes losgekauft hat, für uns zum Fluch geworden ist (Gal 3,13 nach Deut 21,23). Ähnlich wie das Prädikat der Heiligung könnte der Apostel auch die Erlösung mit Jes 53 verbunden haben. Die Wendung *Jes 53,5:* "Er wurde um unserer Frevel willen *durchbohrt*" (mĕhôlal) ließ sich auch als mĕqôlal = 'verflucht' (ἐπικατάρατος, Gal 3,13, vgl. 11Q Miqd 64,12) lesen: Als der gekreuzigte Gerechte (talûj) war Christus der um unserer Frevel willen Verfluchte und so ein Sühne Wirkender (mĕkapper) und Versöhnung Stiftender (mĕshallem). Auch hat der Tod, das Ausschütten der Seele zum Tode (Jes 53,12), das Weggenommenwerden vom Lande der Lebenden (Jes 53,8), eine für die Sünden sühnende Wirkung (vgl. m Sanh 6,2 kapparah). Der Gottesknecht kann als Schuldopfer ('asham) bezeichnet werden (Jes 53,10); Christus ist unser mekapper. Mit 1.Kor. 1,30 läßt sich etwa 1.Kor 6,11 vergleichen: "Aber ihr seid abgewaschen, geheiligt, gerechtfertigt im Namen unseres Herrn Jesus Christus und im Geist unseres Gottes" oder auch Eph 1,4-11, wo die Heiligung (V 4), die Erlösung durch Jesu Blut (V 7), aber auch die Weisheit (V 8) und die Erkenntnis des göttlichen Heilswillens (V 9) als Wirkung des Christusgeschehens gerühmt werden. Freilich ist dort der Bezug zu Jes 53 und den Urteilsformeln nicht mehr so deutlich zu sehen wie in 1.Kor 1,30.

6.3 Dort werden demnach nicht beliebig aneinander gereihte Substantive, *disjecta membra,*[36] geboten oder "große Schlagworte der Erlösungsreligion ohne theologische Distinktion mehr herausgestoßen als logisch klar geordnet".[37] Vielmehr handelt es sich in 1.Kor 1,30 um wohlgeordnete, von Jes 53 inspirierte Prädikate, in denen die Früchte des Keuzes Christi entsprechend dem Leiden des Gottesknechtes in homologischer, ungemein verdichteter, Form folgerichtig und präzis den Glaubenden vor Augen gestellt werden. Hinter den Nomina stehen Partizipien 'kausativer' Art: Christus ist der maskîl, maṣdîq, mĕqaddesh und mĕkapper ha-rabbîm geworden. Man kann damit vergleichen, wie Gott im Gebet der Achtzehn Bitten gepriesen wird: Er ist der mĕhajjeh ha-metîm (2.Bitte), der go'el Israel (7.Bitte), der mĕbarekh ha-shanîm (9.Bitte), der mĕqabbes niddĕhê Israel (10.Bitte), der makhnî'a zedîm (12.Bitte), der boneh Jerushalajim (14.Bitte). Man könnte auch im Blick auf die Kabbala sagen: Paulus hat in 1.Kor 1,30 eine Reihe christologischer Sĕphîrôth gebildet, d.h. 'Abglänze' des Handelns Gottes, die im Bild des Gekreuzigten und Erhöhten sichtbar werden.

6.4 Gerade dieses als Homologie gebotene heilsgeschichtliche Urteil Gottes über Christus offenbart die *Eigenart christlicher Theologie gegenüber dem Judentum:* Weisheit und Gerechtigkeit werden nicht durch Studium und Tun der Tora gewonnen, die Heiligung wird nicht rituell und kultisch vollzogen, die Erlösung meint nicht Befreiung von einem politischen Unterdrücker. Diese Begriffe bezeichnen auch nicht die Qualitäten eines Herrschers von Gottes Gnaden, sondern sind im Glauben sichtbare, geschichtlich erfahrene *Handlungsweisen Gottes erga nos.* Sie werden am Kreuz geoffenbart, durch den stellvertretenden Tod des Messias uns übereignet. Jesus, der den Dienst des Gottesknechtes vollzog, hat die Weisheit Gottes als Gegensatz zur Weisheit der Welt offenbart, die Gerechtigkeit Gottes als iustitia passiva, den Sünder rettende Macht, zur Geltung gebracht und Heiligung und Erlösung als Tilgung der Sündenschuld und als Befreiung von der Macht des Todes vollzogen. Damit wurde ein wichtiger Schritt zum Neuen Bund hin getan.

6.4.1 Auch die *Apostel* werden zu einer Art von maskîlîm und maṣdîqîm. Ihnen wurde das rechte Verstehen des Keuzes durch den Geist geoffenbart (1.Kor 2,9-12). Aber als Verkündiger (1,25), deren Zeugnis von Beweisen des Geistes und der Kraft begleitet ist (2,4), werden sie auch zu Lehrern der Weisheit Gottes (2,1-7). Sie tun das nicht mit Worten menschlicher Weisheit (2,1), denn ihre Sprechweise ist vom Geist gelehrt (2,13f). Dadurch entsprechen die Boten und deren Kunde dem Gegenstand der Botschaft, der Offenbarung der Macht und Weisheit Gottes durch das Kreuz (vgl. 2.Kor 12,8-10). *Paulus* hat sich 1.Kor 9,22 dazu entschlossen, allen alles zu werden, um einige zu retten, Als ein Freier machte er sich zum Knecht, um viele zu gewinnen (V 19); so wird er zu einem maṣdîq, der durch das Evangelium die Vielen zur Gerechtigkeit führt. Derjenige, der einst den Glauben zerstörte, ist zu dessen Verkündiger geworden (Gal 1,23); in diesem Urteil der Christen über Paulus wird der mashmîd ha'âmûnah zu einem mashmî'a ha'âmûnah. Das ist eine auf das Evangelium bezogene Version des mahătî'- maṣdîq-Urteils.

6.4.2 Die christlichen maskîlîm als Verkündiger der Weisheit Gottes wenden sich an die *'Vollkommenen'* (τέλειοι 1.Kor 2,6). Diesen hier überraschend auftauchenden Begriff sollte man nicht etwa dem Kult der Mysterienreligionen oder der Gnosis zuschreiben, genau so wenig wie die Pneumatiker und Psychiker in 1.Kor 2,13-15.[38] Denkt man an einen hebräischen Hintergrund, so bieten sich weniger die temîmê däräkh in Qumran (1 QS 4,23) an, als vielmehr die *shĕlemîm,* das staurologisch gefüllt ist, die Friedensbotschaft des Kreuzes spiegelt (vgl. Eph 2,14). Diese Vollkommenen (shĕlemîm) wissen, daß Christus unser shalôm ist; sie stehen über dem Streit der Parteien in Korinth. Sie und die sie anredenden Verkündiger werden als maskîlîm der Weisheit Gottes zu mashlîmîm, zu Friedensstiftern, die den durch das Kreuz geschenkten Frieden mit Gott auch für das Leben in der Gemeinde fruchtbar machen möchten.

7. Die Weisheit der Welt

7.1 Wie bei den Rabbinen zum Urteil über den Gerechten, der die Vielen zur Gerechtigkeit führt, das Kontrastbild des Gottlosen gehört, der andere zur Sünde verleitet, so erscheint in 1.Kor 1-2 als Gegensatz zur Weisheit Gottes die 'Weisheit der Welt', die Gott mit der Botschaft vom Kreuz als Torheit und Schwäche entlarvt. Als eine *'insaniens sapientia'* (Horaz Oden I,34) ist sie nicht nur töricht als zwischenmenschliche Verhaltensweise, vielmehr hat sie—gerade in der messianischen Zeit—

eine verführende, *ins Verderben führende, Macht*. Die von der weltlichen Weisheit Verblendeten sind ja "solche, die verloren gehen" (1,18). Die 'Weisheit der Welt' wird von den Weisen, Schriftgelehren und Forschern 'dieses Äons' verbreitet (1,20). Ihre bestechenden Argumente sind deshalb nicht nur nichts vor Gott, sondern haben auch für die Menschen eine 'nichtende', das Nicht-Erwählt-Sein offenbarende, Macht: Sie führen ins Verderben, sind mashhîtîm, im Gegensatz zur rettenden (moshîa'), schlicht vorgetragenen, Botschaft vom Kreuz (1,18; 2,13f).

7.2 Hier *korrigiert der Apostel die* jüdische—einst von ihm selbst bejahte—*Tradition*. Denn das mosaische Gesetz steht nun nicht mehr als Stimme der Weisheit Gottes im Gegensatz zum Heidentum, zu der epikuräischen Philosophie, sondern gehört—jüdisch interpretiert—selbst auf die falsche Seite. Und die im Judentum so fest verbundenen Größen des maskîl und masdîq werden voneinander getrennt. Denn die Vertreter des Weisen (maskîl) sind nach 1.Kor 1,20 nicht etwa die großen Männer der Stunde, die das Geheimnis der Endgeschichte kennen (1.Kor 2,1.7) und deshalb die Vielen zur Gerechtigkeit führen; vielmehr sind sie dem Zeitgeist verfallen und auch Werkzeuge des 'Verfalls'. Gott selbst hat die Weisheit der Welt zur Torheit gemacht (ἐμώρανεν 1,20); dieses μωραίνειν ist das Gegenteil vom kausativen hiskîl.[39] Das 'Wort vom Kreuz' erweist die scheinbare Ohnmacht und Torheit Gottes als weiser und stärker als die Qualitäten der Welt, weil sie der Rettung des verlorenen Menschen dienen (1,18).

7.3 Das Urteil Gottes über die Weisheit der Welt und ihre in das Verderben führende Kraft wird besonders an den *Herrschern dieser Welt* und an ihrem Verhalten gegenüber Christus offenbar: Weil sie die im Geheimnis der Heilsgeschichte verborgene Weisheit Gottes nicht erkannten, haben sie den Herrn der Herrlichkeit gekreuzigt (2,7f).[40] Einst hatte der Pharao in Ägypten die Erwählung Israels nicht wahrhaben wollen; ähnlich werden, überrascht von Gottes Handeln an seinem Knecht, Völker und Könige den Mund verschließen (Jes 52,15). Dieser Jesajastelle werden wohl die 'Fürsten dieser Welt' in 2,8 ihre Erwähnung mit verdanken. Dabei spielt es kaum eine Rolle, ob mit ihnen Engelmächte oder irdische Herrscher gemeint sind oder sogar ein 'sowohl-als auch' in Frage kommt.[41] Von Jes 52,15 her wird man eher an *irdische Machthaber* denken, wie sie im Prozeß Jesu erscheinen. Für einen jüdischen Hohenpriester wie Kaiphas war der messianische Anspruch Jesu ein gottteslästerliches Ärgernis, für den Heiden Pilatus eher eine Torheit; beide konnten im gefangenen Jesus keinen 'Herrn der Herrlichkeit' erkennen. Für Kaiphas und Pilatus spricht auch die Aussage des Paulus Apg 13,27f: Die Bewohner Jerusalems und ihre Oberen (ἄρχοντες) verkannten Jesus, "und die Stimmen der Propheten, die an jedem Sabbat vorgelesen werden, haben sie durch ihr Urteil erfüllt. Und obwohl sie keine todeswürdige Schuld an ihm gefunden hatten, baten sie Pilatus, daß er hingerichtet werde".

8. Praeparatio Evangelica: Das Handeln der Weisheit Gottes im Alten Testament und im frühen Judentum

8.1 Die Botschaft von einem leidenden, gekreuzigten Messias war für die Juden, die von einem Messias beglaubigende 'Zeichen', d.h. objektiv sichtbare Beweise seiner Bevollmächtigung durch Gott, erwarteten (vgl. Mk 8,11f; Ex 4,7; Jos Bell 2,259ff), ein 'Ärgernis', ein Stolperstein auf dem Weg zum Heil. Hinsichtlich des Kreuzes konnten sie sich auf Deut 21,23 berufen, wonach 'ein am Holz Hängender' verflucht ist und das Land verunreinigt. Auch der Pharisäer Paulus hatte diese Stelle so verstanden und deshalb die hellenistischen Judenchristen als Gotteslästerer verfolgt. Dennoch gibt es für eine Gottesoffenbarung 'unter dem Gegenteil' schon *Hinweise im Alten Testament*. Ein Jude sollte deshalb nicht allzusehr davon überrascht sein, daß Gottes Wege seltsam aussehen. E. Ellis urteilt richtig, wenn er die von Gott gegebene Weisheit sich an dem prophetischen Zeugnis der Schrift bewähren läßt.[42] 8.2 Nach 1.Kor 1,27 hat Gott das erwählt, was vor der Welt töricht und gering ist; in Korinth sind es nicht viele Weise nach dem Fleisch, nicht viele Mächtige und Edle (1,26). Aber Ähnliches gilt auch vom *Volk Israel*, an dem sich die unbegreifliche Liebe und rettende Gerechtigkeit Gottes bewährt hatten. Obwohl es nicht zahlreich, sondern das Kleinste unter allen Völkern war, hat Gott es auserkoren, und nicht der Vernunft, sondern seiner Liebe und der Treue zu den Vätern ist diese Wahl zuzuschreiben; aus diesem Grunde hat Gott dieses Volk auch aus Ägypten erlöst (Deut 7,6-11). Und nicht wegen dessen Gerechtigkeit gab er ihm das gelobte Land; vielmehr ging dieser heilsgeschichtliche Schritt von Gottes rettender Gerechtigkeit aus (Deut 9,4-7).8.3 Auch die *Qumrangemeinde* wußte etwas vom Geheimnis der Erwählung, das dem Weisheits-und Machtdenken der Welt verborgen bleibt. Denn sie konnte sich als eine Pflanzung im dürren Land verstehen (1 QH 8,4f, vgl. Jes 53,2), verborgen unter Bäumen, die am Wasser stehen, aber fähig, den Schößling für eine immerwährende Pflanzung hervorzubringen (Zeile 6). Dieser Schößling wird zwar in der Gegenwart vom Vieh abgeweidet und zertrampelt, von Vögeln bewohnt und vom hohen Bäumen überragt; er steht verdeckt und unbeachtet, sein 'Siegel', d.h. seine von Gott gegebene Bestimmung, ist unbekannt (Zeile 10f). Aber er wird von Engeln behütet wie das Paradies (Zeile 11f); er ist die wahre, endzeitlich bedeutsame, Größe, die Sammlung der von Gott Erwählten.

8.4 Schließlich konnte *Paulus* dieses wunderbare Erwählungshandeln Gottes mit seiner eigenen Erfahrung bestätigen. Gott hatte ihn ja zum Apostel Christi berufen, obwohl der eifernde Pharisäer dessen Gemeinde verfolgt hatte (Gal 1,3f; 1.Kor 15,8-11). Die Kraft Gottes vollendet sich in unserer Schwäche (2.Kor 12,9); dadurch wird verhindert, daß sich der Mensch vor Gott rühmen kann (1.Kor 1,29f).

Abschluß

1. Die Kap. 1-2 des 1.Kor lassen sich von Jes 52,13-53,12 her als eine gedankliche Einheit erweisen, in der Paulus seine am Kreuz orientierte Christologie und Offenbarungslehre der jüdischen Endzeiterwartung und jeder weltlichen Weise, von der Wirklichkeit Gottes zu reden, schroff entgegenstellt. Von Anleihen bei gnostischen Ideen und von dezidiert antignostischen Argumenten ist dort m.E. nichts zu finden. Vielmehr urteilt der Apostel *von der Schrift her,* wobei er seine Auffassung, Gottes Handeln in der Geschichte vollziehe sich unter dem Gegenteil und habe deshalb im Kreuz des Messias seinen Höhepunkt erreicht, mit dem *Sendungsbewußtsein Jesu* in Einklang bringt: Gott hat seinen Heilsplan vor den Weisen und Mächtigen der Welt verborgen und ihn den Unmündigen geoffenbart (Mt 11,25 nach Jes 44,25; 52,15); der Menschensohn ist dazu gekommen, daß er diene und sein Leben für die Vielen dahingebe (Mk 10,45 nach Jes 43,3f und 53,12). Mit Jesu Weg zum Kreuz wurde die Weissagung vom leidenden Gottesknecht verwirklicht, die auch das Evangelium der Urgemeinde und die Theologie des Paulus geprägt hat. **Gerade die paradoxe These,**

die Botschaft vom Kreuz des Christus sei eine Kraft Gottes, läßt sich von Jes 53 her verständlich machen. In Jes 53,1 wird ja das Evangelium vom Knecht Gottes ausdrücklich auf eine Machtoffenbarung Gottes bezogen; diese wird nur da als solche geglaubt und erkannt, wo man das 'Für uns' des Sühneleidens sieht und bestätigt (Jes 53,4f). Darin liegt das Geheimnis des Kreuzes, an dem die Verkündigung des Evangeliums partizipiert.

2. In der Auslegung von Jes 53 tritt das *Neue, Andersartige des christlichen Glaubens* gegenüber der jüdischen Auffassung vom Weg zum Heil, zur Gerechtigkeit vor Gott und zur messianischen Erlösung deutlich hervor. Der scharfe Gegensatz zwischen dem *sola gratia* aufgrund des Kreuzes und dem *sola lege* der jüdischen Ethik sollte stets erklärt, aber nicht abgeschwächt werden. Er entstand trotz der gemeinsamen Grundlage des *sola scriptura* und trotz der von beiden Seiten vollzogenen messianischen Auslegung des Liedes vom leidenden Gottesknecht. Ja, er trat gerade darum besonders klar hervor. Denn die christliche Theologie vom Kreuz Christi steht deshalb im Gegensatz zur jüdischen Theologie, weil für sie Jes 53 als eine Schlüsselstelle benutzt wurde, wobei man gerade das betonte, was von den jüdischen Exegeten meist übersehen wurde, nämlich die sühnende Wirkung des vom Gottesknecht erlittenen Sterbens.

3. Im Kreuz und in seiner Verkündigung wird die *schöpferische Macht Gottes* den Menschen mitgeteilt, was sich auch in der *Sprache der Verkündigung* ausdrückt. Charakteristisch sind etwa die in den Urteilsformeln verwendeten kausativen Partizipien, die deshalb auch für prädizierende Gebetsaussagen übernommen werden. Auch die auf Christus bezogenen Substantive in 1.Kor 1,24.30 lassen sich ja auf solche Partizipien des Heilshandelns zurückführen. Die Sprache verrät ferner, wie man *vom Alten zum Neuen Bund* hinübergeht. Während der Alte Bund *sprachlich* vom Befehlen Gottes, vom Hören und Gehorchen der Menschen bestimmt ist, erscheinen z.B. bei der Verheißung und Verwirklichung des Neuen Bundes auf seiten Gottes das *Geben und Vergeben*. Das Gesetz wird nicht mehr 'befohlen' (1 QS 8,15, vgl. 1,3; 3,10), sondern ins Herz 'gegeben' (Jer 31,32); die Sünden werden *vergeben* (31,34). Gott wird ein neues Herz und einen neuen Geist 'geben' (Ez 36,26.27). Dementsprechend erscheint Gott als ein gütiger, gebender Vater in der *Verkündigung Jesu* (Mt 7,7.11; 10,8.19; 13,11f; Mk 13,11; Lk 11,13; 12,32; 19,13; vgl Joh 6,31ff; 17,1ff), der auch selbst gibt bis hin zur Selbsthingabe (Mk 6,37.41; 8,6; 10,45). So lebte die christliche Gemeinde von der Gabe des Geistes und den ihr geschenkten Charismen.

4. Was war eigentlich theologisch falsch bei den Korinthern, was wird speziell in 1.Kor 1-2 zurechtgerückt? Sicherlich gehören dazu der Stolz auf die eigene geistliche Reife und Erkenntnis, auf den von Paulus selbst gerühmten Reichtum an Charismen (1,5-7, vgl. 1,29.31; 3,18-21; 4,6f). Dieses Selbstbewußtsein wird durch die Weisung 1,31 gedämpft: "Wer sich rühmen will, der rühme sich des Herrn". Das Kreuz als Offenbarung der Kraft und Weisheit Gottes hat ja gezeigt, daß das, was dem Heil der Menschen dient, nicht durch deren eigene Leistung gewonnen werden kann. Das Rühmen der Gnade Gottes, der alles eigene Vermögen zugeschrieben wird, macht das Wesen des Wortes vom Kreuz Christi aus, hebt es vom Gesetzeseifer der Juden und vom philosophischen Streben der Griechen ab. Die Christen sind eben nicht reich und satt an Weisheit (1.Kor 4,8), sondern deren bedürftig; sie sollen nicht herrschen wollen, sondern einander dienen. Das vom Glaubenden geforderte Werk ist der *Dienst am Leib Christi*, seine Begabung die ihm geschenkte Geistesgabe, die in der

Gemeinde mit anderen Charismen harmonisch zusammenwirkt. Auch das in Korinth wohl besonders geschätzte 'Wort der Weisheit' bzw. 'Wort der Erkenntnis' ist eine Gnadengabe (1.Kor 12,8); es kann deshalb nicht als menschliche Eigenleistung gerühmt, sondern nur dem Herrn der Kirche zugeschrieben werden (1,31). Wichtig ist die praktische Folgerung (ἵνα), die Paulus aus der Homologie 1,30 zieht: Gott hat durch Christus auch deshalb so viel für uns getan, damit jeder Eigenruhm ausgeschlossen sei (1,31). Eben diese *existentielle Konsequenz der Kreuzesbotschaft* wurde wohl in Korinth nicht immer beachtet, sonst hätte der Apostel nicht den Hang zum Herrschen ironisch kritisiert (4,8). Vielmehr führt die Gemeinschaft mit dem gekreuzigten und erhöhten Herrn zum Dienst mit den zugewiesenen Gnadengaben, zur Erbauung der Gesamtgemeinde und nicht zu gegenseitiger Rivalität. In *1.Kor 12,4-6* entwirft Paulus eine Art von *ökonomischer Trinität,* und zwar im Blick auf die Einheit im Wirken der verschiedenen Gnadengaben: Gott als schöpferische Potenz, Christus als Herr der Kirche und der Geist als Quelle der Charismen arbeiten in einer diakonischen Kondesendenz im Leib der Kirche zusammen, deren Begabungen und Dienste somit alle von oben, von dem sich selbst mitteilenden Gott und seiner Gnade, kommen. Dabei ist es bezeichnend, daß Christus als der eine Herr der Kirche ausgerechnet mit den mannigfachen 'Diensten' verbunden wird (12,5). Er ist ja zum 'Knecht' der Menschen geworden (Phil 2,7 vgl. Jes 53), so wie Gott einst Israel gedient hat (Jes 43,23). 1.Kor 12,5 stimmt mit dem zentralen Wort Mk 10,45 überein, in dem sich Jesus auf Jes 53,10.12 und Jes 43,3f.23 bezieht und damit die Aussage von der Herrschervollmacht des Menschensohns (Dan 7,14) korrigiert: Der Menschensohn läßt sich nicht dienen, sondern dient den Vielen bis hin zur Hingabe seines Lebens. Ohne diakonische Liebe wird die Erkenntnis arrogant und damit weltlicher Weisheit gleich (1.Kor 8,1); so kann sie zu Störungen, Spaltungen, Krankheiten im Leibe Christi führen. Dessen Heilung kann nur durch das Wort vom Kreuz geschehen, das Christus als den Gottesknecht verkündigt, der unsere Krankheiten trug und durch die stellvertretend erlittene Strafe Frieden stiftete (Jes 53,3-5). Die Verkündigung der am Kreuz geoffenbarten Weisheit Gottes richtet sich deshalb an die 'Vollkommenen' (shĕlemîm 2,6), die als Glieder der Gemeinde über dem Streit der Parteien stehen. Der apostolische maskîl und Bote der Weisheit des Kreuzes erweist sich so als ein mashlîm: Paulus macht die 'Vollkommenen' (shĕlemîm) zu Menschen des Friedens (Shalôm) in der Gemeinde.

Notes

1. "'Wisdom' and 'Knowledge' in I Corinthians", in E. E. Ellis, *Prophecy and Hermeneutics in Early Christianity*, Tübingen, 1978, 45ff. Vgl. dazu M. Hengel: "It is time to stop talking about 'gnosticism in Corinth'. What happened in the community does not need to be explained in terms of the utterly misleading presupposition of a competing Gnostic Mission" (*Crucifixion*, London 1977, 18, Anm. 10).

2. "Christ Crucified", in A.a.O., 74ff.

3. Nach Hengel (*Crucifixion*, a.a.O. S.19) spricht sich in 1.Kor 1 auch die langjährige Missionserfahrung des Apostels aus, der sich für seine Verkündigung des Kreuzes Spott und Widerspruch zuzog. Daß der Messias und Sohn Gottes die 'mors turpissima crucis', den schändlichen Tod eines Verbrechers erlitten haben sollte, war ein Ärgernis, und die Verehrung eines solchen Mannes ein Eselskult. Der historische Vorgang der Kreuzigung Jesu und dessen theologische Deutung durch die Christen sind nicht voneinander zu trennen.

4. Vgl. dazu den Apologeten Justin in seinem Dialog mit dem Juden Trypho Kap. 32: "Dieser euer sogenannter Christus ist ehrlos und ruhmlos geworden, so wie er auch dem äußersten Fluch im Gesetz Gottes verfiel. Denn er wurde gekreuzigt".

5. Der Prophet hat ja das entsetzliche Leiden des Gottesknechts als weise und heilbringende Veranstaltung Gottes verkündigt und so den christlichen Theologen und Verteidigern des Glaubens eine wichtige Stütze für ihr Wort vom Kreuz in die Hand gegeben. Deshalb konnte auch Justin, als ihm der ehrlose und unter dem Fluch der Tora stehende Tod Jesu von Trypho vorgehalten wurde (Dial. c.Tr. 32,1), diesen speziell auf den Gottesknecht von Jes 53 hinweisen: Seine Gestalt wird ohne Herrlichkeit sein . . . durch seine Wunden sind wir geheilt . . . er ließ sich zur Schlachtbank führen wie ein Lamm . . . (32,2 vgl. 89,1-3). Schon Dial. 13,2-7 zitierte Justin das Lied vom leidenden Gottesknecht, wobei er mit Jes 52,10 begann und erst mit Jes 54,6 endete (13,8-9). Er wollte damit sagen, daß das Leiden des messianischen Knechtes zum Heil führt, und zwar für alle Völker (Jes 52,10). In Dial. c.Tr. 111,3 hat Justin Christus als wahres Passahlamm (1.Kor 5,7) mit Jes 53,7 verbunden.

6. In seiner *Theologie des Neuen Testaments*, Tübingen, 1951, 31f, lehnte R. Bultmann die Möglichkeit ab, daß Jesus selbst sich als den deuterojesajanischen 'Gottesknecht' gewußt habe. Abgesehen von den Bedenken gegen die Geschichtlichkeit der Leidensweissagungen spreche dagegen, daß die überlieferten Jesusworte keine Spur von einer Beziehung zu Jes 53 zeigten. H. W. Wolffs Nachweis dafür (*Jesaja 53 im Urchristentum*, München, 1942) sei schwerlich gelungen. Auch die urchristliche Gemeinde habe Jes 53 relativ spät aufgenommen (Apg 8,32f; 1.Petr 2,22-25; Hebr 9,28); allerdings könne dieses Kapitel auch hinter dem vielleicht vorpaulinischen, credoartigen, Satz Röm 4,25 stehen. Für 1.Kor 15,3f sei nicht auszumachen, ob Paulus bei κατὰ τὰς γραφάς an Jes 53 gedacht habe.

Dieses m.E. völlig unzutreffende Urteil R. Bultmanns, das schon wegen einer fehlenden authentischen Kenntnis der jüdischen Quellen unberechtigt war, wirkte sich lähmend auf die neutestamentliche Exegese und vor allem auf die Beantwortung der Frage aus, wie sich Jesus zur Möglichkeit eines gewaltsamen Todes in Jerusalem verhalten haben könnte.

7. Vgl. dazu meinen Aufsatz 'Jesu Evangelium vom Gottesreich', in: *Das Evangelium und die Evangelien*, ed. P. Stuhlmacher, Tübingen, 1983, 56f.

8. Vgl. dazu die Geschichte von Imma Schalom und dem christlichen Philosophen in b Shabbat 116 a/b und meinen in Anm.7 erwähnten Aufsatz S.56f.

9. Solch eine Zusammenschau vollzog auch Justin, der in Dial. c.Tr. 13,2-9 Jes 52,10–54,6 zitierte.

10. Diesen Hinweis verdanke ich Herrn Prof. Dr. Creech, Houston Baptist University.

11. "Paulus versteht die πίστις primär als ὑπακοή, den Glaubensakt als Gehorsamsakt." (*Theologie des Neuen Testaments, 310*).

12. Das ist ein Fortschritt gegenüber den Kommentaren, die meist nur auf Jes 64,3 (LXX) und Ps 30,20 verweisen.

13. Der Schluß des Zitats 1.Kor 2,9 scheint Deut 7,9 aufzunehmen: Gott übt Gnade an denen, die ihn lieben und seine Gebote halten.

14. W. Grimm, *Weil ich dich liebe*, Frankfurt, 1976, 112-123, besonders S. 120. Jes 52,15 ist auch in aeth Hen 46,4f; 55,3f; 62,1-4 aufgenommen.

15. Mk 9,9 ist nicht etwa eine nachträglich zur Verklärungsgeschichte hinzugefügte Aussage, die der Theorie des Messiasgeheimnisses bei Markus dienen soll, sondern ein Baustein in der auf dem Fundament von Jes 53 auferbauten Verklärungsgeschichte, die auf die dem Leiden folgende Erhöhung und Verherrlichung des Menschensohns hinweist (vgl. Jes 52,13). Auferstehung und Erhöhung Jesu sind das unerhörte Geschehen, das noch aussteht, aber geoffenbart und verkündigt werden soll.

16. Die von p^{46} D, F, G und anderen Textzeugen gebotene Lesart ἴδομεν anstelle von εἴδομεν in 1,Kor 2,12 läßt sich von Jes 52,15b her decken.

17. Der Targum versteht jaslah: Mein Knecht, der Messias, wird Erfolg haben. Dieser Satz ist gleichsam das Thema der folgenden Interpretation, die den Triumph des messianischen Gottesknechtes herausarbeitet. Die LXX sagen dagegen: συνήσει ὁ παῖς μου καὶ ὑψωθήσεται καὶ δοξασθήσεται.

18. In aeth Hen 104,2 werden die verfolgten Gerechten getröstet: "Seid voll Hoffnung: Früher seid ihr durch Übel und Trübsal in Schande versetzt worden. Aber jetzt sollt ihr leuchten wie die Himmelslichter; ihr sollt leuchten und gesehen werden, und die Tore des Himmels sollen für euch offen stehen". Nach Phil 2,15 sollen die Christen wie Lichter in der Welt scheinen und sollen unbefleckte Kinder Gottes in einem verkehrten und verdrehten Geschlecht sein. Wie in Mt 5,13-16 ist hier die apokalyptische Verheißung vergegenwärtigt und ethisch verstanden.

19. LXX und Theodotion haben in ihren Wiedergaben von Dan 11,33 und 12,3 die illuminierende Wirkung und rechtfertigende Tätigkeit weggedeutet (LXX Dan 11,33: οἱ ἐννοούμενοι, Dan 12,3: συνιέντες... οἱ κατισχύοντες τοὺς λόγους μου.Theodotion Dan 11,33: οἱ συνετοί Dan 12,3: οἱ συνιέντες... καὶ ἀπὸ τῶν δικαίων τῶν πολλῶν...

20. Der Begriff 'Maskil' bezeichnet eine wichtige Funktion im Leben der Qumrangemeinde, die sich wie die Asidäer (Chasidim) im Buch Daniel in einer Drangsalszeit zu bewähren hatte (1 QS 3,22f, vgl. Dan 12,1). Die Schüler des Maskil sind die 'Kinder des Lichts' (1 QS 3,13), die auf eine Erlösung durch den Erzengel Michael warten (vgl. Dan 12,2 mit 1 QS 4,20; 1 QM 17,6).

21. Er ist nicht etwa ein maskîl und masdîq, denn die helfende und heilbringende Tätigkeit des Gottesknechts ist hier verschleiert. Er wird kontinuierlich auf die Probe gestellt, leidet und stirbt, aber wird letztlich durch Gottes Urteil zum masliah werden: Er wird Erfolg haben.

22. Dafür wird Deut 32,21 als Beweistext gegeben, die einzige Stelle im Alten Testament, an der die Wendung 'Gerechtigkeit Gottes' (sidĕqat J.) erscheint. Mose tat 'die Gerechtigkeit Gottes und Rechtssätze in Israel'.

23. zakhûth bedeutetnicht etwa 'Tugend' (virtue, so E.P. Sanders). Vgl. dazu das *Wörterbuch von Eliezer ben Jehudah* (Bd II,S.1234), wo die Bedeutungen 'Schuldlosigkeit', 'Verdienst' (mit den meisten Belegen),'Vorzug', 'Recht' genannt werden.

24. Das Urteil über Jerobeam wird in Aboth 5,18 analog zu Jes 53,11 formuliert. Zu Aboth 5,18 gibt es eine Parallele in b Joma 87a: "Es ist nicht genug, daß die Gerechten für sich selbst gerecht sind (zokhîn lĕ'asman), vielmehr machen sie ihre Kinder und Enkel gerecht (mĕzakkîn)". Dafür dienen Mose und Aaron als Beweis. Dann folgt das generalisierende Urteil: "Jeder, der die Vielen gerecht macht, hat keine Sünde in seiner Hand; jeder, der die Vielen zur Sünde verleitet, für den gibt es keine Gelegenheit, Buße zu tun".

25. Der Targum zu Jes 52,13-53,12 ist ungewöhnlich breit geraten. Er verrät das verständliche Bemühen, mit diesem sprachlich schwierigen und theologisch tiefsinnigen Text zurechtzukommen. Nirgendwo wird die Notwendigkeit, eine paraphrasierende Wiedergabe des hebräischen Textes in das Aramäische zu bieten, so evident wie in Jes 53. Auch mußte dieser Text dem alttestamentlichen Sühnedenken und der gängigen jüdischen Messiaserwartung angepaßt werden; schließlich galt es, den Toragehorsam als Voraussetzung für die dort angesprochene Rechtfertigung einzubringen. Vor allem aber kann man in dieser midraschartigen Wiedergabe von Jes 53 eine Widerlegung seiner neutestamentlichen Interpretation sehen.

26. Der Targum sieht wie die urchristliche Exegese im Gottesknecht den Messias. Schon in Jes 52,13 werden die Weichen gestellt: 'abdi mĕshîha'. Der Erfolg des Messias wird aus dem Text herausgelesen; vom Leiden des Knechtes wird der Messias aber möglichst fern gehalten. Die Leidensaussagen des hebräischen Textes werden auf das bedrängte, exilierte, Israel (zu 52,14) und vor allem auf die vom Messias besiegten Gegner verteilt (zu 53,7.9). Der Messias ist der Sieger (zu

53,2), und auch die Gerechten siegen mit ihm (zu 53,2.8). Er ist ferner ein Fürbitter (zu 53,4.12) und vor allem ein Lehrer der Tora, obwohl jaskîl in 52,13 im Blick auf 53,10 als jaṣlaḥ=Erfolg haben 'übersetzt wird'. Vielleicht wirkt auch nach, daß in Jes 42,4 die Tora des Gottesknechts erwähnt wird.

27. Ähnlich sprechen die LXX von der Rechtfertigung der Gerechten (δικαιῶσαι δικαίους, vgl. Gal 3,2).

28. Jes 53,5 wird im Targum so wiedergegeben: "Durch seine Erziehung— musar='Züchtigung', 'Strafe' wird wie von den LXX als 'Erziehung' (παιδεία) verstanden—wird sein Friede zahlreich werden, und wenn wir uns um seine Worte versammeln, wird uns vergeben werden". Tg Jes 53.11 a: "Durch seine Weisheit wird er Gerechte gerecht machen, um Viele dem Gesetz zu unterwerfen". Tg Jes 53,12: "Er unterwirft die Widerspenstigen dem Gesetz". Vergebung gibt es nur bei Umkehr zum Gesetz (Tg Onq zu Ex 34,7).

29. Dadurch, daß alle wie Adam sündigten (Röm 5,12), wurde die Herrschaft von Sünde und Tod über die Menschen aufgerichtet (V 17.21). Jeder wiederholt die Sünde des ersten Menschen. Vgl. Röm 7,7-12: Wie Adam durch das Verbot Gottes dazu verleitet wurde, ungehorsam zu werden, so geschieht das beim Menschen schlechthin: Das an sich gute Gebot Gottes weckt die Begierde und läßt das in den Gliedern ruhende Gesetz wirksam werden, das dem Geist und dem Gebot Gottes widerstreitet.

30. Schon in der Rede des Paulus auf dem Areopag werden Adam und Christus einander gegenübergestellt: Aus einem Menschen (Adam) ließ Gott die ganze Menschheit hervorgehen (V 26), und durch einen von Ihm bestimmten Mann (Christus) wird er den ganzen Erdkreis richten (V 31).

31. Vgl. die Fülle (rôb) der Gnadengaben Gottes nach Ps 106,7.45; Jes 63,7 und die Kraft der Gnade (Ps 103,11). Der reiche Segen der neuen Existenz des Gottesknecht ist in Jes 53,10f mit den Verben ṣalaḥ='gedeihen' und saba'='satt sein' bildlich angezeigt. Der Hinweis auf sein langes Leben (Jes 53,10) könnte das durch Christus geschenkte ewige Leben in Röm 5,21 erklären. In Jes 53,10 sind viele Nachkommen verheißen (Targum: "Sie werden viele Söhne und Töchter haben"). Die Verteilung von Beute (Jes 53,12) ist Ausdruck des Sieges und der königlichen Herrschaft (vgl. Röm 5,17.21).

32. Vgl. dazu Röm 1,19f. Nach Prov 8,22ff war die Weisheit der Werkmeister ('umman V 30), das Prinzip (re'shîth = ἀρχή), mit dessen Hilfe Gott die Welt erschuf.

33. H. Lietzmann, An die Korinther I-II, HNT 9, Tübingen, 1949, 11.

34. Dabei ist die Form ἐγενήθη als ein passivum divinum zu verstehen und auf Kreuz und Auferstehung zu beziehen.

35. Die rechtfertigende Wirkung der Gerechtigkeit des Christus ergibt sich auch aus 2.Kor 3,9, wo dem 'Dienst der Verurteilung' der 'Dienst der Gerechtigkeit' gegenübersteht, der somit auch aktive Bedeutung haben, zur Gerechtigkeit führen muß.

36. E. Fascher, Der Erste Brief des Paulus an die Korinther, ThHK NT 7/1, Berlin, 1975, 112.

37. So J. Weiß. Sie sind auch keine Exegese von σοφία (G. Heinrici), noch Antithesen zu 'töricht, schwach, unedel und nicht seiend' (J. Bohatec), vgl. E. Fascher a.a.O., 109f. Richtiger W. Bauer, ἁγιασμός sei ein abstractum pro concreto: Christus ist in der Tat der Urheber unserer Heiligung (Fascher a.a.O, 111).

38. Vgl. dazu Bultmann, Theologie, a.a.O., 174f; nach R. Reitzenstein, Hellenistische Mysterienreligionen, Leipzig, 1927, 56, 71-73; W. Bousset, Kyrios Christos, Göttingen, 197-199. Vgl. dazu meinen Aufsatz, "Das Problem der Gnosis seit der Entdeckung der Texte von Nag Hammadi", in: VF 2 (1976) 46-80.

39. μωραίνειν ist in der Profangräzität intransitiv; hier hat es aktive ('kausative') Bedeutung. Es könnte auch an ein Wortspiel gedacht sein: Die maskîlîm werden zu mistakkělîm, d.h. verwirrten Narren.

40. Vgl. dazu Sap.Sal. 2,21 von der Verblendung der Gottlosen: ἐπλανήθησαν, ἀπετύφλωσεν γὰρ αὐτοὺς ἡ κακία αὐτῶν vgl. 5,6. Sie erkannten die Geheimnisse Gottes nicht (vgl. 1.Kor 2,7f); wie die Sadduzäer lehnen sie die Hoffnung auf eine künftige Belohnung der Frömmigkeit und auf ein ewiges Leben ab (2,22). Eben diese Verblendung läßt die Gottlosen zu Verfolgern der Frommen werden bis zu deren gewaltsamem Tod.

41. Vgl. dazu O. Cullmann, Études de Theologie Biblique, Neuchâtel, 1968, 105f.

42. Vgl. Jes 44,25. Nach 1.Kor 2,6f ist das heilsgeschichtliche Handeln der Weisheit Gottes in

einem 'Geheimnis' (μυστήριον) verborgen. Auch dieser Begriff hat nichts mit den Mysterienreligionen zu tun. Er findet sich zwar auch nicht in Jes 53, läßt sich aber zum Verbum 'offenbaren' in Jes 53,1 in Beziehung setzen, das 1.Kor 2,10 erscheint.

"Righteousness from the Law" and "Righteousness from Faith": Paul's Interpretation of Scripture in Romans 10:1-10*

James D. G. Dunn

Paul's argument in Romans 10:1-10 involves a number of important issues on which commentators have been divided, literally for centuries. Not least of these is his use of two texts from the Torah in vv 5-8—Lev 18:5 and Deut 30:11-14. The problem here is that Paul seems to set the two text in outright antithesis, whereas, when taken in their most natural sense, the two texts seem rather to speak with one and the same voice. Thus in its original context Lev 18:5 is part of an explicit command by Yahweh to obey the law:

> You shall observe my institutions and my laws: the man who keeps (ποιήσας) them shall have life through them. I am the Lord (NEB).

Similarly Deut 30:11-14 is part of a strong encouragement to keep the law:

> [11]This commandment which I command you this day is not too hard for you, nor is it far off. [12]It is not in heaven, that you should say, 'Who will go up for us to heaven, and fetch it for us, that we may hear and do (ποιήσομεν) it?' [13]Nor is it beyond the sea, that you should say, 'Who will cross to the other side of the sea for us, and fetch it for us, that we may hear and do (ποιήσομεν) it?' [14]The word is very near to you, in your mouth and in your heart, so that you can do (ποιεῖν) it'.

Both texts are clearly exhortations to keep or do the law—both using the same verb (ποιεῖν). But Paul takes the former as a description of "the righteousness which is from the law" and the latter as an expression of "the righteousness from faith", as though the two passages pointed in quite opposite directions—a treatment of Deut 30:11-14 which many have found "purely fanciful", "especially crass" or "arbitrary".[1]

The problem then is one of Paul's integrity: How could he set in opposition what stand in such clear agreement? Or if not his integrity, at least his credibility: How could he hope to persuade those who knew the Torah by such forced exegesis? Such disingenuity hardly does the apostle to the Gentiles any credit and must surely fail in its primary purpose of commending the gospel to the Gentiles.

Can Paul be defended against such a serious charge? Are there reasons for his choice of these texts which help explain why he treats them in the way he does? Is there a logic in his line of argument in Romans 10 which has been lost sight of and which clarifies and perhaps even justifies his use of these texts? The following essay is an attempt to demonstrate that all these questions should be answered in the affirmative. But first we need to clear the ground by reaffirming that there is a real problem here and that persistent attempts to resolve the problem by denying its existence have to be rejected.

I. Is There a Problem?

There have been two major efforts to defuse the problem of Paul seeming to set the two Torah texts in unjustified antithesis.

1. *Is there a quotation?* The first is to deny that Paul intended to quote one of the texts as such. With the quotation from Lev 18:5 there is little difficulty. Despite some uncertainty as regards the text of Rom 10:5[2] and the text form of Lev 18:5, there is no dispute that Paul did intend to quote Lev 18:5: he introduces the sentence as something Moses wrote; and it was a text he had already used in Gal 3:12.

But with 10:6-8 there is much more room for dispute. For what these verses contain is by no means a straightforward quotation from Deut 30:11-14 and could be classified simply as a borrowing of language and imagery also found in the Deuteronomy passage rather than a citation as such.[3] Nevertheless, on closer examination it becomes apparent that Paul did intend to refer to Deut 30:12-14 and to make his point by expounding it.

(1) The text is too close to that of the Deuteronomy passage for the agreement to be accidental. Paul uses the middle part of Deut 30:12 more or less verbatim—"Who will go up . . . to heaven?" And 10:8 follows Deut 30:14 exactly, omitting only the adverb "very" and the final phrase "so that you can do it". The second part of the alleged quotation is more problematic. Deuteronomy asks, "Who will cross the sea for us?"; whereas in Paul the equivalent question runs, "Who will go down to the abyss?" But here the recently published Targum Neofiti provides the likely answer. For it renders Deut 30:13 as follows:

> Nor is the law beyond the Great Sea, that one should say: Would that we had one like Jonah the prophet *who would descend into the depths* of the Great Sea and *bring up* the law for us . . .

This suggests the possibility that there was a form of the Deuteronomy text in which the horizontal contrast (heaven/other side of the sea) had been replaced by the vertical (heaven/sheol).[4] More likely, however, the two contrasts were regarded in Jewish circles as equivalent, so that one could be used in place of the other or to supplement the other without alteration of meaning. This is also implied in Neofiti and in Ps 139:8-9, and the idea that the primeval waters of chaos were under the earth would facilitate the association.[5] Of the two, the heaven/underworld contrast is the more natural (cf. particularly Ps 107:26; also Isa 7:11; Amos 9:2; Sir 16:18; 24:5; Jub 24:31; 4 Ezra 4:8), and, in Paul's case not least, it would certainly bring out the human impossibility of what was envisaged more effectively.[6] In short, the variations between the words used by Paul and the known text forms of Deut 30:11-14 are not significant enough to deny Paul's use of the latter.

(2) More striking is the way Paul uses Deut 30:11-14—(a) by a series of three partial citings, (b) with explanatory notes inserted following each, (c) each introduced by the formula "that is" (τουτ᾽ ἔστιν). Thanks particularly to the discovery of the Dead Sea Scrolls, what seems to modern ears a strange and arbitrary way of dealing

with a scriptural text can now be recognized for what it is—a characteristic Jewish mode of exposition in that period.

(a) The use of a text in a series of partial citations can be paralleled by the use of the very same Deuteronomy passage in other Jewish writings (particularly Bar 3:29-30 and Philo, *Post* 84-85). In all three cases (Baruch, Philo, Paul)[7] the context makes it sufficiently clear that Deuteronomy is being cited, and in all three cases the partial quotations respect and reflect the sequence and significance of Deuteronomy's imagery.

(b) From among the Dead Sea Scrolls the various commentaries and exegetical writings preserved (usually in fragmentary condition) show clearly that such exposition was regularly used by the Qumran covenanters (see especially 1QpHab 5:6-8; 6:2-8; 7:3-5; 10:2-4; 12:2-10).

(c) The explanation offered in the Qumran scrolls is introduced by an identifying formula—"it/he/this is . . ." (as in 1QS 8:14-15; 4QFlor 1:11; 4QpIsa[b] 2:6-7), or "the interpretation is . . ." (repeatedly in the commentaries).[8]

In short, it is doubtful whether anyone familiar with Jewish citation and exegesis at the time of Paul would have been in any doubt: Paul was offering an exegesis of a scriptural text. Incidentally, it would also be observed that Paul carries the explanation forward into v 9, where he deliberately repeats two importants phrases from Deut 30:14—"in your mouth" and "in your heart"—picking them up and explaining them (cf. again 1QpHab 11:17–12:10). Within the rest of the NT the closest parallels would be Eph 4:8-11 and Heb 10:5-10.

(3) Finally we need simply note that the "What does it say?" (τί λέγει) of v 8 is clearly intended as an appeal to an authoritative text (cf. Rom 4:3; 11:2, 4; Gal 4:30).[9] This alone would be sufficient to correct the inference which some have drawn from the absence of an "it is written" or "he/it says" formula at the beginning of the Deuteronomy citation. Paul reserves the "it says" for the most positive part of the text on which he is going to build in the following verses.

We may conclude with confidence therefore that Paul intended Rom 10:6-9 as an exposition of Deut 30:11-14 and that this intention was clearly signalled for his readers.

2. *Is there an antithesis?* The usual view that Paul intended to set the two Torah texts in antithesis to each other poses the issue of Paul's credibility so strongly that some have attemptied to deny it. Lev 18:5 and Deut 30:11-14 are such closely related and parallel passages that Paul surely cannot have intended to see them against each other.[10] The solution which has offered the most attractive alternative is to remove the negative implication attaching to Paul's quotation of Lev 18:5 by referring it to *Christ:* Christ is the man who has kept (= fulfilled) the law (above all in his death) and now lives (= resurrection) as a consequence.[11] Consequently the two Torah passages are *not* set in antithesis but provide equally positive assertions regarding "righteousness", when both are interpreted by reference to Christ.

However, this attempt to cut the knot by denying the problem will not do. (1) When Paul sets righteousness "from faith" alongside righteousness "from" something else, where δέ is the linking word, the most natural conclusion, grammatically and logically, is that he intended to set the two phrases in opposition (as also in 4:16; 9:30,32; Gal 2:16; 3:21-22). (2) Paul gives another indicator of his intention by attributing the first quotation to Moses ("Moses says") and the second to righteousness ("Righteousness says"). Although Moses elsewhere is cited as the author of the Torah quotation (9:15; 10:19; 1 Cor 9:9), in none of these cases is he set alongside a concept like "righteousness", as here. In this case the better parallels are Rom 5:14, 1 Cor 10:2 and 2 Cor 3:7-15, where Moses is put forward as characterizing the old epoch now superseded by Christ. The implication is that Lev 18:5 speaks for the old epoch before Christ, represented by Moses, while Deut 30:12-14 speaks for the new age of God's wider grace introduced by Christ, characterized by "the righteousness from faith" (3:21-26; 10:4), with "righteousness" personified as a way of speaking of God's gracious outreach, as in Ps 85:10-13 and Isa 45:8. (3) A very similar contrast using Lev 18:5 in an even more polemical line of argument is clear in Gal 3:10-12.[12] Consequently, the argument that Paul would not have set scripture against scripture is undermined. He had already done so, using the same Torah passage as here.

We are pushed to the conclusion therefore that Paul did intend the introductions to the two Torah quotations to stand in antithesis to each other and so also to set the two quotations themselves against each other. Since this is so, we cannot meet the problem of Paul's integrity and credibility by denying its existence. On the contrary, we are confronted with it all the more sharply. Why should Paul choose to pull apart so rudely two texts which in their original contexts could sit so comfortably together? And how could he hope to justify such a polarizing exegesis?

II. Why These Texts?

Why should Paul choose Lev 18:5 and Deut 30:11-14 to characterize two contrasting attitudes (as he would understand them to be), two differing understandings of "righteousness"?

So far as Lev 18:5 is concerned, it would not be far from the mark to say that it was a typical expression of Israel's understanding of its responsibilities before God, a characteristic statement of its obligations and promises under the covenant—"do and live" (e.g. Deut 4:1; 5:32-33; 8:1; 30:15-20; Neh 9:29; Ezek 18:9, 21; 20:11; 33:19). Hence the phrase "the law of life" in Sir 17:11 and 45:5. In most of these cases the covenant is explicitly in view—as also in Targum PsJon on Lev 18:5; and "life" means life within the covenant, not the life of the age to come as such—as also in Philo's use of Lev 18:5 in *Cong* 86-87. Paul would certainly have understood the text in the same way, that is, as a characteristic expression, quite possibly one of the most characteristic expressions, of how his fellow Jews understood "righteousness". As Lev 18:5 demonstrates, righteousness for the typically devout Jew of Paul's acquaintance was a matter of doing and living, a matter of "covenantal nomism";[13] righteousness was what the people of the covenant did and how they lived as members of the covenant.

If the reason is clear enough why Lev 18:5 should be used to express what, after all, was its most natural sense, what of Deut 30:11-14, where Paul's interpretation seems to wrest the text away from its most natural sense, not least by his omission of the key final phrase, "so that you can do it"? Why should he choose Deut 30:11-14 on which to wreak his "exegetical violence"? The answer is less obvious, but there are sufficient pointers for us to follow with some confidence.

(1) For one thing an appeal to Deut 30:11-14 would resonate with a diaspora Jewish readership. It is self-evident that the immediately preceding passage, Deut 30:1-10, would be greatly cherished by the devout of the diaspora, with its explicit promise to those scattered among the nations that conversion (return to the Lord) and

obedience would result in restoration and a circumcision of the heart which would produce love of God from the heart. This *a priori* likelihood is confirmed by Philo, *Praem* 163-72, where just such a use of the exhortations and promises of Deut 30:1-10 is made. Also by the clear allusion to Deut 30 in Jewish tomb inscriptions in Asia Minor, where the curse of Deut 30:7 is evoked as something well enough known to protect Jewish tombs from abuse and robbery[14] (cf. again Philo, *Praem* 169). Paul would presumably have seen his ministry in the regions of the diaspora as seeking just that conversion and obedience ("of faith"—1:5; 16:26), and as producing that circumcision of and love from the heart (2:29; 5:5) of which Deut 30 spoke. More important for the issue of Paul's credibility, however, we may deduce that by virtue of its context, Deut 30:11-14 would very likely be recognized as having a special applicability in a diaspora context.

(2) Moreover, there is good evidence that Deut 30:11-14 itself was the subject of considerable reflection among Jewish synagogues both in Palestine and in the diaspora. The LXX already shows some readiness to elaborate the thought, particularly of v 14 ("in your mouth and in your heart and in your hands, so that you can do it"). Neofiti shows a similar willingness to develop the thought, as we saw above. Bar 3:29-30 too is clearly modeled on Deut 30:12-13—"Who has gone up to heaven and fetched it (Wisdom) and brought it down from the clouds? Who has gone across to the other side of the sea and found it, and will gain it with choice gold?" And Philo makes explicit use of the LXX text on no less than four occasions (*Post* 84-85; *Mut* 236-7; *Virt* 183; *Praem* 80) as well as alluding to it several times elsewhere (*Som* 2:180; *SpecLeg* 1:301; *Prob* 68). It would probably cause little surprise among congregations familiar with the diaspora heritage, therefore, when Paul turned to just this text.

(3) Most striking of all is the evidence that this text was interpreted with a considerable degree of freedom. In particular, Baruch and Philo demonstrate that Deut 30:11-14 was widely understood to have a reference which transcended the original more straightforward reference to the Torah. Baruch envisages the object of the impossible quest to heaven and beyond the sea as divine Wisdom—a concept of course larger than the Torah, even though Baruch goes on to identify the Wisdom spoken of as given to Israel in "the book of the commandments of God" (Bar 4:1). Similarly Philo thinks of the object of the search as "the good", and, like Paul, pays little attention to the final clause ("so that you can do it"). We can say, therefore, that Paul's looking through and beyond the immediate sense of Deut 30:11-14 to a more transcendent referent puts him in good Jewish company. Of course, his particular use of the passage and conclusions drawn from it would have been controversial, but not the possibility and propriety of such a free use of the text.

In short, despite our evidence being inevitably restricted, we can nevertheless give a fairly confident answer to the question, Why did Paul choose just these texts to make his point? The answer seems to be that they characterized two Jewish attitudes to the Torah and to use of Torah texts—different attitudes, but both Jewish. Lev 18:5 could be regarded, quite legitimately and recognizably, as an expression of Jewish nomism, as maintained most vehemently within Palestine. Whereas Deut 30:11-14 was widely regarded as looking beyond the Torah to some transcendent category of more universal appeal, particularly in the diaspora. Paul's choice of these texts indicates a recognition of this potential dichotomy and an attempt to exploit it in the service of the gospel. All that being said, however, it nevertheless still remains a hard fact that Paul seems to force these texts into an unnatural opposition unwarranted by anything we have so far seen of the use made elsewhere of these texts. Can any more be said to explain or even justify Paul's interpretation of Lev 18:5 and Deut 30:11-14? The best place to look for an answer is the context in which Paul sets his interpretations, particularly the lead-in to each text.

III. Leviticus 18:5 as an Expression of Israel's Righteousness

The natural tendency to divide the argument of Rom 10 after v 4 and to begin a new paragraph at v 5 obscures the important fact that v 5 grows out of the preceding verses and in effect sums them up. This is particularly evident from the sequence of γάρ ... γάρ ... γάρ ... γάρ which links vv 2-5: each verse serves as some sort of explanation of the antecedent verse, with Lev 18:5 serving as the proof text, at the end as usual, to anchor the line of argument firmly in scripture. To be more precise, we should observe the way in which the contrast in vv 5 and 6-8 matches the contrasts of the preceding verses:

v 2	zeal for God	but not in accordance with knowledge
v 3	sought to establish their own righteousness	did not submit to God's righteousness
v 4	law ... to righteousness	Christ ... to all who believe
vv 5-9	righteousness from the law—Lev 18:5	righteousness from faith—Deut 30:11-14

In the sequence which finds its scriptural documentation in Lev 18:5 the full significance of several of the contrasting elements has been missed.

a) "They have a zeal for God" (v 2). The phrase "zeal for God" is one way of characterizing the ideal of Jewish piety—a passionate zeal focused on God and dominating concern to do his will.[15] On hearing the phrase, most Jews of Paul's time would naturally think of the classic examples of this zeal, heroes of the faith who had been willing to use the sword to defend and maintain Israel's distinctiveness as God's covenant people—Simeon and Levi (Gen 34; Jdt 9:4; Jub 30:5-20), Phinehas (Num 25:10-13; Sir 45:23-4; 1 Macc 2:54; 4 Macc 18:12), Elijah (1 Kgs 18; Sir 48:2; 1 Macc 2:58) and Mattathias (1 Macc 2:19-26). In Maccabean literature this ideal is characterized as "zeal for the law" (1 Macc 2:26, 27, 50, 58; 2 Macc 4:2),[16] and in the Dead Sea Scrolls as "zeal for just ordinances" (1QS 4:4; 9:23; 1QH 14:14). In TAsh 4:5 "zeal for God" is defined as "abstaining from what God ... forbids through his commandments".

As the more immediate context of Paul's language we should recall that these ideals of zealous piety were a potent stimulus to the Zealots in Palestine at the very time Paul was writing this letter,[17] and that "zeal for the law" was the chief characteristic of the Jerusalem Christian congregations according to Acts 21:20. Above all, Paul himself knew the force of such zeal from "inside": it was as just such a "zealot" as Phinehas that he too some years earlier had taken the sword to defend Judaism's distinctive prerogatives (Gal 1:13-14; Phil 3:6; Acts 22:3-4). The obvious conclusion is that it was just such "zeal for God" which Paul had in mind here.

b) "They seek to establish their own righteousness" (v 3). "Their own" (ἴδιος) is usually taken to mean "attained by them"—"a righteous status of their own earning".[18] But ἴδιος has more the sense of "mine (and not yours)", "peculiar to me".[19] So "their own righteousness" most naturally means Israel's righteousness, righteousness which is Israel's alone, theirs and nobody else's—or, alternatively expressed, covenant righteousness, the righteousness which is Israel's by virtue of their being the chosen people of God.[20]

Somewhat surprisingly the significance of the accompanying verb has been almost wholly missed. What they seek to do is to "*establish*" (στῆσαι) their own righteousness. This should certainly be seen as a reflection of the Hebrew הקים and of its characteristic use in relation to the covenant—usually of *God's* action in establishing his covenant (though occasionally also of Israel's responsibility within the covenant).[21] In view of what we have already seen to be involved in the background of Paul's language here we should note Sir 44:20—Abraham (or God?) "established" (ἔστησεν) the covenant in his flesh". And particularly 1 Macc 2:27—Mattathias' summons to defend the covenant: "Let everyone who is zealous for the law and supports (ἱστῶν) the covenant come out after me". It is surely this sort of sentiment and ideal which Paul echoes here—concern to maintain covenant righteousness as Israel's peculiar obligation, zeal to establish by their pattern of daily living the righteousness of the covenant as Israel's distinctive prerogative.

c) "The law as a means to righteousness" (v 4). The exegesis of this phrase is a matter of much greater dispute. But the most obvious way to take it is as a further synonymous variant of what has just been described and which it further explains (note again the linking "for"). It is true that to link "law" directly with "to righteousness" is awkward grammatically, since the word "Christ" comes in between (τέλος γὰρ νόμου Χριστὸς εἰς δικαιοσύνην).But Paul had used precisely the same construction just a few verses earlier—"Does the potter not have authority over the clay?"—where the subject ("the potter") again disrupts the natural phrase ("authority over the clay") (οὐκ ἔχει ἐξουσίαν ὁ κεραμεὺς τοῦ πηλοῦ). In both cases the most obvious explanation is that Paul wanted to juxtapose most closely the words which set up the contrast (potter/clay, law/Christ), even at the cost of some grammatical infelicity. Moreover we need to recall once again that v 5 explains v 4 ("for"). In which case the most obvious way to read the phrase in v 5, "the righteousness which is *from* the law", is as the inverse of the preceding phrase (which it explains in v 4), "the law which (leads) *into* righteousness"—

νόμος εἰς δικαιοσύνην·
δικαιοσύνη ἐκ νόμου

The clear implication is that the law thus spoken of is the law understood as the means of establishing righteousness as Israel's, the law seen as defining the boundary within which and the terms on which righteousness may be claimed, a righteousness bounded by the law and therefore limited more or less by definition to the people of the law.[22]

Thus the line of thought in vv 2-5 confirms that the much disputed word in v 4, τέλος, does indeed mean "end", even if "end" in the sense of "completion". Despite the recent attempt by R. Badenas to argue otherwise, the sense of termination cannot be excluded from the word—as the wider usage clearly confirms, particularly the LXX and Paul himself, where the sense "end" is impossible to escape.[23] The clear message of v 4 therefore is that Christ has brought to an end the phase of God's covenant purpose during which it was focussed on ethnic Israel alone, when righteousness could properly be regarded as a function of the Jewish law and therefore as a possibility only for those within the covenant who lived in the terms laid down by the law.

It thus becomes evident that just this attitude to the law and to righteousness is what Paul sums up and documents by citing Lev 18:5. As we have already seen, Lev 18:5 is the first statement in the Jewish scriptures of what was evidently a typical expression of Israel's sense of obligation under the covenant—"do and thus live". It does not have all the overtones which are present in the talk of "zeal for God" and "establishing righteousness" (vv 2-3). But undoubtedly those who were "zealous for God" and "sought to establish their own (covenant) righteousness" would have seen in Lev 18:5 the scriptural authorization for their attitude. In other words, if we are to understand Paul's use of Lev 18:5 in context, we must see it as having a particular target—*not* as condemning all "doing" or "good works" in general, but as characterizing that Jewish covenant zeal which restricted God's righteousness to ethnic Israel, to those who by doing what the law commanded lived within the law and identified themselves as God's people.[24] Lev 18:5 so understood, as most of his Jewish contemporaries would understand it, Paul regards as *passe,* no longer expressive of God's purpose.

IV. Deut 30:12-14 as an Expression of God's Righteousness

What then of the second scriptural passage—Deut 30:12-14? In contrast to Lev 18:5 Paul obviously regards it as an expression of God's righteousness, God's eschatological righteousness now operative since Christ. But once again the question poses itself: How to justify this pulling of Deut 30 so far away from Lev 18? And once again it is a fuller appreciation of the context of Paul's argument which points most clearly to the answer. In the sequence of contrasts drawn in vv 2-8, just as Lev 18:5 is intended to sum up and document one side of these contrasts, so we may assume Deut 30:12-14 is intended to sum up and document the other.

a) "Not in accordance with knowledge" (v 2); "not knowing the righteousness of God . . . they did not subject themselves to the righteousness of God" (v 3). The implication from the context is that by limiting covenant righteousness in the way they did Israel had failed to understand that in making his promise to Abraham, Isaac and Jacob, God always had the Gentiles in view from the first (4:13-17; Gal 3:7-9). By understanding "the law of righteousness" in terms of "works" they had failed to reach what God wanted (9:31-32).[25] By understanding righteousness as a Jewish prerogative maintained by Jews for Jews they had failed to submit to God's righteousness in its more unrestricted sweep (10:2-3; cf. Gal 3:10-12).[26]

b) The period of a more restricted (understanding of) righteousness has now been ended by Christ, with the consequence that God's righteousness is now open to all through faith (v 4). The acceptance that this is so means faith in Christ, faith both in God's covenant promise *and* in the enlargement of its scope through Christ (Gal 3:13-14).[27] Hence faith (in Christ) stands as the opposing pole to works (of the law), or to the law understood in terms of works (cf. the contrast of Rom 9:32 with that of 10:5-6). The concentration of the key language in these verses (righteousness, faith, law, works—9:30-32; 10:3-6) is obviously intended to recall the major theme of the letter as expounded in 1:16–5:1.

c) Not least of importance here is the opening part of the quotation in v 6—"Do not say in your heart". It has generally been recognized that Paul here deliberately draws Deut 8:17 and 9:4 into his use of Deut 30:12-14; but the full reason for his so doing has not been appreciated. The point of these earlier Deuteronomy references is not simply that in their context both are directed against self-complacency and presumptuous boasting.[28] The point is rather that both passages are directed against the assumption that Israel's righteousness has been the ground of Israel's military triumph and prosperity. For Israel so to speak "in the heart" was to forget that their success was *entirely* God's from start to finish, to forget that it is *God* who confirms (στήσῃ) the covenant (Deut 8:18; 9:5). The echo of 10:3 will certainly not be accidental. Paul in effect underscores his earlier criticism that in seeking to "establish" covenant righteousness as peculiarly theirs (v 3) Israel had shown their failure to appreciate the fact that only God can establish the covenant—and that he does so through faith, which Gentile may exercise as well as Jew, and not in terms of the law understood as that which sets Jew apart from Gentile.

d) It is this line of argument which Paul sums up and takes further with the quotation from Deut 30:12-14 (vv 6-8).

(1) The logic of the interpretation is clear. Deut 30 speaks of two impossible enterprises as a way of emphasizing how near to hand is the commandment and the observance it calls for. The two impossible clauses match two central elements already firmly established in Christian faith—Christ's exaltation to heaven[29] and Christ's resurrection from the dead. Referring the two impossible clauses to Christ's exaltation and resurrection is a nice touch which prepares the reader for what is to follow. But in effect Paul's interpretation is simply making Deuteronomy's point in a more elaborate way—such impossible enterprises are unnecessary. The real point is the equation of the "commandment/word" of Deuteronomy with "the word of faith" (v 8).[30] And since Paul calls for "the obedience of faith" (Rom 1:5; cf. 16:26) and sees faith as the establishment of the law (Rom 3:31) and "faith working through love" as the fulfillment of the law (Gal 5:6, 14; Rom 13:8, 10), he can not unjustifiably claim that his is a quite proper exposition of Deut 30:12-14. The law which defines God's righteousness can be obeyed only "out of faith" (cf. 9:30-32 with 10:3), so it is the "word of faith" which makes such obedience possible, and so it is "the word of faith" to which Deut 30:14 must point, especially when understood eschatologically, in the light of Christ.

(2) Paul's interpretation would have all the greater credibility since there was already a widespread recognition that the language of Deut 30:11-14 pointed to something more mysterious, more ultimate. Whereas Lev 18:5 pointed up a narrow and particularist view of the law as Israel's alone, in both Baruch and Philo Deut 30:11-14 was seen as expressing something which everyone of good will was open to and eager for—divine Wisdom, the good. Of course Baruch and Philo both see that more universal ideal to be focused in the law. But by developing such an apologetic line they opened Jewish thought to the recognition that what Deuteronomy spoke of was capable of more universal expression. Whereas Lev 18:5 expressed Israel's claim to a national monopoly of God's righteousness, Deut 30:11-14 could better express the eschatological breadth of God's covenant purpose.

(3) Finally we may note that Paul makes repeated use of the phrase "in the heart" (vv 6, 8-9). This emphasis (also v 10) was no doubt intended to recall Paul's earlier contrast between his typical Jewish contemporary and "the true Jew" in 2:28-29. The point there was that an emphasis on keeping the law can too easily be corrupted into an emphasis on physical and national identity markers "visible, in the flesh", too easily corrupted into a superficial understanding of circumcision in particular (2:25-28). Whereas what Paul looked for was "the circumcision of the heart" (2:29)—the very

promise, we may recall, of Deut 30:1-10. In Paul's understanding of the gospel it is, of course, the gift of the Spirit which fulfils both that hope (2:29) and the promised blessing of Abraham (Gal 3:14).

In short, what at first appears to have been a forced and unnatural interpretation of Deut 30:11-14 may be seen to have much greater coherence and to have been capable of winning the assent of the interested Jew or proselyte or God-fearer in the Roman congregations where this letter would have been read.

Conclusions

The key to understanding Paul's use of Lev 18:5 and Deut 30:12-14 is the recognition that the contrast he draws between them is essentially a salvation-historical contrast. Lev 18:5 could be taken quite fairly to characterize the period when God's covenant purpose was effectively limited to Israel, a period which Paul saw now to have ended; God's righteousness is no longer to be thought of as limited to those who lived within the boundary defined by the law and marked by such distinctively Jewish practices as circumcision, sabbath and food laws. Deut 30:11-14, on the other hand, could more readily be given a wider, more universal perspective, and thus characterize the eschatological breadth of God's covenant purpose, where righteousness was to be seen in terms of faith, of obedience from the heart, and open to Gentile as Gentile as well as to Jew.

It is important to realize that this salvation-historical contrast is not a straight contrast between the law and faith. It is because commentators have envisaged here a polarized antithesis between the law on one side and faith on the other that Paul's use of Deut 30:12-14 has appeared so strained. But the negative side of the antithesis for Paul was not the law *per se:* it was the law understood as establishing and limiting righteousness as *Israel's* righteousness (v 3). Νόμος in fact could appear on both sides of the contrast, as Paul's use of the phrase "law of righteousness" in 9:31 clearly indicates. The negative sign is provided by Paul when he narrows the definition of "the law of righteousness" by adding ἐξ ἔργων (9:32); but equally "the law of righteousness" could stand on the other side of the contrast by adding the phrase ἐκ πίστεως (9:32). This is why Paul can take a scripture which talks about the word which is God's commandment and see in it a reference to the eschatological word of faith (10:6-9), because he saw the law fulfilled in its eschatological intent only in the obedience of faith.

We may put the point another way. Technically it would have been quite feasible for Paul to take *both* texts either way, since he has already argued for a deeper "doing" (2:12-29) and a more unbounded concept of righteousness (3:21–4:25). But in the normal understanding of Lev 18:5 its language and emphasis invited a more *restricted* understanding of righteousness (or of "the law of righteousness"), or at least made it an obvious and legitimate characterization of the typically Jewish "zeal for God" which limited righteousness to ethnic Israel. Deut 30:11-14 on the other hand was widely understood to invite a much *broader* and more universal understanding of righteousness, such as was appropriate to an eschatological understanding of the law of righteousness no longer limited to ethnic Israel but open to all who believe.

In short, Paul's interpretation of these two Torah texts demonstrates both the *continuity* he saw between the OT and the gospel of Christ, and the *discontinuity* he saw between his people's too restricted understanding of the covenant and the fulfillment of the covenant promise in Christ. The key to a proper exegesis of this passage is to recognize both elements, of continuity and discontinuity, and to find the balance Paul maintained between both.

It gives me great pleasure to offer this essay in honor of one whose work in this area was the first to awaken me to the character and significance of *Paul's Use of the Old Testament*.

Notes

*This paper was also delivered to the NT postgraduate seminars at both Durham and Oxford.

1. C. H. Dodd, *Romans*, Moffatt, London, 1932, 166; E. Gaugler, *Römer,* Zürich, 1952, 2.124; A. T. Hanson, *Studies in Paul's Technique and Theology* London, 1974, 147.

2. Several commentators prefer to read τὴν δικαιοσύνην as the object of ὁ ποιήσας; for details see e.g. C. E. B. Cranfield, *Romans,* ICC, Edinburgh, 1979, 2.520-521; U. Wilckens, *Römer,* EKK 6/2, Zürich, 1980, 224, n. 1003. But the reading of Aland²⁶ has the stronger claims on the principle of *difficilior lectio;* see further B. Metzger, *A Textual Commentary on the Greek New Testament,* London, ²1975, 524-5.

3. So e.g. W. Sanday & A. C. Headlam, *Romans,* ICC, Edinburgh, ⁵1902, 289; C. K. Barrett, *Romans,* London, 1957, 199; see further O. Kuss, *Römer,* Regensburg, 1978, 3.758-61; R. Badenas, *Christ the End of the Law: Romans 10:4 in Pauline Perspective,* JSNTSup 10, Sheffield, 1985, 125-6 with bibliography.

4. Cf. particularly M. McNamara, *The New Testament and the Palestinian Targum,* AnBib 27A, Rome, (1978), 72-8.

5. Cf. Barrett, *Romans,* 199.

6. Cf. Str-B 3.281.

7. The use of Deut 30:11-14 made by Baruch is relatively brief, but the reference to the law in 4:1 confirms that the Deuteronomy passage is in mind.

8. See further, M. P. Horgan, *Pesharim: Qumran Interpretations of Biblical Books,* CBQMS 8, 1979; W. H. Brownlee, *The Midrash Pesher of Habakkuk,* SBLMS 24, 1979.

9. Badenas, *Christ,* 126; see also BAGD, λέγω,I.7.

10. W. S. Campbell, "Christ the End of the Law: Romans 10:4", *Studia Biblica 1978,* ed. by E. A. Livingstone, JSNTSup 3, Sheffield, 1980, 73-81; Cranfield, *Romans,* 521-22; Badenas, *Christ,* 118-33.

11. K. Barth, *Shorter Commentary on Romans,* London, SCM, 1959, 127; Campbell, "Rom 10:4" 77-8; Cranfield, *Romans,* 2.521-2.

12. On Gal 3:12 see further J. D. G. Dunn, "Works of the Law and the Curse of the Law (Gal 3:10-14)", *NTS* 31 (1985) 535-6; against H. Hübner, "Gal 3:10 und die Herkunft des Paulus", *KD* 19 (1973) 217, and Badenas, *Christ,* 249, n. 259, who oppose reference to Gal 3:12 at this point.

13. To use E. P. Sanders' phrase, coined in *Paul and Palestinian Judaism,* London, 1977, 75, 236, and now (too?) much used in the debate which Sanders work has prompted.

14. I owe this observation to my research student, Paul Trebilco, who is investigating the Jewish communities in Asia Minor at this period. The inscriptions referred to are MAMA VI, 335a, MAMA VI, 335 and CIJ 770.

15. Cf. A. Stumpff, *TDNT* 2.878.

16. Cf, *IDB* 4.936-39; M. Hengel, *Judaism and Hellenism,* London, 1974, 1.305-14.

17. E. Schürer, *The History of the Jewish People in the Age of Jesus Christ,* revised and edited by G. Vermes et al. Edinburgh, 1979, 2.598-606 with other literature.

18. Cranfield, *Romans,* 515; more generally see the scathing protest of C. Klein, *Anti-Judaism in Christian Theology,* Philadelphia, 1978, chap. 3.

19. BAGD.

20. G. Howard, "Christ the End of the Law: the Meaning of Romans 10:4", *JBL* 88 (1969) 336; L. Gaston, "Paul and the Torah", in *Antisemitism and the Foundations of Christianity* ed. by A. T. Davies, New York, 1979, 66; E. P. Sanders, *Paul the Law and the Jewish People,* Philadelphia, 1983, 38.

21. Gen 6:18; 9:11; 17:7, 19, 21; 26:3; Exod 6:4; Lev 26:9; Deut 8:18; 9:5; 29:13; Jer 11:5; Sir 17:12; 45:7, 24; but also of Israel's responsibility (Jer 34:18 LXX 41:18; cf. 35:16 LXX 42:16; Sir 11:20).

22. C. T. Rhyne, *Faith Establishes the Law,* SBLDS 55, Chico, CA., 1981, attempts to maintain the dubious and overstrained thesis that νόμος in v 4 has a positive sense even though in (the explanatory) v 5 νόμος has a negative sense (105-6). But see H. Räisänen, *Paul and the Law,* WUNT 29, Tübingen, 1983, 545.

23. Badenas, *Christ,* 38-80; the only reference from the Pauline corpus which gives any real

support to Badenas is 1 Tim 1:5. Badenas provides long lists of scholars who support the differing renderings of τέλος (pp. 156-8).

24. See n. 12.

25. Cf. Cranfield, *Romans*, 509.

26. See again Dunn, "Works of the Law", 533-36.

27. Ibid 536-38.

28. As O. Michel, *Römerbrief*, KEK, Göttingen, [5]1978, 328, and Cranfield, *Romans*, 523 recognize.

29. A reference to Christ's pre-existence is much less likely; see J. D. G. Dunn, *Christology in the Making*, London, 1980, 184-6.

30. *Not* with Christ: Christ is the one whom the word confesses.

"Le Seigneur de tous" (Ac 10:36; Rm 10:12): Arrière-fond scripturaire d'une formule christologique

J. Dupont

Ce n'est pas d'hier que date l'intérêt porté par le Professeur E. Earle Ellis à la manière dont l'Ancien Testament est utilisé par Paul ou dans les discours des Actes;[1] j'espère donc lui être agréable en revenant sur ce sujet dans un volume publié en son honneur, même s'il faut que je me limite à un point très particulier sur lequel mon ambition est de suggérer plus que de démontrer.

Parmi les discours des Actes, le Professeur Ellis n'avait pas à s'arrêter à celui que Pierre adresse au centurion de Césarée (Ac 10: 34-43).[2] Il ne contient en effet aucune citation explicite, et on sait combien est délicate la délimitation entre ce qui est allusion significative à un texte précis et ce qui relève plus largement d'un vocabulaire et d'un style à l'imitation de la LXX. Et il n'y a en tout cas aucun antécédent biblique valable à l'affirmation du v 36 déclarant, après la mention de Jésus Christ, "C'est lui le Seigneur de tous".[3] La rencontre n'en est que plus frappante avec Rm 10,12, seul autre cas dans le Nouveau Testament où le Christ est appelé "Seigneur de tous", et cela dans un contexte qui, comme celui des Actes, nie toute différence faite par Dieu entre les hommes sur la base de leur appartenance ethnique. La même expression a donc bien le même sens: l'universalité de la seigneurie du Christ supprime la distinction qui sépare le Juif du Gentil.

Par rapport à Ac 10:36, l'affirmation christologique de Rm 10:12 présente l'avantage de se situer entre deux citations bibliques explicites dont elle ne prétend que dégager une conséquence. C'est par là que notre examen doit commencer. Il s'agira surtout de mettre en valeur le rapport privilégié qui unit la formulation du v 12 à la citation de Joël 3:5a LXX au v 13. Un détour s'imposera alors pour observer que le même texte de Joël est cité en Ac 2:21, au début du discours de la Pentecôte, et pour s'interroger sur les échos qu'il reçoit dans la suite du discours et dans l'ensemble des premiers chapitres du livre. On disposera ainsi des données en fonction desquelles il devrait être possible d'orienter l'interprétation de la formule d'Ac 10:36.

Romains 10:1-13

Comme souvent, la pensée de Paul se développe au moyen de jeux de contraste. Le plus caractéristique d'entre eux est sans doute dans cette section celui qui, aux vv 5-6, oppose "la justice qui vient de la Loi" et "la justice que vient de la foi". Cette antithèse avait été introduite par les derniers versets du chapitre 9 (vv 30-32a), où elle se trouvait associée à un autre contraste, opposant "Israël" aux "Nations". C'est sur ce second contraste qu'un déplacement se produit en 10:1-13. Paul y insiste précisément sur l'idée que la justice qui vient de la foi est accessible à tous, l'opposant ainsi implicitement à une justice qui serait réservée aux bénéficiaires de la Loi. Les deux affirmations christologiques du passage sont liées à cet élargissement: "Le Christ est la fin de la Loi en vue de la justification de *tout* (homme) qui croit" (v 4), "Le même est Seigneur de *tous,* riche envers *tous* ceux qui l'invoquent" (v 12). Il est tout à fait clair avec ce v 12 que le mot "tous" dépasse l'opposition de 9,30-31 entre Israël et les Gentils et supprime la différence entre "le Juif et le Grec" pour ne conserver de distinction qu'entre croyant et non-croyant.

A cet universalisme, Paul tient à donner une base scripturaire: deux citations explicites terminent en effet le développement. D'abord celle du v 11: "Car l'Ecriture dit: Tout (homme) qui croit en lui ne sera pas confondu" (Is 28:16). Ensuite, après le commentaire personnel de l'Apôtre, celle du v 13: "Tout (homme) qui invoquera le nom du Seigneur sera sauvé" (Jl 3:5 LXX). Le πᾶς qui commence la citation du v 11 ne se trouve ni dans le texte biblique (LXX et TM) ni dans la forme sous laquelle Paul l'a cité quelques lignes plus haut: "Celui qui croit en lui ne sera pas confondu" (9:33). Il est clair que le texte biblique a été retouché en fonction de l'argumentation à laquelle il doit concourir.[4] Mais l'addition n'est pas purement arbitraire: se contenant d'aligner la citation d'Isaïe sur celle que le v 13 fait de Joël. En d'autres termes, le πᾶς du v 11 ne fait qu'anticiper celui du v 13.

S'il est exact qu'au moment où Paul cite Isaïe au v 11, il a déjà en tête le texte de Joël qu'il va citer au v 13, on peut se demander si le même texte n'a pas déjà influencé la formulation des versets précédents. La question se pose particulièrement pour le v 9: "Si (ἐάν) tu professes par ta bouche que Jésus est Seigneur ... , tu seras sauvé." Ne s'agit-il pas d'une application de l'affirmation de Joël: "Tout (homme) qui (ὃς ἄν) invoquera le nom du Seigneur sera sauvé"?[5]

Mais l'important ici est de se rendre compte que le v 12 veut simplement expliciter la pensée que Paul croit pouvoir découvrir dans le texte de Joël cité au verset suivant. Quand il écrit que le Seigneur est "riche envers tous ceux qui l'invoquent" (12c), c'est pour exprimer sans littéralisme excessif que "tout (homme) qui invoquera le nom du Seigneur sera sauvé". Quand il explique en 12a "qu'il n'y a pas de distinction entre Juif et Grec", c'est pour donner toute sa valeur au πᾶς sur lequel commence le texte de Joël. Enfin l'affirmation christologique: "Car le même est Seigneur de tous" (12b), résulte simplement d'un retournement des termes de Joël: là où celui-ci considérait tout homme dans son rapport au Seigneur, Paul considère le Seigneur dans son rapport à tous les hommes. En s'exprimant comme il le fait, l'Apôtre ne veut que mieux dégager le sens qu'il reconnaît à la déclaration sotériologique de Joël.

Il reste à noter le complément ajouté par les vv 14-15: il n'est possible de croire et d'invoquer que là où la bonne nouvelle est annoncée, cete bonne nouvelle dont parle Is 52:7, cité explicitement. Il n'est peut-être pas fortuit que le même verset d'Isaïe trouve un écho dans le texte d'Ac 10:36 dont nous aurons à nous occuper.

Joël 3,5 au début des Actes

Quelques lignes ont suffi à Luc pour rapporter l'événement de la venue de l'Esprit sur les apôtres (Ac 2:1-4). Le récit s'étend bien davantage sur la stupeur de la foule et les questions qu'elle se pose (vv 5-13). L'explication nécessaire est fournie par la grande citation de Joël 3:1-5a LXX qui constitue l'ouverture du discours de Pierre (vv 17-21). La longueur de la citation surprend. En fait, les deux premiers versets sont seuls à avoir rapport avec l'effusion de l'Esprit qui vient de se produire et avec les transports prophétiques qu'elle provoque.[6] Inutile de chercher un rapport avec la situation pour ce qui concerne les deux versets suivants et les prodiges qu'ils évoquent: ". . . du sang, du feu, des colonnes de fumée, le soleil changé en ténèbres et la lune en sang".[7] Luc n'a pas voulu affaiblir le témoignage prophétique en supprimant ces versets qui conduisent à la déclaration à laquelle il attache une importance capitale: "Et il arrivera que tout (homme) qui invoquera[8] le nom du Seigneur sera sauvé" (v 21 = Jl 3:5 LXX).

Le rapprochement s'impose entre cette citation de Joël qui introduit le discours inaugural de Pierre et la grande citation d'Is 61:1-2 qui introduit en Lc 4:18-19 le discours inaugural de Jésus et constitue, d'une certaine manière, le programme de son ministère.[9] Mais l'analogie est plus frappante encore avec la citation d'Is 40:3-5 qui, au début du récit évangélique (Lc 3:4-6), se présente comme la définition de la mission de Jean Baptiste. Ici également, la première partie de la citation est seule à correspondre à la situation concrète; la suite assure la transition[10] permettant d'arriver à l'affirmation: "Et toute chair verra le salut de Dieu" (Lc 3:6), affirmation que Luc rappellera dans la conclusion de son ouvrage (Ac 28:28),[11] dont elle constitue en quelque sorte la clé herméneutique.

La comparaison montre l'importance qu'il convient d'attacher à l'affirmation qui termine la citation de Joël en Ac 2:21. Alors que les paroles du prophète rapportés en 2:17-18 devaient éclairer l'événement auquel les auditeurs de Pierre assistaient et tels qu'ils sont rappelés au v 33, le but essentiel du discours est de dévoiler l'identité de ce "Seigneur" dont il faut invoquer le nom pour être sauvé.[12] Pierre procède par étapes: une première citation lui permet de montrer que Jésus est le "Christ" dont David a parlé dans le Ps 15 (Ac 2:22-31); c'est en tirant ensuite argument du Ps 109 qu'il peut conclure que Jésus est aussi *Kyrios* (2:32-36). Il ne lui reste plus alors qu'à tirer les conséquences pratiques: il parle non plus d'invoquer le nom, mais de "se faire baptiser au nom de Jésus Christ" (v 38) et ainsi de "se sauver" du milieu d'une génération dévoyée (v 40). La manière dont le v 39 "corrige" Joël 3:5b[13] montre bien que la citation initiale est toujours présente à la pensée de l'auteur.

Mais le dévoilement du sens de Joël 3,5a ne se termine pas avec le discours de la Pentecôte. Le même thème se poursuit dans le récit de la guérison de l'infirme par Pierre et Jean "au nom de Jésus Christ" (Ac 3:1-11), guérison dont les explications fournies ensuite par Pierre font, comme le dit bien R. C. Tannehill, "un paradigme du salut qu'on obtient par le nom de Jésus".[14] De là, la manière curieuse dont 3:16 attribue la guérison tout ensemble à la foi (de qui?) et au nom de Jésus; peut-être aussi l'aggravation de la menace de Dt 18:19 au v 23,[15] pour mieux accentuer le contraste avec la promesse de Joël: "Et il arrivera que toute âme qui n'écoutera pas ce prophète sera exterminée du peuple." De là aussi la formulation de la question posée par les Sanhédrites en 4:7: "Par quelle puissance ou en quel nom avez-vous fait cela?", et celle surtout de la réponse de Pierre: "Il n'y a de salut en aucun autre, car il n'y a pas sous le ciel d'autre nom donné aux hommes par lequel nous devions être sauvés" (4:12).

Plus on s'éloigne de la citation-clé d'Ac 2:21, plus le rattachement au texte précis de la prophétie de Joël devient problématique. Mais l'exemple du rappel qu'Ac 28,28 fait d'un texte cité en Lc 3,6 permet au moins de se poser la question de savoir s'il n'y a pas une sorte d'inclusion dans le fait que l'histoire de la période hiérosolymitaine de l'Eglise primitive (Ac 2-7) se termine par une invocation d'Etienne qui semble faire écho à la citation initiale de Pierre: "Tandis qu'on le lapidait, Etienne invoquait et disait: Seigneur Jésus, reçois mon esprit" (7:59).[16]

L'histoire du martyre d'Etienne achève une première période, mais en introduit aussi une seconde, tout particulièrement marquée par la conversion de Paul. Dans le récit de cet événement on trouve deux fois la désignation des chrétiens comme "ceux qui invoquent le nom du Seigneur";[17] elle ne se réfère pas nécessairement au texte de Joël 3:5, mais n'est-ce pas à ce texte d'abord que pensera naturellement le lecteur des Actes? On la trouve d'abord sur les lèvres d'Ananias qui, recevant du Seigneur l'ordre d'aller trouver Saul, objecte aussitôt: "Seigneur, . . . cet homme a ici le pouvoir de la part des grands prêtres pour enchaîner tous ceux qui invoquent ton nom" (9:13-14). Ce sont ensuite les Juifs qui expriment leur étonnement en entendant Saul prêcher dans les synagogues que Jésus est le Fils de Dieu: "N'est-ce pas lui qui, à Jérusalem, malmenait ceux qui invoquent ce nom?" (v 21). L'expression revient avec une nuance différente, liturgique, dans le deuxième récit de l'événement de Damas, quand Ananias conclut son discours à Paul en lui disant: "Fais-toi baptiser et lave-toi de tes péchés en invoquant son nom" (22:16). On remarquera que, dans ce cas comme en 9:21, le lien avec le titre christologique de "Seigneur" n'est plus qu'indirect; mais on voit en même temps reparaître une perspective sotériologique.

Nous retiendrons surtout de cette rapide enquête que la citation de Joël en Ac 2:21 commande l'ensemble du discours de la Pentecôte et étend probablement son influence plus loin encore. Plus précisément, l'affirmation de 2:36, suivant laquelle Dieu a fait Jésus Seigneur, ne doit pas s'entendre seulement comme la conclusion de l'argument tiré du Ps 109 au v 34. Il faut aussi y reconnaître l'application à Jésus du titre *Kyrios* tel qu'il est employé dans la citation de Joël: Jésus est le Seigneur qu'on doit invoquer pour être sauvé.

Le discours de Pierre chez le centurion romain

Il n'y a pas lieu de s'attarder ici sur le corps du discours (10:37-41), constitué par un résumé de l'histoire évangélique.[18] On y reconnaît aisément les deux parties de cette histoire, déjà distinguées dans un résumé antérieur (Lc 23:5): d'abord ce qui est arrivé "dans la Judée tout entière" (Ac 10:37a), c'est-à-dire "dans le pays des Juifs" (v 39a), ensuite ce qui s'est passé "à Jérusalem" (v 39b). Dans la première partie, on identifie d'abord un "commencement" qui se situe en Galilée (v 37b); à cette occasion, Luc rappelle plus précisément la scène de la prédication inaugurale de Jésus à Nazareth et le texte d'Is 61:1-2 au moyen duquel Jésus avait présenté sa mission à ses concitoyens (v 38; cf. Lc 4:17-19). La seconde partie mentionne la crucifixion (v 39b) dans les mêmes termes qu'en 5:30; elle s'étend surtout sur la résurrection et les apparitions à la suite desquelles le Douze sont devenus les témoins attitrés du Ressuscité: Luc résume ici ce qu'il a raconté en Lc 24 et Ac 1 et qui sera rappelé plus brièvement encore en Ac 13:30-31.

L'interprétation des versets qui encadrent ce morceau central doit surtout tenir compte du procédé de parallélisme qui les unit et leur fait jouer le rôle d'une inclusion. L'universalité du salut est affirmée au début et dans la finale: "en toute nation celui que le craint . . ." (v 35a), ". . . tout (homme) qui croit en lui" (v 43b). Le message est destiné directement à Israël: "La parole qu'il a envoyée aux fils d'Israël . . ." (v 36a), "Et il nous a prescrit de proclamer au Peuple . . ." (v 42a). Mais en même temps l'objet immédiat de ce message est christologique: ". . . c'est lui le Seigneur de tous" (v 36b), ". . . c'est lui que a été constitueé par Dieu Juge des vivants et des morts" (v 42b). L'universalité de la fonction du Christ est ainsi envisagée par rapport à deux situations différentes: celle de la division actuelle de l'humanité en deux groupes ethniques, les Juifs et les Nations, et celle qui se vérifiera au moment du jugement auquel les morts devront être soumis aussi bien que les hommes encore en vie.

Le rapprochement qui s'opère ainsi entre les deux titres christologiques n'est manifestement pas très éclairant: non seulement l'universalisme y est envisagé à deux points de vue différents, mais aussi "Juge des vivants et des morts" se situe dans une perspective eschatologique[19] qui n'est pas celle du "Seigneur de tous (les hommes)". Mais un dernier élément de parallélisme mérite encore d'être pris en considération, celui que fournissent, au début et à la fin, les deux précisions introduites par un διά instrumental. Il est surtout frappant de voir comment la finale repasse de la considération eschatologique du v 42 à la réalité présente du salut: "A lui tous les prophètes rendent ce témoignage que, par (le moyen de) son nom, reçoit la rémission de ses péchés[20] tout (homme) qui croit en lui" (v 43). Au début, c'est Dieu lui-même qui, accueillant aux hommes "de toute nation" (v 35), "annonce la bonne nouvelle de la paix par (le moyen de) Jésus Christ", bonne nouvelle qui se résume dans l'affirmation: "C'est lui le Seigneur de tous" (v 36). Dans les deux cas, la précision διά indique la manière dont Jésus Christ réalise son rôle à l'égard d'hommes de "toute nation", à l'égard de "tout (homme) qui croit": il est celui par qui Dieu "annonce la bonne nouvelle de la paix" (dont parle Is 52:7), celui "par le nom de qui tout (homme) croyant en lui reçoit la rémission de ses péchés" (au témoignage de "tous les prophètes").

Explicitant ce que Pierre a finalement compris (v 34) et la portée de l'événement que constitue l'admission du premier non-Juif au baptême, le discours de Césarée contient un message trop important pour qu'on n'en retrouve pas l'écho dans les deux discours qui sont encore attribués à Pierre par les Actes. A son retour à Jérusalem, Pierre observe: "Dieu a accordé à ces gens le même don qu'à nous pour avoir cru au Seigneur Jésus Christ" (11:17). Lors de l'assemblée de Jérusalem, le rappel qu'il fait de l'événement de Césarée se conclut par ces mots avec lesquels s'achève aussi son rôle dans les Actes: "C'est par la grâce du Seigneur Jésus que nous croyons être sauvés, exactement comme eux"(15:11).

Cette dernière affirmation nous ramène à notre problème. Elle s'accorde avec l'oracle de Joël, au moins pour le fond. Là où Joël parle de "tout (homme)", Pierre explicite: "nous comme eux"; au lieu d'"invoquer", il dit "croire"; au lieu du "nom du Seigneur", il mentionne "la grâce du Seigneur Jésus"; enfin l'infinitif aoriste "être sauvé" se substitue à un indicatif futur "sera sauvé". On pourrait fort bien imaginer que l'auteur des Actes ait voulu terminer le dernier discours de Pierre par le rappel de la citation que commençait son discours inaugural. Mais la différence des termes est telle qu'il serait manifestement arbitraire de supposer qu'Ac 15:11 a réellement été écrit sur le modèle de 2:21.

L'examen du discours de Césarée ne révèle pas davantage la trace de l'oracle de Joël. Ici cependant la prudence s'impose en raison non seulement de l'importance accordée par Luc à la citation de 2:21 pour la suite de son récit, mais aussi et surtout en raison des points de contact qu'on découvre entre ce discours et les considérations que Rm 10 fonde sur les termes de Joël 3:5a. Il n'y a pas de doute d'abord que les deux passages se rapportent au même problème: celui que pose la disparition de la distinction que séparait du point de vue religieux les Juifs et les "Grecs". Ces deux passages, ensuite, sont les seuls dans le Nouveau Testament, à désigner Jésus comme "le Seigneur de tous (les hommes)". Paul y arrive en retournant la promesse de salut que Joël adresse à "tout (homme)" invoquant le nom du Seigneur; une association analogue pourrait s'établir dans le discours des Actes entre ce qui est dit de "toute nation" (v 35) ou de "tout (homme) qui croit" (v 43) et le titre christologique "Seigneur de tous" (v 36). Un contact supplémentaire s'établit entre les deux passages par suite de leur rapport avec Is 52:7, cité explicitement en Rm 10:15, probablement évoqué en Ac 10:36.

Ces contacts soulèvent des questions. Celle d'abord de savoir si on peut les considérer comme purement fortuits ou s'ils témoignent d'un lien de dépendance. Toute dépendance littéraire directe devant être exclue, il y aurait lieu de s'interroger sur la mesure dans laquelle il faut faire appel à une tradition commune. Il ne semble pas, en effet, qu'on puisse s'arrêter à l'idée que la formulation d'Ac 10 s'inspire d'une tradition paulinienne: l'argumentation théologique de Rm 10 est trop spécifique pour représenter une expression caractéristique du langage de l'Apôtre. Cette tradition commune s'apparenterait au texte de Joël 3:5a dans sa version grecque; elle relevait donc de communautés où l'on parlait grec.[21] Comme dans Joël, elle devait suggérer, sous un angle sotériologique, un rapport entre "tout (homme)" et "le Seigneur (Jésus)", susceptible de se retourner en une affirmation que Jésus est "le Seigneur de tous (les hommes)"; cette affirmation prenait toute sa force dans le context concret de l'admission des Gentils dans l'Eglise. Associé au titre de "Seigneur", le mot "nom" reparaît assez naturellement (cf. Rm 10:13 et Ac 10:43, 48), tandis que les verbes sont plus facilement remplaçables: "invoquer" peut céder le pas à "confesser" (Rm 10:9, 10) et surtout à "croire" (Ac 10:43;[22] Rm 10:4, 9-11, 14), "être sauvé" (cf. Ac 15:11) peut devenir "recevoir la rémission de ses péchés" (Ac 10:43).

L'emploi du titre "le Seigneur de tous" appliqué à Jésus Christ en Ac 10:36 pose ainsi une série de questions que peuvent mettre en cause la lecture que certains milieux du christianisme primitif de langue grecque faisaient de la sentence de Joël 3:5a. En essayant de préciser ces questions, nous espérons avoir montré notre intérêt pour l'orientation des recherches entreprises naguère par E. E. Ellis, notre souhait aussi de les voir se prolonger.

Notes

1. Nous visons d'abord l'ouvrage *Paul's Use of the Old Testament*, Edinburgh, 1957. Ensuite la vue d'ensemble "Midrash, Targum and New Testament Quotations", dans *Neotestamentica et Semitica. Studies in Honor of M. Black*, ed. E. E. Ellis and M. Wilcox, Edinburgh, 1969, 61-69. Enfin et surtout l'étude "Midrashic Features in the Speeches of Acts", publiée dans *Mélanges Bibliques B. Rigaux*, ed. A. Descamps et R. P. A. de Halleux, Gembloux, 1970, 303-312, puis, sous une forme revue et augmentée: "Midraschartige Züge in den Reden der Apostelgeschichte", *ZNW* 62 (1971) 94-104.

2. Sur ce discours deux articles importants viennent de paraître coup sur coup, en octobre et en décembre 1985: G. Schneider, "Die Petrusrede vor Kornelius. Das Verhältnis von Tradition und Komposition in Apg 10,34-43", dans Id., *Lukas, Theologe der Heilsgeschichte. Aufsätze zum lukanischen Doppelwerk* (BBB 59), Königstein/Ts.-Bonn, 253-279; A. Weiser, "Tradition und Lukanische Komposition in Apg 10,36-43", dans *A cause de l'Evangile. Etudes sur les Synoptiques et les Actes offertes au P. J. Dupont* (LeDiv 123), Paris, 757-767. Nous croyons pouvoir nous autoriser de ces études pour nous dispenser de longues listes bibliographiques et de discussions ne touchant pas directement à notre sujet.

3. Une liste de parallèles fournis par les apocryphes et les pseudépigraphes a été dressée par H. J. Cadbury, "The Titles of Jesus in Acts", dans F. J. Foakes Jackson - K. Lake, *The Beginnings of Christianity*, I/V, London, 1933, 354-375 (362); la 26e édition du Nestle-Aland en a retenu Sg 6,7 et 8,3. L'expression employée là est ὁ πάντων δεσπότης et πάντων n'est au masculin que dans le premier cas. Il s'agit aussi d'un neutre dans l'expression κύριος εἶ πάντων de la prière de Mardochée (Est 4:17 grec). Notons une expression équivalente en Jr 39:27: ἐγὼ κύριος ὁ θεὸς πάσης σαρκός, où κύριος correspond à YHWH (32:27), nom propre que ne saurait être suivi d'un complément déterminatif.

4. Ce point est justement souligné par E. E. Ellis, *Paul's Use*, 139s.

5. Il serait plus hasardeux de soupçonner déjà l'influence du texte de Joël sur le παντί du v 4.

6. Voir F. Bovon, "Le salut dans les écrits de Luc", *RTP*, 3.Ser. 23 (1973) 296-307 (299).

7. D'accord avec G. Schneider, *Die Apostelgeschichte*, I (HThK V,1), Freiburg, 1980, 269: en ajoutant des "signes" aux "prodiges" dont parlait Joël, le v 19 recourt à un "Biblizismus" courant; inutile de chercher un raport avec le miracle de la Pentecôte, ou avec les miracles accomplis par Jésus (v 22) et les apôtres, ou avec les prodiges qui ont accompagné la mort de Jésus (Lc 23:45).

8. Nous n'avons pas affaire à un indicatif aoriste qui marquerait normalement l'antériorité par rapport au temps du verbe principal: "qui aura invoqué". Le subjonctif aoriste est dépourvu de toute idée de temps. En Rm 10:13, le parallélisme avec le participe présent du v 11, ὁ πιστεύων, inviterait à traduire également par un présent: "tout homme que invoque"; mais il peut sembler préférable d'accorder la traduction avec le temps des deux indicatifs futurs de ce verset.

9. Le meilleur indice de la portée programmatique de cette citation se trouve sans doute dans la manière dont Ac 10:38 résume le ministère de Jésus. On peut voir à ce propos notre étude "Jésus annonce la bonne nouvelle aux pauvres", dans: Associazione Biblica Italiana, *Evangelizare pauperibus. Atti della XXIV Settimana biblica*, Brescia, 1978, 127-189 (150-155), ou dans le recueil *Etudes sur les évangiles synoptiques*, I BEThL 70A, Leuven (1985) 46-51. Noter aussi l'article, déjà mentionné, de Weiser, "Tradition und lukanische Komposition . . .", 764-765.

10. Dans la perspective de Luc, la description reprise au v 5 tend à mettre en valeur le "salut de Dieu" dont parle le v 6: E. E. Ellis, *The Gospel of Luke* (CeB New ed.), Edinburgh, 1966, 88.

11. Communément admise aujourd'hui, la relation étroite entre Lc 3:6 et Ac 28:28 avait été soulignée dans notre étude "Le salut des Gentils et la signification théologique du Livre des Actes", dans *NTS* 6 (1959-60) 132-155 (136-138), reprise dans J. Dupont, *Etudes sur les Actes des Apôtres* (LeDiv 45), Paris, 1967, 398-401.

12. C'est ce qui a été fort bien mis en lumière par M. Rese, *Alttestamentliche Motive in der Christologie des Lukas* (StNT 1), Gütersloh, 1969, 46-55, 63-66, 126-127. Notons, dans le même sens: A. Barbi, *Il Cristo celeste presente nella Chiesa. Tradizione e Redazione in Atti 3,19-21* (AnBib 64), Roma, 1979, 175-176; J. Roloff, *Die Apostelgeschichte* (NTD 5^{17}), Göttingen, 1981, 53-55.

13. Le texte du prophète n'évoque les sauvés que comme un petit nombre de rescapés; les Actes insistent au contraire sur le grand nombre.

14. R. C. Tannehill, "The Composition of Acts 3-5: Narrative Development and Echo Effect", dans *SBL 1984 Seminar Papers*, 217-240 (224). Cet auteur élargit à juste titre la perspective dans laquelle Rese soulignait que le *discours* du chapitre 3 prolonge celui du chapitre 2: *Alttestamentliche Motive*, 66-67; voir aussi U. Wilckens, *Die Missionsreden der Apostelgeschichte. Form- und traditionsgeschichtliche Untersuchungen* (WMANT 5), 3e éd., Neukirchen, 1974, 226.

15. Le v 23 ne doit pas être considéré comme une citation de Lv 23:29, ainsi qu'on le répète encore trop souvent: Luc y substitue aux termes de Dt 18:19 une formulation plus dure, très familière au langage biblique. Ce point nous paraît avoir été bien démontré par C. M. Martini, "L'esclusione dall comunità del popolo di Dio e il nuovo Israele secondo Atti 3,23", dans *Bib* 50 (1969) 1-14; version remaniée dans *Communio* 12 (1973) 63-82, réimprimée dans le recueil *La Parola di Dio alle origini della Chiesa*, Roma, 1980, 239-258. Nous avons eu l'occasion de revenir sur ce sujet dans l'ouvrage *Teologiea della chiesa negli Atti degli apostoli* (Studi biblici 10), Bologna, 1984, 69-76.

16. Le v 60 ajoute une seconde invocation: "Seigneur ne leur impute pas ce péché." Ces deux invocations correspondent clairement aux deux prières que Jésus crucifié adresse à son "Père": Lc 23:34, 46.

17. Désignation traditionnelle comme l'attestent 1 Co 1:2; 2 Tm 2:22, outre le passage de Rm 10:12-14 où elle est directement rattachée à Joël.

18. On peut regretter que les deux articles tout récents sur ce discours, celui de Schneider et celui de Weiser cités au début de notre article, omettent de signaler une étude qui reste fondamentale: E. Samain, "La notion de APXH dans l'oeuvre lucanienne", dans F. Neirynck (éd.), *L'Evangile de Luc. Problèmes littéraires et théologiques. Mémorial L. Cerfaux* (BEThL 32), Gembloux, 1973, 299-328 (voir 305-313).

19. La perspective sur laquelle se termine précisément, dans des termes analogues, le discours d'Athènes (Ac 17:31), l'autre grand discours missionnaire adressé dans les Actes à des non-Juifs. En désignant Jésus comme "le Seigneur des morts et des vivants", Rm 14:9 se situe dans une perspective un peu différente.

20. Pour désigner le salut, la "rémission des péchés" est une expression typiquement lucanienne: Luc la doit à Mc 1:4 en Lc 3:3; il l'introduit en Lc 1:77; 24:47; Ac 2:38; 5:31; 10:43; 13:38; 26:18. Son contexte est celui d'une prédication missionnaire.

21. C'est au niveau du grec qu'il est possible de reporter sur Jésus le titre de κύριος, correspondant dans l'original au nom de YHWH. Le même phénomène se vérifie au seuil de l'évangile pour la citation d'Is 40:3 (Lc 3:4). L'analogie n'est sans doute pas dépourvue de signification, comme l'observe Schneider, *Lukas, Theologie der Heilsgeschichte*, 219, n. 37.

22. Ajouter Ac 15:11 où, dans l'expression "nous croyons être sauvés", le verbe "croire" traduit non une simple opinion mais la foi en son plein sens théologique. Voir surtout S. A. Panimolle, *Il discorso di Petro all'assemblea apostolica, III. Legge e grazia (Atti 15,10-11)* (Studi biblici 3), Bologna, 1978, 78-81; J. Nolland, "A Fresh Look at Acts 15.10", *NTS* 27 (1981) 105-115 (112 s.).

Code and Context:
A Few Reflections on the
Parenesis of Col 3:6–4:1

Lars Hartman

During the last decade or so, New Testament scholarly discussions have revealed a renewed interest in the so-called household codes, especially the two NT texts which deserve this designation, viz. Col 3:18–4:1 and Eph 5:22–6:9.[1] One reason is, of course, that the feminist movement has increased the embarassment many exegetes have felt regarding the admonitions that wives be submissive.[2] Another is that new suggestions have been made in terms of background material, viz. the so-called household management traditions, and, as a matter of fact, these have also been used when it has come to grappling with the hermeneutic problems posed by the texts. In this paper some of these new insights will be combined with older suggestions concerning the possible role played by the Decalogue[3] in the context of the Colossian household code. In addition, this will be carried out with respect to the argument of Colossians. I find it natural to dedicate this article to Professor Ellis, as it touches upon a field of research on which he has done so much significant work, viz. the investigation of the use of the OT in early Christian history and traditions.[4]

It has been a widely spread opinion that the household code of Col 3:18–4:1 is a textual unit that was formulated before Col was written. Its style is different from that of the surrounding parenesis, and if one should withdraw it, the text would flow smoothly all the same. If, then, the passage is a loan, from where has it been borrowed? Furthermore, what, if anything, does that tell us about the history of the Early Church and about its relationship to the surrounding world? Finally, how does the household code function within the framework of the letter, and what is its function with regard to the situation of the addressees?[5]

The questions of the preceding paragraph have received different answers among NT scholars.[6] Thus, Martin Dibelius held (1913)[7] that behind the "Haustafeln" lay a "schema", which was originally Stoic and visible in the way such philosophers organized their discussions of what was "fitting" (*kathēkon*) "towards the gods, one's parents, one's brothers, one's country, and towards foreigners" (Epict. 2.17.31). He saw the Church's adoption of this pattern as a sign that it was on the way to abandoning the eschatological perspective which was thought to characterize its attitude from the beginning, and was adjusting itself to a life in this world.

Fifteen years later Karl Weidinger elaborated Dibelius' ideas, presenting more material from the philosphers as well as from Judaism.[8] "Hellenistic Judaism"[9] had also used the "schema", and he thought that it was possibly the milieu from which the Christians got it. But, in addition, the Christians assumed not only the "schema" but also the very texts themselves, at least in the case of the code of Col 3:18–4:1. They merely christianized the code by adding "in the Lord" at suitable places.

Dibelius' and Weidinger's ideas dominated the understanding of the household codes for several decades. In 1972, however, J. E. Crouch went through the material again.[10] He too assumed an "Hellenistic" origin of the codes, and thought that "Hellenistic Judaism" had had a decisive influence.[11] However, he criticized Dibelius and Weidinger for simplifying the problem of the role played by the eschatological expectations. Weidinger was also accused of being too quick to generalize, both in terms of the pre-Christian Stoic-Cynic *and* Jewish material, as well as when it came to the Christian codes.

Others have claimed that the household codes had a purely Christian origin. Thus, K. H. Rengstorf has derived them from an early Christian interest in the *oikos*.[12] A partly similar opinion concerning the origin is held by David Schroeder.[13] He finds the roots of the *form* in OT apodictic law *and* in Stoic lists of the stations in life. But "the content is drawn from the OT, Judaic tradition, although with the addition of certain Greek (what is fitting) and Christian *(agapē)* concepts. The basic ethical conception of the NT codes—that without belonging to the world as such, one has responsibilities within the structure of society—takes us back to the teaching and example of Jesus himself."

The second half of the 1970's brought a new stage in research on the codes: instead of having parallels in the *kathēkon*-lists, the "stations" addressed in the codes, as well as some of the advice found in them, were seen as having clearer parallels in the philosophical treatises from Plato and Aristotle onwards, which dealt with household management, *oikonomia* or *oikonomos*.[14] Regarding the NT household codes in the light of this tradition led to new suggestions of what the Church was actually doing with its household codes. D. Lührmann saw therein a latent claim of the Christians that the Christian house was a model for society.[15] D. C. Balch concluded, having especially 1 Pet in mind, that "the code has an apologetic function in the historical context: the paraenesis is given in light of outside criticism", viz. from persons who "were alienated and threatened by some of their slaves and wives who had converted to the new, despised religion, so they were accusing the converts of impiety, immorality, and insubordination".[16] K. Müller seems to suggest something similar: the early Christians lived in a society, in which some people, including some women, questioned the age-old subordination system of the "house", whereas others wanted to hold on to or to reinforce the good old authoritative pattern. In such a situation "the oldest household code of the NT demonstrates . . . a highly respectable early Christian decision in favor of a middle course of social morality".[17]

After this short review of some answers to the questions raised in the beginning of this paper,[18] let us turn to the text itself, first considering its context in the literary sense of the word.

As I see it, Col has a more hortatory character than one often assumes. This is seen not least from the fact that the author reverts to the second person when summoning the addressees.[19] The Christologically loaded passages of 1:13-20 and 2:9-15 serve as bases for admonition; in 1:21-23 this is indicated indirectly, whereas 2:16-23 is directly addressed to the believers. To concentrate on the second instance, this part of the letter begins with 1:24–2:5. It functions as a *captatio benevolentiae* which is partly realized by tying bonds of affection between "Paul"[20] and the addressees. Then, an introductory exhortation follows in 2:6-8: "walk in him . . . as you were taught . . . See to it that nobody carries you away captive . . . according to the principles of the world *(ta stoicheia tou kosmou)*, not according to Christ". This leads *(hoti)* directly into the Christological basis, 2:9-15, which is applied in the following admonition of

2:16-23: "thus *(oun)*, nobody must judge you in terms of food or drink ... If you died with Christ from the principles of the world, why do you allow rules to be laid on you: do not touch ...". The whole section of 1:24–2:23 becomes the background against which positive ethical teaching is given in 3:1–4:6. In a sense 2:6-7 ("walk in him as you were taught") becomes specified in 3:1-4, and the life with Christ (3:1,3) and the heavenly mind (3:2) are placed over against the human and this-worldly rules (2:8, 14, 16, 20-23) and the earthly mind (3:2), for which the "philosophers" stand.

3:1-4 opens up the general Christologically determined perspective for the ethics. Then, in 3:5–4:6 more particular instructions follow. Regarded in this way, the parenesis in 3:1–4:6 is not only a section added to the theological parts of the letter, but rather something that has been prepared for almost from the beginning of the letter (cf. "knowledge of his will", 1:9).

We need not discuss the details of how the instruction of 3:5–4:6 is construed,[21] but only state that 3:5-17 is largely made up of catalogues of vices and virtues with a tendency of grouping them by fives. 3:16 deals with worship, and 3:17 is often understood as a summarizing conclusion: "whatever you do in word and deed, do it all in the name of Lord Jesus, thanking God the Father through him". However, since the following household code starts without any connecting conjunction or particle, and because of the seven occurrences of "the Lord" in the code, 3:17 also becomes a bridge to the household code; indeed, it might very well be regarded as its introduction.[22]

As already mentioned, however, the code appears like an island in its context. The shift in style is one factor contributing to this effect, viz. the direct address, "You wives", etc., and the shape of the admonitions (address + imperative + motivation). Furthermore, it is tightly held together by its reference to the household.

After the household code, the style in 4:2 is once again more similar to that in 3:5-17, and these admonitions have a concluding character inasmuch as they contain several echoes from the preceding text. Such observations would seemingly confirm Lohmeyer's opinion *(ad loc.)* that "one could hardly surmise that there were a gap if this passage were blotted out".

Of course one could assume, then, as does Lohmeyer, that there must have been something in the Colossians' situation that demanded the insertion of this text. This might very well be so, but that does not make it unnecessary to consider the possibility I mentioned at the outset, viz. that the Decalogue might have something to do with this parenetic section, the household code included.

As a matter of fact, the Decalogue is a structuring factor in several ethical catalogues.[23] Mark 7:21-22 is a Christian example: fornication, theft, murder, adultery, coveting, wickedness, deceit, licentiousness, evil eye, slander, pride, foolishness. The parallel text in Matt 15:19 brings the text even closer to the OT: murder, adultery, fornication, theft, false witness, slander. 1 Tim 1:8-10 is another NT instance:[24] "lawless and disobedient, ungodly and sinners, unholy and profane, murderers of fathers and murderers of mothers, manslayers, fornicators, sodomites, kidnappers, liars, perjurers . . ." There are echoes of the Decalogue in Jewish, non-Palestinian texts as well, e.g. Sib. Or. 4.24-39: "love the great god (in contrast to worshiping idols, 25-30), . . . no murder, . . . no dishonest gain, . . . no desire for another's spouse or for abuse of a male ..." Similarly in the beginning of the ethical admonitions of Pseudo-Phocylides (3-21): "do not commit adultery, homosexuality, treachery, nor stain your hands with blood; do not become rich unjustly, . . . be content with what you have and abstain from what is another's, do not tell lies . . . , honor God foremost, and afterward your parents, . . . flee false witness . . . , do not commit perjury, . . . do not steal seeds . . . , give the laborer his pay."[25] In passing we may note that the order between the commandments is not always the same, and there are more examples of this than Mark 10:19.[26]

With the examples of the preceding paragraph in mind one is immediately prepared to endorse Gnilka's supposition in his commentary on Colossians[27] that the two vice catalogues of Col 3:5 and 8 are dependent on the Decalogue: "fornication, impurity, passion, evil desire, and covetousness, which is idolatry", and: "anger, wrath, malice, slander, foul talk". I would also add the beginning of v 9: "do not lie to (or, about) one another". Counting (with, e.g., Philo) the image-commandment as the second one, and taking hatred and murder as equal (Matt 5:21-22, 1 John 3:15), we see that numbers 2, 6, 7, 8, 9 and 10 of the Decalogue have counterparts in Col 3:5-9.[28] The application and interpretation of the commandments, visible in the lists of Col 3, have several parallels in Jewish texts.[29]

As a contrast, 3:10–4:1 presents the life of the New Man. The description of this New Man begins with the characteristic "neither Greek nor Jew". I find it natural to combine this detail with the abundant epithets applied to the addressees in the subsequent verse, "God's elect, holy and beloved". Commentators state that the author here transfers classical designations of God's people to the addressees.[30] However, in this context it is appropriate to remember that Israel's election and holiness was closely connected with the covenant and the Law (e.g. Exod 19:5-6; Lev 19; Deut 4:37-40), and that the covenant and the Divine Revelation were expressions of God's love for His people (e.g., Deut 4:37; 7:8). In Col 3, however, God's elect are those in the New Man, in whom there is neither Greek nor Jew. But, precisely as in the case of Israel, the election is bound up with duties, with "putting on" a particular sort of life.

Certainly the "put on" of 3:12 is the positive counterpart to the "put off" of 3:5. But one cannot put the virtues of vv 12-14 in a one-to-one contrast to the vices of 3:5-9, i.e., as precise positive instructions implied in the prohibitions as they have been re-phrased and interpreted in the vice lists. Many Christians are used to reading the Decalogue in such a way, and may therefore be too ready to hear echoes from the Decalogue also behind the positive admonitions. Thus, e.g., Lutherans learn in Luther's classical small catechism that the commandment against false testimony means: "We should fear and love God, and so we should not tell lies about our neighbor, nor betray, slander, or defame him, but should apologize for him, speak well of him, and interpret charitably all that he does". In the Office of Instruction of the Episcopal Church we hear of the duties towards one's neighbor as brought forward by the tenth commandment: "Not to covet nor desire other men's goods; But to learn and labor truly to earn mine own living, And to do my duty in that state of life unto which it shall please God to call me".

When Philo comments on the Decalogue, there is not much of this sort of discovery of implicitly commanded virtues, but in the catalogue I just cited from Pseudo-Phocylides we come across a similar tendency to add a "but" to the prohibitions: "do not become rich unjustly, but live from honorable means, . . . do not tell lies, but always speak the truth" (5, 7) (alla and de, respectively).

In Col 3 the virtues are not, as we noted, directly related to the individual items of the vice lists, but nonetheless one could say that they counter the transgressions of the commandments concerning murder, stealth, false witness and covetousness as the author of Col has interpreted them. Like his master, Paul, and following Jesus, he also regards love as the all-embracing commandment (3:14; Matt 5:43-48; Mark 12:28-33; Rom 13:8-10, etc.).

So far we have traced nothing from the first five commandments (except for idolatry in 3:5), including the one concerning parents. Nor has the one on adultery, such as the author interpreted it, been given any positive counterpart in 3:12-17. It seems to me that this lack is met in the household code of 3:18–4:1. But before delineating this let me point to the possibility that even the Sabbath commandment lies behind a piece of the parenesis in Col 3.

The author certainly has nothing but contempt for the "philosophers'" ceremonial rules concerning "a feast, a new moon or a sabbath" (2:16). But there are traces of Jewish speculations on the Sabbath and its deeper meaning, which, in my opinion, a writer who held the sort of cosmic wisdom-Christology we encounter in Col could use for an interpretation of the Sabbath commandment. Thus, Philo explains the meaning of "sabbath" as "rest" (anapausis; see Abr. 28). He finds this very fitting, for number seven "is always free from factions and war and quarrelling and is of all numbers the most peaceful". Indeed, as a matter of fact, to real lovers of wisdom the whole of life is a feast, for they always strive for "a life free from war and peaceful" (Spec. leg. 2.45). Furthermore, to Philo, but even more to Aristobulos, the number seven is something like a basic principle to the All which becomes manifest in the celebration of the seventh day.[31] To a philosophically minded Christian interpreter of the Sabbath commandment this might become a point of departure for a reference to the "peace of Christ" with this followed by some advice that Christ's word should dwell among the addressees and that they should teach each other and praise God. The study and the teaching of the Scriptures are, as is well known, of central importance to Philo when he describes the Sabbath,[32] and to his fellow Jews as well. The picture Philo gives of prayers, singing, and instruction at the Sabbath worship of the Therapeuts[33] is not too distant from Col 3:16.[34]

Whether there be any intimations of the fourth commandment behind 3:15-16 or not, to anyone who has felt that the commandment concerning parents should not be left out of consideration, and that the one on adultery should also be addressed with positive admonitions, this feeling of something lacking would be satisfied in the household code, 3:18–4:1. But did anybody—author and/or reader—feel that lack and then regard 3:18–4:1 as complying with it?

It may be of some importance to an answer to that question that, e.g., Philo understood the fifth commandment as covering the laws which "deal with the relations of old to young, rulers to subjects, benefactors to benefited, slaves to masters" (Decal. 165).[35] He also saw parents and masters as, in some respects, being gods to the other members of the house (Decal. 107-120; Spec. leg. 2.225-27), which gives an extra echo to the references to "the Lord" in the household code: being obedient "pleases the Lord" (3:20), and the slaves are to serve as it were to the Lord (3:23). That is, if 3:20–4:1 somehow represents the fifth commandment, it does so in a way that was found in contemporary Judaism. Also in favor of a positive answer to my question, there is the fact that, when the author of Eph uses Col 3:20,[36] he finds it natural to insert an explicit quotation of the fifth commandment (Eph 6:2-3).[37]

Philo did not include the relationship between wife and husband in that which was covered by the fifth commandment. Nonetheless, it is undeniable that it provides the positive instruction that would give the other side of the coin also in the case of the adultery commandment. On the other hand we have to realize that the contents certainly have some parallels in the surrounding world, but not, as far as I know,[38] in connection with an explanation of the prohibition of adultery. Accordingly, we should either assume that our text represents an innovation in terms of Decalogue interpretation, or that the code derives its contents from reasons other than the author's wish to reinterpret and apply two commandments of the Decalogue.

It is possible that the alternatives are too harshly stated in the preceding paragraph. At least it may seem so, if we supplement our discussion of the contents with some literary and form-critical observations. There are good reasons to assume that the code is a pre-Colossian unit, or, rather, that it is written in accordance with traditional turns of phrase. Its coherence and the difference in style as compared to the context have been mentioned above, and its coherence is not only stylistic, but also caused by the thought pattern of the "house". Accordingly, I would suggest that the author does not draw upon a ready made development of the commandments about honoring parents and not commiting adultery. Rather, when composing this parenesis with all its echoes of and interpretative applications of the Decalogue, he used this (partly pre-formulated?) code which was structured according to the role system of the "house". Thus, in the Col-context it came to fulfill the function of applying parts of the Decalogue to God's elected and beloved people, in whom there was neither Greek nor Jew.[39]

I have argued above that the parenesis of 3:1–4:1 is not merely added to a "theological" part of the letter, but rather that Col as a whole has a more exhortatory character than is often realized. But the echoes of the Decalogue, of the Law in some sense of the word, is something also met with in Paul (Rom 13:8-10).[40] Our author had, however, not simply learned from his master that letters to Christian communities should have a parenesis. The phenomenon was not exclusively Pauline—in the NT 1 Pet, Jas and Heb follow a similar line. It is often held that most of the *material* that is parenetic in a form-critical sense has a non-Christian origin, viz. in Judaism and popular Philosophy.[41] Our deliberations above have not falsified that opinion. I would, however, suggest that the *practice* of admonishing one's addressees to hold on to the morals they had learnt is a tradition from Judaism. Thus, the Epistle of Baruch (2 *Bar* 78-86) is an example of a "letter" which should be read in the assemblies of the addressees (86), and in chapter 84 the author instructs them in different ways to keep faithfully to the Law. This invites us to conclude that the author of Col followed a convention not only when he concluded his letter with a parenesis, but also when he did so by using material that to such a large extent was interpretation and application of the Law, in this case, the Decalogue.[42]

It is now time to return to the questions I asked at the outset. Concerning the question of origin, it seems that we must reckon with a rather developed root-system behind both the household code of Col and the preceding parenesis. *Per se* the code and the other parenesis can have different roots. The tradition behind the preceding parenesis appears to have a Christian *Sitz* before its appearance in Col—the echoes of Jesus' teaching indicate this. But its interpretations of the Decalogue are ultimately inspired by Judaism. The list-form is widely used in Jewish as well as in other Hellenistic circles.[43] On the one hand the household code is also to be related to the Decalogue, but indirectly, although its parallel in Eph explicitly quotes the fifth commandment in relation to a part of it. On the other hand, it regards people in their standard positions in society, i.e. in the "house". This thought pattern of the "house" organizes the code, but it is so general and natural in antiquity that one can hardly use it when asking more particularly for a milieu of origin. The manner of expression in the code reminds one of the so-called apodictic law, and indicates an OT-Jewish inspiration at the very bottom. But this does not necessarily mean that it was directly taken from there. On the contrary, the fact that the addressees have been "taught" (2:7) should indicate that the author makes use of traditions, though not necessarily very fixed ones, which were taught as being based on divine law and not human tradition (cf. 2:8, 22).

Does the presence of the "house" pattern tell us anything particular about the development of the Church, when seen generally? I doubt this—thinking in terms of the "house" was next to inevitable (cf. e.g., Matt 10:35)—and the connection with the Decalogue is only one more sign of the fact that in a way Gentile Christian churches were also Jewish-Christian.[44]

Most of that which has been said in the preceding paragraphs concerns the author's side of the letter's communication: his producing a text is allowed to testify about *his* ways of thinking and *his* background. But we should also ask for the function of the code and of its parenetic context within Col, and, as well, for their function in relationship to the addressees and their situation. As to the first question, I have already intimated an answer: the parenesis is there as a God-given contrast to the precepts advanced by this-worldly "philosophy", and it has been prepared for at least from 2:6 onwards *(peripateite)*. The catalogues of vices and virtues in relation to one's fellowmen stand over against "humility", angelic service, visions (2:18, 23). The worship of 3:16 is different from the observance of feasts, new moon and sabbath (2:16), and the household code, in its practical worldliness,[45] is quite different from "do not touch," etc., of 2:23.[46]

Scholars have suggested several solutions to the problem of the external function of the parenesis, and especially of the household code. I have mentioned some of them above. One such function is implied by the contrast to the "philosophical" rules I just pointed to. Are there also any attempts to temper some sort of emancipation on the part of women and slaves? There are no signs in the letter that the author was disturbed because the women of the Colossian community were caught up in the liberal tendencies of some circles. Also, if the sister church in Laodicea met in a house owned by a woman, Nympha, which is rather probable,[47] nothing in the text indicates that this circumstance called for any remarks. Thus, the Decalogue and "house" structures seem to be sufficient reasons for the wife-husband admonition, the contents of which seems to be what was rather normal in the sort of Jewish circles[48] that have been the original seedbed of both the Decalogue reinterpretation and the wisdom-Christology. But that which is said concerning slaves breaks the frames of style and proportion, as most commentators note. Already A. Deissmann assumed that this reflected the social structure of the church.[49] The situation of house slaves was not to be compared with slavery of more modern times,[50] but possibly the Christian view of masters and slaves as brethren in Christ can have caused problems.[51]

For the rest, even the circumstance that the whole parenesis seems to be making extensive use of traditional material can be regarded in two ways. On the one hand, being standard exhortations and having the Decalogue as a point of departure, the parenesis does not tell us very much about its particular external function. On the other hand, the very fact of its "standard" character might be a point: the "philosophy" seems to have claimed that the "standard" was not enough and that, instead, the perfect should stand in a good relationship also to other powers besides the Lord Jesus and hold to loftier and more particular rules than the standard ones. Against this the author has argued: the Lord Jesus was good enough, and so was the sort of life in him that they had learnt.

Notes

1. Other texts referred to as household codes are: 1 Pet 2:18–3:7 (which does not deal with the whole household). 1 Tim 2:8-15; Titus 2:1-10; *Did* 4:9-11; *Barn* 19:5-7; 1 *Clem* 21:6-9; Pl *Phil.* 4:2–6:3 are no real household codes.

2. E.g., D. L. Balch, "Early Christian Criticism of Patriarchal Authority: 1 Peter 2:11–3:12", *UnSemQuartRev* 39 (1984) 161-173.

3. Contemporary Jews counted the commandments of the Decalogue in such a way that the one against making graven images became number two, and the one on honoring one's parents number five, the last of the first table. In this paper I will follow this way of counting. The Decalogue has been drawn into the discussion of the household code by R. M. Grant, "The Decalogue in Early Christianity", *HTR* 40 (1940) 1-17, and P. Stuhlmacher, "Christliche Verantwortung bei Paulus und seinen Schülern", *EvT* 28 (1968) 165-186, esp. 177-78.

4. E.g., E. E. Ellis, *Paul's Use of the Old Testament,* Edinburgh, 1957; *id., Prophecy and Hermeneutic in Early Christianity. New Testament Essays,* WUNT 18, Tübingen, 1978, Chaps. 9-17.

5. One could use different terms for these two "functions". In another context I have distinguished between a literary (or illocutionary) and a sociolinguistic function (L. Hartman, "Survey of the Problem of Apocalyptic Genre", in *Apocalypticism in the Mediterranean World and the Near East,* ed. by D. Hellholm, Proceedings of the International Colloqium on Apocalypticism, Uppsala, August 12-17, 1979, Tübingen, 1983, 329-343, § 3.3.1 and 3.3.2.), but I here follow the terminology of D. Hellholm, preferring "(text-) internal" and "(text-)- external" (D. Hellholm, "The Problem of Apocalyptic Genre and the Apocalypse of John", in *id., Dispersa Membra,* to be published in ConBNT, 3.3.2.)

6. For a discussion of the scholarly debate see J. E. Crouch, *The Origin and Intention of the Colossian Haustafel,* FRLANT 109, Göttingen, 1972, chap. 1, and D. L. Balch, *Let Wives be Submissive: The Domestic Code in 1 Peter,* SBL Monogr. Ser. 26, Chico, 1981, chap. 1.

7. M. Dibelius, *An die Kolosser, Epheser, an Philemon,* HNT 12, 3rd ed., ed. by H. Greeven, Tübingen, 1953, 48-50.

8. K. Weidinger, *Die Haustafeln. Ein Stück urchristlicher Paränese,* UNT 14, Leipzig, 1928.

9. Although I use this traditional expression (because the cited authors do so), the quotation marks are there to mark that I would rather replace it by "Greek speaking, largely non-Palestinian Judaism" or something similar.

10. Crouch, *Origin and Intention.*

11. E. Lohmeyer (*Die Briefe an die Philipper, an die Kolosser und an Philemon,* MeyerK 9, 9th ed. by W. Schmauch, Göttingen, 1953; the 8th ed., the first one written by Lohmeyer, appeared in 1930) also held the opinion that Col 3:18–4:1 was a pre-Colossian unit, but regarded it as being of purely Jewish origin. In so doing, he did not ask so much for the provenance of a "schema" as for the root system of the ideas.

12. K. H. Rengstorf, "Die neutestamentlichen Mahnungen an die Frau, sich dem Manne unterzuordnen", in *Verbum Dei manet in aeternum: Festschrift O. Schmitz,* ed. by W. Foerster, Witten, 1953, 131-145.

13. D. Schroeder, "Lists, ethical", *IDBSup,* 1976, 546-547. His unpublished Hamburg dissertation from 1959 dealt with the household codes, their origin and their theological meaning. It has not been available to me.

14. D. Lührmann, "Wo man nicht mehr Sklave oder Freier ist", *WortuDienst, NF* 13 (1975), 58-83; *id.,* "Neutestamentliche Haustafeln und antike Ökonomie", *NTS* 27 (1980/81) 83-97; K. Thraede, "Ärger mit der Freiheit", in *"Freunde in Christus werden . . .",* ed. by G. Scharffenorth, K. Thraede, Berlin, 1977, 31-182; *id.,* "Zum historischen Hintergrund der 'Haustafeln' des NT", in *Pietas Festschrift für B. Kötting,* ed. by E. Dassmann, K. G. Frank—*JAC,* Erg. bd. 8, 1980, Munich, 1980, 359-368; Balch, *Wives Be Submissive,* after a Yale dissertation in 1974; K. Müller, "Die Haustafel des Kolosserbriefes und das antike Frauenthema", in *Die Frau im Urchristentum,* ed. by G. Dautzenberg, H. Merklein, K. Müller, QD 95, Freiburg, Basel, Vienna, 1983, 263-319, esp. 284-90.

15. Lührmann, *NTS* 27 (1980/81) 86.

16. Balch, *Wives Be Submissive,* 109.

17. Müller, "Die Haustafel," 290.

18. Müller's article contains a broader and slightly peppered review of the research. The strictly literary and form-critical questions have largely been left aside here. I deal with them in my contribution to the Festschrift to H. C. Kee, forthcoming.

19. See 1:9-12, 21-23, 2:4, 6-8, 10, 16, 18, 20.

20. I assume that the author is a member of Paul's school.

21. See, e.g. the literature referred to and the discussion in J. Gnilka, *Der Kolosserbrief*, HTKNT 10:1, Freiburg, Basel, Vienna, 1980, *ad loc*.

22. As a matter of fact the three cases of *kai* introducing a main clause in vv 15-17 are a little strange (cf. W. Bujard, *Stilanalytische Untersuchungen zum Kolosserbrief als Beitrag zur Methodik von Sprachvergleichen*, SUNT 11, Göttingen, 1973, 42). Gnilka, *Kolosserbrief*, 198, concludes that they are to be explained through the assumption that "in 3:15-17 Einzelmahnungen zusammengestellt sind". It would, however, fit well with my suggestions below, if v 15 begins a re-interpretation of the sabbath-commandment (sabbath—rest—peace). The idea that v 17 introduces the household instruction, which covers "everything" a man could be, is supported by, e.g., Seneca, *ep*. 94.1, in which he describes what is contained in a household management treatise: *eam partem philosophiae, quae dat propria cuique personae praecepta . . .* !

23. K. Berger, *Die Gesetzesauslegung Jesu I*, Neukirchen, 1972, 272-73.

24. See Grant, *HTR* 40 (1940) 7. Cf. A. Vögtle, *Die Tugend-und Lasterkatologe exegetisch, religions- und formgeschichtlich untersucht*, NTAbh 16, 4-5, Münster, 1936, 16; S. Wibbing, *Die Tugend- und Lasterkataloge im NT und ihre Traditionsgeschichte unter besonderer Berücksichtigung der Qumran-Texte*, BZNW 25, Berlin, 1959, 83.

25. Berger, *Gesetzesauslegung Jesu*, 374, is not prepared to hear any echoes from the Decalogue here, but cf. M. Küchler, *Frühjüdische Weisheitstraditionen*, OBO, 26, Freiburg, Göttingen, 1979, 277-79.

26. Berger, *Gesetzesauslegung Jesu*, 275-76.

27. Gnilka, *Kolosserbrief*, 185.

28. The *blasphēmia* of v 8 should hardly be taken as based on the commandment against taking the Name in vain.

29. See Berger, *Gesetzesauslegung Jesu*, chap. 4. There are indications to the effect that the Decalogue had a central place in the synagogue worship in the times of the Early Church. That this position of the Decalogue changed is often assumed to have taken place because of the Christian usage of the Decalogue. See Grant, *HTR* 40 (1940).

30. E.g., E. Larsson, *Christus als Vorbild*, ASNU 23, Lund, 1962, 210; E. Lohse, *Die Briefe an die Kolosser und an Philemon*, MeyerK 9:2, 14th ed. Göttingen, 1968, *ad loc.;* E. Schweizer, *Der Brief an die Kolosser*, EKKNT, Neukirchen-Vluyn, 1976, *ad loc*.

31. M. Hengel, *Judaism and Hellenism I*, Philadelphia, 1974, 166-169.

32. *Decal.* 98, 100; *Spec. Leg.* 2.62; *Omn. Prob. Lib.* 82; cf. Euseb. *Praep. ev.* 8.7, 12-13.

33. *Vit. Cont.* 29, 75-80.

34. A scholar who is more fanciful than I might even be prepared to combine 3:17, about doing everything in the name of the Lord Jesus, with the commandment concerning God's name. I would be hesitant, though, and prefer seeing the verse as introducing the code, which covers "everything" one does as an individual; see note 22 above.

35. Similarly in *Spec. Leg.* 2.226-27. Cf. Crouch, *Origin and Intention*, 78-79, who criticizes Schroeder's thesis concerning the role of the Decalogue. Sib. Or. 2.278, also includes servants who turn against their masters among those who transgress this commandment.

36. Cf. H. Merklein, "Eph 4,1-5,20 als Rezeption von Kol 3,1-17 (zugleich ein Beitrag zur Problematik des Epheserbriefes)", in *Kontinuität und Einheit, Festschrift für F. Mussner*, Freiburg, 1981, 194-210.

37. Some modern authors are positive in finding the Decalogue in the background, see note 3, above.

38. Such a well informed author as Berger *(Gesetzesauslegung Jesu)* does not refer to any interpretation of that kind either.

39. If Crouch *Origin and Intention*, 79, and Balch, *Wives Be Submissive*, 53, cite Schroeder's thesis correctly, the latter binds the code to the Decalogue in a way that is quite different from my approach.

40. Cf. Stuhlmacher, *EvT* 28 (1968) 169-71.

41. P. Vielhauer, *Geschichte der urchristlichen Literatur*, Berlin, New York, 1975, 53-55.

42. See Stuhlmacher, *EvT* 28 (1968) 177-78.

43. See E. Kamlah, *Die Form der katalogischen Paränese im NT*, WUNT 7, Tübingen, 1964, 2:III-IV.

44. H. Koester, *"Gnomai diaphoroi.* The Origin and Nature of Diversification in the History of Early Christianity", in *id.* and J. R. Robinson, *Trajectories through Early Christianity*, Philadelphia, 1971, 114-157, 115.

45. Schweizer *(Brief an die Kolosser)* makes a lot of this "gute und nüchterne Weltlichkeit", 161.

46. Of course I cannot pretend to know, any more than anyone else, what these rules of the "philosophy" actually aimed at.

47. See the commentaries for a discussion of the MSS evidence and of the linguistic problem. I take 4:15 as saying "Nympha . . . in her house", regarding this to be the *lectio difficilior.*

48. Philo, Josephus and Pseudo-Phocylides agree to a large extent in these matters of morality. See further Crouch, *Origin and Intention*, chaps. 5, 6.

49. A. Deissman, *Paul. A Study in Social and Religious History*, 2nd ed., London, 1926, 243.

50. S. Scott Bartchy, *Mallon chrēsai: First Century Slavery and 1 Corinthians 7:21* SBLDS 11, Missoula, 1973, chap. 2, and R. Gayer, *Die Stellung des Sklaven in der paulinischen Gemeinden und bei Paulus. Zugleich ein sozialgeschichtlich vergleichender Beitrag zur Wertung des Sklaven in der Antike*, Europ. Hochschulschr., 23:78, Bern, Frankfurt, 1976.

51. See F. F. Bruce, *The Epistle to the Colossians, to Philemon, and to the Ephesians*, NICNT, Grand Rapids, 1984, *ad loc.*

Der Jakobusbrief als antipaulinische Polemik

Martin Hengel

Die Aporien des Briefes

Der Jakobusbrief stellt—darin hat sich in rund 150 Jahren kritischer Auslegungsgeschichte kaum etwas geändert den Leser vor tiefe, bisher noch nicht befriedigend gelöste Aporien.[1] Er scheint gewissermaßen ein Widerspruch in sich selbst zu sein.

Einmal hat er als einziger neutestamentlicher Brief die Gestalt eines Schreibens *an alle Christen* (außerhalb des Heiligen Landes)—nur diese Deutung des Adressaten: "den 12 Stämmen in der Zerstreuung" scheint mir sinnvoll zu sein[2]—, ein Tatbestand, der ihn zu einer "Enzyklika" an alle Christen macht, die unter den "Völkern" zerstreut leben und ganz überwiegend "Heidenchristen" sind. Er ist der erste, ja der einzige frühchristliche Brief, der mit diesem unerhörten Anspruch auftritt, er wolle von allen gehört werden.

Auf der anderen Seite bleibt unklar, *warum* dieser "Brief" in einer solch lockeren Form und mit einem—zumindest äußerlich—recht unspezifisch erscheinenden, allgemeinen "paränetischen" Inhalt (von z.T. fast trivial anmutendem Charakter) geschrieben wurde. Die Angaben über den Anlaß des Briefes in den Kommentaren sind darum entsprechend vage.

Alle vergleichbaren frühchristlichen, wirkliche und fingierte "Briefe" (die echten Paulinen, Eph, Past, Hebr, Judas, 1.Joh, 1. und 2.Petr, aber auch noch 1. und 2.Clem, Barn und Diognet)—die Frage der Authentizität und der möglicherweise nichtbrieflichen Urgestalt spielt hier keine Rolle—besitzen eine klarere christlich-theologische Thematik und einen übersichtlicheren Gedankengang. Auch wenn man den "Briefcharakter" von Jak völlig leugnet und in der Schrift eine Predigt oder eine dürftig christianisierte jüdische Weisheitslehre[4] vermutet, wird die Aporie nicht gelöst, sondern nur verschoben. Denn abgesehen von der Frage nach dem Sinn einer derartigen Predigt bzw. der vermuteten jüdischen Grundschrift bleibt unerklärt, warum dieser eine solch pompöse Einkleidung gegeben wurde. Was will unsere in ihrem Präskript so anspruchsvoll auftretende, universale "Enzyklika" bezwecken, was ist ihre Ursache (bzw. die ihrer Einkleidung), und was ist ihr Ziel? Und schließlich: Wer steht wirklich als Absender resp. Autor dahinter, und welche Empfänger resp. Leser sollten damit angesprochen werden? All diese Grundfragen sind bis heute ungelöst und zugleich strittig, und eben darum fällt es uns so schwer, dieses seltsame Opus und sein sachlich-theologisches Anliegen zu verstehen.

Die deutsche Forschung ist auch heute noch beherrscht von dem großartigen, jetzt 65 Jahre alten Kommentar von Martin Dibelius. Er nahm nicht nur eine, im Grunde unbestimmbare, m.E. zu späte Abfassung zwischen 80 und 130 an[5] (der einzige einigermaßen sichere Anhaltspunkt ist der Judasbrief, der im Präskript Jak voraussetzt[6]), sondern war darüber hinaus der Meinung, daß ein mittelmäßig begabter Kompilator ohne theologischen Sachverstand[7] eine Anthologie von paränetischen Einzelsprüchen samt einigen größeren dazwischengeschobenen Spruchkompositionen verfaßt, oder besser, aus traditionellem Material zusammengestellt habe. Denn "es fehlt in dem ganzen Schriftstück der gedankliche Zusammenhang".[8] Dies hat erst recht zur Folge, daß die Frage "cui bono" nach dem Sinn und Zweck der ganzen Veranstaltung von Dibelius nicht mehr beantwortet werden konnte. Auch das neue Stichwort "Paränese" löste dabei das Rätsel des Briefes nicht. Denn für Dibelius ist das Motiv der Auswahl[9] aus der Fülle des Traditionsmaterials in keiner Weise befriedigend zu erklären. Um "ein ταμιεῖον, eine Schatzkammer zu sein"—wie Dibelius "die Absicht des Jakobusbriefes" umschreiben möchte[10]—, dazu sind die behandelten Themen zu eingeschränkt oder aber zu künstlich und weit hergeholt, die zahlreichen Polemiken zu kompromißlos und der stilistisch-rhetorische Aufwand zu groß. Auch ist von der "verbürgerlichten" Kirche der Pastoralbriefe und der apostolischen Väter, in deren Nähe Dibelius Jak ansiedeln möchte, da man dort solche "Schatzkammern" zu schätzen begann, hier noch kaum etwas zu spüren.[11] Man vergleiche nur seine rigide Polemik gegen die Reichen mit den moderaten Mahnungen der Hermasapokalypse. Jak ist trotz sprachlicher Anklänge in seiner kompromißlosen Schroffheit von ihr durch einen Graben geschieden.[12] Auch die Wirkungsgeschichte dieses Briefes in der Alten Kirche ab dem 2. Jh. zeigt, daß diese "Schatzkammer" im Gegensatz zu anderen paränetischen Texten— nicht zuletzt wegen ihrer Einseitigkeit und Härte—nicht allzuoft geöffnet wurde. Dem wesentlich späteren und so ganz anderen Hirten des Hermas war hier ein—zunächst—viel größerer Erfolg beschieden.[13]

Die von Dibelius mit Vorliebe herangezogenen "paränetischen" Texte: Bergpredigt, Logienquelle, die Mandata der Hermasapokalypse, 1.Petr, Pastoralbriefe, Mahnreden (bzw. Brief) Henochs, Zwölfertestamente, Sapientia Salomonis, Jesus Sirach oder auch einige Isokrates zugeschriebene Schriften wie ad Demonicum und ad Nicoclem zeigen entweder eine klarere, konzentriertere Thematik, eine bessere Disposition bzw. eine eindeutigere Situationsbezogenheit, oder aber es handelt sich um wirkliche "Spruchsammlungen" von Einzelsprüchen analog zu Ps.Phokylides, Ps.Menander, Sextus, Publilius Syrus, Dicta Catonis etc. Aber ein bloßes "Gnomologion" will dieser "Brief" mit seinem anspruchsvollen Präskript, das sofort durch die geschickte Alliteration χαίρειν–χαρᾶν fest mit dem eigentlichen Text verbunden wird, ganz gewiß nicht sein.

Neuere Ausleger (Mußner, Davids, Baasland und Wuellner)[14] entdeckten in diesem zudem einen literarischen Gestaltungswillen, den man zuweilen fast raffiniert nennen könnte und der mit vielfältigen Stilmitteln arbeitet. Dem Postulat einer ganz lockeren, zumeist zufällig-ziellosen Zusammenstellung traditionellen paränetischen Spruchguts widerspricht das schriftstellerische Geschick des Verfassers, verbindet er doch in einer für das frühe Christentum einzigartigen Weise die überkommene jüdische Form des Weisheitsspruchs bzw. des Lehrgedichts mit einer zuweilen fast gesucht erscheinenden rhetorisch-literarischen Kunst.[15] Diese Einsichten sind nicht neu, sie waren nur geraume Zeit verschüttet. Nach Chr. G. Wilke in seiner Neutestamentlichen Rhetorik "trägt der Brief die Merkmale einer gut griechischen und oratorischen Diktion. Insbesondere zeugt der Vortrag von Agilität der Einbildungskraft und von Lebhaftigkeit des Geistes".[16] J. B. Mayor, der zugleich ein bedeutender klassischer Philologe war, betont, die kurzen Sätze des Briefes seien "better formed and more rhythmical than are to be found elsewhere in the N.T. ...".[17] Rhetorische Bemühung und weisheitliche Form geben so zusammen dem Brief ein fast "poetisch" erscheinendes Gepräge. A. Schlatter, der in seinem

Kommentar 1932 die weisheitlich-poetische Form der Schrift durch den Druck des griechischen Textes in Strophen und Stichen hervorhob, bemerkte dazu: "Der Stil, der die Kunst des Jakobus formte, ist der des Psalms und der Spruchdichtung, die die einander entsprechenden Sätze gleich lang macht".[18] Auf der anderen Seite muß man freilich sehen, daß der strenge Parallelismus membrorum nur noch teilweise durchgeführt ist und häufig typisch griechische Stilfiguren angewandt werden. Schon zu Beginn dieses Jahrhunderts hatte H. J. Cladder aufgrund der Zeilenanordnung und der Schreiberpunkte in den alten Majuskeln eine ganz ähnliche Einteilung wie Schlatter durchgeführt und auf den bei der Rezitation des Textes deutlich spürbaren Rhythmus hingewiesen.[19]

A. v. Harnack hat—ganz im Gegensatz zu Dibelius—diese "Paradoxie" des Textes deutlich gespürt: "Paradox sind endlich auch die Ausdrucksmittel, die Sprache und die Einkleidung der einzelnen Abschnitte. Einzelnes muthet wie eine treue Reproduktion von Sprüchen Jesu an und ist es wohl auch . . . , Anderes ist ebenso hebräisch gedacht aber im Geist der alten Propheten . . . , wieder Anderes kann sich an Kraft, Correctheit und Eleganz der Ausdrucksmittel mit guten Erzeugnissen griechischer Rhetorik vergleichen. . . . Anderes ist das Product eines theologischen Polemikers. Dabei läßt sich—und das ist das Paradoxeste des Paradoxes—doch nicht verkennen, daß eine gewisse Einheitlichkeit sowohl der sittlichen Gesinnung als auch der Sprache vorhanden ist, die dem Ganzen—ähnlich wie gewissen ATlichen Prophetenbüchern—trotz der Zusammenhanglosigkeit eine innere Einheitlichkeit verleiht. Diese Beobachtungen *sicher* zu erklären, fehlen uns die Mittel".[20] Diese— rund 24 Jahre vor Dibelius niedergeschriebenen—Sätze zeigen, daß der Deutungsversuch in dessen Kommentar zu eng ist. Er sieht nur eine Seite und verdrängt die andere.

Die eigenartige, weisheitlich-poetische und zugleich rhetorisch ausgefeilte Form des Briefes verbietet es, dem Werk dieselben Gliederungsgesetze aufzuerlegen wie einem philosophischen oder theologischen Prosatraktat, es ist auch keine Predigt im Stil des 2.Clemens oder des Hebräerbriefes. Schon die auffallende Anhäufung von Imperativsätzen—"von 108 Versen sind 54 als Imperative geformt"[21]—erschwert die Darstellung übergreifender Zusammenhänge. Das fast völlige Fehlen von Satzperioden, des Genitivus Absolutus, des AcI und des Optativ, der sehr eingeschränkte Gebrauch der Partikel und die Vorliebe für das Asyndeton müssen nicht unbedingt als griechische Stilmängel betrachtet werden,[22] sondern hängen mit dieser "autoritären", imperativen Struktur des Briefes zusammen.

Gleichwohl werden *übergreifende Themen* relativ deutlich sichtbar, und zwar durch immer wieder auftauchende beherrschende Stichworte und Metaphern, die beim jeweiligen Erscheinen gerne leicht variiert werden und so einen Gedankenfortschritt anzeigen. Man könnte diese Stichworte mit den bunten Fäden eines Teppichs vergleichen, die kurz sichtbar werden, wieder verschwinden, um später wieder aufzutauchen, deren Zusammenwirken jedoch bei allen Variationen einen relativ geschlossenen Eindruck hervorruft. Man wird diesen inneren Zusammenhängen ihre argumentative Kraft nicht absprechen können.[23] Der Autor hat so gerade für die *Form* seines Werkes erhebliche Mühe aufgewandt. Darf man dann demgegenüber annehmen, daß der *Inhalt* des Ganzen mehr oder weniger zufällig ist und auf relativ geistloser Sammeltätigkeit beruht?

Das Dilemma des verdienstvollen und seinerzeit revolutionären Kommentars von Dibelius liegt nicht zuletzt darin, daß mit Hilfe des Stichworts "Paränese" der Text zu einem wenig sinnvollen, ja im Grunde überflüssigen "Sammelsurium" wird und die Motive seiner Entstehung weitgehend im Dunkeln verschwinden. Erst recht wird die Bedeutung seiner eigenartigen, durchaus kunstvollen Form durch die Stichworte "Sammelwerk" und "Paränese" nicht zureichend erklärt.

Das Dilemma verstärkt sich dadurch, daß der "Brief" nicht nur vor dem Judasbrief (und 2.Petrusbrief) entstanden sein muß (s.v.S. 267, Anm. 6), sondern schon auf den Hirten des Hermas,[24] den 1.Clemens-[25] und den 1.Petrusbrief[26] eingewirkt hat. Offenbar war Jak in Rom zwischen 90 und 120 n.Chr. noch bekannt.[27] Die in ihm verarbeitete Jesustradition setzt außerdem ein früheres Überlieferungsstadium voraus, als es etwa in Mt vorliegt,[28] mit dem der Jakobusbrief theologisch am nächsten verwandt ist. Auch die Probleme des 2.Jh.s, die Abwehr der gnostischen Häresie, die Festigung der Hierarchie, der Gemeindeordnung und Organisation, sowie die Verfolgungen durch die römischen Behörden,[29] werden noch nicht sichtbar, während die Christologie und Soteriologie ganz und gar unterentwickelt sind, einer der Punkte, in dem man den Brief mit der Logienquelle vergleichen könnte, die ja ebenfalls palästinischen Ursprungs ist. Fast alles spricht so für eine relativ frühe und nichts wirklich für eine späte Entstehung.[30] Wo und wie soll man dieses rätselhafte Schreiben einordnen?

Hält man den Brief jedoch für *authentisch,* d.h. für ein Schreiben des Herrenbruders Jakobus an alle Christen außerhalb Palästinas, so wird die Aporie zunächst kaum geringer.

Gewiß, manche Einwände gegen eine frühe jakobäische Herkunft lassen sich heute mit geringerer Mühe als früher widerlegen. So könnte man das gute Griechisch und die rhetorische Form aufgrund unseres besseren Wissens über die Verbreitung "griechischer Bildung" im jüdischen Palästina mit Jakobus als Autor durchaus vereinbaren. Jak konnte in Jerusalem einen rhetorisch geschulten Sekretär dazu herangezogen haben; ja selbst die Möglichkeit, daß er in der ca 6-7 km von Nazareth entfernten langjährigen Hauptstadt Galiläas, Sepphoris, die Grundlagen griechischer Bildung erlernte, wäre nicht auszuschließen. Der etwa eine Generation spätere Galiläer Justus von Tiberias ist in seinem griechischen Stil selbst dem Jerusalemer Josephus weit überlegen.[31] Die Zweisprachigkeit Jerusalems ergibt sich aus der Tatsache, daß mehr als ein Drittel der dortigen Inschriften aus der Zeit des 2.Tempels in griechischer Sprache sind, in der großen Grablege im galiläischen Beth Schearim sind es sogar zwei Drittel. Aus der Zeit des Barkochba-Aufstandes wurden zahlreiche griechische Dokumente in der Wüste Juda gefunden, darunter zwei griechische Briefe von Beamten Barkochbas, von denen einer Barkochba erwähnt und der andere Anordnungen für die Feststräuße zum Laubhüttenfest gibt. Sie haben wie Jak das typisch griechische Präskript Ἀ]ννανος Ἰωναθῇ τῷ ἀδελφῷ χαίρειν. Der zweite Brief scheint anzudeuten, daß der Schreiber leichter Griechisch als Hebräisch (bzw. Aramäisch) schreiben konnte.[32] Eine der neueren Untersuchungen zu Jak und Paulus, die ersteren für ein spätes Pseudonym hält, gibt daher zu: "In der Tat ist die griechische Sprache des Jak das schwächste Argument gegen seine Echtheit".[33] In früheren Zeiten gehörte es noch zu den scheinbar stärksten. Doch die Zeiten ändern sich, und die Argumente werden weniger.

Aber auch bei der Annahme der Echtheit bleibt die Frage: Warum schreibt Jakobus—etwa an Judenchristen—einen derartigen, so wenig spezifischen, allgemeingehaltenen Brief mit scheinbar unverbundenen Einzelmahnungen, die oft dazu noch z.T. recht schlicht klingen? Dies gilt besonders dann, wenn man in 2,14-

26 keinerlei antipaulinische Polemik erkennen möchte, da der Brief noch vor dem "Apostelkonzil" geschrieben sei.[34] Der Brief wird auch hier weitgehend unverständlich. Ein sinnvoller Grund für seine Entstehung läßt sich auf diese Weise so wenig finden wie bei Dibelius.

Diese Aporie gilt selbst dann, wenn man in dem Schreiben einen stärkeren theologischen Zusammenhang entdeckt oder gar in ihm eine ursprüngliche "Predigt" des Jakobus sieht. Vor welcher Gemeinde wurde—mit solcher Kunst—eine derartige "Rede" gehalten, und warum erschien sie dem Verfasser als so wichtig, daß er sie als "Enzyklika" allen Christen in der "Diaspora" mitteilte? Wenn der Brief nach dem Martyrium des Jakobus im Jahre 62 von einem Schüler herausgegeben wurde,[35] muß man fragen: Hatte dieser aus dem Munde seines Meisters, des Bruders, nichts Bedeutsameres mitzuteilen als diese sonderbare "mélange"? Warum geht er nicht auf seinen Märtyrertod ein und überläßt dies dem Josephus und der unglaubwürdigen späteren Legende eines Hegesipp?[36] Soll man gar in 5,6 einen Hinweis auf sein Martyrium und 5,16b eine Anspielung auf Jakobus den "Gerechten" als charismatischen Beter sehen?

Ist der Text aber von Jakobus selbst direkt als Rundschreiben konzipiert, wird der Anlaß noch undurchsichtiger. Man könnte vielleicht noch sagen: Der Verfasser vertritt in allgemeiner Weise ein Christentum der Tat gegenüber einem tatenlosen Schein-Glauben, der Armut gegenüber einem eo ipso frevelhaften Reichtum. Aber warum verwendet er gerade dazu so weithergeholte Beispiele wie die Pläne des reisenden Großkaufmanns 4,13-16, die rhetorisch ausgeschmückten Gefahren der ungezügelten Zunge, den ausbeuterischen reichen Großgrundbesitzer, und schließlich gar die Mahnung zur Krankensalbung und zum Gebet der Ältesten, das Heilung verspricht, wenn jemand seine Sünden bekennt? Klingt dies für einen Aufruf zur Tat nicht z.T. ziemlich weit hergeholt? War das die Paränese, die die "zwölf Stämme" in der Diaspora, seien es nun Juden- oder Heidenchristen, benötigten?[37]

Die Lösing des Problems

Im folgenden wird versucht, diese Aporie durch eine *Hypothese* zu lösen. Da unsere Disziplin bei der relativ schmalen Quellenbasis schon immer auch—auf jeden Fall mehr als sie zugeben will—eine "Vermutungswissenschaft" gewesen und in den letzten Jahrzehnten noch mehr geworden ist, soll eine—m.E. nicht völlig unbegründete—*Vermutung* entwickelt werden. Meine Hypothese (um mehr als einen hypothetischen Lösungsversuch kann es sich nicht handeln) geht in folgende Richtung:

Der Brief könnte vielleicht *doch* von Jakobus dem Gerechten, dem Bruder Jesu, stammen (bzw. von einem Sekretär in seinem Auftrag) und als Rundschreiben an die außerhalb des jüdischen Palästinas liegenden, ganz überwiegend heidenchristlichen Gemeinden einige Zeit nach der Verhaftung des Paulus bzw. seiner Überführung als Angeklagter nach Rom zwischen 58 und 62 verfaßt sein.

Dabei ist zunächst der immer wieder geäußerte Einwand, daß Jakobus doch "Ritualist" oder "Nomist" gewesen, und daß im Brief davon nichts enthalten sei, zurückzuweisen. Das jüdische Ritualgesetz war für diese Gemeinden—auch nach der Ansicht des Jakobus (s. Gal 2,6ff und Apg 15)—kein *heilsentscheidendes* Problem mehr.[38] Hätte Jakobus nach dem Apostelkonzil die Heilsnotwendigkeit der Beschneidung für Heidenchristen vertreten, hätte Paulus ihn nie unter der Aussage

1.Kor 15,11 einbeziehen können und wäre er sicher nicht nach Jerusalem gereist, um die Kollekte zu überbringen. Doch das Tischtuch war nicht ganz zerschnitten.

In Gal 2,11ff geht es zwischen Paulus und Petrus nicht mehr um die Frage der Heilsnotwendigkeit der Einhaltung des Ritualgesetzes—von diesem hatte sich Petrus weitgehend emanzipiert—, sondern um die Tischgemeinschaft zwischen Juden- und Heidenchristen, um das συνεσθίειν beim Herrenmahl. In der Forschung wird fast völig unterschlagen, daß Jakobus und andere Judenchristen 62 n.Chr. als "Gesetzesbrecher" (ὡς παρανομησάντων) hingerichtet wurden.[39] Auch beim sog. "Aposteldekret" geht es nicht um die Heilsfrage, sondern um einen Kompromiß um der gemeinsamen Mahlpraxis willen. Der Standpunkt der späteren Ebioniten war nicht der des Jakobus. Außerdem kann ein Brief, der einen breiten Adressatenkreis ansprechen will, auch Konfliktpunkte übergehen, wenn diese nicht mehr zentrale, heilsentscheidende Bedeutung haben. Auch für den Christen Jakobus war—darin greift er mit dem ganzen Urchristentum auf eine Grundlehre seines Bruders zurück— das "königliche Gesetz" des Liebesgebotes entscheidend (2,8 vgl. 1,25).[40] Auf das Ritualgesetz *mußte* der Verfasser nicht mehr Bezug nehmen, er hätte dem Brief dadurch nur seine Wirkung genommen. Diese Frage war um 60 in den Gemeinden Kleinasiens, Griechenlands und Roms kaum mehr akut, das zeigen die beiden Korintherbriefe, der Römerbrief und das 69/70 in Rom entstandene Markusevangelium.

Inhaltlich enthält der Brief jedoch in seinen wesentlichen Teilen *antipaulinische Polemik,* freilich—wie es antiker Polemik häufig entspricht—in *indirekter Form* und ohne den Namen des Gegners zu nennen. Kritisiert werden sowohl die persönliche Verhaltensweise wie auch theologische Anschauungen des Paulus, und zwar—das ist die Besonderheit des Briefes—in einer "paränetischen", allgemeingültig erscheinenden Weise, die den Brief auch für die Gemeinden noch lesbar, verständlich und—in gewissen Grenzen—"erbaulich" macht, die von der Auseinandersetzung mit Paulus nicht betroffen bzw. über sie nicht informiert waren, jedoch so, daß diejenigen, die Paulus kannten, sehr wohl wissen mußten, gegen wen sich dieser Brief in erster Linie richtete und warum er geschrieben wurde.

Fast möchte ich—ausgehend von dieser Hypothese—den Brief als ein Meisterstück frühchristlicher Polemik bezeichnen. Die Schärfe in der Polemik des Briefes ist den Exegeten schon immer aufgefallen, nur wurde um ihrer angeblichen "Allgemeinheit" willen (und der sich daraus ergebenden Unverbindlichkeit) ihre eigentliche Intention nicht verstanden. Man könnte die antipaulinische Polemik mit Gal und 2.Kor 10-13 vergleichen, wo Paulus seine Gegner ebenfalls nicht bei Namen nennt. Jedoch kämpft Jak im Gegensatz zum Heidenapostel nicht mit offenem Visier, sondern bewußt indirekt mittels allgemein formulierter Mahnungen, und ist nur für von dem Streit Betroffene als Kritiker des Paulus zu erkennen. Der Polemik des Paulus in Gal gegen die Judaisten und in 2.Kor gegen die aus Palästina stammenden Sendboten der Petrusmission (?) tritt innerhalb des neutestamentlichen Kanons ein äußerlich verdecktes Beispiel antipaulinischer Polemik gegenüber. Daß die im 2.Jh. aus der Kirche hinausgedrängten Ebioniten in schärfster Weise gegen Paulus polemisiert haben, bezeugen später Irenäus (adv.haer. 1,26,2), die hinter den Pseudoclementinen stehenden Traditionen und die Nachrichten bei Epiphanius.[41] Im Vergleich dazu erscheint hier eine kunstvolle, subtilere Polemik, die anders als die späteren massiven Verleumdungen wenigstens teilweise theologisch zu argumentieren versucht.[42]

1. In der Forschung weitgehend anerkannt ist die antipaulinische Tendenz von

2,14-23. Sie sollte man nicht mehr bestreiten, denn der Konflikt bzw. Gegensatz zwischen "Glauben und Werken" im Blick auf das Heil ist ein paulinisches Grundproblem, das sich *vor* Paulus nirgendwo nachweisen läßt, weder im Judentum noch bei Jesus und im frühesten Christentum. Der paulinischen These der Rechtfertigung des Gottlosen durch den Glauben ohne des Gesetzes Werke wird von Jakobus das Postulat von der Notwendigkeit der Mitwirkung der Werke zusätzlich zum Glauben, ja vom Vorrang derselben bei der Erlangung des Heils gegenübergestellt.[43]

Spätestens in 1,22 wird diese Blickrichtung sichtbar, ja im Grunde schon in 1,2f, wo die Bewährungsprobe des Glaubens in den Anfechtungen auf das ἔργον τέλειον hinführt.[44] Im Gegensatz zu der paulinischen Relation: Wort (resp. Predigt/Evangelium)—Glaube—Heil (vgl. Rö 10,9ff.17; 1,16f; Gal 3,1ff) ist für Jakobus die Relation: Wort (königliches Gesetz der Freiheit resp. Liebesgebot)—Tat der Liebe—Rechtfertigung im Gericht grundlegend. Einen z.T. auch sprachlich ganz ähnlich formulierten Zusammenhang finden wir bei Paulus in Rö 2,5-12—freilich innerhalb der die rettende Offenbarung der Gerechtigkeit Gottes im Sühnetod Jesu vorbereitenden universalen *Anklagerede* von Rö 1,18–3,20.[45] Was Paulus als eigene menschliche Möglichkeit verwirft, erscheint—in fast naiver Weise—bei Jakobus als Voraussetzung des Heils. Der Fromme kann aus sich selbst das "vollkommene Gesetz der Freiheit" (1,25), "das königliche Gesetz" von Lev 19,18 (2,8) beständig (1,25 καὶ παραμείνας) erfüllen. Im Gericht retten ihn seine eigenen Werke der Barmherzigkeit (2,13). Das bedeutet aber, daß bereits aufgrund des ganzen vorausgehenden Argumentationskomplexes 1,18–2,13 die darauffolgende Verhandlung von 2,14-26 über die Defizienz des "bloßen Gaubens ohne Werke" eine innere Folgerichtigkeit, ja Notwendigkeit besitzt und die polemische Klimax der Auseinandersetzung darstellt. 2,24 wird dabei direkt antipaulinisch formuliert: "Sehet, daß aufgrund von Werken der Mensch gerechtfertigt wird *und nicht aus Glauben allein*".[46] Der Glaubensbegriff des Jakobus ist im Grunde der des Judentums, wo der Glaube als Werk oder Tugend verstanden werden konnte; er steht darin dem des Hebräerbriefs nahe. Er ordnet sich damit nicht in den "Frühkatholizismus" der Apostolischen Väter ein, sondern hängt noch an seinen jüdischen Wurzeln. In diesem Sinne gilt die Feststellung A. Lindemanns: "Das πίστις-Verständnis des Jak ist bereits als solches antipaulinisch".[47]

Aber 2,14-26 ist bei weitem nicht der einzige Text in Jak, der an paulinischen Aussagen und Verhaltensweisen Kritik übt. Es gibt m.E. noch wesentlich mehr solcher Stellen.

So könnte möglicherweise bereits in der 1,13ff beginnenden Polemik, die ältere weisheitliche Parallelen besitzt (Sir 15,11-20; s. Anm. 46) ein antipaulinischer Ton anklingen. Während Jakobus jeden Gedanken daran, daß Gott den Menschen versuche, zurückweist, alle Versuchung auf die eigene sündige Begierde im Menschen zurückführt und im Anschluß daran bekennt, daß nur gute, vollkommene Gabe von Gott komme und es bei diesem "keine Veränderung oder Verfinsterung durch Wechsel gibt" (1,17), konnte Paulus davon sprechen, daß Gott den Pharao verhärtet habe (Rö 9,17f), daß er "Gefäße des Zorns, bestimmt zum Verderben schaffe", ja daß er Israel "einen Geist der Betäubung" (Rö 11,8 nach Jes 29,10 vgl. Dtn 29,3) gab. Daß Gott in den Gläubigen das "Wollen und das Vollbringen wirkt" (Phil 2,13), ist ganz und gar unjakobäisch. Bei ihm gilt entsprechend jüdisch-alttestamentlicher Tradition: ἐγγίσατε τῷ θεῷ καὶ ἐγγιεῖ ὑμῖν (4,8).

Freilich darf man bei Jakobus wohl kaum ein tiefergehendes Studium der

Martin Hengel | 255

Paulusbriefe voraussetzen; er argumentiert aufgrund mündlicher Kenntnisse der paulinischen Theologie, die ihm im ganzen fremd und verdächtig ist. Es besteht so eine *Verstehensbarriere* zwischen den beiden—offenbar extrem verschiedenen— großen Gestalten des Urchristentums. Wenn man freilich liest, wie ein so klar formulierender Theologe wie R. Bultmann ständig darüber klagte, er werde von seinen Kritikern mißverstanden, darf man bei einem so abgründig-leidenschaftlichen Denker wie Paulus schwerlich weniger gegnerische Mißverständnisse erwarten. Bereits in dem im Winter 56/57 entstandenen Römerbrief verteidigt er sich erbittert gegen schlimme Fehlinterpretationen.[48]

Wenn aber in Jak das Zentrum der paulinischen Theologie in so direkter Weise angegriffen wird, dürfte man in diesem Brief *noch weitere Ansätze zur Pauluskritik* vermuten, die sich in einer ganz überwiegend paränetisch-praktisch und nicht "dogmatisch" argumentierenden Schrift natürlich auch *gegen das persönliche Verhalten* des Apostels und gegen damit entstehende Gefahren richten könnten, da der führende Heidenmissionar als eine leidenschaftliche, facettenreiche Persönlichkeit gewiß eine breite Angriffsfläche bot. Nun sind wir freilich über die Auseinandersetzungen zwischen Jerusalem und Paulus nur durch relativ wenige Hinweise in den Paulusbriefen und einige Andeutungen in der Apg unterrichtet. Sehr viel läßt sich daraus nicht erschließen. Hinzu kommen die Angaben des Paulus über seine Pläne und Taten, die ihn als aggressiven Polemiker und aktiven Missionar mit einem nicht geringen Selbstbewußtsein erweisen. Aber vielleicht lassen sich daraus doch mehrere sonst schwer verständliche Passagen in Jak besser erklären, als dies bisher der Fall war.

2. Im frühesten Christentum des 1.Jh.s spielen *Großkaufleute* mit Städte und Provinzen überspannenden Geschäftsinteressen und entsprechenden weiträumigen und langandauernden Geschäftsreisen noch kaum eine Rolle. Der reiche Reeder Marcion aus Sinope deutet auf eine neue Epoche in der Kirchengeschichte hin, die mit den Antoninen beginnt. In einem berühmten Text bei Cicero, de officiis 1,151, hat "das Handelsgewerbe . . . , wenn es groß und umfangreich ist, viele Güter von überall herbeischafft und ohne Betrug an viele verteilt", Ansehen; während der Kleinhandel als verächtlich erscheint. Diese kleinen Gewerbetreibenden und Händler, die in den tabernae ihre z.T. selbst gefertigten Waren feilboten, mögen dagegen in den christlichen Stadtgemeinden der frühesten Zeit häufiger gewesen sein, während wir von reisenden christlichen Unternehmern kaum etwas hören.[49] Der paränetische Sinn der Polemik von *Jak 4,13-16,* bezogen auf "christliche (Groß-)Kaufleute" und ihre profitablen Geschäftsreisen in ferne Städte, mit längeren Aufenthalten, erscheint auf diesem Hintergrund recht zweifelhaft zu sein, denn es wird hier ein Phänomen angesprochen, das in den Gemeinden des ausgehenden 1.Jh.s kaum schon *wesentliche* Bedeutung besaß. Der Brief aber wendet sich ja an alle Christen und nicht an wenige vereinzelte Glieder, die der heidnischen Oberschicht nahestehen.[50] Was soll daher eine derartige Polemik in einem "Ökumenischen Rundbrief"? Um vor der Gefahr der "Verweltlichung" zu warnen (1,27; 4,4), gab es wahrlich bessere Beispiele. Dagegen finden wir *eine Metropolen und Provinzen umfassende, langfristig geplante "globale" Reisestrategie, mit monate- ja jahrelangen Aufenthalten in einzelnen Großstädten, mit dem Ziel, Heiden und Juden zu "gewinnen", zuerst und zugleich in einzigartiger Weise bei Paulus* (und seinen Missionshelfern wie Prisca und Aquila, wobei sich gerade bei letzteren Missionsarbeit und Ökonomie offenbar in einzigartiger Weise verbunden hat). Paulus weiß sich in dieser ganze Provinzen übergreifenden Strategie allen missionarischen Konkurrenten überlegen. In der

späteren Zeit hören wir dagegen nichts mehr von vergleichbaren Plänen und Strategien. Schon für Lukas ist darum Paulus der von Stadt zu Stadt, von Provinz zu Provinz reisende "Weltmissionar". Sollte der so eigenartig in kein Schema christlicher Paränese passende "unternehmerische" Plan Jak 4,13: σήμερον ἢ αὔριον πορευσόμεθα εἰς τήνδε τὴν πόλιν καὶ ποιήσομεν ἐκεῖ ἐνιαυτὸν καὶ ἐμπορευσόμεθα καὶ κερδήσομεν, etwa in diese Richtung weisen? Das Ganze klingt nach *Missionsmetaphorik*. Zu analogen Reiseplänen mit zeitlichen Aufenthaltsangaben finden wir zahlreiche Parallelen in der Schilderung der paulinischen Mission in der Apg, aber auch bei Paulus selbst.[51] Das Verb κερδαίνειν begegnet uns 1.Kor 9,19-22 viermal *im Sinne des missionarischen "Gewinnens" von Menschen*. Die ganze Existenz des Paulus ist darauf ausgerichtet.[52] Man könnte weiter auf 1.Petr 3,1, die Gewinnung des ungläubigen Ehegatten, und Mt 18,15, die (Wieder-)Gewinnung des irrenden Bruders, verweisen. C. Spicq bemerkt dazu: "κερδαίνειν est devenu un terme religieux, voire apostolique et missionnaire".[53] Auch das Verb ἐμπορεύεσθαι kann in polemischem Kontext einen religiös-missionarischen Bezug erhalten. 2.Petr 2,3 polemisiert gegen die Irrlehrer: "und in Habgier werden sie euch mit erkünstelten Worten kaufen" (ἐμπορεύσονται). K. H. Schelkle schreibt zur Stelle: "Auch Paulus hat diesen Vorwurf hören müssen, und er verteidigt sich heftig gegen ihn", und verweist dabei auf 1.Thess 2,5; 2.Kor 7,2 und 8,20.[54] Die Didache nennt später den christlichen Reisenden, der sich durchfüttern läßt und nicht arbeitswillig ist, einen χριστέμπορος und fügt hinzu, daß man sich vor solchen Reisenden in acht nehmen soll.[55] Wie nahe die Verwendung der polemischen Metapher des "Geschäftemachens" bei der missionarischen Arbeit und den damit verbundenen Reiseplänen liegt, zeigt ihr Gebrauch bei Paulus selbst: "Denn wir treiben nicht wie die Vielen einen Handel mit dem Worte Gottes . . .". Der Vorwurf des "καπηλεύειν mit geistigen Gütern" (Lietzmann z.St. 2.Kor 2,17) war, wie die Parallelen bei Wettstein und späteren Kommentatoren und jetzt besonders die gründliche Untersuchung von S. J. Hafemann zeigen, überaus geläufig.[56] Während καπηλεύειν hier eher den nach Cicero "schmutzigen" Kleinhandel meint, deutet im Kontext von Jak 4,13 das Verb ἐμπορεύεσθαι auf ein—missionarisches—"Geschäftemachen" im großen Stil hin—wie man es Paulus und seinen Gehilfen wohl vorwerfen konnte.[57]

M.a.W.: Die große geographische und zeitliche Räume übergreifenden Reisepläne, die Paulus selbst in seinen Briefen entwirft, nicht zuletzt im Zusammenhang seines kombinierten Jerusalem-, Rom- und Spanienprojekts (vgl. Rö 15,14ff; 2.Kor 10,13ff), kommen jenen Vorhaben, die Jakobus seinen pläneschmiedenden, die (Groß-)Städte bereisenden "Kaufleuten" unterstellt, verdächtig nahe. Man muß bei ihm von einer großräumigen "Missionsstrategie" sprechen, die im Blick auf die einzelnen Wirkungsorte über längere Zeit vorbereitet wurde und die auch mit *ökonomischen* Überlegungen verbunden sein mußten. So bereiten seine Freunde Prisca und Aquila, wohl selbst erfolgreiche Geschäftsleute mit verschiedenen Niederlassungen, seine Wirksamkeit in Ephesus und dann auch in Rom vor,[58] d.h. Paulus war bei seiner Strategie auf die Hilfe vermögender Freunde angewiesen, u.a. etwa um die relativ hohe Miete für die "Schule des Tyrannus" in Ephesus (Apg 19,9), für Schiffspassagen mit mehreren Teilnehmern oder für die Wohnung in Rom (Apg 28,30) aufzubringen. Schon zu Caesars Zeiten betrugen die niedrigsten Wohnungsmieten pro Jahr in Rom 2000 Sesterzen. Der Tagelohn für einen einfachen Handarbeiter schwankte etwa zwischen zwei und vier Sesterzen (= 1/2 - 1 Drachme),[59] wobei er immer mit längeren Zeiten der Arbeitslosigkeit rechnen mußte. Nach Juvenal konnte man sich für die Jahresmiete einer Wohnung in Rom außerhalb der Stadt ein kleines Landgut erwerben.[60] Der karge Arbeitslohn eines σκηνόποιος reichte hierfür sicherlich nicht aus.[61] Das von Paulus mehrfach gebrauchte προπέμπειν hat nach W. Bauer nicht nur die Bedeutung "geleiten", sondern konkreter *"zur (Weiter-)Reise ausstatten* m. Lebensmitteln, Geld, durch Stellung v. Begleitern, Beschaffung v. Fahrgelegenheit usw., *auf den Weg bringen, weiterbefördern.*"[62] Ohne derartige Hilfe wäre die paulinische Missionsarbeit unmöglich gewesen—auch wenn er selbst keine Unterstützung von den eben gegründeten Gemeinden *forderte*. Wurde sie unaufgefordert gegeben, nahm er sie, wie der Philipperbrief zeigt, gerne an.

Daß die so erfolgreiche missionarische Planung und Arbeit des Paulus zugleich sein apostolisches Sendungsbewußtsein stärkte und daß seine Hinweise darauf, daß er erfolgreicher gearbeitet habe als alle anderen Apostel, d.h. daß er als Missionar diesen allen überlegen sei, auch als "Selbstruhm" mißdeutet und verurteilt werden konnten, läßt sich kaum bezweifeln. Die Hinweise auf seine apostolischen Taten und Vorhaben sind ja in fast allen Briefen zu finden.[63] Daß dem Paulus im Blick auf seine Missionserfolge und Reisepläne solches καυχᾶσθαι direkt vorgeworfen wurde, zeigt 2.Kor 10,8.13-15. Der scharfe Tadel Jak 4,16: νῦν δὲ καυχᾶσθε ἐν ταῖς ἀλαζονείαις ὑμῶν· πᾶσα καύχησις τοιαύτη πονηρά ἐστιν richtet sich darum m.E. nicht so sehr gegen frühchristliche, von Stadt zu Stadt reisende Großkaufleute—die gab es noch kaum—als gegen Missionare, die in einem großräumigen Stil planten und sich ihrer Erfolge rühmten wie Paulus. Er hatte diesen Missionsstil als erster eingeführt und mit ihm findet dieser im Grunde auch schon wieder sein Ende.[64]

Auch die sich anschließende in eigenartiger Weise sehr allgemein gehaltene paränetische Konsequenz: εἰδότι οὖν καλὸν ποιεῖν καὶ μὴ ποιοῦντι, ἁμαρτία αὐτῷ ἐστιν, die durch οὖν als Folgerung aus der vorhergehenden Polemik ausgewiesen ist, aber im paränetischen Kontext wenig Sinn ergibt,[65] läßt sich am ehesten auf diesem Hintergrund erklären. An sich würde man ja eher eine konkrete soziale Mahnung ähnlich wie in 1,27 oder 2,15f erwarten. Nicht Pläne schmieden oder Gewinne machen, sondern den Armen helfen ist Gottes Wille. Denn daß der "christliche" (Groß-)Kaufmann mit seinen Reise und Profitplänen eo ipso Gutes zu tun weiß und es bewußt unterläßt, ist schwer einzusehen. Zu fragen wäre, ob Paulus wegen oder bei seinen ehrgeizigen heidenchristlichen Missionsplänen in den Augen der Jerusalemer "Gutes", das er hätte tun sollen, unterlassen hat. Geht es um die Verweigerung der Anerkennung des die Einheit zwischen Juden- und Heidenchristen wiederherstellenden Aposteldekrets? Freilich spielt die Frage nach Juden- und Heidenchristen im Brief überhaupt keine Rolle, man hat vielmehr den Eindruck, daß der Autor dieses in früherer Zeit heiße, aber in der Zeit um 60 bereits abgekühlte Eisen ganz bewußt vermeidet. Selbst bei einem späteren Pseudepigraphon, das Jakobus zugeschrieben wurde, hätte man eigentlich ein Eingehen auf diese Frage erwarten können, denn auch die lukanische Apostelgeschichte, die Pseudoclementinen und der Epheserbrief behandeln diesen Punkt sehr wohl. Man wußte darüber auch später noch Bescheid.[66] Oder geht es darum, daß Paulus sich über seinen Missionsplänen trotz seines apologetisch klingenden, im Bericht vom Apostelkonzil nachhinkenden: ὃ καὶ ἐσπούδασα αὐτὸ τοῦτο ποιῆσαι (Gal 2,10) nicht genügend bzw. nicht in der von den Jerusalemern gewünschten Weise um die Kollekte für die Armen und Heiligen in Jerusalem gekümmert hat? Es fällt auf, daß Paulus nur spät und zunächst nur am Rande von der Kollekte spricht. 1.Kor 16.1 erwähnt er sie—vermutlich im Herbst/Winter 55/56—erstmals und sagt, daß er dieselbe den Gemeinden in Galatien aufgetragen habe. Achaia ist später dran, dort geht die Sammlung "auf das Vorjahr" (2.Kor 8,10; 9,2), d.h. etwa das Frühjahr/Sommer 55, zurück. Die Anfrage der Korinther (1.Kor 16,1) zeigt, daß sie noch recht ahnungslos sind. Makedonien folgt noch später. Paulus scheint sich bei der Einrichtung der Kollekte während des langen Aufenthalts in Ephesus viel Zeit gelassen zu haben. Das "Konzil" fand aber schon etwa im Jahr 48/49 statt. Von der Sammlung in Galatien hören wir nichts mehr, auffallend ist dabei, daß der Galaterbrief selbst die Durchführung derselben Kollekte nicht behandelt. Paulus weist nur auf das "Daß" seiner Bemühung hin.

Auch über Asia schweigt Paulus, nur in Makedonien und Achaia wird sie plötzlich energisch betrieben, wobei Paulus weiß, daß es mit der Aushändigung in Jerusalem Probleme geben wird. Wir können hier freilich nur Vermutungen äußern. Lukas weiß um die Kollekte, schweigt aber dort darüber, wo er sie erwähnen sollte (21,15ff), und läßt sie im nachhinein bei der Verteidigung gegen die Anklagerede des Rhetors Tertullus vor Felix aufblitzen: "nachdem ich durch Jahre hindurch Almosen für mein Volk eingezogen hatte . . ." (24,17). Weiß Lukas darum, daß sie zurückgewiesen wurde? Vielleicht weil Paulus oder die Jerusalemer oder beide Bedingungen damit verbunden hatten, die unerfüllbar waren? Weil Paulus zwar wußte, was er Gutes zu tun hatte, aber es doch nicht so ausführte, wie er es hätte tun sollen? Die sonderbare Mahnung des Jakobus *könnte* in diese Richtung gehen.

Auch die conditio Jacobaea: ἐὰν ὁ κύριος θελήσῃ καὶ ζήσομεν καὶ ποιήσομεν τοῦτο ἢ ἐκεῖνο "wenn der Herr (es) will, so werden wir leben und dies oder jenes tun" paßt vorzüglich in den Kontext missionarischer Planung und ihrer Imponderabilien; die Einleitung "so der Herr will" konnte Paulus selber verwenden.[67] Offenbar hatten die Gegner Paulus bei seiner Reiseplanung Eigenwilligkeit, aber auch Furcht und andere menschliche Motive vorgeworfen. Er beruft sich dagegen auf den Gotteswillen. Auch bei Lukas wird dieser Konflikt sichtbar: Apg 18,21 legt Lukas diese Formel in den Mund des Paulus, wie er sich von den ihm noch freundlich gesonnenen Juden in Ephesus gegen Ende der "2. Reise" verabschiedet: "Ich werde wieder zu euch zurückkommen, wenn Gott will!", was sich dann auch erfüllt. Dagegen läßt Lukas den Paulus bei seinem Abschied von den Ältesten von Ephesus in Milet 20,22-25—in der Form eines vaticinium—eine ganz andere, sehr in Moll getönte Prognose vortragen: Der heilige Geist nötige ihn, nach Jerusalem zu reisen, obwohl er wisse, daß ihn dort Gefangenschaft und Leiden erwarten, er werde daher die Gemeinde in Ephesus nicht mehr sehen. In dem im Winter 56/57 in Korinth geschriebenen Rö 15,14-32 erklingt dagegen immer noch das helle Dur des Missionsstrategen, obwohl sich Paulus bewußt ist, daß in Jerusalem Lebensgefahr droht und er nicht sicher sein kann, daß seine Kollekte akzeptiert wird. Sollte Lukas mit seinen sich steigernden vaticinia den Apostel verteidigt haben, während das offensichtliche Scheitern der weltweiten Pläne des Paulus und seine in Jerusalem beginnende Gefangenschaft in manchen judenchristlichen Kreisen als Strafe für sein ungebührliches Rühmen verstanden wurde? Obwohl Lukas, wie Apg 19,21 zeigt, die weiteren Pläne des Apostels, die nach Rom führen, sehr wohl kannte, legt er Wert darauf, immer wieder zu betonen, daß Paulus in der festen, immer stärker bekräftigten Gewißheit seiner Verhaftung nach Jerusalem gereist sei.[68] Lukas gibt sich weiter größte Mühe, auch den Weg des Paulus nach Rom und die dortige freie Missionsverkündigung des Gefangenen als *Gottes Willen* darzustellen. Man konnte es auch ganz anders sehen: Trifft auf den als Gefangenen nach Rom überführten Paulus, der dort das letzte Urteil des Kaisers zu erwarten hatte und dessen hochfahrende, bis nach Spanien reichende Missionspläne zerbrochen waren, trifft auf ihn, den größten christlichen "Pläneschmied", nicht jenes Urteil zu: ἀτμὶς γάρ ἐστε ἡ πρὸς ὀλίγον φαινομένη, ἔπειτα καὶ ἀφανιζομένη . . . (Jak 4,14)? Ist bei ihm, dem vom Todesurteil Bedrohten, nicht mit dem ζήσομεν auch das ποιήσομεν in Frage gestellt? Lukas will durch das διδάσκων . . . μετὰ πάσης παρρησίας ἀκωλύτως gerade das Gegenteil erweisen.[69]

Jak 4,13-16 wird so m.E. in seiner Rätselhaftigkeit als paränetisches Unikum in der frühchristlichen Literatur dadurch am besten verständlich, daß es auf das plötzliche Scheitern der Missionspläne des Apostels durch seine Gefangennahme und seine anschließende lange Haftzeit mit der drohenden Todesstrafe hinweist. Der Brief wäre dann in der Spätzeit beider Kontrahenten, während der paulinischen Gefangenschaft in Cäsarea oder vielleicht noch eher in Rom (d.h. zwischen 58 und 62) entstanden. Schon Wettstein hatte ihn mit historischem Scharfsinn im Grunde richtig eingeordnet: "Scripsit (scil. Jacobus) autem post Pauli Epistolam ad Romanos et ad Galatas, quibus in speciem contra dicere videtur (ich glaube freilich nicht, daß der Verfasser die Briefe wirklich kennt); et ante Primam Petri (für uns heute ein Pseudepigraphon aus der Zeit Domitians), in quam multa ex Jacobo translata leguntur."[70] Möglicherweise starben Paulus und Jakobus im selben Jahr 62 n.Chr. den Märtyrertod, jeder auf seine Weise als "Gesetzesbrecher" (s.o.Anm.39). Der Jakobusbrief hätte dann vor allem den Zweck, die durch den Kapitalprozeß gegen ihren Heros und Gründer verunsicherten, überwiegend heidenchristlichen Missionsgemeinden der griechischsprechenden Diaspora auf die Gefahren einer—gewiß mißverstandenen—paulinischen Theologie, die nach Meinung der Gegner des Paulus zu einer libertinistischen Gesetzlosigkeit, zu einem Glauben ohne Werke führen konnte, hinzuweisen und zugleich gewisse fragwürdige Züge im Verhalten des verehrten Lehrers bloßzustellen.

3. Der Hinweis zu Beginn des Briefes (1,2ff) auf die *"vielfältigen Anfechtungen"*, die ja doch nur ein Bewährungsmittel für den echten (Tat-)Glauben darstellen, bei dem der, ganz anders als für Paulus, durch seine Werke gerechtfertigte (2,21ff) Abraham das erste und größte Paradigma darstellt, erhielte damit seinen guten Sinn: Die durch das Schicksal ihres Gründers betroffenen, ja erschütterten Gemeinden sollen sich über die von Gott mit Recht auferlegte Bewährungsprobe freuen und nach der (nicht unverschuldeten) Verhaftung ihres Lehrers jene Standhaftigkeit erlernen, die allein zu dem von Gott geforderten "vollkommenen Werk" führt (1,2ff).

Die dazu notwendige *"Weisheit"*,[71] die bei Jakobus an die Stelle des paulinischen πνεῦμα tritt, will dazu freilich erbeten sein (1,5ff). Voraussetzung dazu ist ein noch ganz an der alten Jesustradition orientierter (Gebets-)Glaube, der seiner Sache frei von allen Zweifeln gewiß ist.[72] Diese friedfertige, freundliche, gehorsame und liebevolle Weisheit von oben hat nichts gemein mit jener dämonisch-irdischen Weisheit von unten (3,13-18), die böse Begierden weckt (4,1f) und durch Neid bzw. Eifer- und Selbstsucht (3,14ff) nur *Unordnung* (ἀκαταστασία) *und Streitigkeiten* (πόλεμοι καὶ μάχαι) hervorrufen (4,1f), wie wir sie aus den paulinischen Gemeinden durch die Briefe des Apostels nur allzu gut kennen.[73] Der von der göttlichen Weisheit Erleuchtete und Verständige (3,13f) erweist den Besitz dieser Gabe, die nur durch Gebet aus ungeteiltem Herzen erlangt wird (1,17), aufgrund seines friedfertigen Wandels und der daraus resultierenden Frucht der Gerechtigkeit (3,18). Sollte der Verfasser des Briefs eben diese Gabe bei dem so streitbaren Heidenapostel und seinen Parteigängern vermißt haben, so daß der Zustand seiner Gemeinden auf den Gründer zurückfällt (4,1f)?

4. Unmittelbar auf die eindeutig antipaulinischen Ausführungen über Glaube und Werke folgt—noch vor der Abrechnung mit dem streitsüchtigen und rechthaberischen Weisen 3,13ff und gewissermaßen als Hinführung dazu—eine hochrhetorische Warnung vor der *Gefährdung des Lehrers durch den Mißbrauch und die Macht der Zunge* 3,1-12. Zunächst wird von dem Ehrgeiz Lehrer zu werden gewarnt (3,1a). War Paulus—nach seinem eigenen Urteil nicht durch solchen Ehrgeiz gefährdet,[74] ja hatte er sich nicht, im Urteil seiner Gegner, in das Amt des apostolischen Lehrers gedrängt? Blieb sein Apostolat—trotz Gal 2,9—nicht umstritten? Am Anfang (3,1) wie auch am Ende (3,12) steht—fast könnte man von einer inclusio reden—die *Warnung vor Gottes endzeitlichem Gericht.* Vor ihm muß sich der Lehrer, der seine Zunge nicht in Zaum halten und größtes Unheil damit anrichten kann (3,5ff), wie auch der, der seine Brüder schmäht und schändet, oder gar verflucht, verantworten (3,1b und 4,11ff vgl 3,9). Man kann hier auf die nicht wenigen *Maßlosigkeiten paulinischer Polemik* hinweisen, bei der sich der Apostel durch seine Leidenschaft—gewiß um der "Wahrheit des Evangeliums willen" (Gal 2,5.14)—zu schärfsten Invektiven gegen seine Widersacher hinreißen läßt, wobei Paulus in der mündlichen Auseinandersetzung gewiß noch schärfer werden konnte als in seinen Briefen, wo er die Namen der Gegner verschweigt.[75] Man müßte in diesem Zusammenhang etwa die Frage stellen, wie wohl die τίνες ἀπὸ Ἰακώβου, deren Erscheinen in Antiochien den Zwischenfall zwischen Petrus, Barnabas und den Judenchristen auf der einen Seite und Paulus auf der anderen verursacht hat, das Auftreten des Heidenapostels bei ihrer Rückkehr in Jerusalem dargestellt haben: Das um der "Wahrheit des Evangeliums willen" (2,14) gewiß notwendige κατὰ πρόσωπον αὐτῷ ἀντέστην, ὅτι κατεγνωσμένος ἦν wird bei der Emotionalität des Paulus durchaus mit persönlich verletzenden Angriffen verbunden gewesen sein, die sich im Blick auf die 1. Antithese Mt 5,21f schwerlich noch rechtfertigen ließen. Der matthäische Jesus sagt ja nicht, daß beim Kampf um die Wahrheit des Glaubens seine Aussage nicht mehr gelte. Wir wissen nicht, wie die Vertreter der Gegenseite die Invektiven wie Gal 5,12, die ans Obszöne grenzten, aufgenommen haben: Lag hier nicht eine Antwort wie Jak 1,20—unter verfremdendem Anklingen paulinischer Sprache—nahe: ὀργὴ γὰρ ἀνδρὸς δικαιοσύνην θεοῦ οὐκ ἐργάζεται? Die Verstimmungen waren entsprechend nachhaltig, und sie wirken in den großen Briefen des Apostels, vor allem im 1. und 2.Korintherbrief, schmerzhaft fort. Den den Zwiespalt lösenden Kompromiß des Aposteldekrets fanden Jakobus, Petrus und die Antiochener offenbar ohne, ja vielleicht gegen Paulus, der dasselbe u.W. nie anerkannte. Die Geschichte gab der anderen Seite nicht die Chance, daß ihr Paulusbild erhalten blieb. Die wenigen späten und völlig entstellten Spuren, die uns aus den Pseudoclementinen und dem kurzen Hinweis des Epiphanius auf die ebionitische Kampfschrift Ἀναβαθμοὶ Ἰακώβου erhalten sind (s.o.Anm.13), können vielleicht noch durch das sehr viel ältere und u.E. ursprüngliche Zeugnis des Jakobusbriefes ergänzt werden.

Neben die Warnung vor der Verfehlung mit der Zunge tritt in 5,12, wieder im Zusammenhang mit der Warnung vor dem Gericht, das *Verbot des Schwörens,* dessen Form gegenüber der nah verwandten Fassung Mt 5,34-37 ursprünglicher ist. In keinem frühchristlichen Werk des 1. und 2.Jh.s finden wir so viele schwurähnliche

Beteuerungen (und Verfluchungen) wie in den Paulusbriefen.[76] Gegen Angriffe wegen nicht eingehaltener Reise-bzw. Besuchszusagen wehrt er sich z.B. mit der Anrufung Gottes als Zeugen (Rö 1,9; 2.Kor 1,23). Offenbar floß dem Apostel derartiges relativ leicht aus der Feder. Die drastische Szene Apg 23,3 gibt dazu die nötige Anschauung. Vielleicht hat Lk den Apostel doch besser gekannt, als wir gemeinhin annehmen. Man hat daher in der Forschung zuweilen vermutet, Paulus hätte das Schwurverbot der Bergpredigt nicht gekannt.[77] Auch hier tritt wieder die Leidenschaftlichkeit des Apostels hervor, die er selbst in 2.Kor 11,29 mit dem knappen Satz umschreibt: τίς σκανδαλίζεται καὶ οὐκ ἐγὼ πυροῦμαι;

5. Daß—in der ungewissen und bedrängten Situation nach der Verhaftung des Paulus—die verwaisten heidenchristlichen Gemeinden die abschließende *Mahnung zur Geduld inder Erwartung der nahen Parusie des Herrn* wohl gebrauchen konnten (5,7ff), wobei auch die Warnung vor dem gegenseitigen Murren übereinander und der Hinweis auf "die Geduld Hiobs" angebracht waren, ist verständlich. Im Blick auf den nahen Richter 5,9, der "vor der Tür steht",[78] haben die fortdauernden Streitigkeiten und Anklagen jegliches Recht verloren. Damit hätte eigentlich der Brief abschließen können. Es folgt jedoch außer dem ganz unvermittelten, aber gerade im Blick auf Paulus verständlichen Hinweis auf das Schwurverbot (s.o.) eine weitere Sonderbarkeit: Was bedeutet am Ende dieser einzigartige, ebenfalls völlig unmotivierte Hinweis auf das rechte *Verhalten des Kranken?*[79] Er soll die Ältesten der Gemeinde rufen—ein Bischofsamt ist offenbar noch unbekannt—, damit sie über ihm beten und ihn im Namen des Herrn mit Öl salben, damit er gesund werde (5,13-16). Denn das aus echtem Glauben kommende, nicht durch Zweifel beeinträchtigte Gebet (1,6f; 4,2)—auch hier handelt es sich wieder um eine inclusio—und insonderheit das "Gebet des Gerechten" hat große Wirkungen. Freilich, der Sünder muß in diesem Zusammenhang seine Sündebekennen. Krankheit, vollmächtiges Gebet, Ölsalbung und Sündenbekenntnis und Heilung stehen in einem unmittelbaren Zusammenhang; 15b setzt dabei das Sündenbekenntnis voraus, auch wenn es erst in der generalisierenden Zusammenfassung v 16 erwähnt wird. Man könnte hier zunächst auf Jakobus als interzessorischen, charismatischen Beter und "Zaddik" hinweisen, wie er uns von Hegesipp und Epiphanius nach der späteren ebionitischen Legende geschildert wird.[80] Aber vielleicht wäre auch daran zu erinnern, daß wir—nachdem uns aus dem frühen Christentum kaum etwas von schwerer, bzw. unheilbarer Krankheit bei Christen berichtet wird[81]—allein von Paulus das sehr persönliche Zeugnis besitzen, daß er an einer uns nicht näher bekannten schlimmen Krankheit litt, "dem Pfahl (oder Splitter) im Fleisch", "dem Satansengel, der mich mit Fäusten schlägt", die vom Herrn selbst auferlegt ist, "damit ich mich nicht überhebe" (!). Trotz dreimaligem Gebet wurde dieses—gewiß drückende—Leiden nicht von ihm genommen. Er muß es nach dem Willen des Herrn weiter tragen. Diese Krankheit war den Gemeinden bekannt.[82] Mußte sie nicht—vor allem von judenchristlichen Gegnern—in traditionell jüdischem Sinne als Gottesstrafe interpretiert werden? Ist nun dieser Hinweis am Ende des Jakobusbriefes auf den Kranken, der die "Ältesten der Gemeinde" rufen soll, damit sie ihn durch Gebet und Ölsalbung heilen, nachdem er—das wird man aufgrund des Nachsatzes vermuten dürfen—seine Sünden bekannt hat, reiner Zufall bzw. verbreiteter, selbstverständlicher christlicher Brauch,[83] von dem wir sonst freilich keine Nachricht mehr haben? Eigenartig ist die Gewißheit, mit der dieses "Rezept" vorgetragen wird. Hier wirkt noch der alte jesuanische Gebetsglauben nach.[84] Oder wird hier den heidenchristlichen Gemeinden gesagt,

wie auch ein "hoffnungslos Kranker" (wie Paulus), wenn er nur wollte, von seiner dämonischen Krankheit hätte befreit werden können, wenn er sich dem Gebet samt exorzistischer Salbung durch die Ältesten (oder gar dem Gebet des "Gerechten": 5,16?) anvertraut und seine Sünde bekannt hätte? Gewiß, dieser gute Brauch, den der Schreiber für seine eigene Gemeinde als heilsam voraussetzt, soll in allen Gemeinden gelten. Aber welchen Sinn hat dieser ausführliche, etwas umständliche Hinweis, nachdem mit der Berufung auf den bald kommenden Richter die Paränese des Briefes im Grunde abgeschlossen ist?

Vielleicht darf in diesem Zusammenhang noch darauf hingewiesen werden, daß das—ursprünglich jüdische—Ältestenamt vermutlich von Jerusalem ausging[85] und zumindest dort nach der Apg zuerst bezeugt ist, während es die echten Paulusbriefe noch nicht kennen. Es ist darum abwegig, die Erwähnung der Ältesten als Zeichen einer späteren Zeit ins Feld zu führen. Sowohl Paulus wie Lukas zeigen, daß die unter der Leitung des Jakobus stehende Urgemeinde in Jerusalem feste "institutionalisierte" Formen aufweist. M.E. ist das Ältestenamt—wie auch der monarchische Episkopat—von Osten nach Westen gewandert.[86]

6. Der Schluß des Briefes ist *versöhnlich*. Der, der sich von der Wahrheit abgewandt hat, soll zurückgewonnen werden. Wer dies tut, rettet ein Leben vom Tode und "wird die Menge der Sünden bedecken".[87] Nach urchristlicher Anschauung war es Christus, der die menschliche Sünde tilgt (Joh 1,29; 1.Joh 2,2f; 1.Kor 15,3 u.ö.). Darüber weiß der Jakobusbrief nichts zu sagen. Christus wird bezeichnenderweise nur zweimal genannt: im Präskript und 2,1. Dort bezieht sich der "Glaube an unseren Herrn Jesus Christus, (den Herrn) der Herrlichkeit" auf die Erwartung des kommenden Herrn und Richters in seiner himmlischen Glorie (2,1). Bei ihm ist es die gute Tat, die rettende Wirkung besitzt und eigene und fremde Verfehlung entschärft (5,20 und 2,13.16).

Auch hier bei der Schlußmahnung 5,19f, die nach allen Gerichtsdrohungen und harter Polemik friedlich klingen soll, kann man noch einmal fragen: Gilt das einfach für jedermann und alle? Oder steht dahinter nicht zugleich ein ganz besonderer Fall, ein Paradigma, das sich die heidenchristlichen Gemeinden zu Herzen nehmen sollten? Ein "Sünder", vor dessen "Irrweg" zu warnen ist und um dessen Rettung man bemüht sein müßte? Geht es gar um den, der das Wort allein auf den Glauben bezieht, der das Heil nicht vom Gesetz, sondern vom Evangelium erwartet, der verkündigt, daß Gott allein durch den Glauben ohne Werke des Gesetzes rechtfertigt, und dafür Abraham als Zeugen zu benennen wagt, der sich für einen ganz großen Lehrer hält, doch in maßloser Polemik seine Zunge nicht im Zaum zu halten vermag, der sich weise dünkt, bei dem aber von der friedfertigen himmlischen Weisheit wenig zu spüren ist, der vielmehr Streit und Kämpfe in den Gemeinden verursacht und der gar zu gerne über andere richtet? Der sich weltweiter Missionsreisen und -erfolge rühmt und immer weitergreifende Pläne macht, jetzt aber in seinem Rühmen gescheitert ist und als Gefangener der Hinrichtung entgegensieht, der zudem krank ist, sich aber nicht von den Ältesten der Muttergemeinde aller Christen helfen lassen will?

7. Auch die *schroffe Polemik gegen die "Reichen"* ohne alle Abstriche und Vermittlung läßt sich hier vorzüglich einordnen. Paulus war, wie ich schon sagte, bei seiner "weltweiten" Missionsstrategie und seinen Gemeindegründungen ständig auf die Mithilfe und Opferbereitschaft relativ wohlhabender Christen angewiesen. Nur mit ihrer Hilfe konnten "Hausgemeinden" gegründet, Lehrsäle und Mietwohnungen

angemietet, die Kosten für teuere Schiffsreisen bezahlt, Briefe befördert und Übergriffe von fremder Seite abgewehrt werden. In den Paulusbriefen und erst recht in der Apg des "Armen-Theologen" Lukas haben wir zahlreiche Beispiele für wohlhabende Christen und deren Hilfe.[88] Aktive Mission kostete viel Geld, auch dann, wenn man für sich selbst auf die Forderung des persönlichen Unterhalts durch die Gemeinden verzichtete. Darüber hinaus mußte man auch noch die Kollekte für "die Armen" in Jerusalem einsammeln.[89] Als Organisator einer sich über das ganze Römische Reich erstreckenden Missionsbewegung konnte sich Paulus keine sozial-revolutionären Experimente und grundsätzlichen Aversionen gegen die ökonomisch Bessergestellten leisten.[90] Jakobus ist gerade in diesem Punkt *unerbittlich*. Sein Haß gegen die Reichen zeigt keine Spur von Kompromißbereitschaft. Schon das unterscheidet ihn von Lukas, den Pastoralbriefen oder dem Hirten des Hermas. Die Reichen scheinen, auch wenn sie Christen sind, vom Heil ausgeschlossen zu sein. Ein Reicher kann nicht wirklich Christ sein.[91] Das entspricht der Situation der Gemeinde der Armen in Jerusalem und Judäa, die von Anfang an durch die sadduzäische Oberschicht, bestehend aus dem hochpriesterlichen Adel und den Großgrundbesitzern, die das Synhedrium beherrschten, unterdrückt und z.T. blutig verfolgt wurden. Dem entsprechend sind die κριτήρια Jak 2,6 nicht die römischen, sondern die jüdischen Gerichte, die von den Vertretern des sadduzäischen Adels beherrscht waren.[92] Schon Jesus selbst wurde durch diese dem Tode ausgeliefert.[93] Gerade für die letzten zehn Jahre vor Ausbruch des jüdischen Krieges bezeugt Josephus schwerste soziale Spannungen in Judäa.[94] Die Christen standen hier auf der Seite der Verarmten und Unterdrückten, sie gehörten ja selbst zu dieser Gruppe. Durch die gescheiterte "Gütergemeinschaft" ohne geordnete Produktion,[95] eine Folge des Enthusiasmus der frühesten Naherwartung, mit dem auch Paulus etwa in Thessalonich zu kämpfen hatte,[96] durch die Hungersnöte unter Claudius und wohl auch durch Unterdrückung und Boykott im eigenen Volk waren sie auch ökonomisch "die Armen" geworden. Die neuen, blühenden heidenchristlichen Gemeinden erschienen ihnen gegenüber "reich" (und hochmütig), um so mehr, als sie in der Lage, ja dazu verpflichtet waren, die Armen in Jerusalem zu unterstützen, von denen sie—wie Paulus selbst betont—die "geistlichen Güter" (Rö 15,27) erhalten hatten. Die eingebildeten "Starken" in Korinth, die ja wohl überwiegend aus den besser gestellten Schichten stammten, werden nicht nur auf die beschränkten "Schwachen" in Korinth mit Verachtung herabgesehen haben, sondern auch auf die "gesetzlichen" Judenchristen in Jerusalem. Auch in Rom regte sich ähnlicher Hochmut.[97]

In den heidenchristlichen Missionsgemeinden war es—nach der Vorstellung der Jerusalemer christlichen *'äbjonim* und ihres Führers—wahrscheinlich, daß *ein vornehmer* Besucher der Gemeindeversammlung mit goldenem Siegelring und prächtigem Gewand einen Ehrenplatz erhielt, denn von dem Einfluß und der Unterstützung solcher Leute konnte man sich einiges erhoffen: politisch-rechtlichen Schut—wie es z.B. Lukas im Zusammenhang mit dem Aufruhr des Silberschmieds Demetrius in Ephesus schildert—, ein geräumigeres Versammlungslokal, Hilfe in Gemeindeangelegenheiten, eine effektivere Armenversorgung . . . u.a.m. Welch eine unschätzbare Hilfe bedeutete es etwa in einer der antiken Großstädte wie Antiochien, Ephesus, Korinth und erst recht in Rom, wo die abscheulichen Mietskasernen häufig und Einzelhäuser selten waren, wenn ein reicher Hausbesitzer seine villa oder seine domus der Gemeinde zur Verfügung stellte? Durch einen solchen Akt wurde oft erst die Möglichkeit einer dauerhaften Gemeindebildung geschaffen. Die frühesten

"Ämter" der Vorsteher, Episkopen und Diakone in den paulinischen Gemeinden, die Charismata der ἀντλήμψεις und κυβερνήσεις beziehen sich nicht so sehr auf geistliches als auf organisatorisches und ökonomisches "Vermögen".[99] Ihre Bedeutung und die damit verbundenen Talente wurden bis in die jüngste Zeit hinein in Deutschland (dem Land der Kirchensteuer) notorisch unterschätzt. Es ist verständlich, daß die armen Judenchristen in Jerusalem und Judäa, die ab der Verfolgung durch Agrippa I. auch ökonomisch mehr und mehr deklassiert und unterdrückt wurden, auf die sozial günstigere Situation in den heidenchristlichen Gemeinden, auf deren Hilfe sie teilweise angewiesen waren, mit Mißtrauen herabsahen und fürchteten, daß hier—vollends in der Verbindung mit Gesetzesverachtung und einem werkelosen Glauben—die Gefahr der Verweltlichung drohte. Dies würde die schroffe Zurückweisung des Reichtums, ohne jeden Kompromiß, bei Jakobus erklären. Die wahre, reine "Religion" (θρησκεία)—ein eigenartig förmlicher Begriff[100]—besteht in der sozialen Fürsorge gegenüber "Witwen und Waisen in ihrer Trübsal" und in der radikalen Abwendung von der Welt (1,27). Auch hier könnte man wieder eine Distanzierung von dem großen Missionar vermuten, der trotz seines hohen religiösen Anspruchs εἴ τις δοκεῖ θρησκὸς εἶναι (vgl. das Thema ab 3,1ff) seine Zunge nicht im Zaume zu halten vermag (1,26), d.h. der zu überscharfer Polemik neigte und der selbst seinen missionarischen Dienst als "Priesterdienst" (Rö 15,16: λειτουργός, ἱερουργεῖν) verklärte. Der mit einer beträchtlichen Summe (2.Kor 8,20) und zahlreichen heidenchristlichen Begleitern[101] herangereiste Paulus erschien gewissermaßen als der Repräsentant dieser "reichen", "weltlichen", vom Wohlleben verwöhnten oder zumindest bedrohten Gemeinden. Armut und Reichtum sind ja Relationsbegriffe. Dies wäre um so mehr verständlich, wenn man davon ausgehen darf, daß die Anschuldigungen gegen Paulus, er schaffe in seinen Gemeinden libertinistische Verhältnisse und mißachte Gottes Gebote, nicht nur nach Rom (Rö 3,8; 6,1), sondern auch nach Jerusalem gedrungen waren.

Summa: Der Jakobusbrief ist nach dieser *Hypothese* kein spätes, dürftiges Zufallsprodukt. Er ist mit Überlegung konzipiert und mit rhetorischem Geschick verfaßt. Die dahinterstehende Gedankenwelt ist die der jüdischen Weisheit, verbunden mit profetischem Pathos und in engster Verflechtung mit der Jesustradition, wie sie uns in Q, bei Mt und Mk begegnet.

Der Verfasser steht dabei seinem leiblichen Bruder so nahe, daß er es nicht nötig hat, sich ständig auf ihn zu berufen oder gar zu zitieren. Das völlige Fehlen eines Hinweises auf "Herrenworte" ist ein Zeichen seiner frühen Entstehung und der profetischen Autorität des Schreibers. Sein Brief ist als sein Wort zugleich "Wort des Herrn".[102] Er spricht als die von ihm eingesetzte Autorität, d.h. als δοῦλος Θεοῦ καὶ κυρίου Ἰησοῦ Χριστοῦ eo ipso in seinem Namen, wobei δοῦλος hier ganz im Sinne des hebräischen 'äbäd zu verstehen ist.[103] Fast ist man versucht, vom "Stellvertreter" zu sprechen. In solcher Vollmacht wendet er sich an die Christen in der griechischsprechenden Diaspora. Theologisch kann man an dem Brief erkennen, in welche Problematik eine auf das Ethos reduzierte, "vereinfachte" Jesusüberlieferung hineinführt, wenn man sie gegen die paulinische Rechtfertigungslehre ausspielen will. Providentia Dei hat die frühe Kirche in Paulus, nicht in Jakobus *den* ἀπόστολος, gesehen. Man kann auch das Zögern der Kirche im 3., ja 4. Jh. bei der Kanonisierung sehr wohl verstehen.[104]

Die Besonderheit des Briefes ergibt sich aus seinem Doppelcharakter. Er spricht—in gekonnter Weise—auf *zwei Ebenen* und setzt gewissermaßen zwei Empfängergruppen voraus.

1. Erscheint er als eine lockere, weisheitlich-rhetorisch stilisierte Mahnrede mit verschiedenen, zumindest zum Teil traditionellen Themen, die im Brief wie Fäden eines Teppichs auftauchen und wieder verschwinden, aber dabei doch in einem gewissen inneren Zusammenhang zueinander stehen. Sie will alle Christen ansprechen, erscheint jedoch durch Wahl der Motive und Anordnung des Stoffes als rätselhaft, da die eigentliche Intention des Briefes unklar bleibt und den Exegeten bis heute seine Einordnung unmöglich machte.

2. Gleichwohl enthält der Brief im weisheitlich-paränetischen Gewande und vielfältig variiert eine gezielte antipaulinische Polemik, die mit dem persönlichen Verhalten des Paulus, seiner Missionspraxis und gefährlichen Tendenzen seiner Theologie abrechnet. Der Verfasser setzt voraus, daß die Gemeinden, die Paulus kennen bzw. gar von ihm gegründet sind, diese Polemik sehr wohl verstehen und sich dadurch warnen lassen. Unter Voraussetzung dieser Hypothese könnte es vielleicht doch möglich sein, diese eigenartige Schrift im Blick auf ihren historischen Ort und ihren Inhalt besser zu verstehen und historisch einzuordnen.

Notes

*Der Aufsatz ist aus einem Seminar über den Jakobusbrief herausgewachsen, das ich zusammen mit Herrn Kollegen Baasland, Oslo, abhielt. Ihm verdanke ich wertvolle Anregungen, auch wenn er meiner—etwas radikalen—These nicht zustimmen konnte. Der Studie liegen weitere Seminare zugrunde, die im Trinity-College Dublin und den theologischen Fakultäten in Durham, Leeds und Glasgow abgehalten wurden. Seine jetzige Fassung erhielt er für einen Vortrag vor der neutestamentlichen Sozietät in Tübingen. Im folgenden zitiere ich die Standardkommentare nur mit Verfassertitel, Auflage und Seitenzahl, die anderen Abkürzungen verwende ich nach S. Schwertner. Theologische Realenzyklopädie, Abkürzungsverzeichnis, 1976. Für das Schreiben des komplizierten Manuskripts, die Überprüfung der Zitate und manchen wertvollen Hinweis danke ich meiner Assistentin Frau Anna Maria Schwemer.

1. Die Aporie geht im Grunde schon auf die alte Kirche zurück, wo ihn erst Origenes, der den Verfasser mehrfach "Apostel" nennt, und Dionysios von Alexandrien eindeutig als "Schrift" zitieren. Clemens Alexandrinus mag ihn in seinen Hypotyposen kommentiert haben, doch haben wir in seinem erhaltenen Werk kein eindeutiges Zitat aus ihm—im Gegensatz zu dem von Jak abhängigen Judasbrief. Gerne übersehen wir seine Verwendung in der Syr. Didaskalia, Anf. d. 3.Jh.s n.Chr.(?): s. c.5 (CSCO 407 p.51 Üs. von A. Vööbus), wo 1,12 als "Schrift" zitiert wird, und die eindeutigen Anspielungen c.1 Anf. = 2,8 (op.cit. p.9); c.12 Schluß = 2,2f (CSCO 408 p.134); c.20 = 2,19 (op.cit. p.182). Zu beachten sind auch die Papyri P[20] 3.Jh. und P[23] Ende 3.Jh. s. W. Grunwald/K. Junack, Das NT auf Papyrus I, ANT 6, 1986, 11-14.35ff. Auch die altlateinische Übersetzung sollte man nach Meinung des besten Sachkenners W. Thiele nicht zu spät ansetzen, s. VL 26,1 Epistulae Catholicae, 58.66* und briefliche Mitteilung vom 14.8.1986: "m.E. ist die alte lateinische Üs. von Jac genau so früh, wie sie für 1 Pt belegt ist, d.h. da bei Cyprian 1 Pt belegt ist, setze ich Jac auch um 200 an, da Cyprians Text schon eine Entwicklung zeigt. Die meisten Forscher setzen allerdings (m.E. zu Unrecht) Jac/lat später". Die "kanonische" Geltung des Jak setzte sich dagegen nur langsam durch und zog sich bis ins 4.Jh. hin s. J. B. Mayor,[3] LXVI-LXXIV; Th. Zahn, Gesch. d. ntl. Kanons, I,1, 321ff; M. Dibelius,[6] 74ff. Die Aporie bricht in der Reformationszeit aufgrund der Neuentdeckung des paulinischen Evangeliums wieder auf und ist seit den ersten kritischen Stellungsnahmen im vorigen Jahrhundert bis heute wirksam: s. W.M.L. de Wette, Lehrbuch der hist. krit. Einleitung in die kanon. Bücher des NTs, [1]1826, 306; F. K. Kern, Der Charakter und Ursprung des Briefs Jakobi, TZTh (1835), 2.H., 1-132 (65ff) vermutete schon einen unbekannten Autor des 2.Jh.s, änderte aber dann in seinem auch heute noch lesenswerten Kommentar, Der Brief Jakobi untersucht und erklärt, 1838 gründlich seine Meinung und trat für den Herrenbruder ein. Wesentliche Streitpunkte der Diskussion bis heute wurden von ihm vorweggenommen. Auch de Wette tendierte später in seinem Kommentar eher für die Wahrscheinlichkeit der Authentizität s. Kurzgefaßtes exegetisches Handbuch z. NT III,1, [3]1865, bear. v. E. Brückner, 193, vgl. dazu auch das zurückhaltende Urteil in der 6.Aufl. seines Lehrbuchs bearbeitet v. H. Messner/G. Lüdemann, 1860, 373: "Jedoch muß anerkannt werden, dass der Brief vortheilhaft absticht gegen die Erzeugnisse der nachapostolischen Litteratur, und nicht (mit Schwegler) zu tief herabgesetzt werden muss". Ähnlich bei A. Ritschl, Die Entstehung der altkatholischen Kirche, s. den Unterschied zwischen der 1.Aufl. 1850, 150f und der 2.Aufl. 1857, Vorrede 109f. und bei G. V. Lechler, Das apostolische und nachapostolische Zeitalter . . . , Preisschrift v.d. Teylerschen Theol. Gesellschaft, Haarlem, 1851, und die letzte 3. Aufl. 1885, 244ff. Zum Ganzen s. J. B. Mayor,[3] CLXXVII. Die Liste der Retractationes ließe sich fortsetzen. Zu den kontroversen Meinungen über Autorschaft und Datierung seit der Jahrhundertwende s. die Übersicht bei P. H. Davids, 1982, 4. Ähnlich disparat beurteilt wird die Frage der antipaulinischen Polemik s. A. Lindemann, Paulus im ältesten Christentum, BHTh 58, 1979, 240ff.
2. Die seit der alten Kirche vorherrschende Beschränkung auf die Judenchristen, wie sie von Th. Zahn, Wohlenberg und heute in moderierter Form von Mußner, Davids (zu 1,1) vertreten wird, engt den Kreis der Adressaten zu sehr ein. Erst recht ist die Vermutung jüdischer Adressaten (Mayor, Schlatter) abwegig. Die zwölf Stämme sind die Christen als das wahre Israel, das "in der Zerstreuung" spricht diese dagegen nicht als Fremdlinge auf der Erde und himmlische Bürger an (von der himmlischen Welt ist herzlich wenig die Rede), sondern ist als die "Zerstreuung unter den

Völkern" außerhalb des heiligen Landes zu verstehen. Der Vf. verwendet nicht das in frühchristlichen Briefpräskripten so häufige Motiv der irdischen Fremdlingsschaft (dazu M. Hengel, Die Evangelienüberschriften, SHA.PH 1984, H.3, 46 Anm.109). Der von Jak abhängige 1.Petr 1,1 führt dieses Motiv neu ein und kombiniert es mit dem geographisch näher bestimmten Diasporabegriff. Bei den Apostolischen Vätern fehlt der Begriff διασπορά ganz; bei Justin, dial 117,2.4.5 aber auch 113,3; 121,4 ist die jüdische Diaspora gemeint.

3. Das kritische Urteil Luthers betraf auch die Form: "und wirfft so unordig eyns yns ander" WA.DB 7,386; "Dazu ist da kein ordo noch methodus" WA.TR 5,157. Vgl. auch das Zugeständnis de Wettes, Ex.Hb. (Anm.1), III,1, 103: "Dieser Standpunkt und Zweck des Briefes ist ein bloß vermuthlicher; denn dieser ist ohne Plan geschrieben".

4. S. die trotz ihrer Irrtümer eindrucksvolle Untersuchung von A. Meyer, Das Rätsel des Jacobusbriefes, BZNW 10 (1930), sowie die älteren Untersuchungen von L. Massebieau, L'epitre de Jacques est-elle l'oeuvre d'un chrétien?, RHR XVI (32) (1885), 249-283 und F. Spitta, Der Brief des Jakobus untersucht, 1896. S. auch A. Jülicher/E. Fascher, Einleitung in das NT, [7]1931, 211f; H. Thyen, Der Stil der jüdisch-hellenistischen Homilie, FRLANT 65, 1955, 14ff; R. Bultmann, Theologie d. NTs[9]1984, 515.

5. Dibelius,[6] 67; ältere Autoren 33 Anm.1; s. auch die Aufstellung bei P. Davids, 4: Die meisten Autoren sehen heute in Jak ein späteres Pseudepigraphon.

6. Dibelius,[6] 52: "Das Präskript des Jud scheint den Jak vorauszusetzen". Vgl. A. Meyer, op.cit. (Anm.4), 82-85. Dabei deutet der erhebliche inhaltliche Unterschied auch auf eine zeitliche Distanz hin. Judas kämpft am Ende des 1.Jh.s gegen eine frühe Form der "Gnosis" mit libertinistischen Neigungen, s. den Kommentar von E. Fuchs/P. Reymond, La deuxième épître tre de Saint Pierre. L'épître de Saint Jude, 1980, 143 dazu den Forschungsbericht von R. Heiligenthal, ThR 51 (1986), 117-129. Jud wird wieder von 2.Petr ausgeschrieben, der seinerseits die wahrscheinlich z.Z. Bar Kochbas entstandene Petrus-Apokalypse beeinflußte s. F. Spitta, Die Petrusapokalypse und der zweite Petrusbrief, ZNW 12 (1911), 237-242. Vgl. auch die Zusammenstellung der Texte bei A. v. Harnack, Bruchstücke des Evangeliums und der Apokalypse des Petrus, [2]1893, 87f, der freilich—zu Unrecht—die Reihenfolge umstellen will. Die früh bezeugte Petrusapokalypse (Clem.Alex., Can.Mur.) ist wahrscheinlich während oder bald nach dem Bar-Kochba-Aufstand 132-135 anzusetzen, s. dazu c.2 der äth. Fassung und Chr. Maurer bei Hennecke/Schneemelcher, NTA 2, 469. Eine Datierung von Jak vor 80/90 ergibt sich auch aus der Tatsache, daß 1.Petr und 1.Clem von ihm abhängig sind und seine Jesustradition älter ist als die des Mtevg s.u.S. 251.

7. Dibelius,[6] 19: "Man wird gut tun, den Anteil des Verf. an der Gedankenbildung nicht zu überschätzen. Mit dieser Erkenntnis verliert natürlich die Autorfrage überhaupt an Bedeutung". Die Parallele zu seiner—m.E. verfehlten—Beurteilung der synoptischen Autoren als "Sammler, Tradenten, Redaktoren", Die Formgeschichte d. Ev., [2]1933,2, ist offensichtlich. Dibelius liebt in diesem Zusammenhang das Wort "harmlos" s. 40 Anm.4: τέλειος wird harmlos und keineswegs gnostisch verwendet"; 42: "Gesetz wird nicht polemisch, "sondern harmlos, ohne Definition (gebraucht)". 34: "die große Harmlosigkeit dieser Pseudonymität . . .". Der Brief zeigt "keinerlei bestimmte ›Theologie‹" 41 vgl. 36, nur "seine Gesinnungen . . . sind . . . von einheitlichem Charakter". S. dagegen neue Untersuchungen, die zeigen, daß hier eine mit Überlegung und Kunst verfaßte "Weisheitsschrift" mit weisheitlicher "Theologie" vorliegt: E. Baasland, StTh 36 (1982), 119-139; U. Luck, ZThK 81 (1984), 1-30 u.a.

8. Dibelius,[6] 14 vgl. 21: . . . "auf weite Strecken hin des gedanklichen Zusammenhangs völlig entbehrt". S. jedoch die Einschränkung: . . . "dabei soll dem Jak nicht jede einheitliche Note abgesprochen werden". Sollte Jak vielleicht ein anderes Verständnis von "Einheitlichkeit des Gedankengangs" besitzen, dem unseres eher zu schlicht und indirekt erscheint? Vielleicht ist die "Planlosigkeit", "die Wiederholung des gleichen Motivs an verschiedenen Stellen" (op.cit. 22), bewußt gewollt?

9. Zum Eklektizismus des Jak s. op.cit. 19f. S.42 wird "eine große eigene Belesenheit" des Autors geleugnet. Doch wird man neben der Kenntnis der Bibel (deren Kanon noch nicht streng abgegrenzt war) auch eine gute Kenntnis der Weisheitsliteratur (Sir, T.XII etc.) voraussetzen müssen. Freilich hat sich der Vf. nicht—wie ein antiker Literat (oder moderner Professor)—"Sammlungen von Lesefrüchten" (42) angelegt; dafür war sein Gedächtnis zu gut und der eigene Gestaltungswille zu groß.

10. Op.cit., 23 vgl. 42: "Jak (ist) also nicht Denker, Prophet, geistiger Führer, sondern Pädagog,

einer unter vielen, nehmend und austeilend aus dem allen gemeinsamen Besitz." Damit wird er
verkannt und verharmlost. Der Brief ist gerade nicht völlig profillos. Das hat Harnack klarer
gesehen s.u.S. 250 Anm.20.

11. Die hinter der Deutung von Dibelius stehende Hypothese von der fortschreitenden Verweltlichung und Verbürgerlichung der Gemeinden (vgl. op.cit. 62-66; 69-73) überzeugt nicht; sie
ist zu einfach. Die Gefahr der "Verweltlichung" war—wie der Streit in Korinth zeigt—in den
neugegründeten Missionsgemeinden des Paulus am größten, und reichere Christen und soziale
Konflikte gab es gerade schon dort (s.u.S 263f.). Das Schlagwort der "Konventikelethik" (op.cit.
71) trifft das ganze Urchristentum, der Gegensatz zwischen den "Höhen des Paulus-Glauben" und
den "Alltagsmenschen" mit ihrer Kleinbürgerlichkeit und Weltscheu, die Jak vertrete (op.cit. 73),
weist auf den Protestantismus des ausgehenden 19.Jh.s zurück. Interessant ist, daß der Neukan-
tianer A. Ritschl (op. cit. Anm. 1) zu einer sehr viel positiveren Wertung kommt.

12. S. dazu C. A. Osiek, Rich and Poor in the Shepherd of Hermas, Diss. Washington D.C.
1983. Hermas, ein Freigelassener aus dem Mittelstand, stammt aus einem völlig anderen Milieu als
der Vf. des Jak (sozialethisch bereitet er den Kompromiß des Clemens Alex. vor), s. R. Staats, TRE
16, 1986, 100-108 (103.105). S. auch M. Hengel, Eigentum und Reichtum in der frühen Kirche,
1973, 54ff.63f.

13. Zur Wirkungsgeschichte des Hermas s. R. Staats, op.cit. (Anm.12), 106f; von seiner Be-
liebtheit zeugen auch die zahlreichen frühen Papyri ab der 2.H d. 2.Jh.s, s. C. H. Roberts, Manuscript, Society and Belief in Early Christian Egypt, SchL 1977, 1979, 14.21f.42.59. Es war "outside the Bible the most widely-read book" (63). Jak wurde zwar noch vor 1.Petr, 1.Clem und
Hermas verwendet, dann aber taucht er erst wieder *eindeutig* in der Syrischen Didaskalia und bei
Origenes auf. Eigenartig ist, daß ungefähr einen Tatbestand entsprechend Jakobus der Herrenbruder noch bei Lk erscheint, und in den anderen Evangelien die Brüder Jesu in negativem Kontext stehen, die Apostolischen Väter, Apologeten und Apostelakten ganz über ihn schweigen und
erst Hegesipp um 180 und Clemens Alex. ausführlicher über ihn berichten. Erst Nag Hammadi
brachte mit Ev Thom Log 12, dem Jak-Apokryphon, den beiden Jak-Apokalypsen ebionitische
Überlieferung ans Licht. Zur Jak-Tradition s. M. Hengel, Jakobus der Herrenbruder—der erste
»Papst«?, in: Glaube und Eschatologie. Festschrift für W. G. Kümmel zum 80. Geburtstag, 1985,
71-104.

14. Zu Baasland s.o.Anm.7. Vgl. auch W. H. Wuellner, Der Jakobusbrief im Licht der Rhetorik
und Textpragmatik, LingBibl H.43 (1978), 5-66: "Die Anordnung der Argumente hat ergeben, daß
die opinio communis der Exegeten betreffs der fehlenden Gedankenführung auf falschen Voraus-
setzungen beruht" (65).

15. Dibelius[6] hat diesen Zwiespalt gesehen, aber zu wenig berücksichtigt: "Der Jak enthält zum
gutenTeil gemeinsame alte Tradition, und doch macht sein Sprachgewand einen verhältnismäßig
einheitlichen Eindruck".

16. Die neutestamentliche Rhetorik ein Seitenstück zur Grammatik des neutestamentlichen
Sprachidioms, 1843, 484: "Das Augenfälligste sind die Zeichen der Lebhaftigkeit, welche sein
Vortrag an sich trägt . . . Er macht Schilderungen, die an das Poetische anstreifen" (485).

17. CCLVI. S. überhaupt die ausführliche Darstellung der stilistischen Eigentümlichkeitn
CCVI-CCLIX: "I should be inclined to rate the Greek of this Epistle as approaching more nearly
to the standard of classical purity than that of any book of the N.T. with the exception perhaps of
the Epistle to the Hebrews" (CCXLIV). Dibelius[6] 53-57; Schlatter, 77-84; Mußner, 26-33. S. auch
A. Wifstrand, Stylistic Problems in the Epistles of James and Peter, StTh 1 (1948), 170-182 hebt
den Zusammenhang mit der gehobenen literarischen Koine der griechischsprechenden Synagoge
hervor: "the principal origin is the edifying language of the hellenized Synagogue" (181); zugleich
warnt er vor einem schlagwortartigen Gebrauch des Begriffs der Diatribe.

18. Op.cit. 84f. Schon A. Ritschl, op.cit. (Anm.1), 116 spricht von der "Anlehnung des Jakobus
an die didaktische Poesie des A.T.".

19. Der formale Aufbau des Jakobusbriefes, ZThK 28 (1904), 295-333 (312f); s. schon den
Gliederungsversuch: Die Anlage des Jakobusbriefs, op.cit. 37-56.

20. Die Chronologie der altchristlichen Litteratur bis Eusebius, 1897, I,1, 487f; zitiert bei H. J.
Cladder, op.cit. (Anm.19), 43, der freilich den "theologischen Polemiker" mit einem Fragezeichen
versieht. M.E. liegt hier der Schlüssel zur Erklärung des Paradoxons. Indem Harnack jedoch Jak

einem anonymen Autor zuschreibt, das Präskript als späte Zutat erklärt (s. dazu u. S. 250) und aufgrund einer falschen Deutung von 2,6f "principielle Christenverfolgungen und *christliche Denunciationen*" (486) um 120 oder später ansetzt, kommt er zu einer Fehlbeurteilung seines historischen Ortes (s.u.S. 252f.). Jak unterscheidet sich durch das Fehlen einer Christologie und Ekklesiologie und durch seine völlige Unabhängigkeit von den synoptischen Evangelien grundsätzlich von "Hermas, Clemens, Justin, II.Clemens", er steht näher bei Q und der jüdischen Weisheitstradition. Vgl. die ähnliche Beurteilung des Charakters des Autors und seines Werks bei Mayor, CCXLIX und CCLIX: "Still in its rough abruptness, in the pregnant brevity of its phrases, in its austerity of its demand upon the reader, in concentrated irony and scorn, this Epistle stands alone among the Epistles of the New Testament".

21. Mußner, 33 im Anschluß an Eichholz.

22. Dazu Th. Zahn, Einl. in d. N.T. I, ^{3}1906, 83; Schlatter, 84.

23. Die von Dibelius aufgrund seines "Vor-Urteils" vollzogene, nahezu völlige Bestreitung aller sachlichen und argumentativen Zusammenhänge müßte in der Einzelexegese widerlegt werden. Ch. Burchard, Zu Jakobus 2,14-26, ZNW 71 (1980), 27-45 versucht daher—gegen die vorherrschende Exegese, die "Martin Dibelius Kontextverbot" folgt—mit gutem Recht, diesen Text "im Kontext zu lesen" (27f); vgl. auch 27 Anm.2 zum "Gedankengang" in der Diatribe, der oft hinter "Knappheiten und Unausgesprochenem" zu entdecken ist. Zum selben Text R. Heiligenthal, Werke als Zeichen, WUNT 2.R. 9, 1983, 27f.

24. Zu Hermas s. Th. Zahn, op.cit. (Anm.22), 97 (ältere Literatur); instruktiv zur Arbeitsweise von Hermas s. C. Taylor, The Didache Compared with the Shepherd of Hermas, JP 18 (1890), 297-325, speziell zu Jak 320ff. Zurückhaltender urteilt F. Spitta, op.cit. (Anm.4), 382-391, eindeutig dagegen A. Meyer, op.cit. (Anm.4), 60-68; Mayor, LXXIVff; Mußner, 37f. Auch Dibelius,[6] 49f betont, daß die eng inhaltlich verwandte Paränese der Mandata "auf fortgeschrittenere Verhältnisse berechnet (ist), als sie es sind, für die Jak schreibt". Er lehnt jedoch weitere Schlüsse auf eine literarische Abhängigkeit—m.E. zu Unrecht—ab. Da Hermas außer dem obskuren Eldad und Modad-Zitat (Vis 2,3,4=7,4) nicht zitiert, sondern alle Texte, die er übernimmt "einschmilzt", kann man keine größeren Zitate erwarten. Die zahlreichen Anklänge und Berührungen kann man jedoch kaum allein auf bloße gemeinsame Tradition zurückführen. Wenig befriedigend ist die Untersuchung von O. J. F. Seitz, Relationship of the Shepherd of Hermas to the Epistle of James, JBL 63 (1944), 131-140, der sich auf das von Jak zweimal verwendete δίψυχος beschränkt und eine gemeinsame Quelle annimmt, aus der auch 2.Clem noch geschöpft haben soll. Der Sprachgebrauch von δ. kommt aus der Synagoge, s. das verwandte διπρόσωπος T.Dan 4,7 und mehrfach in T.Asser. Auch Seitz muß die auffallend engen Beziehungen zwischen Jak 1,8; 4,8 mit ihrem Kontext und Hermas, mand. 9 zugeben.

25. F. Spitta, op.cit. (Anm.4), 230-236; Mayor LXXf; A. Meyer, op.cit. (Anm.4), 68-72; Mußner, 35f; zurückhaltend Dibelius,[6] 51f. Vgl. jedoch die Einschränkung 67!

26. Hier ist die Beziehung besonders auffallend s. F. Spitta, op.cit. (Anm.4), 183-202 mit einer ausführlichen Tabelle der Parallelen. Dabei ist bedeutsam, daß sie zu einem guten Teil in beiden Briefen in der gleichen Reihenfolge verlaufen. S. auch schon Jak 1,1.2.3.10f.18.21 und 1.Petr 1,1.6.7.24.23; 2,1 etc. Das kann nicht allein durch gemeinsame paränetische Tradition weggedeutet werden s. Dibelius,[6] 48f. Der Begriff der "literarischen Entlehnung" müßte hier geklärt werden. Natürlich hat 1.Petr Jak nicht ausgeschrieben, wohl aber gelesen und später "verarbeitet". Ein umgekehrtes Abhängigkeitsverhältnis ist unmöglich, der 1.Petr hat die jakobäische Tradition sehr viel stärker "verchristlicht". Vgl. auch A. Meyer, op.cit. (Anm.4), 72-82; A. Schlatter, 67-73; bei Mußner, 34f wird der Vergleich sehr oberflächlich durchgeführt. Die πειρασμοὶ ποικίλοι 1,2 = 1,6, die mit dem darauffolgenden Vers eine Einheit bilden, sind z.B. weggelassen. S. schon Wettstein u.S. 275 Anm.70.

27. A. Meyer, op.cit. (Anm.4), 59f. Diese Wirksamkeit im Westen bricht ab, dagegen erscheint der Brief ab Clemens bzw. der Syr. Didaskalia u. Origenes im Osten. Vgl. A. Jülicher/E. Fascher, op.cit. (Anm.4), 212: "Die Benutzung durch 1.Pt und I.Clem lassen die Zeit vor 95 als geraten erscheinen". Er erwägt auch Rom als Abfassungsort.

28. Schon A. Ritschl betont, daß Jak "unter allen neutestamentlichen Schriften die nächsten Anklänge an die Reden Jesu enthält" op.cit. 2.Aufl. (Anm.1), 109; vgl. F. Spitta, op.cit. (Anm.4), 155-183; A. Schlatter, 19-29. Die Evangelien werden dabei noch nicht vorausgesetzt, s. A. Meyer,

op.cit. (Anm.4), 85f. Eine schöne Übersicht gibt F. Mußner, 47-52: Der Brief weist über die vorevangelische Jesus-Tradition auf Jesu ethische Verkündigung zurück. S. auch P. Davids, 47ff und W. D. Davies, The Setting of the Sermon of the Mount, 1964, 401-405.

29. Die Vermutung einer antignostischen Tendenz, so bei H. Schammberger, Die Einheitlichkeit des Jakobusbriefes im antignostischen Kampf, Gotha 1936, und H. J. Schoeps, Theologie und Geschichte des Urchristentums, 1949, 343-350 wird heute kaum mehr vertreten. Schoeps bringt jedoch einige gute Beobachtungen zum judenchristlichen Milieu des Briefes, das noch nicht "ebionitisch" ist; in 2,7 geht es um die jüdischen Hierarchen und nicht um römische Behörden s.u.S. 277, Anm. 92.

30. S. dagegen die Verteidigung des heute vorherrschenden Spätansatzes bei K. Aland, Der Herrenbruder Jakobus und der Jakobusbrief, ThLZ 69 (1944), 97-104 = Neutestamentliche Entwürfe, 233-245 gegen G. Kittel, Der geschichtliche Ort des Jakobusbriefes, ZNW 41 (1942), 71-105. In seiner Antwort, Der Jakobusbrief und die Apostolischen Väter (1950/51), 54-112 hat G. Kittel m.E. überzeugend gezeigt, daß Jak in Glaubensvorstellung, Eschatologie und Verwendung von Jesustradition nicht einfach an die apostolischen Väter angeglichen werden kann. Nur die Didache hat eine ähnliche Zahl von Anklängen an Herrenworte, setzt dabei freilich eindeutig das Mtevg voraus. Irreführend sind bei Kittel sein zu früher Ansatz vor 48 (ZNW 41 [1942], 99f) und die judenchristlichen Adressaten (103f). Der historische Ort wird *zwischen* Kittel und Aland zu suchen sein.

31. Zu Sepphoris s. E. Schürer/G. Vermes/F. Millar, The History of the Jewish People in the Age of Jesus Christ, 2, 173: Nach seinem Wiederaufbau durch Antipas hatte es eine gemischte Bevölkerung und stand 66 auf Seiten der Römer. Bis zur Gründung von Tiberias ca 26 war es galiläische Hauptstadt und Residenz. Zu Justus s. Jos. Vita 40.336. Zur griechischen Sprache im jüdischen Palästina s. op.cit., 2, 52-80; vgl. auch M. Hengel, Zwischen Jesus und Paulus, ZThK 72 (1975), 151-206 (173f) und J. N. Sevenster, Do You Know Greek, 1968. Weitere Literatur bei J. A. T. Robinson, Redating the New Testament, 1976, 133 Anm. 46.

32. E. Schürer . . . , op. cit. 2, 79; 29 Anm. 118 (Lit.) s. auch SB 8, 9843/44. Zum Briefpräskript vgl. Apg 15,23. Die Grußformel sollte daher nicht mehr als Argument gegen die Authentizität herangezogen werden, dasselbe gilt von der Verwendung der LXX, so z.B. K. Aland, op.cit. (Anm.30), 236 gegen Kittel. Bei englischen Vorträgen liegt es für den deutschen Autor oder den Übersetzer ja auch nahe, für Schriftzitate die Revised Standard Version zu verwenden. Für Jakobus wäre hier die Rücksicht auf die ganz überwiegend heidenchristlichen Empfänger entscheidend. Man schreibt auf "griechische" Weise mit dem üblichen Präskript, dem den Empfängern gewohnten Bibeltext und in gutem Stil, damit der Brief positiv aufgenommen und nicht schon wegen seiner "barbarischen Form" abgelehnt wird. Bezeichnenderweise hat der pseudonyme Judasbrief, obwohl er Jak voraussetzt, wieder auf das übliche, christliche Präskript zurückgegriffen. Das ungewohnte "nicht christliche", profane Präskript spricht gegen einen Spätansatz.

33. A. Lindemann, op.cit. (Anm.1), 241 Anm.57. Ein eindrückliches, relativ neues Argument für die Zweisprachigkeit in gut jüdischen Familien z.Z. des Jakobus ist die Grablege von 3 Generationen einer jüdischen Familie aus der Zeit des Jakobus zwischen 10 und 70 n.Chr. aus Jericho (!) s. R. Hachili, The Goliath Family in Jericho, BASOR 235 (1979), 31-70 vgl. besonders 32ff.46.60f. Von 32 Inschriften auf 14 Ossuarien sind 17 in griechischer und 15 in jüdischer Quadratschrift. Die Namen der Familie sind gleichwohl alle jüdisch bis auf die Hauptfigur Theodotos, die auch den hebräischen Namen Nathanael führt und als ἀπελεύθερος βασιλίσσης Ἀγριππίνης, d.h. der Frau des Claudius 50-54 und Mutter Neros, ausgewiesen ist; vgl. dazu Apg 6,9 die Synagoge der "Libertinoi" in Jerusalem u. M. Hengel, op.cit. (Anm.31), 182ff. Seine Freilassung muß wohl in die Jahre 50-54 fallen. "The inscriptions in general testify to the usage of Greek by the Jews of the Second Temple period and inscriptions 3 and 14 may indicate that Greek was more common than Aramaic at this time". Der "Hellenismus" im Urchristentum hat seine Wurzeln in Jerusalem selbst, wenn nicht gar in Galiläa.

34. Siehe die Zusammenstellung von Autoren, die einen derartigen Frühansatz zwischen 40 und 50 vertreten, bei P. Davids, 4, sie reicht von Knowling und Zahn über Mayor bis zu Guthrie und J. A. T. Robinson, zu seiner ausführlichen und originellen Begründung s. op.cit. (Anm.31), 118-139, dort 138f noch weitere Autoren. Davids, 21f spricht diesem Ansatz selbst gute Gründe zu, entscheidet sich aber dann doch für eine spätere Datierung, 55-65 oder 75-85.

35. Vgl. P. Davids, loc.cit.: Das Material stammt vom Herrenbruder, die Redaktion geschah mit

fremder Hilfe oder nach dem Tode des Jak durch einen Judenchristen. Vgl. schon F. Schleiermacher, Einleitung ins Neue Testament, hg. von G. Wolde, Sämmtliche Werke 1.Abt. Zur Theologie, Bd. 8, 1845, 428f: "Wenn wir uns denken, daß Jemand unseren Brief im Namen des palästinischen Apostels Jakobus geschrieben und Erinnerungen aus seinen Vorträgen nicht auf die glücklichste Weise und in einer Sprache zusammengestellt hat, die ihm selbst nicht geläufig war: so erklärt sich Alles auf eine Weise, welche durch die älteste patristische Annahme unterstützt wird."

36. Ant 20,200-203; Euseb, h.e. 2,23,4-18 dazu M. Hengel, op.cit. (Anm. 13), 73ff.

37. Vgl. etwa die Kritik von F. Schleiermacher, op.cit. (Anm.35), 427: "Manches ist darin, was durchaus einen äußerlichen wunderlichen Typus hat ohne einen inneren Gehalt und eigentliche Kraft". Zu 5,1-6 und 3,1ff wird zweimal der rhetorische "Wortschwall" kritisiert. "Es entsteht die Ansicht, daß der Brief ein späteres Product und ein eigentliches Machwerk ist, d.h. ohne zugleich eine That zu sein, und ohne, daß sich der Verfasser ein bestimmtes Publicum gedacht hat". Sicher hat Schleiermacher auch an der schroffen Polemik des Briefes Anstoß genommen. Zu seinem negativen Urteil über die Sprache s.o.S. 270, Anm.35. Er tut durch seine stark ästhetisch bestimmte Kritik dem Jak gewiß unrecht, (s.o.S. 280 die ganz andere Beurteilung durch A. Ritschl und A. v. Harnack), doch sieht er *ein* Problem des Briefes in aller Schärfe.

38. Die Gesetzesfrage erscheint in der neueren Kritik als der Hauptanstoß. S. schon A. Jülicher/E. Fascher, op.cit. (Anm.4), 205f; K. Aland, op.cit. (Anm.30), 237 in der Auseinandersetzung mit G. Kittel, s. dessen Antwort ZNW 43 (1950/51), 56-58; W. G. Kümmel, Einleitung in das Neue Testament, [20]1980, 364 unter 2; Ph. Vielhauer, Geschichte d. urchristlichen Literatur, 1975, 579.

39. Josephus, ant 20,200. Lediglich bei A. T. Cadoux, The Thought of St. James, 1944, 100 fand ich einen entsprechenden Hinweis.

40. Diese neue "Gesetzesauffassung" ist nicht erst eine Errungenschaft von 1. und 2.Clemens, Hermas, Barnabas und Justin, sondern findet sich auch bei Mk und Mt und ist überhaupt typisch für breite Kreise des Urchristentums, abgesehen von den "Judaisten", zu denen nach Gal 2,6ff Jakobus gerade nicht zu rechnen ist. M.E. könnte sie mit den Hellenisten in Verbindung stehen. Dann würde Jak eine Vorstellung aufnehmen, die auch im nichtpaulinischen Heidenchristentum verbreitet war, s. M. Hengel, op.cit. (Anm.31), 175. Bei Jak nimmt sie holzschnitthaft vergröberte Konturen an. Gleichwohl spricht er noch nicht von καινὸς νόμος (Barn 2,6), den καινὴ ἐντολή (Joh 13,34) oder dem καινὸς νομοθέτης (Justin, dial 14,3; 18,3). Der νόμος τέλειος τῆς ἐλευθερίας wird sachlich am besten durch einen Text wie Lk 10,25-37 illustriert!

41. S. dazu A. Lindemann, op.cit. (Anm.1), 102-109; G. Lüdemann, Paulus der Heidenapostel II. Antipaulinismus im frühen Christentum, FRLANT 130, 1983, 228-260; M. Hengel, op.cit. (Anm.13), 76f.

42. Bezeichnenderweise erheben sich gegen diese Vermutung einer direkten Polemik gegen Paulus je und je *moralische* Bedenken: s. A. Jülicher/E. Fascher, op.cit. (Anm.4), 207f: "Hätte dagegen Jakobus der Gerechte ca 60 oder 64 Jak 2,14-26 geschrieben, so könnte der bekämpfte Feind nicht eine Entartung des Paulinismus, sondern nur P. selber sein, und die Polemik gegen ihn, welcher nicht der Milderungsgrund einer veränderten religiösen Situation zugute kommt, *wäre in ihrer Unwahrhaftigkeit lediglich empörend;* denn Jakobus hätte dann verheimlicht, was ihm die Hauptsache war, die Fortdauer des Mosegesetzes". Eben das bestreite ich: Für die Heidenchristen hat dieses auch nach der Meinung des Jak kaum heilsrelevante Bedeutung. Im übrigen ist die verletzende Polemik in den Briefen des Pls kaum "moralischer" als die indirekte des Jak. S. auch Th. Zahn, op.cit. (Anm.22), 1, 89: Die Vermutung einer antipaulinischen Polemik "ließe sich nur so aufrecht erhalten, daß man zugleich behauptete, Jk habe die Lehre des Pl *in einer geradezu unglaublichen Weise mißverstanden oder boshafterweise verdreht und überdies mit feiger Hinterlist bestritten.* Dem widerspricht aber der Eindruck, welchen jeder urteilsfähige Leser von dem intellektuellen und moralischen Charakter des Vf.s aus seiner Schrift empfängt". Es war bezeichnend, daß in der Diskussion unserer neutestamentlichen Sozietät dieser Anstoß eine wichtige Rolle spielte. Wir sollten uns jedoch davor hüten, in den Männern des frühesten Christentums Perfecti und "Heilige" zu sehen. Für sie und uns alle gilt Rö 4,5. Von welch erfrischender Realität ist hier doch das Jüngerbild des Mk! Es ist aus dem Leben geschöpft, denn dahinter steht ein Petrusschüler. Man übersehe selbst bei dem "harmonisierenden" Lk nicht Stellen wie Apg 6,1f; 11,2; 15,1f.7.39 (παροξυσμός: ein herbes Wort); 21,20b/21.

43. Zur neueren Diskussion um diesen am meisten umstrittenen Text in Jak s. die interessante Darstellung von A. Lindemann, op.cit. (Anm.1), 240-252: "Der Vf. des Jak wollte die paulinische Theologie treffen und widerlegen, und zwar mit ihren eigenen Mitteln. Deshalb wählte er das Pseudonym des Jakobus, um eine Gegenautorität ins Feld führen zu können" (249). Aber warum hat er dann die Würde dieser Gegenautorität in so unverständlicher Weise unterdrückt? Interessant ist auch die Vermutung S. 244: Die "noch wirksame Kraft der paulinischen Rechtfertigungslehre, die es den Vertretern eines expliziten Antipaulinismus . . . nicht erlaubte, offen gegen Paulus aufzutreten, sondern sie . . . dazu zwang, in der Maske des "klassischen" Paulus-Gegners Jakobus . . . gleichsam abstrakt und theoretisch gewisse Lehren anzugreifen, *wobei dem Eingeweihten natürlich klar war, um wessen Lehre es hier ging*" (Sperrung von mir). M. E. greift Jak Pls durchaus konkret und praktisch an, freilich in verallgemeinerter weisheitlicher Form. Und: Warum soll dieser Angriff nicht von einem Zeitgenossen stammen? S. 250: "Der Vf. des Jak hat Paulus durchaus verstanden. Gerade deshalb protestiert er gegen die paulinische Theologie". Ich würde hinzufügen: noch ohne die Briefe zu kennen, aufgrund von Nachrichten über die Verkündigung des Paulus samt ihren Wirkungen. Vgl. auch S. 251 Anm.123 in Ablehnung der These von Kümmel und Vielhauer über den "sachlichen Abstand" zu den Paulusbriefen: "eine antipaulinische Theologie hat es natürlich auch und gerade zu Lebzeiten des Paulus gegeben (womit keine Frühdatierung des Jak behauptet werden soll); der Widerspruch gegen Paulus ist überhaupt kein Anhaltspunkt für eine Datierung". Wie wahr!

44. S. R. Heiligenthal, op.cit. (Anm.23), 27ff vgl. 1,2f und 2,22b! Freilich wertet Jak—was H. nicht wahr haben will—damit den Glauben ab: Wenn dieser durch die Werke erst "vollendet werden" muß (2,22b), so deutet er auf einen "unvollkommenen Zustand" hin, der erst durch die hinzutretenden Werke vollkommen wird s. die von H. zitierte Bedeutung von τελειόω bei W. Bauer, WBNT 1602. Die von H. abgelehnte Deutung bei Chr. Burchard ZNW 71 (1980), 42 besteht zu Recht: "V.22 soll nicht bei Abraham eine lebendige . . . Synthese von Glauben und Werken . . . als heilsnotwendig setzen (Mußner), sondern den Glauben herunterspielen". Burchard stellt gleichwohl gegen Lindemann eine antipaulinische Haltung bei Jak in Frage: 44 Anm.o.

45. Es gibt eine ganze Reihe von sprachlichen Anklängen zwischen Jak und Paulus, insbesondere zu Rö: Vgl. z.B. Jk 1,3f und Rö 5,3-5; Jk 2,1 und Rö 2,11; Jk 1,22; 4,11 und Rö 2,13. Th. Zahn, op.cit. (Anm.22), 1, 91-95 vermutete, daß schon "Pl zur Zeit der Abfassung des Rm Stellen des Jk im Sinn hatte" (91); vgl. auch F. Spitta, op.cit. (Anm.4), 209-225; A. Meyer, op.cit. (Anm.4), 86-108, der die Berührungen aus der "gemeinsame(n) Herkunft des Jac und Paulus aus dem hellenistischen Judentum" erklären will (107). Daß Jak durch Gespräche und Mitteilungen Dritter paulinische Formeln und Gedanken kannte, ist selbstverständlich, ja es ist nicht auszuschließen, daß er über den Inhalt des Römerbriefs, der wohl im Winter 56/57 in Korinth, ca 4-6 Monate vor der Jerusalemreise, geschrieben wurde, orientiert worden war. Was er nicht verstand und ablehnte, ist die Dialektik des paulinischen Denkens. Doch wo in der frühen Kirche wurde Pls wirklich ohne Einschränkung verstanden und akzeptiert?

46. Daß sich Jk 2,24 gegen einen paulinischen Kampfsatz wie Rö 3,28 wendet, sollte nicht mehr bestritten werden. Dabei hat Jak das Rö 3,28 sachlich vorausgesetzte μόνον zu Recht eingetragen; entsprechend besteht auch Luthers Übersetzung zu Recht: ". . . das der Mensch gerecht werde/on des Gesetzes werck/*alleine* durch den Glauben". S. dazu A. v. Harnack, Geschichte der Lehre von der Seeligkeit allein durch den Glauben in der alten Kirche, ZThK 1 (1891), 87-178 (97): in Jak 2,24 u. 20-23 "ist der schärfste Gegensatz gegen den Paulinismus ausgesprochen". Jak kommt es entscheidend auf das συνήργει 2,22 an, was Pls entschieden ablehnen mußte. Das Argument, daß dabei nicht zwischen dem auf das Liebesgebot konzentrierte "Gesetz" bei Jak und den "Gesetzeswerken" bei Pls, die sich vor allem auf das Ritualgesetz bezögen, unterschieden werde, geht an der Sache völlig vorbei. Für Paulus fällt auch das Liebesgebot, ja gerade dieses, unter den Satz von Rö 4,15: "denn das Gesetz bewirkt Zorn" vgl. Rö 8,7f. Das Heil wird dagegen bei Jak an vom Menschen zu leistende Bedingungen, eben die "Werke" geknüpft. Daß die "Frucht des Geistes" allem Gottes Werk ist, wird auch in 3,18 gerade nicht gesagt, vielmehr ist dort die "Frucht der Gerechtigkeit" als Lohn τοῖς ποιοῦσιν εἰρήνην vorbehalten. Im Gegensatz zu Pls hat Jak eine "optimistische", "naive" Anthropologie. Es ist der weisheitliche und pharisäische "Synergismus", der hier fortwirkt. S. dazu M. Hengel, Judentum und Hellenismus, WUNT 10, ²1973, 254ff; vgl. Josephus, bell 2,163; ant 18,13f und G. Maier, Mensch und freier Wille, WUNT 12, 1971, dazu

W. Bousset/H. Greßmann, Die Rel. d. Judent. im späthell. Zeitalter, ³1926, 403, der Sir 15,14 mit Jak 1,13-15 vergleicht und G. F. Moore, Judaism, 1927, 2, 453-459.
47. Op.cit. (Anm.1), 249 Anm.111. Vgl. auch D. Lührmann, Πίστις im Judentum, ZNW 64 (1973), 19-38; ders., Glaube im frühen Christentum, 1976, 78ff und besonders den Schlußsatz über Jak 84. Zum Glauben im Judentum und Jak s. die ausführliche Darstellung bei A. Meyer, op.cit. (Anm.4), 123-141. Die zweimalige Rede vom toten Glauben 2,17.26 ist ein polemisches Oxymoron, das sich gegen das paulinische ἐκ πίστεως μόνον wendet. Das Judentum kannte jedoch gegen Meyer die Antithese Glauben-Werke noch nicht.
48. Zu Lk s. einerseits Lk 18,9-14; 15; Apg 13,38f; 20,24.28 vgl. 15,9 und andererseits Apg 10,2ff.35; 17,30f; 24,14-16; 26,20. Im 1.Clem, der mehrere Paulusbriefe kennt, s. den Gegensatz zwischen paulinisch klingenden Formeln wie 32,4; vgl. 8,5; 50,2 und 5,7 und dagegen 30,3 oder 33.1.7. Ein derartiger Gegensatz wie in 1.Clem findet sich im Jak—noch—nicht. Er ist in diesem Punkt "eindeutig".
49. Dibelius,⁶ 279 sieht das Problem und meint, daß "für die Christen eine Gefahr befürchtet (wird), die mit geschäftlichen Plänen und Absichten zusammenhängt". "Die Sache ist anschaulich, aber durchaus nicht spezialisiert gesagt". Das Ungewohnte dieser Polemik ergibt sich aus dem Fehlen der Parallelen. Hermas, sim 6,3,5=63,5 über die ἀκαταστατοῦντες ταῖς βουλαῖς, die vielerlei unternehmen, wegen ihrer bösen Taten aber nichts zuwegebringen und den Herrn beschuldigen, ist sehr viel allgemeiner formuliert und geht in eine andere Richtung. Hermas spricht dabei aus eigener bitterer Erfahrung s. vis 1,3,1f = 3,1, denn er geriet als Freigelassener und (Bau?-) Unternehmer in geschäftliche Schwierigkeiten. H. J. Drexhage, Wirtschaft und Handel in den frühchristlichen Gemeinden, RQ 76 (1981), 1-72 beginnt sein Kapitel "Christen und Handel" (40ff) mit der Purpurhändlerin Lydia, die mit einem ausgesprochenen Luxusgut für die Reichen handelte und springt sofort zu Markion über. Plinius, ep 10,96,9 spricht zwar ca 112 n. Chr.—wohl etwas übertreibend, er muß ja die Gefährlichkeit der Situation hervorheben, um sein Verhalten ins rechte Licht zu stellen—davon, daß multi . . . omnis ordinis gefährdet waren, aber damit ist noch nichts über die Verbreitung christlicher Handelsreisender gesagt. Zur sozialen Rolle des Handels in der frühen Kaiserzeit s. John H. d'Arms, Commerce and Social Standing in Ancient Rome, 1981, dort 23ff zu dem bekannten Cicero-Text.
50. Dibelius,⁶ 274 sieht darin einen an 4,1ff anknüpfenden "Spezialfall weltlicher Gesinnung", wobei der Abschnitt "im Stil prophetischer Ansprache gehalten" ist. "Der Prophet ruft seine Worte unter die Menge ohne Rücksicht darauf, ob seine Anklagen das Ohr der Beschuldigten erreichen". Man dürfte hier keinesfalls Schlüsse auf den Leserkreis ziehen. Im Gegensatz zu der verbreiteten Warnung V.14, daß man nicht wisse, was das Morgen bringt, kann Dibelius zu der recht konkreten Beschreibung V.13 keine Parallele beibringen.
51. Zur Apg s. 15,36-40; 18,21-23; 19,21; 20,1 und 19,1 westl. Text; 20,22: δεδεμένος ἐγὼ τῷ πνεύματι πορεύομαι εἰς Ἰ.; 19,21: δεῖ με καὶ Ῥώμην ἰδεῖν und dazu 23,11 und 28,14. Lk legt großen Wert darauf, die paulinischen Reisepläne nicht als eigene Entschlüsse darzustellen. Zur Zeitdauer vgl. schon Apg 13,2; 16,6-10; 20,3: ποιήσας δὲ μῆνας τρεῖς; 18,11.33; 19,10; 20,31. Zu Pls s. Rö 1,11-15; 15,19.24:ὡς ἂν πορεύωμαι εἰς τὴν Σπανίαν;25:νυνὶ δὲ πορεύομαι εἰς Ἰ.; 1.Kor 4,18-21; 11,34; 16,4-8; 2.Kor 1,15-17; 2,3; 13,1.10; Phil 1,25; 2,24; Phm 22. In den Pastoralbriefen wird dieses fast hektische Planen auch auf die Missionsgehilfen übertragen: 1.Tim 1,3; 2.Tim 4,9-13.20f; Tit 1,5; 3,12. Es gehörte auch später noch zu dem Bild des Pls; vgl. 1.Clem 5,6f. Die späteren Apostelakten haben sich die Apg mit dem rastlos reisenden Pls zum Vorbild genommen.
52. Vgl. 1.Petr 3,1; Mt 18,15. Dieser "missionarische" Sprachgebrauch verschwindet bei den Apostolischen Vätern und Apologeten, vgl. noch Justin, apol. 1,44,13 hier jedoch in etwas anderem Sinn. In Lampe, A Patristic Greek Lexicon ist das Verb nicht mehr aufgeführt.
53. Notes de Lexicographie néo-testamentaire, OBO 22,1,1978, 1, 342. Auch das Gleichnis Mt 25,19-23, wo κερδαίνειν 4 mal für erfolgreiche Bankgeschäfte verwendet wird, könnte von Mt her im Sinne des missionarischen Einsatzes gedeutet werden, vgl. Mt 28,19f: "Im Zusammenhang des Matthäusevangeliums sagt das Gleichnis: In der treuen Verwaltung der anvertrauten Lehre, die . . . in Wort und Werk der Liebe weitergegeben wird, daß sie andere zu ihrem Heil empfangen und gewonnen werden, soll die Zeit ausgefüllt werden bis zur Ankunft des Sohnes des Menschen . . ." W. Grundmann, Das Evg. n. Mt., 1968, 523.

54. Die Petrusbriefe. Der Judasbrief, HThK XIII,2, [3]1964, 205. Vgl. noch Tit 1,11: διδάσκοντες ἃ μὴ δεῖ αἰσχροῦ κέρδους χάριν und 1.Petr 5,2.

55. 12,5 s. dazu M. Hengel, Die Arbeit im frühen Christentum, Theologische Beiträge 17 (1986), 174-212 (203).

56. Suffering and the Spirit, WUNT 2.R.19, 1984, 106ff. Es wird von Platon vor allem den Sophisten zum Vorwurf gemacht.

57. Op.cit., 112. Platon unterscheidet den Kleinhändler (κάπηλος/καπηλεύειν) und den Händler in grössem Stil (ἔμπορος/ἐμπορεύεσθαι). Der Unterschied verwischt sich zwar schon im 4.Jh., s. jedoch W. Bauer, WB, 509 zu ἔμπορος.

58. Rom/Korinth: Apg 18,2; Korinth/Ephesus: 18,18.26; 1.Kor 16,19; Ephesus/Rom: Rö 16,3 und sekundär 2.Tim 4,19. S. dazu W.-H. Ollrog, Paulus und seine Mitarbeiter, WMANT 50, 1979, 24-27 und Index 273 s.v. "(sie) gaben . . . seiner Missionstätigkeit eine gewisse materielle Grundlage". Zur Annahme von Unterstützungen s. 117 Anm.41.

59. Sueton, Caes. 38,2. Zum Tageslohn s. R. Duncan-Jones, The Economy of the Roman Empire, 1974, 54; vgl. auch zur Situation des Lohnarbeiters in der Antike G.E.M. de St. Croix, The Class Struggle in the Ancient Greek World, 1981, 179-204; speziell zu Rom s. D. Nörr, Zur sozialen und rechtlichen Bewertung der freien Arbeit in der sozialen Welt, ZSRG.R 82 (1965), 67-105; John Crook, Law and Life in Rome, 1967, 180.195-200.221ff.

60. Sat 3,223. S. dazu J. Carcopino, Rom. Leben und Kultur in der Kaiserzeit, [2]1979, 74f. 377 Anm.41.

61. Zum Beruf des Paulus s. R. F. Hock, Paul's Tentmaking and the Problem of his Social Class, JBL 97 (1978), 555-564; ders., The Social Context of Paul's Ministry. Tentmaking and Apostleship, 1980.

62. W. Bauer, WB, 1406f; προπέμπειν: Rö 15,24 die Römer nach Spanien; 1.Kor 16,6 und 2.Kor 1,16 die Korinther nach Judäa; Apg 15,3 die Antiochener nach Judäa; vgl. Tit 3,13; 3.Joh 6; Polykarp 1,1. S. dazu A. J. Malherbe, The Inhospitality of Diotrephes, in: God's Christ and His People. Studies in Honour of N. A. Dahl, 1977, 222-232 (230 Anm.11), ihm folgt W. A. Meeks, The First Urban Christians, 1983, 66.

63. 1.Kor 15,10; 2.Kor 10,4ff.12-18; 11,5.21-33; 12,1-5; vgl. auch Rö 1,1; 1.Kor 9,1f; 4,15; selbst die Peristasenkataloge und die aufgezwungene "Narrenrede" in 2.Kor 11 konnten von seinen Gegnern als besonders raffinierter "Selbstruhm" ausgelegt werden. Vorwurf stand hier gegen Vorwurf. Vgl. auch Phil 2,16; 1.Thess 2,19; Rö 1,9-17 und vor allem 15,14-23.

64. S. dazu M. Hengel, Die Ursprünge der christlichen Mission, NTS 18 (1971), 15-38 (17ff) = Between Jesus and Paul, 1983, 48-64 (49ff). Welch ortsgebundenen, lokalen Eindruck macht dagegen die Mission des Hellenisten Philippus in Samaria und der Küstenebene Palästinas, s. M. Hengel, Der Historiker Lukas und die Geographie Palästinas in der Apostelgeschichte, ZDPV 99 (1983), 147-183 (164ff) = Between Jesus and Paul, 1983, 96ff (110ff).

65. S. Dibelius z.St.: "Welche Gründe den Autor hier zur Einfügung des Wortes veranlaßten, ist schwer zu sagen" (275). Der Spruch stehe "isoliert zwischen zwei verwandten Texten".

66. Auf der anderen Seite erscheint das Problem *innerhalb* der paulinischen Gemeinde als strittige Frage nach Ausweis der Briefe nicht mehr. In den Paulusbriefen hören wir expressis verbis nichts mehr von Streitigkeiten zwischen beiden Gruppen in den angeschriebenen Gemeinden selbst. Die Judaisten in Galatien kamen von außen. Vielleicht wird für diese Zeit zwischen 55 und der Zerstörung Jerusalems die Brisanz der Gesetzesfrage *in den Missionsgemeinden* selbst überschätzt. Auch im ca 69/70 entstandenen Markusevangelium ist die Frage nicht mehr von zentraler Bedeutung (s.o.S. 253).

67. Die Übersetzung folgt Windisch, 28; zur Begründung s. Dibelius,[6] 278. Zu Paulus s. gleichlautend 1.Kor 4,19 vgl. 16,7; Rö 1,10; 15,32 gerade im Blick auf seine Reisepläne. Die Hinweise zu den Paulusbriefen zeigen, welche Rolle dieses Motiv in der urchristlichen Diskussion spielt, und wie empfindlich man an diesem Punkt war. Es ging hier um mehr als nur um eine bloße Redensart. Heidnische Parallelen bei Dibelius,[6] 278. Vgl. auch A. Deißmann, Licht vom Osten, [4]1923, 175 Anm.10. Windisch verweist auf Min.Felix, Oct. 18,10f wo das: *si deus dederit* des *consensus omnium* als *vulgi naturalis sermo* bezeichnet wird.

68. Apg 20,38; 21,4; 21,11ff; s. schon Rö 15,31 in Korinth: Paulus scheint geahnt zu haben, daß sein Leben in Jerusalem bedroht war. Ganz anders dagegen noch 1.Kor 16,6: Vielleicht hatte er gegen Ende seines Aufenthalts in Ephesus die Möglichkeit erwogen, von Korinth aus erst nach

Rom weiterzureisen, dies aber dann aufgegeben vgl. Rö 1,13. Dieses ständige "weltweite" Planen und Abwägen könnte einem Lehrer, der bewußt an der stabilitas loci in Jerusalem, dem "Mittellpunkt der Welt", vgl. Hes 38,5; 5,5; Jub 8,19; Hen 26,1; Sib 5,250; Josephus, bell 3,52; bSanh 37a u.ö., festhielt, als vermessen erscheinen.

69. Apg 28,31. Die Apg wurde m.E. zu einer Zeit verfaßt, als man sich in den Gemeinden an Paulus noch erinnerte, d.h. kaum sehr viel später als 80 n.Chr., das Evangelium entstand einige Jahre früher. Das legt auch die noch relativ positive bzw. hoffnungsvolle Beurteilung der römischen Behörden nahe. Prozesse gegen Christen mit Verurteilungen nominis causa kommen erst unter der Herrschaft Domitians auf: 1.Petr 4,15. Jak 2,6f setzt dies noch nicht voraus, s.u.S. 277 Anm.92.

70. Novum Testamentum Graecum II, 1752, Nachdr. Graz 1962, 659. Zum Spätansatz des Jak zu Lebzeiten des Herrenbruders s. die Tabelle bei P. Davids, 4. Vgl. etwa P. Feine/J. Behm, Einleitung in das NT,[9]1950, 244f: "um 65 (!)..., nicht lange vor dem Tode des Jk"; R.St.J. Parry, A Discussion of the General Epistle of St. James, 1903; R. V. G. Tasker, The General Epistle of James, TNTC, 1957 (Nachdr. 1969), 33: "The most probable date of the Epistle would seem to be *circa* A.D. 60." (Kursiv vom Vf.).

71. 1,5 vgl. 3,13 dazu 3,15.17: ἡ ἄνωθεν σοφία. In Jak 2,5 und dem schwierigen "Zitat" 4,5 ist πνεῦμα der nach Gen 2,7 dem Menschen von Gott eingehauchte Lebensodem; s. E. Schweizer, ThWNT VI, 1959, 445. Auch dieser eigenartige Sprachgebrauch ist eines der vielen Indizien für eine frühe Entstehung. Bei den Apostolischen Vätern hat sich diese Relation völlig verschoben. Sie entspricht jedoch jüdischem Sprachgebrauch, etwa der Sap.Sal. 7,22ff. 27; vgl. auch das Gebet Salomos um die Weisheit 9,1ff. Man wird zugleich an die Weisheit in der synoptischen Überlieferung: Mk 6,2 = Mt 13,54; Lk 21,15 vgl. auch Q: Lk 7,52 = Mt 11,19; Lk 11,31 = Mt 12,42 erinnert.

72. Zum Gebet s. Mt 7,11; Gutes = Lk 11,13 (hl. Geist).

73. Vgl. 2.Kor 7,5 ἔξωθεν μάχαι. Die—späteren—Pastoralbriefe machen dafür theologische Diskussionen (mit Irrlehrem) verantwortlich 2.Tim 2,23 vgl. Tit 3,9: davon spricht Jak gerade nicht. Jak: ζῆλος καὶ ἐριθεία (3,14.16 zum letzteren s. W. Bauer, WB 612); Pls: 1.Kor 3,3; 2.Kor 12,20; Gal 5,20; 1.Kor 1,10f: σχίσματα, ἔριδες vgl. 11,18; Gal 5,15; Phil 1,17. Daß die paulinische Verkündigung in Verbindung mit der leidenschaftlichen Persönlichkeit des Apostels auch Gräben aufreißen und zu Spannungen führen konnte, ist offensichtlich. In 1.Clem 3-5 erscheinen ζῆλος καὶ φθόνος; (5,5; 6,4 ζῆλος καὶ ἔρις) als jüdisch- hellenistische Topoi, beziehen sich aber dann doch auf ganz konkrete Vorgänge in der Gemeinde in Korinth. Das Motiv des Streits durchzieht in vielfältiger Variation fast den ganzen Brief—aber bei aller paränetischen Gestaltung mit einem sehr praktischen Ziel: der Wiedereinsetzung der alten Presbyter 47,6; 54,2; 57,1.

74. 2.Kor 12,7; Gal 1,14; 1,Kor 4,16; 11,1; vgl. 1,Kor 9,15 (!) u.a. Zum Apostolat s. 1.Kor 9 und 15,8f.

75. Phil 3,2.18f; Gal 2,4; 3,1; 5,12; 2.Kor 11,5.13ff.20. Vgl. auch Apg 15,39; 13,10f; 1.Kor 5,3f; 4,21; 2.Kor 10,2; 12,21; 13,2.

76. 1.Thess 5,27: ἐνορκίζω ὑμᾶς τὸν κύριον: Man sollte diese "Beschwörung" nicht vorschnell als "dringliche Bitte" abschwächen, so M. Dibelius, 1. und 2.Thess., HNT, 32. Die Frage bleibt doch, warum Paulus so rasch Schwurformeln verwendet. 2.Kor 1,23:ἐγὼ δὲ μάρτυρα τὸν θεὸν ἐπικαλοῦμαι vgl. Rö 1,9; Phil 1,8; 1.Thess 2,5.10 dazu 1.Sam 12,6. Vgl. auch Rö 9,1; 2.Kor 11,31; Gal 1,20; Verfluchungsformeln: 1.Kor 16,22; Gal 1,8; Rö 3,8; vgl. dagegen 12,14 und Jak 3,9f.

77. E. Käsemann, Rö, HNT, 15.

78. Vgl. Mk 13,29 = Mt 24,33; Phil 4,5. Wir haben hier und in 5,8 einen deutlichen Hinweis auf die lebendige Naherwartung des Briefs, den das Gerichtsmotiv wie ein roter Faden durchzieht s. 1,10f.15; 2,12f; 2,24; 3,1; 4,12; 5,5.8.

79. 5,12 schließt an 5,10-13 an und bildet mehr schlecht als recht den Übergang zu der Perikope über den Kranken, Gebet und Sündenbekenntnis. Zugleich weist 5,13a auf 1,2f zurück. Hier könnte man natürlich an den gefangenen Apostel denken. In eigenartiger Nähe und zugleich im Gegensatz dazu Apg 16,25; Hier wird von Lk das κακοπαθεῖν und εὐθεμεῖν in eins zusammengefaßt. Die Gefangenen beten und singen zugleich.

80. M. Hengel, op.cit. (Anm.13), 78. Die Ölsalbung von Kranken ist jüdischer bzw. judenchristlicher Brauch s. Billerbeck 3,51 und H. Windisch, 33. Mk 6,13 weist wohl auf einen Brauch der frühesten palästinischen Gemeinde zurück.

81. Wenn von konkreter Krankheit einzelner Christen berichtet wird, wird sie in der Regel geheilt vgl. Apg 9,32-35. Die andere Möglichkeit besteht in der Krankheit als Strafe und Mittel des göttlichen Gerichts Apk 2,22f; 1.Kor 5,5; 11,30f; pragmatisch Hermas, vis 3,9,3 = 17,3; sim 6,3,4 = 63,4. Eine Ausnahme bildet die Erzählung von der Tochter des Petrus in den koptischen Petrusakten, Hennecke/Schneemelcher, NTA 2, 188f: Sie war halbseitig gelähmt, um sich und andere vor Sünde zu bewahren. Vgl. noch die allgemeine Mahnung 1.Thess 5,14 ἀντέχεσθε τῶν ἀσθενῶν; dazu das Gebet 1.Clem 59,4; Mt 25,36.43. Zum Ganzen s. A. v. Harnack, Mission und Ausbreitung des Christentums, [4]1924, 129ff.147ff.151ff. Eine so distinkte Heilungsverheißung wird jedoch sonst nicht gegeben; s.u. Anm.83.

82. 2.Kor 12,6-10; vgl. Gal 4,13-15; 6,17.S. dazu H. Windisch, 2.Kor., 382-393.

83. Soweit ich sehe, ist dieser Text einzigartig. Das Judentum kennt das Gebet des Zaddiq oder auch des Gelehrten für den Kranken vgl. H. Windisch, Die kath. Briefe, [3]1951, 33. Vgl. A. Meyer, op.cit. (Anm.4), 164f. Nach Koh.R. 1,8 heilt R. Jehoschua seinen von den Judenchristen in Kapernaum "verhexten" Neffen mit Öl, Billerbeck 1, 529. Die Verbindung von Krankenheilung und Sündenvergebung geht auf das Handeln Jesu zurück vgl. Mk 2,5ff; vgl. auch Ps.Clem., ep.Clem. ad Jac. 15,5 (GCS 42,18 ed. Rehm), wo freilich die Krankheit nur eine Metapher für die Sünde ist, von der man durch das Bekenntnis befreit wird. Polykarp, Phil 6,1 spricht in seinem Pflichtenkatalog nur davon, daß die Presbyter die Kranken besuchen; vgl. ähnlich bei Justin, ap. 1,67,6, die Beziehung zu Mt 25 ist offensichtlich. In Jak 5,14 geht es um mehr als um bloße Fürsorge.

84. Vgl. Jak 1,6. Es ist eigenartig, daß wir die nächsten Parallelen zu diesem ganzen Komplex: Gebetsglaube, Sündenvergebung und Heilung bei Jesus finden. Er geht auf das Wirken Jesu zurück: vgl. Mk 9,23f.29; 5,24; 10,52; 11,22f; 2,5-12; 6,5. Zum Sündenbekenntnis vgl. auch Mk 1,5.

85. Vgl. dazu G. Bornkamm, Artk. πρεσβύτερος, ThWB VI, 1959, 664 zu Jak 5,14: die Presbyter erscheinen hier als "einziges Amt" in einem hellenistischen Judenchristentum, das sich nicht mehr lokalisieren läßt (vgl. dazu auch 2,2 εἰς συναγωγὴν ὑμῶν): "So sehr diese Presbyter nach Art eines Synagogen-Vorstandes zu denken sind, so hat die Selbstverständlichkeit der Annahme, daß sie als solche u[nd] insgesamt zum heilkräftigen Gebet befähigt sind, im Judt doch keine Entsprechung, sondern setzt die urchristliche Charismen-Erfahrung voraus". Soweit ich sehe, gibt es dazu auch im Christentum keine eindeutige Parallele. M.E. machte diese Vollmacht das Spezifikum der Presbyter in Jerusalem aus, die sich als Nachfolger der (zwölf) Apostel betrachten konnten, für die die Heilgabe nach der Aussendungsüberlieferung Mk 6,7.13 (Heilung mit Ölsalbung) inhärent war. Auch dieser archaische Zug spricht gegen einen Spätansatz.

86. Vgl. Apg 11,30; 15,2ff: auffallend ist in c.15 das formelhafte οἱ ἀπόστολοι καὶ οἱ πρεσβύτεροι; ohne Apostel 21,18. Auch in Gal 2,1-10 macht die Jerusalemer Gemeinde mit ihren drei "Säulen" den Eindruck, daß hier die "Institutionalisierung" besonders weit fortgeschritten ist. S. auch M. Hengel, op.cit. (Anm.13), 92ff. 102ff.

87. 5,20: ὁ ἐπιστρέψας ἁμαρτωλὸν ἐκ πλάνης ὁδοῦ αὐτοῦ σώσει ψυχὴν αὐτοῦ ἐκ θανάτου καὶ καλύψει πλῆθος ἁμαρτιῶν. Dahinter steht ein beliebtes Zitat aus dem masoretischen Text von Prov 10,12 entspricht: wᵉ'al kol pᵉšā'îm tᵉkassäh 'ahᵈbā. Wir finden es im Gegensatz zu Jak unverändert in 1.Petr 4,8; 1.Clem 49,5; 2.Clem 16,4. In der Didaskalia 2,3 erscheint es als Herrenwort s. A. Resch, Agrapha, [2]1967, 310f. Von Jak wird es als alttestamentliches Wort in eigenwilliger Weise abgewandelt.

88. Rö 16,1f. die Briefbotin Phöbe; 16,4: die Bürgschaftsleistung von Prisca und Aquila; 16,22f: der—selbstbewußte—Briefschreiber Tertius, der Gastgeber Gaius und der Aedil Erastus in Korinth; 1.Kor 1,11: die Leute der Chloe; 16,15-18: Stephanas und sein Haus; Phil 2,25ff; 4,15ff: die Unterstützung durch die Gemeinde in Philippi; 4,22: Angehörige der familia Caesaris vgl. auch 2.Kor 12,13ff; Phm 1ff.18f. Bei Lk ist die Ambivalenz zwischen der positiven Hervorhebung der Armut und des Eigentumsverzichts und der ständigen Erwähnung vornehmer Christen auffällig. Das Werk, das selbst einem Glied der Oberschicht gewidmet ist, verkörpert den Gegensatz zwischen—moderierter—palästinischer Armenfrömmigkeit und der Hochschätzung vornehmer Christen, die für die Gemeindebedürfnisse sorgen. Das Problem findet sich schon in der "Petrusmission": Apg 9,36ff.43; 10,1ff, aber noch viel mehr bei Paulus: 13,12; 16,14.27-34; 17,4f.34; 18,7f; 19,31: Paulus hat φίλοι unter den "Asiarchen", d.h. den Mitgliedern des Provinzlandtages. Zum sozialen Status der paulinischen Missionsgemeinden s. A. Malherbe, Social Aspects of Early Chris-

tianity, 1977; W. A. Meeks, op.cit. (Anm.62), 51-66 und zu den Hauskirchen s. J. Klauck, Hausgemeinde und Hauskirche im frühen Christentum, 1981, 21-68.

89. Paulus geht von einer realen Armut der Jerusalemer Gemeinde aus: "Denn in der jetzigen Zeit (vgl. Rö 3,26; 11,5) soll euer Überfluß für den Mangel jener (in Jerusalem verwendet werden)" 2.Kor 8,14; denn wenn die "Armen der Heiligen in Jerusalem . . . von ihren geistlichen Gütern den Heiden Anteil gegeben haben, so sind diese auch verpflichtet, jenen mit den materiellen Gütern zu dienen" (Rö 15,26f vgl. 2.Kor 9,12). Der Rat von 1.Kor 16,2 setzt voraus, daß die meisten Christen in Korinth ein relativ geregeltes Einkommen hatten.

90. In seinen echten Briefen tritt darum auch die heute so hochgeschätzte "Sozialkritik" ganz zurück. In 1.Kor 1,26 ist das dreifache οὐ πολλοί zu beachten. Paulus sagt nicht "keine".

91. Jak 1,9f. Die Aufforderung 1,10, der Reiche solle sich seiner Niedrigkeit rühmen, ist ironisch gemeint: Er ist ein Nichts, das vergeht. 1,11f: Von Buße und guten Werken ist gegenüber dem Reichen nicht die Rede. Entsprechend ist der Vornehme 2,2ff in der christlichen Versammlung fehl am Platz, er verführt nur Christen zur προσωπολημψία. Der arme Glaubende ist dagegen von Gott erwählt, 2,5; die Reichen sind die Verfolger 2,6f. Für sie, die eo ipso sozial ungerecht sind (5,4), bleibt nur die Klage über das kommende Gericht 5,1ff.

92. Apg 4-7; 12; 1.Thess 2,14f; Jos., ant 20, 200; vgl. auch Mk 13,9 = Mt 10,17: Die palästinischen συνέδρια waren von Vertretern der Oberschicht besetzt; das gilt besonders für das sadduzäische Synhedrium, das Hannas II. im Jahr 62 zusammenrief, um Jakobus und andere Judenchristen zum Tode zu verurteilen. M. Hengel, op.cit. (Anm.13), 73f. Der "gute Name" ist nicht die Bezeichnung χριστιανοί (Apg 11,26; 1.Petr 4,16), sondern der Name Christi, auf den die Christen getauft werden (vgl. 1,18). Er wird über dem Täufling ausgerufen, dagegen von den jüdischen Gegnern verlästert; s. dazu Mt 12,32; Joh 8,48; Mk 15,29 = Mt 27,28; Lk 22,65; Apg 13,45; 18,6; 26,11 = Justin, apol 1,31,6; Apk 2,9.

93. Wenn man Jak 5,5f, wie K. Aland, op.cit. (Anm.30), 243 im Anschluß an die altkirchliche Auslegung (s. dazu Theophylaktos, MPG 125, 1184) vornehmlich auf Jesus bezieht, wird dieser historische Zusammenhang noch deutlicher. Die, die Jesus, den δίκαιος, am Rüsttage vor dem Passamahl (Joh 18,28; 19,14) zu Tode brachten, sie unterdrücken und verfolgen auch die Gemeinde der "Armen" in der darauffolgenden Zeit (2,6). Zu δίκαιος als altertümlichem christologischem Titel s. Apg 3,14; 7,52; 22,14 vgl. Sap 2,10.12.18; Jes 3,10. Bei Jak kann sowohl Jesus wie der Märtyrer gemeint sein. Der eschatologische Bezug von 5,1-11 ist damit nicht aufgehoben.

94. Jos., ant 20, 180f.199f.205ff; s. auch die Klage des Abba Schaul über das Verhalten der führenden hochpriesterlichen Familien TMen 13,21 (Zuckermandel 533) = Pes 57a, dazu J. Jeremias, Jerusalem zur Zeit Jesu, ³1962, 220ff s. auch 258ff.263f. Die sich verschärfenden sozialen Spannungen waren auch eine der Ursachen, die seit dem Tode Agrippas I., 44 n.Chr., allmählich zum jüdischen Krieg führten s. M. Hengel, Die Zeloten, ²1976, 359f. 368f.394f. S. dazu vor allem Jos., bell 2,427. Zum Ganzen s. R. P. Martin, The Life-Setting of the Epistle of James in the Light of Jewish History, in: Biblical and Near Eastern Studies, Essays in Honour of William Sanford LaSor, ed. G. A. Tuttle 1978, 97-103.

95. Dazu M. Hengel, Eigentum und Reichtum in der frühen Kirche, 1973, 39ff.

96. 1.Thess 4,10ff vgl. 2.Thess 3,10ff. Dazu M. Hengel, Die Arbeit im frühen Christentum, Theologische Beiträge 17 (1986), 174-212 (195ff).

97. 1.Kor 4,8; 8,1; 10,23f; Rö 11,18f; 15,1f.

98. Die Formel εἰς συναγωγὴν ὑμῶν ist im urchristlichen Sprachgebrauch, wo man schon sehr früh zwischen ἐκκλησία und συναγωγή unterschied, doch ungewöhnlich s. W. Schrage, Artk. συναγωγή, ThWNT VII, 836. Im NT erscheint es nur hier als Bezeichnung für eine christliche Versammlung bzw. deren Versammlungsort. Die von Schrage aufgeführten patristischen Belege, die sich nur teilweise mit Jak 2,2 berühren, sind nicht gerade zahlreich. Hinter der Formel steht der geläufige jüdische Sprachgebrauch.

99. 1.Kor 12,28 werden die Gaben der "Hilfeleistung" und der "Leitung" bzw. "Organisation" zwar erst an 6. und 7. Stelle genannt, es fällt aber auf, daß gegenüber den von Offenbarungs- und Zungenrede, Weisheit und Erkenntnis faszinierten Korinthern solche prosaischen Gaben überhaupt genannt werden. Es wäre zu überlegen, ob Paulus das ganz ungewöhnliche σὺν ἐπισκόποις καὶ διακόνοις im Philipperpräskript 1,1, das ökonomische "Verwalter" und "Helfer" bedeutet, deswegen hinzufügte, weil er von den Philippern mehrfach tatkräftig unterstützt worden war. Die

κοπιῶντες und προιστάμενοι 1.Thess 5,12 (vgl. 1.Kor 16,16; Rö 12,8; 16,6.12) waren ja doch in der Regel solche Gemeindeglieder, die a) Zeit für die Gemeinde hatten, weil sie nicht durch ihren täglichen Broterwerb gebunden waren, und b) die—wie es im antiken Gemeindewesen viel verbreiteter war als heute—ihr Vermögen für den gemeinen Nutzen einsetzen konnten.

100. Er findet sich im NT nur noch negativ in Kol 2,18 (vgl. 23) und in dem "offiziellen" Gespräch des Paulus mit Agrippa II. Apg 26,5 für die jüdische Gottesverehrung. Die Vulgata übersetzt in allen vier Fällen mit religio. Der palästinische Priestersohn und Hellenist Josephus verwendet dagegen das Wort besonders gerne. Jak 1,27 für sich genommen könnte eine Distanz gegenüber dem Kult zum Ausdruck bringen, wie wir ihn bei Mt etwa 9,13 u. 12,7 finden. Bei den Apostolischen Vätern haben wir den Begriff bezeichnenderweise nur bei dem Römer Clemens, 1.Clem 45,7; 62,1 (lat.: cultus), Justin meidet ihn ganz. Erst bei Melito und Tatian taucht er wieder auf. Auch dieser Sprachgebrauch stammt aus der hellenistischen Synagoge.

101. Vgl. 1.Kor 16,3f; 2.Kor 1,6; 8,19ff; und die Liste Apg 20,4f, die noch unvollständig ist s. 21,29, auch Lk wird dazuzurechnen sein. Allein die Reisekosten der Gruppe waren beträchtlich. Die Jerusalemer mögen diese Fremden aus der "Diaspora" angestaunt haben wie arme Christen der dritten Welt die reichen Besucher des kirchlichen Jet-Set aus Europa oder Nordamerika.

102. S. dazu M. Hengel, op.cit. (Anm.13), 85-88: Zur späteren Funktion des Jak als "Offenbarungsmittler" in der ebionitischen Tradition.

103. Bei einem späteren Pseudepigraphon hätte seine Würde als Bruder des Herrn kaum gefehlt. Die pseudepigraphischen Paulus- und Petrusbriefe (1.u.2.Tim; Tit; ad Laodic. Text bei J. B. Lightfoot, St. Paul's Epistles to the Colossians and Philemon, 1875, 359 haben den Aposteltitel. Daß er in der epistula Petri ad Jac (Ps.Clem. Hom. GCS 42 p.1) fehlt, ist verständlich: bei der unterwürfigen Anrede Πέτρος Ἰακώβῳ τῷ κυρίῳ καὶ ἐπισκόπῳ τῆς ἁγίας ἐκκλησίας ist für den Aposteltitel des Schreibers kein Platz mehr. Der Judasbrief kopiert das Jakobuspräskript, erläutert den eigenen Namen durch ein ἀδελφὸς δὲ Ἰακώβου; ähnlich hat Ps.Titus in seinem Brief über die Keuschheit in der Subscriptio die Erläuterung "Titus, der Schüler des Paulus" s. Hennecke/Schneemelcher, NTA 2, 109.

104. Sie ist kaum ein Argument gegen einen relativ frühen Ansatz. Daß der Brief in den heidenchristlichen Gemeinden trotz aller stilistischen Bemühung—aufgrund seines schweren christologischen Defizits und seines harschen Tones—wenig Anklang fand, ist verständlich. Für die paulinischen Gemeinden war er zu verletzend, für die anderen zu wenig konkret und zu allgemein. In Rom war er immerhin bis zur Zeit des Hermas noch bekannt. Der im antignostischen Kampf brauchbare sekundäre Judasbrief hat ihn überholt. Man bedenke, wie vollständig die noch in das 2.Jh. zurückgehende Epistula ad Diognetum trotz ihres theologischen Gehalts in der alten Kirche übersehen wurde, so daß man auch heute noch fragen kann, ob es sich nicht um eine geschickte humanistische Fälschung handelt (was ich nicht glaube). Der Hirte des Hermas hat dagegen—trotz seiner späten Entstehung—rasch weite Verbreitung gefunden. Es ist verständlich, daß der eher großbürgerliche Clemens Alex., selbst wenn er den Jakobusbrief in seinen Hypotyposen erklärte, ihm distanziert gegenüberstand, während ihn der Asket Origenes geschätzt hat.

The Opponents of Paul in 2 Corinthians: An Old Issue Revisited

Ralph P. Martin

I. Introduction

The sub-title of this short essay is meant to remind us that as early as the Marcionite Prologues to the *corpus paulinum* the question of how the Corinthian church was beset by controversy has been discussed. The Prologue writer comments:

> The Achaeans heard the word of truth *(verbum veritatis)* from the apostle and were in several ways *(multifarie)* perverted by false apostles, some by the verbal eloquence of philosophy, other led on by the sect of the Jewish law.

R. J. Hoffmann[1] has recently remarked on this text as evidence of a surprisingly "modern" recognition that Paul had to face a variety of opponents at Corinth. In an area of debate which has evoked the widest range of possibilities, of identities and counter-proposals, there is general agreement[2] that a distinct shift in the nature of the opposition that appeared at Corinth from the evidence in 1 Corinthians to the situation described in 2 Corinthians may be seen. In 1 Corinthians the internal divisions are occasioned by Corinthian factionalism (1:10-16; 3:21, 22) and aggravated by notions of a "realized" eschatology (4:8; 15:12) that Paul judged to be erroneous. Enthusiastic practices in worship and libertine morality seem clearly to stem from the false idea of a baptismal resurrection which conferred an exalted status exploited by some of the church people.

When 2 Corinthians was written—whether it was composed in stages or as a whole—Paul is on the defensive for other reasons. To be sure, there is a verbal link between ἐγὼ δὲ Χριστοῦ in 1 Cor 1:12 and the expression Χριστοῦ εἶναι in 2 Cor 10:7, and the charismatic and spiritual phenomena on display according to the canonical first letter may well have paved the way for the problems which came to the surface and were addressed in the second letter. But the locus of the debate has evidently moved. In 1 Corinthians the defense of Paul is conducted in terms of his gospel of the resurrection hope that requires an interim between the "already" and the "not yet" elements (cf. 1 Cor 15:23, 36), and there is no *direct* evidence that his apostolate was under suspicion, even if certain parts of 1 Cor 15 may contain hints that he was disdained, e.g. 1 Cor 15:8, 9. When we turn to the later correspondence it is apparent that Paul's entire mission to Corinth as "an apostle of Christ Jesus by the will of God" (2 Cor 1:1) is being seriously questioned and denied. So far there would seem to be a unanimous opinion. The Marcionite prologue writer joins all the evidence together and speaks only of "false apostles." Modern scholars see a development from one part of the Pauline correspondence to the later.

It is also a well-considered view, stated by the honoree of this *Festschrift*, that the identity of Paul's opponents at Corinth comes into clearer focus when we consider 2 Cor 10–13. E. E. Ellis writes:[3]

> Of the various Pauline letters in which opponents or false teachers appear, 2 Cor 10–13 presents perhaps the most detailed picture. The section gives both Paul's accusations against the opponents and, in one or two instances, their own perception of their status and mission.

The aim of what follows is to use this citation as a "text," and to submit that it could be enriched in one particular way. The four chapter letter which, in our view, represents a later response to developments at Corinth and was sent subsequent to the dispatch of 2 Cor 1–9 (or conceivably 2:14–7:4) holds much valuable information not only of the opponents' "own perception of their status and mission" but *also of their perception of Paul's claim to apostleship as well.* We are indeed fortunate, in our reading of this complex document, to overhear, in addition to the claims registered by Paul's rivals, their own estimate and evaluation of his apostolic office— or rather, of the ways they found that apostolate to be deficient and discredited. A further presupposition of this study, which acknowledges the stimulus received from Earle Ellis' remarkably full and provocative essay on "Paul and his Opponents", is that not only does the seriousness of Paul's attitude to his rivals increase when it comes to his composing 2 Cor 10–13, but it is possible to detect an increasingly stronger tone emerging within the flow of the four chapters. We propose that a turning point is seen at 11:1-4, and that Paul's cognizance of the danger increased as he committed his highly charged and emotional thoughts to written form. The thesis offered is that Paul came to see that the fundamental issue before the church at Corinth was his understanding of the kerygmatic nature of the Christian message, embodied not only in proclamation but just as tellingly in the lifestyle of its accredited messengers. For Paul it was his apostleship that was on trial at Corinth, and a threat to his mission strategy that made his base at Corinth of vital consequence for the next phase of what he planned (a visit to Jerusalem with the collection, a long-desired trip to Rome, a projected expansion of mission work westward to Spain) was indeed a serious issue. He needed to win Corinth over to his side for these pragmatic, practical (and eschatological; see Rom 15:23-29) reasons. But, even more importantly, Paul must make it clear that his version of the kerygma is the only one that gives validity to an apostolic authority whose strength is determined by "the word of the cross." Such a "word" is more than can be expressed by verbal preaching, important as that may be; it is an authority that sets forth a way of life which carries its own validating force (6:4-10; 11:22-24). The apostle was not only a preacher of the Passion story; he also lived it out.[4]

C. K. Barrett's reminder that what Paul faced at Corinth is "one of the crucial questions for the understanding of the New Testament and the origins of Christianity" is in order.[5] He goes on to explain why this is so. Paul's adversaries claimed ultimate authority for their beliefs, which ran diametrically opposite to Paul's both in content and application. "No exposition of New Testament theology that by-passes this problem (of theological conflict) can be satisfactory, and it is one that runs deep, not only into formal Christology, but into the meaning of history and the nature of authority."[6]

This quotation sets an imposing agenda which this modest contribution is not adequate to address. All it seeks to do is to shed some little light, we hope, on a series of baffling verses in Paul's letter and to etch a little more sharply the profile of Paul's opponents at Corinth.

II. Paul's Opponents as "Judaizers"

Since F. C. Baur was the first to find in the opposition Paul encountered the decisive key to the apostle's writings,[7] it is both convenient and appropriate to begin with his views of the Corinthian scene. Building on the datum of 1 Cor 1:12, Baur found the identity of Paul's opponents in those who came to the city as emissaries of Peter and claimed to be "of Christ" (2 Cor 10:7). In more recent times this link between the rival mission and a Petrine group has been advocated by D. W. Oostendorp[8] who maintains that the opponents advocated a "Jewish Christian superiority" and C. K. Barrett who gives a more nuanced definition of their relationship to Peter. The latter regards the intruders as Jews from Jerusalem who came on to the scene as Judaizers, i.e. they were intent on fomenting trouble for Paul and his cause since they claimed to represent the mother church and to draw upon the prestige of Peter, whether with or without his consent. Barrett's phrase to qualify the relationship is: "Peter, in the hands of those who made use of him, was on the way to ruining Paul's work at Corinth."[9] He is thus able to deflect the obvious objections that (1) Peter's name does not occur in 2 Corinthians, even if there are some cryptic allusions to a person (or persons) who could conceivably be linked with him; (2) Paul does not repudiate the ὑπερλίαν ἀπόστολοι (11:5, 12:11) whom Barrett equates with the Jerusalem leaders but, on the contrary, speaks in mild tones of their status, while opposing virulently the men spoken of in 11:13-15; and (3) Paul never utters a word of denunciation throughout these chapters of the features which marked his debate with Judaizers in Galatia and (presumably) at Philippi: circumcision, sabbath rites, dietary codes and above all obedience to Torah as salvific. Barrett's response to the last point is to plead that Jewish Christianity was not monolithic but sufficiently broad to include Jewish missionaries who did not insist on circumcision.

Barrett's position has been subjected to criticism on many grounds. For one thing, the importance he gives to Peter as a presence at Corinth has been faulted.[10] Then, it has been argued that his distinction between the ὑπερλίαν ἀπόστολοι and those branded as ψευδαπόστολοι cannot be sustained, and in fact it is an unnecessary distinction since it is James, not Peter, who is the anti-Paul figure represented by these intruders.[11] They arrived at Corinth with a portfolio of missionary recruitment which aimed at attacking Paul for his (alleged) subverting of Mosaic authority (cf. Acts 21:21, 25, 26) and his abandoning of the decree (Acts 15:19-21) as well as espousing a wrongheaded christology (11:4: the "other Jesus" in this view is ebionite). Yet again, Barrett's reconstruction has been judged defective because it keeps the ὑπερ–λίαν ἀπόστολοι and the "false apostles" separate, whereas (it is argued) they are to be equated and identified with Peter and the close associates who looked to him as their model. There was, according to this alternative, a rift between Paul and Peter who comes in for the severe rebuke of 11:13-15 because he acted through his representatives as the mouthpiece of Satan at Corinth as at Galatia (Gal 2:11-14), and stood condemned. Paul is not sure whether this defection from his gospel has occurred at Corinth or whether Peter himself is implicated, so he defended his apostolic status and issued a fierce judgment on the intruders "just in case some of the original apostles might be included amongst his opponents."[12]

None of these counter-proposals is really convincing. A group linked with Peter, at least in the background of 10:12-18, seems pretty well assured, given the debate over the territorial limits of mission which in turn can only be made comprehensible in the light of the missionary concordat of Galatians 2:7-10 involving Peter. To appeal to the witness of James in Acts 21:20-25 and to trace at Corinth the echoes of a debate over the writ of the Apostolic decree and circumcision is to run against the argument that these rituals and proscriptions are singularly absent from 2 Cor 10–13. Nor is the bringing in of Rom 16:17-20[13] really illuminating in spite of some verbal agreements, given the problematic provenance of that part of the Roman letter and our uncertainty as to the church situation the text there has in view, whether at Rome or Ephesus. It has hardly a direct bearing on the Corinthian scene.

Finally, the attempt to make Peter into the "bogeyman" of 2 Cor 10–13 is no more successful and turns the wheel of criticism a full circle, reverting to F. C. Baur in the last century. To moderate the Baur hypothesis by conceding that Paul was not altogether sure of Peter's presence or influence or that Peter's opposition in the person of his followers was only temporary or that Paul's language in 11:13-15 may be treated as "exaggerated"[14] scarcely inspires conviction that a definite identity-label for the opponents has been found.

So Barrett's basic premise convincingly argued for by E. Käsemann[15] that there were two groups in Paul's mind: οἱ ὑπερλίαν ἀπόστολοι and οἱ ψευδαπόστολοι, seems well-founded, though we may reserve judgment on his more ambitious effort to affirm confidently that they were "Jews, Jerusalem Jews, Judaizing Jews."[16]

III. The Opponents as "Hellenists"

Perhaps the most disquieting element in the proposal that Paul is answering "Judaizing Jews" in his apologia of 2 Cor 10–13 lies in the ground on which he confronts them. C. K. Barrett slips in an aside which he does not seem to justify when he writes: "the Corinthians, confronted by these rival apostolates, proceeded to compare and to judge between them *on essentially hellenistic grounds.*"[17] The question is raised, why did the debate over apostleship center on the struggle between two types of legitimation and be expressed in fundamentally Greek idioms, so that recent interpreters are able to see in Paul's struggle the defense of the "fool" against the "wise" patterned on the contest between the philosopher and the sophist in Greek society? In reviewing the nature of his engagement with its free use of such rhetorical devices as exaggeration, parody, sarcasm, irony, mock humility, and "comparison" *(synkrisis)*[18] we seem to have moved a long way from the debate involving Paul and the Judaizers in Galatia. Barrett's only response is that the intruding apostles themselves were obligated to the Corinthians for the terms in which the dispute was conducted (he thus explains the abrupt transition from 11:4 to 11:5, 6). This concession leads to the unusual conclusion that it is the Corinthians who are dictating the procedures to be followed by the two rival apostolic representatives.[19] It is noted by Käsemann[20] as a compelling reason why the "bearers of satanic deception" in 11:4 (cf. 11:13-15) cannot be the same as the super-apostles of 11:5 with whom Paul favorably compares himself, given the "erratic" *(sprunghaft)* transition from v 4 to v 5. The conclusion is "unusual", because repeatedly Paul charges his readers with the accusation that it is they who have given hospitality to the encroaching teachers who have come on the scene from the outside—a datum which Barrett has done so much to argue for with cogency. See 11:4 (λαμβάνετε . . . ἐδέξασθε . . . ἀνέχεσθε),19 (ἀνέχεσθε), 20 (ἀνέχεσθε . . . λαμβάνει).

Discontent with the hypothesis of the Baur-Barrett-Thrall axis has led to some fresh proposals, all of which introduce features drawn from the hellenistic world. One of the early proponents of a view, diametrically opposed to Baur, was W. Lütgert[21] whose influence may be seen on R. Bultmann[22] and W. Schmithals[23] as well as in a measure on W. G. Kümmel[24] and H. Windisch.[25] Lütgert described the enemies in Paul in terms of pneumatics who had recourse to their possession of gnosis to account for their "inspiration," and thereby their libertine practices. They claimed to represent an advance on Paul's teaching and a pushing of his position of *sola fide sola gratia* to an antinomian extreme which he disavowed. Bultmann[26] developed his overall viewpoint by describing the adversaries as "Gnostic pneumatics" who falsified Paul's gospel—as he would judge them—by exercising their ἐξουσία, by taking pride in their status, and generally by adopting an overbearing attitude in regard to the congregation. Schmithals[27] elaborates this understanding, mainly in the direction of finding the root disagreement in christology, i.e., the false teachers were docetics who despised the earthly Jesus in favor of their confidence in the powerful aeon, the heavenly Christ. Kümmel[28] was content to see only affinities with the gnosticizing groups opposed in 1 Corinthians and, while those groups may have emerged from Palestine, they did not necessarily come from Jerusalem. Windisch[29] agreed on their Jewish character and found their genius in what Paul deemed to be pride in their "enthusiasm"—an echo of Lütgert. This was a trait to be picked up and made the linchpin of an elaborate model in the hands of D. Georgi[30] and G. Friedrich,[31] to whom we now turn.

At the center of Georgi's presentation is the postulating of a group of itinerant hellenistic Jewish missionaries whose appeal was in their christology and its associated lifestyle. They patterned their own preaching and way of life on the figure of a"divine man" linked with their perception of a charismatic wonder-working Jesus. But this character of a powerful presence and miracle-activity is equally to be seen in the great men of the Old Testament like Abraham and Moses as these characters were romanticized in hellenistic Judaism (e.g., by Philo Judaeus). They also came to Corinth with a "missionary self-consciousness"[32] seen in their letters of accreditation (3:1-3) and insistence on the right to maintenance by the congregation (12:13). The latter practice is taken to stem directly from their connection with the Jerusalem leaders who, in turn, were responsible for the claim that apostolic ministry is validated by imposing on the congregation. Such validity was also supported by an appeal to miracles, visions and demonstrations of the Spirit (12:12). The tracing back of charismatic phenomena as a sign of a valid ministry to Palestinian Christianity is not a new discovery. T. W. Manson[33] argued exactly for this point. It has recently been put on a firm exegetical basis from the Gospel and Corinthian studies of G. Theissen,[34] and with an appeal to the history of Jewish prophets with their "signs and wonders" to accredit them by P. W. Barnett.[35]

Two observations in Georgi's novel reconstruction are worth a mention, even if the final verdict may have to be a negative one on the ground that the identifiable "type" of the hellenistic θεῖος ἀνήρ has an inbuilt ambiguity and there is no certain evidence that the "divine man" persona was ever such a wonderworker[36] as Georgi's theory required. On one issue, Georgi's study has proved illuminating, namely that he has taken seriously the earlier innovative proposal of Käsemann to do with the main issue debated at Corinth. The nub of the discussion which polarized the apostle and his opponents is the "principle of legitimation" *(Traditionsprinzip)* by which the claims of the true apostle are certified to the congregation.[37] The issue turns on the question, what are the authentic evidences to be weighed and who at Corinth can lay claim to such credentials? This argument over "criteria of legitimacy" is plain in 13:1-6; and, according to Käsemann,[38] it lies in the center of the apologetic argument in 2 Cor 10–13, Georgi has put a sharper point on this, while H.-D. Betz[39] has given it an even clearer definition with his setting of the issue of δοκιμή in the framework of the philosopher-sophist encounter. The opponents' appeal to their charismatic powers and their claim to be the mouthpiece of divine revelation are the central matters underlying Paul's response as he seeks to defend himself and his ministry against the charge that it is ineffectual (10:10; 11:6) and (ironically) lacking in the very gifts on which they prided themselves (12:11, 12).

The second major contribution of Georgi's study stems from his assertion that "the distinction [between Paul and his opponents] is above all in christology."[40] In this statement attention is focused on a text that is often regarded as too enigmatic for much use to be made of it, viz. 11:4 and the witness to a gospel proclaiming "a rival Jesus" (ἄλλον Ἰησοῦν) and "a different spirit" (πνεῦμα ἕτερον). For Georgi these designations are taken with all solemnity to mean a characterization of Jesus which Paul regarded as anathema, i.e., a pneumatic, non-crucified Jesus who was a stranger to suffering, failure and weakness. As these missionaries based their apostolic life on such a role model they too took a stance on their lordly bearing in the congregation, and so (in Paul's eyes) manifested an "alien spirit" that ran counter to his gospel. By contrast, he could point only to his weakness and humiliation, which in turn were patterned on the incarnate and self-denying Jesus who was "crucified in weakness" (13:4; see, too, 4:10-12; 8:9). Paul's experiences of personal shame (11:23-33) and the painful thorn that "spoilt" his ecstatic gift (12:6-10) are rehearsed as part of his set piece of apology, and turn a pretentious aretalogy into a telling parody to illustrate the axiom: "When I am weak, then I am filled with power" (12:10). His deportment marked by ὑπομονή qualified his entitlement to having "the signs of an apostle" (12:12).

Not the least merit in proposing this setting of christology as the crux of the debate is that Georgi is able to appeal to the entire second letter, especially the key verses of 2:17; 3:1-18 and 5:16, though he does concede that the argument moves forward in stages until its climax in the last four chapters.

As a refinement of Georgi's proposal we may cite G. Friedrich's line of reasoning which strikes out in a new way. Instead of building too much on figures drawn from the world of hellenistic religiosity (the θεῖοι ἄνδρες), he bids us to consider examples in early Christianity.[41] In particular, there are Stephen and Philip (Acts ch. 6–8) who fill the role of "enthusiastic" leaders, charged with obvious charisma and evidently key figures in early Christianity, who in turn gathered followers (Acts 6:9, 10; 8:2; cf. Philip in 8:6; 11:19, 20; 21:8, 9). Stephen is said to have had dramatic power in speech and reasoning (λόγος; cf. 2 Cor 10:10, 11) and Philip performed "signs" (σημεῖα) and "deeds of power" (δυνάμεις, 8:5-13). "Wonders and signs" are attributed to Stephen (6:8) and there are visions and prophecies (7:55; 21:9) and one example of an ecstatic experience (8:39). Stephen's speech began with the note of "glory" (7:2) and his life closed with the same theme (7:55, 56), with Moses characterized as a divinely appointed and wonderworking leader an important point in his speech (7:20-36). Friedrich's conclusion is that from the circle around Stephen which revered Jesus as a second Moses, not the suffering servant of God, a mission came to Corinth to challenge Paul's gospel and to extol the virtues of a hellenized version of the kerygma evident both in theological/christological emphases and in a power-laden lifestyle.

This imaginative hypothesis has to overcome a series of objections such as the reason why Paul did not more closely identify the opponents[42] if they represented envoys who carried the torch of Stephen and Philip. The former, of course, did not survive the ordeal of lynch-law to approve or disapprove of these men; and, according to Acts 21, Paul's later relations with Philip and his prophetically gifted family were cordial. But Luke's tendency is to overlook serious rifts in Paul's attitude to Jerusalem-Palestine and vice versa. Then there is the witness of 2 Cor 11:22 where the opponents' claims are based on their being Ἑβραῖοι. But this is an ambiguous term, and seems to mean no more than Jews speaking Aramaic (or Hebrew) as their "mother tongue," while not ignorant of Greek.[43] The objection that Paul would not have challenged them on this point if they were "hellenists" loses much of its force, however, once we recall that, whatever their precise self-designation may have been, he too entered that claim to identity for himself (11:22); and from all that we know Paul's roots were in the hellenized Jewish world of the Dispersion just as Stephen's were.

IV. Paul's Opponents: A Proposal

Without reviewing the strengths and weaknesses of the rival identities—and in this field of inquiry all we can do is to try to frame a theory that takes in as much of the data as we may—let us offer a tentative proposal. Three exegetical questions seem to be the most intractable, but they are essential to any reconstruction.

(1) A major issue centers on the relationship between "the (exalted) apostles" (οἱ [ὑπερλίαν] ἀπόστολοι of 11:5; 12:11), texts which are both heavily weighted by irony, and the ψευδαπόστολοι who in 11:13-15 are fiercely lambasted as Satan's agents for pretending to be what they palpably are not, i.e., ἀπόστολοι Χριστοῦ, and so they are exposed to divine judgment. Paul's attitude to the former group is deferential and respectful; to the latter he is implacably hostile. The former may rightly be called ἀπόστολοι; but Paul will not dignify the second group in 11:13-15 with any such title. Their title is διάκονοι —to which he supplies αὐτοῦ, sc. "of Satan." This is consistent with 11:22, 23 where the reply to the set of rhetorical questions is, in reference to διάκονοι Χριστοῦ εἰσιν; not "I am too" (κἀγώ), but "I am more one than they (ὑπὲρ ἐγώ)—even if I am out of my senses in claiming this."[44] Yet Paul's claim to be ἀπόστολος Χριστοῦ 'Ιησοῦ beginning with 1:1 is a *leitmotif* in the entire letter. So there are two distinct groups, however related, in ch. 11, as Käsemann and Barrett have maintained. And the simplest view is that the "'exalted' apostles" represent the Jerusalem leaders, while the "false apostles" may be identified as emissaries either sent with or claiming to be sent with their support. Again, it is more natural to suppose that the ψευδαπόστολοι were acting *ultra vires* in coming to Corinth. They then constituted a rival mission, and posed a threat to Paul's work.

(2) The Pauline apostolate at Corinth is the theme of the complex section found in 10:12-18. The most plausible interpretation of the phrase τὸ μέτρον τοῦ κανόνος[45] is that Paul is defending his "sphere of service" demarcated by the accord of Gal 2:7-

10, and is insisting that he has every right to be in Corinth which was in the *Missionsgebiet* of his "preaching to the Gentiles." But while Paul is on the defensive and is resisting the charge that he is no genuine apostle, he is content to grant that there is a proper sphere of service which "another" (10:16) may rightfully occupy, and he will respect that allocation. That "division of labor," again reflecting the working agreement in Gal 2 is important for Paul because only as his mission at Corinth is seen to be valid and his competency (ἱκανότης, 2:14–3:6)[46] respected can he plan to venture out in further missionary work to the Gentiles (10:16).

We may trace here the awareness in Paul's mind of the strategic importance of Corinth as a power base from which he intended to launch a westward extension of his work as a prelude to the end-time. The obverse side of this mission strategy, as we have suggested, is the sad fact that he had become alienated from Antioch and had lost the support of fellow believers in the Syrian province and the holy land of Israel. His energy devoted to raising the "collection for the saints" may be understood on this basis, namely as a fervent effort on his part to cement relations between his congregations and the mother church, and a plea for his acceptance by the Jewish wing of the church, as he came to Jerusalem bearing gifts (2 Cor 8:12-15; Rom 15:25-33).

(3) The exegetical crux in 2 Cor 11:4, 5 must now be addressed afresh. Käsemann, as we saw, noted the sudden "jump" from v 4 with its exposé of false teaching to v 5 and its moderate tone.[47] Some scholars such as Bultmann find the leap too much to explain, and conclude that Paul's writing requires an identity between the men in 11:4, 5 and the "messengers of Satan" in 11:13-15. Barrett finds an easing of the tension in his suggestion—if I understand it—that v 5 brings in the "pillar" apostles at Jerusalem as "referees"[48] to test the claims of the rival gospel and their respective preachers (Paul, the ψευδαπόστολοι).

Perhaps a variation of this offers a solution and a way out of an impasse. Paul needed to adopt an ambivalent attitude, given the delicacy of the situation at Corinth and the prospect he cherished of future mission service. He must keep good relations with Jerusalem and pay respect to the "pillar" leaders whom he puts in their place in a slightly derogatory way, while mindful of their status and cognizant of the claim they have to occupy their sphere of mission work (10:13-18). When, however, in the sequential flow of the letter, a threatened danger from the Antiochian hellenistic faction appears on the scene, heralded clearly in 11:4 by ὁ ἐρχόμενος and with as a new factor a triadic description of "another Jesus, a rival gospel, an alien spirit" which gives evidence of how serious the threat was, Paul appeals to "the 'exalted' apostles" over the heads of the intruders. While he seems to be answering the accusations that he is inferior to the *Urapostel* he is really using them to defeat the real enemy, the proponents of a "gospel" he regards as antithetical to his own.

The reasons for Paul's virulent antagonism to those whose chief disgrace (in his sight) was that they claimed to be the sort of Christian leaders they were not, and asserted that they were "like us" (11:12) show how much was at stake. At issue was nothing less than an attack on his apostleship as ineffective and bogus, a falsifying of his gospel of the crucified Jesus whose "strength is perfected in weakness" (interpreting 12:10 in the light of 13:1-4), and a portrayal of the Christian life as assertive and domineering, far removed from humiliation, shame and frailty. These three accusations which we know from Paul's counter-arguments may all be summed up in the contrast between a *theologia gloriae* and Paul's adhering to an embodiment of a *theologia crucis*. If that is the case, C. K. Barrett's assessment of the nature of this

Auseinandersetzung[49] at the heart of 2 Corinthians quoted earlier is exactly to the point and in no way exaggerates. At the heart of Paul's theology as *verbum veritatis* is the cross of Jesus and the weakness of Paul his suffering, sick apostle.[50] The *carmen Christi* of Phil 2:6-11 in its first draft seen as a triumph song of the enthroned Lord and powerful cosmocrat and not too imaginatively traced to hellenistic Christianity and Stephen's school[51] needed the Pauline insertion of θανάτου δὲ σταυροῦ (v 8c), "the death of the cross," to give it its authentically Christian rationale.[52] It both set the standard as the central element of Paul's kerygma and gave the pattern of his Christian living and service. It was his response to his opponents at Corinth (and Philippi), and now offers paradigm for all subsequent Christian ministry, a theme to which Earle Ellis has also devoted considerable attention.[53]

288 | The Opponents of Paul in 2 Corinthians

Notes

1. R. J. Hoffmann, *Marcion: On the Reconstitution of Christianity.* An Essay on the Development of Radical Paulinist Theology in the Second Century. AAR Academy Series 46, Chico, CA, 1984, 88.

2. Expressed by C. K. Barrett, "Christianity at Corinth," in *Essays on Paul*, London, Philadelphia, 1982, 2. Originally in *BJRL* 46 (1964) 269-97.

3. E. Earle Ellis, "Paul and his Opponents. Trends in [the] Research," cited from his *Prophecy and Hermeneutic in Early Christianity.* New Testament Essays, WUNT 18, Tübingen, 1978 = Grand Rapids, 1978, 102. Originally in *Christianity, Judaism and Other Greco-Roman Cults . . .* for Morton Smith, ed. J. Neusner. 4 vols. Leiden, 1975, 1, 264-298.

4. So G. Friedrich, "Die Gegner des Paulus im 2 Korintherbrief" in *Abraham unser Vater.* Festschrift für Otto Michel, ed. O. Betz, M. Hengel & P. Schmidt, Leiden/Köln, 1963, 189, appealing to A. Schlatter, *Paulus, der Bote Jesu,* Stuttgart, 1969, 553.

5. C. K. Barrett, "Paul's Opponents in 2 Corinthians," in *Essays on Paul* (as in n. 2) 60. Originally in *NTS* 17 (1970-71) 233-254.

6. Ibid.

7. F. C. Baur, *Paul the Apostle of Jesus Christ.* Tr. E. Zeller, London, 1876. See Ellis, "Paul and his Opponents" (as in n. 3) 88.

8. D. W. Oostendorp, *Another Jesus. A Gospel of Jewish Christian Superiority in II Corinthians,* Kampen, 1967.

9. C. K. Barrett, "Cephas and Corinth," *Essays on Paul,* (as in n. 2) 38. Originally in *Abraham unser Vater* (as in n. 4) 1- 12.

10. Hoffmann, *Marcion* (as in n. 1) 90 n. 51.

11. P. W. Barnett, "Opposition in Corinth," *JSNT* 22 (1984) 3-17.

12. M. E. Thrall, "Super-Apostles, Servants of Christ, and Servants of Satan," *JSNT* 6 (1980) 42-57 (49).

13. Cf. Barnett (as in n. 11) 6, 7.

14. Thrall (as in n. 12) 55.

15. E. Käsemann, *Die Legitimität des Apostels.* Eine Untersuchung zu II Korinther 10-13, Darmstadt, 1956, 12-30. Originally in *ZNW* 41 (1942) 33-71.

16. Barrett, "Opponents" (as in n. 5) 80 (italics added).

17. Barrett, "Opponents" (as in n. 5) ibid.

18. See for these rhetorical features, J. Zmijewski, *Der Stil der paulinischen "Narrenrede."* *Analyse der Sprachgestaltung in 2 Kor 11, 1-12, 10 als Beitrag zur Methodik von Stiluntersuchungen neutestamentlicher Texte,* Köln-Bonn, BBB 52, 1978.

19. Barrett, "Opponents" (as in n. 5) 71; cf. C. Kruse, *New Testament Foundations of Ministry,* London, 1983, 105.

20. Käsemann, *Die Legitimität des Apostels* (as in n. 15) 21.

21. W. Lütgert, *Freiheitspredigt und Schwarmgeister in Korinth,* Gütersloh, 1908.

22. R. Bultmann, *Der zweite Brief an die Korinther,* ed. E. Dinkler Göttingen, KEK 6, 1976. ET. *The Second Letter to the Corinthains.* trans. R. A. Harrisville, Minneapolis, 1985.

23. W. Schmithals, *Die Gnosis in Korinth,* Göttingen, FRLANT 48, 1956. ET. *Gnosticism in Corinth,* trans. J. E. Steely, Nashville, 1971.

24. W. G. Kümmel in H. Lietzmann, *An die Korinther I-II,* Tübingen, HzNT 9, 1969.

25. H. Windisch, *Der zweite Korintherbrief,* Göttingen, KEK 6, 1924.

26. Bultmann, *The Second Letter,* 203.

27. Schmithals, *Gnosticism in Corinth* (as in n. 23) 124-135.

28. W. G. Kümmel in H. Lietzmann, *An die Korinther I-II* (as in n. 24) 211.

29. Windisch, *Der zweite Korintherbrief* (as in n. 25) 328.

30. D. Georgi, *Die Gegner des Paulus im 2 Korintherbrief,* Neukirchen-Vluyn, WMANT 11, 1964.

31. G. Friedrich, "Die Gegner des Paulus im 2 Korintherbrief," in *Abraham unser Vater* (as in n. 4) 181-221.

32. Georgi, *Die Gegner* (as in n. 30) 76-82; see too Zmijewski, *Der Stil der paulinischen "Narrenrede"* (as in n. 18) 241.

33. T. W. Manson, "The Corinthian Correspondence," in *Studies in the Gospels and Epistles,* Manchester, 1962, 190-224.

34. G. Theissen, *The Sociology of Early Palestinian Christianity,* trans. J. Bowden, Philadelphia, 1978; *The Social Setting of Pauline Christianity,* trans. J. H. Schütz, Philadelphia, 1982.

35. P. W. Barnett, "The Jewish Sign Prophets," *NTS* 27 (1981) 679-97.

36. For this observation see C. H. Holladay, *Theios Aner in Hellenistic Judaism.* A Critique of the Use of this Category in New Testament Christology, Missoula, MT, SBLDS 40, 1977, 237-41.

37. Käsemann, *Die Legitimität des Apostels* (as in n. 15) 29. Georgi, *Die Gegner des Paulus im 2 Korintherbrief* (as in n. 30) 329 n. 3 qualifies this statement by remarking that a *Traditionsprinzip* in the legal sense is not found among the opponents. But see J. H. Schütz, *Paul and the Anatomy of Apostolic Authority,* Cambridge, SNTSMS 26, 1975, 171; Hoffmann, *Marcion* (as in n. 1) 95 n. 75.

38. Käsemann, *Die Legitimität des Apostels* (as in n. 15) 34.

39. H.-D. Betz, *Paulus und die socratische Tradition,* Tübingen, BHT 45, 1972, 132-37.

40. Georgi, *Die Gegner des Paulus im 2 Korintherbrief* (as in n. 30) 285.

41. Friedrich, "Die Gegner des Paulus im 2 Korintherbrief," in *Abraham unser Vater* (as in n. 4) especially 156-208. See too for a general discussion of Stephen's role (at least in Acts), M. Hengel, *Between Jesus and Paul,* London, trans J. Bowden, 1983, 19-23, concluding that "Stephen . . . presumably appeared [in Luke's source] as a paradigm of the earliest Christian spirit-inspired enthusiasm" (23).

42. The problem raised by Paul's refusal to name the opponents may well be solved by P. Marshall, "Invective: Paul and his Enemies in Corinth," in *Perspectives on Language and Text,* Festschrift for F. I. Andersen, ed. E. Condrad (Winona Lake, forthcoming), who sees in this silence a rhetorical device designed to accomplish several objectives, namely to make an effective comparison *(synkrisis),* expose the opponents to caricature, and to lead them to shame (cf. 11:21a).

43. Hengel, *Between Jesus and Paul* (as in n. 41) 10, 11.

44. The retort ὑπὲρ ἐγώ, "I am more" (11:23a), is ambiguous. We prefer to interpret it as adverbial in a superlative or elative sense.

45. On the question of what is behind the phrase μέτρον τοῦ κανόνος see E. A. Judge in *New Documents Illustrating Early Christianity, 1977,* North Ryde, NSW, 1982, #55. Cf. J. F. Strange, "2 Cor 10:13-16: Illuminated by a Recently Published Inscription," *BA* 46 (1983) 167, 168.

46. As Bultmann noted, *The Second Letter* (as in n. 22) 169 n. 1.

47. So Schütz, *Paul and the Anatomy of Apostolic Authority* (as in n. 37) 169 n. 1.

48. Barrett, "Paul's Opponents in 2 Corinthians," (as in n. 5) 81.

49. To use Käsemann's term, *Die Legitimität des Apostels* (as in n. 15) 29.

50. J. Jervell, "Der schwache Charismatiker" in *Rechtfertigung.* Festschrift für Ernst Käsemann zum 70 Geburtstag, ed. J. Friedrich, W. Pohlmann & P. Stuhlmacher, Tübingen, Göttingen, 1976, 185-198 (197: is there an intended pun in the designation based on 2 Cor 10:10; 12:5 of Paul as *der Heillose?* That is, Paul is both an ailing apostle and an ineffectual miracle-worker).

51. We may appeal to R. P. Martin *Carmen Christi: Phil 2:5-11,* Grand Rapids, 1983[2], xxxiii-xxxix, 312-319, with reference to D. Georgi, "Der vorpaulinische Hymnus Phil. 2, 6-11," in *Zeit und Geschichte.* Dankesgabe an Rudolf Bultmann zum 80 Geburtstag, ed. E. Dinkler, Tübingen, 1964, 292, 293.

52. H. Weder, *Das Kreuz Jesu bei Paulus,* Göttingen, FRLANT 125, 1981, 212, 213 has so identified the function of θανάτου δὲ σταυροῦ: "The insertion of the 'death of the cross' has then far-reaching consequences for the interpretation of the entire hymn. It becomes its center, from which the other statements (of the hymn) appear in a new light."

53. See Ellis's several essays in his collected work, *Prophecy and Hermeneutic in Early Christianity* (as in n. 3) chs. 1, 2, 8.

Judgment and the Brother:
Romans 14:1–15:13

Wayne A. Meeks

The Letter to the Romans is, by ancient epistolary standards as well as our own, very long. No wonder the latter chapters have often been neglected. In the early church, a shortened version circulated, presumably because the document seemed more universally applicable if one removed all those names and personal greetings of chapter 16. Some modern scholars have performed the same surgery. More often, commentators have treated Paul's discourse about the status of Israel in chapters 9–11 as a kind of personal excursus, interesting for insights into Paul's problems but not of much relevance to ours. The real message of Romans was found, of course, in the rich theological arguments about the law, faith, grace, and justification in the first eight chapters. Many a course on Romans has ended with chapter eight, and some commentaries might as well have done so.

In recent years the latter half of Paul's letter has begun to receive more attention. More and more readers are recognizing that the argument about Israel in chapters 9–11 is, far from being an excursus, the climax of the letter, as Stendahl boldly asserted some years ago.[1] Harry Gamble showed that chapter 16 was an integral part of the letter;[2] those greetings are important not only for our understanding of Paul's missionary and epistolary strategy and of the social form of the earliest churches, but also for understanding Paul's theology of the church. Indeed, the rediscovery of the latter half of Romans goes hand-in-hand with a returning awareness that Paul's theology and his practice can hardly be understood correctly when they are separated.

But what of chapters 12–15? Are they not "mere parenesis," a kind of ethical appendix tacked on after the real theological teaching of the letter is complete? It is not uncommon to find in handbooks and introductions a statement to the effect that the typical Pauline letter divides into two parts, a theological or didactic section and an ethical or parenetic section, the latter introduced by the verb παρακαλῶ. In fact, it is difficult to fit any other of Paul's letters precisely into that scheme; Romans seems to be the tacit model. In this essay I will argue that, even in the case of Romans, the bipartite pattern encourages misreading. Paul's advice about behavior in the Christian groups cannot be rightly understood until we see that the great themes of chapters 1–11 here receive their denouement. And we do not grasp the function and therefore the meaning of those theological themes in their epistolary context unless we see how Paul wants them to work out in the everyday life of the Roman house communities.

In these chapters, before discussing his own travel plans in 15:14-33 (verses which themselves form an inclusion with 1:8-15), Paul has exemplified the manner of life for which he appeals at the beginning of chapter 12 by adducing a number of parenetic topics. The last and longest of these, 14:1–15:13, has to do with the relations between those who have scruples about food and the calendar and those who do not—the "weak" and the "strong." It is commonly recognized that here Paul draws upon the response he worked out in 1 Cor 8–10 to a specific problem raised by Corinthian Christians. On the face of it, this topic thus seems remote from the epistolary situation of Romans[3] and from the letter's main themes, although those who see the "weak" as "Jewish Christians" and the "strong" as "Gentile Christians" obviously recognize some connections between the two parts of the letter. Those connections are in fact much tighter than is commonly perceived, and they remain intact even if one calls into question the simple identificaiton of the two factions just mentioned.

Paul's Argument in Rom 14:1–15:13

Paul's admonition is framed by the two parallel imperatives of 14:1 and 15:7, each of which is backed by an explanation, the one simple, the other elaborate.

τὸν δὲ ἀσθενοῦντα τῇ πίστει προσλαμβάνεσθε (14:1)
διὸ προσλαμβάνεσθε ἀλλήλους (15:7)

The imperatives are identical, but their objects are not, and the differences reflect the movement of the intervening argument. Paul begins by assuming an unequal relationship; the "strong" are urged to "accept" those who are "weak with respect to faith"[4] (cf. 15:1). However, 14:2 already introduces a series of statements in antithetical form (ὃς μὲν ..., ὁ δὲ + ptcp and the like), which introduce a pattern of reciprocity. We recall that also in 1 Cor 8–10 there is a broad alternation of viewpoints—to the confusion of some commentators; here, however, the alternation is much more compact and explicit.

The imperative of 14:1 is followed by a qualification: μὴ εἰς διακρίσεις διαλογισμῶν. Here we see the first pejorative use of a word on the root κριν-, which becomes a leitmotif of our text. There are limits on the strong person's obligation toward the weak, and these limits imply at the same time obligations upon the weak: not to be disputatious and judgmental. The qualification is not repeated in 15:7, for it is implicit in the way Paul has worked out the dialectic of the situation in chap. 14. That discussion is summed up in 15:1-6 with (1) a reprise of 14:1 in the explicit terms of the obligation which "we the powerful" have toward "the powerless" (v 1); (2) a warrant for that obligation in the form of a christological statement backed by a citation of scripture (vv 3-4); and (3) a wish or prayer that the recipients of the letter be granted unity and mutuality (τὸ αὐτὸ φρονεῖν ἐν ἀλλήλοις κατὰ Χριστὸν Ἰη-σοῦν, ἵνα ὁμοθυμαδὸν ἐν ἑνὶ στόματι δοξάζητε τὸν θεόν, κτλ. vv 5-6). The ἀλλήλους of v 7 thus replaces the qualification of 14:1, which has been superseded by the preceding appeals for reciprocal acceptance. Instead of a qualifying clause, the imperative of 15:7 is supported by another christological warrant, this time cast in language specific to the parenetic appeal: "Therefore welcome one another, as indeed Christ welcomed you." That warrant is similar in use and meaning to the one in v 3, and like it is backed by scripture, this time in the form of a catena of texts that provides a formal conclusion to the parenesis and culminates in another wish/prayer more general than that in vv 5-6.

There is one odd thing about this catena of texts. What is common to the four quotations is that all refer to the ἔθνη, and specifically to the Gentiles "confessing" and "praising" Israel's God—joining with Israel, μετὰ τοῦ λαοῦ αὐτοῦ, as the quotation in v 10 from Deut 32:43 LXX puts it. That, too, is the point which Paul emphasizes in his introduction to the catena (vv 8-9): Christ's "receiving" the Gentile Christians of Rome is identified with his having become "circumcision's servant for the sake of God's truth, to confirm the promises of the fathers, that the Gentiles would glorify God for mercy." Note the indirection of this claim: Christ accepted the *Gentile* Christians by being a διάκονος of the *Jews,* in order to fulfill promises made in the Jewish scriptures to Jewish patriarchs about Gentiles. This extraordinarily compact statement consitutes a reprise of the themes Paul has developed in chaps 9–11 and, more than that, in the whole letter, leading up to Paul's restatement of the goal of his own mission, which follows in the remainder of this chapter (n.b. 15:16, 18, 27). But what has the theme of the unity of Jews and Gentiles to do with disputes between meat-eaters and abstainers? The "weak" cannot be simply identified with "Jewish Christians" and the "strong" with "Gentile Christians," as Paul's inclusion of himself among the strong makes plain (15:1: ἡμεῖς οἱ δυνατοί).

To be sure, the way Paul characterizes the issue between strong and weak does embrace specifically Jewish categories, and those are probably the starting point in his mind. Nevertheless he avoids halakic language, for example, about *kashrut* and Sabbath. The nearest he comes is in 14:14. It is in this part of the discussion (14:13–15:6) that the parallels with 1 Cor 8–10 are closest, but the differences are important. The term εἰδωλόθυτα does not appear in Romans, and indeed the whole question of idolatry goes unmentioned in the present context. Rather, it is a question of food being deemed "profane," κοινός, or not. In the synoptics and Acts, the term is used as the opposite of "clean" and thus equivalent to the Hebrew *tame'*, or perhaps *stam*.[5] Paul's statement, "I know and am convinced in the Lord Jesus that nothing is κοινόν of itself," is roughly equivalent to the synoptic Jesus-saying, "There is nothing that, entering a person from without, can κοινῶσαι him" (Mark 7:15 par.; cf. Acts 10:15; 11:19). The question in Rom 14:14 thus seems broader than in 1 Cor 8–10; not only meat from pagan markets, but *kashrut* or at least some modified food taboos, like those in Acts 15:20, 29; 21:15, are at issue.

We may be surprised that the Paul who so indignantly opposed the "Judaizers" in Galatia should here so irenically urge acceptance of people who keep food-purity rules. There are, however, at least two significant differences in the circumstances of the two letters.[6] First, the Roman house-churches were not founded by Paul; he is very much conscious of being an outsider to them, who must carefully introduce "his gospel" before he visits them (note the polite and rhetorically correct disclaimer that follows immediately on our text, 15:14-33). Second, there is no evidence, despite many attempts at "mirror-reading" by commentators, of any present crisis around this issue in the Roman groups. Paul takes up the topic out of his experience, not theirs, because it is well suited to show in behavioral terms the outworking of the main themes of the letter.

Furthermore, Paul takes pains to state the issue in terms general enough that a former Jew is not necessarily on one side and a former Gentile on the other, as we have seen. Thus 14:2 speaks of those who "eat everything" and those who "eat (only) vegetables," and 14:21 suggests that "it is good neither to eat meat nor to drink wine" if such things would trip up a brother. To be sure, there is a certain degree of rhetorical hyperbole in these sentences, but it is nevertheless significant that Paul chooses expressions that are broader than either the εἰδωλόθυτα of Corinth or food purity-rules. Similarly in the other kind of example that he gives in 14:5-6, Sabbath observance is perhaps the most obvious instance of someone who "judges one day in contradistinction from another," but that need not be the only case. Anyone who has read Theophrastus' or Plutarch's description of the superstitious person[7] will see that there were many reasons for a pagan to judge one day more auspicious or more dangerous than another, and some of those concerns could (and doubtless did) persist in people who were converted to Christianity. Thus, throughout the argument, Paul is describing concerns that every diaspora Jew faced, but using language general enough to include Gentiles, too.

What then are the major points that Paul wants to get across in this paradigmatic address to the scrupulous and the enlightened? We may see them more clearly if we sum up the main outline of the steps that this passage shares with the argument of 1 Cor 8–10 and then look more closely at one further way in which the two arguments differ. (1) Paul identifies himself with the position of "the strong" (a designation explicit only in Rom 15:1, but implicit in both passages; cf. also 1 Cor 1:26), which is based on *knowledge* given in the Christian proclamation (Rom 14:14 οἶδα, cf. 1 Cor 8:1-6 οἴδαμεν). (2) He insists that those who have this liberating knowledge should nevertheless forego exercising their resultant rights if such exercise would harm the "weaker" brother who has not come to this insight (14:15, 20, 21; 15:1; cf. 1 Cor 8:7-13; 9 *passim;* 10:28). (3) However, the strong are not to permit their own free conscience to be "slandered" or "judged" by a (weaker) conscience (1 Cor 10:19-30; cf. Rom 14:16). (4) Thus mutual love (ἀγάπη) and upbuilding (οἰκοδομή) are the fundamental guides (e.g. 14:15, 19; 15:2; cf. 1 Cor 8:1, 10; 10:23). (5) What finally counts is God's will and rule, and "food" or "food and drink" do not affect our relationship to him (14:17; cf. 1 Cor 8:8).

Obviously this is not the place to go into details of either passage,[8] but examining one further apparent difference between them will bring us back to our main question. One of the key terms of 1 Cor 8–10, συνείδησις, "conscience," does not appear in this part of Romans. The person who is described in 1 Cor 8:7, 12 as having a "weak conscience" is in Rom 14:1 called "weak with respect to *faith.*" However, the difference in substance is not great. There are expressions in Romans 14 that are functionally equivalent to συνείδησις: λογίζομαι (14:14) and ὁ μὴ κρίνων ἑαυτὸν ἐν ᾧ δοκιμάζει, as opposed to ὁ δὲ διακρινόμενος (14:22-23). I have already called attention to Paul's predilection in this passage for verbs of "judging," which is illustrated again here. In anticipation of God's eventual judgment, the Christian is advised to judge his own behavior, but not to judge fellow Christians. In 1 Cor 8–10 Paul does not use quite those terms, but he does elsewhere in 1 Corinthians, especially 4:3-5 (about which I shall say more in a moment) and 11:27-34. In Romans the theme of God's impartial judgment, before which there is "no distinction" among humans, has been prominent since the beginning, and the careful listener to a reading of the letter will have noticed sharp reminders of Paul's first use of that theme. Before turning to those reminders, however, let us widen our net a bit by noticing some similar uses of this motif elsewhere in the New Testament.

God's Judgment Relativizes Our Own

While the argument that God's judgment ought to preempt our own judging of each other is only hinted at in 1 Cor 8–10 (particularly in 10:29: "For why is my freedom to be *judged* by a conscience not mine?"), it is prominent elsewhere in that letter, as noted above. The elementary lesson (probably that is the meaning of the quasi-proverbial μὴ ὑπὲρ ἃ γέγραπται)[9] that Paul wants the Corinthians to learn in 1 Cor 1–4 is "that you not be puffed up, one for the one and against the other" (4:6). Their partisanship, exemplified in choosing between Paul and Apollos, is wrong because it entails inappropriate and untimely acts of judgment. As builders and planters and "stewards of God's mysteries" (4:1), Paul and Apollos will indeed be judged by "the Day" of God's judgment (3:10-16; 4:1-2). For that very reason, though, Paul will not submit to their premature judging. "For me to be judged by you or by a human day is a negligible matter. Indeed, I do not even judge myself—for I have nothing on my conscience, but that fact does not acquit me—the one who judges me is the Lord. Therefore do not judge before the time when the Lord comes" (4:3-5). Now obviously this expected judgment by God and the Lord does not eliminate *all* present acts of mutual judgment within the community, as chapters 5 and 6 make clear in different ways. The problem of the coherence of these parts of the letter, which I believe can be solved by careful attention to context and Paul's strategy, need not concern us for our present purposes, however.[10]

Colossians 2:16 may be an application of Paul's rule by a disciple; it could almost be taken as a concise summary of one pole of the advice in Rom 14:1–15:13: μὴ οὖν τις ὑμᾶς κρινέτω ἐν βρώσει καὶ ἐν πόσει ἢ ἐν μέρει ἑορτῆς ἢ νεομηνίας ἢ σαββάτων. However, there is no hint in the immediate context of Paul's eschatological warrant for such advice, though one does not have to read far to find a related statement in 3:3-4. Again, the thought is that the real life of the Christian is "hidden with Christ" and only to be revealed at his coming. Special claims by individuals or groups within the community, by which claims they "judge" or "disqualify" other Christians, are therefore to be resisted. What counts in the present is what all believers alike received in their baptism. This is true to the concerns of Paul in 1 Corinthians as well as Romans, but the emphasis is different. In 1 Corinthians Paul played down baptism as such, presumably because the elitist movements at Corinth were making a special point of it, while in Colossians his disciple emphasizes baptism but does not make much of the eschatological motif of final judgment.

Paul was not the only leader of the early Christian groups to use the expectation of God's judgment to try to restrain judgmental and divisive tendencies in those groups. He also may not have been the first, though that is harder to decide. The most striking parallel to Paul's repeated apostrophe to the "judging" brother of Rom 14:4, 10 comes from what we usually take to be the opposite end of early Christianity's theological spectrum, the letter of James: σὺ δὲ τίς εἶ ὁ κρίνων τὸν πλησίον; (4:12). The formulation with πλησίον instead of Paul's ἀδελφός suggests that we may have a Jewish theologoumenon, alluding to Lev 19:18, and that would accord with the affinities of much of the other material in James. However, it is hard to find any precise parallel in Jewish sources.[11] Pseudo-Phocylides 10-11 is close: "Cast the poor not down unjustly, judge not partially. If you judge evilly, God will judge you thereafter."[12]

On the other hand, gnomes of this sort were also used independently in later Christian parenesis, as the third-person formulation in Sentences of Sextus 183 shows: ὁ κρίνων ἄνθρωπον κρίνεται ὑπὸ θεοῦ.[13] Perhaps independent use of such gnomes has also affected the manuscript tradition of James 4:12, producing the substitution of ἕτερον for πλησίον in the majority text, though it is also possible that scribes thought of Rom 2:1. None of these formulations of the gnome or admonition seems likely to have been derived directly from the form most familiar to us from the synoptic tradition, "Judge not, lest you be judged" (Matt 7:1; the parallel in Luke 6:37 is somewhat different). Thus we find hints that the sentiment may have been more widespread than our extant sources demonstrate and therefore reasons to doubt that Paul was the first to express it. His use of it in Romans, however, is special, and to that use we now return.

"Who are you to judge?"

Let us look more carefully at the first part of Paul's address to the strong and the weak, Rom 14:1-12/13, the part in which he plays variations on the theme of judgment. At the beginning and end of this section, immediately after the introductory admonition and immediately before the concluding warrant with its scripture backing, there are surprising intrusions into the parenetic style. These two intrusions, as they seem, are addresses to an imaginary interlocutor—characteristic of diatribe but unusual and calling particular attention to themselves when they appear, as here and in James 4:12, in parenesis.[14] The force of the apostrophe depends upon the abruptness of its shift to the second person singular and the sharpness of its indictment of the behavior that it portrays. "You—who are you (to be) judging someone else's houseslave?" (v 4). Is this addressed only to the "weak," since that is who is urged not to "judge" in v 3? Not likely, for the next sentence (v 5) uses κρίνει on both sides of the antithesis. The two verbs in v 3, ἐξουθενεῖν and κρίνειν, are equivalent, though the nuances are appropriate to the two sides, and they are taken up again in the second apostrophe, v 10, which balances v 4.

The first apostrophe introduces the dominant theological warrant for Christians' not judging one another; more precisely, it specifies the context of the warrant already stated in v 3: "God has received" the other precisely as the ultimate Judge, before whom each "stands or falls." Verse 4 states that context in a vivid metaphor: the judgment of a possibly miscreant slave is in the hands of his or her master, and another private person (especially, as is implicitly the case here, a fellow slave!) has no right to intrude. Moreover, in this case we are told that the master will certainly vindicate the slave, having the power to establish him (as acceptable). The warrant that follows the reiterated apostrophe in v 10 ("For all of us will present ourselves before the tribunal of God") translates the metaphor into direct theological language. Equally important, the one who is called "someone else's slave" in v 4 now becomes "your brother," and the single apostrophe becomes a merism, reprising the two verbs of v 3, "despise" and "judge," in reverse order.

The rhetorical circle established by these two parallel apostrophes clearly sets the terms for the expansion of the argument that follows. Verse 13, shifting the verb into the plural and, initially, to the first person, returns us from the indicting address of the apostrophe to the mutual appeal proper to the parenetic context: "Let us then no longer judge one another; rather come to this judgment (τοῦτο κρίνατε), not to set a stumbling block or obstacle in the way of your brother." In the further argument, Paul once again employs apostrophe in 14:22; "You—the faith that you have, keep it your own before God."[15] Like the other two, this address to an imagined interlocutor also turns on the theme of judgment (vv 22-23), but here in the sense of a believer privately judging his own conduct "before God." Paul appears to be using πίστις here in a rather special sense to refer to the whole shape of one's relation to God, which may vary according to the different insights of different groups or individuals within the church. (Most likely he has the same special sense in mind when he uses the dative to qualify "being weak" in 14:1, as the use of the verb πιστεύει in 14:2

shows.)[16] To act in a way that is out of accord with that faith, διακρινόμενος, misses the mark and is condemned. The exact point remains less than lucid, but the general contours of Paul's argument are clear enough.

Once we recognize how central and forceful these apostrophes are in this last of Paul's admonitions in Romans, it becomes surprising that commentators, as far as I can see, have paid no attention to the striking parallel in form, substance, and function with the apostrophe that startles every reader in the middle of the first argument in the letter, 2:1: "Therefore you are without excuse, O man, everyone who judges, for by judging the other you condemn yourself." The abruptness of the change to the second person singular has led most editors of texts and translations to put a paragraph here, and most commentators speak of a turn from the indictment of Gentile sins in 1:18-32 to "judgment on the Jews."[17] However, once we recognize that the abruptness of the apostrophe is typical of its use in diatribe, as Stowers has shown,[18] there is no longer any reason to try to explain away the normal inferential force of the διό in 2:1.[19] The address to "the hypocritical judge," which even has close parallels in the diatribes of pagan philosophers,[20] thus functions "to bring home, to concretize and to sharpen the indictment in 1:18-32 (especially vv 28-32) for Paul's audience."[21] Far from marking a sharp break from the previous chapter, 2:1 requires rather that we read the indictments of that chapter in an inclusive sense and connect them closely with 2:1-11 (ὦ ἄνθρωπε πᾶς ὁ κρίνων, 2:1, corresponds with πᾶσαν ἀσέβειαν καὶ ἀδικίαν ἀνθρώπων, 1:18; ἀναπολόγητος picks up ἀναπολογήτους, 1:20, to mention only the most obvious links).

We can therefore acknowledge the correctness of a minority view of 1:18–2:11 that has been argued with increasing force in recent years. The exposé of idolatry in 1:18-32, though it does obviously employ elements typical of Jewish polemic against paganism, is not directed exclusively against paganism. Verse 23 contains unmistakable allusions to Ps 106:20 and Jer 2:11, which speak of Israel's idolatry in the incident of the Golden Calf.[22] And in chapter 2, it is not until v 17 (another apostrophe!) that the Jew is addressed directly. There is therefore good reason to take Paul's ἄνθρωπος in 1:18; 2:1, 3, 9, 16 as deliberately inclusive, of "the Jew first and also the Greek" (1:16; 2:9, 10).[23] The "pivot" of the argument in 1:16–2:29 is, as Bassler says, 2:11: "For there is no partiality with God."[24] And the human implication of that "theological axiom" is that "there is no distinction, for all have sinned and are lacking the glory of God, yet they are justified as a gift by his grace, through the redemption that is effected in Christ Jesus" (3:22-23). Paul's summation in 3:27-31 of his first, foundational argument shows that in fact the axiom of 2:11 is pivotal of the whole argument, not only the first part. For the appeal here, again in vivid diatribal style, to the even more fundamental axiom, "God is one," recalls for the reader again the impartiality of the one God, who is obviously therefore not the God of Jews only but also of the Gentiles and "will justify circumcision on the basis of faith and uncircumcision through faith" (3:30).

It is the just, impartial judgment of the one God, therefore, that eliminates the distinction (or separation, διαστολή) between Jew and Gentile within the community of faith and, as we learn from Rom 9–11, in God's ultimate plan, though without abolishing the special gifts and promises which the Jew received (3:1; 9:4-5; 11 passim). It was that righteousness, which can be enacted only by the God who characteristically makes something out of nothing, which Abraham obtained by his trust (chap. 4). That is the righteousness that brings liberty (in the paradoxical form of servitude to God and righteousness, 6:12-23) to all the children of God in hope, awaiting a final liberation to be shared by "the creation itself" (chap. 8). Again it is the impartial judging by God that renders human distinctions invalid: "It is God who acquits; who is it who condemns?" (8:33b-34a). Even the hard case, the apparent rejection by God of his own people Israel (since they do not on the whole accept the crucified Jesus as Messiah), is not what it appears, for there is "no injustice with God" (9:14). Of course, as creator of us all, he has absolute power to behave as arbitrarily as he wishes. Again an apostrophe to the foolish human judge makes the point: "O man, who are you to be answering back to God?" (9:20). Yet rightly understood, God is not acting inconsistently at all; the same rules apply, in God's hidden wisdom, to Jew and Gentile alike. "The end and goal of the Law" is none other than Christ (10:4).[25] The boasting that is excluded by the law of faith (3:27) includes not only the boasting of Jew over Gentile, but also of Gentile Christian over Jew (11:18). Just as, contrary to all "natural" expectation, Gentiles have been grafted into the people of God, so also, contrary to what now seems evident to Gentile Christians, "all Israel will be saved." If the Jews are now disobedient (to the righteousness of God revealed in Messiah Jesus), then they are in just the same position as the Gentiles before that revelation, and again the impartiality of God will triumph: "For God confined all to disobedience, that he might enact his mercy to all" (11:32). Precisely how God is going to bring that about, Paul does not tell us, for the way is hidden in the "unsearchable judgments (κρίματα) of God" (11:33).

Conclusion

Even this cursory review of some central themes of the Letter to Romans should suffice to show that Paul chose the topic of his final sample of admonition with deliberate thought and shaped his rhetorical presentation of it with great care, as an altogether fitting conclusion to his great protreptic exhibition of "his gospel." The crucifixion and resurrection of Jesus the Messiah reveals the impartial righteousness of the one God, "himself just and justifying" (3:26) without respect of human distinctions. The debate over the eating of meat at Corinth has helped Paul to see what he here explains to the Roman Christians: those acts of judging one another that divide the people of God run directly contrary to the universal judgment of the one God. Until the strong accept the weak and the weak the strong, the liberated and the scrupulous each other, they do not yet understand the implication of the fact that "Christ has accepted us."[26] Paul's care to put the issue in general terms, including but not limited to either the specific matter of sacrificed meat or the related question of Jewish food rules, should warn us against limiting the object of his admonitions in 14:1–15:13 to relations between former Jews and former Gentiles in the Christian groups. Still less is he laying down general rules for "tolerant coexistence between Jews and Gentiles."[27] We may even venture further than that. We may hope to go beyond "tolerant coexistence," reaching out to the Jews not to "convert" but to work out with them implications of our shared confidence in the one God whose promises and mercy will not finally be thwarted by our prejudices. Indeed Christians will not have betrayed Paul's vision if they reach out not only to the Jews, though their election remains the trunk that supports our branches, but to "every human being" (πᾶς ἄνθρωπος), as we wait in hope, with all the creation, for the revealing of "the children of God," not all of whose names are in our rollbooks. As Paul saw so clearly, however, such a universal outreach is only pious talk unless it begins when those of us who already acknowledge that God is judge of us all therefore cease to judge one another.

Notes

1. K. Stendahl, *Paul Among Jews and Gentiles and Other Essays,* Philadelphia, 1976, 4.

2. H. A. Gamble, Jr., *The Textual History of the Letter to the Romans: A Study in Textual and Literary Criticism,* Grand Rapids, 1977.

3. I remain unconvinced by any of the attempts by modern scholars to connect Paul's admonitions to specific issues in the Roman churches of which he is supposed to have become aware, though no doubt he had enough information to convince him that what he had learned from the "idolatry" controversy in Corinth would be relevant in Rome. For a representative sample of arguments on both sides, see *The Romans Debate,* ed. by K. P. Donfried, Minneapolis, 1977.

4. All translations in this essay are mine.

5. For the difficulty in taking κοινός = שׂמא and a possible alternative, (κοινός = סחם), see M. Smith, *Tannaitic Parallels to the Gospels,* SBLMS, 6, Philadelphia, 1951, 51-52.

6. See J. P. Sampley, "Romans and Galatians: Comparison and Contrast," in *Understanding the Word: Essays in Honor of Bernhard W. Anderson,* ed. by J. T. Butler, E. W. Conrad, and E. C. Ollenburger, JSOT Sup 37, Sheffield, 1985, 315-39.

7. Theophrastus, *Char.,* 16; Plutarch, *De superst. (Mor.* 164E-171F).

8. See the comparison of the two passages in U. Wilckens, *Der Brief an die Römer,* Vol. 3: *Rom 12-16,* EKKNT 6.3; Zürich, 1982, 115.

9. J. Fitzgerald, "'Cracks in an Earthen Vessel': An Examination of the Catalogues of Hardships in the Corinthian Correspondence," Ph.D. Dissertation, Yale University, 1984 [revised version forthcoming in SBLDS], 224-35.

10. David Kuck is presently writing a dissertation at Yale on Paul's use of judgment language, particularly in 1 Cor 1-4, and I refer to that for further discussion of these passages. In general I have been greatly aided in my understanding of this motif in Paul's letters by Mr. Kuck's preliminary work. On the question of chap. 6 in its context, see A. C. Mitchel, S.J., "1 Corinthians 6:1-11: Group Boundaries and the Courts of Corinth," Ph.D. dissertation, Yale University, 1986.

11. See chap. 2 of the dissertation by Kuck cited in the previous note.

12. μὴ ῥίψῃς πενίην ἀδίκως, μὴ κρῖνε πρόσωπον· ἢν σὺ κακῶς δικάσῃς, σὲ θεὸς μετέπειτα δικάσσει. *The Sentences of Pseudo-Phocylides, with Introduction and Commentary,* ed. by P. W. van der Horst, Studia in Veteris Testamenti Pseudepigrapha, 4, Leiden, 1978.

13. *The Sentences of Sextus,* ed. and trans. by R. A. Edwards and R. A. Wild, S.J. Texts and Translations: Early Christian Literature Series, 5; Chico, CA: 1981. See also Sent. 184.

14. See S. K. Stowers, *The Diatribe and Paul's Letter to the Romans,* SBLDS, 57; Chico, CA: 1981, 79-118.

15. The variant reading that omits the relative is strongly supported; if we adopt it, we might better punctuate the first clause as a rhetorical question (cf. H. Lietzmann, *An die Römer,* Handbuch zum NT, 8; 4th ed., Tübingen, 1933, 118), like the other two apostrophes in this chapter and very often in other literature: "Do you have faith? Keep it to yourself. . . ." Cf. Jas 2:14, 18, 19.

16. Against Wilckens, *Der Brief an die Römer,* ad loc.

17. E. Käsemann, *Commentary on Romans,* trans. and ed. by G. W. Bromiley, Grand Rapids, 1980, 52.

18. Stowers, *Diatribe,* chap. 2.

19. Käsemann, *Commentary,* 54, following numbers of others, identified by Stowers, *Diatribe,* 214 n. 21, as dependent on E. Molland, "Dio: Einige syntaktische Beobachtungen," *Serta Rudbergiana: Symbolae Osloenses,* Suppl. 4 (1931) 43-52.

20. Stowers, *Diatribe,* 103, cites Epictetus, *Diss.* 2.21.11-12; 3.2.14-16; Plutarch, *Curios. (Mor.)* 515D; Seneca, *Vit. beat.* 27.4.

21. Stowers, *Diatribe,* 110.

22. J. M. Bassler, *Divine Impartiality: Paul and a Theological Axiom,* SBLDS, 59; Chico, CA., 1982, 249 n. 3 and Appendix C.

23. For a list of scholars who have argued for the unity of Paul's exposition in 1:16-2:11, see Bassler, *Impartiality,* 250 n. 8; her own argument to this purpose is pp. 123-37.

24. Ibid., 153.

25. On this most controverted verse, see P. W. Meyer, "Romans 10:4 and the 'End' of the Law"

in *the Divine Helmsman: Studies on God's Control of Human Events, Presented to Lou H. Silberman*, ed. by J. L. Crenshaw and S. Sandmel, New York, 1980, 59-78.

26. Bassler is thus quite correct when she says that Rom 14-15 show the "actual sociological ramifications" (she means, I think, "social ramifications") of Paul's understanding of divine impartiality (*Impartiality*, 162).

27. Against R. Jewett, "The Law and the Coexistence of Jews and Gentiles in Romans," *Int* 39 (1984) 354.

Gospel Traditions in the Church in Corinth (with Apologies to B. H. Streeter)

Peter Richardson

Introduction

The work of Earle Ellis has included substantial contributions on 1 Corinthians and the traditions lying behind that letter. Many of these have been printed together in *Prophecy and Hermeneutic in Early Christianity,* including his essay for the Conzelmann *Festschrift,* "New Directions in Form Criticism," where Ellis argues for "an extensive complex of written Gospel material . . . [in] the pre-Markan period, i.e. pre-65."[1] This present essay juxtaposes an homage to Ellis with a celebration of the work of Burnett Hillman Streeter. At the time of Ellis's birth (March 18, 1926), New Testament scholars were hailing the appearance of Streeter's great book on *The Four Gospels,* the first edition of which appeared in 1924 and the second soon after in 1926.[2]

Streeter summarized brilliantly the long lines of scholarly work on the text traditions of the New Testament, the sources of the synoptic gospels, and the nature of the Fourth Gospel. He added to the whole a particular concern for the geographic aspect of New Testament study. The result was a neatly dovetailed—perhaps too neatly dovetailed—argument about the geographical origins of the various text-traditions and the geographical setting of the sources lying behind the gospels. This led, in another work, to a strong stress on local variation in matters of gospel traditions, church order, and theological emphases.[3]

Despite its greatness the long-term impact of Streeter's work has not been as profound as might have been expected. Indeed, the most imaginative part of his conception—the Proto-Luke hypothesis—has not found much support. Streeter proposed a novel and significant thesis concerning the development of the Gospel of Luke, that Luke was not built out of Q and L materials inserted into the Markan framework, but that Markan materials were inserted into an existing document (Proto-Luke) already constructed out of Q and L materials.[4]

Ellis himself has rejected this hypothesis.[5] And recent studies render more difficult too simple assumptions about the nature and extent of sources such as Proto-Luke, or even Q. There is a challenge to advocates of Proto-Luke to show that this hypothesis is a more cogent explanation of the data than other hypotheses. This present contribution does not do this; it makes large assumptions about the nature of Proto-Luke and of Q, in the interest of exploring one question only: is there a setting in the Pauline mission that might account for a "gospel" such as Proto-Luke?

1. *Paul, Luke, and Proto-Luke.* Streeter argued that the various gospel layers were influenced strongly by the spread of the churches' mission into the Gentile world. He seems to have wondered little, however, about the affinities between his Proto-Lukan document and Paul's message. It is frequently said that Luke's theology is influenced

by Paul: handbooks refer to Luke's universalism, his interest in God's love for sinners, his stress on joy, his interest in Gentiles and Gentile mission.[6]
This claim may be correct, but is unexceptional. Can one go beyond these claims of theological influence to a more specific claim? The argument I will attempt to defend is this: Paul was familiar with a sayings or *logia* source related to the Q-traditions, disliked some important features of these, and encouraged the writing of a document that is more or less what Streeter identified as Proto-Luke.

The claim may be too bold, but it may be helpful to be still bolder and to make the following additional claims: there is evidence in 1 Corinthians for Paul's knowledge of Jesus-traditions similar to the *logia* source; some of Paul's difficulties in Corinth stemmed from disagreements about that source;[7] some features of Proto-Luke resemble features of Paul's message.

The main point I wish to explore, then, is the linkage of two stages in the complex development of gospel traditions to the vigorous debates in one center of the Pauline mission.[8]

2. *On Q and Proto-Luke.* I begin by assuming the essential correctness of Streeter's hypothesis concerning Proto-Luke. I will also assume more or less his view of the extent of material included in that hypothetical document, without attempting either justification of these views or greater precision. To do this inevitably requires also accepting some form of Q-hypothesis as a prior collection of *logia* material. To a first approximation Proto-Luke is then the material drawn from the *logia* of the Q materials, however modified and re-shaped by the author, plus material usually known as L representing traditions circulating separately and also known to the author. Put another way, and less accurately, Proto-Luke comprises the present gospel of Luke minus the Markan additions.

Such a description does not do justice to the hypothesis itself, which requires a running commentary that has never yet been provided. The potential importance of the Proto-Luke hypothesis is that it would present us with an early gospel, independent of Mark, and with a quite different story-line from that of Q, Mark, or Thomas.

To be persuasive, the hypothesis requires a completely fresh analysis and explication. But one or two considerations might be sketched. First, the resulting Proto-Luke is a remarkably coherent document, not the mish-mash one would expect upon removing the other possible backbone—Mark—upon which the present gospel of Luke might be constructed. Some aspects of this coherence will emerge below. Second, it has a structure of its own which is strongly geographical. The important transitions are marked by generalizing editorial statements. The structure seems to be: Introduction (3:1-20); Beginning of the Account of Jesus (3:23); Galilee, dealt with in four parts (Nazareth in 4:16; Gennesaret in 5:1; Capernaum in 7:1; and Nain in 7:11); On the way to Jerusalem, dealt with in three or four parts (first in 9:51; second in 10:38?; third in 13:22; and fourth in 17:11); in Jerusalem (19:37); at the Tomb and beyond (23:55; cf. 24:13, 36, 50). One consequence of this structure is to obviate the usual queries over the role and character of the so-called "travel narrative" in 9:51–18:14.

While it is not a necessary corollary, I will assume that Proto-Luke and Luke are from the same person (whom I will call Luke), and that it is unimportant for the limited purpose of this paper to identify precisely what editorial alterations took place between the two redactions.

The variations between Q and Proto-Luke are, however, important though not the main subject of this paper. I follow the usual definition of Q's extent and character. Q is basically a sayings-source with almost no narrative material. It is heavily eschatological with a strong Son of Man christology. There are no passion or resurrection narratives, and no birth narrative. It has a special interest in John the Baptist, and most of the "wisdom" emphases in the gospels are to be identified with Q.

Proto-Luke as it is usually reconstructed adds narrative material to Q's sayings-material; most significantly, it rectifies the absence of both passion and resurrection accounts. Proto-Luke also introduces redactional emphases not found in or different from those in Q. It modifies the strong sense of imminence in Q's eschatology. It balances a Son of Man christology against a christology focussing on "the Lord," alongside which it also includes some other important christological motifs (Mosaic prophet, Son of God, and Messiah especially). The wisdom emphasis continues. The position of John the Baptist has been modified. Finally, a rather powerful interest in Gentile mission emerges.

There is more than one possible explanation of these data, but this paper will show that the best interpretation of the important variations between Q and Proto-Luke is that these reflect the Pauline mission, and more especially the controversies in Corinth. This is not to say that Proto-Luke's theology is merely a pale reflection of Pauline theology, for the author is a theologian, too. His task is to supplement the existing collection of sayings-materials with other appropriate Jesus-traditions. He is not working from whole cloth. So Proto-Luke shows a mixture of influences: the inheritance from Q, additional oral traditions, his own theological concerns, and some of Paul's special interests. It is essential to insist on this mixed set of factors at work in Proto-Luke.

The Problems in Corinth and the Revision of Q

The evidence of 1 Corinthians shows that important tensions have arisen in Corinth, involving claims by or on behalf of Paul, Apollos, and Cephas. A sketch of the major issues in contention in Corinth will have to suffice.

The thanksgiving in 1 Corinthians underlines the related problems of knowledge, gifts, and eschatological expectation. It is not stated whether there is a close link between one or other of these issues and the divisions in Corinth (1:10-13). It is a reasonable conjecture, however, that the divisions are very closely related to questions of baptism, the centrality of the cross, and differing attitudes to wisdom (1:13–2:16). The roles of Paul, Apollos and Cephas in the church of Corinth are also disputed but it is clear that Paul and Apollos are the main actors (3:1–4:7). The question of an over-realized eschatology (1 Cor 4:8) has surfaced. The response topics concern sexual morality together with the need for communal judgment of the offenders, and marital relations in the context of a near expectation of the end. Eating practices involving several separate problems also surface: idol-food; support for the apostles; table fellowship; the Lord's supper and community meals. The problem of gifts receives a detailed treatment and questions about death and resurrection occupy the prominent closing position.

It would be folly, of course, to claim that all these problems in Corinth are reflected in Proto-Luke. My hypothesis involves, rather, two complementary suggestions. (1) Some of the problems of which we have evidence in 1 Corinthians are caused by differences of opinion over the interpretation of sayings of Jesus circulating at the time of the disputes between Paul and Apollos in Corinth, a collection more or less like Q. (2) Proto-Luke as a revision of Q can be accounted for in part by some of the distinctly Pauline concerns expressed in 1 Corinthians.

To put it too simply, the situation of 1 Corinthians is a kind of middle term between Q and Proto-Luke, being shaped by the one and shaping the other. Essential to this hypothesis is the possibility that Paul would find Q to be inadequate, that the author of Proto-Luke would have access to other Jesus- traditions, and that there were sharp differences of opinion over the nature of "gospel."[9]

The dominant issues suggesting this interaction among Q, 1 Corinthians and Proto-Luke (or, to put it differently, among Apollos, Paul, and the redactor of Proto-Luke) may be summarized as follows.

(1) Paul's stress in 1 Corinthians on the cross and resurrection is characteristic of him. In its present form it may be prompted by Apollos's view of the priority of wisdom over cross and resurrection, a view related to the theological tendencies of hellenistic Jewish wisdom speculation. But Apollos's views are consistent with the absence of a passion narrative from Q and its interest in wisdom. Apollos and Q do not share Paul's view of the centrality of cross and resurrection, and the passion narrative of Proto-Luke may be seen to correct this lack.

(2) Paul downplays baptism—the first item to be mentioned following the description of divisions in Corinth. In Q John the Baptist plays an important role, but in Proto-Luke there is a substantial re-writing of that role to minimize the importance of John.

(3) Paul is deeply involved in mission, which is long recognized as an interest of Luke as well. Almost all Luke's mission-oriented material is either in the special L material that has been added to Q, or is found in Lukan revisions to earlier Q-material.

(4) There are a number of other suggestive similarities between Q and 1 Corinthians and between 1 Corinthians and Proto-Luke. Two of the more unusual ones will be explored below: the stress on communal judging in a Christian setting, and the concern about the proper place of wisdom.

Finally, there are two especially significant theological shifts that can be seen to take place between Q and Proto-Luke: (5) the shift from a heavily imminent eschatology to a balance between future and present concerns, and (6) the shift from a dominantly "Son of Man" christology to one which is unique among the gospel layers—a "Lord" christology. Both bear upon Paul's hypothesized dissatisfaction with Q and his influence upon a revision of it such as may be found in Proto-Luke.

In what follows, each of these issues will be explored in turn.

1. *Aspects of the Trial, Death and Resurrection in Proto-Luke*. The obvious place to begin is with Proto-Luke's passion narrative, and the observation—widely agreed upon—that Q did not have one. The trial in Luke is often—I think correctly—seen as almost completely different from and independent of Mark, though it has some Markan insertions. Since the resurrection accounts also do not derive from Mark or Q, Luke's Passion Narrative, less some Markan additions, is attributable to Proto-Luke.

Proto-Luke's simple addition to Q of accounts of the trial, death and resurrection of Jesus is itself no more startling than the fact that the earliest Jesus-traditions are *logia*. The addition of a passion narrative to Q is obvious, not specially "Pauline," and unsurprising. Is is startling, however, that the Proto-Lukan passion narrative has a number of very important resonances with the Pauline material, especially with 1 Corinthians, and that in almost every case the similarity does not extend to Matthew or Mark.

(a) In both Paul and Proto-Luke (1 Cor 15:3-4; Luke 24:46, cf. 24:26) there is the unusual combination of something being "written" about the "Messiah" "dying" and "rising." None of the other gospels has this combination of ideas.[10]

(b) In Proto-Luke (Luke 24:34) Jesus appears to Simon *(ōphthē Simōni)*, the only gospel reference to such an appearance.[11] This is very like Paul's report of the first appearance, though with a variant name for Peter (1 Cor 15:5, *ōphthē Kēpha*).

(c) In Proto-Luke (Luke 24:9, 33, 36) Jesus appears to the Eleven. This is the only gospel to mention the number of the disciples in connection with the resurrection and compares with Paul's formalized reference (1 Cor 15:5) to an appearance to the Twelve. In none of the other gospels does Jesus "appear" to the Eleven or Twelve; it is generally to "the disciples."[12]

(d) In Proto-Luke (Luke 24:10) the women tell the news to the "apostles." This, too, might be compared with Paul's early kerygma (1 Cor 15:7) where "all the apostles" are listed as recipients of a resurrection appearance. None of the other gospels mentions "apostles" in connection with the resurrection.

(e) In both Paul and Proto-Luke women are not witnesses of the resurrection. In Proto-Luke women are involved as witnesses of the empty tomb and as (untrustworthy) messengers to the apostles (so also Mark 16:1-8, but cf. Mark 16:9). Paul's list of resurrection appearances, of course, has no mention of women.

These five points of similarity create a strong presumption that the Proto-Lukan resurrection narrative is related to the tradition Paul passes on to the Corinthians about the resurrection. It is also, of course, related to the other synoptists' narratives, but those narratives are not connected in the same way with Paul's kerygma.

In addition, other similarities should be noted in the trial and death scenes.

(f) It is well known that the longer text of the Supper liturgy in Luke 22:19 is very similar to Paul's account in 1 Cor 11:23-24. For this reason its authenticity has often been questioned; but if the text is original it is a dramatic case of similarity between the two writings.[13]

(g) In Proto-Luke Jesus celebrates a Passover meal with his disciples (Luke 22:15). Paul, too, makes this connection in 1 Cor 5:7 where Christ is described as the paschal lamb (cf. also, perhaps 1 Cor 10:18). This emphasis is not, however, unique to Proto-Luke (it is also found in Mark 14:12 pars.).

(h) In some MSS, a prayer is ascribed to Jesus on the cross (Luke 23:34), not found in the other gospels: "Father, forgive them, for they know not what they do." If it be an authentic part of the text it has a curious resemblance to 1 Cor 2:8: "None of the rulers of this age understood this, for it they had they would not have crucified the Lord of glory."[14]

(i) In a unique christological statement Proto-Luke refers to Jesus as "the Christ of God, his Chosen One" (Luke 23:35). The nearest resemblance to Luke's *ho christos tou theou* is to be found in 1 Corinthians, though admittedly it is not very close (3:23, *hymeis de christou, christos de theou).*[15]

(j) Perhaps relevant is the fact that Jesus' promise in Proto-Luke to a criminal concerning "paradise" is reflected only in Paul's own experience of "being caught up into Paradise" (2 Cor 12:3; cf. also Rev 2:7).

These points of similarity are all between the Proto-Lukan passion narrative and the Corinthian correspondence, almost exclusively with 1 Corinthians. While the passion narrative in Proto-Luke is very similar in broad outline to the Markan narrative, their independence from each other shows the stereotyped character of the tradition of the passion. Nonetheless, the similarities between this one version of the narrative and Pauline concerns begins to demonstrate the mutual influence of Jesus-traditions on Paul, and of Paul on one of the redactional layers of the gospels, and other features of Proto-Luke reinforce a perception of this mutual influence.

2. *A Revisionist View of John the Baptizer.* When Paul first describes the tensions in Corinth (1 Cor 1:10-13) he moves immediately into a discussion of baptism (1 Cor 1:13-17), then almost imperceptibly shifts into a consideration of Christ and the cross (1 Cor 1:17-19), and then to a consideration of wisdom. The association of baptism, cross, and wisdom reflects Paul's assessment of the key issues dividing him from the other leaders in the Corinthian Church. Apollos is probably the source of this particular set of concerns for he reflects a variant position on baptism ("the baptism of John," Acts 18:25), he is untutored in the Christian way (he had to have "expounded to him the way of God more accurately," Acts 18:24-28), and he debates with lofty words (as Acts 18:24 says, he is "eloquent").[16]

This intriguing conjunction between 1 Corinthians and Acts is relevant to our purpose because Q, like Apollos, is strong on John and weak on the cross. Indeed Q is not only lacking the passion narrative but also any reference to the cross in passion predictions. Apollos's stance then might be more than incidentally related to Q's. Apollos could well have aligned himself with that form of Jesus-traditions found in Q, but not with the further theological development reflected in Paul's clear focus on cross and resurrection. This difference between Paul and Apollos would well explain the otherwise perplexing description of Apollos in Acts 18:25-26—that he "taught accurately the things concerning Jesus" but inaccurately "the way of God." We may surmise also that Apollos is too tied to his earlier understanding as a disciple of John. And now that he knows the Q traditions, he is confirmed in his views by the importance given to John and his baptism.

The relevance of this speculation concerning Apollos and Paul is that between Q and Proto-Luke an important reconsideration of the place of John has occurred. Proto-Luke presents a revisionist view of John which modifies his prominence in the collection of sayings in Q, and which is consistent with Paul's attempt to downplay the importance of the role of baptizers in 1 Corinthians. This devaluation of John is seen in the following features of Proto-Luke.

(a) Proto-Luke rearranges the narrative so that John is removed from the scene formally (though he reappears in the narrative later, of course) before Jesus is even mentioned (3:21). In 3:19-20 Herod is charged with shutting up John in prison, an incident that is found in Mark 6:17-18 // Matt 14:3-4. This is followed in 3:21 by report of Jesus' baptism which avoids saying—even though it maintains the implication—that Jesus was baptized by John. This combination of alterations leads to the inference that John is only a forerunner. He is quickly removed from the scene, after which Jesus controls and dominates the action. Proto-Luke is here counteracting a tendency of the redaction of Q to elevate John to a position beside Jesus.[17]

(b) Proto-Luke contains the only pericope in the synoptic gospels that raises the question whether John is the Christ (3:15, cf. also John 1:25). A similar question is raised in the Markan material (Mark 8:27-28 pars.), but about Jesus. This question about John in Proto-Luke is all the more remarkable since it is the only time in this redaction that this christological title is used until the trial, and in the trial (22:67) the question has an almost identical form. Further, it is only Proto-Luke who in the trial keeps the two christological questions about "Christ" and "Son of God" separate, as they ought to be. Proto-Luke underlines the claim that Jesus alone is the proper holder of the title "Christ," and he may see that particular question as one of the key issues of the gospel. Following the trial the term is used four times: in the Sanhedrin's summary of the accusation against Jesus (23:2), in the criminal's confession from the cross (23:39), and twice by the risen Jesus of the Messiah's suffering (24:26, 46).

(c) When a short Markan insertion in the Proto-Lukan narrative in 3:1-6 is removed, the Baptist's ministry is described in the following terms: "the word of God came to John the son of Zechariah in the wilderness; and he went into all the region about the Jordan, as it is written in the book of the words of Isaiah the prophet, 'The voice of one crying in the wilderness . . . .' " The Markan insertion into this pericope refers to John preaching a baptism of repentance for the forgiveness of sins, and John's demand for repentance is echoed in a later Q saying (Luke 11:32 // Matt 12:41; Luke 10:13 // Matt 11:20-21), but the introductory statement of Proto-Luke makes John's preaching simply a preparatory wilderness mission.

(d) The next Proto-Lukan pericope after the baptism (excluding the geneaology) stresses that Jesus is full of the Spirit (4:1, 14, 18), the obvious complement to John's reported statement in 3:16 ("I baptize you with water . . . he will baptize you in Holy Spirit and fire") and another instance of Proto-Luke's heightened contrast of Jesus and John.[18]

(e) Proto-Luke likens Jesus to Elijah (and Elisha) in Luke 4:24-27. The other gospels compare John to Elijah. For example, in Matt 11:14, a Matthean redactional addition to a Q pericope, John is Elijah who is to come; in the Proto-Lukan version of this pericope (Luke 16:16) there is no reference to Elijah at all. Instead there is the well-known variation between Matthew and Luke on the implied chronology of the breaking in of the Kingdom.

(f) In another Proto-Lukan pericope we find a strange conjunction of ideas: "I came to cast fire upon the earth; and would that it were already kindled! I have a baptism to be baptized with; and how I am constrained until it is accomplished! Do you think I have come to give peace on earth?" (12:49-51). The association of fire, violence and baptism invites comparison with Luke's version of John's statement in 3:16, "he will baptize you with the Holy Spirit and with fire," and with another reference to John in 16:16, that "every one enters [the kingdom of God] violently." These three pericopae taken together seem another revisionist tactic, implying more than just that Jesus fulfills John's expectation: Proto-Luke seems to urge that Jesus' real baptism is not John's baptism at all, but rather his coming agony.[19]

(g) Luke 7:18-28 presents the Q account of John's disciples going to Jesus. It is noteworthy that John is not in prison (cf. (a) above, Matt 11:2), and that John sends his disciples to "the Lord," not "the Christ" as in Matthew. (Jesus is not yet "the Christ" in Proto-Luke.) Jesus dazzles John's messengers "in that hour" by curing many. The pericope is bracketed in Proto-Luke on the one hand by references to Jesus as "the Lord" (editorially) and "a great prophet," and by "God has visited his people" (both in the crowd's mouth), and on the other hand by a description of John as "a prophet" and as Jesus' "messenger." All of these heighten the contrast between Jesus and John and increase the sense of John's subordination.

These redactional motifs show that the differences between John and Jesus have been heightened in Proto-Luke. In terms of timing, function, and position Proto-Luke enhances the position of Jesus and, where he alters the picture of John, he tends to lessen his role. The Corinthian situation would provide some reasons for these alterations, as I have suggested.

3. *Missionary Aspects of Proto-Luke.* The Gospel of Luke has a special interest in the Gentiles and Gentile mission.[20] This missionary emphasis derives from Proto-Luke and is one of its dominant characteristics. The material can be classified under two main headings: places where minor changes in Proto-Luke's use of the Q material show an increased interest in mission; places where there are major variations, with which this section begins.

(a) Proto-Luke chooses to use as the introduction to Jesus' ministry the Preaching of Nazareth where one finds the dual motif of acceptance and rejection (4:16-30). This pericope is introduced by the revealing phrase, "their synagogues," in 4:15. Jesus quotes Isaiah to underline his mission to "poor," "captives," "blind," and "oppressed" (cf. also 7:22; 14:13; 14:18; 14:21); when giving examples of his prophetic ministry he likens himself to Elijah who went not to Israel but to a Sidonian woman, and to Elisha who went not to Israel but to a Syrian; as a result Jesus is thrown out and "went away." It is difficult to see this as anything other than a statement about the church's mission to those beyond the synagogue. This motif is held in tension with Luke's interest in the synagogue: Jesus is in the synagogue six times in Proto-Luke (plus two questionable, plus seven drawn from Mark), eight times in Mark, and nine times in Matthew.

(b) In the introduction to Proto-Luke, a Gentile emphasis may also be present. In 3:6 the quotation from Isaiah concludes with "all flesh shall see the salvation of God," and in 3:7; 3:10; 3:15; 3:18; 3:21, a generalizing noun is used consistently: multitudes, people, all the people.[21] In no case, of course, does the phrase need to imply Gentiles; but Gentile readers might well be expected to see themselves pictured here.

(c) This *Tendenz* is found in Luke 21:23-24 where the unusual eschatological word *anagkē* is used (elsewhere in the New Testament as an eschatological term only at 1 Cor 7:26) of the "distress . . . upon the earth and wrath upon this people." Whether the clause, "Jerusalem will be trodden down by the Gentiles until the times of the Gentiles are fulfilled," refers to a Gentile inheritance of the place of "this people" is not clear, but it is consistent with a Gentile mission.

(d) Alongside this can be put Proto-Luke's distinctive form of the Q parable of the Great Banquet (Luke 14:15-24). Though not as heavily allegorized as the Matthean form, the missionary motif is more clearly present. Mission takes place in two stages: to the city, and beyond the city. The negation of the invitation to "those who were invited" is cast in different terms from the Matthean form, terms strongly suggestive of the Gentile mission.

These examples juxtapose an emphasis on Jesus' mission with Israel's rejection of its proper place. There are other minor instances of the same tendency.

(e) In 6:22 Proto-Luke inserts "when they exclude you," and in 6:23 he replaces Q's neutral "men" with "their fathers." Both variants heighten the tension between Jews and the Christian messengers.

(f) The account of the Centurion (7:1-10) adds to Q's strong emphasis on lack of faith in Israel another dimension. A non-Jew "loves our nation and he built us our synagogue"; he even can get "elders of the Jews" to intercede with Jesus on his behalf—all missing from Matthew's account and probably from Q.

(g) The evidence from the Commissioning of the Seventy (Luke 10:1-12) is not as clear as one would expect from a pericope so obviously connected to mission. Indeed its most interesting evidence has to do with the eating practices of those sent: only Luke's version provides instructions to eat and drink whatever a householder provides, and even repeats that those sent in the gospel are to "eat what is set before you." These instructions are reflective of a mission among Gentiles, and easily bear comparison with 1 Cor 8-10.[22]

(h) In the Q saying about persecution there is probably another reference to missionary activity (11:49). It seems likely that Q contained a reference to "wise men" and possibly also "scribes," which Proto-Luke has replaced with "prophets and apostles" (cf. also 6:13). In the immediately following saying Proto-Luke is more specific than Matthew about the lawyers' "hindering those who were entering" (11:52).

Enough has been said to show that in Proto-Luke there is a strong emphasis on Gentile mission and that this mission involves a shadow aspect, the rejection of the Jews. In some places Proto-Luke seems almost to have historicized Paul's own missionary experiences: the exclusion from the synagogues; being brought "before synagogues and the rulers and authorities" (12:11); and possibly even the fascinating aside in 8:3 about the Twelve being provided for out of the women's means.[23] But the similarities are found not only in experience but also in thought: the Gentile mission according to both Paul and Proto-Luke occupies an important interim place ("until the times of the Gentiles") during which time the place of the Jews is questionable, to say the least.[24] Both 1 Corinthians and Proto-Luke retain an imminent eschatology, but they both also stretch out the time so that there is an important "present"—the time of the Gentile mission. The eschatological understanding of the Gentile mission shared by Paul and Proto-Luke is expressed by Paul more clearly in 1 Thess 2:16 and Rom 11, but it also underlies 1 Corinthians (see below).

4. *Suggestive Similarities: Judging and Wisdom in Proto-Luke.* These two themes are assessed together because of their bearing on the question of a link with 1 Corinthians. Both are minor themes in Proto-Luke, but in both cases their shape in Proto-Luke bears out my hypothesis. I will comment first on "judging statements" in Q, Proto-Luke, and 1 Corinthians.

(a) A Q saying, as reported in Luke 6:37, reads "Judge not and you will not be judged." Is it possible that in this Q saying there is to be found a partial, or even complete, explanation of the Corinthians' refusal to judge (1 Cor 5-6)?[25] If someone in Corinth, perhaps Apollos as I have suggested, knew the Q-traditions, one might well imagine this saying used to urge the course of action that Paul must contend against in 1 Cor 5:1-5 and 6:1-6. The Q saying, however, is modified in Proto-Luke first by the inclusion of parallel references to not condemning and to forgiving, and secondly, by the inclusion of other Q materials, found elsewhere in Matthew, that modify the force of the original saying: you can't play blind man (6:39) or you will both fall in a pit; you must be like your teacher (6:40). And thirdly, Proto-Luke omits, immediately after the "judge not" sayings, the complementary saying in Matthew, which I suspect was found in Q, "for with the judgment you pronounce you will be judged." This redactional setting softens—albeit slightly—the force of the saying, in ways compatible with Paul's concerns in 1 Corinthians.

(b) To this pericope should be added a reference to the Q pericope on judging the twelve tribes of Israel (22:28-30). This saying is the only possible synoptic background to Paul's statement in 1 Cor 6:2 about the saints judging the world. With Paul's strong introductory statement, "Do you not know . . . ," it may be that he is alluding to another *logia* from Q to offset the effect of the one found in Luke 6:37.

(c) Luke 12:57 is also noteworthy: "Why do you not judge for yourselves what is right?" This Proto-Lukan addition prefaces a Q pericope which describes a disciple going with an accuser before a magistrate. Because it presupposes a setting very much like that described by 1 Cor 6, the addition could have been generated by the Corinthian dispute, and supports Paul's demands of the Corinthians.

With respect to "Wisdom" in Q, Proto-Luke and 1 Corinthians, three points may be summarized. First, all the relevant wisdom passages are in Q; there are a few important Proto-Lukan variations in them but no totally new material. Second, in the variations Proto-Luke tends to omit the references to "wise" men. Third, Proto-Luke enhances slightly the references to wisdom.

(d) The most important pericope is the notorious "thunderbolt from the Johannine sky" in Luke 10:21-24, which in Proto-Luke lands firmly in a mission context. I have worked out the connections between this pericope and 1 Cor 1-2 elsewhere.[26] Here it will suffice to say that the wisdom traditions in Q bear upon the disputes in Corinth, for they provide a basis for Apollos' and others' wisdom approach to the good news. Paul refers only indirectly to this "thunderbolt" because of the use of Q by Apollos, but in Paul's allusive reference to the saying he particularly reinforces the negation: "These things [are hidden] from the wise and understanding."[27] The Proto-Lukan form of the saying is closer to the original than the Matthean form. Apart from the addition of the editorial phrase "and turning to the disciples," no other alterations were called for in Proto-Luke.[28]

(e) In Luke 6:48 the word "wise" is dropped in the context of a man laying a foundation. The foundation metaphor figures prominently in 1 Cor 3 as a part of Paul's view of the divisions in Corinth; there it is Paul who lays the foundation on which another builds. In a similar fashion "wise men" is dropped from the Q saying in Luke 11:49, and is replaced by "apostles" (Matt 23:34 has "prophets, wise men, and scribes"). This pericope was introduced in Q by a reference to "the Wisdom of God";[29] what Proto-Luke has done is to retain the theological hypostasization, but eliminate the reference to current "wise men" in favor of "apostles."

(f) Another revision in the Proto-Lukan view of the wise man occurs in 12:42-46. Q has, and Proto-Luke retains, the "wise steward" who is the subject of the story (considerably expanded in Proto-Luke by the addition of 12:47-48 and 12:49-53 [cf. Matt 10:34-36]). The Matthean form distinguishes between two servants by the insertion of a "wicked servant," who shares the final end of the "hypocrites." In Proto-Luke, however, the servant in verse 45 is the same servant as in verse 42: the wise and faithful steward has become unfaithful (cf. 1 Cor 4:1-6). It is possible that this form is nearer Q's original, but there can be no doubt that it is also a form of the pericope more relevant to Paul's controversies in Corinth, where the problem is explicitly what Proto-Luke implies. Paul says "it is required of stewards that they be found trustworthy" (*pistos*, cf. Luke 12:46, *meta tōn apistōn*), and he goes on to say, "I have applied all this to Apollos and myself."

(g) Proto-Luke does not always delete references to wisdom; it retains "wisdom" found in a Q saying in Luke 7:35 // Matt 11:19. And Proto-Luke also retains a reference to wisdom in a Q pericope where Matthew does not have it. The Proto-Lukan statement in Luke 11:52 charges the lawyers (Matthew = scribes and Pharisees) with having "taken away the key of knowledge *(kleida tēs gnōseōs)* and hindering "those who were entering." This is probably a case where Matthew has shifted the saying to refer to the kingdom of heaven.

When this evidence is put together it appears that both judging and wisdom have caused problems in Corinth, that Q pericopes concerning judging and wisdom would support positions Paul opposes in Corinth, and that the Proto-Lukan variations of these Q pericopes are patient of the interpretation that they are intended to avoid some of the misunderstandings created in a context like that in Corinth. In sum, Proto-Luke like Paul in 1 Corinthians heightens the need for judgment and minimizes the wisdom element.

5. *Christology in Proto-Luke.* Proto-Luke's theology, which can here only be hinted at in this section on christology and the next on eschatology, is clear and distinct. It differs from the theology of Q, and may differ somewhat from the theology of Luke in its final form.

Proto-Luke is woven around a "Lord" christology.[30] In this it is unique among the gospels or gospel sources. This one motif dominates proto-Luke and gives a clear indication of the purpose behind the compiling of this collection of Jesus materials. A table is appended that will show this and other christological data.

The dominant christological emphasis inherited from Q is "Son of Man." Proto-Luke expands their number through his use of the L material. This added material does not alter or expand significantly the range of Son of Man sayings. The majority of the references are earthly; there are a number of apocalyptic sayings; but there is only one suffering Son of Man reference, and that in a resurrection pericope (24:7), where it is cast in the mouth of the two men in dazzling apparel, quoting a saying of Jesus. There is a double strangeness to this: not only is it found on the lips of someone other than Jesus (cf. perhaps Acts 7:56, re. Stephen), but more significantly there is no saying in Proto-Luke to which this can refer.[31]

Proto-Luke is also strongly flavored by three other motifs. There is a fascinating "messiah" strain, introduced in 3:15 with reference to John, referred to glancingly in 4:18 (the Spirit *echrisen me*), and then strongly evident from the trial on (22:67; 23:1; 23:39; 24:26; 24:46). As suggested earlier, one of the reasons for the writing of Proto-Luke may have been to refute the notion that John is a messianic figure, and to demonstrate how, in the trial and resurrection, Jesus is demonstrated to be the Messiah. Alongside this runs a "Son of God" christology. It is introduced in the temptation (4:3, a Q passage), is present in the transfiguration if the words of the voice from the cloud are Proto-Lukan (9:35) and in a rare form in 10:22 where there is an absolute use of Son, and then reappears in the Trial, where Luke is careful to keep Son of God separate from Messiah. Figuring more strongly in the early portions of the narrative is a "prophet" christology (4:24; 7:16; 7:39; 13:31-33; 24:19).

But it is "Lord" who dominates Proto-Luke. Of all the sayings, only two seem to be drawn from Q; the rest are from special Lukan materials. Peter, the disciples, the Seventy, Martha, Zacchaeus, the Centurion and other unnamed persons all refer to Jesus as *kyrie*. The author frequently finds *kyrios* the appropriate term to use when referring to Jesus, sometimes in missions- related contexts (10:1; 7:13), sometimes in instructional settings (10:39; 17:5-6; 19:8).[32]

This combination of motifs—Lord, earthly Son of Man, Messiah, Son of God,

Mosaic Prophet—has a unique flavor. The emphasis on the Lord is strongly dominant. And the juxtaposition of an early prophet motif, replaced by Son of God and Messiah, is unusual. Many of the Proto-Lukan instances of the designation of Jesus as "Lord" occur in the narrative, or in the mouths of others (see table). Since the sayings materials will be more influenced by the need for fidelity to oral tradition, and the narrative materials will show the editorial stance of Proto-Luke most clearly, the "Lord" christology of Proto-Luke is thus shown even more strongly.

This unique Proto-Lukan emphasis on a "Lord" christology is easily assimilable to Pauline theology, and strongly supports the hypothesized influence of Paul on the Proto-Lukan redaction of Q.

6. *Eschatology in Proto-Luke.* Proto-Luke inherited from Q a strongly imminent expectation of the breaking in of the Kingdom. The additions to and revisions of this eschatology generally move it in two complementary and compatible directions: towards a longer period of time before the end, and towards a greater stress on the significance of the present. A few examples will suffice for our purpose here.

(a) In the Beatitudes (Luke 6:20-26) Proto-Luke's emphasis in four places (two of them Q, two L) is on "now." Indeed Proto-Luke's point is the eschatological significance of the present, since, unlike Matthew, Luke does not spiritualize the Beatitudes (e.g. poor, not poor in spirit; hunger, not hunger and thirst for righteousness).

(b) In the sayings on earthly care and watchfulness, there are several minor alterations to be noted. In Luke 12:32 Proto-Luke's version of the Q saying specifically refers to the "little flock" who will inherit the Kingdom. In 12:41 Luke adds Peter's question whether the parable is "for all." In 12:45 he adds "in coming" to the words "My master is delayed." In 12:49 there is one of three important references to "fire," here explicitly noting that the fire is not yet kindled (the other two references are 9:54 and 17:29). And in 12:56 Luke's version of a Q saying replaces "signs of the times" with "the present time."

(c) In Luke 13:6-9 (the Parable of the Fig Tree) the Proto-Lukan message is that there is more time before the tree is cut down.

(d) Proto-Luke includes a statement in 17:20 that "the kingdom of God is not coming with signs to be observed" and follows that immediately with a unique statement that "the kingdom of God is in the midst of you" (17:21). There are two further additions (17:23-24), both putting the Son of Man's coming farther away: ". . . in his day. But first he must suffer many things and be rejected by this generation" (cf. also 17:30).

(e) The most outstanding case is Proto-Luke's addition to the Q material found at Luke 19:11: "because they supposed that the Kingdom of God was to appear immediately." This is given as one of two reasons for the telling of the Parable of the Pounds, but is transparently addressed to the situation of the redaction. For this reason one should take seriously as an important Proto-Lukan secondary conclusion the additional sentence in Luke 19:27 ("But as for these enemies of mine, who did not want me to reign over them, bring them here and slay them before me"). With this we might compare 1 Cor 15:25, or 4:8.

(f) The question of the Proto-Lukan form of the Little Apocalypse is very difficult and will not be raised here.[33] But the saying in 21:24 about Jerusalem being "trodden down until the times of the Gentiles are fulfilled" is a very important Proto-Lukan emphasis. Alongside this it is important to underline another saying in 21:28 (found only in Luke): "when these things *begin* to take place . . . your redemption is drawing near."

These represent the more important Proto-Lukan variations to the imminent Q eschatology which still dominates Proto-Luke. In every case the emphasis of the alteration is on the importance of the present time, and the need to recognize more time before the end.

The relationship between Proto-Luke's and Q's eschatology is paralleled by the relationship between Paul's and a competing group's eschatology in Corinth. The eschatologies are not identical, neither Q's and the competing group's, nor Proto-Luke's and Paul's. In Corinth, for example, it appears that someone is arguing that the Kingdom has already come and that the saints are already reigning (1 Cor 4:8; cf. 15:12). What is important to observe, however, is that Proto-Luke's additions and alterations to Q's imminent eschatology are similar to Paul's retention of an imminent eschatology (1 Cor 7:26, 31) with a strong stress on more time before the end.

Conclusion

What I hope to have shown is that there is a consistent correlation at a wide variety of points. The pattern of the correlation is this: disagreement between Q and Paul, with a possibility at some points that problems experienced in Corinth could have been prompted by Q materials; agreement between Proto-Luke and Paul's attitude to the issues raised in Corinth.

I have not systematically addressed methodological problems in reconstructing Proto-Luke, or problems in distinguishing Proto-Lukan features from those of the final redaction. Nonetheless, some conclusions concerning these issues have been supported. I suspect it to be the case that most of the emphases generally attributed to Luke are, in fact, emphases of Proto-Luke. If Streeter is correct that the Markan material is later inserted into Proto-Luke, then the characteristics and purpose of the final Lukan redaction need to be sought elsewhere than in the redactional motifs of Proto-Luke. It is likely the case that the final version of Luke is motivated by a desire to build a bridge between the churches lying behind Mark's gospel and those in the Pauline mission lying behind Proto-Luke.[34]

Streeter's hypothesis of the existence of an earlier edition of Luke independent of Mark's gospel opens up some interesting avenues of exploration when considering the question of Paul and Jesus-traditions. Streeter's emphasis on local diversity is an important contribution to our understanding of the early church, and is also a much more congenial notion in today's scholarly world. That the Pauline mission, in particular, was characterized by a very hesitant attitude to existing collections of Jesus material, I have no doubt. That other attitudes existed alongside Paul's views is also very likely. And that these varying attitudes came into conflict, and ultimately needed to be reconciled, seems to me altogether probable. Streeter contributed substantially to pointing us in one good direction for attacking these issues.

Let me add one other curious support to these tentative conclusions. The so-called Anti-Marcionite prologue to the Gospel of Luke says in part: "Though the gospels were already in existence, that according to Matthew composed in Judea and that according to Mark in Italy, he [Luke] was prompted by the Holy Spirit and composed this gospel entirely in the regions about Achaia . . . it was necessary to set forth for Gentile converts the accurate account of the (new) dispensation that they might not be distracted by Jewish fables or deceived by heretical and foolish fantasies, and so miss the truth itself. . . ."[35]

A recognition of the mystery surrounding the composition of Luke is perhaps the right place to stop. Yet, while Luke's association with Corinth cannot be sure, the evidence highlighted in this paper, the anti-Marcionite prologue, and the Proto-Luke hypothesis all lead in the same direction.

Notes

1. E. E. Ellis, *Prophecy and Hermeneutic in Early Christianity,* Grand Rapids, 1978, 237-53; the quotation is from 240. In a more recent homage to M. Hengel, "Traditions in 1 Corinthians," *NTS* 32 (1986) 481-502, Ellis has surveyed very succinctly a wide range of data, including "Jesus-Traditions" (485-90). He cites approvingly M. Dibelius's view that "collections which contained exclusively sayings of Jesus . . . were given to the missionaries orally or fixed in writing" in the context of an argument that Paul had a collection of Jesus-traditions that he passed on, including prominently traditions about the "body of Christ" and the "temple of God."

2. B. H. Streeter, *The Four Gospels: A Study of Origins, Treating of the Manuscript Tradition, Sources, Authorship, & Dates,* London, 1924; references to the second edition (1926).

3. B. H Streeter, *The Primitive Church Studied with Special Reference to the Origins of the Christian Ministry,* London, 1929, was written as a sequel to *The Four Gospels* and explicitly argues from wide evidence for local diversity.

4. His closest and best known follower is V. Taylor, *Behind the Third Gospel: A Study of the Proto-Luke Hypothesis,* Oxford, 1926. J. Jeremias, in his own way, has also adopted this stance. More independently, see L. Gaston, *No Stone On Another,* Leiden, 1970. A handy summary of the arguments against the hypothesis can be found in J. A. Fitzmyer, *The Gospel According to Luke 1-9,* Garden City, N.Y., 1981, 89-91. Most of the arguments that he uses fall on closer inspection.

5. E. E. Ellis, *The Gospel of Luke,* London, 1966, 21-27.

6. For example, W. G. Kümmel, *Introduction to the NT,* revised edition, Nashville, 1975, 149.

7. See P. Richardson and P. Gooch, "Logia of Jesus in 1 Corinthians" in *Gospel Perspectives 5: The Jesus Tradition Outside the Gospels,* ed. by D. Wenham, Sheffield, 1985, 39-62; P. Richardson, "The Thunderbolt in Q and the Wise Man in Corinth," in *From Jesus to Paul,* ed. by P. Richardson and J. C. Hurd, Waterloo, 1984, 91-111. For a somewhat different suggestion, see J. M. Robinson, "Basic Shifts in German Theology," *Int* 16 (1962) 82-86; "Kerygma and History in the New Testament," in *The Bible in Modern Scholarship,* ed. by H. P. Hyatt, London, 1965, 127-31; and also H.-W. Kuhn, "Der irdische Jesus bei Paulus," *ZTK* 67 (1970) 295-320. D. L. Balch, from a very similar concern, comes closest to the thesis of this paper when he says: "Paul then gave this saying [scil. Luke 14:26] the same ascetic interpretation as Luke later did. I conclude that the Corinthians' asceticism was formed by certain sayings of the Lord that were under discussion at Corinth." ("Backgrounds of 1 Corinthians 7," *NTS* 18 (1972) 351-64; the quote is from 358).

8. A similar attempt has been made by several people, most notably R. P. Martin, *Mark: Evangelist and Theologian,* Grand Rapids, 1973, 156-62, who suggests that Mark derives from the need to correct an exaggerated Pauline type of Christianity unconcerned with Jesus' humanity. See also H. C. Kee, *Jesus in History, An Approach to the Study of the Gospels,* New York, 1977; J. M. Robinson, "Logoi Sophon: On the Gattung of Q," in *Trajectories Through Early Christianity,* Philadelphia, 1971. C. M. Tuckett, "1 Corinthians and Q," *JBL* 102 (1983) 607-19, argues explicitly against an influence of Q on 1 Corinthians. In his nicely nuanced article, Tuckett in fact summarizes a good bit of data that support the contention of an influence (e.g. work by Koester, Kuhn, and Balch). He distinguishes carefully between Paul's knowledge of Q and the Corinthians' knowledge of Q. The main difference between what Tuckett argues against and what I argue for is that I contend that not only is Q a factor influencing one part of the opposition to Paul, but that one can find reflections in a later strand of the synoptics (Proto-Luke) of the same kind of tension. It is the synchronism between the disputes in Corinth and the differences between Q and Proto-Luke that are the strongest arguments in favor of some knowledge of Q in the Corinthian setting.

9. It is worth recalling here Martin's argument (*Mark,* 24-28, 156-62) that Mark, as the earliest gospel, is the first to apply to this new genre of literature the term "gospel," taken over from Paul's emphasis on "gospel" as an oral message about the crucified and risen Lord. Proto-Luke does not begin with "gospel" (indeed the word never appears in Luke and only twice in Acts), and this absence is carried over into the final form of Luke's introduction (Luke 1:1-4). Perhaps this is because for Luke "gospel" is reserved for the Pauline kerygma.

10. Luke 24:46, *hoti houtōs gegraptai pathein ton christon kai anastēnai ek nekrōn tē tritē hemera.* 1 Cor 15:3-4, *hoti christos apethanen hyper tōn hamartiōn hēmōn kata tas graphas, kai hoti etaphē kai hoti egēgertai tē hēmera tē tritē kata tas graphas.*

11. In John, Simon Peter is a witness of the empty tomb (John 20:2, 6) and is the key actor in the account of John 21 set by the Sea of Galilee, an appearance to seven "disciples."

12. The "Eleven" do appear in one Matthean pericope (28:16). It is primarily a commissioning account, not a resurrection account, though it does refer to their "seeing" *(idontes)* him. The late Markan longer ending (16:14) also contains a reference to the "Eleven."

13. See the discussion in B. M. Metzger, *A Textual Commentary on The Greek New Testament,* London/New York, 1971, *ad loc.*

14. The authenticity of the logion is quite doubtful in the text of the final version of Luke. It is possible that it properly belongs to the Proto-Lukan stage of the pre-history of Luke and was subsequently deleted, in most MSS, because of an increasing degree of "anti-Judaism" in Luke. See L. Gaston, "Anti-Judaism in the Passion Narrative in Luke and Acts," in *Anti-Judaism in Early Christianity,* ed. by P. Richardson, Waterloo, 1986, 127-53, especially 152; cf. S. G. Wilson's essay in the same volume.

15. Cf. Mark 15:32, *ho christos ho basileus Israēl;* Matthew 27:42, *basileus Israēl.* For "chosen one," see John 1:34.

16. The first word of the quotation in 1 Cor 1:19 *(apolō)* is probably a deliberate pun on the name Apollos *(apollō).*

17. In this section of the paper I am indebted to J. Kloppenborg, now of the University of Windsor, for a number of helpful suggestions. His recent work on Q provides very helpful analyses of the redaction of Q; see especially "Tradition and Redaction in the Synoptic Sayings Source," *CBQ* 46 (1984) 34-62; "Wisdom Christology in Q," *Laval théologique et philosophique* 34 (1978) 129-47.

18. It is unclear to me whether the account of the descent of the Spirit after Jesus' baptism in Luke 3:22 is a part of Proto-Luke. It looks Markan. And it is also unclear to me if the genealogy belongs in Proto-Luke. The narrative may have jumped from 3:21 to 4:1 in this fashion: "Now when all the people were baptized and when Jesus also had been baptized . . . the Holy Spirit descended upon him in bodily form . . . and Jesus, full of the Spirit returned from the Jordan . . . ."

19. It is tempting to suggest with respect to 12:49-51 that the final clause in 12:51 "No, I tell you, but rather division . . ." is related to the divisions in Corinth. While such a suggestion may be too far-fetched, yet the word "division" is missing in Matthew's parallel of this Q pericope (Matt 10:35), and the pericope in Proto-Luke is found in a context of stewardship and servanthood, the very issue that dominates the early chapters of 1 Corinthians.

20. See S. G. Wilson, *The Gentiles and Gentile Mission in Luke-Acts,* Cambridge, 1973, esp. 29-58. For a perspective on Mark see D. Senior, "The Struggle to be Universal: Mission as a Vantage Point for New Testament Investigation," *CBQ* 46 (1984) 63-81.

21. The noun *laos* used here in three places would be understood by Jews to mean the people of Israel. See my *Israel in the Apostolic Church,* Cambridge, 1970, Appendix B). It may be doubted whether Luke understood "Jews" by this term (cf. Acts 15:14; 18:10).

22. Matthew's version—"the laborer deserves his food" (10:10)—seems an awkward reworking of the more obvious Lukan "the laborer deserves his wages," and probably indicates Matthew's attempt to remove the offensive instructions concerning food. See Tuckett, 612.

23. P. Richardson, "From Apostles to Virgins: Romans 16 and the Roles of Women in the Early Church," *Toronto Journal of Theology* 2/2 (1986), 232-61.

24. Wilson, *Gentiles,* 249-55.

25. P. Richardson, "Judgment in Sexual Matters in 1 Corinthians 6:1-11," *NovT* 25 (1983), 37-58.

26. Richardson, "Thunderbolt" (as in note 7, above).

27. See also the pericope in Luke 12:1-4 where everything is to be revealed and made known. The Proto-Lukan form of the pericope has moved the emphasis away from Jesus and put it on the speech of his disciples (or is it the Pharisees?).

28. See Kloppenborg, "Wisdom Christology" (as in note 17, above), 135.

29. See S. Schulz, *Q: Spruchquelle der Evangelisten,* Zürich, 1972, 336 and n. 96.

30. On the Proto-Lukan character of *kyrios,* see H. Schürmann, "Protolukanische Spracheigentümlichkeiten," *Traditionsgeschichtliche Untersuchungen,* Düsseldorf, 1968, 209-27, esp. 224-25.

31. This may, in fact, indicate that this saying, and perhaps the whole pericope, should be attributed to the final redactor's hand.

32. Streeter uses this christological usage to a different effect. Pointing out that many of the instances are in a Q context, but not in Q, he argues that *kyrios/kyrie* demonstrates that the Q and L materials were joined before the Markan material was added, hence this becomes a strong argument for the correctness of the Proto-Luke hypothesis. See *The Four Gospels,* 212-14.

33. See Gaston, *No Stone.*

34. See also my comments in "Thunderbolt" (as in note 7, above), especially 110-11.

35. English translation from J. A. Fitzmyer, *The Gospel According to Luke,* 1981, 38; Greek text in Aland, *Synopsis;* discussion in R.G. Heard, *JTS,* n.s. 6 (1955) 7. Nothing that I am aware of in the New Testament would naturally suggest to a later editor that Luke wrote in Achaia. Why then? I would not wish to claim that he actually wrote in Achaia, only that there was a vague tradition connecting the gospel with Achaian "fables . . . and . . . fantasies."

Appendix: Addresses/Titles for Jesus in Proto-Luke

([ ] doubtful; <u>underline</u> = Q; rest are L)

	In Jesus' Mouth	*In Others' Mouths*	*In Narrative*
kyrios	<u>6:46</u> (why do you call me *kyrie*)	5:8 (Peter)	7:13 (Lord saw her)
	(10:2, 22, Jesus' title for God)	9:54 (disciples)	10:1 (Lord appointed)
		9:61 (another)	10:39 (sat at the Lord's feet)
	(3:4, quote from Isaiah)	10:17 (the 70)	
	[12:36f] (parable of the servants waiting)	10:40 (Martha)	10:41 (Lord answered)
		11:1 (disciples)	11:39 (Lord said)
	[12:42ff] (parable of the wise and faithful steward)	13:23 (someone)	13:15 (Lord answered)
		13:25 (someone)	17:5 (said to Lord)
		17:37 (disciples)	17:6 (Lord said)
		19:8 (Zaccheus)	18:6 (Lord said)
		22:33 (Peter)	19:8 (said to Lord)
		22:38 (disciples)	7:19 [Q?] (sent to Lord)
		22:49 (disciples)	
		24:34 (disciples)	
		<u>7:6</u> (Centurion)	
huios tou anthrōpou	<u>6:22</u> (not Mt)	24:7 (men at tomb "quoting" Jesus)	
	<u>7:31</u>		
	<u>7:34</u>		
	<u>9:58</u>		
	<u>11:30</u>		
	<u>12:8</u> (not Mt)		
	<u>12:10</u>		
	<u>12:40</u>		
	17:22		
	<u>17:24</u>		
	<u>17:26</u>		
	<u>17:30</u>		
	18:8		
	19:10		
	21:36		
	(22:27, replaces Son of Man)		
	22:48		
	22:68		

	In Jesus' Mouth	*In Others' Mouths*	*In Narrative*
christos	(3:15 re: John the Baptist) [4:18] the Spirit *echrisen* 24:26 (should suffer) 24:46 (should suffer)	22:67 (council) 23:2 (council) 23:35 (rulers 23:39 (criminal)	
huios tou theou	10:22 (no one knows) [22:29] (my Father) [22:42] (Father) [23:46] (Father)	22:70 (council) [9:35] prob. Mark 4:3 (devil) 4:9 (devil)	3:38 (genealogy)
prophētēs	4:24 (no prophet) 13:33 (prophet perish)	7:16 (crowd) 7:39 (Pharisee) 24:19 (disciple)	
didaskalos	6:40 (disciple not above)	7:40 (Pharisee) 11:45 (lawyer) 12:13 (someone) 19:39 (Pharisee) 10:25 (lawyer)	5:3 (*edidasken*) 13:22 (*didaskōn*)
Others	*basileus*, 19:38 (disciples); [23:42] (criminal) *dikaios*, 23:47 (centurion) *iatros*, 4:23 (Jesus) *kēryx*, 4:18 (Jesus, quoting Isaiah); 8:1 (narrative)—cf. *euangelistēs*		

Nochmals: Paulusakten und Pastoralbriefe*

W. Rordorf

Am VIII. Internationalen Patristiker-Kongress in Oxford (1983) habe ich nicht nur die Apostelgeschichte, sondern auch die Pastoralbriefe mit den Paulusakten konfrontiert.[1] Ich bin zum Schluss gekommen, dass der Verfasser der Paulusakten weder von der Apostelgeschichte noch von den Pastoralbriefen abhängig ist, sondern in seinem Werk z.T. gleiche Traditionen, wie sie hinter der Apostelgeschichte und den Pastoralbriefen stehen, verwertet und selbständig verarbeitet hat.

Zur selben Zeit hat D. R. MacDonald sein Buch *The Legend and the Apostle. The Battle for Paul in Story and Canon*, Philadelphia, 1983, veröffentlicht. Was das Verhältnis zwischen den Pastoralbriefen und den Paulusakten betrifft, kam er zum genau gleichen Resultat wie ich.[2] Er ist aber noch einen Schritt weitergegangen: aufgrund von eingehenden Studien über die Gesetze der mündlichen Tradierung, die er in den Paulusakten wiederfindet, wagt er die kühne These aufzustellen, die Pastoralbriefe seien in der Absicht verfasst worden, emanzipatorischen Tendenzen, wie sie sich in den mündlichen Legenden, die vor der Abfassung der Paulusakten schon in Kleinasien in Frauenkreisen umliefen, entgegenzutreten.[3]

Ich möchte nun auf dieser Linie noch etwas weiter voranzukommen versuchen. Es muss ja auffallen, dass die Pastoralbriefe gegen die *persönlichen Umstände* der Missionstätigkeit des Paulus, wie sie in den Paulusakten geschildert sind, *nicht* polemisieren, sondern im Gegenteil ungefähr dieselben Umstände voraussetzen. Daraus wird man wohl schliessen dürfen, dass in *dieser* Beziehung die Pastoralbriefe und die Paulusakten nicht nur von der gleichen Tradition abhängen, sondern sie auch stillschweigend als glaubwürdig hinnehmen und als solche überliefern.

Mein Aufsatz gliedert sich dementsprechend in folgende Teile: I. Zuerst möchte ich nochmals kurz die zwischen Pastoralbriefen und Paulusakten übereinstimmenden Traditionen zusammenstellen. II. Dann wird vor allem die Frage aufzuwerfen sein, ob und wie diese Traditionen eventuell im Leben des Paulus unterzubringen wären.

Als Auftakt ist es wohl das beste, wenn ich gleich meine Ansicht über die "Historizität" der Pastoralbriefe bekanntgebe. Mit der Mehrheit der Exegeten teile ich die Auffassung, dass die Briefe in ihrer *jetzigen* Form kaum von Paulus stammen können. Dagegen spricht das konstrastreiche, z.T. judaistische, z.T. gnostische Profil der Häresie, die von den Pastoralbriefen bekämpft wird und die am besten ans Ende des 1. Jahrhunderts zu situieren ist.[4] Zum gleichen Resultat gelangt man, wenn man die ekklesiologischen Verhältnisse in den Pastoralbriefen untersucht.[5] Trotzdem hält es schwer, den sogenannten persönlichen Notizen in den Pastoralbriefen jeglichen authentisch-biographischen Charakter abzusprechen.[6] Da die Fragmenten-Hypothese allerdings auch auf Schwierigkeiten stösst,[7] bin ich geneigt, P. Dornier[8] zuzustimmen, der zu folgendem Schluss kommt:

> Paul aurait bien écrit deux lettres à Timothée et une à Tite; cette édition, aujourd'hui perdue, était sans doute plus courte, plus spontanée et plus représen-

tative de la théologie de l'Apôtre. Après la mort de celui-ci, un disciple ... aurait repris (vers 70-80) les trois lettres et en aurait donnée une édition plus développée et répondant mieux aux besoins de l'Eglise de son temps. Il ne s'agirait pas là de l'oeuvre d'un 'faussaire', composant de toutes pièces un pastiche plus ou moins heureux, mais d'une nouvelle rédaction d'écrits authentiquement pauliniens.

I

Die Uebereinstimmungen zwischen den Paulusakten und den Pastoralbriefen sind hauptsächlich in den vorkommenden Personennamen zu finden. Nehmen wir sie der Reihe nach durch!

1. *Demas und Hermogenes* (der Kupferschmied[9]) treten in den Theklaakten (die bekanntlich ein Teil der Paulusakten sind) als Reisegefährten des Paulus bei seiner Ankunft in Ikonium auf, die von Paulus im christlichen Glauben unterrichtet worden sind, ihm aber nur aus Heuchelei anhangen (Kap. 1) und darum auch von Onesiphorus nur widerwillig als Brüder anerkannt werden (Kap. 4). Bald werden sie denn auch zu offenen Gegnern des Apostels, indem sie dem enttäuschten Thamyris, dem Bräutigam Theklas, raten, Paulus den Behörden als Christen zu denunzieren (Kap. 11-14). Bei dieser Gelegenheit sagen sie zu Thamyris: "Und wir werden dich belehren, dass die Auferstehung, von der dieser (sc. Paulus) sagt, dass sie geschehe, schon in den Kindern geschehen ist, die wir haben, und wir auferstanden sind, indem wir den wahren Gott erkannt haben".[10]

Nun ist es auffälig, dass wir diese beiden Männer auch im 2. Timotheusbrief in ungünstigem Licht antreffen. In Kap. 1, Vers 15 lesen wir: "Du weisst es, dass alle, die in Asia sind, sich von mir abgewendet haben, unter denen Phygelus ist und Hermogenes".[11] In Kap. 4, Vers 10 heisst es dann ferner: "Denn Demas hat mich im Stich gelassen, weil er die jetzige Welt liebgewann, und ist nach Thessalonich gereist", und in Vers 14f.: "Alexander, der Schmied, hat mir viel Böses zugefügt; der Herr wird ihm nach seinen Werken vergelten". Ist es ein purer Zufall, dass hier nochmals ein Schmied erscheint?[12] Im gleichen Brief finden wir genau die von Demas und Hermogenes in den Theklaakten vertretene Lehre, dass die Auferstehung bereits stattgefunden hat, allerdings hier mit den Namen Hymenäus und Philetus verbunden (2.Tim. 2,17f.).[13]

2. *Onesiphorus.* Er wird schon zu Beginn der Theklaakten als Christ eingeführt, der von Titus eine Beschreibung der Gestalt des Apostels Paulus erhalten hat und ihn darum sofort auf der Strasse erkennt (Kap. 2-4). Offensichtlich versammelt sich die Gemeinde von Ikonium im Hause des Onesiphorus (Kap. 5); in ihm hört auch Thekla Paulus Predigen (Kap. 7) undkehrt darum später an diesen Ort ihrer Bekehrung zurück (Kap. 42). Onesiphorus, dessen Frau Lektra und dessen Kinder Simmias und Zeno[14] namentlich erwähnt werden (Kap. 2), zieht nachher mit seiner Familie Paulus nach, der sich in einer Grabanlage versteckt hat. Dort haben sie nichts zu essen. Der Text kommentiert: "Und sie hatten nichts, wovon sie Brote hätten einkaufen können; denn Onesiphorus hatte die weltlichen Dinge verlassen und war dem Paulus mit seiner ganzen Familie gefolgt" (Kap. 23). Darauf entlässt Paulus den Onesiphorus mit seiner Familie und zieht mit Thekla nach Antiochien (Kap. 26).

Auch Onesiphorus wird im 2. Timotheusbrief zweimal erwähnt. In Kap. 1,16ff. lesen wir:

Der Herr schenke Barmherzigkeit dem Hause des Onesiphorus; denn er hat mich oft erquickt und sich meiner Ketten nicht geschämt, sondern als er nach Rom gekommen war, hat er mich eifrig aufgesucht und gefunden. Der Herr gebe ihm, dass er Barmherzigkeit finde von seiten des Herrn an jenem Tage. Und wieviele Dienste er in Ephesus geleistet hat, weisst du besser als ich.

Und in 4,19 wird er von Paulus zusammen mit Priscilla und Aquila, also vermutlich auch in Ephesus, gegrüsst.

Hier ist die Vergleichsbasis also auch relativ schmal. Sowohl in den Theklaakten als auch im 2. Timotheusbrief wird uns gesagt, dass Onesiphorus mit seiner ganzen Familie Paulus viele Dienste erwiesen hat, aber die Ereignisse, auf die sich die Theklaakten beziehen, geschehen in Ikonium, während der 2. Timotheusbrief Onesiphorus und seine Familie mit Ephesus und Rom in Zusammenhang bringt.

3. *Titus*. In den Theklaakten, Kap. 2, erscheint Titus schon als Vorgänger von Paulus: er hat Onesiphorus das Porträt des Apostels schon vor dessen Ankunft in Ikonium beschrieben. Nachher hören wir dann nichts mehr von Titus, bis zum Martyrium Pauli in Rom, wo es heisst: "Es erwarteten aber den Paulus in Rom Lukas, der aus Gallien, und Titus, der aus Dalmatien (gekommen war)" (Kap. 1). Die beiden, Titus und Lukas, sind dann auch beim Grabe des Paulus, wo sie den Soldaten Longus und Cestus die Taufe geben (Kap. 5/7).

Die letztere Nachricht trifft sich wieder einigermassen mit einer Stelle im 2. Timotheusbrief. In Kap. 4,10-11 lesen wir: "Crescens ist nach Galatien (= Gallien[15]), Titus nach Dalmatien gereist. Lukas ist allein bei mir". Der 2. Timotheusbrief sezt ja voraus, dass Paulus als Gefangener in Rom weilt.[16] Lukas ist also nach dieser Voraussetzung bei ihm in Rom; es ist allerdings nicht er, der mit Gallien in Verbindung gebracht wird, sondern Crescens. Und Titus ist nicht wie im Martyrium Pauli von Damatien hergekommen, sondern dorthin abgereist.[17]

II

Lassen sich die von den Pastoralbriefen und den Paulusakten vorausgesetzten Ereignisse im Leben des Paulus unterbringen?

Was die Pastoralbriefe betrifft, haben die Exegeten, welche an der Glaubwürdigkeit wenigstens der persönlichen Notizen, die in diesen Briefen enthalten sind, festhielten, natürlich immer wieder versucht, diese Frage zu bejahen. Sie sind aber zu sehr verschiedenen Resultaten gelangt.[18] Und es ist merkwürdig, dass niemand[19] auf die Idee kam, für diese Untersuchung auch die Paulusakten heranzuziehen. Offensichtlich hat man ihr Zeugnis nicht genügend ernstgenommen, da es sich um eine apokryphe Schrift handelt, die mit den kanonischen Pastoralbriefen nicht auf eine Stufe gestellt werden darf.

Ich sage gleich, dass mich die Versuche, die von den Pastoralbriefen und den Paulusakten vorausgesetzten Ereignisse *im Rahmen der von der kanonischen Apostelgeschichte geschilderten Zeitepoche* unterzubringen, nicht überzeugen.

1. Eine erste Variante wurde in letzter Zeit vor allem von B. Reicke nachdrücklich und mit Erfolg vertreten.[20] Der 1. Timotheusbrief wäre zwischen Sommer 56 und 57 geschrieben; der Titusbrief im Jahre 58, und der 2. Timotheusbrief während der zweijährigen Gefangenschaft des Paulus *in Cäsarea* (laut Apg. 24-26). Ich will gleich auf den letzten Punkt eingehen, der mir der schwächste an der ganzen Rekonstruk-

tion zu sein scheint. Denn nach Reickes Ansicht muss die Gefangenschaft des Paulus, die in 2. Tim. 1,16f. vorausgesetzt ist, als diejenige in Cäsarea, welche Apg. 24-26 schildert, gedeutet werden. Das ist aber doch wohl eine gewaltsame Exegese der betreffenden Stelle:

> Die kurze Notiz über die Ankunft des Onesiphorus in Rom (2.Tim 1,16f.) soll nicht dahin verstanden werden, dass sich Paulus zur Zeit des 2. Tim in einem römischen Gefängnis befand . . . Onesiphorus ist . . . nicht mit Eifer nach Rom gefahren, um Paulus im Gefängnis zu besuchen, sondern der Eifer setzte ein, als er Paulus in Rom zunächst nicht antraf, wie er offenbar erwartet hatte. Dann werden der Eifer beim Suchen und der Besuch im Gefängnis als grossartige Leistungen des Onesiphorus dargestellt, indem es heisst, dass sie vom Herrn am jüngsten Tage ganz besonders zu belohnen seien (1,18). Hätte es sich um Rom gehandelt, wäre gar kein Suchen nötig gewesen, denn jeder hätte Onesiphorus den Weg zum Gefängnis zeigen können, und ein Besuch beim verhafteten Apostel wäre ein selbstverständlicher Liebesdienst gewesen. Indem hingegen die übrigen Ortsangaben des 2.Tim auf Cäsarea als Gefängnisort hinweisen, ergibt sich eine weniger triviale Perspektive: Onesiphorus hatte den ohne sein Wissen verhafteten Apostel in Rom erwartet, musste ihn suchen, tat das mit Eifer und hat ihn dann in Cäsarea gefunden. So erscheint sein Barmherzigkeitswerk des überschwenglichen Lobpreises würdig.[21]

2. Eine zweite Variante wird von S. de Lestapis[22] vertreten. Nach ihm sind der 1. Timotheusbrief und der Titusbrief hintereinander im Frühjahr 58 geschrieben, während der 2. Timotheusbrief aus der zweijährigen *römischen* Gefangenshaft stammt, die Apg. 28 geschildert ist. Wieder ist es der letzte Punkt, welcher der Annahme dieser These Schwierigkeiten bereitet. Denn schon immer haben die Exegeten hervorgehoben, dass von einer "custodia libera", wie sie Apg. 28 vorausgesetzt ist, im 2. Timotheusbrief nichts mehr verlautet: Paulus ist in Ketten und wird wie ein Schwerverbrecher behandelt.

So bleibt—wenn man auf das biographische Material der Pastoralbriefe nicht verzichten will—nur der Ausweg übrig, anzunehmen, *die Pastoralbriefe würden auf den Lebensabschnitt des Paulus Bezug nehmen, der auf Apg. 28 gefolgt ist:* m.a.W., wir müssten postulieren, dass Paulus aus einer ersten Gefangenschaft in Rom nochmals freigekommen ist. Der profilierteste Vertreter dieser These in neuerer Zeit ist und bleibt C. Spicq.[23] Ich bin schon aus den bisher angegebenen Gründen bereit, seiner Ansicht zu folgen. Nun hoffe ich aber zeigen zu können—und darin besteht mein persönlicher Beitrag—, dass das Zeugnis der Paulusakten die These von C. Spicq einerseits zwar stützt, andererseits aber auch modifizieren hilft.

C. Spicq[24] hat die Gründe zusammengestellt, die für die Annahme einer Freilassung des Paulus nach einer ersten Gefangenschaft in Rom sprechen. Ich komme nicht auf sie zurück; sie scheinen mir persönlich stichhaltig zu sein.

Wie steht es nun aber mit den Reisen des Apostels in den Orient nach seiner Entlassung aus der ersten römischen Gefangenschaft?[25] Der Freiburger Exeget, aufgrund der persönlichen Notizen in den Pastoralbriefen, entwirft folgendes Bild:

> Il est impossible de reconstituer ses itinéraires, de déterminer leurs étapes, encore moins de leur assigner une date précise. Le plus clair est que l'Apôtre a fait de la

métropole d'Asie Mineure—où il réside avec Timothée et Trophime l'éphésien—
le centre le plus fixe, sinon permanent, de son ministère. Il a certainement visité
Colosses, où Philémon se préparait à le recevoir (*Philém*. 22). Il est passé rapide-
ment en Crète où il laisse Tite organiser les communautés locales (*Tit*. I,5) avant
de le rejoindre à Nicopolis en Epire, où il compte passer l'hiver (III,12). Lorsqu'il
s'absente d'Ephèse pour aller en Macédoine et revoir ses chers Philippiens (cf.
Philip. II,24), il confie la direction de l'Eglise à Timothée (*I Tim*. I,3); mais ce sera
un bref intérim (III,14; IV,13), car c'est au retour à Ephèse, semble-t-il,
qu'Onésiphore lui manifestera un attachement si généreux (*II Tim*. I,18; IV,19).
Contraint, enfin, de quitter définitivement les éphésiens, Paul leur envoie Tychi-
que (*II Tim*. IV,12), qui avait peut-être été l'auxiliaire de Tite en Crète (*Tit*.
III,12). C'est au cours de l'une ou l'autre de ces allées et venues que, descendant
à Troas, chez Carpos, l'Apôtre y a laissé une pèlerine et des manuscrits qu'il
réclamera plus tard.[26]

Dazu habe ich nichts zu sagen. Denn derjenige Teil der Paulusakten, der von
diesen Ereignissen gehandelt haben mag, ist verloren. Man kann höchstens aufgrund
der Titusakten vermuten, dass nach den Paulusakten der Apostel in Begleitung von
Titus tatsächlich auch auf Kreta evangelisiert hat.[27]

Präzisere Informationen bieten die Paulusakten über die Umstände der *zweiten
Romreise des Paulus*. In dieser Beziehung glaube ich nämlich über meine in Oxford
geäusserte Ansicht hinausgehen zu müssen. Ich hatte dort—unter dem Einfluss der
Autorität C. Schmidts—angenommen, die im Hamburger Papyrus erzählte
Reiseroute des Apostels, die von Ephesus über Mazedonien nach Korinth und Rom
führt, gehöre demselben Zeitraum an, von dem auch der letzte Teil der Apostelgeschichte berichtet. Ich musste mich dann mit der Tatsache abfinden, dass Paulus nach
den Paulusakten—im Gegensatz zur Apostelgeschichte—also nicht nach Jerusalem
gefahren und in Rom als freier Mann angekommen war, was ich im Anschluss an
C. Schmidt als "starkes Stück" bezeichnete.[28] Ich machte zwar den Versuch, den
Autor der Paulusakten vor dem Vorwurf einer ins Blaue hinein fabulierenden Be-
richterstattung zu retten, aber ohne Erfolg.[29] Nun glaube ich aber die Lösung gefunden zu haben.

Schon C. Schmidt musste zugeben, dass der Hamburger Papyrus der Paulusakten
auch in seinen erhaltenen Partien den ursprühglichen Text nicht vollständig wiedergibt. Die Ueberschrift oben auf Seite 6 des Papyrus "Von Philippi nach Korinth" gibt
zu verstehen, dass Paulus in Philippi Station gemacht hat; der erhaltene Text—der
hier lückenlos überliefert ist—berichtet aber nur im Rückblick von einem Aufenthalt
des Paulus in Philippi. Dieses Stück, das im koptischen Papyrus von Heidelberg enthalten ist und in dem auch der berühmte sogenannte 3. Korintherbrief überliefert
ist,[30] wurde also im Hamburger Papyrus—aus welchem Grund auch immer—über-
gangen. Nun hat C. Schmidt als selbstverständlich angenommen, dass das übersprun-
gene Stück, das über Philippi handelte, einer Episode *derselben* Reise angehört, die
auf den Seiten 1-5 und dann auf den Seiten 6-11 des Hamburger Papyrus erzählt wird.
Diese Annahme möchte ich nun bestreiten. Ich behaupte nun, dass die Lücke viel
grösser sein muss: während wir uns mit den Seiten1-5 des Hamburger Papyrus in
einem Kontext befinden, welcher sich auf der sogenannten 3. Missionsreise des
Paulus (nämlich dem in Apg. 19-20 Erzählten) abgespielt hat, sind die Seiten 6-11
dem Lebensabschnitt des Apostels zuzuordnen, welcher *nach* Apg. 28, also nach

seiner Befreiung aus der ersten römischen Gefangenschaft, zu stehen kommt.[31] Ich habe für meine neue Sicht der Dinge vor allem 3 Gründe anzuführen:

1. C. Schmidt musste alles, was er im koptischen Papyrus von Heidelberg über Philippi verzeichnet fand, in diese Lücke des Hamburger Papyrus, die nach ihm von einem einzigen Aufenthalt in dieser Stadt sprach, "hineinbeigen". Man sieht aber wirklich nicht ein, wie so verschiedene Episoden, wie die auf den Seiten 41-44 und 45-50 des Heidelberger Papyrus erzählten, einander entsprechen sollen.[32] Wenn es sich aber um zwei verschiedene Aufenthalte des Apostels in Philippi handelt, dann fallen alle Schwierigkeiten mit einem Schlag dahin.

2. Im Hamburger Papyrus (S. 6), wo wir Paulus in Korinth antreffen, wird mit keinem Wort auf den Brief Bezug genommen, den Paulus doch vor kurzem von Philippi aus an die Korinther geschrieben hätte. Das ist schlechterdings unerklärlich.[33] Zudem sind im 3. Korintherbrief ganz andere Personen erwähnt als im Hamburger Papyrus.[34] Auch hier empfiehlt es sich anzunehmen, dass es sich um zwei verschiedene Episoden handelt: die Korrespondenz mit den Korinthern situiert sich zu einem andern Zeitpunkt als der Aufenthalt des Paulus in Korinth nach dem Hamburger Papyrus.[35]

3. Das gewichtigste Argument ist—wie schon erwähnt—die Romreise, wie sie im Hamburger Papyrus (Seite 7,18ff. und 8) geschildert wird. Sie ist von A bis Z von der Romreise, die in der Apostelgeschichte geschildert wird, verschieden: Paulus kommt von Korinth, als freier Mann, auf einem Schiff, dessen Kapitän Artemon heisst und von dem gesagt wird,dass Petrus ihn getauft habe. Offensichtlich begleiten den Apostel noch andere Brüder, denn es wird erzählt, Paulus habe mit ihnen Fasten und Nachtwachen gehalten. In einem Traum sieht der Apostel Christus auf dem Meere wandeln, mit betrübter Miene, so dass Paulus ihn fragt, warum er leide? Darauf erhält er die Antwort vom Herrn, er sei im Begriff, von neuem gekreuzigt zu werden.[36] Paulus solle nach Rom gehen, um die Brüder zu stärken. In Italien angekommen, geht Paulus mit Artemon in das Haus eines gewissen Claudius, wo andere Brüder versammelt sind und voll Freude einer langen Ansprache des Paulus zuhören.[37]

Diese Reiseschilderung—das dürfte klar sein—hat nichts mit der in der Apostelgeschichte erzählten Reise zu tun. Dann dürfen wir sie aber wohl als mögliche Quelle für die Rekonstruktion der zweiten und letzten Reise des Apostels nach Rom benutzen, wie sie C. Spicq postuliert. Dieser sagt dazu folgendes:

> Lorsque saint Paul rédige *II Tim.*, il est à Rome, à nouveau prisonnier (I,12,16-17; II,9), et il envisage sa mort come prochaine (IV,17-18). Que s'est-il passé? On en est réduit à des conjectures, que l'on peut évoquer avec vraisemblance. Si l'Apôtre a réalisé son projet de retour à Ephèse, c'est dans cette ville qu'a dû se passer l'incident qui a amené son arrestation. Il y comptait, en effet, des ennemis acharnés (cf. *Act.* XIX,23–XX,1,3; XXI,27; II Cor.I). Parmi eux, Alexandre le forgeron—qu'il avait livré à Satan (*I Tim.* I,20)—devait, semble-t-il, chercher à se venger: 'il a fait preuve à mon endroit d'une grande méchanceté'. Y eut-il complot, échauffourée, émeute plus ou moins spontanée, une forme quelconque de provocation? Toujours est-il que la police locale est intervenue. Les conjonctures sont telles que les chrétiens ou amis du prévenu refusent de se compromettre en sa faveur et se désolidarisent de lui: 'tous les Asiates m'ont abandonné' (*II Tim.* I,15; cf. *Mt.* XXIV,10).[38]

Man kann natürlich dieser phantasiereichen Rekonstruktion folgen, wenn man will. Ich für meinen Teil neige dazu zu denken, die Paulusakten hätten hier womöglich eine glaubwürdige Tradition aufbewahrt; diese Variante ist jedenfalls durch einen aus dem 2. Jahrhundert stammenden Text verbürgt, was C. Spicq von seiner Rekonstruktion nicht behaupten kann.

Damit kommen wir zum *Martyriumsbericht* der Paulusakten,[39] der z.T. Uebereinstimmungen mit dem 2. Timotheusbrief aufweist. Wenn wir diesen Martyriumsbericht ernstnehmen, dann werden einige Fragen geklärt, die aufgrund des 2. Timotheusbriefs allein unbeantwortet bleiben.[40] Paulus kommt, wie gesagt, als freier Mann in Rom an. Dort erwarten ihn Lukas, der aus Gallien, und Titus, der aus Dalmatien gekommen war (Kap. 1; vgl. 2. Tim. 4,10f.). Er mietet eine Scheune ausserhalb Roms, wo er mit beachtlichem Erfolg Missionsreden hält. Der Mundschenk des Nero, Patroklus mit Namen, sowie weitere Leute vom kaiserlichen Hof, interessieren sich auch für die neue Botschaft. Patroklus stösst ein ähnliches Missgeschick zu wie Eutyches in der Apostelgeschichte:[41] er stürzt rücklings vom Fenster, kommt aber dank des Apostels Fürbitte mit dem Leben davon. Dieser Zwischenfall wird zum Anlass, dass Nero von der Bekehrung mehrerer seiner Bediensteten zum Christenglauben erfährt und ein Edikt erlässt, die Soldaten des Christkönigs, die durch ihre subversive Einstellung die Reichssicherheit gefährden, ausfindig zu machen (Kap 2[42]). Im Zuge dieser Fahndung wird auch Paulus dem Kaiser vorgeführt, bei welcher Gelegenheit er eine Verteidigungsrede hält. Obwohl zur Enthauptung verurteilt, wird er einstweilen noch am Leben gelassen, da die Christenverfolgung überhaupt momentan suspendiert wird (Kap. 3; vgl. 2. Tim. 4,16-17 und 4,6). Später wird Paulus dann noch ein zweites Mal vor den Kaiser zitiert, wo sein Fall reexaminiert wird, Nero aber am Todesurteil durch Enthauptung festhält. Dieses Mal wird das Urteil auch vollstreckt (Kap. 4-7).

Um zum Schluss zu kommen: Die in den Pastoralbriefen (vor allem im 2. Timotheusbrief) und in den Paulusakten verarbeiteten Traditionen, die sich zu ergänzen scheinen, würden also durchaus im Leben des Paulus unterzubringen sein, falls man sich dazu entschliessen kann, sie in einem Zeitabschnitt, der auf Apg. 28 folgt, anzusiedeln. In diesem Fall würden die Paulusakten eine willkommene Stütze und Ergänzung für das sonst ganz auf sich allein gestellte Zeugnis der Pastoralbriefe bieten.[43]

Notes

*Die folgende Studie ist meinem langjährigen Freund Earle Ellis gewidmet. Ich möchte ihn bei dieser Gelegenheit ermuntern, sein geplantes grösseres Werk bald zum Abschluss zu bringen. Wir warten darauf!

1. "In welchem Verhältnis stehen die apokryphen Paulusakten zur kanonischen Apostelgeschichte und zu den Pastoralbriefen?"; erscheint in Band 3 der Kongressakten (Kalamazoo, MI).

2. "The *Acts of Paul* and the Pastoral Epistles", 59-66.

3. "Chapter III: The Pastoral Epistles against 'Old Wives' tales", 54-77. Vgl. meine Rezension des Buchs von D. R. MacDonald, in : *Cristianesimo nella storia* 6 (1985) 148-151, sowie meinen Forschungsbericht "Tradition and Composition in the *Acts of Thecla*", in *Semeia* 38, ed. D. R. MacDonald, 1986, 43-52.

4. Gute Zusammenfassung von G. Haufe, "Gnostische Irrlehre und ihre Abwehr in den Pastoralbriefen", in: *Gnosis und Neues Testament*, Berlin 1973, 325-339. Zur Einordnung der Häresie siehe P. Prigent, "L'hérésie asiate et l'Eglise confessante de l'Apocalypse à Ignace", *VigChr* 31 (1977) 1-22.

5. Vgl. z.B. A. Lemaire, *Les ministères aux origines de l'Eglise*, Paris, 1971, 123-138; H. v. Lips, *Glaube - Gemeinde - Amt*, Göttingen/Zürich, 1979.

6. Trotz N. Brox, "Zu den persönlichen Notizen der Pastoralbriefe", in: *Pseudepigraphie in der heidnischen und christlich-jüdischen Antike*, Darmstadt, 1977, 272-294.

7. Vgl. z.B. M. Carrez, "Les Epîtres pastorales", in: *Introduction à la Bible. Nouveau Testament III*, Paris, 1977, 197f.

8. *Les Epîtres pastorales*, Paris, 1969, 25.

9. Diese Berufsbezeichnung fehlt in einem Teil der handschriftlichen Überlieferung.

10. W. Schneemelcher, in: *Neutestamentliche Apokryphen*, II, Tübingen, 1964[3], 245, übersetzt etwas anders.

11. Und gleich anschliessend, in Vers 16, wird sehr viel Gutes von Onesiphorus gesagt.

12. B. Reicke, "Chronologie der Pastoralbriefe", *ThLZ* 101 (1976), 86, bringt ihn sogar mit dem in Apg. 19,33 erwähnten Alexander zusammen.

13. Aber Hymenäus und Alexander erscheinen andererseits zusammen in 1. Tim 1,19-20 als Männer, die Paulus dem Satan übergeben hat.

14. Die handschriftliche Überlieferung ihrer Namen ist sehr schwankend. Sie finden sich auch in 2 Minuskelhandschriften (Nr.181 und 460) zu 2. Tim 4,19.

15. Es handelt sich um Gallien; vgl. C. Spicq, *Les Epîtres pastorales*, II, Paris, 1969[2], 811-813.

16. Siehe dazu unten.

17. D. R. MacDonald, *The Legend and the Apostle*, Philadelphia, 1983, 61, möchte noch zwei weitere Übereinstimmungen zwischen Paulusakten und Pastoralbriefen festhalten.

(1) 2. Tim 3,10-11 berichtet von einer Verfolgung des Apostels in Antiochien, Ikonium und Lystra. MacDonald sieht hier keine Anspielung auf Apg 13-14, sondern auf die in den Theklaakten erzählte Verfolgung in Ikonium und Antiochien, weil Timotheus sie "beobachtet" habe, was erst nach Apg. 16, also zu einem späteren Zeitpunkt als Apg. 13-14, möglich sei. Damit nimmt er aber das Verb *parakoloutheo* zu wörtlich; es schliesst nicht ein, dass Timotheus bei diesen Verfolgungen zugegen war.

(2) 2. Tim 4,16-19 versteht MacDonald als eine Anspielung auf eine *ephesinische* Verfolgung, wie wir sie am Anfang des Hamburger Papyrus der Paulusakten finden (siehe auch Seite 23 seines Buches, und seinen Artikel "A conjectural emendation of 1 Cor 15:31-32; Or the case of the Misplaced Lion fight", *HThR* 73 [1980] 265-276). Es ist aber viel wahrscheinlicher, dass 2. Tim 4,16-19 sich auf eine *römische* Gefangenschaft des Paulus bezieht; siehe unten.

18. Vgl. den ausführlichen Forschungsbericht von S. de Lestapis, *L'énigme des Pastorales de saint Paul*, Paris, 1976, 33-79.

19. Ausser W. Michaelis, *Die Apokryphen Schriften zum Neuen Schriften zum Neuen Testament*, Bremen, 1958[2], 272-282, der es aber nicht genug systematisch machte; siehe unten Anm. 31.

20. "Chronologie der Pastoralbriefe", *ThLZ* 101 (1976) 81-94; ders., "Caesarea, Rome, and the Captivity Epistles", in: *Apostolic History and the Gospel. Biblical and Historical Essays presented*

to F. F. Bruce, 1970, 275-286. J. A. T. Robinson, *Redating the New Testament*, London/Philadelphia, 1976, hat diese These zu der seinen gemacht.
21. Art.cit. (*ThLZ*), Sp.90.
22. Op.cit. (Anm. 18), 83-177.
23. *Les Epîtres pastorales*, I-II, Paris, 1969²; speziell I, 126-146. Vgl. auch W. Metzger, *Die letzte Reise des Apostels Paulus*, Stuttgart 1976.
24. Op.cit., 126-129.
25. Ich möchte in diesem Zusammenhang nicht auf die Diskussion von C. Spicqs These eingehen, Paulus sei nach seiner Freilassung zuerst nach Spanien gereist (op.cit., 129-138). Gerade sie wird jedenfalls von den Paulusakten nicht gestützt!
26. Op.cit., 138f.
27. Vgl. mein Oxforder Referat (Anm. 1).
28. Der Hamburger Papyrus der Paulusakten ist von C. Schmidt und W. Schubart herausgegeben worden; vgl. dazu E. Hennecke- W. Schneemelcher, *Neutestamentliche Apokryphen*, II, Tübingen 1964³, 222-224; 254-257; 261-268.
29. Siehe die Anm. 29 meines Oxforder Referates (Anm. 1).
30. Siehe dazu Hennecke-Schneemelcher, *Neutestamentliche Apokryphen*, II, 222-224; 257-261.
31. W. Michaelis, op.cit. (Anm. 19), 273f., hatte schon in dieser Richtung gesucht, aber die Zäsur zwischen den Seiten 8 und 9 gesucht, was das eigentliche Problem nicht löst.
32. Einmal (S. 41-44) ist Paulus im Metallbergwerk (darauf ist vielleicht auf Seite 6 des Hamburger Papyrus angespielt), das andere Mal (S. 45-50) schreibt Paulus, wegen einer gewissen Stratonike gefangen, seinen berühmten Brief an die Korinther.
33. Die Bemühungen C. Schmidts, *Praxeis Paulou. Acta Pauli*, Hamburg 1936, 98-100, das Rätsel verständlich zu machen, wirken sehr gekünstelt.
34. Im 3. Korintherbrief sind es Stephanus, Daphnus, Eubulus, Theophilus, Xenon, Theonoe, Threptus und Eutychus; im Hamburger Papyrus sind es Epiphanius, Kleobius und Myrte.
35. Das Postulat von Schmidt, dass sich nach den Paulusakten der Apostel in einer Stadt immer nur einmal aufhielt, ist—schon gerade wegen des 3. Korintherbriefs—nicht aufrecht zu halten.
36. Dieses Jesus-Logion ist von Origenes, Johanneskommentar XX,12, zitiert worden.
37. Zu dieser Ansprache besteht eine auffallend grosse Parallelüberlieferung auf Papyrusfragmenten.
38. Op.cit., 141.
39. Der Martyriumsbericht ist gut überliefert; vgl. Hennecke-Schneemelcher, *Neutestamentliche Apokryphen*, 225; 265-268.
40. Vgl. C. Spicq, op.cit., 141-145, dessen Ausführungen ich im folgenden stillschweigend korrigiere.
41. Siehe dazu mein Oxforder Referat (Anm. 1).
42. Ich habe an anderer Stelle versucht, den Bericht der Paulusakten als Quelle für Tertullians Erwähnung des "institutum Neronianum" zu identifizieren und den historischen Hintergrund dieser Tradition im Lichte der neronischen Verfolgung vom Jahre 64 zu verdeutlichen: vgl. *NTS* 27-28 (1982), 365-374.
43. Seit der Niederschrift dieses Aufsatzes (Sommer 1986) hat E. E. Ellis, "Traditions in the Pastoral Epistles", in *Studies in Memory of W. H. Brownlee*, Decatur 1987, 237-253, speziell 248ff., sich selber zu diesem Thema geäussert; es wird ihn freuen festzustellen, dass ich unabhängig von ihm zu den gleichen Ergebnissen gelangt bin.

The Hermeneutical Significance of 1 Cor 2:6-16

Peter Stuhlmacher

Translated by Colin Brown

At the present time critical exegesis has very little to say on the hermeneutical significance of 1 Cor 2:6-16. Apart from Hans Weder's investigation of *Das Kreuz Jesu bei Paulus* (1981) and Gerd Theissen's study of *Psychologische Aspekte paulinischer Theologie* (1983) [Eng. tr. *Psychological Aspects of Pauline Theology*, 1987], there has been hardly any public reflection on the hermeneutical relevance of this passage in the exegetical and theological debates of recent decades. This state of affairs is unfortunate, and fails to match the hermeneutical heritage of the Reformation era and the obligation which it lays upon us. It is therefore time to attempt to renew the discussion.

I

For the Reformers 1 Cor 1:18–2:16 was of the utmost importance. In the Heidelberg Disputation of 1518 Luther developed his celebrated *theologia crucis* on the basis of 1 Cor 1:18ff. When seven years later in *De servo arbitrio* he disputed with Erasmus of Rotterdam about the appropriate method of interpreting Holy Scripture, he again proceeded from the testimony of Paul. Luther's hermeneutical thesis concerning the twofold clarity (and twofold obscurity) of Scripture corresponds exactly to the apostle's position. According to Luther, only those who are moved by the Holy Spirit and whose hearts are not darkened by Satan (cf. 2 Cor 4:4; 1 Cor 2:15) attain inward understanding of Scripture and the certainty of faith. "No one on earth will understand Scripture or even the slightest thing in Scripture without the Holy Spirit."[1] On this insight there was no real difference between Luther and Erasmus. What was disputed, however, was whether Scripture by its external testimony and wording enables the gospel to be so clearly recognized, that preachers and teachers can appeal to it, refer to Scripture as the measure of faith, and hope to bring about spiritual understanding through proclamation and teaching of the externally clear word. Whereas Erasmus remained skeptical on this, Luther vehemently argued for the external clarity of Holy Scripture (citing as support 1 Tim 3:16 and 2 Pet 1:19). On the authority of 1 Cor 1:23, 2:8, 14, 3:20 Luther rejected every intellectual counter-argument. Holy Scripture remains outwardly obscure with regard to the gospel only to those who want to understand the Word of God by their own free will, their own reason, and their own strength.[2] Luther summed up both aspects of his teaching in the *Small Catechism:*

I believe that I cannot by my own reason or strength believe in Jesus Christ, my

Lord, or come to Him; but the Holy Spirit has called me by the Gospel, enlightened me with His gifts, sanctified and kept me in the true faith. . . .[3]

On this issue Calvin shared the same view as Luther. Adopting Luther's hermeneutical approach, he developed on the basis of Eph 1:13-14 the celebrated doctrine of the *testimonium Sancti Spiritus internum [arcanum]*. In the *Institutes* of 1559 he wrote: "As God himself in his word is the sole, truly authentic witness of himself, so too this word will not find faith in human hearts until it has been sealed by the internal testimony of the Holy Spirit."[4] As scriptural proof of this Calvin also cited 1 Cor 2:14.[5] Good exegete that he was, he explained both in the *Institutes* and in his *Commentary* on 1 Cor 1:18–2:16, that sealing by the Holy Spirit is not only a matter of the illumination of the understanding but also of the strengthening of the heart. Hence according to Paul, the knowledge of faith and the life of faith belong inseparably together.[6] On 1 Cor 1:20 Calvin vividly wrote: "Both these points are to be observed with care, that knowledge of all academic disciplines is mere smoke where the heavenly wisdom of Christ is lacking, and that a man on his own with all his wits is as incapable of understanding the mysteries of God as an ass is unsuited for music."[7]

Hermeneutically these insights were cherished right down to the hermeneutics of pietism and the biblical interpretation of J. G. Hamann. In his posthumously published *Erläuterung über seine eigene Institutiones Hermeneuticae Sacrae*[8] Johann Jacob Rambach took up Calvin's saying about the ass and explained that, for the purpose of a truly insightful exposition of Holy Scripture, the *animus profanus* "must be removed and laid aside, so unsuited it is for exegesis as the ass is for the lyre *[ut asinus ad lyram]*."[9] Rambach went on to say:

One must put on the *sanctum animi habitum,* so that there must be *vera & sincera pietas;* but this cannot happen without special assistance of the Holy Spirit. The exegete must find himself *in statu gratiae,* and stand as it were in a right, mysterious familiarity with the Holy Spirit, through whose inspiration Holy Scripture was composed, and who as *optimus verborum suorum interpres* is the surest and highest interpreter of his own words. There are indeed also many things in Scripture *historica, genealogica, chronologica* and *geographica* which even a profane mind can explain, which one can indeed understand without a special illumination of the Holy Spirit, and which can be made known through industry and application of the necessary *subsidiorum.* But the chief *contenta* of Holy Scripture are *ta tou pneumatos tou theou,* the things of the Spirit of God, which concern the Spirit of God and his secret working in the soul of man. . . . These cannot possibly be understood *sine spiritu sancto salutariter.* The truth of this will indeed remain standing, as 1 Cor 2:14 states: *psychikos anthrōpos ou dechetai ta tou pneumatos tou theou.* . . . On the other hand, David says in Psalm 25:14 that the secret of the Lord is among them that fear him, and he lets them know his covenant.[10]

In his *Tagebuch eines Christen* Johann Georg Hamann stated that the reading of the introductory chapter of 1 Corinthians sums up the insight that the power and wisdom of God in the preaching of the cross "puts to shame the wit of all human beings with all spirits." He added: "What an irresistible spirit is the testimony of Paul in verses 27 and 28 [of 1 Cor 1]."[11]

Hamann's pronouncement is astonishing, because in the meantime a quite different way of thinking had gained ascendancy in scholarly exegesis which was moving towards Neology. In his *Abhandlung von freier Untersuchung des Canons* which appeared between 1771 and 1775 Johann Salomo Semler equated without more ado Calvin's *testimonium Spiritus Sancti internum* with man's inner conviction of rational, moral truths. He thereby eliminated the distinction between the Holy Spirit and rational insight that was characteristic of Paul and the Reformers. According to Semler, the worth of the canonical books of the Old and New Testaments was now only determined "by their moral, general value."[12] He wrote: "The sole proof which provides complete satisfaction for the sincere reader is inward conviction through truths which are found in this piece of Holy Scripture (but not in all parts and individual books); which to put it briefly was formerly called by a biblical and somewhat obscure expression, the testimony of the Holy Spirit in the soul of the reader."[13]

With this a mighty chord was struck which resounded for more than a century. Ferdinand Christian Baur may be taken as representative of many. Stamped philosophically by Hegel's Idealism, Baur took 1 Cor 2:11 as occasion to interpret the Holy Spirit as "Christian consciousness," and to stress that in Christian consciousness God's Spirit and the human spirit become identical.

> The spirit of Christian consciousness is also identical with the Spirit of God himself, the same Spirit who in the same way as the human spirit is the principle of human self-consciousness, in God is the principle of divine self-consciousness, so that in this same unity man's knowledge of the content of his Christian consciousness is knowledge of God himself. In the content of his Christian consciousness, as essentially spiritual, the Christian therefore knows himself to be identical with the Spirit of God, because only the Spirit, the Spirit of God, the absolute Spirit can know the divine which is the content of Christian consciousness.[14]

This harmony of God's Spirit and human spirit, stabilized by Idealism, was permanently shattered by Hermann Gunkel's first published work *Die Wirkungen des heiligen Geistes nach der populären Anschauung der apostolischen Zeit und nach der Lehre des Apostels Paulus* (1888) [Eng. tr. *The Influence of the Holy Spirit: The Popular View of the Apostolic Age and the Teaching of the Apostle Paul*, 1979]. Gunkel showed that for the early church "the relationship between divine and human activity is that of mutually exclusive opposition. The activity of the Spirit is thus not an intensifying of what is native to all. It is the absolutely supernatural and hence divine."[15] According to Gunkel, wisdom in 1 Cor 2:6-10 is to be understood as revelation through the Holy Spirit.[16] Then in 1903 Gunkel advocated a thoroughgoing "history-of-religions understanding" of the New Testament.[17] In it he defended among other things the thesis *"that Christianity, born out of syncretistic Judaism, shows strong syncretistic traits."*[18]

Paradoxically this (in approach correct) history-of-religions viewpoint contributed in fact to casting doubt on the hermeneutical significance of 1 Cor 2:6-16 in German exegesis. Following in Gunkel's footsteps, Wilhelm Bousset then discovered that in our passage from Paul "the basic outlook of the ancient mystery cults flows into Christianity." Bousset ominously added: "When Paul introduced this basic idea of a hidden wisdom into the Christian church, he took the first step towards that binding of the gospel with forms of religion coined in the realm of Hellenistic culture which one day would become very harmful for Christianity."[19]

Some years later this view of the text prompted Rudolf Bultmann in critical dialogue with Karl Barth's exposition of 1 Corinthians to stress that it seemed "certain" to him that Paul in 1 Cor 2:6–3:2 was "thinking along the lines of the mystery cults."[20] The assimilation of Paul's thought to the concepts of the mystery cults had led the apostle to deviate from his insight into the paradoxical wisdom-character of the cross (cf. 1 Cor 1:24, 30). Content criticism *[Sachkritik]* therefore "rightly objects to the use of the concept of 'wisdom' in 1:18-26 as a basis for the interpretation of the concept of 'wisdom' in 2:6ff. In 2:5–3:2, it is Paul's pride which declares that Christians, too, have a 'gnosis' which can compete with the gnosis of the heathen."[21] In his *Theologie des Neuen Testaments* Bultmann further expanded this content criticism of 1 Cor 2:6ff. with the announcement that "The Gnostic idea that Christ's earthly garment of flesh was the disguise in consequence of which the world-rulers failed to recognize him—for if they had recognized him, they would not have brought about their own defeat by causing his crucifixion—lurks behind 1 Cor 2:8."[22]

Ernst Käsemann[23] and Ulrich Wilckens[24] have adopted the view of 1 Cor 2:6-16 taken by Bultmann. It is still echoed in Hans Conzelmann's commentary on *1 Corinthians*[25] as well as in Hans Weder's independent reflections on our passage.[26] It is precisely Paul's statements, which gave decisive impetus to the Reformed distinction between the external and internal clarity of Scripture and between philological-historical and spiritual-biblical interpretation, that have been subjected to theological content criticism in the history-of-religions oriented critical exegesis of our century. The apostle's argument in 1 Cor 1:18ff. with its theology of the cross is recognized and praised, but its epistemological consequences in 2:6ff. are still drawn only with hesitation or no longer at all.

Fortunately this curious exegetical constellation has not prevented Karl Barth,[27] Otto Weber,[28] Hermann Diem,[29] Friedrich Mildenberger,[30] and Wilfried Joest[31] from insisting on the necessity of spiritual-theological biblical interpretation as opposed to merely historical-critical exegesis. But despite the efforts of Ernst Fuchs on behalf of an understanding of the biblical texts[32] that transcended historical criticism, critical exegesis has not kept pace with dogmatics with regard to our principal Pauline passage. This has made it easy for evangelical opponents of historical criticism to reclaim the domain of spiritual interpretation for themselves.[33] Under these circumstances it is high time for historical exegesis to speak up for itself again on the subject of spiritual, biblical interpretation.

In the meantime yet another turn in exegesis was announced. Already in his celebrated book *Paul*, Günther Bornkamm refused to go along with Bultmann's criticism of 1 Cor 2:6-16. He stressed that the passage "in which at the first glance, by trimming his gospel to suit the Christian 'gnostics' Paul is apparently untrue to himself, makes plain that he knows no higher or deeper mysteries transcending the gospel than that comprised *in* 'the word of the cross.' Thus, the arguments which seemed to be taking him beyond himself come back to where they started, and are not only polemic, but also a very positive exposition of the gospel of the cross."[34] Then in 1979 Bornkamm's pupil Ulrich Wilckens published in the *Festschrift* for Erich Dinkler an essay "Zu 1 Kor 2, 1-16,"[35] in which he made a radical change of position. 1 Cor 2:6-16 is no longer understood by Wilckens (as in his earlier work on the passage)[36] in the sense of a wretched (from the standpoint of *Sachkritik*) accommodation of Paul to the gnostic thought-world. The passage is now understood "as interpretation of the *logos tou staurou* in direct continuation of the antithetical theme of the previous argument."[37] The background of the apostle's statements are early Jewish wisdom traditions and primitive Christian passion tradition (cf. 1 Cor 2:8 with Acts 3:17; Luke 23:13, 35; 24:20; and 1 Thess 2:15).

Gerd Theissen has emphasized (with reference to Wilckens) in his book published in 1983 on *Psychologische Aspekte paulinischer Theologie* that in 1 Cor 2:6-16 Paul "unmistakably draws on Jewish wisdom traditions" and was himself "an important factor" in the process of developing wisdom tradition into gnostic Sophia.[38] A parallel determination of the background of the passage causes Gerhard Sellin to hear in 1 Cor 2:6-16 theologically reflected "meta-language" of the apostle's preaching of the cross,[39] and to discover in 2:10b-16 a "pneumatic theory of knowledge" which Paul developed in critical dialogue with the Corinthian pneumatics.[40]

Friedrich Lang has taken up and put together all these approaches in his new commentary on the Corinthian letters. In his exposition of the "almost confessionally" shaped passage[41] he is guided by the observation that "Jewish-Hellenistic wisdom tradition, bound up with apocalyptic understanding of revelation, is to be regarded as the religious-historical background of the passage 2:6-16. The merging of wisdom and apocalyptic traditions was already common at the time of Paul."[42] According to Lang, it is critical to see how Paul interprets "these Jewish-Hellenistic traditions in a new sense, i.e. from the standpoint of the wisdom and power of God in the cross and resurrection of Christ. This has as its consequence a reduction and strong concentration of wisdom and apocalyptic ideas into the Christ-event."[43] This "new christological interpretation" provides for Lang the explanation of the "certain tension between the theological statement of content and the linguistic means of expression," which repeatedly alienated exegetes of 1 Cor 2:6-16. Lang can even see in "the mysterious wisdom which Paul and his co-workers proclaim among the perfect (2:6) 'a more penetrating interpretation of the word of the cross' (U. Wilckens) which Paul has not yet presented to the Corinthians in this way."[44]

With this account of the background of Paul's argument and with the understanding of 1 Cor 2:6-16 as the logical continuation of Paul's discussion in 1:18–2:5, German exegesis has caught up with the plea made long ago by E. Earle Ellis that interpretation of the Corinthian correspondence should not be guided by a hypothetically constructed picture of Gnosticism, but by Jewish wisdom tradition.[45] But at the same time it has gone beyond Ellis' assumption that the issue in 2:6-16 has to do solely with a previously formulated exegetical midrash taken over by Paul on the subject of "wisdom" with a central (v 9) and a concluding (v 16) quotation from Scripture.[46]

Interestingly enough when the passage is seen in the framework of Israelite wisdom thinking (and early Christian passion tradition) and is understood as relevant Pauline teaching, the hermeneutical problem, which 1 Cor 2:6-16 bequeathed to the Reformers, returns. It is in fact the question whether we have before us in these verses a spiritual theory of knowledge which is absolutely basic for understanding the revelation of God in the gospel of the crucified (and risen) Christ. It is this question which must now be investigated.

II

First, let us envisage the train of thought in which 1 Cor 2:6-16 stands.[47] After the opening address (1:1-3) in which Paul introduces himself as "called by the will of God to be an apostle of Christ Jesus" (1:1), and the proem (1:4-9), Paul begins by admonishing the Christians at Corinth whom he addresses directly as *adelphoi* (1:10-17). He exhorts them to unity (v 10) and criticizes the formation of factions (evidently in rivalry with each other), which Chloe's people had brought to his attention. Their followers had declared themselves variously as belonging to Paul, Apollos, Kephas, or even directly to Christ. Paul returns to speak about divisive factions in 3:1-4. Thus from the standpoint of the structure of the text, 1:18–2:16 is inserted into the apostle's admonition about party divisions at Corinth, and therefore is to be understood as part of this exhortation.

The section 1:18-25 takes its key words from 1:17: "cross," "Christ," "wisdom [of speech]," and "preach the gospel" (proclaim the message/Christ). It contrasts the gospel as the word of the cross—which is folly to those who are perishing but which is the saving power of God to those who are being saved, namely "us" (those at Corinth addressed by Paul as "brothers," he himself, and his co-workers)—with the wisdom of the world. The verses are carefully structured. Verse 18a is commented on by vv 19-22, and verse 18b by vv 23-25. This structuring of the text shows that we have before us in 1:18-25 a carefully considered, didactic argument of the apostle. Verses 26-31 fit into this train of thought by illustrating what Paul has said in vv 18-25 with the example of the make-up of the church. The church is drawn from the most ordinary sociological strata, and yet it may be seen as the event of divine election and new creation, which God has wrought at Corinth through the crucified and risen Christ. According to 1:30, Christ has been appointed to "us" (cf. v 18) by God as wisdom, and more precisely righteousness, sanctification, and redemption. The crucified one (v 23), proclaimed by Paul in the "word of the cross," is therefore for the apostle and his believing readers the creative wisdom of God in person who includes in himself the entire redemptive action of God. In 2:1-5 Paul follows with a second example, parallel to 1:26-31 (and again by way of illustration to vv 18-25). He now speaks of himself and his work as an apostle in Corinth. He has proceeded on his mission conscious only of knowing of Christ as crucified. His kerygma, presented in human weakness and in the fear of God ("fear and trembling"), has proved to be the authoritative Spirit-event, which established the faith of the Corinthians.

The verses which now follow and which particularly concern us (2:6-16) do not deviate from the apostle's previous line of argument, employing teaching and example at the same time. They present its continuation from the standpoint of wording (note the key words given earlier in 1:18–2:5: "wisdom," "crucify [cross]," "Spirit," "foolishness," and "know"), content, and structure. The section corresponds to 1:18-25 and is no less carefully constructed than those verses. Verses 6a and 6b set out the structure as a whole. In chiastic sequence of thought v 6b is commented upon and developed by vv 7-9 and then 6a by vv 10-16. In his carefully constructed wisdom discourse Paul presents now what he had initially only alluded to as a theme in 1:24-25. The message of the crucified Christ which appears to unbelievers as foolishness is in truth the revelation of God's wisdom. Verses 2:6-16 enlarge upon 1:18-25, and do not contradict those verses.[48]

With 3:1-4 Paul returns to the level of direct argument against party strife in the church (cf. 1:10-17). In the next section (3:5-17) he uses the example of himself and Apollos to deal with true service in the building up the (one) church. After this he again speaks of the situation at Corinth in 3:18-23. In direct application of 1:18-25 he calls upon those in the church who are ostensibly wise to become fools, in order really to attain to wisdom (in the sense of 2:6ff.). In 4:1-13 there follow renewed applications to Paul (4:1-5) and Apollos (4:6-13) of what has been said. 4:14-15 give a summary with reference to the particular situation, in which the apostle stands as "father" over against the church. In 4:16-21 the typically Pauline "ring composition" is rounded off with an exhortation to imitate Paul, a reference to the visit of Timothy that he has authorized, and the announcement of the apostle's forthcoming visit. When he comes he will find out the truth, and if need be, put his critics in their place.

When we review the total structure of the four introductory chapters of 1 Corinthians, 1:18–2:16 appear as the first major argumentative part of the apostle's exhortation. In it 1:18-25; 1:26-31, and 2:1-5 are not set in contrast with 2:6-16, but are expanded and confirmed by these verses. In 2:6-16 Paul shows in what way the word of the cross of Christ, who is God's wisdom in person (1:30), can be called the revelation of the original saving wisdom of God revealed in the gospel. This wisdom can be understood by none but those who are illuminated by the Holy Spirit and brought to the full knowledge of faith. If we compare 2:6 with 1:5-6 and 3:1-2, we see the apostle's reproachful sorrow over the fact that the spiritually richly gifted Corinthians had not yet attained (on account of their strife and divisions) this full knowledge, which is there for all believers by virtue of the Spirit. The wisdom discussion for the "mature" in 2:6ff. has the practical aim of leading the Corinthians, who in practice still fell short of their wealth of knowledge, into complete insight into the gospel. This is why "we," i.e. Paul, his co-workers, and all Christians at Corinth, have received "the Spirit which is from God" (through preaching which establishes faith, and baptism), "that we might understand the gifts bestowed on us by God" (2:12). The apostle's discussion of wisdom is intended to lead to spiritual knowledge of the gifts of God's grace which are included in Christ, i.e. to spiritual knowledge of righteousness, sanctification, and redemption, which are included in the Christ-event (1:30).

According to 2:6-16, spiritual recognition of the Christ-event means understanding the event of the cross as God's creative, redemptive act. The first actual commentary on 1 Cor 1:30 and 2:12 is to be found in Rom 3:24-26. If we see this, there is no reason at all to set the understanding of the manifestation of the righteousness of God in Christ's atoning death (according to 1 Cor 1:30 and Rom 3:24-26) in opposition to spiritual recognition of the mysterious depths of God's redemptive action in Christ (according to 1 Cor 2:6-12). The Pauline gospel as "the word of the cross" (1 Cor 1:18) is at the same time "the word of reconciliation" (2 Cor 5:19). For Paul it has its basis in the knowledge of Christ which illuminated him on the way to Damascus, which he describes in 2 Cor 4:5-6; 5:16; and Phil 3:7ff.[49] What was given and revealed to Paul himself by God in the crucified, risen Christ, Paul now proclaims and teaches to the Corinthians. He hopes that they too will soon be able to grasp the implications of the apostolic teaching that he proclaims to them.

III

The hermeneutical situation from which resulted 1 Cor 1:18–2:16 is constituted by a three-cornered relationship. The apostle, the church founded by him, and those "servants of Christ" (4:1) who worked in Corinth with Paul and after him, stand in a relationship to each other. Without propounding any wild hypotheses, the following may be said.

It is easy to understand how, in the syncretistic situation of first-century Corinth the women and men who made their way to the Christian church from the Jewish community, the world of the synagogue, and from the pagan populace of Corinth, understood the teaching presented by Paul, his co-workers and the "apostles of Christ" (who figure especially in 2 Corinthians and were opposed by Paul, cf. 2 Cor 11:13), as revelatory knowledge which enabled them to ascend to God and praise him in their own strength. (We can see a clear example of what knowledge of revelation meant for people of that time in the Hermetic tractate *Poimandres*.) This process resulted at Corinth in the self-reliant "wisdom of this world," rebuked by Paul in 1:19ff., 3:19f., and 2 Cor 10:3f. Not only did it affect Jews and Greeks who stood outside the church (cf. 1:20-22), it also threatened to bring down some of the Christians at Corinth.

It is difficult to see what special part Christian preachers working after Paul and along with him had in the growth of this worldly wisdom. It is easy enough to make Apollos, the Jewish born Christian from Alexandria (cf. Acts 18:24ff.), the chief culprit for this development at Corinth which caused Paul's disapproval. Nevertheless, he should not be made the key figure in the process. There is no hint of any special polemic against him or any other apostle in 1 Cor 1-4. "Throughout the apostle addresses the whole church. He attacks the formation of factions as such (H. Conzelmann), and rejects exclusive claims in all four groups as an offense against the unity of the body of Christ. His rebuke is not directed primarily against the missionaries themselves whom he names, but against the false estimation of leaders by their supporters."[50]

Paul's own contribution to the development at Corinth through his teaching should not be underestimated. If we take the testimony of the Corinthian letters together with Luke's account of the apostle's activity at Corinth, unless we cast wholesale doubt on Luke's description, we can form a vivid picture of Paul's activity in the city.[51] Paul found lodging and work with the "enterprising married couple" (M. Hengel), Priscilla and Aquila, who had been expelled from Rome by the Edict of Claudius (A.D. 48). He thus was living with Jewish-Christian fellow believers. At first Paul taught and disputed each sabbath in the synagogue. But when this resulted in violent disputes, Paul provocatively moved his missionary and teaching work to the house of the God-fearing Gentile, Titius Justus, adjoining the synagogue. In the meantime, Paul received energetic support from Silas and Timothy and material help through the gift from Thessalonica and Philippi (mentioned in Phil 4:15f.) Paul "stayed a year and six months, teaching the word of God" (Acts 18:11) next door to the synagogue. He finally left the city after the Jewish community had brought fruitless charges against him before the tribunal of Gallio. On the basis of Acts 18:11, the parallel account of the apostle's missionary instruction "in the school of Tyrannus" at Ephesus which went on for two years (Acts 19:9-10), and the elements of tradition in the Corinthian letters, Hans Conzelmann has concluded (in my opinion rightly) that Paul himself was engaged in "theology as schooling in wisdom."[52]

If we ask about the principal contents of Pauline missionary instruction, we can identify with some certainty three elements. First, there are gospel and faith traditions, for example, like those Paul refers to and comments on in 1 Cor 15:1-11. To these traditions belong the various Christ-formulae to be found in Paul (e.g., 2 Cor 5:21; Rom 3:25-26; 4:25), the Christ-hymns (see especially Phil 2:6-11 and Col 1:15-20), as well as a certain amount of Jesus-tradition (see below). Secondly, Paul teaches that the Holy Scriptures (the Old Testament in the canonically open form that he then had) were to be expounded with reference to Christ who is the Spirit (2 Cor 3:12-18; 1 Cor 10:11; Rom 1:1ff.). Thirdly, we find in Paul's letters detailed instruction on how one "ought to live and please God" (1 Thess 4:1). If we take all three components together, we can designate Paul as the apostolic teacher of the wisdom of God revealed in the gospel. In 2 Cor 10:3-6 Paul argues as "a wise man" in Christ (cf. 2 Cor 10:5 with Prov 21:22). Our passage, together with didactic passages like 1 Cor 13, and the apostle's rational style of argument discussed by Folker Siegert[53] with reference to Rom 9-11, provide documentary support which shows that our characterization is not without substance. The fact that the Corinthians turned the apostle's teaching into their own high-handed version of wisdom, just as they did the instruction of his co-workers and opponents, is a misfortune which Paul shares with other Christian teachers of all ages.

If we return from the three basic elements of Paul's teaching that we have just mentioned to 1 Cor 2:6-16, we can see that they are all reflected in Paul's wisdom teaching for the "mature."

1. First of all there is Holy Scripture in the form which in Paul's day was still open to the so-called apocryphal writings. As Hans Peter Rüger has shown, the proof-text in v 9 cited as Scripture draws on Isaiah 64:3 (4) and a primitive Jewish tradition of expounding the prophet. However, according to Origen's thoroughly credible testimony, it comes from a now lost Apocalypse of Elijah.[54] Verse 16 presents a quotation of Isa 40:13 which is supported by the Septuagint.

2. We know already that the entire section of the epistle is based on the thought forms and manner of speaking of late Old Testament and early Jewish wisdom. In view of the references to Sirach and the Wisdom of Solomon which will be noted later, attention may now be drawn to the fact that at the time of the apostle both of these books did not merely represent the legacy of Hellenistic-Jewish tradition, but were counted as Holy Scripture. This had its *Sitz im Leben* in the Jewish "wisdom schools," which existed both in Palestine as well as in the Diaspora.[55]

When in 1 Cor 1:18–2:16 (and likewise Rom 1:18ff. and elsewhere) Paul took up and referred to wisdom traditions, he was speaking of situations and texts which he himself (and part of his audience) already knew from Jewish school instruction. It is possible that Sirach, the Wisdom of Solomon and other related books were read and learned in the Christian school of Paul. The outstanding feature of Paul's wisdom teaching in 1 Cor 1:18–2:16 is the antithetical form in which the wisdom of God, hidden and at the same time revealed in the gospel, is set over against the wisdom of the world. This is pressed even into the sociological dimension. Paul no longer simply distinguishes, as was common in wisdom, between the wise and the foolish, the righteous and the wicked. From the standpoint of the gospel, the distinction for Paul is between "those who are perishing" and "those who are being saved," between "us" (as illumined believers) and those who reject the gospel who are not illumined. Christians (as the minority and community of faith) stand over against unbelievers.

The roots of this Christian juxtaposition of believing wisdom and worldly wisdom, of those who receive revelation and Jews and Greeks, who are in truth foolishness, lie apparently in the Jesus-tradition. Here mention may be made above all of Luke 10:21f./Matt 11:25-27[56] and Mark 4:11-12 par., for the echoes of Luke 10:21-22 in 1 Cor 1:26ff. and 2:10 are remarkable.[57] In post-Easter Christian texts like 1 Cor 8:6, Col. 1:15-20, and the Johannine Prologue, the contrast is continued between (creative and saving) wisdom in Christ and the wisdom of the world, as it presents itself in the Law of Moses. If Gerd Theissen is correct, in Jas 3:15-17 Christian "anti-wisdom" has also something to say as paraenesis. According to Theissen,

Paul's argument in 1 Cor 2:6ff. and Jas 3:17ff. probably both "go back to early Christian wisdom traditions independently of each other. Both document the sharpening of revelatory wisdom to a dualism of wisdom, and allow the social background of this process in the history of the tradition to become visible."[58]

3. As is well known, it is disputed how far Paul himself acted as a teacher of the Jesus-tradition.[59] In my opinion, 1 Cor 11:23 speaks for it rather than against it. The fact that one can no longer read out of 2 Cor 5:16 a theologically based disinterest in the earthly Jesus on the part of Paul has been stressed by Otto Betz, followed recently also by Nikolaus Walter.[60] If we pursue the traces of the Jesus-tradition as they lead to our text, it is noteworthy that (in addition to the echoes of Luke 10:21f. already mentioned) 1 Cor 2:8 is explained most simply and clearly by reference to Acts 3:17 (4:5, 8, 26), 13:27, and Luke 23:13, 35 (see Wilckens[61] and Sellin[62]). Later Gnostic traditions need not be pressed in aid of understanding this verse. Paul alludes to the passion story. "With the execution of Jesus as a political messianic pretender the representatives of the Jewish and Roman authorities have proved that they did not recognize his true identity. Here Paul calls the crucified Jesus 'the Lord of glory,' because he understands the crucified and exalted Jesus Christ as the same person. 'Lord of glory' in Judaism is a divine title (Ethiopic Enoch 22:14; 63:2 and often.)"[63]

If this explanation is correct, which was urged already by Julius Schniewind,[64] it raises the interesting question whether the contact of 1 Cor 2:8, 12 and 11:23ff. with Lucan or proto-Lucan tradition is accidental, or whether it indicates particular knowledge of that tradition. Since there are particular points of contact between Rom 13:1-7 and Luke 20:20-26, this possibility is not to be rejected out of hand. In our context, however, it is sufficient to be aware of the fact that 1 Cor 1:26ff. and 2:8, 12 can be more readily understood by reference to the Lucan Jesus-tradition than without it.

When after this review of Pauline teaching we finally proceed to the primary hermeneutical thesis of the apostle in 2:10ff., the first thing to be noted is this. Even for understanding the "depths of God" revealed by the Spirit (v 10), we must not press into service in the first instance late Gnostic tradition. An adequate understanding can be gained from the standpoint of Dan 2:22 and 2 Bar 14:8f. The Holy Spirit as the power of illumination teaches us to explore the otherwise unfathomable depths of God's way of salvation.[65] The decisive factor is to see that the principal pronouncements of the apostle in vv 11-16 carry on from the Hellenistic-Jewish wisdom tradition right down to the details. The identification of Holy Spirit and wisdom (as the God-given power of insight into the ways and will of God) is found in Wis 7:22-30 and 9:9-18.[66] Gerd Theissen has pointed out that in Wis 9:13-18 "soul" *(psychē)* and Spirit *(pneuma)* stand antithetically over against each other as in 1 Cor 2:14. "Here *psychē* and *nous*, on the one hand, and the mortal *sōma*, on the other hand, stand in opposition to each other. God himself has to communicate wisdom. Mind and soul are not of themselves able to achieve wisdom. The step from experiential to revelatory wisdom is unmistakable."[67]

That Spirit can only be known through Spirit and wisdom only through wisdom corresponds to the ancient tenet that like can only be known through like. Philo appeals to this idea in explaining his doctrine of knowledge of wisdom wrought by the Spirit (cf. Gig 9; Mut Nom 6 and 56; Spec Leg 1, 46; Mig Abr 39 and 40).[68] Paul takes up this sapiential school tradition, and makes it the medium of his Christ-Spirit theory of knowledge, which proceeds from the experience of Pentecost and baptism.

338 | The Hermeneutical Significance of 1 Cor 2:6-16

"Verse 12 is stamped by grateful joy over the fact that God has bestowed upon believers the knowledge of his saving work in Jesus Christ by the gift of the Holy Spirit, which all Christians have received in baptism (1 Cor 12:13; Acts 2:38)."[69] What Christians gain with the gift of the Spirit as the power of illumination is insight into the mysteries of revelation, but above all the understanding of the gracious gifts bestowed by God in Christ in the form of justification, sanctification and redemption (cf. 2:12 with 1:30). To this is added the capacity to interpret and identify this Spirit-given knowledge to other Christians who are filled with the Spirit. *Synkrinein* in v 13 is best rendered by "interpret" and *pneumatikois* is best understood personally. Verse 13 speaks therefore about the process of Christian preaching and instruction by Christians of other Christians.

This point is readily illustrated by 2:4-5. What Paul has achieved by his preaching and teaching at Corinth is an excellent example of interpreting spiritual things for those who are filled with the Spirit in words which the Spirit has taught. What he now writes in 2:6ff. continues the earlier teaching and expands it. Verse 13 therefore deals with preaching and teaching the gospel of the crucified Christ as the event of salvation and revelation. It was Paul's missionary experience, confirmed also at Corinth, that this preaching and teaching appears as folly to the "unspiritual" *(psychikoi)*, i.e., unbelievers who are not filled by the Holy Spirit.[70]

The apostle writes about them in 2 Cor 4:4: "In their case the god of this world has blinded the minds of the unbelievers, to keep them from seeing the light of the gospel of the glory of Christ, who is the likeness of God." The revelation of God's glory in the crucified Christ can be perceived and admitted as God's self-disclosure for the salvation of the lost only by someone who is finished with self-reliant knowledge and will before God, i.e., the *pneumatikos* who is chosen and illumined by God (cf. 1:18, 27f.; 2:14). Again Paul presents himself as the prime example of this process of election and illumination (see below), which the apostle regards as typical for every believer (cf. 1:26ff.; 3:18f.).

Comparison with 4:3-4 shows that v 15 is likewise intended to be exemplary and typical. Paul's critics at Corinth are already in view. But Paul refuses to allow anyone coming from outside, who does not have the Spirit, to pass binding judgment on himself, his co-workers, or even any Spirit-filled Christian. The discussion of wisdom concludes in v 13 with an expression of certainty. No earthly being can understand God's Spirit and mind or act as God's counselor. This is attested by Isa 40:13 (on the formulation cf. Wis 9:13). However, God has revealed himself in Christ (as his wisdom in person) to those who hear the gospel. The gift of obedient hearing is (according to Gal 3:2) the Holy Spirit, by whose power believers can reach an understanding of the mysteries of God's saving wisdom and take them to heart. The concluding words in v 16 read: "But we have the *mind* of Christ." The wording reflects the christological application of the previous quotation from Isa 40:13, and is yet another instance of the sapiential way of speaking. According to Wis 7:22, wisdom is a matter of being filled with an "understanding, holy spirit," and is in fact identical with it. From a Christian standpoint, this means that the Holy Spirit is not least active and present, when Christians are delivered from bondage to a blinded and base mind (cf. Rom 1:28) and are liberated through the obedience of faith in Christ, their Lord, to a new way of thinking which is capable of discerning revelation and the will of God (cf. 1 Cor 2:9f., 16 with Rom 12:2).

In 1 Cor 2:6-16 we are indeed presented with a theory of knowledge shaped by the wisdom traditions of Scripture, the Jesus-tradition, and the Christian experience of the Spirit. If he himself had not passed through the school of wisdom and not himself been a teacher of the revelation of wisdom in Christ, Paul would not have been able to have formulated it. The hermeneutical significance of the theory can be measured fully, if we venture to take two further reflective steps. First, we must consider more explicitly than we have done so far the fact that Paul applies to the Corinthians the very same faith cognition that brought illumination to him on the Damascus road. Secondly, we must relate this same cognition to the specifically Israelite wisdom maxim: "The fear of the LORD is the beginning of wisdom" (Prov 1:7).

IV

Paul begins 1 Corinthians with the self-designation: "Paul, called by the will of God to be an apostle of Christ Jesus" (1 Cor 1:1). He concludes the argument of 1:10–4:21 with the summons to imitate (mimēsis) his own thought and behavior, which he has already described in 2:1-5, 3:5-17, and 4:1-5 by way of practical commentary on his teaching. For this reason we do not treat Paul's testimony in 1 Cor 1:18–2:16 as analytically "retrogressive" (H. Weder). Rather, we are following the apostle's example, if we too elucidate what was for Paul spiritual knowledge of the crucified and risen Christ by means of his own accounts of the knowledge of Christ granted him on the way to Damascus. We are all the more justified in doing this in view of Paul's own repeated allusions to his call in the two Corinthian letters. In 1 Cor 9:1 he refers to his vision of the Lord (on the way to Damascus), and in 9:16 he alludes to the inescapable obligation to preach the gospel that was bound up with it. In 15:8-10 he likewise tells of the appearance of Christ granted to him and the gracious election of God which pulled him back from persecuting the church. In his missionary journeying Paul saw himself as the vanquished enemy of God, led along in God's triumphal procession as a public spectacle. Instead of being led off to death, he had been pardoned out of pure mercy to serve God henceforth as the apostolic messenger of the wisdom contained in Christ (cf. 2 Cor 2:14-16 with Sir 24:15; 39:13f.).[71]

Although illumination through his gospel remained hidden to those blinded by Satan, the apostle's gospel preaching, criticized by Paul's opponents at Corinth, still taught that the glory of God was to be seen in the face of Christ crucified and exalted at the right hand of God. God, the Creator of light, has endowed Paul the vessel of his grace with the illuminating knowledge that his glory rests in the face of Christ (2 Cor 4:4-6). In the proclamation of the gospel with which Paul was charged, God's creative primal light is revealed.[72] It proceeds from the glorified Christ in virtue of his sacrificial offering in which God has reconciled the world to himself. Whereas Paul as persecutor of the church had a carnal, polemical view of Christ, he now saw in him the reconciler and Lord, and proclaimed the gospel as the "word of reconciliation." For believers it introduces here and now the day of final salvation (2 Cor 5:14–6:2). The proclamation of such saving revelation by an apostle who was almost overwhelmed by affliction and suffering (cf. 2 Cor 4:7ff.; 6:3ff.; 11:21bff.) is no contradiction of the gospel. It only demonstrates that God's power in Christ comes to full effect just where human beings perish in their own strength (cf. 2 Cor 12:9 with 1 Cor 1:28f.; 2:3; 3:18f.). As the word of reconciliation, the word of the cross thus becomes the means of insight. It illuminates with the knowledge of God's revelation in the way of the cross of his Christ those who—like Paul—have suffered the loss of every item of knowledge and advantage, which prior to their encounter with the gospel was their security and pride (cf. Phil 3:7ff. with 1 Cor 1:26-29; 2:1-5; 3:18-23).

For Paul the persecutor, life and thought changed on the way to Damascus. God himself had (in the language of 2 Cor 10:5) taken "captive in the obedience of Christ" the mind and heart of this Pharisee zealous for the tradition of the fathers. In the face of Christ, crucified by the Jewish court at Jerusalem as a pseudo-Messiah and deceiver who led others astray,[73] Paul beheld the mighty splendor of the one God (cf. Deut 6:4). God who raises the dead had already raised from the dead this one man Jesus Christ, and had invested him with the rights of the messianic Son, which his earthly enemies denied him (cf. Gal 1:13-17). It was this vision that enabled Paul to look back and recognize that the place of deepest shame—the cursing of Jesus of Nazareth, the cross on Golgotha (cf. 2 Cor 13:4; Gal 3:13)—was none other than the scene and action of God's redemption. The cross is the event and place of the reconciliation willed by God and enacted by the atoning death of Christ. It brings about redemption for the new people of God (Rom 3:24-26; 1 Cor 1:30). The resurrection of Jesus confirms this event, but it cannot and may not overshadow it. It was on the basis of this insight that Paul proceeded at Corinth specifically and only from the knowledge of the crucified One (cf. 1:23; 2:2). It led him to condemn as Satanic deception all preaching of Christ that sounded different (cf. 2 Cor 11:4, 13f.; Gal 1:8f.).

With this we come full circle. What Paul says in 1 Cor 1:18–2:16 concerning the gospel of the crucified (and risen) Christ and his understanding corresponds in detail to the compelling knowledge of Christ bestowed on him by God on the Damascus road. For Christians, including those at Corinth, there is therefore in the encounter with the Pauline gospel a repetition of that revelation that was granted to Paul outside Damascus, which leads life and thought captive in obedience to Christ. It is repeated whenever Christians encounter the message of the gospel as Paul encountered the Christ revealed by God, namely as reconciler and Lord in one person. Since his call the Christ who appeared to Paul was the prior, unconditioned gift of God which determined his life. Likewise for Christians the gospel can and should be the prior gift of their lives, by which and from which they should take direction. However, they can accept and take this direction to heart only when God has won them to faith, as he did Paul, and filled them with the Spirit of the knowledge of Christ. By the power of the Holy Spirit he enables them also to believe, and gives them to know that in the crucified and risen Christ "are hid all the treasures of wisdom and knowledge" (Col 2:3; cf. 1 Cor 1:30; 2:7ff.).

V

The wisdom formulations of 1 Cor 1:18ff., 30, 2:6ff., and Col 2:3 themselves demand comparison with the epistemological precept that was particularly characteristic of Israel: "The fear of the LORD is the beginning of wisdom" (Prov 1:7). This precept is repeated with variations in Prov 9:10; 15:33; Ps 111:10; and Job 28:28. It is therefore of fundamental significance for the wisdom tradition of ancient Israel. In his monograph *Weisheit in Israel* (1970; Eng. tr. *Wisdom in Israel*, 1972), Gerhard von Rad draws attention to the fact that "Non-Israelite wisdom is unaware of this kind of almost programmatic rooting of wisdom in the fear of God."[74] On Prov 1:7 he writes: "The thesis that all human knowledge comes back to the question about commitment to God is a statement of penetrating perspicacity. . . . It contains in a nutshell the whole Israelite theory of knowledge."[75] Knowledge of God and turning to him are the starting point for knowledge of all the ordinances in life which is the theme of wisdom. "Faith does not—as is popularly believed today—hinder knowledge; on the contrary, it is what liberates knowledge, enables it really to come to the point and indicates to it its proper place in the sphere of varied, human activity."[76] Interestingly enough, Paul speaks of Christ and the gospel in 1 Cor 1:18–2:16 and Col 2:3 in a similar fashion. It is therefore no exaggeration to say that we have before us in these Pauline statements the New Testament counterpart to Prov 1:7 and parallels. A faith theory of knowledge is also present in nutshell form in 1 Cor 2:6-16, where faith is not a hindrance but liberation to realistic thought. The fact that capacity for this new thought grows out of the gift of the Holy Spirit does not separate Paul from the wisdom tradition of Israel. It binds him to it.

Our contention that 1 Cor 1:18–2:16 and Col 2:3 are counterparts to the precept in Prov 1:7 and parallels appears to be contradicted by the fact that neither Prov 1:7 nor any of the Old Testament variants are cited in Paul or anywhere else in the New Testament. Since the question is, as we saw, that of the New Testament preaching of the wisdom of God hidden in Christ over against the wisdom of the world, the absence of these quotations is easily explained. In his work *Law and Wisdom from Ben Sira to Paul* (1985) Eckhard J. Schnabel observes that the wisdom saying about the fear of God as the beginning of wisdom was well known to Sirach (Sir 1:11-20). Schnabel demonstrates that from then on it was applied almost exclusively to the Torah and the appropriation of its teaching.

> If you desire wisdom, keep the commandments,
>   and the Lord will supply it for you.

> For the fear of the Lord is wisdom and instruction,
>   and he delights in fidelity and meekness (Sir 1:26-27).

See further Sir 2:15f.; 6:37; 15:1; 19:20; 21:11 and other similar passages. Parallel exhortations to the fear of God are given in Test Levi 13:1; Test Gad 3:1-3; Test Joseph 11:1; and also 2 Bar 46:4-6. In the Pharisaic Psalms of Solomon the fear of God is the special characteristic of the righteous man who cleaves to the law (Pss Sol 4:23; 5:18; 13:11f.; 15:13).[77]

As the persecutor of the Christian church Paul could easily have pursued this link between Prov 1:7 and parallels and obedience to the Torah. As the chosen apostle he could no longer do this. Like Jesus before him and the Johannine school contemporary with him and after him (cf. Luke 10:21-22/Matt 11:27-30; John 1:1-18), Paul sets the wisdom that is embodied in Christ over against that contained in the law. Those who wish to understand God's revelation in sending Christ and to overcome the world with the "mind of Christ" must turn to the gospel in the obedience of faith and make the "law of Christ" (Gal 6:2) the standard of their lives. Faith as life turned to God in and through Christ (Gal 2:20), the prior gift of God's wisdom in Christ, and the Holy Spirit as God's illuminating gift of grace belong together for Paul, just as in Israelite wisdom tradition the fear of God, the revelation of the law and illumination by the Holy Spirit as the gift of wisdom constituted a unity. In this way Paul taught that the wisdom tradition of Israel was to be seen and appraised anew in the light of the revelation of Christ. What this means from the standpoint of the theory of knowledge is made clear by 1 Cor 2:6-16. The apostle's pen was not guided in these verses by charismatic enthusiasm but by the perception of Christ as the embodiment of the original wisdom of God that redeems all sinful existence.

VI

When this situation is properly seen, the issue in 1 Cor 2:6-16 is about the fundamental problem of the Christian understanding of the revelation of God in Christ. Theological *Sachkritik* must thus remain silent with regard to this passage. Rather stress must be laid on the critical significance of Paul's statements for theological thought and life. The text is thus transposed from being an item of tradition subject to critical questioning into a witness which subjects us to criticism and before which believers are hermeneutically answerable. In the circumstances Paul's text requires of the theologian at least three admissions.[78]

1. It is not we who have to determine critically and selectively what the gospel may or may not say. Rather, the gospel, already given to us by Paul with formulated dogmas and teaching, demands to be received as such and have its thoughts explored. Spiritual understanding of the gospel means receiving the gospel in its Pauline and biblical linguistic form as (following 1 Thess 2:13) the Word of God. This means receiving it as God's prior gift and seeing what lies at the heart of it for thought and life.

2. Theological thought is not to be equated without more ado with critical thought, and the historical critical method is not simply to be exalted as *the* theological method. Rather, theological thought is in the first instance listening thought, and only then critical thought. It proceeds from faith, and is pleased to be set before a biblical testimony, whose external clarity can be examined with all the appropriate scholarly exegetical tools, but whose internal clarity is not open to such critical analysis.

3. The way to the internal clarity of the biblical gospel testimony is found only by those who, as interpreters of Scripture, let themselves be interpreted by Scripture, and who share in the faith and walk of Christ's church. This is true insofar as, according to Paul, the gift of the Holy Spirit is shared by all those and only those who hear the gospel and share in the life of the church through baptism (Gal 3:2; Rom 10:17; 1 Cor 12:13). Put simply (and again fully in the spirit of the wisdom tradition), it may be formulated as follows. Spiritual knowledge of the gospel is not only a matter of the intellect; it is at the same time also a matter of the heart. It is not only a concern of mental effort; it requires the practical dedication of one's life (1 Cor 13:1-3; John 7:16f.).

The exegetical situation that we sketched at the beginning has led to an unfortunate misconception which extends far beyond the German-speaking world. To take to heart Paul's statements in 1 Cor 2:6-16 and to seek a spiritual understanding of Scripture have been taken to mean the repudiation of critical, scholarly thinking in theology and in the life of faith at large. Anyone who advances this opinion has not understood either Paul or even Luther's hermeneutical thesis about the twofold clarity and obscurity of Scripture. The intellectually demanding Pauline epistles whose interpretation requires great effort on the part of the exegete were themselves the product and result of the apostle's reason subjected to the obedience of Christ! It is a specific task, enjoined upon those who esteem and love Holy Scripture, that they apply themselves with all their scholarly seriousness and gifts to the clarification of the linguistic form of Paul's letters and the biblical books in general.

Paul himself had to wrestle with others about the understanding of the gospel in all his letters. He found himself in critical conflict over the truth of the gospel before the assembled church of Antioch with none other than Peter (Gal 2:11ff.). Over and over again he was ready to fight for the truth of the gospel. It is therefore both dangerous and wrong to abandon critical thought and judgment in interpreting Scripture and in deciding matters of faith in general (cf. 1 Pet 3:15). Theological thinking must proceed from the gospel. As such it must be—and continue to be—critical in the light of its subject matter. What is truly needed and will always be needed is the recognition that critical thought in the sense outlined above is not the key to faith. It is merely a special human talent that may be put to the service of faith. As long as he knows this, it is an honor for the theologian to join with Luther in his confession of Scripture: "We are beggars. *Hoc est verum.*"[79]

Notes

1. Luther, *De servo arbitrio* (1525) in *Werke,* WA 18: 609, 11-12: "Spiritus enim requiritur ad totam scripturam et ad quamlibet eius partem intelligendam." The translation given above in the text is based on the somewhat modernised version of Justus Jonas in Luther's *Ausgewählte Werke,* ed. H. H. Borcherdt and G. Merz, Munich, 1939, Ergänzungsreihe 1: 15.

2. WA 18, 653, 13-659, 36.

3. *Small Catechism,* Explanation of the Third Article of the Creed, following the translation given in *Triglot Concordia: The Symbolical Books of the Ev. Lutheran Church,* Saint Louis, 1921, 545.

4. "Nam sicuti Deus solus de se idoneous est testis in suo sermone: ita etiam non ante fidem reperiet sermo in hominum cordibus quam interiore Spiritus testimonio obsignetur," *Institutio christianae religionis* 1. 7. 4.

5. *Institutio* 2. 2. 20.

6. *Institutio* 3. 2. 33. In his *Commentary* Calvin observed with reference to 1 Cor 1:30: "Non posse nos gratis iustificari sola fide, quin simul sancte vivamus. Istae enim gratiae quasi individuo nexu cohaerunt: ut qui eas separare nititur, Christum quodammodo discerpat" (*Iohannis Calvini in omnes Paul Apostoli Epistolas atque etiam in Epistolam ad Hebraeos Commentarii,* ed. A. Tholuck, Halle, 1831, 1: 232).

7. "Utrumque istorum diligenter notandum, quod fumus est omnium scientarum cognitio, ubi abest coelestis Christi scientia: et homo cum toto suo acumine perinde est stupidus ad intelligenda per se Dei mysteria, atque asinus ineptus est ad symphoniam" (*Commentarii,* 1: 227).

8. The full title of this work is *D. Johann Jacob Rambachs . . . ausführliche und gründliche Erläuterung über seine eigene Institutiones Hermeneuticae Sacrae aus der eigenen Handschrift des seligen Verfassers mit Anmerkungen und einer Vorrede von der Vortrefflichkeit der Rambachischen Hermeneutik ans Licht dargestellt von* D. Ernst Friedrich Neubauer, Giessen, 1738.

9. *Erläuterung,* 64.

10. *Erläuterung,* 64-65. On the problems of pietistic hermeneutics see P. Stuhlmacher, *Vom Verstehen des Neuen Testaments. Eine Hermeneutik,* Grundrisse zum Neuen Testament, Das Neue Testament Deutsch, Ergänzungsreihe 6, Göttingen, 2nd ed., 1986, 137-40.

11. J. G. Hamann, *Sämtliche Werke,* ed. J. Nadler, Vienna, 1949, 1: 234-35.

12. Quoted from W. G. Kümmel, *Das Neue Testament. Geschichte der Erforschung seiner Probleme,* Freiburg and Munich, 2nd ed. 1970, 75.

13. Quoted from Kümmel, *Das Neue Testament,* 76.

14. F. C. Baur, *Paulus, Der Apostel Jesu Christi. Sein Leben und Wirken, seine Briefe und seine Lehre,* Zweite Auflage nach dem Tode des Verfassers besorgt von Dr. Eduard Zeller, Leipzig, 1867, 2: 139.

15. H. Gunkel, *Die Wirkungen des heiligen Geistes,* Göttingen, 1888, 24; cited from the Eng. tr. by R. A. Harrisville and P. A. Quanbeck II, *The Influence of the Holy Spirit: The Popular View of the Apostolic Age and the Teaching of the Apostle Paul,* Philadelphia, 1979, 34.

16. *The Influence,* 25.

17. H. Gunkel, *Zum religionsgeschichtlichen Verständnis des Neuen Testaments,* FRLANT 1, Göttingen, 1903, 3rd unaltered ed. 1930.

18. Gunkel, *Zum religionsgeschichtlichen Verständnis,* 35 (words set in emphasis in Gunkel's text).

19. W. Bousset, *Der erste Brief an die Korinther,* Die Schriften des Neuen Testaments 2, 3rd ed. edited by W. Bousset and W. Heitmüller, Göttingen, 1917, 84.

20. R. Bultmann, "K. Barth, 'Die Auferstehung der Toten,'" in *Glauben und Verstehen,* Tübingen, 2nd ed., 1954, (1: 38-64), 42; Eng. tr. by L. P. Smith, "Karl Barth, *The Resurrection of the Dead,*" *Faith and Understanding,* London, 1969, 1: 71.

21. Bultmann, *Faith and Understanding,* 1: 72.

22. R. Bultmann, *Theologie des Neuen Testaments,* Tübingen, 3rd ed. 1958, 179. cf. pp. 184-85; Eng. tr. by K. Grobel, *Theology of the New Testament,* New York, 1951, 1: 175, cf. 1: 181-82.

23. E. Käsemann, Meditation on 1 Cor 2:6-16 in *Exegetische Versuche und Besinnungen,* Göttingen, 1960, 1: 267-76.

24. U. Wilckens, *Weisheit und Torheit. Eine exegetisch-religionsgeschichtliche Untersuchung*

zu 1 Kor 1 und 2, Beiträge zur historischen Theologie 26, Tübingen, 1959, 52-54 and passim; cf. also Wilckens, *sophia, TDNT* 7: 519-22.

25. H. Conzelmann, *Der erste Brief an die Korinther*, KEKNT 5, Göttingen, 2nd ed. 1981, 77-79; Eng. tr. by J. W. Leitch, *1 Corinthians*, Hermeneia, Philadelphia, 1975, 58-61.

26. H. Weder, *Das Kreuz Jesu bei Paulus*, FRLANT 125, Göttingen, 2nd ed., 1981, 165-67.

27. See Barth's Preface to the Second Edition of K. Barth, *The Epistle to the Romans*, in Eng. tr. of the Sixth Edition of E. C. Hoskyns, London, 1933, 2-15; K. Barth, *Church Dogmatics*, Eng. tr. by G. T. Thomson and H. Knight, Edinburgh, 1956, 1/2: 515-18; K. Barth, *Evangelical Theology: An Introduction*, Eng. tr. by G. Foley, London, 1963, 171-83.

28. O. Weber, "Inspiration der hl. Schrift, dogmengeschichtlich," *RGG*[3] 3: 775-79; O. Weber, *Foundations of Dogmatics*, Eng. tr. by D. L. Guder, Grand Rapids, 1981, 1: 313-14, 319-30.

29. H. Diem, *Dogmatics*, Eng. tr. by H. Knight, (Edinburgh; 1959), 164-78; H. Diem, "Zur Problematik theologischer Wahrheitsfindung," *ThLZ* 95 (1970) 161-72.

30. F. Mildenberger, *Gotteslehre*, Tübingen, 1975, 114ff.; F. Mildenberger, *Theology of the Lutheran Confessions*, Eng. tr. by E. L. Lueker, ed. R. C. Schultz, Philadelphia, 1986, 211-37; F. Mildenberger, *Kleine Predigtlehre*, Stuttgart, 1984, 9-11, 27-36.

31. W. Joest, *Fundamentaltheologie*, Stuttgart, 1974, 167ff., 181ff., 200ff.; W. Joest, *Die Wirklichkeit Gottes*, Göttingen, 1984, 76ff.

32. E. Fuchs, *Marburger Hermeneutik*, Hermeneutische Untersuchungen zur Theologie 9, Tübingen, 1968, 205-7, 245-48.

33. Cf. G. Maier, *Heiliger Geist und Schriftauslegung*, Wuppertal, 1983. Unfortunately there is nothing in German which corresponds to the fair discussion of the fundamentalist approach to Scripture given by P. J. Achtemeier in *The Inspiration of Scripture: Problems and Proposals*, Philadelphia, 1980.

34. G. Bornkamm, *Paulus*, Stuttgart, 1969, 171; cited from the Eng. tr. by D. G. M. Stalker, *Paul*, London, 1971, 163-64. See also G. Bornkamm, *mystērion, TDNT* 4: 802-28, especially 819-22.

35. U. Wilckens, in *Theologia Crucis-Signum Crucis. Festschrift für Erich Dinkler zum 70. Geburtstag*, edited by C. Andresen and G. Klein, Tübingen, 1979, 501-37.

36. See above, n. 24.

37. Wilckens, in *Theologia Crucis-Signum Crucis*, 513.

38. G. Theissen, *Psychologische Aspekte paulinischer Theologie*, FRLANT 131, Göttingen, 1983, 349-50; Eng. tr. by J. P. Galvin, *Psychological Aspects of Pauline Theology*, Philadelphia, 1987, 353-54.

39. G. Sellin, "Das 'Geheimnis' der Weisheit und das Rätsel der 'Christuspartei' (zu 1 Kor 1-4)," *ZNW* 73 (1982) (69-96) 81.

40. Sellin, *ZNW* 73 (1982) 86.

41. F. Lang, *Die Briefe an die Korinther*, NTD 7, Göttingen, 1986, 38.

42. Lang, *Die Briefe an die Korinther*, 40-41.

43. Lang, *Die Briefe an die Korinther*, 41.

44. Lang, *Die Briefe an die Korinther*, 41.

45. E. E. Ellis, *Prophecy and Hermeneutic in Early Christianity: New Testament Essays*, WUNT 18, Tübingen, 1978, 47-50.

46. Ellis, *Prophecy and Hermeneutic*, 25-26, 59-60, 156-57.

47. On the structure of 1 Cor 1-4 see Conzelmann, *1 Corinthians*, 6-12, 56-57, 82-93; Wilckens in *Theologia Crucis-Signum Crucis*, 501- 504; Sellin, *ZNW* 73 (1982) 72-73; and Lang, *Die Briefe an die Korinther*, 27-59.

48. So Bornkamm, *Paul*, 159-64; Sellin, *ZNW* 73 (1982) 81. Wilckens observes that "the entire section 2:6-16 proves in fact to be a deeper interpretation of the initial *logos tou staurou* than Paul had yet presented to the Corinthians" (in *Theologia Crucis-Signum Crucis*, 513). Lang states that "the apostle's sequence of thought in 1:18–3:4 is fully comprehensible without the assumption of a break in conception or a later interpolation" (*Die Briefe an die Korinther*, 41).

49. Cf. S. Kim, *The Origin of Paul's Gospel*, WUNT 2/4, Tübingen, 2nd ed., 1984; Grand Rapids, 1982, 78-99.

50. Lang, *Die Briefe an die Korinther*, 24.

51. Cf. J. Roloff, *Die Apostelgeschichte*, NTD 5, Göttingen, 1981, 268-74.

52. H. Conzelmann, "Paulus und die Weisheit," in *Theologie als Schriftauslegung. Aufsätze zum Neuen Testament*, Munich, 1974 (177-90) 179; cf. also H. Conzelmann, *Die Apostelgeschichte*, HNT 7, Tübingen, 2nd ed., 1972, 115, 120.

53. F. Siegert, *Argumentation bei Paulus, gezeigt an Röm 9-11*, WUNT 34, Tübingen, 1985.

54. In an advanced seminar in the Winter semester 1985-86 conducted by H. P. Rüger and myself, Rüger showed that the puzzling quotation of Isa 64:3 in 1 Cor 2:9, may be shown as a Jewish formulation relating to Targ Isa 64:3, Mid Prov on 13:25, expounding Isa 64:3. From this standpoint the allusion in Asc Isa 11:34 (Lib Ant 26:13) is understandable, as also is the remark of Origen in his Matthew commentary on 27:9: "in nullo enim regulari libro hoc positum invenitur nisi in secretis Eliae prophetae" (Migne, *PG* 13: 1769C). Therefore, E. Earle Ellis can maintain his view that 1 Cor 2:6-16 contains a pre-Pauline midrash (see above, n. 46), only because he questions the origin of v 9 in a Jewish apocryphon. See also E. E. Ellis, *Paul's Use of the Old Testament*, Grand Rapids, 2nd ed. 1981, 34-37. In my view the conclusion of O. Michel is more apposite: "We do best to remain with the conclusion that the formal points of contact between 1 Cor 2:9 and Isa 64:4 LXX do not suffice to overthrow the church tradition that there is here an apocryphal quotation" (*Paulus und seine Bibel*, Darmstadt, 2nd ed. 1981, 36).

55. On these wisdom schools see M. Hengel, *Judaism and Hellenism: Studies in their Encounter in Palestine during the Early Hellenistic Period*, Eng. tr. by J. Bowden, London, Philadelphia, 1974, 1: 78-83, 169-75, 207-10, 247-54. H. Stadelmann has shown the likely use of Jesus ben Sirach in school education (*Ben Sira als Schriftgelehrter. Eine Untersuchung zum Berufsbild des vor—makkabäischen Sōfer unter Berücksichtigung seines Verhältnisses zu Priester—, Propheten—, und Weisheitslehrertum*, WUNT 2/6, Tübingen, 1980), 27-30. D. Georgi has rightly drawn attention to the fact that the Wisdom of Solomon is a "school product," which "grew and was formed in a collective process" (*Weisheit Salomos*, JSHRZ 3/4, Gütersloh, 1980, 393). It depends on one's definition of Gnosis whether, as Georgi thinks (p. 394), the Wisdom of Solomon is the oldest Gnostic text "that we possess." This question cannot be resolved here.

56. For analysis and the place of this text in the teaching of Jesus and the primitive Jewish tradition see M. Hengel, "Jesus als messianischer Lehrer der Weisheit und die Anfänge der Christologie," in E. Jacob, ed., *Sagesse et Religion*, Paris, 1979 (147-88) 152f., 160ff.; and H. Gese, "Die Weisheit, der Menschensohn und die Ursprünge der Christologie als konsequente Entfaltung der biblischen Theologie," *SEÅ* 44 (1979) 77-114, see especially pp. 98ff.

57. See R. Riesner, *Jesus als Lehrer. Eine Untersuchung zum Ursprung der Evangelien-Überlieferung*, WUNT 2/7, Tübingen, 2nd ed. 1984, 336.

58. Theissen, *Psychological Aspects of Pauline Theology*, 361.

59. See on the one hand, P. Stuhlmacher, "Jesustradition im Römerbrief?", *Theologische Beiträge* 14 (1983) 240-50, and on the other hand N. Walter, "Paulus und die urchristliche Tradition," *NTS* 31 (1985) 498-522.

60. O. Betz, "'Fleischliche' and 'geistliche' Christuserkenntnis nach 2 Kor 5, 16," *Theologische Beiträge* 14 (1983) 167-79; Walter, *NTS* 31 (1985) 503 (see above, n. 59).

61. In *Theologia Crucis-Signum Crucis*, 508-510.

62. Sellin observes: "By the 'rulers of this age' are not meant demons or gnostic *archontes* of the fallen world, as was thought largely in the interest of a gnostic-mythic interpretation, but the political and religious leaders who were responsible for the crucifixion of Jesus" (*ZNW* 73 [1982] 84-85; see above n. 39). Sellin rightly concludes from the synonymity of "wisdom of this age" (2:8) and "wisdom of men" (2:5) that the "rulers of this age" (as representatives of the wisdom of this age) are "*human beings*" (p. 85, n. 55, Sellin's italics). The interpretation of v 8 in the light of the Lucan texts is therefore to be preferred over the anthropological-demonological interpretation which is already present in Ambrosiaster (Migne *PL* 17: 204-5).

63. Lang, *Die Briefe an die Korinther*, 43-44.

64. J. Schniewind, "Die Archonten dieses Äons, 1 Kor 2, 6- 8," in *Nachgelassene Reden und Aufsätze*, edited by E. Kähler, Berlin; 1952, 104-9.

65. Sellin refers to 2 Bar 14:9 (*ZNW* 73 [1982] 83, n. 47). The text of 2 Bar 14:8-9 reads: "O Lord, my Lord, who can understand your judgment? Or who can explore the depth of your way? Or who can discern the majesty of your path? Or who can discern your incomprehensible counsel? Or who of those who are born has ever discovered the beginning and the end of your wisdom?"

(translation by A. F. J. Klein in J. H. Charlesworth, ed., *The Old Testament Pseudepigrapha*, Garden City, NY, 1983, 1: 626).

66. On the identification of wisdom and Spirit see J. A. Davis, *Wisdom and Spirit*, Lanham, MD, 1984.

67. Theissen, *Psychological Aspects of Pauline Theology*, 367-8.

68. On Philo see Sellin, ZNW 73 (1982) 87.

69. Lang, *Die Briefe an die Korinther*, 45.

70. On the relation of Gen 2:7 to the distinction in 1 Cor 15:45-49 between "physical" and "spiritual" human beings see Lang, *Die Briefe an die Korinther*, 46. His comment should also be noted: "The contrast between the earthly minded and those who are led by the Spirit is prepared in Paul theologically by the OT contrast between God who is 'Spirit' and man who is 'flesh' (Isa 31:3). What comes from the Spirit of God can be received and understood only by those who are themselves filled by the Spirit of God."

71. On the interpretation of 2 Cor 2:14-16 see S. J. Hafemann, *Suffering and the Spirit: An Exegetical Study of II Cor 2:14–3:3 within the Context of the Corinthian Correspondence*, WUNT 2/19, Tübingen, 1986, 41-87.

72. On the connection between wisdom and the primal light in creation see Hengel, *Judaism and Hellenism* 1: 165-69.

73. For the basis of this interpretation of the grounds for the condemnation of Jesus by the Sanhedrin see A. Strobel, *Die Stunde der Wahrheit. Untersuchungen zum Strafverfahren gegen Jesu*, WUNT 21, Tübingen, 1980; and P. Stuhlmacher, "Warum musste Jesus sterben?", *Theologische Beiträge* 16 (1985) 273-85.

74. G. von Rad, *Wisdom in Israel*, Eng. tr. by J. D. Martin, London, Nashville, 1972, 66.

75. von Rad, *Wisdom in Israel*, 67.

76. von Rad, *Wisdom in Israel*, 68.

77. See E. J. Schnabel, *Law and Wisdom from Ben Sira to Paul: A Tradition Historical Enquiry into the Relation of Law, Wisdom, and Ethics*, WUNT 2/16, Tübingen, 1985, 81-82, 162-65.

78. On the following arguments see especially E. Jüngel, *God as the Mystery of the World: On the Foundation of the Theology of the Crucified One in the Dispute between Theism and Atheism*, Eng. tr. by D. L. Guder, Grand Rapids, 1983, 154-55. At the same time I am seeking to do justice to Diem's demand that in the discovery of theological truth the "biblical way of knowledge" must be borne in mind and adhered to. Accordingly human knowledge of God follows being and becoming known by God (cf. Gal. 4:9; 1 Cor 9:3). According to Diem, "this prior ordering of the knowledge of human beings by God before the knowledge of God by human beings is irreversibly decisive for the biblical way of knowledge. Knowledge never begins with human beings. Therefore it is not tied to any precondition of human knowledge of reality, nature, history, or even self-knowledge of human beings and their nature. Rather knowledge follows our being known by God as an act of the loving activity of God, through which he gives himself to be known. Thus God can never be the mere object of knowledge. Rather, as its originator he is at the same time also its subject" (*ThLZ* 95 [1970] 167-68 [see above, n. 29]).

79. *Werke*, WA Tischreden 5: 318, 2 (# 5677); cf. *Luther's Works* 54, *Table Talk*, Eng. tr. by T. G. Tappert, (Philadelphia, 1967), 476. [Tr.: This remark was among Luther's last utterances on the day before he died.]

Index of Scripture References

The Dead Sea Scrolls

Index of Modern Authors